THE OFFICIAL GNOME™ 2
DEVELOPER'S GUIDE

THE OFFICIAL GNOME™ 2 DEVELOPER'S GUIDE

by Matthias Warkus

NO STARCH
PRESS

San Francisco

Publisher: William Pollock
Managing Editor: Karol Jurado
Cover and Interior Design: Octopod Studios
Technical Reviewer: Michael Meeks
Copyeditor: Judy Ziajka
Compositor: Wedobooks
Proofreader: Stephanie Provines
Indexer: Brian Ward

The Official GNOME 2 Developer's Guide is an English version of *GNOME 2.0: Das Entwickler-Handbuch*, the German original edition (3-89842-182-1), published in Germany by Galileo Press (Bonn), copyright © 2002 by Galileo Press, GmbH. English translation prepared by Brian Ward.

For information on book distributors or translations, please contact No Starch Press, Inc. directly:

No Starch Press, Inc.
555 De Haro Street, Suite 250, San Francisco, CA 94107
phone: 415-863-9900; fax: 415-863-9950; info@nostarch.com; http://www.nostarch.com

Library of Congress Cataloguing-in-Publication Data

Warkus, Matthias.
  The official GNOME 2 developer's guide / Matthias Warkus.
      p. cm.
  ISBN 1-59327-030-5
 1. Graphical user interfaces (Computer systems) 2. Computer programming. 3. Computer software--
Development. I. Title.
   QA76.9.U83 W375 2004
   005.4'38--dc22

                                                              2003023351

BRIEF CONTENTS

Introduction
1

Chapter 1
GLib
5

Chapter 2
GObject
59

Chapter 3
GTK+
111

Chapter 4
The GNOME Libraries
245

Chapter 5
Glade and libglade
303

Chapter 6
Additional Software
Development Tools
323

Chapter 7
GConf
343

Chapter 8
GnomeVFS
377

Chapter 9
Where to Go from Here
429

Appendix A
Stock Item Reference
437

Appendix B
Glossary
445

Appendix C
Bibliography
459

Appendix D
Getting the GNOME
Development Software
461

Appendix E
Creative Commons
NonCommercial-ShareAlike
License
467

Index
473

CONTENTS IN DETAIL

INTRODUCTION

Limits 2
Conventions 2
Platform 3
Programming Examples 4
Functions and Macros 4
Counting 4
Pathnames 4
Pointers and Addresses 4

1
GLIB

1.1   Introduction 5
1.2   GLib Naming Conventions 6
1.3   Basic Types 6
1.4   Basic Utilities 7
      1.4.1   Memory Management 7
      1.4.2   Quarks 11
      1.4.3   C Strings 13
      1.4.4   Unicode and Character Encodings 15
      1.4.5   Timer 23
      1.4.6   Message Logging 24
      1.4.7   Debugging Functions 27
      1.4.8   Exception Handling with Error Reporting 28
1.5   Data Structures 33
      1.5.1   Strings 33
      1.5.2   Lists 36
      1.5.3   Arrays 44
      1.5.4   Trees 46
      1.5.5   Hash Tables 52
      1.5.6   Creating Hash Tables 52
1.6   Further Topics 57

2
GOBJECT

2.1   Object-Oriented Programming Basics 60
      2.1.1   Objects as Instances of Classes 60
      2.1.2   Inheritance 61

2.2 Defining Classes 64
    2.2.1 Structure Definitions 64
    2.2.2 Utility Macros 65
    2.2.3 Initializing Type Identifiers 67
    2.2.4 The Base Class: GObject 69
2.3 Methods 72
2.4 Properties 72
    2.4.1 Declaring Parameters 73
    2.4.2 Tangent: Generic Containers for Values 75
    2.4.3 Installing Properties 77
2.5 Using Objects 81
    2.5.1 Using Properties 82
    2.5.2 Strong and Weak Object References 83
2.6 Signals 84
    2.6.1 Defining Signals and Installing Handlers 85
    2.6.2 Emitting Signals 88
    2.6.3 Marshallers 89
    2.6.4 Signal Accumulators 92
    2.6.5 Attaching Handlers to Signals 93
    2.6.6 Details 95
    2.6.7 Emission Hooks 96
    2.6.8 More Signal Utilities 98
2.7 Inheritance 99
    2.7.1 Interfaces 104
2.8 Further Topics 109

3
GTK+

3.1 What Is GTK+? 111
    3.1.1 Widgets and Containers 112
    3.1.2 Event-Driven Programming 114
    3.1.3 An Elementary Example 114
    3.1.4 Widget Fundamentals 118
    3.1.5 Methods 118
    3.1.6 Properties 119
    3.1.7 Signals 120
3.2 Windows 120
    3.2.1 Icons 122
3.3 Display Widgets 122
    3.3.1 Labels and Pango Markup 127
    3.3.2 Images and GDK Pixbufs 129
    3.3.3 Progress Bars 138
3.4 Container and Layout Widgets 138
    3.4.1 Boxes 144
    3.4.2 Tables 146
    3.4.3 Paned Widgets 148
    3.4.4 Notebooks 148
    3.4.5 Alignment Containers 150
    3.4.6 Sensible Widget Arrangement 151

3.5 Button Widgets 151
3.6 Data Entry Widgets 156
    3.6.1 Option Menus 162
    3.6.2 Entry Boxes 162
    3.6.3 Combo Boxes 164
    3.6.4 Adjustment Objects 165
    3.6.5 Slider Widgets 166
    3.6.6 Spin Button Widgets 167
    3.6.7 Color Chooser Widgets 168
    3.6.8 Font Chooser Widgets 168
    3.6.9 File Browsers 169
    3.6.10 Chooser Examples 170
3.7 Dividers and Decorations 174
    3.7.1 Frames 177
    3.7.2 Separators 178
    3.7.3 Arrows 178
3.8 Tooltips and Keyboard Control 178
    3.8.1 Tooltips 178
    3.8.2 Keyboard Operation 181
3.9 Scrolling 183
    3.9.1 Scrolled Window Properties 186
3.10 Dialogs 186
3.11 Tree and List Widgets 191
    3.11.1 List and Tree API Reference 196
    3.11.2 Tree Views 201
    3.11.3 Selecting Rows 207
    3.11.4 An Extended Example 210
3.12 Text 217
    3.12.1 Text Buffers 224
    3.12.2 Text View Widgets 240
3.13 Further Topics 242

4

THE GNOME LIBRARIES

4.1 What Characterizes a GNOME Application? 245
    4.1.1 "Take This GNOME and Shove It" 246
4.2 libgnome 247
    4.2.1 Initializing GNOME 247
    4.2.2 Utility Functions 249
    4.2.3 Sound 254
    4.2.4 Scores 256
4.3 libgnomeui 257
    4.3.1 Application Windows 257
    4.3.2 Context Menus 269
    4.3.3 Enhanced Data Entry Widgets 270
    4.3.4 Text Entry Widgets with History 275
    4.3.5 File Choosers 276
    4.3.6 Font Pickers 277
    4.3.7 Color Pickers 278

    4.3.8   Icon Pickers 278

    4.3.9   Image Pickers 279

    4.3.10   Date/Time Widgets 280

    4.3.11   Hyperlinks 281

    4.3.12   High Scores 282

    4.3.13   About (Credits) Windows 283

    4.3.14   GNOME Stock Item Additions 286

    4.3.15   Druids 286

    4.3.16   Session Management 298

4.4 Further Topics 302

5

GLADE AND LIBGLADE

5.1 Glade 303

    5.1.1   Create a Project 304

    5.1.2   The Widget Palette 305

    5.1.3   Property Editor 306

    5.1.4   The Widget Tree 311

    5.1.5   Clipboard 311

5.2 Using the Interface 312

    5.2.1   Reading Glade Files 315

    5.2.2   Accessing Widgets 316

    5.2.3   Automatically Attaching Signals 316

    5.2.4   Associative Functions 317

    5.2.5   The Complete Temperature Converter 317

5.3 Further Topics 321

6

ADDITIONAL SOFTWARE DEVELOPMENT TOOLS

6.1 pkg-config 323

    6.1.1   Package Lists, Versions, and Descriptions 325

    6.1.2   Determining Compiler and Linker Options 325

    6.1.3   Using pkg-config in a Makefile 326

6.2 The GNU Autotools 326

    6.2.1   Overview 327

    6.2.2   configure.ac 328

    6.2.3   Makefile Templates 331

    6.2.4   Extra Tools 333

    6.2.5   aclocal and m4 Libraries 334

    6.2.6   autoheader 334

    6.2.7   automake and Standard Package Files 334

    6.2.8   autoconf 335

    6.2.9   configure 335

    6.2.10   Standard Targets 335

    6.2.11   autogen.sh 336

6.3 Menu Items 336

6.4 Help Documents 337
      6.4.1 Installing Documentation 338
6.5 Supporting Locale Options with gettext and intltool 339
      6.5.1 intltool 341

7

GCONF

7.1 Overview 344
7.2 The User End 345
      7.2.1 Configuration Database Keys and Values 345
      7.2.2 The GConf Configuration Editor 345
      7.2.3 gconftool-2 347
7.3 Programming with GConf 350
      7.3.1 Initializing and Finalizing GConf 350
      7.3.2 Reading and Writing GConf Values 352
      7.3.3 GConf Value Change Notification 362
      7.3.4 The GConf Cache 364
      7.3.5 Error Handling 364
      7.3.6 Schemas 366
      7.3.7 A Complete Example 368
      7.3.8 Preferences Guidelines 375
7.4 Further Topics 375

8

GNOMEVFS

8.1 Transparency with URIs 377
8.2 Initializing and Shutting Down GnomeVFS 379
8.3 Synchronous Access 380
      8.3.1 Opening, Creating, and Closing Files 383
      8.3.2 Reading, Writing, and Seeking 384
      8.3.3 Extracting and Changing File Information 385
      8.3.4 File Management 388
8.4 Directory Operations 389
      8.4.1 Directory Navigation 389
8.5 Asynchronous I/O 391
      8.5.1 Opening and Closing Files 392
      8.5.2 Reading and Writing 393
      8.5.3 Retrieving and Setting File Information 394
      8.5.4 Miscellaneous Operations 394
      8.5.5 An Example 396
8.6 Transfers 409
      Step 1: 410
      Step 2: 410
      Step 3: 411
      8.6.1 Additional Transfer Functions 412

8.7   File Types 413
       8.7.1   Declaring MIME Types 414
       8.7.2   Declaring Application Support for a MIME Type 415
8.8   URI Structures 417
       8.8.1   Building URI Paths 417
       8.8.2   Extracting Path Information from a URI 418
       8.8.3   Accessing URI Connection Information 419
       8.8.4   URI Lists 419
8.9   Miscellaneous Utilities 420
8.10   Result/Error Codes 420
8.11   Portability Notes 422
8.12   File Information Example 422
8.13   Further Topics 427

9
WHERE TO GO FROM HERE

9.1   Reading, Discussing, and Collaborating 429
       9.1.1   Real Life 430
       9.1.2   WWW 430
       9.1.3   Mailing Lists 433
       9.1.4   IRC 434
9.2   The Future 434
       9.2.1   libegg 434
       9.2.2   Toolbars 434
       9.2.3   Trees and Lists 435
       9.2.4   Date/Time Widgets 435
       9.2.5   Icon Themes 435
       9.2.6   Recent Files 435
       9.2.7   File Browser 435
       9.2.8   System Sound 436
9.3   Conclusion 436

A
STOCK ITEM REFERENCE

GTK+ Stock Items 437
GNOME Stock Items 442

B
GLOSSARY
445

C
BIBLIOGRAPHY
459

D
GETTING THE GNOME DEVELOPMENT SOFTWARE

System-Specific Packages 461
GARNOME 461
CVS 463
     JHBuild 464
Conventional Source Archives 465

E
CREATIVE COMMONS NONCOMMERCIAL-SHAREALIKE LICENSE
467

INDEX
473

FOREWORD

The Gnome project began in 1997 as a way to bring free software to the computer desktop. At the time, the scene looked a bit like this: Microsoft had released Windows 95, which was a very big improvement over their previous OS, and they were fiercely competing with Netscape for the browser space. Linux and BSD Unix were increasingly being used to run servers and were the source of most of the server-based innovation at the time. But at the time, the free software story of desktop software was looking pretty bad. Oh, there were a few proprietary desktop environments, and the KDE effort, but even KDE was, sadly, built on top of a proprietary platform.

Gnome was an attempt to produce the missing pieces needed to make the open source Unix (and in particular Linux) suitable for use on desktop computers. But we had to solve various problems first: We had to create the basic desktop software as well as a set of desktop-related services (like printing and configuration) as well as a common development platform to factorize the common tasks performed by these applications.

The Gnome project spans many domains, from the development platform to the actual visual components that make up the desktop. It includes the design process, implementation, translation, documentation, architecting, bug fixing, and managing the release and quality assurance processes. But unlike the traditional software development process, Gnome has been developed by individuals and companies distributed around the world, on a non-stop basis. This process of distributed software development has posed numerous challenges, but it brings with it plenty of benefits: Gnome is multi-cultural, and benefits from the input of many experts in various fields worldwide.

Today Gnome is one of the most used desktops in the world. In fact, the end of 2003 saw very large deployments of the Gnome desktop in Spain, Brazil, China, and the United Kingdom. And Gnome as a desktop is continuously evolving. It continues to improve and to incorporate the best usability ideas from the industry, and has also proven to be a vessel for distributing innovative applications.

In 2000, the various developers and companies involved in the Gnome project launched an initiative to create a Gnome Foundation. The Foundation was to be responsible for engineering releases, integrating new components into Gnome, establishing partnerships with other projects, and liaising with other nonprofits, corporations, governments, developers, and users. Gnome 2.0 was the first release of the desktop under the umbrella of the Gnome Foundation. It featured an improved user interface and an improved development platform. Since the release of Gnome 2.0, the team has been able to deliver reliable releases of the platform every six months, with the schedule allowing for the code to be properly internationalized and tested before each release.

Gnome is unique because, from the very beginning, it has had a strong focus on creating a development platform to provide services for applications; services that developers typically expect to find on their operating system. *The Official Gnome 2 Developer's Guide* will show you how to use this platform. Matthias Warkus wrote this book based on the new Gnome 2 platform, and it has been available in German for quite some time. I am very happy to see this book translated into English, thanks to the efforts of Brian Ward. Michael Meeks performed the technical review of the translation for accuracy, and updated the book as necessary to reflect the latest changes in Gnome.

Since the early days of the Gnome project, we have understood the need for a programming language that would help programmers to be more productive. Thus, the Gnome APIs were designed to accommodate the needs of the various programming languages. The information in this book is focused on the C API, but it is equally applicable to the various language bindings included with Gnome: C++, Java, Perl, Python, and the .NET bindings (which include C# and Visual Basic). This language-neutral policy is one of the great strengths of the Gnome APIs, because they accommodate system programmers as well as developers who choose to use the more agile programming systems. In fact, all of the GUI code I write these days is done in C# using the concepts explained in this book, and all of the new GUI software that we are producing is being built on the C#/Gnome combination. Once you become familiar with the development APIs, I suggest that you read the Gnome "Human Interface Guidelines" document published by the Foundation. This document summarizes the conventions and policies used when developing for the desktop to create applications that are easy to use, that reuse the Gnome framework, and that are visually integrated with the rest of the desktop.

Miguel de Icaza
Gnome Project Founder

TECHNICAL REVIEWER'S NOTE

It was with some surprise and trepidation that I received the task of technical review of a book on the GNOME platform. As I started to read it, however, it became obvious that the selection of topics to keep the bulk down, along with some great explanations and examples, make for easy reading and comprehension. Thus it was, in the end, more of a privilege than a chore.

This book packs a punch greater than its weight by providing useful examples showing good design patterns and avoiding extranous distractions or mechanically extracted, exhaustive API listings. It is light on patronizing screenshots and high on raw content.

Matthias Warkus' diligent research and genius provided the original German text, informed by his long association with GNOME. Mercifully, Brian Ward stepped forward to translate and update it in an English version, and did an amazing job. It was a pleasure to work with someone so patient and talented; we owe Brian a great debt.

And so I come to the end, as you come to the beginning — may you enjoy working with GNOME, learning from the insights and bending them to your purpose. Happy hacking with GNOME, and I look forward to seeing your name in some ChangeLogs.

Michael Meeks

PREFACE TO THE
ORIGINAL EDITION

"Why are *you* writing a *developer's guide* to GNOME 2? I thought you were a translator . . ."

A somewhat stunned colleague asked me something like this at the GNOME Project booth as the plans for this book began to take shape at LinuxTag (Linux Day) 2001 in Stuttgart. And because I had the insolence to undertake this task without any actual extensive GNOME programming experience, I should probably prepare for a series of sleepless nights.

When I started fooling around with GNOME in 1998 (around version 0.30), I don't think that I would have dreamed it would go this far. Apart from curiosity, the main reason that I started using GNOME was that it was the only modern user interface that the slightly outdated hardware on my Linux system could deal with, if only barely.

One thing led to another: Sometime or other, I decided to subscribe to several mailing lists, translated GNOME software into German, spent day upon day compiling the latest GNOME source trees, demonstrated GNOME at trade shows, did some talks about it, and wrote articles. The one thing that I hadn't done yet was to program GNOME, not just because I didn't have the time, but because I was somewhat lacking in inspiration.

Therefore, writing a comprehensive GNOME 2 programming guide was quite a daring undertaking, and it would have never gotten to this point without the support of Judith Stevens-Lemoine. Judith deserves my special thanks — I couldn't have hoped for a better editor. Without her, this book wouldn't exist, and the compromise of content breadth versus limited space and time wouldn't have come out so well.

The same thanks go to Jens "triqster" Finke, Christian "chrisime" Meyer, and Thomas "chip" Ziehmer, who reviewed the book for correctness and clarity. I have them and a large number of other members in the GNOME community to thank for motivation; their expressed desire for this book ensures that it indeed has the practical value that I had strived for.

I hope that you share this view. If you have some constructive criticism or ideas for revisions, feel free to send them directly to me.

And now I'd like to use this opportunity to make some further remarks and thanks:

The names in Chapter 2 come from a Usenet posting by Peter Bouillon. Many thanks to him and the founders of Netdigest (`de.alt.netdigest`) who have archived his posts. [tr.ed.: The terms in the German edition are Flippe and Qwurxel; these have been "translated" into Flipper and Slop.]

I have my sister (Iris) to thank for many more things than are possible to mention in this preface.

Tuomas "Tigert" Kuosmanen, GNOME's "head artist," gets thanks not just for his wonderful images, but also for providing me with several special versions of the GNOME logo.

Jeff "jdub" Waugh has not been the release coordinator of GNOME 2, but also saved me a lot of time with his GARNOME system that allows an entire GNOME build with just a few commands. Before this, a new system could take days to build, and I was happy to invest the time that would otherwise be spent installing GNOME in writing.

This book's work was also supported by music from (among others): The Alan Parsons Project, Amorphis, Antrum Nequam, Tori Amos, Ayreon, Johann Sebastian Bach, Ludwig von Beethoven, Black Sabbath, Blue Öyster Cult, Bluescream, Eric Burdon and The Animals, Eric Burdon and The New Animals, Eric Burdon and War, B. Where, Miles Davis, DDT, Deep Purple, Derek and The Dominos, Dio, The Doobie Brothers, The Doors, Ekseption, Duke Ellington, Emerson Lake and Palmer, Peter Frampton, Herbie Hancock, Iron Butterfly, J.B.O., Maria João, Billy Joel, Judas Priest, Led Zeppelin, Bob Marley, Massive Attack, John Mayall and The Blues Breakers, Meat Loaf, John Miles, The Modern Jazz Quartet, Thelonious Monk, Carl Orff, Pink Floyd, Queen, Sergei Rachmaninov, Seal, Arnold Schönberg, Simon and Garfunkel, Paul Simon, Jimmy Smith, The Specker Davis Group, Star One, The Steve Miller Band, Toto, Uriah Heep, Van Halen, and Hannes Wader — and let's not forget the people who have shown that you really can find friends of music in the Internet: the wonderful collection of musicians in `de.rec.music.machen`.

I hope that you have as much fun working with this book as I had writing it.

Matthias "mawa" Warkus
`mawarkus@gnome.org`
Korborn, July 2001-October 2002

PREFACE TO THE
ENGLISH EDITION

To many, GNOME seems like an American phenomenon, even though it's pointless
to assign this sort of label to a free software project. You could write to your heart's
content about how the project came about and which project outgrowths produce
the various pieces that make up GNOME. At the same time, you encounter people
who feel that they need to view company acquisitions and other developments in free
software not only as conflicts, but also in terms of their "nationality" — a point of
view that's so senseless that it would be a waste of time to explain any further. Free
software makes the best sense when thought of as international, and with that,
transatlantic. This book, written by a German and now appearing in America, shows
that GNOME is no exception. That's perhaps the biggest reason that I'm thrilled
about this translation.

You might notice that this is a good translation. That could have something to
do with Brian Ward being a good translator — so good that I couldn't find one single
thing to fix in his translation. In addition, working with Karol Jurado (managing
editor of No Starch Press) went very smoothly.

I'm especially delighted to have the service of GNOME guru Michael Meeks as a
technical reviewer. Anyone who knows GNOME a little from the inside can
understand why. With the help of Michael and Brian, this book not only has been
translated, but also revised and improved.

To the petty politickers mentioned earlier, I'd recommend that instead of
partaking in silly discussions, you use your time to become GNOME programmers,
because (among other things), I still don't have the time to be a full-fledged
GNOME programmer.

I wish the readers of this edition just as much fun as I did to the readers of the
original German version. Even though there's probably some sort of ocean between
us, we might just come across each other one day.

Matthias "mawa" Warkus
mawarkus@gnome.org
Marburg, November 2003

INTRODUCTION

 You need some programming experience to take advantage of this book. If you were starting from scratch, the book would require an especially large and sturdy binding to contain all of the pages, and you probably wouldn't be able to lift it.

To be more specific, you should have:

- Firm programming experience in C, including pointers, dynamically allocated data structures, and pointers to functions. You should also be familiar with enumeration types and bit fields [Kernighan].

- A solid grasp of pointers to pointers (** types), where to use them, and how to extract and use the address of a pointer.

- Understanding of C macros and the C preprocessor.

- Fundamental understanding of Unix: processes, libraries, search paths, and so on.

- Practical Unix experience, including how to use a text editor, shell scripts, and make.
- Basic familiarity with GNOME (as a user). You should know how GNOME 2.0 applications look and feel and how to work with graphical user elements such as control panels and dialog boxes.

In addition, some understanding of GUI programming is helpful. Knowledge of what callbacks (event handlers) are and how they work goes a long way. This isn't absolutely necessary, but you'll probably need a little more time to work through the book if you have never touched a user-interface API.

You do *not* need experience in:

- GTK+ or GNOME programming.
- Programming languages other than C.
- Object-oriented programming.
- Model-View-Controller (MVC) programming.

Limits

This book's content lies somewhere between a tutorial and a reference. To keep it from becoming too bloated, some restrictions were imposed:

- This book does not contain a complete API reference. In particular, you won't find seldom-used or obsolete functions and classes here.
- This book omits certain implementation details, such as data structures and libraries and functions that are purely internal or pertain only to further development of GNOME libraries. If you are interested in this sort of thing, have a look at Appendix D for information on how to obtain the GNOME source code. This software is distributed as open source under GNU LGPL [FSF 1999] and GPL [FSF 1991].
- To make more space for the most frequently used classes and functions, this book includes some reference material for obscure API components, but no examples.
- You won't see how to go from an idea to a complete, robust, elegant GUI application in excruciating detail. This is a book on GNOME as a tool for building applications; its goal is not software engineering. The programming examples are meant to demonstrate classes and functions, not full applications.

Conventions

The typographical style of this book is similar to that of other programming books:

- **File, library, GConf keys, and URLs**, such as *gobject.h*, */apps/gconfdemo/pictures_as_words*, and *http://www.gnome.org/* are set in italic.
- **Glossary terms** appear in ***boldface italic*** at first mention.

- **Menu commands** are in **boldface**, separated by an angle bracket (>): for example, **File > Open** or **Help > Info**.

- **C code, shell commands, function names, and variable names** are in a monospaced typeface:
  `GtkWidget *foo = gtk_widget_new();`
  Note that you can distinguish a function by its trailing parentheses:
  `g_timer_new()`

- Class names like **GtkWidget** are set in boldface.

- Object names also appear in monospace. Therefore, you might see phrases like "The object gconf belongs to the **GConfClient** class" and "gconf is a GConfClient." However, you will frequently see "a **GConfClient** object" used to refer to an indefinite object of a class.

- Parameters such as *object* in `G_OBJECT(object)` are in *monospaced italic*.

- Properties and signals such as `changed`, `set-size`, and `shadow-type` appear in **monospaced bold**.

- Pseudocode such as `<< save humanity >>` is monospaced between two sets of angle brackets. You will often see `<< ... >>`. This means that there's no reason to say what this pseudocode does, because it's either obvious or undefined.

- **References** to literature such as [Wirth] and [Pennington] appear in brackets. Appendix C is a bibliography.

NOTE *There are note indicators in the margin to denote material that is particularly helpful or important.*

WARNING *Likewise, if you see a warning in the margin, you should read the material carefully, or there's a good chance that you might shoot yourself in the foot.*

Because the text in this book has a maximum width of 83 monospaced characters, all programs and file listings that exceed this limit must be split. A backslash (\) at the end of a line indicates that the next line is a continuation. Unfortunately, not all C compilers understand line continuation in the same way, and some programs that work with the other file listings in this book don't support it at all. You should always consider split lines to be a single line, other than notable exceptions such as Makefiles and shell scripts.

Platform

GTK+ and GNOME have gradually become platform independent. In spite of this, the primary working environment for this book is Unix. When there is a difference among Unix systems, this book leans toward a GNU system with a Linux kernel (otherwise known as GNU/Linux or just Linux). In general, this book tries to avoid operating system dependencies, but in the interest of space and clarity, it leans toward the GNU platform because it has the overwhelming majority of GNOME installations.

Programming Examples

The examples in this book are quite important. At the very least, you should skim them, acquiring a good idea of what they do and a fundamental understanding of how they work. This text presents many concepts that seem somewhat awkward in words alone but are clear when presented in conjunction with an example.

In the continuing effort to keep this book's page count down, many of the examples here are not complete valid C programs. The first few chapters contain primarily short multiline fragments, demonstrating function calls described in the surrounding text. There are many full programs within the text, though, and you can get them at *http://www.nostarch.com/gnome.htm.*

If you come across a variable that doesn't seem to have a declaration and you don't know its type or significance, take a look at the previous pages; you should find it there. For instance, the listings accompanying the description of GList don't always contain the line

```
GList *list;
```

When a preprocessor directive such as #include appears just before some function calls, then you must use the directive somewhere at the beginning of your source code. This is similar to the style of the online Unix programming manual; run man gethostbyname and look at the SYNOPSIS section.

Functions and Macros

Remember that you can only *call* a function. A macro application often looks very similar to a function call, but it is an *expansion* that takes place before the compiler converts the source into object code. However, in most APIs, it isn't often clear which elements are functions and which are macros, so this text doesn't draw a strict line between the two.

Counting

In C, indices for arrays and fields start at 0. To avoid errors, this book carries this convention to other areas, but especially to lists. One notable example is GLib's list element indexing.

Pathnames

The system for pathnames in this book follows the automake rules. The name $(prefix) refers to the installation prefix for your GNOME installation (for example, /usr or /opt/gnome2).

Pointers and Addresses

GTK+ and GNOME use pointers to pointers extensively. This book sometimes refers to a pointer to a pointer as the *address* of a pointer, because you normally use parameters such as &ptr, where ptr is a pointer.

1

GLIB

1.1 Introduction

The letter *G* is ubiquitous in the world of open-source software; it stands for GNU (Richard Stallman's "GNU's Not Unix"). You'll see it throughout this book in names like GTK+, GLib, GObject, and GNOME, as well as in many other software packages such as Ghostscript and gcc.

To understand the later chapters in this book, you need to learn about a fundamental library called GLib (*libglib-2.0*). It provides basic data structures and utility functions for the GTK+ widget set and GNOME applications in general. This chapter deals with GLib's architecture and introduces the API. You'll see GLib's object system (GObject) in Chapter 2.

You can't really avoid GLib when using GNOME and GTK+. Other libraries such as ORBit use GLib, and many don't depend on any other libraries. The abstractions and utilities that GLib provides are handy for nearly any programming task and simplify ports to other platforms.

This chapter contains no graphical code. It is a concise, point-by-point guide to the most important GLib functions and data structures. You may find this material a bit dry, so you can go directly to Chapter 3 to get started with GTK+. However, you may find yourself regularly looking back to these first two chapters for reference.

1.2 GLib Naming Conventions

As with many other libraries, GLib has naming rules for consistency and readability:

- Function names are always in lowercase, with an underscore between each part of the name: g_timer_new(), g_list_append(). In addition, all function names begin with g_.
- All functions in a library start with a common prefix. In GLib, this prefix is g_.
- Type names contain no underscores, and each component inside starts with a capital letter: GTimer, GList. The names start with G. The notable exceptions to these rules are the elementary types in Section 1.3.
- If a function operates primarily on a certain type, the prefix of this function corresponds to the type name. For example, the g_timer_* functions work with the GTimer type, and g_list_* functions go with GList.

It sounds more complicated than it is.

1.3 Basic Types

To get started with GLib, you should adjust to its elementary types. You might wonder why it is important to use guchar instead of unsigned char. There aren't any real differences as long as you stay on the same platform. However, if you decide that you want to import, export, and interface your software between, say, Windows and Unix, then you'll be thankful that GLib can abstract the basic data types for you.

For example, if you want to do something unpleasant such as define an unsigned integer variable that is exactly 16 bits wide on any potential platform, things can start to look a little ugly in C. Fortunately, GLib takes care of this so that you don't have to get your hands too dirty. The basic types are listed in the table on the opposite page.

To use GLib and all of its types, include the *glib.h* header file in your source code:

```
#include <glib.h>
```

The gpointer and gconstpointer types appear frequently when interacting with the GLib data structures, because they are ***untyped pointers*** to memory. In GLib, functions that use these pointers take responsibility for verifying the type, not the programmer or the compiler. These can be especially handy for type abstraction in callback functions and equality operators used in sorting and iteration.

The GLib header file defines the constants TRUE and FALSE for the gboolean type. However, it's bad style to use equivalence operators with these constants; that is, use if (my_gboolean), not if (my_gboolean == TRUE).

GLib Type	Corresponding Type in C
gchar	char
guchar	unsigned char
gint	int
guint	unsigned int
gshort	short
gushort	unsigned short
glong	long
gulong	unsigned long
gfloat	float
gdouble	double
gint8	int, 8 bits wide
guint8	unsigned int, 8 bits wide
gint16	int, 16 bits wide
guint16	unsigned int, 16 bits wide
gint32	int, 32 bits wide
guint32	unsigned int, 32 bits wide
gint64	int, 64 bits wide
guint64	unsigned int, 64 bits wide
gpointer	void *, untyped pointer
gconstpointer	const void *, constant untyped pointer
gboolean	Boolean value, either TRUE or FALSE

1.4 Basic Utilities

GLib has a number of utilities that simplify everyday interaction with the C
programming language and the system that your program runs on. For functions
dealing with GLib data structures, see Section 1.5.

1.4.1 Memory Management

If you employ GLib's memory management routines, you can save yourself
some headaches — GLib provides additional error checking and diagnostic
functionality. As in C, there isn't much to learn; the table on the next page
provides a reference for the C programmer.

Instead of malloc(), realloc, and free(), you can use g_malloc(), g_realloc(),
and g_free(); they operate in an identical fashion. To allocate memory and
zero out any previous content, use g_malloc0(). Note that its syntax is like malloc,
not calloc().

The advantage of these functions over those in the standard C library is the
built-in error handling. If a problem occurs during runtime, g_error() can step in
to examine it (see Section 1.4.6). With the usual C library, you might be faced
with a core dump if you fail to check the return codes carefully every time you
allocate memory.

GLib Function	Corresponding C Function
gpointer g_malloc(gulong n_bytes)	void *malloc(size_t size) with error handling
gpointer g_malloc0(gulong n_bytes)	like malloc(), but initializes memory as in calloc()
gpointer g_try_malloc(gulong n_bytes)	like malloc() without error checking
gpointer g_realloc(gpointer mem, gulong n_bytes)	void *realloc(void *ptr, size_t size) with error checking
gpointer g_try_realloc(gpointer mem, gulong n_bytes)	realloc() without error checking
void g_free(gpointer mem)	void free(void *ptr)

NOTE *If you have some special reason for inspecting the return code by hand, you can do so with the GLib functions* g_try_malloc() *and* g_try_realloc(), *which work just like their C counterparts — that is, they return* NULL *upon failure. You could use this in a place where the allocated memory isn't critical (for example, in extra buffers meant to improve performance) or when you're running some sort of probe.*

Naturally, if you choose to override GLib's protection mechanism, you need to know exactly what you're doing. For most applications, the normal functions like g_malloc() can save you a lot of code, frustration, and time.

Normal practice dictates that you do not specify the requested memory block size for functions like malloc() and g_malloc() as a concrete number. Instead, you make the compiler or runtime system figure it out from a type size multiple, usually with sizeof(). To make the data types agree, you must apply a cast to the malloc() return value. All of this makes for a mess of parentheses and stars, so GLib offers the macros g_new(), g_new0(), and g_renew(), as demonstrated in this code fragment:

```
typedef struct _footype footype;
footype *my_data;

/* Allocate space for three footype structures (long version) */
my_data = (footype *) g_malloc(sizeof(footype)*3);

/* The abbreviated version using g_new */
my_data = g_new(footype, 3);

/* To initialize the memory to 0, use g_new0 */
my_data = g_new0(footype, 3);

/* Expand this block of memory to four structures (long version) */
my_data = (footype *) g_realloc(my_data, sizeof(footype)*4);

/* Shorter version */
my_data = g_renew(my_data, 4);
```

You can clearly see how g_new() abbreviates g_malloc() and g_renew() is a short form of g_recalloc() in this fragment. In addition, g_new0() is a brief form for invoking g_malloc0().

Remember that you need to use a type with g_new()*, just as you would with* sizeof()*. Something like* b = g_new(a, 1) *(where a is a variable) yields a compilation error. It will be an ugly error because* g_new() *is a macro.*

Memory Chunks

GUI applications tend to repeatedly allocate memory in identically sized blocks (***atoms***). Furthermore, there are relatively few kinds of atoms. GLib uses a mechanism called ***memory chunks*** (GMemChunk) to provide applications with atoms. A chunk consists of several atoms; its block size is the total byte length of the component atoms. Therefore, the block size must be a multiple of the atom size.

Here is an example of how to use g_mem_chunk_new() to request a new memory chunk:

```
GMemChunk my_chunk;

my_chunk = g_mem_chunk_new("My Chunk",          /* name */
                           42,                  /* atom size */
                           42*16,               /* block size */
                           G_ALLOC_AND_FREE);   /* access mode */
```

The g_mem_chunk_new() function has four arguments: a name for the memory chunk that you can use for diagnostics, the size of each atom (here, 42), the overall block size (it's easiest to write this as a multiple of the atom size), and the access mode (see below). The return value is a pointer to the new GMemChunk structure.

A GMemChunk *isn't a data structure. It's a management system for memory fragments that can contain data structures.*

The access mode (or type) gives you control over how to create and deallocate the atoms. There are two modes:

- G_ALLOC_AND_FREE allows you to return individual atoms to the memory pool at any time.
- G_ALLOC_ONLY permits deallocation of atoms only when you dispose of the entire memory chunk. This mode is more efficient than G_ALLOC_AND_FREE.

Here is how an example of how to allocate and free memory atoms in the chunk created in the preceding example:

```
gchar *data[50000];
gint i;

/* allocate 40,000 atoms */
for(i = 0; i < 40000; i++)
{
  data[i] = g_mem_chunk_alloc(my_chunk);
}
```

```
/* allocate 10,000 more atoms and initialize them */
for(i = 40000; i < 50000; i++)
{
   data[i] = g_mem_chunk_alloc0(my_chunk);
}

/* free one atom */
g_mem_chunk_free(my_chunk, data[42]);
```

Here, g_mem_chunk_alloc() and g_mem_chunk_alloc0() make the individual atoms available. They work like g_malloc() and g_malloc0(), returning a pointer to the atom's memory, but they take a GMemChunk structure as the argument instead of a size specification. The g_mem_chunk_free() function takes a pointer to an individual atom, returning it to the unallocated pool of memory.

WARNING   *Remember that you can use* g_mem_chunk_free() *only on atoms of a memory chunk that was created with the* G_ALLOC_AND_FREE *access mode. In addition, never use* g_free() *to free an atom — this will inevitably lead to a segmentation fault, because one of the memory chunk deallocation functions will cause a double* free().

Several functions clean and dispose of atoms in memory chunks, working on an entire memory chunk at once. Here is an example of how to use these functions:

```
/* free up any unused atoms */
g_mem_chunk_clean(my_chunk);

/* free all unused atoms in all memory chunks */
g_blow_chunks();

/* deallocate all atoms in a chunk */
g_mem_chunk_reset(my_chunk);

/* deallocate a memory chunk */
g_mem_chunk_destroy(my_chunk);
```

- g_mem_chunk_clean(*chunk*) examines *chunk* and deallocates any unused memory. This procedure gives you some manual control over the underlying memory management. The g_mem_chunk_free() function doesn't necessarily deallocate an atom's memory immediately; GLib does this when convenient or necessary. g_mem_chunk_clean() forces immediate deallocation.

- g_blow_chunks() runs g_mem_chunk_clean() on *all* outstanding memory chunks in your program.

- g_mem_chunk_reset(*chunk*) frees all atoms in *chunk*, including those in use. Be careful when using this function, because you might have a few lingering pointers to previously allocated atoms.

- g_mem_chunk_destroy(*chunk*) deallocates all atoms of *chunk* and the memory chunk itself.

As is the case for general memory management, GLib provides some macros that can save you some typing:

```
typedef struct _footype footype;
GMemChunk *pile_of_mem;
footype *foo;

/* create a memory chunk with space for 128 footype atoms */
pile_of_mem = g_mem_chunk_new("A pile of memory",
                              sizeof(footype),
                              sizeof(footype)*128,
                              G_ALLOC_AND_FREE);

/* the same thing, with g_mem_chunk_create */
/* the name will be "footype mem chunks (128)" */
pile_of_mem = g_mem_chunk_create(footype, 128, G_ALLOC_AND_FREE);

/* allocate an atom */
foo = (footype *) g_mem_chunk_alloc(pile_of_mem);

/* the same thing, with g_mem_chunk_new */
foo = g_mem_chunk_new(footype, pile_of_mem);

/* the same thing, but zero out the memory */
foo = g_mem_chunk_new0(footype, pile_of_mem);
```

The macros' purposes should be fairly obvious from the code. Note that g_mem_chunk_create() is a shorter way to use g_mem_chunk_new() if you know the atom data type. Note, too, that each macro automatically pieces together the chunk's name. Furthermore, g_mem_chunk_new() and g_mem_chunk_new0() are the memory chunk counterparts of g_new() and g_new0().

If you want to see some statistics on your current memory chunks, use g_mem_chunk_print(chunk) for a brief report on one chunk or use g_mem_chunk_info() to see detailed information for all chunks.

1.4.2   Quarks

To label a piece of data in your program, you usually have two options: a numeric representation or a string. Both have their disadvantages. Numbers are difficult to decipher on their own. If you know roughly how many different labels you need beforehand, you can define an enumeration type and several alphanumeric symbols. However, you can't add a label at run time.

On the other hand, you can add or change strings at run time. They're also easy enough to understand, but string comparison takes longer than arithmetic comparison, and managing memory for strings is an extra hassle that you may not wish to deal with.

GLib has a data type called GQuark that combines the simplicity of numbers with the flexibility of strings. Internally, it is nothing more than an integer that you can compare and copy. GLib maps these numbers to strings that you provide through function calls, and you can retrieve the string values at any time.

To create a quark, use one of these two functions:

```
GQuark quark;
gchar *string;

quark = g_quark_from_string(string);
quark = g_quark_from_static_string("string");
```

Both functions take a string as their only parameter and return the quark. The difference between the two is that g_quark_from_string() makes a copy of the string when it does the mapping, and g_quark_from_static_string() does not.

Be careful with g_quark_from_static_string(). *It saves a tiny bit of memory and CPU every time you call it, but may not be worthwhile because you create an additional dependency in your program that can cause debugging problems later.*

If you want to verify that *string* has a quark value, call

```
g_quark_try_string(string)
```

This function returns the string's quark if the program has already defined the string as a quark. A return value of zero (0) means that no quark corresponds to that string (there are no quarks with a numeric value of zero).

To recover the string from a quark, use

```
string = g_quark_to_string(quark);
```

If successful, this function returns a pointer to the *quark* string. Make sure that you don't run any free() calls on that pointer — it isn't a copy.

Here is a short quark demonstration program:

```
GQuark *my_quark = 0;

my_quark = g_quark_from_string("Chevre");

if (!g_quark_try("Cottage Cheese"))
{
  g_print("There isn't any quark for \"Cottage Cheese\"\n");
}
g_print("my_quark is a representation of %s\n", g_quark_to_string(my_quark));
```

NOTE GQuark *values are numbers assigned to strings and are efficient when tested for equality. However, they have no set numeric order. You can't use the quark values to test for alphabetic order, and thus, you can't use them as sorting keys. If you want to compare the strings that quarks represent, you must extract the strings with* g_quark_to_string() *and then apply an operation like* strcmp() *or* g_ascii_strcasecmp() *to the result.*

1.4.3   C Strings

GLib offers several string functions that interoperate with strings in the standard C library (not to be confused with GString, a GLib-specific string type described in Section 1.5.1). You can use these functions to augment or supplant functions like sprintf(), strdup(), and strstr().

The following functions return a pointer to a newly allocated string that you must deallocate yourself:

- gchar *g_strdup(const gchar *str)
  Copies *str* and returns the copy.

- gchar *g_strndup(const gchar *str, gsize n)
  Copies the first *n* characters of string and returns the copy. The copy always contains an additional character at the end: a NULL terminator.

- gchar *strnfill(gsize *length*, gchar *fill_char*)
  Creates a string that is *length* characters long and sets each character in the string to *fill_char*.

- gchar *g_strdup_printf(const gchar *format*, ...)
  Formats a string and parameters like sprintf(). However, you don't need to create and specify a buffer as you would in sprintf(); GLib does this automatically.

- gchar *g_strdup_vprintf(const gchar *format*, va_list *args*)
  Like the preceding function, but is the analog to vsprintf(), a function that uses C's variable argument facility described on the stdarg(3) manual page.

- gchar *g_strescape(const gchar *source*, const gchar *exceptions*)
  Translates special control characters, backslashes, and quotes in *source* to the normal ASCII range. For example, this function converts a tab to \t. The translations performed are for the backspace (\b), form feed (\f), line feed (\n), carriage return (\r), backslash (\ becomes \\), and double quotes (" becomes \"). Any additional non-ASCII characters translate to their octal representation (for example, escape becomes \27). You can specify any exceptions in the string *exceptions*.

- gchar *g_strcompress(const gchar *source*)
  The reverse of g_strescape(); that is, converts an ASCII-formatted string back to one with real escape characters.

- gchar *g_strconcat(const gchar *string1*, ..., NULL)
  Takes any number of *strings* as parameters and returns their concatenation. You *must* use NULL as the final argument.

- gchar *g_strjoin(const gchar *separator*, ..., NULL)
  Joins a number of strings, adding *separator* between each string. For example, gstrjoin("|", "foo", "bar", NULL) yields "foo|bar". As with g_strconcat(), you must place NULL at the end of the argument list. With a NULL separator, gstrjoin() operates like g_strconcat().

For the following functions, you may need to allocate space for the result; GLib won't make a copy for you. These functions work much like their C counterparts, where one of the arguments contains a buffer large enough for a processed string.

- `gchar *g_stpcpy(gchar *dest, const gchar *src)`
  Copies *src* to *dest*, including the NULL terminator. Upon success, this function returns a pointer to the copy of this terminator in *dest*. This function is useful for efficient string concatenation.

- `gint g_snprintf(gchar *string, gulong n, const gchar *format, ...)`
  Like sprintf(); you must ensure that there is enough space for *string* in the result. However, you must specify the length of this buffer with *n*. The return value is the length of the output string, even if the output is truncated due to an insufficient buffer. This is the C99 standard, *not* the traditional snprintf() behavior that your machine's C library may exhibit.

- `gint g_vsnprintf(gchar *string, gulong n, const gchar *format, va_list list)`
  Like the preceding function, but with variable arguments.

- `gchar *g_strreverse(gchar *string)`
  Reverses the order of the characters in *string*. The return value is also *string*.

- `gchar *g_strchug(gchar *string)`
  Eliminates whitespace from the beginning of *string*, shifting all applicable characters to the left in *string*. Returns *string*.

- `gchar *g_strchomp(gchar *string)`
  Eliminates whitespace from the end of *string*. Returns *string*.

- `gchar *g_strstrip(gchar *string)`
  Eliminates whitespace from the beginning *and* end of *string*. Returns *string*.

- `gchar *g_strdelimit(gchar *string, const gchar *delimiters, gchar *new_delimiter)`
  Changes any characters found in *delimiters* to *new_delimiter*. If *delimiters* is NULL, this function uses "_-|<>."; this is the standard set found in G_STR_DELIMITERS. Returns *string*.

- `gchar *g_strcanon(gchar *string, const gchar *valid_chars, gchar *substituter)`
  Replaces any character in *string* that isn't in *valid_chars* with *substituter*. Returns *string*. Note that this function complements g_strdelimit().

With the exception of g_ascii_dtostr(), these string functions do not alter their arguments:

- `gchar *g_strstr_len(const gchar *haystack, gssize haystack_len, const gchar *needle)`
  Looks through the first *haystack_len* characters of *haystack* for *needle*. This function stops when it finds the first occurrence, returning a pointer to the exact place in *haystack_len*. When this function fails to find *needle*, it returns NULL.

- `gchar *g_strrstr(const gchar *haystack, const gchar *needle)`
  Like g_strstr_len, except that this function returns the *last* incidence of *needle* in *haystack*, and it does not take a size parameter.

- gchar *g_strrstr_len(gchar *haystack, gssize haystack_len, gchar *needle)
  Identical to g_strrstr, except that it searches only the first haystack_len characters of haystack.

- gsize g_printf_string_upper_bound(const gchar *format, va_list args)
  Examines format and args, returning the maximum string length required to store printf() formatting.

- gdouble g_ascii_strtod(const gchar *nptr, gchar **endptr)
  Converts string to a double-length floating-point number. If you supply a valid pointer address for endptr, this function sets the pointer to the last character in string that it used for the conversion. The difference between this function and strtod() is that this function ignores the C locale.

- gchar *g_ascii_dtostr(gchar *buffer, gint buf_len, gdouble d)
  Converts d into an ASCII string, writing into buffer of maximum length buf_len and ignoring the C locale so that the output format is always the same. The resulting string is never longer than G_ASCII_DTOSTR_BUF_SIZE. This function returns a pointer to buffer.

NOTE   *Use g_ascii_strtod() and g_ascii_dtostr() to write to and read from files and data streams, not for anything that people read. Because these functions use a unified, locale-independent format, you'll be protected from certain problems. For example, if someone sets a German locale and runs your program, you won't have to worry about the fact that its locale reverses the meanings of the comma and dot for numbers.*

Finally, here are a few functions that handle arrays of strings (gchar **). NULL pointers terminate these arrays.

- gchar **g_strsplit(const gchar *string, const gchar *delimiter, gint max_tokens)
  Uses delimiter as a guide to chop string into at most max_tokens parts. The return value is a newly allocated array of strings that you must deallocate yourself. If the input string is empty, the return value is an empty array.

- gchar *g_str_joinv(const gchar *separator, gchar **str_array)
  Fuses the array of strings in str_array into a single string and returns it as a newly allocated string. If separator isn't NULL, g_str_joinv() places a copy of it between each component string.

- gchar **g_strdupv(gchar **str_array)
  Returns a complete copy (including each component string) of str_array.

- void **g_strfreev(gchar **str_array)
  Deallocates the array of strings str_array and the strings themselves.

WARNING   *Don't use anything other than g_strfreev() to free up an array of strings returned by a function like g_strsplit() or g_strdupv().*

1.4.4   Unicode and Character Encodings

The traditional C string functions and those in the previous section are byte strings. These functions don't need to worry about the length of an individual character because each gchar is one byte long.

The functions in this section are different, because they work with **Unicode** characters and strings. Unicode is an extensive, unified character set that can encode any character in any language using the Universal Character Set (UCS; see ISO 10646). Unicode was originally a 16-bit encoding. GLib supports three different encoding schemes (see also man utf-8):

- **UCS-4** is the full 32-bit UCS-compatible encoding. Every character is 4 bytes long, with the Unicode character occupying the lower 2 bytes (the other 2 are typically zero). The GLib data type for UCS-4 is gunichar. It is 32 bits wide and is the standard Unicode type. Some functions use UCS-4 strings (gunichar *).

- **UTF-16** is the native encoding (UTF stands for Unicode Transformation Format). Every character is 2 bytes wide. GLib uses the gunichar2 type for characters in UTF-16. As with UCS-4, you will see UTF-16 strings (gunichar2 *).

- **UTF-8** is important in practice, because it is compatible with ASCII. Normal ASCII characters use 8 bits, but other characters may require 2 or more bytes. Therefore, every file in ASCII format contains valid UTF-8 text, but not the other way around. A significant disadvantage is that the nonuniform character width of UTF-8 renders random access in a text file next to impossible; to get to a certain part, you must start from the beginning and iterate over the characters. GLib doesn't have a type for UTF-8 because the characters don't have uniform sizes. However, you can encode UTF-8 strings with normal character strings (gchar *).

GLib generally uses the 32-bit UCS-4 gunichar type as its Unicode standard. The following functions test individual Unicode characters:

- gboolean g_unichar_validate(gunichar c) returns TRUE if c is a valid Unicode character.

- gboolean g_unichar_isdefined(gunichar c) returns TRUE if c has a Unicode assignment.

- gboolean g_unichar_isalnum(gunichar c) returns TRUE if c is a letter or numeral.

- gboolean g_unichar_islower(gunichar c) returns TRUE if c is a lowercase letter.

- gboolean g_unichar_isupper(gunichar c) returns TRUE if c is an uppercase letter.

- gboolean g_unichar_istitle(gunichar c) returns TRUE if c is titlecase.

NOTE *Titlecase doesn't appear much in English (or many other languages, for that matter). A titlecase letter is usually some sort of composite character or ligature where the first part of the composite goes to uppercase when the letter is capitalized at the start of a word. An example is the* Lj *in the Croatian word* Ljubija.[1]

- gboolean g_unichar_isalpha(gunichar c) returns TRUE if c is a letter.

- gboolean g_unichar_isdigit(gunichar c) returns TRUE if c is a base-10 digit.

- gboolean g_unichar_isxdigit(gunichar c) returns TRUE if c is a hexadecimal digit.

- gboolean g_unichar_ispunct(gunichar c) returns TRUE if c is some sort of symbol or punctuation.

---

[1] Thanks to Roman Maurer for this example.

- gboolean g_unichar_isspace(gunichar c) returns TRUE if c is a form of whitespace, including spaces, tabs, and newlines.

- gboolean g_unichar_iswide(gunichar c) returns TRUE if c normally requires twice the space of a normal character to draw on the screen.

- gboolean g_unichar_iscntrl(gunichar c) returns TRUE if c is a Unicode control character.

- gboolean g_unichar_isgraph(gunichar c) returns TRUE if you can print c; that is, if it's not a control character, format character, or space.

- gboolean g_unichar_isprint(gunichar c) is like g_unichar_isgraph(), but also returns TRUE for spaces.

If you have a gunichar character c and want to know its classification in Unicode, you can run

---

g_unichar_type(c)

This function returns one of the following constants (more information in [TUC]):

- G_UNICODE_LOWERCASE_LETTER: Lowercase letter

- G_UNICODE_UPPERCASE_LETTER: Uppercase letter

- G_UNICODE_TITLECASE_LETTER: Titlecase letter

- G_UNICODE_CONTROL: Unicode control character

- G_UNICODE_FORMAT: Unicode formatting character

- G_UNICODE_MODIFIER_LETTER: Modifier (odd-looking letters that modify pronunciation)

- G_UNICODE_SURROGATE: A composite of two 16-bit Unicode characters that represents one character

- G_UNICODE_UNASSIGNED: Currently unassigned character

- G_UNICODE_PRIVATE_USE: Character reserved for private, internal use

- G_UNICODE_OTHER_LETTER: Any miscellaneous letter

- G_UNICODE_COMBINING_MARK: Mark that may be combined with another letter

- G_UNICODE_ENCLOSING_MARK: Mark that contains another letter

- G_UNICODE_NON_SPACING_MARK: Mark that usually requires no space to print; its position depends on another base character

- G_UNICODE_DECIMAL_NUMBER: Digit

- G_UNICODE_DECIMAL_LETTER_NUMBER: Numeral made from a letter

- G_UNICODE_OTHER_NUMBER: Any other numeral

- G_UNICODE_CONNECTION_PUNCTUATION: Binding punctuation

- G_UNICODE_DASH_PUNCTUATION: Dashlike punctuation

- G_UNICODE_OPEN_PUNCTUATION: Opening punctuation (such as a left parenthesis)

- G_UNICODE_CLOSE_PUNCTUATION: Closing punctuation

- G_UNICODE_INITIAL_PUNCTUATION: Starting punctuation

- `G_UNICODE_FINAL_PUNCTUATION`: Terminal punctuation
- `G_UNICODE_OTHER_PUNCTUATION`: Any other punctuation
- `G_UNICODE_CURRENCY_SYMBOL`: Monetary currency symbol
- `G_UNICODE_MODIFIER_SYMBOL`: Modifier symbol (for example, an accent)
- `G_UNICODE_MATH_SYMBOL`: Mathematic symbol
- `G_UNICODE_OTHER_SYMBOL`: Any other odd symbol
- `G_UNICODE_LINE_SEPARATOR`: A line break (for example, a line feed)
- `G_UNICODE_PARAGRAPH_SEPARATOR`: Divides paragraphs
- `G_UNICODE_SPACE_SEPARATOR`: An empty space

Here are some functions for converting single `gunichar` characters:

- `gunichar g_unichar_toupper(gunichar c)`
  Converts c to uppercase if possible and returns the result. It does not modify the character if it has an uppercase version.

- `gunichar g_unichar_tolower(gunichar c)`
  Converts c to lowercase if possible.

- `gunichar g_unichar_totitle(gunichar c)`
  Converts c to titlecase if possible.

- `gint g_unichar_digit_value(gunichar c)`
  Returns the numeric equivalent of c. If c isn't a numeral, this function returns −1.

- `gint g_unichar_xdigit_value(gunichar c)`
  Same as the preceding function, but with hexadecimal numerals.

Now that you know how to do some interesting things with `gunichar` characters, you probably want to know how you can get your hands on this kind of data. For the most part, you must extract Unicode characters from UTF-8-encoded strings, and in the process, you'll want make certain that these strings are valid, navigate them, and read the individual characters.

NOTE *In the functions you're about to see, you can provide a NULL-terminated string, but this isn't always necessary. If a function takes a gssize parameter, you can specify the number of bytes in the UTF-8 string that the function should process. If you want to tell a function to process an entire NULL-terminated string, use -1 as the size.*

- `gboolean g_utf8_validate(const gchar *str, gssize max_len, const gchar **end)`
  Reads at most *max_len* bytes of the UTF-8 string *str*, returning TRUE if the string is valid UTF-8 text. This function returns FALSE upon failure, and you can also specify an address to a gchar pointer as the *end* parameter. The function sets this *end* to the first invalid character in the string when there is a problem. Otherwise, *end* goes to the end of a valid string.

- `gunichar g_utf8_get_char_validated(const gchar *p, gssize max_len)`
  Tries to extract the byte sequence at *p* from a UTF-8 character as a gunichar UCS-4 character, making sure that the sequence is valid UTF-8. This func-

tion returns the converted character upon success. Upon failure, there are two possible return values: (gunichar) –2 if the function ran out of data to process, or –1 if the sequence was invalid.

- gunichar g_utf8_get_char(const gchar *p)
  Converts the UTF-8 character at *p* to a gunichar character and returns this result.

g_utf8_get_char() *doesn't check the validity of its parameters. Use this function for strings that you have already verified with* g_utf8_validate()*. Using these two functions is faster than running* g_utf8_get_char_validated() *on every single character in the string.*

The rest of the functions in this section assume that their input is valid UTF-8. Unpleasant circumstances arise if the string is not UTF-8.

- gchar *g_utf8_next_char(gchar *p)
  Returns a pointer to the character in the UTF-8 string following *p*. Therefore,

```
p = g_utf8_next_char(p);
```

advances a pointer by one character. The pointer should not be at the end of the string. (This is actually a macro in the current GLib implementation, not a function.)

- gchar *g_utf8_find_next_char(const gchar *p, const gchar *end)
  Same as the preceding function, but with *end* pointing to the end of the UTF-8 string *p*. If *end* is NULL, this function assumes that *p* ends with a NULL value. The return value is NULL if *p* already points the end of the string.

- gchar *g_utf8_prev_char(gchar *p)
  Same as the preceding function, but looks back to the previous character. There is no error check, and *p* should not point the start of a string.

- gchar *g_utf8_find_prev_char(const gchar *str, const gchar *p)
  Also returns the character previous to *p*, but provides an additional error check when you specify the start of the string with *str*. This function returns NULL upon failure.

- glong g_utf8_pointer_to_offset(const gchar *str, const gchar *pos)
  Returns the offset (that is, the character index) of *pos* in the UTF-8 string *str*.

- gchar *g_utf8_offset_to_pointer(const gchar *str, const gchar *pos)
  Returns a pointer to the *pos*-th character in the UTF-8 string *str*.

Because the traditional C string library doesn't work on UTF-8 strings, GLib provides some equivalents:

- glong g_utf8_strlen(const gchar *str, gssize max)
  Computes the length (in characters) of *str*. You can specify a maximum byte length with *max*.

- gchar *g_utf8_strncpy(gchar *dest, const gchar *src, gsize n)
  Copies *n* UTF-8 characters from *src* to *dest*. Note that you must allocate the necessary space at *dest*, and that *n* is the number of characters, *not* bytes.

- `gchar *g_utf8_strchr(const gchar *str, gssize len, gunichar c)`
  Returns a pointer to the first occurrence of *c* in *str*, or NULL if the character is not present. Note that *c* must be in the UCS-4 encoding.

- `gchar *g_utf8_strrchr(const gchar *str, gssize len, gunichar c)`
  Same as the preceding function, but looks for the last occurrence of *c* in *str*.

- `gchar *g_utf8_strup(const gchar *str, gssize len)`
  Returns a new copy of *str*, translated to uppercase. This string could have a different length; characters such as the German scharfes S go from one character (ß) to two (SS) when converted to uppercase. You are responsible for deallocating the new string.

- `gchar *g_utf8_strdown(const gchar *str, gssize len)`
  Same as the preceding function, but converts uppercase letters to lowercase. Don't expect a string like NUSSDORFER STRASSE to become Nußdorfer Straße, though; your locale software probably isn't smart enough to get this right.

- `gchar *g_utf8_casefold(const gchar *str, gssize len)`
  Changes the mixed-case version of *str* into a case-independent form and returns the result as a new string. This result isn't suitable for printed output, but works for comparison and sorting.

- `gchar *g_utf8_normalize(const gchar *str, gssize len, GNormalizeMode mode)`
  Produces a *canonical* version of *str*. In Unicode, there are several ways of representing the same character, such as the case of a character with an accent: It can be a single character or a composition of a base character and an accent. To specify *mode*, use one of the following:

    G_NORMALIZE_DEFAULT: Normalize everything that doesn't affect the text content.

    G_NORMALIZE_DEFAULT_COMPOSE: Same as the preceding, but attempt to make composed characters as compact as possible.

    G_NORMALIZE_ALL: Change everything, including text content. For example, this would convert a superscripted numeral to a standard numeral.

    G_NORMALIZE_ALL_COMPOSE: Same as the preceding, but attempt to make composed characters as compact as possible.

NOTE *Before you compare UTF-8 strings, normalize them with the same mode. The strings might have the same value but slightly different encoding styles that a comparison function won't recognize.*

- `gint *g_utf8_collate(const gchar *str1, const gchar *str2)`
  Compares the UTF-8 strings *str1* and *str2* linguistically (at least as much as possible). If *str1* is less than *str2* in the sort order, the return value is –1; if the strings are equal, 0 is the result; and if *str2* comes before *str1*, this function returns 1.

- gchar *g_utf8_collate_key(const gchar *str, gssize len)
  Returns a sorting key for str. If you compare two of these keys with strcmp(), the result will be the same as a comparison of their original strings with g_utf8_collate().

NOTE *If you compare a number of UTF-8 strings frequently (for example, if you're sorting them), then you should obtain keys for all of the strings and use strcmp() as your comparison function. This approach is much faster than using g_utf8_collate() every time, because that function normalizes its parameters every time it runs, and that involves not only a bit of computation, but also memory management time.*

Several conversion functions translate strings among the different Unicode encoding schemes. In general, they take a string str as input and produce a freshly allocated NULL-terminated string with the same content in a different format. Some of these functions have an items_read parameter, which is actually a pointer to an integer; it can write the number of base units converted to this integer (here, base units refers to the number of bytes in UTF-8, 16-bit words in UTF-16, and 32-bit words in UCS-4). Therefore, if you want a function to store this count in a variable i, you would pass &i as the items_read parameter to the function. Similarly, you can employ the items_written parameter to record the number of characters written to the output stream. You can use NULL for both of these parameters if you don't care about this information.

If the input is in UTF-8 format, and items_read is NULL, an error will occur when an incomplete character occurs at the end of the input string (str). If you want to find out what this (or any other) error is, use the address of a GError pointer as the error parameter (see the "Error Codes" section on the next page; the error class is G_CONVERT_ERROR). These functions return NULL on failure:

- gunichar2 *g_utf8_to_utf16(const gchar *str, glong len, glong *items_read, glong *items_written, GError **error)
  Converts a UTF-8 string to a UTF-16 string.

- gunichar *g_utf8_to_ucs4(const gchar *str, glong len, glong *items_read, glong *items_written, GError **error)
  Converts a UTF-8 string to a UCS-4 string.

- gunichar *g_utf8_to_ucs4_fast(const gchar *str, glong len, glong *items_written)
  Same as the preceding function, but roughly twice as fast, because it doesn't perform any error checking. Consequently, this function doesn't have the items_read and error parameters.

- gunichar *g_utf16_to_ucs4(const gunichar2 *str, glong len, glong *items_read, glong *items_written, GError **error)
  Converts UTF-16 to UCS-4.

- gchar *g_utf16_to_utf8(const gunichar2 *str, glong len, glong *items_read, glong *items_written, GError **error)
  Converts UTF-16 to UTF-8.

- gunichar2 *g_ucs4_to_utf16(const gunichar *str, glong len, glong *items_read, glong *items_written, GError **error)
  Converts UCS-4 to UTF-16.

- `gchar *g_ucs4_to_utf8(const gunichar *str, glong len, glong *items_read, glong *items_written, GError **error)`
  Converts UCS-4 to UTF-8.

- `gint *g_unichar_to_utf8(gunichar c, gchar *outbuf)`
  Stores the UCS-4 character *c* as a UTF-8 character in *outbuf*. You must reserve at least 6 bytes in this buffer. The return value is the number of bytes written to the buffer. If *outbuf* is NULL, this function doesn't perform any translation; it simply reports the size of *c* in UTF-8.

Finally, a number of functions perform translations between Unicode and other character encodings:

- `gchar *g_locale_to_utf8(const gchar *str, glong len, glong *items_read, glong *items_written, GError **error)`
  Changes a string from your current locale's character encoding to UTF-8. This function (and those that follow) work just like the previous conversion functions.

- `gchar *g_filename_to_utf8(const gchar *opsysstring, glong len, glong *items_read, glong *items_written, GError **error)`
  Converts the filename *opsysstring* from your operating system to UTF-8.

- `gchar *g_filename_to_uri(const char *filename, const char *hostname, GError **error)`
  Combines *filename* and *hostname* into a UTF-8-encoded URI (Uniform Resource Identifier; URLs are a subset of these). The *filename* string must be a full pathname. You can specify NULL for *hostname*.

- `gchar *g_locale_from_utf8(const gchar *utf8string, glong len, glong *items_read, glong *items_written, GError **error)`
  The opposite operation of g_locale_to_utf8(); this function translates *utf8string* into your current locale.

- `gchar *g_filename_from_utf8(const gchar *utf8string, glong len, glong *items_read, glong *items_written, GError **error)`
  Same as the preceding function, but the result is a filename that your operating system understands.

- `gchar *g_filename_from_uri(const gchar *uri, char **hostname, GError **error)`
  Takes a *uri* value in UTF-8 encoding and produces its filename. If there is a hostname in *uri* as well, this function will extract it and set the pointer *hostname* to the hostname. If you don't care about the hostname, you can set this parameter to NULL.

Error Codes

The G_CONVERT_ERROR error class contains the following conditions:

- `G_CONVERT_ERROR_NO_CONVERSION`: The requested conversion is impossible.
- `G_CONVERT_ERROR_ILLEGAL_SEQUENCE`: The input string contains an invalid byte sequence.
- `G_CONVERT_ERROR_FAILED`: The translation failed for an unknown reason.
- `G_CONVERT_ERROR_PARTIAL_INPUT`: The input string isn't complete.

- G_CONVERT_ERROR_BAD_URI: The input URI isn't valid.

- G_CONVERT_ERROR_NOT_ABSOLUTE_PATH: A path given as input wasn't an absolute path, as required by a function like g_filename_to_uri().

1.4.5   Timer

The Gtimer is nothing more than a stopwatch that is as accurate as your system clock. Here is a demonstration:

```
/* gtimerdemo.c -- demonstration of GTimer */

#include <glib.h>
#define DURATION 200000

int main(int argc, char **argv)
{
  GTimer *clock = NULL;
  gint i;
  gdouble elapsed_time;
  gulong us;  /* microseconds */

  clock = g_timer_new();
  g_timer_start(clock);
  g_print("Timer started.\n");

  g_print("Loop started.. ");
  for (i = 0; i < DURATION; i++) { ; }
  /* wasting CPU time like this is only allowed in programming examples */

  g_print("and finished.\n");
  g_timer_stop(clock);
  g_print("Timer stopped.\n");

  elapsed_time = g_timer_elapsed(clock, &us);
  g_print("Elapsed: %g s\n", elapsed_time);
  g_print("         %ld us\n", us);

  g_timer_destroy(clock);

  return 0;
}
```

This small program illustrates everything that you need to know about GTimer. The clock variable is a pointer to a GTimer structure, initially set to NULL. To create one of these structures, the program calls g_timer_new(); it sets clock to the return value (a GTimer pointer to the new structure).

The g_timer_start() function starts the stopwatch. The program runs through a loop that does nothing but waste processor time.[2] Afterward, it uses g_timer_stop() to halt the timer.

To retrieve the current state of the timer, call

```
time = g_timer_elapsed(timer, us_ptr);
```

The return value is the elapsed time in seconds, represented as a double-width floating-point number. In addition, you can obtain the fractional part of the elapsed time in microseconds (millionths of a second) with g_timer_elapsed() if you provide a pointer to a gulong variable as *us_ptr*. Because this number does *not* include the whole numbers of seconds, you must multiply the integral part of the second count (obtained by a type cast) by one million and add it if you want a total number of microseconds.

NOTE   *If you don't care about microseconds, set* us_ptr *to* NULL.

You can reset a GTimer structure with g_timer_reset(timer), and you can remove one that is no longer needed with g_timer_destroy(timer).

1.4.6   Message Logging

To help with runtime error diagnosis, GLib offers several utilities for logging messages to the system console. These are, in order of the priority levels:

1. g_message() for informative messages indicating normal runtime behavior
2. g_warning() for warnings or problems that won't cause errant operation (at least not yet)
3. g_critical() for warnings that likely *are* going to matter
4. g_error() for fatal errors; calling this function terminates your program

These utilities take parameters like printf() — that is, a format string followed by a list of substitution parameters. You don't need to put a newline at the end of the format, though. To ensure that you and your users know that these messages come from your software, you should set the G_LOG_DOMAIN macro when you compile. This can be a short identification string that identifies the application or library. Most GNOME-based programs define G_LOG_DOMAIN with a compiler option like -DG_LOG_DOMAIN=\"*name*\".

This program shows all four message logging types:

```
/* messagedemo.c -- show logging features */

#include <glib.h>

#define NR 42

int main(int argc, char **argv)
```

---

[2] If you compile this program, disable your optimizer so that it doesn't eliminate this loop.

```
{
  g_message("Coffee preparation engaged");
  g_warning("Bean canister #%d empty", NR);
  g_critical("Water flow failure");
  g_error("Heating element incinerated");

  /* this program shouldn't reach this point */
  return 0;
}
```

The output should look something like this:

```
** Message: Coffee preparation engaged

** (process:3772): WARNING **: Bean canister #42 empty

** (process:3772): CRITICAL **: Water flow failure

** ERROR **: Heating element incinerated
aborting...
```

Marking Levels as Fatal

The g_error() call in the preceding program yields an error message telling you that the program is about to abort (and perhaps produce a core dump). You can configure other log priority levels as fatal so that they behave in the same way. For example,

```
g_log_set_always_fatal(G_LOG_LEVEL_WARNING|G_LOG_LEVEL_CRITICAL)
```

sets this behavior for warning and critical messages. This function's argument is a bit mask that you create by applying bitwise OR to any of the following constants:

- G_LOG_LEVEL_CRITICAL
- G_LOG_LEVEL_WARNING
- G_LOG_LEVEL_MESSAGE
- G_LOG_LEVEL_INFO
- G_LOG_LEVEL_DEBUG

NOTE   *If an application uses GTK+ or GNOME libraries, you can also supply --g-fatal-warnings as a command-line option to make all warning levels fatal.*

Free-Form Messages

If you have have a message that doesn't fit the mold or tone of the preformatted logging utilities, you can send it to the console with g_print() or g_printerr(). The g_print() function works like printf(), sending its output to the standard output (stdout). g_printerr() sends to the stderr, the standard error.

Unlike message logging tools like g_message(), g_print() *and* g_printerr() *require that you specify your own line break at the end of your message.*

You may be wondering why you can't just use fprintf() with the desired output stream to do this work. Believe it or not, this function may not work well on a Windows system. Another reason is that you can define your own message-processing functions that can alter the log messages and send them output to any place that you want (such as a dialog window or log file). Here is an example:

```c
/* printhandlerdemo.c */

#include <stdio.h>
#include <glib.h>

#define N 1

/* print messages in ALL CAPS */
void my_printerr_handler(gchar *string)
{
  GString *msg;

  msg = g_string_new(string);
  msg = g_string_ascii_up(msg);
  fprintf(stderr, "%s\n", msg->str);
  g_string_free(msg, TRUE);
}

int main(int argc, char **argv)
{
  /* print to stdout */
  g_print("If you lie %d time, no one believes you.\n", N);

  /* print to stderr */
  g_printerr("Ouch.\n");

  /* but if you lie all of the time... */
  g_set_printerr_handler((GPrintFunc)my_printerr_handler);
  g_printerr("%d. Ouch. Ouch. Ouch. (Hey, that really hurts.)", N);

  return 0;
}
```

You'll see how the string functions in my_printerr_handler() work in Section 1.5.1. Here is this program's output:

```
If you lie 1 time, no one believes you.
Ouch.
1. OUCH. OUCH. OUCH. (HEY, THAT REALLY HURTS.)
```

As you can see, you set print handlers with g_set_print_handler() and g_set_printerr_handler(). Their only argument is a GPrintFunc function. The type definition is as follows:

```
typedef void (*GPrintFunc) (const gchar *string);
```

Therefore, your handler must be a void function with a single string argument.

There are two more functions that you should know about when constructing your own error messages: g_strerror() and g_strsignal(). These are platform-independent implementations of strerror() and strsignal(). The g_strerror() function takes an error code such as EBADF or EINVAL and converts it to a slightly more comprehensible message such as "Bad file descriptor" or "Invalid argument." Similarly, g_strsignal() returns the name of a signal when given a numeric signal code.

The advantages of these functions over strerror() and strsignal() are not just that they're platform independent, but that they also create UTF-8 output suitable as input for other libraries, such as GTK+.

1.4.7 Debugging Functions

GLib has several facilities that can help you find bugs in your program. Two of these are macros that take the place of normal return statements. In addition to breaking out of the function, they log a G_LOG_LEVEL_CRITICAL message. Therefore, you can use them in places that your program should not reach in normal operation:

- g_return_if_reached() for void functions.
- g_return_val_if_reached(val) for other functions, where you need to return a value val.

Two other similar convenience macros are

```
g_return_if_fail(test)
g_return_val_if_fail(test, val)
```

If test is false, the function returns, logging a message in the process. You often see these at the beginning of GNOME functions, checking for valid parameters.

There are two more macros that carry out the rudimentary *contract* concept — the assertion, where a certain condition must hold in order for a program to proceed in any meaningful sense:

- g_assert() halts the program with g_error() if its parameter evaluates to FALSE.
- g_assert_not_reached() doesn't take a parameter; it simply stops the program with an error message.

You'll find assertions throughout this book, as well as in most GNOME applications. In addition, most of the functions in the GNOME platform libraries use these safety features to protect against inappropriate arguments.

If your program is far enough along that you're sure that you don't need any assertions, you can set the G_DISABLE_ASSERT macro when you compile (for example, give the compiler a -DG_DISABLE_ASSERT flag). This disables all assertions and saves a little processor time, because it eliminates the tests.

1.4.8 Exception Handling with Error Reporting

The routines in the previous section help diagnose and eliminate serious runtime errors. However, these won't help you much with nonfatal errors that your program can overcome, ignore, or treat in a special way. For example, if a graphical application can't open a file selected from a pop-up file browser, you normally don't want the whole application to abort. Instead, you prefer it to find out just what the problem was, perhaps put up a dialog box, and do whatever it would do if you clicked the file browser's Cancel button.

People tend to refer to these types of errors as *exceptions* and ways to compensate for them as *exception handling* (the online GLib manual uses the term *error reporting*). The traditional C style is for functions to return special error codes to test after a call; some functions provide additional details (for example, through the errno global variable). Higher-level languages often provide special syntax, such as try{}, throw(), catch(){}, and the like in C++ and Java.

GLib doesn't have any complex features like these because it uses C. However, it does provide a system called GError that's a little easier to use than the usual do-it-yourself method in C. The GError data structure is at the core; how you use this structure is just as important as its implementation.

GError and GError Functions

Functions that use GError take the *address* of a GError pointer as their last parameter. If you want to use a variable err declared with GError *err, you must pass it as &err. In addition, you should set the pointer's value to 0. You can specify NULL as this parameter if you like; in that case, the function will disable its error reporting.

A GError structure has the following fields:

- domain (type GQuark): The domain or class of the error; a label for the module or subsystem where the error occurs. Every error domain must have a macro definition with the format *PREFIX_MODULE*_ERROR (for example, G_FILE_ERROR). The macro expands to a form that returns the quark's numeric value.

- code (type gint): The error code; that is, the specific error inside the error domain. Every possible error code requires a corresponding symbol of the form *PREFIX_MODULE*_ERROR_*CODE* in an enumeration type called *PrefixModule*Error (for example, G_FILE_ERROR_TYPE in GFileError).

- message (type gchar *): A complete description of the error, in plain language.

The following fragment demonstrates how to read an error condition from a function (do_something()) that uses GError:

```
GError *error = NULL;

/* use this GError variable as last argument */
do_something(arg1, arg2, &error);

/* was there an error? */
if (error != NULL)
{
  /* report the message */
  g_printerr("Error when doing something: %s\n", error->message);

  /* free error structure */
  g_error_free(error);
}
```

You can see from this code that you need to deallocate the error structure with g_error_free() after you're finished. Therefore, if you supply a GError parameter to a function, you should always check it; otherwise, you risk a memory leak.

If you want to do something other than report the error, you'll probably want to know the error domain and code. Instead of checking this by hand, you should use g_error_matches(), a function that matches errors against domains and codes. The first argument is the GError structure, the second is an error domain, and the third is a specific error code. If the error matches the domain and code, the function returns TRUE; otherwise, it returns FALSE. Here is an example:

```
GError *error = NULL;
gchar *filename;
BluesGuitar *fender, *bender;

<< .. >>

filename = blues_improvise(fender, BLUES_A_MAJOR, &error);
if (error != NULL)
{
  /* see if the expensive guitar is broken */
  if (g_error_matches(error, BLUES_GUITAR_ERROR, BLUES_GUITAR_ERROR_BROKEN))
  {
    /* if so, try the cheap guitar */
    g_clear_error(&error);
    filename = blues_improvise(bender, BLUES_A_MAJOR, &error);
  }
}

/* if nothing's working, default to Clapton */
if (error != NULL)
```

```
{
  filename = g_strdup("clapton-1966.wav");
  g_error_free(error);
}

blues_play(filename);
```

In this example, `blues_improvise()` runs, returning a filename if there wasn't a problem. However, if an error occurs, the program checks to see if the code was `BLUES_GUITAR_ERROR_BROKEN` in the `BLUES_GUITAR_ERROR` domain. If this was the problem, the program tries one more time with different parameters. Before this attempt, it clears error with `g_clear_error()`, a function that frees the `GError` structure and resets the pointer to `NULL`.

If there is something in error after this second try, indicating that something still isn't working right, the program gives up. Instead of trying any more `blues_improvise()` calls, it uses a default filename (`"clapton-1966.wav"`) so that `blues_play()` can do its thing.

WARNING   *After you use a `GError` * structure, immediately deallocate it and reset the pointer. GError-enabled functions can't use the same pointer to several errors at the same time; there's space for only one error. As mentioned earlier, your program will have a memory leak if you do not free the `GError` memory.*

Defining Your Own Error Conditions

To use the GError system to report errors in your own functions, do the following:

1. Define an error domain by creating an appropriately named macro that expands to a unique `GQuark` value.
2. Define all of the error code symbols with an enumeration type.
3. Add a `GError` ** argument at the end of each of the functions where you want to use GError (that is, this argument is a pointer to a pointer to a `GError` structure). If the function uses variable arguments, put this parameter just before the va_args list (...).
4. In the places where your function has detected an error, create a fresh `GError` structure and fill it in accordingly.

Here is a definition of an error domain and some codes:

```
/* define the error domain */
#define MAWA_DOSOMETHING_ERROR (mawa_dosomething_error_quark())

GQuark mawa_dosomething_error_quark(void)
{
  static GQuark q = 0;
  if (q == 0)
  {
    q = g_quark_from_static_string("mawa-dosomething-error");
```

```
  }
  return(q);
}

/* and the error codes */
typedef enum {
  MAWA_DOSOMETHING_ERROR_PANIC,
  MAWA_DOSOMETHING_ERROR_NO_INPUT,
  MAWA_DOSOMETHING_ERROR_INPUT_TOO_BORING,
  MAWA_DOSOMETHING_ERROR_FAILED   /* abort code */
}
```

Take a close look at the definition of mawa_dosomething_error_quark() in the preceding example. It creates new quark for the error domain if none exists, but stores the result in a static variable q so that it doesn't have to perform any additional computation on successive calls.

This fragment illustrates how to use the new domain and codes:

```
void mawa_dosomething_simple(GError **error)
{
  gint i;
  gboolean it_worked;

  << do something that sets it_worked to TRUE or FALSE >>

  if (!it_worked)
  {
    g_set_error(error,
                MAWA_DOSOMETHING_ERROR,
                MAWA_DOSOMETHING_ERROR_PANIC,
                "Panic in do_something_simple(), i = %d", i);
  }
}
```

This function "does something," and if it fails, it uses g_set_error() to set the error condition before it returns. This function takes the error pointer address as its first argument, and if that isn't NULL, sets the pointer to a newly allocated GError structure. The g_set_error() function fills the fields of this structure with the third and fourth arguments (the error domain and code); the remaining arguments are the printf() format string and a parameter list that become the GError's message field.

If you want to use the error code from another function, you need to take special care:

```
void mawa_dosomething_nested(GError **error)
{
  gint i;
  gboolean it_worked;
```

```
GError *simple_error = NULL;

<< do something >>

if (!it_worked)
{
    g_set_error(error,
                MAWA_DOSOMETHING_ERROR,
                MAWA_DOSOMETHING_ERROR_PANIC,
                "Panic in do_something_nested(), i = %d", i);
    return;
}

do_something_simple(&simple_error);
if (simple_error != NULL)
{

    << additional error handling >>

    g_propagate_error(error, simple_error);
}
}
```

In mawa_dosomething_nested(), a similar error initialization occurs if the first part of the function fails. However, this functoin goes on to call do_something_simple() if the first part worked. Because the function can set an error condition, it would make sense to send that error condition back to the original caller. To do this, the function first collects the do_something_simple() condition in simple_error; then it uses g_propagate_error() to transfer the GError structure from simple_error to error.

WARNING *Never pass a GError ** pointer that you got as a parameter to any other function. If it happens to be NULL, your program will crash when you try to dereference (access) anything behind it.*

To send an error obtained from a function to some other place, use

g_propagate_error(*error_dest, error_src*)

Here, *error_dest* is the destination of the error as a GError **, and *error_src* is the source as GError *. If the destination isn't NULL, this function simply copies the source to the destination. However, if the destination is in fact NULL, the function frees the source error.

You might have noticed by now that GError tries hard to achieve transparency with respect to NULL, so that you don't have to worry about memory leaks or extra GError pointers when you don't care about the specific nature of the error. In addition, if one of your functions encounters NULL as the error condition, you can take this as a hint that the user doesn't desire any special error treatment and perhaps wants the function to patch up the problem as much as possible.

You should always keep in mind that GError is a fairly workable tool for dealing with exceptions, but only if you stick to the conventions.

1.5   Data Structures

GLib has a number of standard implementations for common data structures, including lists, trees, and hash tables. As is the case for other GLib modules, the names for each data type's functions share a common prefix (for example, g_list_ for lists).

1.5.1   Strings

The standard fixed-length, NULL-terminated strings in C are occasionally error prone, not terribly easy to handle, and not to everyone's taste. Therefore, GLib provides an alternative called GString, similar to the length-tracked string in most Pascal implementations. A GString data structure grows upon demand so that there's never a question of falling off the end of the string. GLib manages its length at all times, and therefore, it doesn't need a special terminating character when it contains binary data. GLib functions that use this data type begin with g_string_.

NOTE   *The processing functions for GLib lists, arrays, and strings use a pointer to the data structure as their first parameter and return a pointer to the data structure as their return value. A typical statement might look like this:*

```
foo = g_string_do_something(foo, bar);
```

You should always remember to reassign the pointer to whatever the function returns, because you can lose track of the data if the function decides to alter its memory location.

This code shows how to create and initialize the GString type:

```
#include <glib.h>

GString *s1, *s2;

s1 = g_string_new("Shallow Green");
s2 = g_string_sized_new(50);
s2 = g_string_assign(s2, "Deep Purple");
g_print("%s\n", s2->str);
```

Here, g_string_new() takes a normal C string as a parameter and returns a pointer to a new GString string. On the other hand, if you want to assign a C string to a GString string that already exists, use

```
string = g_string_assign(string, c_string);
```

The str field in GString points to the current contents of the string. As illustrated in the preceding example, you can use it just as you would a regular C string. GLib manages the NULL terminator for you.

If you have a fairly good idea of how much text you're going to store in a GString structure, use

```
g_string_sized_new(size)
```

to reserve size bytes in advance. This can save some time later if you have a string that slowly grows.

As mentioned earlier, a GString string can contain binary data, including NULL bytes. Naturally, when you initialize these strings, you need to specify the length of the data along with the data itself, because there is no universal terminating character. To allocate such a string, use

```
g_string_new_len(initial_data, length)
```

Adding Characters

All of the functions below return GString *:

- g_string_append(GString *gstring, const gchar *str)
  Adds a str value to the end of gstring.

- g_string_append_c(GString *gstring, gchar c)
  Adds c to gstring.

- g_string_append_unichar(GString *gstring, gunichar c)
  Adds the Unicode character c to gstring.

If you want to insert something at the very beginning of a string, use the g_string_prepend functions; their names are otherwise as described in the preceding list.

The g_string_insert functions are the same, except that they take an additional index argument (for the index of where to insert in the string; the first index is 0):

- g_string_insert(GString *gstring, gssize pos, const gchar *str)
- g_string_insert_c(GString *gstring, gssize pos, gchar c)
- g_string_insert_unichar(GString *gstring, gssize pos, gunichar c)

The following code demonstrates five of these functions on a string called s1.

```
s1 = g_string_assign(s1, "ar");
s1 = g_string_append(s1, "gh");
s1 = g_string_prepend(s1, "aa");
s1 = g_string_prepend_c(s1, 'A');
```

```
s1 = g_string_insert(s1, 4, "rr");

g_print("%s\n", s1->str);          /* prints "Aaaarrrgh" */
```

To insert binary data into a GString string, use these functions:

- g_string_append_len(GString *gstring, gssize pos, const gchar *str, gssize length)

- g_string_prepend_len(GString *gstring, gssize pos, const gchar *str, gssize length)

- g_string_insert_len(GString *gstring, gssize pos, const gchar *str, gssize length)

Removing Characters

You can pull characters out of a GString string at an arbitrary location with

```
g_string_erase(string, index, num_to_remove)
```

To chop a string down to a certain length, use

```
g_string_truncate(desired_length)
```

where *desired_length* is the final length of the string. If you try to truncate a string to a size that is actually larger than the string, nothing happens. If, however, you also want the string's allocated size to grow to that length, this function can truncate and expand:

```
g_string_set_size(desired_length)
```

NOTE   *The new data at the end of such a newly expanded string is undefined. This result typically doesn't make a difference in practice, because GLib terminates the original string with a NULL byte.*

Here are some examples of these functions in action:

```
s1 = g_string_assign(s1, "Anyway");
s1 = g_string_erase(s1, 4, 1);
/* s1 should now be "Anywy" */
s1 = g_string_truncate(s1, 3);

g_print("%s\n", s1->str);          /* prints "Any" */
```

Miscellaneous String Functions

The following are miscellaneous string functions:

- g_string_equal(*string1*, *string2*)
  Compares *string1* and *string2* and returns TRUE if they match. Note that this function is not like strcmp().

- g_string_hash(*string*)

  Returns a 31-bit hash key for *string*. See Section 1.5.5 for more information on hash keys.

- g_string_printf(*string, format, ...*)

  Similar to sprintf(), except that it stores the output in GString *string*. The return value is a GString string and like the other string manipulation functions.

- g_string_append_printf(*string, format, ...*)

  Same as the preceding function, but appends the result to *string* instead of replacing the previous value.

Deallocating Strings

Deallocate GString *string* with

g_string_free(*string, free_orig*)

Here, *free_orig* is a gboolean value that indicates whether the string should be completely deallocated. If you do want to return all of the data to the free memory pool, g_string_free() returns NULL. However, if you want to keep the actual string data in memory, use FALSE as *free_orig*; the function returns the str field of the structure that you just destroyed. Just remember that you're now responsible for deallocating that data as well with g_free(). Here are two examples:

```
gchar *orig_str;

orig_str = g_string_free(s1, TRUE);
/* s1 and all of its fields are now gone;
   orig_str is NULL */

orig_str = g_string_free(s2, TRUE);
/* s1 is gone;
   orig_str points to its old str field */
```

1.5.2 Lists

One of the simplest but most important data structures is the linked list. Implementing linked lists along with their elementary operations is more or less a finger exercise for experienced programmers.

That doesn't mean that their implementations are bug free, though, and who wants to write yet another linked-list library? GLib provides a GList data type and functions for doubly linked lists. (It also provides a GSList data type for singly linked lists, but this book doesn't cover those.)

Creating Lists

Creating a list is easy:

```
#include <glib.h>

GList *list = NULL;
```

In all of the examples that follow, list will be the general pointer to the list or the list's handle. You must initialize all new, empty lists to NULL.

NOTE *There's no special function to create a list; the NULL GList pointer is all you need.*

A list consists of linked *elements*, sometimes called *nodes*. Each element is a GList structure that contains an untyped pointer (gpointer) to a block of data. Make sure you always know which pointer goes to an element and differentiate it from the pointer *in* the element that points to the actual data.

You can use any type that you like; the compiler won't care as long as you use the proper type cast. Most lists contain data of only one type; mixing types in lists requires an additional layer of bookkeeping and is somewhat inefficient and problematic.

NOTE *GLib manages the whole list with the pointer to the first node. However, a GList pointer also serves as a list iterator. When you program with GList structures, make sure that you keep careful track of your pointers.*

Adding List Elements

To append a node to the end of a list, use g_list_append():

```
gint *data_ptr;

data_ptr = g_new(gint, 1);
*data_ptr = 42;
list = g_list_append(list, (gpointer)data_ptr);
```

This fragment declares a new pointer data_ptr and sets it to a newly allocated data block. It then sets the memory block to the integer 42. Then g_list_append() takes the list handle as the first argument and the data pointer as the second; note that you must cast the data pointer to gpointer.

NOTE *All of the list examples in this section use integer data types.*

As you might suspect from the name, g_list_prepend() operates just like the append function, except that it places the new element at the beginning of the list instead of the end.

NOTE *Keep in mind that g_list_prepend() doesn't need to run through the entire list from the list handle to find the end, and therefore is more efficient than its appending counterpart. If you need to add a lot nodes to a list, it is often faster to prepend them and then perhaps use g_list_reverse() if they are not in the desired order.*

You can also insert elements at any arbitrary place in the list with

```
g_list_insert(list, data, index)
```

Here, *list* and *data* are as usual, but the third parameter is an index. Note that the new element goes into the place just *after index*, not before. Here's an example:

```
GList *tmp;

/* Insert 2003 after the third element */
data_ptr = g_new(gint, 1);
*data_ptr = 2001;
list = g_list_insert(list, data_ptr, 3);

/* Find the list element that was just inserted... */
tmp = g_list_find(list, data_ptr);

/* ...and insert 2000 before that element */
data_ptr = g_new(gint, 1);
*data_ptr = 2000;
list = g_list_insert_before(list, tmp, data_ptr);
```

If you'd rather have a new element put in place before a certain element, try

```
g_list_insert_before(list, node, data)
```

Notice that the parameters are different; here, the second parameter *node* is an element in list, *not* an index. The third parameter is the new data block; it will occupy a new node preceding *node*.

Navigating a List

The previous example used

```
g_list_find(list, data)
```

to find the node for *data* in *list*. This function searches the list and returns a pointer to a GList node that contains the same data block address if one happens to exist in the list (upon failure, it returns NULL). This process is not particularly efficient, because a list may require complete traversal before the function finds (or fails to find) a certain node.

There are several other functions for moving around a list. It's perhaps best to illustrate how they work with an example:

```
GList *list, *ptr;
gint *data_ptr;
```

```
gint pos, length;

   << create a list in "list" variable >>

/* point to element at position 3 */
ptr = g_list_nth(list, 3);

/* point to the element _before_ position 3 */
ptr = g_list_nth_prev(list, 3);

/* advance to the next element in the list */
ptr = g_list_next(ptr);

/* record current position of ptr in list */
pos = g_list_position(list, ptr);

/* move back one element */
ptr = g_list_prev(ptr);

/* access the data in position 4 */
data_ptr = g_list_nth_data(list, 4);

/* record position of data_ptr */
pos = g_list_index(list, data_ptr);

/* change data in first and last elements to 42 */
ptr = g_list_first(list);
*(gint *)(ptr->data) = 42;
ptr = g_list_last(list);
*(gint *)(ptr->data) = 42;

/* also change the next-to-last element to 42 */
*(gint *)(ptr->prev->data) = 42;

/* record the length of the list */
length = g_list_length(list);
```

The random-access functions in the preceding program are as follows:

- g_list_nth(*list*, *n*): Returns the node at position *n*.
- g_list_nth_prev(*list*, *n*): Returns the node just before position *n*.
- g_list_nth_data(*list*, *n*): Returns a pointer to the data block of the node at position *n*.
- g_list_first(*list*): Returns the first node in a list.
- g_list_last(*list*): Returns the last node in a list.

NOTE *Keep in mind that a list's first position is 0.*

If you have a pointer to *node* in a list, you can use it as the parameter for the following functions:

- g_list_next(*node*): Returns the next node.
- g_list_prev(*node*): Returns the previous node.

These operations pertain to a node's position (or index):

- g_list_position(*list, node*): Returns the position of a node in a list.
- g_list_index(*list, data*): Returns the position of a node in *list* that contains *data* — basically, the reverse of g_list_nth_data().
- g_list_length(*list*): Returns *list* length.

If you know what you're doing, you can move list nodes around by following the pointers that make up a node, as the last few parts of the example code show. In addition to changing the memory behind data, you can follow the next and prev pointers to access adjacent nodes. Notice that the preceding example uses ptr->prev->data. You can use this approach only if you are absolutely sure that ptr->prev isn't NULL.

Removing Elements

Deleting elements from a list is a little different than you might expect. Remember that you are responsible for the management of each node's data, and just as you created space for each data block, you must also free this space when you're done with it. However, you don't have to worry about the actual nodes.

The functions for removing elements from a *list* are

```
g_list_remove(data)
g_list_remove_all(data)
```

Notice that they do not take an index or a pointer to a node as the node to remove; instead, they want a pointer to the target node's *data block*. The idea is that because you probably need to do something with the data block anyway, you should always be able to find it after you delete a node that pointed to it.

This short example shows the functions in action:

```
/* create a 42 */
data_ptr = g_new(gint, 1);  *data_ptr = 42;

/* place three identical 42s at the beginning of a list */
list = g_list_prepend(list, (gpointer)data_ptr);
list = g_list_prepend(list, (gpointer)data_ptr);
list = g_list_prepend(list, (gpointer)data_ptr);

/* remove the first 42 */
list = g_list_remove(list, (gconstpointer)data_ptr);

/* remove the rest of them */
list = g_list_remove_all(list, (gconstpointer)data_ptr);

/* free the 42 */
g_free(data_ptr);
```

If the list contains more than one instance of the data pointer, g_list_remove()
deletes only the first node that contains the pointer; g_list_remove_all() removes
all of them.

Iterating Through Lists

You can run a function on every element of a list at once, similar to mapping in a
language like Lisp. This is called *iteration*; the GList utility is

```
g_list_foreach(list, func, user_data)
```

It's helpful to see an example first:

```
void print_number(gpointer data_ptr, gpointer ignored)
{
  g_print("%d ", *(gint *)data_ptr);
}
```

```
g_list_foreach(list, print_number, NULL);
```

As usual, *list* is a list. *func* is a function with a prototype matching GFunc, and
user_data is an untyped pointer. The GFunc definition is

```
typedef void (*GFunc) (gpointer data, gpointer user_data);
```

When you put everything in this example together, g_list_foreach() steps
through each element *e* of list, running print_number(*e*->data, NULL). Notice that
the GType function takes the data of the element as the data argument, *not* the
element itself. The second argument corresponds to the *user_data* parameter of
g_list_foreach(). In this example, it is NULL and completely ignored by
print_number().

 This example *does* involve user_data:

```
void plus(gpointer data_ptr, gpointer addend_ptr)
{
  *(gint *)data_ptr += *(gint *)addend_ptr;
}
```

```
gint *num_ptr;
/* Add 42 to each element */
num = 42;
num_ptr = (gpointer)&num;
g_list_foreach(list, plus, num_ptr);
```

```
/* Subtract 65 from each element */
num = -65;
num_ptr = (gpointer)&num;
g_list_foreach(list, plus, num_ptr);
```

The only tricky part of this example is that `plus` accesses the actual addend data in a roundabout way; it takes a pointer in the form of `addend_ptr` and then dereferences it to get the value of the addend data. The example here uses this approach mostly to avoid loss of sign due to type casting.

WARNING *When iterating over a list, don't add or delete any nodes from the list — that is, unless you enjoy dancing with segmentation faults.*

Of course, you may find this style of iteration excessive. It's fine to iterate like this instead:

```
GList *l;
gint *data_ptr;

for(l = list; l; l = l->next)
{
  data_ptr = l->data;
  ...
}
```

Sorting Lists

If you have experience with the standard C library function qsort(), you'll have no problems with

```
g_list_sort(list, comp_function)
```

The return value is *list* sorted by *comp_function*. Here's a small example:

```
gint gint_compare(gconstpointer ptr_a, gconstpointer ptr_b)
{
  gint a, b;
  a = *(gint *)ptr_a;
  b = *(gint *)ptr_b;

  if (a > b)  { return (1); }
  if (a == b) { return (0); }
  /* default: a < b */
             return (-1);
}

list = g_list_sort(list, gint_compare);
```

Here's the type definition for the comparison function:

```
typedef gint (*GCompareFunc) (gconstpointer a, gconstpointer b);
```

To be specific, it takes two pieces of data as parameters (we'll call them *a* and *b*) and returns one of the following:

- A value less than 0 if *a* is less than *b*
- 0 if *a* is equal to *b*
- A value greater than 0 if *a* is greater than *b*

As was the case with iteration, this function receives the elements' data block pointers as its parameters.

A second list sorting variant allows you to pass additional data to a comparison function. To use it, call

```
g_list_sort_with_data(list, compare_func, user_data)
```

In this case, the comparison function has the GCompareDataFunc type and takes an additional data pointer argument.

Miscellaneous List Operations

Three functions take care of a few odds and ends with respect to lists:

```
GList list2 = NULL;

/* copy list into list2 */
list2 = g_list_copy(list);

/* append list2 to the end of list1 */
list = g_list_concat(list, list2);
list2 = NULL;

/* reverse list */
list = g_list_reverse(list);
```

- g_list_copy(*list*)
  Creates a new copy of *list* and returns the copy.

WARNING *This function creates copies of the nodes but does not copy the data blocks. Keep track of that memory.*

- g_list_concat(*list*, *list2*)
  Appends *list2* to *list* and returns the result. *This function does not make copies of any nodes; it uses the existing nodes.* Therefore, be careful what you pass, and set the second list to NULL after running this function.

- g_list_reverse(*list*)
  Reverses the order of the nodes *list*.

Deallocating Lists

To return all of a list's nodes to the free memory pool, use g_free_list(*list*). Use this deallocation function *only* on the list's first element.

WARNING *Keep in mind that GLib has no idea how you created the data blocks of your list elements; you're responsible for them and any memory holes that might have to do with them. If you're sure that each data block appears only once in the list, you can come up with a solution using g_list_foreach(). Just make sure you know what you're doing.*

1.5.3 Arrays

GLib arrays (GArray) are like their C counterparts, except that they don't have a fixed size. They are much faster than GList structures for random access, but the potential cost of inserting data at various points within the array is higher, because they are just a set of contiguous blocks of memory in the actual implementation.

You can create an array with no particular starting size, or if you have an idea of how much space you need, you can preallocate it:

```
#include <glib.h>

GArray *array, *array2;

/* array of integers, unspecified size */
array = g_array_new(TRUE,                  /* use null terminator */
                    FALSE,                 /* don't blank memory */
                    sizeof(gint));         /* element size */

/* array of unsigned chars, size 50 */
array2 = g_array_sized_new(FALSE,          /* no null terminator */
                           TRUE,           /* zero memory */
                           sizeof(guchar), /* element size */
                           50);            /* create space for 50 */
```

Create an array with one of these functions:

```
g_array_new(null_terminated, clear, element_size)
```

```
g_array_sized_new(null_terminated, clear, element_size, reserved_size)
```

Here, *null_terminated* indicates the use of a NULL terminator, *clear* tells the function to zero out the memory before returning the array, and element_size is the byte length of each element in the array; *reserved_size* in g_array_sized_new() is the array's initial size. Upon success, these functions return the newly allocated array.

NOTE   *It doesn't make too much sense to set the first two parameters to* TRUE, *because if you want to terminate your array with* NULL, *you don't want to have any* NULL *bytes that aren't actually the end of the array.*

To access an element in an array, use the macro

```
g_array_index(a, type, i)
```

where *a* is the array, *type* is the array's element type, and *i* is the index. Because this is a macro, you can write code like so (for example, to set the element at index 1 to 37):

```
g_array_index(array, gint, 1) = 37;
```

WARNING *This looks quite wrong in many ways, and you do need to be careful. In particular, you must be absolutely sure that the index exists in your array. Look at the* len *field of an array to check its length (for example,* array->len *in the preceding example). Also, although* g_array_sized_new() *preallocates space, its initial length is still zero.*

To *create* elements in a GArray, you need to add them with a function or use g_array_set_size().

Adding Elements

To add things to your GArray, you need to fill a regular C array with your data. You can add elements to an array in three places:

- At the end: Use g_array_append_vals().
- At the beginning: Use g_array_prepend_vals().
- In the middle: Use g_array_insert_vals().

This code illustrates how these functions work:

```
gint c_array[3];

c_array[0] = 42; c_array[1] = 23; c_array[2] = 69;
/* add the elements in c_array to the end of the GArray array */
array = g_array_append_vals(array, (gconstpointer)c_array, 3);

/* insert 220 and DEADBEEF at index 1 */
c_array[0] = 220; c_array[2] = 0xdeadbeef;
array = g_array_insert_vals(array, 1, (gconstpointer)c_array, 2);
```

There is a way to add a single item to an array, but you must have a variable that contains the data handy. Unfortunately, the names are confusing — they are like the three macros in the preceding code, but end in val instead of vals. Because these are macros (and hence not terribly smart), you can't use a constant like 42. In any case, here is a demonstration of g_array_prepend_val():

```
gint tmp;

tmp = 380;
/* insert 380 at the beginning of the array */
array = g_array_prepend_val(array, tmp);
```

NOTE *Of the functions here, only* g_array_append_vals() *has reasonable performance. The others must shift memory around; therefore, the characteristics of* GArray *in this respect are the opposite of* GList.

If you want to create multiple elements in an array at once, use

```
g_array_set_size(array, size)
```

You can then set the individual elements with g_array_index().

Deleting Elements

You can remove elements in two ways. You can use g_array_remove_index(), which does what you would expect: It pulls an element at a given index out of the array:

```
/* delete element at index 2 */
g_array_remove_index(array, 2);
```

This approach isn't terribly quick, so there is an alternative that replaces the deleted element with the last element in the array. However, if you care about the order of your array, this isn't for you:

```
/* replace index 1 with last element and shorten array */
g_array_remove_index_fast(array, 1);
```

Sorting Arrays

If you perhaps called one too many g_array_remove_index_fast() functions, you can use g_array_sort() and g_array_sort_with_data(). These functions work just like their g_list_sort* counterparts; see Section 1.5.2.

Deallocating Arrays

As was the case with GString (see Section 1.5.1),

```
g_array_free(array, preserve)
```

the *preserve* Boolean value indicates whether you want to preserve the actual data in *array* or not. It returns a pointer to the data (type: gchar *) if you use TRUE as the second parameter; you are responsible for deallocating this later with g_free().

1.5.4 Trees

Another classic data structure is the tree. There are more types of trees than you probably want to know about (splay trees, threaded trees, red-black trees, and so forth), and if you really want to know about them, have a look at [Knuth] and [Cormen]. However, if you just want to use one of them, GLib's GTree type is a complete implementation of balanced binary trees.

Creating Trees

One of the most noteworthy things about GTree is that it doesn't just contain simple elements like GList and GArray. A leaf of a (search) tree not only contains some data, but also a key corresponding to that data. That key is available to help GLib sort through the tree and find the data. For example, you could use the customer number as a key in a customer database, a telephone number as the key for telephone information, the name of a participant spelled phonetically — well, you get the idea.

You must define a comparison relation for your keys (greater or less than) so that the tree can be balanced. If you define it as GCompareFunc (see Section 1.5.2), you can call

```
g_tree_new(compare_func)
```

to create your tree. However, if you opt for GCompareDataFunc instead, use

```
g_tree_new_with_data(comp_func, comp_data)
```

One step further is

```
g_tree_new_full(comp_func, comp_data, key_destroy_func, value_destroy_func)
```

which can also take care of your data's memory management with a pair of
GDestroyNotify function definitions. You have to create these functions yourself;
GLib calls *value_destroy_func()* when it needs to deallocate the data in a node,
and *key_destroy_func* when it needs to free a node's key. It's a simple function
prototype — just a void function that takes a single untyped pointer as a
parameter:

```
typedef void (*GDestroyNotify) (gpointer data);
```

NOTE *In all of the functions described in this section, when you see something like "this or that will
be freed," it means that GLib will do it, and only on the condition that you created the tree
with* g_tree_new_full(). *Otherwise, you need to worry about it yourself. You probably don't
want to think about that, though, because trees can get complicated.*

As usual, GLib manipulates only the keys and data with untyped pointers.
Furthermore, you do not reassign your GTree variables after every function
call, as with the other types.

Enough talk; let's look at some actual code.

```
#include <glib.h>

GMemChunk *key_chunk;
GTree *tree;

/* compare gints; ignore extra data parameter */
gint key_cmp(gconstpointer a_ptr, gconstpointer b_ptr, gpointer ignored)
{
  gint a, b;
  a = *(gint *)a_ptr;
  b = *(gint *)b_ptr;

  if (a < b)    { return (1); }
  if (a == b)    { return (0); }
  /* if a > b */  return (-1);
}

void free_key(gpointer key)
```

```
{
  g_mem_chunk_free(key_chunk, key);
}

void free_value(gpointer value)
{
  g_string_free((GString *)value, TRUE);
}

/* prepare memory for keys and values */
key_chunk = g_mem_chunk_create(gint, 1024, G_ALLOC_AND_FREE);

/* create tree */
tree = g_tree_new_full(key_cmp,
                       NULL,        /* data pointer, optional */
                       free_key,
                       free_value);
```

This program draws storage for the tree's keys from memory chunks and uses GString strings for its values. The three functions are the comparison, key deallocator, and value deallocator. You can see that once you have these three utility functions, you need only run a single function — g_tree_new_full() — to create the tree.

Adding and Replacing Nodes

Insert a new node into a tree with key *key* and value *value* with

```
g_tree_insert(tree, key, value)
```

If *key* already exists in the tree, this function replaces the old value, and if the tree was created with deallocation functions, returns that value to the memory pool. It does not free the old key; instead, it frees the key that you just passed.

Therefore, you need to be careful if you want to use the key that you passed to g_tree_insert() after the function call. You may want to use this instead:

```
g_tree_replace(tree, key, value)
```

It works just the same as insertion, but when it finds a node with a matching key, it deallocates the old value *and* the old key, replacing them with the new ones. Of course, if you use this version, you must make sure that the old key hasn't wandered somewhere else in your program.

Because both functions have pitfalls, the easiest way to avoid a core dump when using these functions is to reset any pointers to the key and value after placing them in a tree.

Here is an example:

```
gint *key_ptr;
GString *value;

/* insert 42 into the tree */
key_ptr = g_chunk_new(gint, key_chunk);
*key_ptr = 42;
value = g_string_new("forty-two");

g_tree_insert(tree, key_ptr, value);
```

To create the node, you need to get a new memory chunk for the key and then a new GString for the value. Notice how this works in tandem with free_key() and free_value(), discussed earlier.

Finding Nodes

To find a node in *tree* matching *key*, use

```
g_tree_lookup(tree, key)
```

The return value is a pointer to the matching node's value if successful, or NULL if *key* isn't in the tree.

There's a slightly more complicated version:

```
g_tree_lookup_extended(tree, key, key_ptr_addr, value_ptr_addr)
```

Upon a match, this function sets the pointer behind *key_ptr_addr* to the key of the matching node, and likewise with *value_ptr_addr* and the matching value. The return value is TRUE if there's a match, and FALSE otherwise. Use this function only if you need to access the key in the tree for some reason (for example, if you didn't define a function to deallocate keys and need to do it by hand).

WARNING   *With* g_tree_lookup_extended(), *you can change keys that are in trees. Don't do this; GLib's tree navigation system won't be able to cope with the change.*

Here are the functions in action:

```
gint *key_ptr, *key_ptr2;

/* look up 37 in the tree */
key_ptr = g_chunk_new(gint, key_chunk);
*key_ptr = 37;

value = (GString *) g_tree_lookup(tree, key_ptr);
if (!value)
```

```
{
  g_print("%d not found in tree.\n", *key_ptr);
} else {
  g_print("%d found; value: %s.\n", *key_ptr, value->str);
}

/* See if 42 is in there */
*key_ptr = 42;
if (!g_tree_lookup_extended(tree, key_ptr,
                            (gpointer)&key_ptr2,
                            (gpointer)&value))
{
    g_print("%d not found in tree.\n", *key_ptr);
} else {
    g_print("%d found; value: %s.\n", *key_ptr, value->str);
}

g_mem_chunk_free(key_chunk, key_ptr);
```

WARNING *If you choose not to provide key and value memory management functions when you create the tree, you need to know exactly what the keys and values look like in memory, and it's particularly important to keep track of your keys. For example, keys with pointers to any other data invite memory leaks.*

Deleting Nodes

To completely remove a node from a tree, including its key and value, use

```
g_tree_remove(tree, key)
```

However, if you want to preserve the key and value, or you want to remove a node from a tree only temporarily, use

```
g_tree_steal(tree, key)
```

However, make sure that you have pointers to the *original* key and value before you run this, or you'll lose track of them. One way to do this is with g_tree_lookup_extended(); the following code builds on the function call that you saw earlier:

```
/* pull a node from the tree */
g_tree_steal(tree, key_ptr2);

/* key_ptr2 and value contain the key and value (see above)--
   now we'll throw them right back into the tree */
g_tree_insert(tree, key_ptr2, value);

/* this time get rid of the node for good */
g_tree_remove(tree, key_ptr2);
```

Traversing a Tree

As with lists and arrays, you can iterate over a GTree tree. This is called *traversing* the tree, and you typically want to do it in the sort order of the nodes' keys. Use

```
g_tree_foreach(tree, func, data)
```

to call *func* on every node in *tree*. Note that *func* has the GTraverseFunc definition:

```
typedef gboolean (*GTraverseFunc)
        (gpointer key, gpointer value, gpointer data);
```

The traversal goes in the order of the keys, with the smallest element first. The GTraverseFunc can halt the traversal at any time by returning TRUE; otherwise, it returns FALSE to keep things moving (you could use this feature when looking for something). Here's an example that prints every node in the tree:

```
/* print a node in a traversal */
gboolean print_node(gpointer key, gpointer value, gpointer ignored)
{
  g_print("[%d %s] ", *(gint *)key, ((GString *)value)->str);
  return FALSE;
}

g_tree_foreach(tree, print_node, NULL);
```

This example uses the third parameter of the GTraverseFunc:

```
/* add the keys; ignore the value */
gboolean sum_keys(gpointer key, gpointer value_ignored, gpointer sum)
{
    *(gint *)sum += *(gint*)key;
    return FALSE;
}

gint sum = 0;

g_tree_foreach(tree, sum_keys, &sum);
```

Tree Statistics

The following functions report on the size of a tree:

- gint g_tree_nnodes(*tree*)
  Returns the total number of nodes in *tree*.
- gint g_tree_height()
  Returns the height of *tree*.

Removing a Tree

To return a tree and its nodes to the free memory pool, use

---

g_tree_destroy(*tree*)

Notice that this function doesn't end in _free like many of the other functions. If you provided deallocation functions for keys and values, this function also completely frees the keys and values. Otherwise, you're responsible for that memory.

1.5.5 Hash Tables

The last GLib data structure that this book covers is another perennial favorite: the hash table. These tables assign keys to values, and using an efficient internal representation, allow you to quickly access values using the key. The GLib data type for a hash table is GHashTable.

As with trees, you can choose any data type that you like for the keys and values of hash tables. An entry in a hash table consists of two untyped pointers: one for the key and the other for the type. GNOME software makes broad use of GHashTable because it can associate data between any two types.[3]

1.5.6 Creating Hash Tables

Use

---

g_create_hash_table_new(*hash_func, equal_func*)

---

to create a new hash table, returning the result as GHashTable. The two parameters are functions. The first is the *hash function*, with a type of GHashFunc. Following this is an equality test function (type GEqualFunc) that determines whether two keys are equal. Although you can probably use the built-in default functions, it never hurts to know the types of the following parameters:

---

typedef guint (*GHashFunc)(gconstpointer key);

typedef gboolean (*GEqualFunc)(gconstpointer a, gconstpointer b);

The equality function is simple; it takes two keys as parameters and, if they are equal, returns TRUE, or FALSE if they aren't equal.

Hash functions are a little trickier. They take a key as input and (efficiently) return a *hash value*, a guint integer that characterizes the key in some way. This isn't a unique mapping like a quark; you can't get a key back from a hash value. The important part about hash values is that they return values that are well distributed throughout the guint domain, even for similar keys.

---

[3] This sets GLib hash tables apart from the hash tables (or dictionaries) of many interpreted languages; those typically allow only strings as keys.

If you want to know about the theory of hash values and algorithms, have a look at the algorithms books in the bibliography. For the most part, you will probably find that one of the following default hash functions fits your needs:

- g_str_hash(*string*) processes gchar * *string* into a hash value. If your keys are strings, use this function.
- g_int_hash(*int_ptr*) treats *int_ptr* as a *pointer* to a gint value and generates a hash value from the gint value. Use this function if your keys are of type gint *.
- g_direct_hash(*ptr*) uses *ptr* as the hash value. This function works when your keys are arbitrary pointers.

If you use one of these hash functions, there are corresponding key equality functions at your disposal: g_str_equal(), g_int_equal(), and g_direct_equal().

Here is an example:

```
GHashTable *hash1;

hash1 = g_hash_table_new(g_direct_hash, g_direct_equal);
```

You are responsible for the memory management with hash tables created with g_hash_table_new(). However, just as in the case of trees in Section 1.5.4, the

```
g_hash_table_new_full(hash_func, equal_func, key_destroy, value_destroy)
```

function can deallocate your hash table entries automatically if you provide it with GDestroyNotify functions:

```
GHashTable *hash2;
hash2 = g_hash_table_new_full(g_str_hash, g_str_equal, g_free, g_free);
```

In this example, the keys and values of the hash table could be dynamically allocated C strings, because g_free() returns these to the free memory pool.

NOTE *You can combine a string and integer hash values with XOR into a hash function like this:*

```
struct vpair
{
  gchar *str;
  int value;
};

GHashFunc (struct vpair *p) {
  return(g_str_hash(p->str)^p->value);
}
```

Inserting and Replacing Values

Most GLib programmers add new values to a hash table with this function:

```
g_hash_table_replace(hash_table, key, value)
```

Here is an example:

```
SomeType *key;
AnotherType *value;

key = g_new(SomeType, 1);
value = g_new(AnotherType, 1);

  << ... >>

g_hash_table_replace(hash1,
                key,                /* key */
                value);             /* value */

g_hash_table_replace(hash2,
                g_strdup("foo"),    /* key */
                g_strdup("bar"));   /* value */
```

As with many other GLib functions, the key and value are untyped pointers. If the key is already in the hash table, this function replaces the value corresponding to that key. However, if you created the table with deallocation functions to manage the key and value memory, g_hash_table_replace() frees the old key's memory because it isn't needed.

There is a seldom-used alternative to g_hash_table_replace():

```
g_hash_table_insert(hash_table, key, value)
```

This function works just like g_hash_table_replace(), except that it deallocates the *new* key if an old key in the hash table matches the new key. Therefore, you must be careful if you still have a pointer to *key* somewhere.

If you want to be completely safe, NULL out any pointers to the key (and value) that you add with either of these functions.

NOTE   *The difference between these two functions with respect to the actual content of your keys is an issue only when the key equality function doesn't take all of the data in the key into account. If your keys use a simple data type, such as an integer or string, there is no difference.*

To find out how many entries are in a hash table (that is, the number of key-value pairs), use

```
g_hash_table_size(table)
```

Finding Values

The easiest way to find something in a hash table is to use

```
g_hash_table_lookup(table, key)
```

The return value is a pointer to the value, or NULL if the key isn't in any of the hash table's entries.

```
gchar *key, *value;

value = (gchar*)g_hash_table_lookup(hash2, "foo");
if (value)
{
  g_print("hash2{\"foo\"} = %s\n", value);
} else {
  g_print("foo isn't in the hash table\n");
}
```

If you need access to the keys and values in the hash table, try

```
g_hash_table_lookup_extended(table, key, key_addr, ptr_addr)
```

Here's an example:

```
if (g_hash_table_lookup_extended(hash2,
                                 "foo",
                                 (gpointer)&key,
                                 (gpointer)&value))
{
  g_print("hash2{\"%s\"} = %s\n", key, value);
} else {
  g_print("foo isn't in the hash table\n");
}
```

This function takes two pointer addresses as the third and fourth parameters: one for a key and the other for a value. If the given key (the second parameter) is in the hash table, this function sets those pointers to the key and value *inside* the hash table. It returns TRUE upon success.

This function is useful when you need to deallocate your key and value manually.

WARNING　g_hash_table_lookup_extended() *gives you direct access to the keys in the table entries, meaning that you also have the ability to change them around. That's a really bad idea — you risk inaccessible entries and key duplication.*

Deleting Entries

To delete an entry in a hash table, use

```
g_hash_table_remove(table, key)
```

where *table* is the hash table and *key* is the entry's key. When successful, this function returns TRUE, and if you created the hash table with automatic key and value deallocation functions, it also frees the key and value memory. Note that this procedure does not try to deallocate the key that you gave as a parameter, so you can write statements with constants, such as this:

```
g_hash_table_remove(hash2, "this");
```

You can also prevent the GLib hash table from trying to deallocate the key and value with

```
g_hash_table_steal(table, key)
```

Iterating Through Hash Tables

You can call a function on every single entry in a hash table, just as you can for lists, arrays, and trees. There are three ways to iterate:

* void g_hash_table_foreach(GHashTable *table, GHFunc func, gpointer user_data)
  Runs *func* on every entry in *table*. This function passes *user_data* as the third parameter to *func*.

* void g_hash_table_foreach_remove(GHashTable *table, GHRFunc func, gpointer user_data)
  Same as the preceding function, but removes the entry if *func* returns TRUE. This approach includes running any deallocation functions on the key and value that you might have specified when you created the hash table. This function is useful if you need to filter a hash table.

* void g_hash_table_foreach_steal(GHashTable *table, GHRFunc func, gpointer user_data)
  Same as the preceding function, but when removing entries, this function doesn't ever try to deallocate the key and data. This function is useful for moving entries to other hash tables or data structures.

Here is the type definition for GHFunc (GHRFunc is the same, except that it returns gboolean):

```
typedef void (*GHFunc)(gpointer key, gpointer value, gpointer user_data);
```

The following is a short example. If you need to see something that involves the user_data parameter, check out the example for trees in Section 1.5.4.

```
void print_entry(gpointer key, gpointer data, gpointer user_data)
{                                         /* user_data not used */
    g_print("key: %-10s     value: %-10s\n",
            (gchar *)key, (gchar *)data);
}

g_print("Hash table entries:\n");
g_hash_table_foreach(hash2, print_entry, NULL);
```

Deleting Hash Tables

To completely remove a GHashTable, call

```
g_hash_table_destroy(hash_table)
```

This approach includes the key and value data if you supplied deallocation functions when you created the hash table. Otherwise, you'll have to take care of the key and value in each entry yourself; g_hash_table_foreach() is a handy means of doing this.

1.6 Further Topics

GLib has many capabilities that aren't covered here because there just isn't enough space. These include the following:

- **Date and time functions:** Would you like to know how many days elapsed between the end of the Thirty Year War and your grandmother's birthday? GLib makes quick work of this type of problem with its conversion utilities.

- **Message logging:** Behind g_message(), g_error(), and their friends are several macros that send a log domain and log level along with the usual parameters to the g_log() function. You can define new log domains and log levels, and with g_log_set_handler(), what to do when a message comes through.

- **Quicksort:** g_qsort_with_data() is like C's qsort() function, but accommodates an additional data parameter.

- **Singly linked lists:** GSList saves a few bytes per node if you don't need to be able to navigate backward in the list.

- **Pointer arrays:** If you just want an array of gpointer elements that can grow automatically like GArray, GPtrArray offers a simpler API without all of the element size parameters.

- **Byte arrays:** GByteArray arrays are identical to pointer arrays, but with guint8-size elements.

- **String chunks:** For efficient allocation and cleanup of a large number of C strings (not GString strings), GStringChunk is available with an API like those of memory chunks.

- **N-ary trees:** If you want trees where a node can have more than two children, GLib enables you to build them yourself with the GNode data type.

- **Queues:** The popular first in, first out (FIFO) approach is available with GQueue. There are additional routines for double-ended queues.

- **Shell and file utilities:** GLib has a number of facilities for working with files, pipes, and processes.

- **Threads:** GLib offers portable implementations of threads, thread pools, and interprocess communication (mutual exclusion, async queues, and so on).

- **Dynamic module loader:** GModule is a system for loading shared objects into running processes. If you want your program to support plug-ins, take a look at this.

As you can see, GLib is a powerful tool that can't be completely documented in a book like this. However, an experienced programmer can easily get a good sense of how to use everything else by rooting around in the extensive API reference documentation that comes with GLib.

2

GOBJECT

Contrary to any grousing you may have heard, GNOME is just
as object-oriented as other modern GUI platforms. The primary
difference between GNOME and its "competitors" is that the
GNOME library source is in plain C, so you can also program it
in C. Libraries such as GTK+ and GNOME rest on the GObject
object system. By contrast, other systems rely on the object-oriented
features of their programming languages, as in the case of KDE's C++
implementation.

NOTE   *This chapter is dry and dense; it covers several complex topics in a relatively small space. This
chapter is the second in the book because it reflects aspects of the entire GNOME API. You don't
need to fully comprehend this material to move on to the next chapters, especially because many of
the techniques appear throughout the book. At the very least, learn how to create objects, manipulate properties, and install signal handlers (Sections 2.5, 2.5.1, and 2.6.5). You do not need to
know how to create your own classes.*

If you are already familiar with object-oriented programming and its terminology,
you can skip the first section and go right to the implementation details in
Section 2.2.

2.1 Object-Oriented Programming Basics

Most programmers agree that programs consist of algorithms and data structures [Wirth]. That's all fine and good, but experience over the years has indicated that algorithms tend to depend on data structures, rather than the other way around.

In other words, nearly every algorithm operates on a specific data structure. If a clearly written C program defines data structures such as struct Flipper and struct Slop, you can expect to see associated functions like flipper_insert(), flipper_shift(), flipper_status(), slop_create(), slop_blocksize(), and slop_destroy(). The functions "belong" to their data structures and always take parameters of a specific data structure. You will not be able to run flipper_status() on a Slop structure.

Take a look at the names above. You should recognize GLib's naming convention from Section 1.2. One tenet of object-oriented programming is that data types, variables of these types, and their algorithms belong together. It's just a way of thinking, but it does help if you have tools that can help you with the day-to-day organizational details. This tool can be the programming language itself; the most prominent object-oriented languages are C++ and Java, and nearly all popular scripting languages offer some sort of object system, even though not everyone chooses to use these features.

C isn't an object-oriented language by any stretch of the imagination, but that's not a problem, because the GLib's GObject library (*libgobject-2.0*) provides object-oriented programming features for C.

2.1.1 Objects as Instances of Classes

Let's get back to Flippers and Slop.

You can think of the Flipper and Slop types as *classes*, and you can think of variables of these types as *instances* of those classes. Because classes are data structures, they contain various data fields (*attributes*; later in this book, you will see the term *property* — see Section 2.4). A class also has several functions that operate on object attributes. These are called *methods*, and you can just think of them as functions that are attached to certain classes. For example, the Flipper and Slop classes have methods that start with flipper_ and slop_.

An *object* is a data structure in memory that conforms to the class or an *instance* of a class. The process of creating an object from a class is called *instantiation*; you invoke the *constructor* of a class to create objects. You can have as many objects as you like, and you can set their attributes any way you like. For example, you can have two objects named red_car and blue_car of the **Car** class, where the only difference between the two objects is in the color attribute.

GObject manipulates its objects with object references: typed pointers to objects that you create and invalidate with special functions. You may have more than one reference to the same object, and therefore, objects have *reference counts* to keep track of their references in the currently running program. If the reference count goes to zero, GObject detects that you no longer need the object and performs the following actions:

1. GObject enters the *dispose* phase to get rid of any references to other objects.

2. GObject *finalizes* the object, marking the memory as ready for reuse.

3. A garbage collector returns the memory to the free pool somewhere down the line.

Constructors and destructors allow custom code that runs when you create or destroy an object. Therefore, an object can be more than just a coupling of data structures and algorithms; it can represent a process. For example, you could define **FilmShort** class to show an animated cartoon. When you create an object from this class, the constructor places the animation on your screen and starts playing the animation. Finalizing the object stops the animation and removes it from your monitor.

2.1.2   Inheritance

Because an object belongs to a class, it has a type. This is sometimes called a *membership relation*; an object my_flipper might belong to the **Flipper** class because you created it with the **Flipper** constructor, and therefore, the class and object have a membership relation.

Now let's assume that you need to something a little trickier; for example, you want to write a program to manage your bloated CD collection. First, you create a **CD** class with several attributes, such as the storage location (location), the title (title), and an inventory number (inv_nr). However, pedant that you are, you have some CD-ROMs on your shelves in addition to audio CDs. Therefore, you decide on two classes, **AudioCD** and **CDROM**. There are some differences in the attributes: **AudioCD** has an artist name and track list; **CDROM** has an operating system and version.

Meanwhile, your CD collection grows so large that you have to store it on different planets, and therefore, you must add a planet attribute to both classes. Isn't it a little clumsy to add that to both classes?

Well, yes. **AudioCD** and **CDROM** share several attributes that were in your original **CD** class. Furthermore, audio CDs and CD-ROMs are both CDs, so they should have a membership relation reflecting this fact. It would make sense if **AudioCD** objects and **CDROM** objects were also **CD** objects.

It's possible to implement this approach. You can dig out your old **CD** class and define **AudioCD** and **CDROM** as *subclasses* of **CD**. They *inherit* attributes from their parent class (or superclass) and add some attributes of their own. The whole system is known as *inheritance*.

Subclasses also inherit methods from their parents. All of the methods from the **CD** class work on **AudioCD** and **CDROM** objects; a **CD** method doesn't care about the specific subclass membership of an object.

You can create subclasses of subclasses. For example, **CDROM** could have a **SoftwareCD** subclass for CDs containing programs and a **RecordsCD** subclass for your archived documents. These subclasses would inherit their attributes and methods from **CDROM** and add their own. If you had a **RecordsCD** object called my_disc, its membership relations would be as follows:

- my_disc is a **RecordsCD** object.
- my_disc is a **CDROM**, object.
- my_disc is a **CD** object.

Figure 2.1 shows the entire *class hierarchy* as a tree.

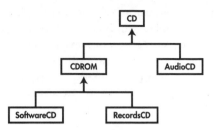

Figure 2.1: CD class hierarchy.

If you implement **RecordsCD** in GObject, Figure 2.1 isn't the complete story. The GObject system has a *base class* called **GObject**. Therefore, you have the following membership relations:

- my_disc is a **RecordsCD** object.
- my_disc is a **CDROM** object.
- my_disc is a **CD** object.
- my_disc is a **GObject** object.

See Figure 2.2 for the whole tree diagram.

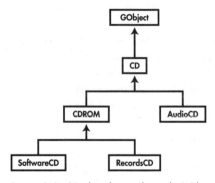

Figure 2.2: CD class hierarchy with GObject base class.

If your collection doesn't contain any exotic CD formats, every CD is a CD-ROM (some subclass of **CDROM**) or an audio CD (**AudioCD**). The **CD** class serves only for the derivation of subclasses; you wouldn't instantiate **CD** objects. Such a class is called an *abstract class*. Some real-life examples of abstract classes are "building," "vehicle," and "work of art." Nothing is just a work of art, but rather, a painting, installation, sculpture, or whatever.

Interfaces

Let's say that you've finished with your CD inventory program. Now you decide that CDs are too small and so add some tapes and records. Organized person that you are, you decide to expand the inventory system to include some new classes: **Media** as a new abstract class that has your old **CD** as a subclass, as well as two other new subclasses, **Tape** and **Vinyl**. Furthermore, these last two have their own subclasses: **EightTrack**, **StudioTape**, **EP**, and **LP** (see Figure 2.3 for the exact positions).

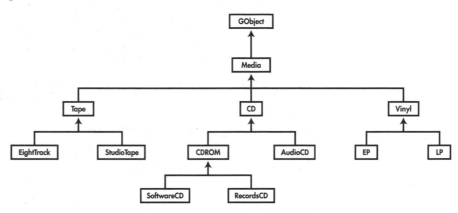

Figure 2.3: Media hierarchy.

With this archival business out of the way, you now want to enable a robot to retrieve audio CDs, 8-track tapes, and records from their storage slots and play them on your designer stereo system. Therefore, the functions that control this system must be able to deal with objects from the **AudioCD**, **Vinyl**, and **EightTrack** classes. This would be practical if they all belonged to a common superclass somewhere, and there is one: **Media**. Unfortunately, this class also includes objects like CD-ROMs and studio tapes, which don't work with your fancy stereo. Therefore, you can't add the support at this level, because the whole idea of a superclass is that *all* of its methods and attributes are supposed to work with its subclasses.

In other object models, it's possible to define classes that inherit from several other classes at once, not just a parent class. This is called *multiple inheritance*, and it tends to confuse a lot of people.

GObject and many other object systems use a similar concept called an *interface*. In the ongoing example, all audio CDs, records, and 8-track tapes have one characteristic in common: They fit in the stereo system. In object-oriented terminology, you would say that they all implement the same interface — that is, you can play all of them in a stereo.

Interfaces contain only methods and therefore reflect the capabilities of these objects. Typical interface names often end in *-able*. You could use **Playable** to label the interface to play something on the stereo. Figure 2.4, on the following page, shows the new interface's relationships.

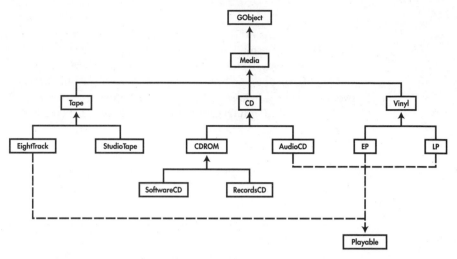

Figure 2.4: Hierarchy of media types, with Playable interface.

All functions that work with **Playable** objects see the methods from only those objects that are defined in the interface. The location of the object classes in the class hierarchy doesn't matter.

What you have just seen sounds easy enough, but now you're about to see the GObject implementation. The rest of this chapter demonstrates how to define classes, create objects, and build interfaces.

2.2   Defining Classes

To put it bluntly, defining a class in GObject isn't easy. If you're used to programming languages like C++, Java, and Smalltalk, this procedure is going to look quite awkward.[1] However, you should try to look at it from an unbiased perspective.

To use GObject, you must include the *glib-object.h* header file and invoke g_type_init() somewhere in your program initialization to set up the GObject type system (GType). Keep in mind that some other function might call g_type_init(), such as gtk_init(), as you'll see in Chapter 3.

2.2.1   Structure Definitions

A GObject class consists of two structures. First, the *instance structure* (or *object structure*) holds the class attributes and is the basis for an object in memory. The other structure, the *class structure*, contains prototypes for certain methods and all signals that the object can provide (you will encounter signals in Section 2.6).

For the **Media** class in Section 2.1.2, you could define Media as the instance structure and MediaClass as the class structure:

---

[1] It might be some consolation that C++ and most scripting languages have GNOME bindings.

```
/* instance structure */
typedef struct _Media
{
  GObject parent_instance;

  guint inv_nr;
  GString *location;
  GString *title;
  gboolean orig_package;
} Media;

/* class structure */
typedef struct _MediaClass
{
  GObjectClass parent_class;

  /* Signals */
  void (*unpacked)(Media *media);
  void (*throw_out)(Media *media, gboolean permanent);
} MediaClass;
```

The attributes in the instance structure include inv_nr, location, title, and orig_package (this last attribute indicates whether the item is still in the original package). The class structure includes handler prototypes for two signals: **unpacked** and **throw-out**. Ignore them for now; they will reappear in Section 2.6.

NOTE *As you may have noticed by now, there are no prototypes for methods in this class definition. As you will see in Section 2.3, most method prototypes appear outside the class structure.*

There is a parent_instance pointer at the beginning of the instance structure, as well as a corresponding parent_class pointer in the class structure. These two definitions are necessary for inheritance; without them, you wouldn't be able do much with your objects (all classes inherit important common features from a base GObject class).

2.2.2   Utility Macros

The following macros are practically essential for smooth operation (you could theoretically write them out by hand each time that you wanted to use these features, but it would test your patience):

```
#define TYPE_MEDIA (media_get_type())

#define MEDIA(object) \
  (G_TYPE_CHECK_INSTANCE_CAST((object), TYPE_MEDIA, Media))

#define MEDIA_CLASS(klass) \
  (G_TYPE_CHECK_CLASS_CAST((klass), TYPE_MEDIA, MediaClass))

#define IS_MEDIA(object) \
  (G_TYPE_CHECK_INSTANCE_TYPE((object), TYPE_MEDIA))

#define IS_MEDIA_CLASS(klass) \
  (G_TYPE_CHECK_CLASS_TYPE((klass), TYPE_MEDIA))

#define MEDIA_GET_CLASS(object) \
  (G_TYPE_INSTANCE_GET_CLASS((object), TYPE_MEDIA, MediaClass))
```

These are somewhat difficult to digest at once, so let's go over them one by one. Note the ongoing difference between the instance and class structures.

- TYPE_MEDIA returns the class type identifier, a GType assignment for the **Media** class. It calls media_get_type() — see Section 2.2.3 for more details. You'll use this macro in any place that calls for an object or type identifier. When you see the term *(class) type identifier* in this section, you need to remember that this is different from a C type.

You will use TYPE_MEDIA when creating **Media** objects.

- MEDIA() is a *casting macro* that casts an *object* (the instance structure) to the **Media** type, or, in other words, the Media structure. This is often simply known as a cast, like its C counterpart.

  Casting macros are useful when calling a method from an object's superclass.

- MEDIA_CLASS() is another casting macro. This one operates on the *class structure*, returning a casted MediaClass structure.

- IS_MEDIA() checks the membership of an object for the Media structure. It is TRUE if the object belongs to the class, and FALSE otherwise.

- IS_MEDIA_CLASS() checks the membership of a class for the MediaClass structure.

- MEDIA_GET_CLASS() yields the class structure of **Media** when given an object (again, an instance) of the Media structure.

As you can see, these macros build on other macros:

- G_TYPE_CHECK_INSTANCE_CAST(*object, type_id, name*)
  If *object*, a class type identifier *type_id* (for example, TYPE_MEDIA), and the instance structure *name* match, this macro expands to a casted pointer to *object*'s instance structure for *type_id*. Note that matching includes superclasses of *object*.

- G_TYPE_CHECK_CLASS_CAST(*klass, type_id, class_name*)
  Same as the preceding, but for class structure pointers.

NOTE name *and* class_name *are the type names from the C structure definitions. Make sure that you understand that these are very different from* type_id, *a runtime identifier for the entire class.*

The preceding macros provide warnings when you attempt to make invalid casts.

- G_TYPE_CHECK_INSTANCE_TYPE(*object, type_id*)
  Returns TRUE if *object* belongs to *type_id*'s class.

- G_TYPE_CHECK_CLASS_TYPE(*klass, type_id*)
  Returns TRUE if *klass* belongs to *type_id*'s class.

- G_TYPE_INSTANCE_GET_CLASS(*object, klass*)
  Returns the class structure for object, casted as the C type class_name.

NOTE *These macros use the parameter* klass *instead of* class. *That's because* class *is a reserved C++ keyword; if you tried to use one of these macros in C++ source code, your program would not compile. The GLib, GTK+, and GNOME source distributions reflect this. However, with parameters to functions in regular C code, this is not a problem, because you wouldn't use a C++ compiler on that. You can always use* class *if you never plan to use C++, or if you just feel like being mean to C++ people.*

To keep C++ compatibility at link time, use G_BEGIN_DECLS and G_END_DECLS to encapsulate your C code:

```
G_BEGIN_DECLS

  << header code >>

G_END_DECLS
```

2.2.3   Initializing Type Identifiers

The previous section made many references to the GObject class type identifier, with the macro TYPE_MEDIA expanding to a media_get_type() call to return the **Media** class type identifier. As mentioned before, the type identifier is an actual piece of runtime data that conforms to the GType standards.

This is perhaps easier to understand when you look at the actual definition of media_get_type():

```
GType media_get_type(void)
{
  static GType media_type = 0;

  if (!media_type)
  {
    static const GTypeInfo media_info = {
      sizeof(MediaClass),                /* class structure size */
      NULL,                              /* base class initializer */
      NULL,                              /* base class finalizer */
      (GClassInitFunc)media_class_init,  /* class initializer */
      NULL,                              /* class finalizer */
      NULL,                              /* class data */
      sizeof(Media),                     /* instance structure size */
      16,                                /* preallocated instances */
      NULL,                              /* instance initializer */
      NULL                               /* function table */
    };

    media_type = g_type_register_static(
                    G_TYPE_OBJECT,       /* parent class */
                    "Media",             /* type name */
                    &media_info,         /* GTypeInfo struct (above) */
                    0);                  /* flags */
  }

  return media_type;
}
```

The return value of media_get_type() is the C type GType — a type of a type (if that makes any sense). This function returns the same class type identifier every time, because the variable used to store and return the class identifier has a static declaration (media_type). Because of the if statement, media_get_type() does some work to initialize media_type upon first invocation, but needs to return the value of this variable only on subsequent calls.

media_type gets its actual value from

---

g_type_register_static(*parent_id, name, type_info, options*)

These arguments are as follows:

- *parent_id*: The parent type identifier. In this case, it's the **GObject** base class (G_TYPE_OBJECT).

- *name*: A name (a string) for the type.

- *type_info*: A GTypeInfo structure containing class details (see the following paragraphs).

- *options*: Option flags (using bitwise OR), or zero if you don't need any. For example, G_TYPE_FLAG_ABSTRACT indicates an abstract class.

WARNING *The type name must be at least three characters long.*

The fields of the GTypeInfo structure are as follows (in this order):

- class_size (guint16): Size of the class structure. In this case, it's easy: sizeof(MediaClass).

- base_init (GBaseInitFunc): The base class initializer. When you create a new class, GObject calls the base initializers of all classes in the hierarchy chain leading up from the class. This is normally necessary only if there is some dynamically allocated part of the class (*not* object) that GObject must copy to a derived class, and therefore, you need it only when your class has such data and is the parent of some other class. Normally, it isn't necessary, and you can use NULL.

- base_finalize (GBaseFinalizeFunc): The base class finalizer; essentially, the reverse operation of the base class initializer. You almost certainly need it when you have a base class initializer; otherwise, use NULL.

- class_init (GClassInitFunc): The class initializer. This function prepares class variables, in particular, properties (see Sections 2.4) and signals (Section 2.6). Note that this is not the constructor for the objects; however, the property definitions in the class initializer set up many of the defaults for the constructor. The class initializer appears throughout this chapter; it is instrumental in figuring out how classes work.

- class_finalize (GClassFinalizeFunc): The class finalizer. You normally won't need to do anything when GObject gets rid of a class, unless you have a very complicated mechanism for saving the state over program invocations.

- `class_data (gconstpointer)`: GObject passes the class data to the class initializer and class finalizer. One example of a situation in which you might use this function is when you want to use the same initializer for several classes. Of course, that could make things even more complicated than they already are.

- `instance_size (guint16)`: The size of the instance structure is an allocated object structure's memory requirement; `sizeof(Media)` shown earlier in the code is typical.

- `n_preallocs (guint16)`: The number of instances to preallocate depends on the number of instances that you think a typical program will use. If you specify 0, GObject allocates memory when it needs to. Be careful when using this function, because you can waste a lot of memory if you go nuts with many different kinds of classes.

- `instance_init (GInstanceInitFunc)`: The instance initializer runs every time you create a new object of the class. It's not strictly necessary, because the constructor is also at your disposal. This field is present because it is a part of GType; GObject doesn't need it.

- `value_table (const GTypeValueTable *)`: This function table can map certain kinds of values to functions, and it is really important only if you're doing something very involved with the type system, such as creating your own object system. This book does not cover that topic, and it's probably best if you forget that this function even exists.

Here are the type definitions for the various function prototypes you just saw:

```
typedef void (*GBaseInitFunc)     (gpointer g_class);
typedef void (*GBaseFinalizeFunc) (gpointer g_class);
typedef void (*GClassInitFunc)    (gpointer g_class, gpointer class_data);
typedef void (*GClassFinalizeFunc) (gpointer g_class, gpointer class_data);
typedef void (*GInstanceInitFunc) (GTypeInstance *instance, gpointer g_class);
```

NOTE *You can get rid of the* GTypeInfo *structure as soon as you're finished with it —* g_type_register_static() *makes a complete copy for itself. So in the media example, you could free up any dynamically allocated parts of* media_info *that you like.*

Try not to get tangled up in the initializers and finalizers. Normally, you won't be dealing with dynamically allocated data in the classes themselves, so you won't need anything except a class initializer; you'll see that in Section 2.4.1. You should not need to bother with the instance initializer, because you can use properties.

2.2.4 The Base Class: GObject

This section illustrates the makeup of the base class, **GObject**. All GObject classes inherit from this class. Not only do you need some of the utility macros to create new classes, but it helps to know the methods that you'll come across later.

Macros

In Section 2.2.2, you defined several utility macros for the **Media** class. Here are the **GObject** versions:

- G_TYPE_OBJECT returns **GObject**'s type identifier. Don't confuse this with G_OBJECT_TYPE.
- G_OBJECT(*object*) casts *object* to the GObject instance structure.
- G_OBJECT_CLASS(*klass*) casts an object class structure *klass* to the GObjectClass class structure.
- G_IS_OBJECT(*object*) returns TRUE if the *object* parameter is an instance of a **GObject**. This should return TRUE for any object that you define with GObject, unless you're very daring and decide to make your own base object.
- G_IS_OBJECT_CLASS(*klass*) returns TRUE if *klass* is a class structure. It should return TRUE for any class structure within the GObject system.
- G_OBJECT_GET_CLASS(*object*) returns the class structure (GObjectClass) corresponding to any instance structure.

Of these, you will encounter G_TYPE_OBJECT and G_OBJECT() the most: G_TYPE_OBJECT when you need to know the type identifier of **GObject** (for instance, when defining a class like **Media**), and G_OBJECT() when you need to pass an object instance as a GObject instance to a function.

NOTE *Many common functions that take **GObject** parameters don't require class type casts, but rather just expect an untyped* gpointer *pointer and do the casting work on their own. Although this approach isn't terribly consistent, it can save you an awful lot of typing. The functions that do this include* g_object_get(), g_object_set(), g_object_ref(), g_object_unref(), *and the entire* g_signal_connect() *family.*

Base Class Methods

Here is the part of the **GObject** class structure that contains public methods and a signal handler prototype. You will see some of these time and again. (This definition comes straight from the *gobject.h* header file.)

```
typedef struct _GObjectClass GObjectClass;
typedef struct _GObjectConstructParam GObjectConstructParam;

<< ... >>

struct _GObjectClass
{
  GTypeClass g_type_class;

<< ... >>

  /* public overridable methods */
  GObject* (*constructor) (GType type,
                           guint n_construct_properties,
                           GObjectConstructParam *construct_properties);

  void (*set_property) (GObject *object,
                        guint property_id,
```

```
                      const GValue *value,
                      GParamSpec *pspec);

  void (*get_property) (GObject *object,
                        guint property_id,
                        GValue *value,
                        GParamSpec *pspec);

  void (*dispose) (GObject *object);

  void (*finalize) (GObject *object);

  << ... >>

  /* signals/handlers */
  void (*notify) (GObject *object, GParamSpec *pspec);

  << ... >>

};

struct _GObjectConstructParam
{
  GParamSpec *pspec;
  GValue     *value;
};
```

The methods are as follows:

- constructor: This is the object's constructor, called when you create an instance of a class. It takes a type identifier parameter (type), the number of properties to create (n_construct_properties), and an array of property descriptions (construct_properties). You'll read about properties and the GValues that they employ in Section 2.4.

  The constructor creates the object and initializes its data. If you want to create your own constructor, you should always run the constructor of the parent class first and then extend the resulting parent class object by yourself, so that your object isn't missing anything. Keep in mind, though, that you do not usually need to make your own constructors; there is a further example of inheritance in Section 2.7 that provides an alternative.

- set_property: Writer function for properties.

- get_property: Reader function for properties.

- dispose: The destructor; GObject calls this when removing an object that is no longer in use (see Section 2.5.2). Destructors take a single parameter: the object to destroy. Destructors clean up after signal handlers and sort out other internal matters.

- finalize: GObject calls the finalizer when an object's reference count goes to zero (again, see Section 2.5.2), before it gets around to calling the destructor. Use this for housekeeping functions that require immediate attention, such as removing dynamically allocated memory. You should always call an object's parent finalizer at the end of your own finalizers. After running the finalizer, the object is officially dead, and you should do nothing more with the data.

- notify: GObject calls this special method for property change signals (see Section 2.6). There is no reasonable default, and you should not touch this (that is, inherit notify from the parent).

2.3 Methods

Although you haven't seen the class initializer for **Media** yet, you can now see how to define a simple method. Here are some important things to remember about methods:

- Methods usually do *not* appear in class structure. Instead, method prototypes usually appear somewhere soon after the class structure.
- A method's name should reflect the class name (for example, media_*() for **Media**).
- A method's first parameter is always an object (a structure of the instance class). Any remaining parameters are up to you.
- In public methods, always check that the first parameter is actually a valid object of the method's class.
- In addition, cast this object parameter after you do the check, because the object you get could be in a subclass.
- Be careful about setting an object's attributes. Standard GTK+/GNOME practice dictates that all attributes are properties (see Section 2.4); use that system for setting attributes.

These considerations sound like a lot of fuss, but this example shows that it doesn't amount to much:

```
void media_print_inv_nr(Media *object)
{
  Media *media;

  g_return_if_fail(IS_MEDIA(object));

  media = MEDIA(object);
  g_print("Inventory number: %d\n", media->inv_nr);
}
```

Most public methods contain everything here but the last line (g_print(...);).

2.4 Properties

You should set and retrieve attribute data on your GObject instances using the *property* system so that other programmers can get at data through a uniform interface, rather than going through a series of custom access functions.

Properties have names and descriptions, so they are self-documenting to a certain extent. In addition, exposing a GObject's data with properties allows you to employ an object design tool (such as Glade, see Chapter 5).

You'll encounter properties *ad infinitum* in GTK+ when you read Chapter 3, primarily when manipulating widget settings.[2]

2.4.1 Declaring Parameters

You must define each property in a class as a GObject *parameter*. To get started, you should obtain a GParamSpec structure in your class initialization function (described in Section 2.2.3).

You'll need the following information to create a GParamSpec structure:

- An **identifier**. A short string will do, such as `inventory-id`.
- A **nickname**. The full name of the parameter, such as `inventory number`.
- A **description**. A concise explanation, such as `number on the inventory label`.
- **Options**, such as read-write access.
- Type-specific information, such as

> Minimum value
>
> Maximum value
>
> Default value
>
> A secondary type if you're encapsulating parameters (for example, `G_TYPE_BOXED`, `G_TYPE_ENUM`, `G_TYPE_FLAGS`, `G_TYPE_OBJECT`, `G_TYPE_PARAM`).
>
> Sizes of arrays.

Because it is somewhat complicated, you don't create a GParamSpec structure by hand. Instead, use one of the g_param_spec_ functions in the following table to allocate the structure and set its fields.

Function	Type
g_param_spec_boolean()	gboolean
g_param_spec_boxed()	GBoxed
g_param_spec_char()	gchar
g_param_spec_double()	gdouble
g_param_spec_enum()	GEnumClass, GEnumValue
g_param_spec_flags()	GFlagsClass
g_param_spec_float()	gfloat
g_param_spec_int()	gint
g_param_spec_int64()	gint64
g_param_spec_long()	glong
g_param_spec_object()	GObject
g_param_spec_param()	GParamSpec

---

[2] Unfortunately, some GTK+ classes do not have property interfaces; hopefully, that's not a permanent situation.

Function	Type
g_param_spec_pointer()	gpointer
g_param_spec_string()	gchar *
g_param_spec_uchar()	guchar
g_param_spec_uint()	guint
g_param_spec_uint64()	guint64
g_param_spec_unichar()	gunichar
g_param_spec_value_array()	Array of some other type

Typically, you place the call to a g_param_spec_ function in your class initializer function. You may recall that the class initializer for the **Media** example is media_class_init(). Therefore, using parameters for **inventory-id** and **orig-package**, media_class_init() would look something like this:

```
static void media_class_init(MediaClass *class)
{
  GParamSpec *inv_nr_param;
  GParamSpec *orig_package_param;

  << ... >>

  /* create GParamSpec descriptions for properties */
  inv_nr_param = g_param_spec_uint("inventory-id",     /* identifier */
                                   "inventory number", /* nickname */
                                   "number on inventory label",
                                                       /* description */
                                   0,                  /* minimum */
                                   UINT_MAX,           /* maximum */
                                   0,                  /* default */
                                   G_PARAM_READWRITE); /* flags */

  orig_package_param = g_param_spec_boolean("orig-package",
                                            "original package?",
                                            "is item in its original package?",
                                            FALSE,
                                            G_PARAM_READWRITE);

  << ... >>

}
```

Although the actual inv_nr and orig_package fields from the Media instance structure aren't in this function, you will need to come back to them when you actually install the property in the class. The GParamSpec structure serves to *describe* the property: its purpose, type, and permissible values.

The last parameter to a g_param_spec_ function is a bit mask that you can specify with a bitwise OR of any of the following:

- G_PARAM_CONSTRUCT indicates that GObject will assign a value to the property upon object instantiation. At the moment, this works only in conjunction with G_PARAM_CONSTRUCT.

- G_PARAM_CONSTRUCT_ONLY indicates that the property may take on a value *only* when an object is instantiated.

- G_PARAM_LAX_VALIDATION disables type checks when you write to this property. Set this only if you know exactly what you're doing.

- G_PARAM_READABLE allows read access to the property.

- G_PARAM_WRITABLE allows write access to the property.

- G_PARAM_READWRITE is shorthand for G_PARAM_READABLE|G_PARAM_WRITABLE.

NOTE   *As this chapter progresses, the* media_class_init() *function code in this section will grow.*

2.4.2   Tangent: Generic Containers for Values

Before you get to Section 2.4.3, where you see how to activate a property in the class initializer, you need to familiarize yourself with how GObject moves the property values from place to place.

Untyped gpointer-style pointers normally take on the task of setting and retrieving function parameters of an arbitrary type. However, you need to store and check the type information at run time so that you don't try to do something disastrous, like attempting to copy a string into a memory location that corresponds to a random integer.

GObject has a mechanism for holding a value along with its type into a single "container," so that you can pass the container along as a parameter and pull its value and type out when necessary. This system is called GValue, with function names that start with g_value_.

The actual container is the GValue data structure. If you need to create one, you can do it with GLib's elementary memory management utilities; there aren't any special functions just for GValues.

WARNING   *That said, you must use* g_malloc0(), g_new0(), *or some other similar allocation function that sets all of the new memory bytes to zero. You'll get an error when you try to initialize a* GValue *structure with random bytes.*

After creating a GValue structure gvalue, initialize it with

---

g_value_init(*gvalue*, *type*)

---

where *type* is an identifier such as G_TYPE_INT (see page 78 for a full list). For each type identifier, the following are available:

- A verification macro, G_VALUE_HOLDS_*TYPE*(*gvalue*), that returns TRUE when *gvalue* contains the type.

- A writer function, g_value_set_*type*(*gvalue*, *value*), to place *value* into the *gvalue* container.

- A reader function, g_value_get_*type*(*gvalue*), to fetch the value from *gvalue*.

NOTE   *If you can't decide on how often to verify the type inside a container, err on doing it too often instead of one time too few when you go to read or write a value.*

The standard types are listed below. Here is a small GValue demonstration:

```
/* gvaluedemo.c -- demonstrate GValue */

#include <glib-object.h>
#include <stdio.h>

int main(int argc, char **argv)
{
  GValue *value;

  g_type_init(); /* initialize type system */

  /* allocate new GValue, zero out contents */
  value = g_new0(GValue, 1);

  /* initialize GValue type to gint */
  g_value_init(value, G_TYPE_INT);

  /* set the value to 42 and read it out again */
  g_value_set_int(value, 42);
  g_print("Value: %d\n", g_value_get_int(value));

  /* is the type of the GValue a GObject? */
  if (G_VALUE_HOLDS_OBJECT(value))
  {
    g_print("Container holds a GObject\n");
  } else {
    g_print("Container does not hold a GObject\n");
  }
  /* expect "Container does not hold a GObject" */

  g_free(value);

  return 0;
}
```

There are two special access functions for GValue structures of G_TYPE_STRING: g_value_set_static_string(*gvalue*, *str*) transfers a string pointer *str* into a *gvalue*, and g_value_dup_string(*gvalue*) returns a copy of a string in *gvalue* (you will need to deallocate that copy when you're done with it, though).

Otherwise, the names are uniform. For each of the types in the following list, there is a verification macro and a reader and writer access function, as described earlier. For example, G_TYPE_CHAR comes with G_VALUE_HOLDS_CHAR(), g_value_get_char(), and g_value_set_char().

G_TYPE_BOOLEAN	G_TYPE_FLOAT	G_TYPE_POINTER
G_TYPE_BOXED	G_TYPE_INT	G_TYPE_STRING
G_TYPE_CHAR	G_TYPE_INT64	G_TYPE_UCHAR
G_TYPE_DOUBLE	G_TYPE_LONG	G_TYPE_UINT
G_TYPE_ENUM	G_TYPE_OBJECT	G_TYPE_UINT64
G_TYPE_FLAGS	G_TYPE_PARAM	G_TYPE_ULONG

It might be prudent to note that GObject also defines a gchararray type that stands for gchar *. The advantage of using gchararray over a simple gchar pointer is in name only; when you have a gchararray array, you can be certain that it's a string and not some other type that you've cast to gchar *.

To reset a GValue to its original state — that is, the zeroed memory that you had just before you ran g_value_init() — use g_value_unset(gvalue). This frees up any extra memory that gvalue is currently using and sets its bytes in memory to zero. At that point, it's ready to be used again.

2.4.3 Installing Properties

Now you're ready to install some properties. Recall that in Section 2.4.1 you came up with the GParamSpec structures for the *Media* class properties in the media_class_init() function. The property installation continues in that function, with a call to

```
g_object_class_install_property(class, id, param)
```

where *class* is the class structure, *param* is the property's GParamSpec structure, and *id* is a unique identifier obtained with an enumeration type. This identifier should begin with PROP_.

WARNING   *The property identifier must be greater than zero, so you will need to place a dummy value like* PROP_MEDIA_0 *at the head of your enumeration type.*

The code for media_class_init() should make things clear:

```
enum {
  PROP_MEDIA_0,
  PROP_INV_NR,
  PROP_ORIG_PACKAGE
};

static void media_class_init(MediaClass *class)
{
  GParamSpec *inv_nr_param;
  GParamSpec *orig_package_param;
  GObjectClass *g_object_class;

  /* get handle to base object */
  g_object_class = G_OBJECT_CLASS(class);

  << param structure setup from Section 2.4.1 >>

  /* override base object methods */
  g_object_class->set_property = media_set_property;
  g_object_class->get_property = media_get_property;
```

WARNING   *Notice that you must set the* set_property *and* get_property *methods before installing the class properties.*

```
<< ... >>

/* install properties */
g_object_class_install_property(g_object_class,
                                PROP_INV_NR,
                                inv_nr_param);

g_object_class_install_property(g_object_class,
                                PROP_ORIG_PACKAGE,
                                orig_package_param);

<< ... >>
}
```

NOTE *The code in Section 2.4.1 and here accesses* GParamSpec *structures with the temporary variables* inv_nr_param *and* orig_package_param *before installation with* g_object_class_install_property(). *Programmers normally omit these temporary variables, using the entire call to* g_param_spec_boolean() *as a parameter when they install the property.*

To use the property system in the new class, media_class_init() must cast the new **Media** class structure (class) pointer to a **GObject** class structure named g_object_class. When you get a handle from a cast like this, you can override the set_property and get_property methods in the **GObject** base class. This is exactly what you must do to install the new properties such as **inventory-id** and **orig-package**. Remember that the base object knows nothing about the properties and instance structures of its subclasses.

The example overrides the base class methods with media_set_property() and media_get_property(), and therefore, you must supply prototypes before media_class_init(). These are straightforward, and because they are replacements for methods in the base class structure, they must conform to the prototypes in the base class structure:

```
static void media_set_property(GObject *object,
                               guint prop_id,
                               const GValue *value,
                               GParamSpec *pspec);

static void media_get_property(GObject *object,
                               guint prop_id,
                               GValue *value,
                               GParamSpec *pspec);
```

NOTE *You can avoid prototypes for static functions by placing the actual functions (described below) before* media_class_init().

Now that you've set up all of this infrastructure to handle the properties, you can write the functions that actually deal with the inv_nr and orig_package fields in the instance structure. The implementations consist of some busywork; to set a field, media_set_property() does the following:

1. Determines the property to set.
2. Removes the new property value from the GValue container from its parameter list.
3. Sets the field in the instance structure (*finally!*).

Here is the actual code:

```
static void media_set_property(GObject *object,
                               guint prop_id,
                               const GValue *value,
                               GParamSpec *pspec)
{
  Media *media;
  guint new_inv_nr;
  gboolean new_orig_package;

  media = MEDIA(object);

  switch(prop_id)
  {
    case PROP_INV_NR:
      new_inv_nr = g_value_get_uint(value);
      if (media->inv_nr != new_inv_nr)
      {
        media->inv_nr = new_inv_nr;
      }
      break;

    case PROP_ORIG_PACKAGE:
      new_orig_package = g_value_get_boolean(value);
      if (media->orig_package != new_orig_package)
      {
        media->orig_package = new_orig_package;
      }
      break;

    default:
      G_OBJECT_WARN_INVALID_PROPERTY_ID(object, prop_id, pspec);
      break;
  }
}
```

The media_get_property() code is similar, except that it needs to put one of the instance structure fields into the container rather than the other way around. No notification is necessary. (It would be very nosy of your program to tell the object every time someone looked at a property, but you can do it if you really want to.)

```
static void media_get_property(GObject *object,
                               guint prop_id,
                               GValue *value,
                               GParamSpec *pspec)
```

```
{
  Media *media;

  media = MEDIA(object);

  switch(prop_id)
  {
    case PROP_INV_NR:
      g_value_set_uint(value, media->inv_nr);
      break;

    case PROP_ORIG_PACKAGE:
      g_value_set_boolean(value, media->orig_package);
      break;

    default:
      G_OBJECT_WARN_INVALID_PROPERTY_ID(object, prop_id, pspec);
      break;
  }
}
```

Take a close look at the `default` case in each of these functions. The default comes into play only when the function encounters an invalid property, and it runs `G_OBJECT_WARN_INVALID_PROPERTY_ID()` on the object, invalid property, and parameter structure. The resulting warning message will hopefully be strong enough to get you to check your property access function calls.

Why Properties?

You may be wondering why you need such a complicated system just to set a bunch of fields in your instance structure. After all, you could write access methods to do this, or you could even just tell the programmer to set the fields. However, you want a uniform system such as properties for the following reasons:

- You need a *dynamic* system. Subclasses can add their own properties with little effort, as you will see in Section 2.7.

- You want to define behavior for when properties change. This capability is extremely important in GUI programming, where you want the program to react to changes in buttons, check boxes, and other elements. If you haphazardly set instance structure fields instead of using properties, you would need to define a "reaction" function and make sure that any code that sets a field also calls that function. Even with access methods, this can get out of hand very quickly, especially if your "reaction" function needs to set other fields.

- You want a system that's easy to document. It's easy to list property names with their possible values and descriptions. Access method APIs are considerably harder to describe, especially if the methods aren't uniform.

But What About Those Access Methods That I Keep Seeing?

In practice, you might see access methods for a class that correspond to properties in the class, especially with older code. Functionally, there is no difference; it's just one more layer of indirection.

Let's say that you have this to set the **Media orig-package** property:

```
void media_set_orig_package(Media *object, gboolean new_value)
{
  Media *media;
  g_return_if_fail(IS_MEDIA(object));
  media = MEDIA(object);

  if (media->orig_package != new_value)
  {
    media->orig_package = new_value;
    g_object_notify(G_OBJECT(media), "orig-package");
  }
}
```

This does all of the work that you see under case `PROP_ORIG_PACKAGE:` in media_set_property() from page 81. Therefore, you can rewrite that part:

```
    case PROP_ORIG_PACKAGE:
       new_orig_package = g_value_set_boolean(value);
       media_set_orig_package(media, new_orig_package);
       break;
```

This is primarily a matter of convention and a function of the age of the code. When reading API documentation, you may see an object with more properties than access function pairs, indicating that someone may have added more properties to some older code without bothering to use access functions (developers don't usually remove access functions for fear of breaking third-party applications). In that case, *class_set_property*() contains a mix of access function calls and field assignments/notifications.

Direct access function calls are slightly faster because they do not have to look up the property identifier and encapsulate any values. However, this speedup usually doesn't matter.

2.5   Using Objects

So far, you have seen a quite a bit of preparatory work with objects. This work is admittedly complex, and you are probably hoping that *using* the objects is easier. Thankfully, it is.

To create an object, use g_object_new(*type*, ..., NULL), where *type* is the object's class type identifier. For example, to create a **Media** object with the default property values, use

```
Media *media;

media = g_object_new(TYPE_MEDIA, NULL);
```

If you want to set some of the properties when you create the object, try something like the following instead:

```
/* create an object, setting some properties */
media = g_object_new(TYPE_MEDIA,
                     "inventory-id", 42,
                     "orig-package", FALSE,
                     NULL);
```

NOTE   *The property list always ends with* NULL.

If you decide to follow tradition and write a generator function to create an object for you, conventions dictate that the generator name should be *type*_new(): for example, media_new(). You can always define a macro for this, but be careful with the variable arguments; not all C preprocessors support variable arguments.

If you did a tidy job of programming your classes — in particular, if every attribute in your instance structure corresponds to a property, with the appropriate code in your initialization functions — you don't need a generator function. If you stick to g_object_new(), you can specify properties in any order that you wish, easily add and delete properties, and in general, will not need to remember an additional set of function names. Furthermore, if you avoid generator functions, you will have a much easier time creating bindings for other programming languages.

2.5.1 Using Properties

Now that you know how to create an object and initialize its properties, you probably want to know how to set and retrieve those properties. The two functions for this are g_object_set() and g_object_get(); their parameters are very similar to those of g_object_new(), as you can see in this example:

```
guint nr;
gboolean is_unpacked;

<< ... >>

/* set new values */
g_print("Setting inventory-id = 37, orig-package = TRUE\n");
g_object_set(media,
             "orig-package", TRUE,
             "inventory-id", 37,
             NULL);

/* double-check those new values */
g_print("Verifying.. ");
g_object_get(media,
             "orig-package", &is_unpacked,
             "inventory-id", &nr,
             NULL);
g_print("inventory-id = %d, orig-package = %s\n",
        nr, is_unpacked ? "TRUE" : "FALSE");
```

To retrieve parameters with g_object_get(), you need to specify the address of the target memory location; g_object_get() fills the memory with the new values. Examples in the preceding code are &is_unpacked and &nr.

Be careful not to mix up your types when accessing properties. That is, don't code something like g_object_get(media, "my-double", &my_int). *You may also need to cast certain constants when using them in conjunction with* g_object_set(). *This is one area where access functions may be a somewhat preferable option.*

Here are a few more functions that work with properties:

- g_object_set_property(*object*, *name*, *value*)
  Sets a single property *name* in *object* to *value*.

- g_object_get_property(*object*, *name*, *addr*)
  Stores the property *name* from *object* in the memory at *addr*.

- g_object_set_valist(*object*, *name*, *varargs*)
  Like g_object_set_property(), but operates with variable arguments.

- g_object_get_valist(*object*, *name*, *varargs*)
  Same as the preceding function, but retrieves the arguments instead of storing them.

2.5.2   Strong and Weak Object References

GObject uses a reference count to keep track of its objects. When you call g_object_new(), you're actually getting a reference to the object, and GObject makes a note with the reference count. If you want another reference to the same object, use g_object_ref(*object*) to return another reference.

To remove a reference, call g_object_unref(*object*). All references to a single object are equal; there is no special treatment for an original reference, and as mentioned before, GObject removes an object when the reference count goes to zero.

Such references are sometimes known as *strong* references, because they determine when GObject destroys an object. However, there are also *weak* references that can be present when GObject performs its garbage collection. GObject manages these references to a certain extent; it has a list of the object pointers in memory. To create a weak reference, use

---

g_object_add_weak_pointer(*object*, *weak_ptr_addr*)

Here, *object* is a casted existing reference to an object, and *weak_ptr_addr* is the *address* of the new weak pointer. If GObject removes the object behind the weak reference, it sets the weak reference to NULL. Use g_object_remove_weak_pointer() with the same arguments to remove a weak pointer.

NOTE *You still must assign the weak pointer by hand.*

Here are some examples of how to use references that build on the examples in the previous section:

```
Media *media2, *media_weak;

    << ... >>

media_weak = NULL;

/* set media2 to a strong reference from media */
```

```
media2 = g_object_ref(media);

/* set media_weak to a weak reference to media2 */
media_weak = media2;
g_object_add_weak_pointer(G_OBJECT(media2), (gpointer) &media_weak);

/* remove one strong reference */
g_object_unref(media2);

/* see if media_weak is NULL, meaning that object is gone */
if (media_weak == NULL)
{
   g_print("media_weak is NULL; object is gone\n");
} else {
   g_print("media_weak is not NULL; object is still in memory\n");
}

/* remove another reference */
g_object_unref(media);

/* check the weak pointer again */
if (media_weak == NULL)
{
   g_print("media_weak is NULL; object is gone\n");
}
```

Don't confuse g_object_*_weak_pointer() with g_object_weak_*ref(). The latter function enables you to call a notification function when the GObject is destroyed, but will not be covered in this book. The weak pointer functions here just set the object pointer to NULL.

2.6 Signals

Signals are events that can happen to an object during the course of the object's life. Signals serve as a means of communication between objects; when an object gets a signal, it can react in some way. The signal system in GObject is called GSignal.

NOTE *In written language, a signal can be the act of sending a message or the message itself. In GObject, a signal is the sender's version of the message. A GObject signal has one source and multiple potential recipients.*

A signal *handler* is a callback function with a prototype that you declare when you initialize a class (for example, media_class_init() from Section 2.4.1). When some other part of a program *emits* a signal, GSignal calls the handler on the object. You can alter the characteristics of an object with a signal handler. You can specify the order of the handler invocations on a per-signal basis.

NOTE *You add signal handlers on a per-object basis. When you add a handler to one object, it does not apply for any other objects in the class.*

You can pass parameters along with signals and receive return values from handlers with the *marshalling*[3] mechanism. Each signal usually has a function pointer in an object's class structure. The function behind this pointer is called the *default handler.* You can link additional functions into a signal, so that if there is more than one return value per signal emission, the object may process all of the return values back with the help of an *accumulator.* Otherwise, GSignal returns the value of only the last signal handler.

2.6.1 Defining Signals and Installing Handlers

A signal isn't a data structure; it's just a `guint` identifier managed by GObject. You should define some names for these identifiers with an enumeration type (for caching purposes later); a good place to do this is somewhere before your class initialization function (for example, `media_class_init()`). Here is an example for two signals: one that removes an item from its package, and another that throws out an item.

```
/* Signal indices */
enum {
  UNPACKED,
  THROW_OUT,
  LAST_SIGNAL
};
```

As you can see, these names correspond to indices. Furthermore, common practice says that you should create a cache array as a static variable. Later, you will set each array element to a GObject signal identifier.

```
/* Signal identifier map */
static guint media_signal[LAST_SIGNAL] = {0, 0};
```

Note how `LAST_SIGNAL` indicates the size of the array.

Now you need to think about the signal handlers. You may recall from Section 2.2.1 that you already provided some infrastructure in the `MediaClass` class structure for signal handlers: function pointer fields called `unpacked` and `throw_out`. The actual functions that correspond to these are `media_unpacked()` and `media_throw_out()`, so you need to provide their prototypes:

```
/* Prototypes for signal handlers */
static void media_unpacked(Media *media);
static void media_throw_out(Media *media, gboolean permanent);
```

With this, you are close to completing the `media_class_init()` function first started in Section 2.4.1. Continue by setting the function pointers in the class structure to the actual signal handlers as shown on the next page:

---

[3] There are two spellings of this word: *marshaling* and *marshalling.* The text in this book uses the double-l variants, but you may see files and API elements with a single l.

```
/* Initialize the Media class */
static void media_class_init(MediaClass *class)
{
  GObjectClass *g_object_class;

  << parameter/property code >>

  /* set signal handlers */
  class->unpacked = media_unpacked;
  class->throw_out = media_throw_out;
```

Then install the **unpacked** signal and its default handler with g_signal_new():

```
/* install signals and default handlers */
media_signal[UNPACKED] =
    g_signal_new("unpacked",                       /* name */
              TYPE_MEDIA,                          /* class type identifier */
              G_SIGNAL_RUN_LAST|G_SIGNAL_DETAILED, /* options */
              G_STRUCT_OFFSET(MediaClass, unpacked), /* handler offset */
              NULL,                                /* accumulator function */
              NULL,                                /* accumulator data */
              g_cclosure_marshal_VOID__VOID,       /* marshaller */
              G_TYPE_NONE,                         /* type of return value */
              0);
```

That's a mouthful, to say the least, so here's how the code breaks down:

- The **return value** of g_signal_new() is GObject's identifier. You should store it in the mapping array from earlier.
- The **name** is a short string to identify the signal.
- The **type identifier** is the GObject class type identifier macro.
- **Options** may include one or more of the following as a bitwise OR:

  G_SIGNAL_DETAILED: The signal supports details (see Section 2.6.6).

  G_SIGNAL_NO_HOOKS: You may not use emission hooks with the signal (see Section 2.6.7).

  G_SIGNAL_NO_RECURSE: If GSignal gets another signal emission for this signal handler when the handler is still active, the signal handler restarts — it does not call the signal handler from within the signal handler.

  G_SIGNAL_RUN_FIRST: Signal emission has several stages. This flag indicates that the handler should run in the first stage (see Section 2.6.2).

  G_SIGNAL_RUN_LAST: The signal handler runs in the third stage (use this if you're not sure what to do).

  G_SIGNAL_RUN_CLEANUP: The signal handler runs in the last stage.

  G_SIGNAL_ACTION: If some code emits an **action signal**, it doesn't need to do any extra housecleaning around the target object. You can use this to interconnect code from different sources.

- The **offset** is an ugly way to tell g_signal_new() where the class signal handler function is. It is an offset from the memory location of the class structure, and luckily, you have the G_STRUCT_OFFSET macro to do the work for you.

- The **accumulator** is a callback function that collects various return values (see Section 2.6.4).

- The **accumulator data** is where to put the accumulator's data.

- The C **Marshaller** for the signal is described in Section 2.6.3.

- The **return value** is the return value of the marshaller.

- The **number of parameters** specifies how many extra parameters to pass along with the marshaller. If this number is greater than zero, you must specify the GValue types (see the **throw_out** example that follows).

Having learned all of this, you can install the signal and default handler for **throw_out** (the difference is that **throw_out** takes a gboolean parameter) and *finally* put media_class_init() to rest.

```
media_signal[THROW_OUT] =
    g_signal_new("throw_out",
                TYPE_MEDIA,
                G_SIGNAL_RUN_LAST|G_SIGNAL_DETAILED,
                G_STRUCT_OFFSET(MediaClass, throw_out),
                NULL, NULL,
                g_cclosure_marshal_VOID__BOOLEAN,
                G_TYPE_NONE,
                1,
                G_TYPE_BOOLEAN);
```

The signal handlers are fairly simple:

```
/* unpacked signal handler */
static void media_unpacked(Media *media)
{
  if (media->orig_package)
  {
     g_object_set(media, "orig-package", FALSE, NULL);
     g_print("Media unpacked.\n");
  } else {
     g_print("Media already unpacked.\n");
  }
}

/* throw_out signal handler */
static void media_throw_out(Media *media, gboolean permanent)
{
  if (permanent)
  {
     g_print("Trashing media.\n");
  } else {
     g_print("Media not in the dumpster quite yet.\n");
  }
}
```

Notice the additional parameter to `media_throw_out()`, and that these functions have no return values.

2.6.2 Emitting Signals

One way to emit a signal is with

---

g_signal_emit_by_name(*object*, *name* [, *parms* ..] [, *return*])

The arguments are as follows:

- *object* (gpointer): The target object.
- *name* (const gchar *): The signal identifier (for example, "unpacked").
- *parms*: Signal handler parameters (if any).
- *return*: Location of return value (if any).

Therefore, if you have a signal with a signature of VOID:VOID, you need only two parameters; otherwise, you need at least three. Here are some examples with the signals defined in Section 2.6.1:

```
g_signal_emit_by_name(media, "unpacked");
/* expect "Media unpacked." */

g_signal_emit_by_name(media, "unpacked");
/* expect "Media already unpacked." */

g_signal_emit_by_name(media, "throw-out", TRUE);
/* expect "Trashing media." */
```

Many programmers prefer to emit signals based on the numeric signal identifier to avoid a lookup on a string. This function is the manual equivalent of g_signal_emit_by_name():

---

g_signal_emit(gpointer *object*, guint *signal_id*, GQuark *detail*, ...)

You should use this function in conjunction with cached signal identifiers. Recall from Section 2.6.1 that `media_signal[]` holds the cache for the ongoing media example. Therefore, this example sends the **unpacked** signal to media:

```
g_signal_emit(media, media_signal[UNPACKED], 0);
```

NOTE *This book primarily uses* g_signal_emit_by_name() *because it requires less coding baggage. However, if you continuously emit signals, you should consider caching the signal identifiers as described above.*

If you set the **throw-out** handlers to return gboolean, the following code would retrieve that value and place it into a return_val variable:

```
gboolean return_val;
```

    « ... »

```
g_signal_emit_by_name(media, "throw-out", TRUE, &return_val);

if (return_val)
{
   g_print("Signal (throw-out): returned TRUE.\n");
} else {
   g_print("Signal (throw-out): returned FALSE.\n");
}
```

When you emit a signal, the GSignal runs through the following stages of handler calls:

1. **Default handlers** installed with the G_SIGNAL_RUN_FIRST option
2. **Emission hooks** (see Section 2.6.7)
3. **User-defined handlers** installed *without* the after option (see Section 2.6.5)
4. **Default handlers** installed with the G_SIGNAL_RUN_LAST option
5. **User-defined handlers** installed *with* the after option
6. **Default handlers** installed with the G_SIGNAL_RUN_CLEANUP option

Here are a few additional functions for emitting signals:

- g_signal_emitv(const GValue *object_and_parms*, guint *signal_id*, GQuark *detail*, GValue **result*)
  To use this function, you must store the target object and signal parameters in a GValue array *object_and_parms* and provide a place for the return value at result.

- g_signal_emit_valist(gpointer *object*, guint *signal_id*, GQuark *detail*, va_list *va_args*)
  This function works just like g_signal_emit, but with a previously prepared variable argument list *va_list* for the handler arguments and return value. With this call, you can create your own signal emission functions that take variable arguments.

2.6.3 Marshallers

When some code emits a signal, GSignal uses a marshaller to transport a list of parameters to the signal handler and to collect and propagate any return values.

Marshallers have names that reflect the parameter types and return values. The format is:

prefix_RETURNTYPE__PARM1TYPE[_PARM2TYPE_...]

For example, the marshaller for media_unpacked() was g_cclosure_marshal_VOID__VOID because this handler takes no parameters other than the object and returns nothing.

GObject comes with a number of marshallers for one parameter and no return value, as shown in the table on the next page.

Marshaller	Parameter Type
g_cclosure_marshal_VOID__BOOLEAN	gboolean
g_cclosure_marshal_VOID__BOXED	GBoxed*
g_cclosure_marshal_VOID__CHAR	gchar
g_cclosure_marshal_VOID__DOUBLE	gdouble
g_cclosure_marshal_VOID__ENUM	gint (enumeration types)
g_cclosure_marshal_VOID__FLAGS	guint (options)
g_cclosure_marshal_VOID__FLOAT	gfloat
g_cclosure_marshal_VOID__INT	gint
g_cclosure_marshal_VOID__LONG	glong
g_cclosure_marshal_VOID__OBJECT	GObject*
g_cclosure_marshal_VOID__PARAM	GParamSpec* or derived
g_cclosure_marshal_VOID__POINTER	gpointer
g_cclosure_marshal_VOID__STRING	gchar* or gchararray
g_cclosure_marshal_VOID__UCHAR	guchar
g_cclosure_marshal_VOID__ULONG	gulong
g_cclosure_marshal_VOID__UINT	guint
g_cclosure_marshal_VOID__VOID	void (no parameters)

WARNING   *Using the wrong marshaller will probably cause your program to crash.*

If you don't see the marshaller you need in the preceding list (that is, your signal handler returns a value and/or takes more than a single parameter), you have to provide your own. Your marshaller names should resemble the following:

```
_my_marshal_INT__VOID
_my_marshal_VOID__OBJECT_INT
_my_marshal_UINT__BOOLEAN_BOOLEAN
```

where _my_marshal is your prefix.

Thankfully, you don't have to actually write the marshaller code; there's a utility called glib-genmarshal to do the dirty work for you. For example, to create the marshallers above, put the following in a file called my_marshaller.list:

```
INT:VOID
VOID:OBJECT,INT
UINT:BOOLEAN
```

The file format is fairly obvious; each line is a *signature* defining a new marshaller, starting with the return type. After a colon, you list the parameter types. You should be able to determine the valid types from the table earlier in this section.

To create the actual code, run these two commands:

```
glib-genmarshal --prefix _my_marshal --header my_marshaller.list > my_marshaller.h
glib-genmarshal --prefix _my_marshal --body my_marshaller.list > my_marshaller.c
```

You now have a new source file, *my_marshaller.c,* and a *my_marshaller.h* header file.

You don't have to supply a prefix. The default is `g_cclosure_user_marshal`, *but if you choose to accept this, be aware that you risk duplicate symbols at link time, especially if you are combining several different pieces of code.*

You must include *my_marshaller.h* in the source file that includes your class initialization function (or any other place where you install signal handlers). The *my_marshaller.h* file should look something like this:

```
#ifndef ___my_marshal_MARSHAL_H__
#define ___my_marshal_MARSHAL_H__

#include <glib-object.h>

G_BEGIN_DECLS

/* INT:VOID (my_marshaller.list:1) */
extern void _my_marshal_INT__VOID
    (GClosure      *closure,
     GValue        *return_value,
     guint          n_param_values,
     const GValue *param_values,
     gpointer       invocation_hint,
     gpointer       marshal_data);

/* VOID:OBJECT,INT (my_marshaller.list:2) */
extern void _my_marshal_VOID__OBJECT_INT
    (GClosure      *closure,
     GValue        *return_value,
     guint          n_param_values,
     const GValue *param_values,
     gpointer       invocation_hint,
     gpointer       marshal_data);

/* UINT:BOOLEAN (my_marshaller.list:3) */
extern void _my_marshal_UINT__BOOLEAN
    (GClosure      *closure,
     GValue        *return_value,
     guint          n_param_values,
     const GValue *param_values,
     gpointer       invocation_hint,
     gpointer       marshal_data);

G_END_DECLS

#endif /* ___my_marshal_MARSHAL_H__ */
```

If you're building a Makefile, rules for creating the marshallers would look something like this:

```
my_marshaller.h: my_marshaller.list
        glib-genmarshal --prefix _my_marshal --header \
        my_marshaller.list > my_marshaller.h

my_marshaller.c: my_marshaller.list
```

```
glib-genmarshal --prefix _my_marshal --body \
my_marshaller.list > my_marshaller.c
```

NOTE *Remember that the whitespace in the preceding listing actually consists of tabs.*

You may also want to add a dependency for `glib-genmarshal`, but this is probably best done with the help of GNU autoconf (see Chapter 6).

2.6.4 *Signal Accumulators*

If GSignal runs several signal handlers for one signal, the handler calls run in succession, and the marshaller propagates the return value from the last handler back to the code that emitted the signal.

In rare cases, though, you may want to know what all of the handlers returned. You can define an accumulator to collect and process all of the return values.

To install an accumulator along with a signal, supply a GSignalAccumulator callback function as the fifth argument to g_signal_new(). Here is the callback type definition:

```
typedef struct _GSignalInvocationHint GSignalInvocationHint;

« ... »

typedef gboolean (*GSignalAccumulator)
    (GSignalInvocationHint *ihint,
     GValue                *return_accu,
     const GValue          *handler_return,
     gpointer               data);

« ... »

struct _GSignalInvocationHint
{
  guint        signal_id;
  GQuark       detail;
  GSignalFlags run_type;
};
```

GSignal calls your accumulator right after it runs each signal handler. As you can see from the preceding code, accumulator functions have four arguments:

* ihint (GSignalInvocationHint *): A structure containing the signal identifier signal_id, a detail (see Section 2.6.6) and the signal options from g_signal_new().

* return_accu (GValue *): The accumulator that GSignal eventually returns to the code that emitted the signal. You can do anything you like with this container.

- `handler_return` (const `GValue` *): Contains the return value from the last signal handler.
- `data` (gpointer): Any accumulator data that you set up with `g_signal_new()`.

Your accumulator should return TRUE if you want GSignal to continue calling signal handlers for this particular signal emission, or FALSE if it should stop.

An accumulator typically may be used to look over Boolean values that signal handlers return. As soon as one of the handlers returns TRUE, the accumulator propagates TRUE as a return value and stops the emission process.

This book doesn't have an example of an accumulator (there's only so much space), but it's easy enough to find one: Unpack the GTK+ source code, change to the distribution's top-level directory, and run this command:

```
grep GSignalInvocationHint */*
```

This command prints lines from the source files that have accumulators.

2.6.5 Attaching Handlers to Signals

As you will see with widget objects in Chapter 3, you want to be able attach different signal handlers to the same kind of object (for example, if you have two button objects, you don't want the buttons to do the exact same thing).

This code attaches a new handler called `meep_meep()` to the **unpacked** signal on media, using `g_signal_connect()`:

```
static void meep_meep(Media *media)
{
  guint nr;
  g_object_get(media, "inventory-id", &nr, NULL);

  g_print("Meep-meep! (Inventory number: \%d)\n", nr);
}
  << ... >>

gulong handler_id;

/* connect new handler */
handler_id = g_signal_connect(media,
                              "unpacked",
                              (GCallback) meep_meep,
                              NULL);

/* test the new handler */
g_signal_emit_by_name(media, "unpacked");
/* expect "meep-meep" message, plus output of other handler(s) */
```

In this example, GSignal calls `meep_meep()` before the default signal handler, because the default was not installed with `G_SIGNAL_RUN_FIRST`.

The most common way to attach a handler is to use

```
gulong handler_id;

handler_id = g_signal_connect(object, name, function, data);
```

- *object* (gpointer): The target object.
- *name* (const gchar *): The signal name.
- *function* (GCallback *): The new signal handler. This callback function must have the same prototype as in the instance structure, but you may need to cast to get a fit as an argument.
- *data* (gpointer): Optional data for the signal handler.

You'll see plenty of uses for the optional data pointer later in this book, such as the one described in Section 3.3. Normally, GSignal attempts to pass the data to the signal handler as the last argument. However, if you want to use a handler that takes a data pointer as its *first* parameter, use

```
g_signal_connect_swapped(object, name, function, data)
```

You might want to do this if your handler is a library function that takes only one argument. An example is in Section 3.6.10.

```
g_signal_connect_after(object, name, function, data)
```

is nearly identical to g_signal_connect(), except that function runs in stage 5 listed in Section 2.6.2 rather than in stage 3. The idea is that you can make the handler run after the default handler, but as you can see from that section, you can also override that behavior when you install the default handler.

All g_signal_connect*() calls return an identifier for the handler binding. If you store the identifier as *handler_id*, you can check the status of a binding with

```
g_signal_handler_is_connected(object, handler_id)
```

To remove a binding, invoke

```
g_signal_handler_disconnect(object, handler_id)
```

Here are some examples:

```
/* test and disconnect handlers */
if (g_signal_handler_is_connected(media, handler_id))
{
    g_print("meepmeep is connected to media. Detaching...\n");
}

g_signal_handler_disconnect(media, handler_id);

if (!g_signal_handler_is_connected(media, handler_id))
```

```
{
  g_print("meepmeep no longer connected:\n");
  g_signal_emit_by_name(media, "unpacked");
}
```

NOTE *Remember that any handlers that you connect to an object are on a per-object basis and do not apply for the rest of the class. You can also connect, disconnect, and block signal handlers during emission.*

2.6.6   Details

Signal details are further subdivisions of signals. To specify a detail in a signal name, append two colons and the detail name (for example, `unpacked::ding`).

You can add detail information when you connect a handler or emit a signal. When you emit a signal with a detail, GSignal calls the handlers with that detail and those completely without details. GSignal does not call a handler with a detail that does not match the given emission. In addition, if you emit a signal *without* a detail, GSignal will not call any handler connected *with* a detail. You should get the idea from the following example:

```
static void ding(Media *media)
{
  g_print("Ding.\n");
}

static void dong(Media *media)
{
  g_print("Dong.\n");
}

  << ... >>

/* connect handlers with ding and dong details */
g_signal_connect(media, "unpacked::ding", (GCallback)ding, NULL);

g_signal_connect(media, "unpacked::dong", (GCallback)dong, NULL);

g_signal_emit_by_name(media, "unpacked::ding");
/* expect "Ding," then "Media ... unpacked" */

g_signal_emit_by_name(media, "unpacked::dong");
/* expect "Dong," then "Media ... unpacked" */

g_signal_emit_by_name(media, "unpacked");
/* expect only "Media ... unpacked" */
```

NOTE *Signal details work only when you install a signal with the* G_SIGNAL_DETAILED *option (see Section 2.6.1).*

2.6.7 Emission Hooks

User-defined signal handlers connect only to single objects. However, you can also define *emission hooks* that apply to a GSignal identifier instead of an object. When you emit a signal that has a hook, GSignal calls the hook regardless of the target object. Therefore, you can make user-defined hooks at run time that apply to all objects in a class rather than just one object. You can attach details to hooks, just as you did with regular signals and their handlers.

Hook functions have the GSignalEmissionHook type and look a bit different than normal signal handlers. Here is the function type definition:

```
typedef gboolean (*GSignalEmissionHook) (GSignalInvocationHint *ihint,
                                         guint n_param_values,
                                         const GValue *param_values,
                                         gpointer data);
```

As with the accumulators in Section 2.6.4, each hook receives a GSignalInvocationHint structure and a user-defined untyped data pointer. The other parameters are as follows:

- n_param_values is the number of signal emission parameters.
- param_values is an array of GValues, each containing the parameters from the signal emission. The first parameter is the target object. To get to the others, you need to do some pointer arithmetic (as the example in this section will imply).
- data is a pointer to any user-defined data.

Hooks return gboolean. If a hook returns FALSE, GSignal removes the hook from the signal emission sequence. Make sure to return TRUE if you want your hook to run more than once.

The following example is a little difficult to read at first, but it does very little. Essentially, the hook verifies that its parameter is a Media object and prints the inventory number. After GSignal calls the hook for the third time, the hook returns FALSE and therefore requests removal from the signal.

```
static gboolean my_hook(GSignalInvocationHint *ihint,
                        guint n_param_values,
                        const GValue *param_values,
                        gpointer *data)
{
  static gint n = 0;
  guint inv_nr;
  Media *m;
  GObject *obj;

  g_print("my_hook(): ");

  /* check for a valid Media object */
  if (n_param_values > 0)
```

```
{
    obj = g_value_get_object(param_values + 0);
    if (IS_MEDIA(obj))
    {
        m = MEDIA(obj);
        g_object_get(m, "inventory-id", &inv_nr, NULL);
        g_print("inventory number = %d.\n", inv_nr);
    } else {
        g_print("called with invalid object\n");
    }
} else {
    g_print("called with invalid parameters\n");
}

n++;
g_print("my_hook(): invocation #%d", n);

if (n == 3)
{
    g_print(" (last time)\n");
    return(FALSE);
} else {
    g_print("\n");
    return(TRUE);
}
}


<< ... >>

gulong hook_id;
Media *m2, *m3;

<< create one more media object, m2 >>

/* add an emission hook */
    hook_id = g_signal_add_emission_hook(media_signal[UNPACKED],
                                    0,
                                    (GSignalEmissionHook)my_hook,
                                    NULL, NULL);

/* test the hook on three different objects */
g_signal_emit_by_name(media, "unpacked");
g_signal_emit_by_name(m2, "unpacked");
g_signal_emit_by_name(media, "unpacked");

/* this time, the hook should no longer be active */
g_signal_emit_by_name(media, "unpacked");
```

Notice that g_signal_add_emission_hook() uses the signal identifier map from Section 2.6.1.

To remove a hook, run g_signal_hook_remove() on the hook identifier that g_signal_add_emission_hook() returns.

NOTE   *You won't find too much use for hooks in common practice. Before you install a hook into a class, you might ask yourself if it's really necessary.*

2.6.8 More Signal Utilities

A number of tools are available to monitor and control signals and their emissions. For example, you can get the options specified at installation, the after flag, and handler bindings. In addition, you can block signal handlers and interrupt a signal emission.

Blocking Signal Handlers

- g_signal_handler_block(gpointer *object*, gulong *handler_id*)
  Disables a signal handler temporarily. GSignal will not call the handler for object until further notice.

- g_signal_handler_unblock(gpointer *object*, gulong *handler_id*)
  Enables a signal handler.

NOTE *You can disable a signal handler as many times as you like; the effect is like putting an extra latch on a door. Therefore, if you block a handler three times in succession, you must enable it three times to get it working again.*

Aborting Signal Emissions

- g_signal_stop_emission_by_name(gpointer *object*, const gchar *signame*)
  Ends the current signal emission. Note that signame is the signal's name, including any detail. If there is no such signal emission, this function prints a warning message.

- g_signal_stop_emission(gpointer *object*, guint *signal_id*, GQuark *detail*)
  Same as the preceding function, but uses a signal identifier and a separate detail name.

Identifier Functions

To help you manage signals, names, and identifiers, GSignal provides the following:

- guint g_signal_lookup(gchar *name*, GType *class*) returns the signal identifier corresponding to *name* for the *class* class type identifier.

- gchar *g_signal_name(guint *signal_id*) returns the signal name for *signal_id*.

- guint *g_signal_list_ids(GType *class*, guint *num_sigs*) returns an array of signal IDs for *class*, writing the number of signals in *num_sigs*. You must deallocate this memory by yourself.

Here is a small demonstration:

```
guint i, nr, *sigs;

sigs = g_signal_list_ids(TYPE_MEDIA, &nr);
g_print("ID     Name\n");
g_print("----   ------------\n");
i = 0;
while (i < nr)
{
  g_print("%-4d  %s\n", *sigs, g_signal_name(*sigs));
```

```
  i++;
  sigs++;
}
g_print("\nTotal signals: %d\n", nr);
g_free(sigs);
```

Miscellaneous Functions

Here are several more functions that work with signals that you might find useful. Refer to the online API documentation for a detailed list of the parameters.

- g_signal_newv() is like g_signal_new(), except that here you supply the handler parameter types in an array.

- g_signal_valist() wants a va_list of the handler parameter types. This function is suitable for building your own signal installers.

- g_signal_connect_data() is the full-blown function for installing signal handlers. The rest of the g_signal_connect functions in this chapter are macros based on this function.

- g_signal_query() asks for detailed information about a signal and fills a GSignalQuery structure with the information. If the utilities in the previous subsection weren't enough for you, check out this one.

- g_signal_handlers_block_matched() blocks all signal handlers that match criteria in a given GSignalMatchType structure.

- g_signal_handlers_unblock_matched() is like the preceding function, but it enables the signal handlers.

- g_signal_handlers_disconnect_matched() is like the preceding function, but it removes the signal handlers from their objects.

- g_signal_handler_find() looks for a signal that matches the criteria in a GSignalMatchType structure.

- g_signal_handlers_block_by_func() disables signal handlers based on a pointer to the handler function.

- g_signal_handlers_unblock_by_func() is the opposite of the preceding function.

- g_signal_handlers_disconnect_by_func() is like the preceding function, but removes the handler.

2.7 Inheritance

After digesting the material in the previous sections, you should be quite familiar with the creation and use of classes and signals. This chapter's final topic is inheritance.

In principle, you already saw inheritance when you created the **Media** class, because it is a subclass of **GObject**. Here are the details of how to build a subclass:

1. Define the **instance structure** with a pointer for the parent instance structure at the beginning.

2. Define the **class structure** with a pointer to the parent class structure at the beginning.

3. In the function that returns the new subclass, use the **parent class type identifier** as the first argument to g_type_register_static().

4. In the **class initializer**, install any new properties and signals. You may also install new default handlers for inherited signals.

The greater part of this section illustrates these steps, creating a **CD** class from **Media**. There is only one additional property, **writable**. A small demonstration of how to work with the new subclass follows the definitions.

To start, you need the usual instance and class structure definitions introduced in Section 2.2.1, as well as the macros from Section 2.2.2. Notice that writable is in the instance structure, but you need nothing else. Items such as set_property and get_property come from the parent structures.

```
/******** CD (class derived from Media) **********/

typedef struct _CD {
  Media media_instance;
  gboolean writable;
} CD;

typedef struct _CDClass {
  MediaClass media_class;
} CDClass;

#define TYPE_CD (cd_get_type())
#define CD(object) \
    (G_TYPE_CHECK_INSTANCE_CAST((object), TYPE_CD, CD))

#define CD_CLASS(klass) \
    (G_TYPE_CHECK_CLASS_CAST((klass), TYPE_CD, CDClass))

#define IS_CD(object) \
    (G_TYPE_CHECK_INSTANCE_TYPE((object), TYPE_CD))

#define IS_CD_CLASS(klass) \
    (G_TYPE_CHECK_CLASS_TYPE((klass), TYPE_CD))

#define CD_GET_CLASS(object) \
    (G_TYPE_INSTANCE_GET_CLASS((object), TYPE_CD, CDClass))

static void cd_class_init(CDClass *class);
```

Now you must provide a function to return the new class type identifier (TYPE_CD), as in Section 2.2.3. Note the parent class type identifier from the **Media** class (shown in boldface):

```
GType cd_get_type(void)
{
  static GType cd_type = 0;
  const GInterfaceInfo cleanable_info;

  if (!cd_type)
```

```
{
    static const GTypeInfo cd_info = {
        sizeof(CDClass),
        NULL,
        NULL,
        (GClassInitFunc)cd_class_init,
        NULL,
        NULL,
        sizeof(CD),
        16,
        NULL
    };

    const GInterfaceInfo cleanable_info = {
        cd_cleanable_init, NULL, NULL
    };

    /* Register type, use ID of parent class TYPE_MEDIA */
    /* "CD" is too short, use "CompactDisc" instead */
    cd_type = g_type_register_static(TYPE_MEDIA, "CompactDisc", &cd_info, 0);

    /* add interface */
    g_type_add_interface_static(cd_type, TYPE_CLEANABLE, &cleanable_info);
  }
  return cd_type;
}
```

Now you are almost ready to write the cd_class_init() class initializer, but first, you must provide some dependencies:

```
/* CD constants and prototypes for properties */
enum {
  PROP_0_CD,
  PROP_WRITABLE
};

static void cd_get_property(GObject *object,
                           guint prop_id,
                           GValue *value,
                           GParamSpec *pspec);

static void cd_set_property(GObject *object,
                           guint prop_id,
                           const GValue *value,
                           GParamSpec *pspec);
```

NOTE   *By now, the pedantic C programmer may be wondering why you would ever make prototypes*
for static functions. The prototypes just shown are not necessary if you define the functions
before the cd_class_init()*. In this book, it's primarily a matter of organization — we didn't*
want to go into detail about properties before explaining the role of the class initializer.

For the sake of demonstration, this subclass replaces **Media**'s default signal handler for **unpacked** with this:

```
/* a new default signal handler for unpacked */
static void unpacked_cd()
{
  g_print("Hi!\n");
}
```

The class initializer is fairly straightforward; notice how replacing the default signal handler is a simple assignment after you get the parent class structure:

```
/* CD class initializer */
static void cd_class_init(CDClass *class)
{
  GObjectClass *g_object_class;
  MediaClass *media_class;

  media_class = MEDIA_CLASS(class);
  media_class->unpacked = unpacked_cd;

  g_object_class = G_OBJECT_CLASS(class);
  g_object_class->set_property = cd_set_property;
  g_object_class->get_property = cd_get_property;

  g_object_class_install_property(
      g_object_class,
      PROP_WRITABLE,
      g_param_spec_boolean("writable", "Writable?",
                           "Is the CD writable?", FALSE,
                           G_PARAM_READWRITE|G_PARAM_CONSTRUCT_ONLY));
}
```

You set and retrieve **writable** as described in Section 2.5.1, but you may wonder how this works. After all, the preceding code overrides the set_property() and get_property() methods for the base class, and there is no mention of the parent's properties in the functions the follow.

The key to understanding this is that GObject initializes parent classes first. When a class installs its properties, GObject associates those properties with the class, and therefore, it can also look up the appropriate *property() functions based on that class.

```
static void cd_set_property(GObject *object,
                            guint prop_id,
                            const GValue *value,
                            GParamSpec *pspec)
{
  gboolean writable;
  CD *cd = CD(object);

  switch(prop_id)
```

```
{
    case PROP_WRITABLE:
        writable = g_value_get_boolean(value);
        if (cd->writable != writable)
        {
            cd->writable = writable;
        }
        break;

    default:
        G_OBJECT_WARN_INVALID_PROPERTY_ID(object, prop_id, pspec);
        break;
    }
}

static void cd_get_property(GObject *object,
                            guint prop_id,
                            GValue *value,
                            GParamSpec *pspec)
{
    CD *cd = CD(object);

    switch(prop_id)
    {
        case PROP_WRITABLE:
            g_value_set_boolean(value, cd->writable);
            break;

        default:
            G_OBJECT_WARN_INVALID_PROPERTY_ID(object, prop_id, pspec);
            break;
    }
}
```

Now we're ready to use the new subclass. For the purposes of demonstration, assume that you also created another new subclass of **Media** called **EightTrack** for 8-track tapes. It adds a `minutes` property to **Media**, representing the total playing time of a tape.

You create objects and access properties as you would expect:

```
Media *media;
CD *cd;
EightTrack *eighttrack;
guint nr;
gboolean is_unpacked;

    << create a new media object >>

/* create a new CD object */
cd = g_object_new(TYPE_CD,
                  "inventory-id", 423,
                  "writable", FALSE,
                  NULL);

/* verify data in the object */
```

```
g_object_get(cd,
             "inventory-id", &nr,
             "writable", &is_unpacked,
             NULL);

g_print("cd: writable = %s, inventory-id = %d\n",
        is_unpacked? "true":"false", nr);

/* create an EightTrack object */
eighttrack = g_object_new(TYPE_EIGHTTRACK, "minutes", 47, NULL);
```

The following tests the signal handlers. Remember that the **unpacked** handler for
CD is different now.

```
/* EightTrack's unpacked handler; same as Media's */
g_signal_emit_by_name(eighttrack, "unpacked", NULL);

/* CD's unpacked handler; expect "Hi!" instead */
g_signal_emit_by_name(cd, "unpacked", NULL);
```

Finally, you can test various objects for membership in classes:

```
/* is cd in Media? (subclass in parent; expect true) */
g_print("cd is %sMedia object\n", IS_MEDIA(cd)? "a " : "not a ");

/* is eighttrack in Media? (subclass in parent; expect true) */
g_print("eighttrack is %sMedia object \n", IS_MEDIA(eighttrack)? "a " : "not a ");

/* is media in CD? (parent in subclass; expect false) */
g_print("media is %sCD object\n", IS_CD(media)? "a " : "not a ");

/* is cd in EightTrack? (expect false) */
g_print("cd is %sEightTrack object\n", IS_EIGHTTRACK(cd)? "an " : "not an ");
```

NOTE   *You sometimes need access to the internals of the parent object in your object initialization
and manipulation functions. If you want the **Media** parent object of* cd, *use the* MEDIA()
casting macro to get a Media *object. Likewise, you can get at the parent class with*
MEDIA_CLASS(). *The class initializer function* cd_class_init() *used this to override the*
unpacked *signal handler.*

2.7.1 Interfaces

In principle, an interface is nothing but a class with no objects and no regard for
class hierarchy. Interfaces consist only of methods, and an object *implements* the
interface when its class has all of these methods.

An interface's infrastructure includes an abstract interface type with a class
structure, but no instance structure. Interfaces inherit all of their base
characteristics from a base interface **GTypeInterface** (type identifier
G_TYPE_INTERFACE), much like a regular class inherits from **GObject**.

Defining an Interface

This section illustrates an interface called **Cleanable** that **CD** and **EightTrack** implement. **Cleanable** will include only one method: void clean(Cleanable *object).

The structures are fairly trivial — the instance structure is empty, and the class structure contains the parent interface and a pointer to the clean method:

```
/* empty declaration for instance structure */
typedef struct _Cleanable Cleanable;

/* Cleanable class structure */
typedef struct _CleanableClass {
  GTypeInterface base_interface;
  void (*clean) (Cleanable *object);
} CleanableClass;
```

Next, you must define a type identifier, casting, membership, and interface macros for **Cleanable**. Following the naming conventions in Section 2.2.2, TYPE_CLEANABLE() returns the result of cleanable_get_type(), IS_CLEANABLE() verifies that an object implements the interface, and CLEANABLE() casts an object to a cleanable type. CLEANABLE_GET_CLASS() returns the interface class, *not* the class of the object.

Another deviation from normal classes and objects is that you don't need CLEANABLE_CLASS or IS_CLEANABLE_CLASS, again, because there are no objects that belong strictly to the **Cleanable** interface.

```
GType cleanable_get_type() G_GNUC_CONST;

#define TYPE_CLEANABLE (cleanable_get_type())

#define CLEANABLE(object) \
  (G_TYPE_CHECK_INSTANCE_CAST((object),  TYPE_CLEANABLE, Cleanable))

#define IS_CLEANABLE(object) \
  (G_TYPE_CHECK_INSTANCE_TYPE((object), TYPE_CLEANABLE))

#define CLEANABLE_GET_CLASS(object) \
  (G_TYPE_INSTANCE_GET_INTERFACE((object), TYPE_CLEANABLE, CleanableClass))
```

The type initializer (cleanable_get_type()) is very similar to that of a class (see Section 2.4.1). However, there are a few differences:

- You need only three fields in the GTypeInfo structure.
- Base initializer and base finalizer functions are not NULL.

The code you're about to see also includes the base initializer and finalizer for the **Cleanable** interface. These do nothing more than manipulate a global variable that serves as a reference counter. When the counter goes from 0 to 1, or from 1 to 0, you may want to do something special with the interface. In the following examples, empty code blocks indicate where to place this code.

This process is somewhat clumsy, but it's necessary because interfaces are not derived from **GObject** and thus have no common class initializer.

```
static guint cleanable_base_init_count = 0;

static void cleanable_base_init(CleanableClass *cleanable)
{
  cleanable_base_init_count++;

  if (cleanable_base_init_count == 1)
  {
    /* "constructor" code, for example, register signals */
  }
}

static void cleanable_base_finalize(CleanableClass *cleanable) {
  cleanable_base_init_count--;

  if (cleanable_base_init_count == 0)
  {
    /* "destructor" code, for example, unregister signals */
  }
}

GType cleanable_get_type(void)
{
  static GType cleanable_type = 0;

  if (!cleanable_type)
  {
    static const GTypeInfo cleanable_info = {
      sizeof(CleanableClass),
      (GBaseInitFunc) cleanable_base_init,
      (GBaseFinalizeFunc) cleanable_base_finalize
    };

    cleanable_type = g_type_register_static(G_TYPE_INTERFACE,
                                            "Cleanable",
                                            &cleanable_info,
                                            0);
  }

  return cleanable_type;
}
```

Implementing and Installing an Interface

Every class that implements an interface must advertise the implementation. The relevant function call here is

```
g_type_add_interface_static(class_type_id, interface_type_id, info)
```

Place this call in your type registration function (for example, cd_get_type()). The arguments here are as follows:

- *class_type_id* (GType): The implementing class type identifier.
- *interface_type_id* (GType): The interface type identifier.
- *info* (const GInterfaceInfo *): Contains these fields:

> interface_init (GInterfaceInitFunc): GObject calls this function to initialize the interface when you cast an object from the implementing class to the interface.
>
> interface_finalize (GInterfaceFinalizeFunc): GObject runs this function when the interface is no longer needed.
>
> interface_data (gpointer): Optional data that you may pass to either of the preceding functions.

The code for installing the interface in cd_get_type() follows; eighttrack_get_type() is similar.

```
static void cd_cleanable_init(gpointer interface, gpointer data);

GType cd_get_type(void)
{
  static GType cd_type = 0;

  if (!cd_type)
  {
    const GInterfaceInfo cleanable_info = {
      cd_cleanable_init, NULL, NULL
    };

    << type initializing code >>

    /* add interface */
    g_type_add_interface_static(cd_type, TYPE_CLEANABLE, &cleanable_info);
  }
  return cd_type;
}
```

Here are the type definitions for GInterfaceInitFunc and GInterfaceFinalizeFunc from the GLib header files:

```
typedef void(*GInterfaceInitFunc) (gpointer g_iface, gpointer iface_data);
```

```
typedef void(*GInterfaceFinalizeFunc) (gpointer g_iface, gpointer iface_data);
```

Normally, this *class-specific* interface initialization function does nothing other than verify that the interface is ready and then install the actual interface implementation function. For the **CD** class, this function is named cd_clean().

When verifying the interface, recall from the previous section that the **Cleanable** class used a cleanable_base_init_count global variable to keep track of reference counts. If the interface is ready, that count is greater than zero:

```
void cd_clean(Cleanable *cleanable);
```

```
static void cd_cleanable_init(gpointer interface, gpointer data)
```

```
{
  CleanableClass *cleanable = interface;

  g_assert(G_TYPE_FROM_INTERFACE(cleanable) == TYPE_CLEANABLE);
  /* is the interface ready? */
  g_assert(cleanable_base_init_count > 0);

  cleanable->clean = cd_clean;
}
```

Here is the implementation of cd_clean():

```
void cd_clean(Cleanable *cleanable)
{
  IS_CD(CD(cleanable));

  g_print("Cleaning CD.\n");
}
```

The interface code for **EightTrack** is nearly identical.

One issue remains: how to bring the **Cleanable** implementations for **CD**
and **EightTrack** into a single method called clean(). This method takes one
Cleanable * object argument (an untyped pointer, of sorts) and runs the
implementation that matches the class behind the object. The general
procedure is as follows:

1. If the argument doesn't implement the interface, abort.
2. Retrieve the class-specific interface from the object.
3. Add a reference to the object, so that GObject doesn't delete the object in
   the process of running the interface.
4. Call the class-specific interface function.
5. Remove the extra reference to the object.

Here is the code:

```
void clean(Cleanable *object)
{
  CleanableClass *interface;

  g_return_if_fail(IS_CLEANABLE(object));

  interface = CLEANABLE_GET_CLASS(object);
  g_object_ref(object);
  interface->clean(object);
  g_object_unref(object);
}
```

This short survey of the inner workings of interfaces is probably far more than you will ever need to know. In practice, you will use standard interfaces, not build your own. Therefore, this section concludes with a short demonstration of how to use the new interface on the cd and eighttrack objects created earlier in this chapter:

```
clean(CLEANABLE(cd));
clean(CLEANABLE(eighttrack));
```

2.8 Further Topics

As with GLib, the topic of GObject and its API is rather broad. Here are some more topics that aren't covered in this chapter:

- GBoxed: A data type and API that allows you to wrap C structures into opaque data types. The most prominent boxed typed is GValue.

- GValueArray packs several GValue elements into an array. Its API is similar to that of GList.

- GClosure: GSignal calls unnamed functions with the help of *closures*; GClosure functions start with g_closure_.

- g_enum_*, g_flags_* are several functions and types that involve finite sets such as enumeration types and bitwise options.

3

GTK+

3.1   What Is GTK+?

GTK+ is a *toolkit* for programming graphical user interfaces. In the earlier days of the X Window System (version 11, or X11), the only toolkit that looked halfway decent and had any sort of popularity was *Motif*. Other toolkits came and went, but when Spencer Kimball and Peter Mattis decided to write an image-processing program in 1995, Motif was handy, so they used it.

This program (later to be called The GIMP) was distributed as free software and soon gained a small following. However, Motif was a commercial library, preventing widespread use. Therefore, Kimball and Mattis decided to do what John Bradley had done with XV: write their own toolkit, GTK (The GIMP Toolkit). GTK debuted in July 1996 [Bunks]. At the beginning, it had three library components: GLib as a fundamental library, *GDK* as an interface to X11, and GTK on top of these.

Somewhere along the line, GTK acquired object-oriented capabilities. Graphical components could now inherit from others, and the basic signal system that we have today was introduced. In honor of the new object-oriented features, the developers decided to rename the toolkit GTK+ [Amundson].

In GTK+ version 2.0 (March 2002), the object-oriented pieces left GTK+, forming the more general GObject system. In addition, GTK+ became platform independent by adding more back ends to GDK. Two new components appeared, *Pango*, a powerful library for text rendering, and *ATK*, an accessibility toolkit. At that point, GTK+ had no reason to be shy in comparisons to any other toolkit.

GTK+ has been free software from day one, distributed under the terms of the GNU LGPL. This is part of the reason that it was chosen as the toolkit for the GNOME project. Not every GTK+ application is a GNOME application (see Section 4.1), but all GNOME applications use GTK+. Therefore, this chapter is a point-by-point explanation of GTK+'s features; the later chapters show how GNOME builds on GTK+.

This chapter does not cover GTK+ components with an equivalent in the GNOME libraries. In addition, the material and examples follow GNOME Usability Project guidelines [GUP].

GUI programming has one principal concept regardless of the particular toolkit: *Widgets* are pieces that the user normally manipulates or views (for instance, scrollbars and buttons are widgets; however, not all widgets are visible). All widgets are GObjects and expose many of their features with the help of GObject properties. *Containers* organize widgets into groups. Furthermore, *events* are emitted as signals in response to user input. In GTK+, you can attach signal handlers to trap these events.

NOTE   *This book tries to cover as few API functions as possible, explaining only the functions that do something that you cannot otherwise achieve by manipulating properties. GTK+ is full of access functions that do nothing other than change properties, and you can do that with the GObject API.*

Keep in mind that properties always have some underlying code. When you change a widget property, the widget changes (as long as the property isn't write protected, that is).

3.1.1 Widgets and Containers

Containers are widgets that hold other widgets and are responsible for the layout of the user interface. The most obvious containers are *windows* — most widgets in an application go into a window.

Other containers include box and table widgets that organize other widgets into a particular place or order. After nesting several containers, you get an application or dialog box look and feel. The act of putting a widget into a container is called *packing*, and a widget inside of a container is the container's *child*. An entire hierarchy of containers and widgets is a *widget tree*.

NOTE   *A widget may not be in more than one container at a single time. In other words, it may not be the child of several containers.*

You can't see a widget when you create the object; you must explicitly request that it appear. You can manipulate and combine widgets without seeing them on your monitor. It isn't a good idea to show a window and then put in every widget; instead, you should work out the representation details when the window is invisible, and then show everything with one shot when you are finished.

It's also possible to hide visible widgets without losing their representation in memory. For example, you might want to hide tool palettes, property windows, and certain dialog boxes. If you hide rather than destroy these widgets, you won't have to worry about creating new instances when you want to show the windows again.

Figure 3.1: GNOME Run Program dialog box in the Default theme.

NOTE   *A widget's precise appearance depends on your current GTK+ theme. Themes vary greatly in implementation and details — anything is possible, from a new set of colors to an entire new code module that controls what the window draws. Figures 3.1, 3.2, and 3.3 illustrate three different themes. (See Figure 3.3 on the next page.) All other screenshots in this book use the GTK+ Default theme.*

Figure 3.2: GNOME Run Program dialog box in the Crux theme.

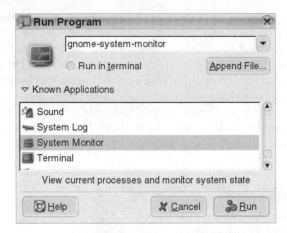

Figure 3.3: GNOME Run Program dialog box in the Grand Canyon theme.

3.1.2 Event-Driven Programming

In contrast to the traditional top-to-bottom programs that you typically run on the command line, graphical programs usually consist of a collection of objects that wait for actions (from a user, the network, and so on). The actions trigger small pieces of code that often manipulate other objects.

This system is called *event-driven programming*. The windowing system transmits events such as key presses and mouse clicks when GTK+ is in a *main event loop*. GTK+ determines the corresponding widget and then emits an appropriate signal. The actual mechanism is GSignal, covered in Section 2.6.

It's important to recognize the difference between events and signals. Events come from outside GTK+ and typically enter through the main loop, where they reach a widget. Ordinary signals are internal to the application. Of course, every event usually leads to a signal emission. Certain signals that end with **-event** are called event signals; GTK+ emits these directly when it gets an event. A handler for an event signal returns a Boolean value; if this is TRUE, the signal emission immediately halts.

3.1.3 An Elementary Example

GTK+ resides primarily in a library that reflects the back end. For X11, the library is *libgtk-x11-2.0*, with a number of auxiliary subsystem libraries. Sometimes it can be hard to tell what libraries you need, so use the pkg-config command with your compiler command to do all of the hard work for you (see Section 6.1). The only header file you need for GTK+ is *gtk/gtk.h*; this file subsequently includes all of GLib, GObject, and anything else you need.

The classic first example, derived from the first program in [Kernighan], is a program that prints Hello, World. Your first GTK+ example should be as grandiose. Here it is:

```c
/* -*-coding: utf-8;-*- */
/* gtkhello.c -- traditional GTK+ Hello program */

#include <gtk/gtk.h>

void hello(GtkWidget *widget, gpointer data)
{
  g_print("Hello, World!\n");
}

gint delete_event(GtkWidget *widget, GdkEvent event, gpointer data)
{
  /* when this function returns FALSE, the delete-event
     signal becomes a destroy signal */
  return FALSE;
}

void end_program(GtkWidget *widget, gpointer data)
{
  /* End the main loop */
  gtk_main_quit();
}

int main(int argc, char **argv)
{
  GtkWindow *window;
  GtkButton *button;

  /* Initialize GTK+ */
  gtk_init(&argc, &argv);

  /* create window, set default height and width to 200 pixels */
  window = g_object_new(GTK_TYPE_WINDOW,
                        "default-height", 200,
                        "default-width", 200,
                        "border-width", 12,
                        "title", "GtkHello",
                        NULL);

  /* add signal handlers for window */
  g_signal_connect(window,
                   "delete-event", G_CALLBACK(delete_event),
                   NULL);

  g_signal_connect(window,
                   "destroy", G_CALLBACK(end_program),
                   NULL);

  /* create a button */
  button = g_object_new(GTK_TYPE_BUTTON,
                        "label", "_Hello, World!\nClick Here.",
```

```
                            "use-underline", TRUE,
                            NULL);

    /* install signal handlers for button */
    g_signal_connect(button,
                        "clicked", G_CALLBACK(hello),
                        NULL);

    g_signal_connect_swapped(button,
                                "clicked", G_CALLBACK(gtk_widget_destroy),
                                window);

    /* pack the button into the window, show all of its contents */
    gtk_container_add(GTK_CONTAINER(window), GTK_WIDGET(button));

    gtk_widget_show_all(GTK_WIDGET(window));

    /* start main event loop */
    gtk_main();

    return 0;
}
```

Compiling

To compile this simple program, use

```
gcc -o gtkhello gtkhello.c `pkg-config --cflags --libs gtk+-2.0`
```

Naturally, you want to create a Makefile or use autoconf for larger applications.

Program Behavior

The gtkhello program opens a window, creates a big button labeled "Hello, World! Click Here" in the window and waits for events (not just button clicks, but also things like window resizing). When you click the button, gtkhello prints Hello, World! on the console, closes the window, and terminates. You can also close the window (and stop the program) with the window manager — that is, click whatever button corresponds to Close in the title bar. See Figure 3.4 to see the final application.

Figure 3.4: Result of **gtkhello** *program.*

Program Structure

The gtk_init(*argc_addr, argv_addr*) function performs several GTK+ initialization tasks, for example, it runs g_type_init() for you. The parameters are the addresses to argc and argv, the main program's command-line options. The gtk_init() function removes anything that it recognizes so that you don't have to deal with the standard GTK+ options yourself.

Then gtkhello does the following:

1. Creates a new window by asking g_object_new() to create a **GtkWindow** widget (returned as a pointer to the window variable). This call sets several properties: **default-width**, **default-height**, **border-width**, and **title**; these set the window size to 200 pixels square, supply a 12-pixel border, and set the title of the window to GtkHello.

2. Attaches new signal handlers for **delete-event** and **destroy**: delete_event() and end_program().

3. Creates a new button object (button) of the **GtkButton** class, with the "Hello World" string as a label.

4. Attaches hello() to the **clicked** signal handler for button.

5. Uses g_signal_connect_swapped() to attach gtk_widget_destroy() to the same **clicked** signal, so that GSignal can pass window to the handler as a parameter. It also packs the button into the window with gtk_container_add(), displays the window and button with gtk_widget_show_all(), and calls gtk_main() to start the main event loop.

Binding Code to Signals

Some signal handler names are nearly identical to their signals: gtkhello binds delete_event() to the similarly named **delete-event**. GTK+ emits **delete-event** with a **GtkWindow** object when the window manager requests removal of the window. As mentioned in Section 3.1.2, this is an event signal, so the handler must return a Boolean value. If this return value is FALSE, the emission continues, and GTK+ destroys the window. The end_program() handler is also bound to **delete-event**; this function calls gtk_main_quit() to stop the main event loop (and consequently, the whole program).

NOTE *When you define handlers like this for* delete-event, *you can determine whether a window removal halts your program. For example, if your application contains unsaved data, you can ask users whether they really want to terminate the application.*

GTK+ also offers gtk_widget_hide_on_delete() that you can employ as a handler for **delete-event**. With this function, GTK+ hides a window in case you want to use it again. This is ideal for tool palettes and similarly recurring windows.

NOTE *GSignal treats - and _ as the same character, so you may see* **delete-event** *and* **delete_event** *used for the same purpose. This book follows the online API documentation, using -.*

The gtkhello program attaches hello() as a handler to button's **clicked** signal. It sends Hello, World! to the console and does nothing else. It is interesting that gtk_widget_destroy() is a second handler for this widget, receiving window as a parameter: Upon emission of this signal, gtkhello prints the message, destroys the window, and halts the program.

NOTE *This function indirectly causes a **destroy** signal emission and therefore, a call to end_program(). In spite of this, it wouldn't be wise to attach end_program() directly to **clicked**, because a program with a GUI should shut down only when it has cleaned up after all of its widgets. By using this indirection, you don't have to override the **destroy** handler, and therefore, you won't have to worry about any trash on the beach (so to speak).*

If you understood this small example and explanation, you probably also see that GTK+ programming is a fairly straightforward, clean matter, guided by clear concepts. Everything else is just a matter of knowing the details.

Character Encoding

You probably noticed this line at the very top of the program:

```
/* -*-coding: utf-8;-*- */
```

This UTF-8 indicator is important if your program contains accents or other characters that aren't 7-bit ASCII, and you happen to use Emacs. Pango works on UTF-8 strings.

Most GTK+ and GNOME programs are in 7-bit ASCII and contain English strings. You can add translations for other languages; see Section 6.5.

3.1.4   Widget Fundamentals

All GTK+ widgets are **GtkWidget** class (type identifier: GTK_TYPE_WIDGET) objects and are therefore also members of the **GtkObject** class (GTK_TYPE_OBJECT), the base class for all GTK+ classes.

One particular technical curiosity of **GtkObject** widgets is that the reference counters work a little differently than in normal **GObject** objects. A newly created widget object has a *floating reference* that the container widget takes over when you pack the widget. This reference ensures that GTK+ sweeps up the widget upon destruction of the container without removing extra references in your setup code.

The base **GtkWidget** class includes GTK+'s visible operational elements (methods, properties, and signals). The next three sections outline the most important.

3.1.5   Methods

To show a widget, use

```
GtkWidget *widget;

gtk_widget_show(widget);
```

However, it's much more practical to use

```
gtk_widget_show_all(widget)
```

to show the widget and all of its children. You can see a widget only if all of its ancestors in the widget tree are also visible.

NOTE   *When you show a widget or perform any other sort of operation that alters the appearance of a widget, GTK+ doesn't change the widget on the screen immediately; instead, it normally waits until the program is in the main loop. If these miniscule fractions of sections actually matter to you, call*

```
gtk_widget_show_now(widget)
```

This function returns only after everything on the screen appears as it should.

WARNING   *Calling* `gtk_widget_show_now()` *is akin to running the main loop, so GTK+ can process events and emit signals unrelated to the widget at hand during this time.*

The converse of showing a widget is hiding the widget; use one of these two methods:

```
gtk_widget_hide(widget)
gtk_widget_hide_all(widget)
```

To completely eradicate a widget, use

```
gtk_widget_destroy(widget)
```

Widget destruction is an important part of several of this book's examples.

3.1.6 Properties

The most important gboolean widget properties are:

- **visible**: TRUE if the widget is visible.
- **sensitive**: FALSE if the widget is inactive (dimmed). When inactive, a widget does not respond to input.
- **can-focus**: TRUE if the widget can grab the input *focus*.
- **has-focus**: TRUE if the widget has the input focus.
- **can-default**: TRUE if the widget is allowed to become its window's default widget.
- **has-default**: TRUE if the widget is its window's default widget.
- **receives-default**: TRUE if the widget becomes the default widget when its window gets the input focus.

The *default widget* receives the input after its window opens and should therefore be one of the least "dangerous" widgets. In dialog boxes, this is normally the button at the lower right. The default widget's purpose is to enable better keyboard operation; for example, the user can operate a default button on a dialog box by pressing the ENTER key.

3.1.7 Signals

GtkWidget objects have plenty of associated signals; most applications ignore the vast majority of them. Here are the three most practical signals, along with their handler prototypes:

- `delete-event`
  `gboolean handler(GtkWidget *widget, GdkEvent *event, gpointer data)`
  This is an important signal for windows, because GTK+ emits this when the window manager wants to delete `widget` (for example, when you click a Close button in the title bar). As with other event signals, the handler gets the actual event through the event parameter. You can safely ignore the event. Your handler should return `TRUE` if you want the signal emission to stop immediately.

- `show`
  `void handler(GtkWidget *widget, gpointer data)`
  GTK+ emits this signal when `widget` becomes visible.

- `hide`
  `void handler(GtkWidget *widget, gpointer data)`
  GTK+ emits this signal when `widget` is hidden.

3.2 Windows

There is a window in Section 3.1.3's example program; you can see that it is a container widget object of the **GtkWindow** class (type identifier: `GTK_TYPE_WINDOW`).

To set a window's title, write a string into its **title** property. The user should be able to distinguish the window's title in a list of windows (for example, in a window manager menu). An application window's title ideally stems from the document currently in that window — a filename, directory, or similar. If you insist on including the application name in the title, place it *after* the document name, but GNOME guidelines advise even against this. Any other information in the title bar is essentially a waste of space.[1]

Here are several versions of the same title and how they rank:

- **Good:** Order.mtx
- **Not so great:** Order.mtx - MiracleText
- **Poor:** MiracleText: Order.mtx
- **Really bad:** MiracleText 0.16.7 (CVS BUILD #1247)

---

[1] GNOME has functions to keep application window titles consistent — see Section 4.3.1.

If a window doesn't contain a document, the naming conventions are somewhat different:

- **Application windows:** *Name of the application* (LavaLamp).
- **Property windows:** *Name of object* - Properties (Table 3.1 - Properties).
- **Preferences windows:** *Name of the application* - Preferences (MiracleText - Preferences).
- **Warnings:** No title. Windows containing warnings should display their information as a short blurb inside the window; if you put the same thing in the title bar, it would show up twice on the screen and look a little confusing. Well, that's what the guidelines say, at least. *My* opinion is that a short title such as Warning or Info never hurt anyone. Furthermore, nameless windows look a little odd in a window manager's list. Section 3.10 covers dialog boxes and the titles that GTK+ may automatically supply.
- **Druids (assistants):** *Name of the druid* (Configure Coffee Machine); for more information on druids, see Section 4.3.15.

Significant **GtkWindow** properties and their types include the following:

- `resizable` (gboolean): If TRUE, the user may change the window's size.

NOTE *It's practically never a good idea to set this property to* FALSE, *thereby making it impossible for users to adjust the window to their preferences. If you set up your container layout properly, the contents remain usable and in proper order at any size.*

- `modal` (gboolean): When TRUE, this is a *modal* window. None of the application's other windows respond to input as long as the modal window exists.

WARNING *In most modern applications, modal windows are completely unnecessary. You should try to do without modal windows, because users tend to become frustrated when a window ignores their input due to some hidden dialog box.*

- `window-position` (GtkWindowPosition): This property determines where the window will appear on the display. The possible values are:

    GTK_WIN_POS_NONE: Let the window manager decide where it wants to put the window. This is the default.

    GTK_WIN_POS_CENTER_ON_PARENT: Place the window on top of the parent, using the parent's center as its center.

    GTK_WIN_POS_CENTER: Put the window in the center of the monitor, at least as much as possible.

    GTK_WIN_POS_CENTER_ALWAYS: Try to keep the window centered, even if the window size changes.

    GTK_WIN_POS_MOUSE: Place the window as close to the mouse pointer as possible.

    All of these values assume that the window manager cooperates — that is, it understands and follows NET_WM *hints*[XDG].

- `default-width` (gint): The default width, as seen in the previous example.
- `default-height` (gint): The default height.

If you decide to force the size of a window, at least use some sensible proportions: for example, a 1:1.6 ratio (the golden section).

- **destroy-with-parent** (gboolean): If TRUE, GTK+ will destroy this window upon the destruction of the window's parent.

- **icon** (GdkPixBuf; see Section 3.3.2): The window's icon. The icon should closely resemble that of its menu item or any other graphical means of starting the application.

3.2.1   Icons

In any polished application, you should outfit your window with an icon that appears in the window list and other places. These routines install icons:

- gboolean gtk_window_set_icon_from_file(GtkWindow *window, const char *filename, GError **error)
  Sets the icon for *window* to the image in *filename*, returning TRUE upon success.

- void gtk_window_set_icon(GtkWindow *window, GdkPixbuf *pixbuf)
  Like the preceding function, but uses *pixbuf* instead of a filename and does not return a value.

- void gtk_window_set_icon_list(GtkWindow *window, GList *pixmap_list)
  Like the preceding function, but uses the first available pixmap in the *pixmap_list*.

- gboolean gtk_window_set_default_icon_from_file(const char *filename, GError **error)
  Sets *all* of the current application's icons to the image in *filename*.

3.3   Display Widgets

Among the most elementary widgets, display widgets do nothing other than show something to the user — for example, text, pictures, and progress.

- **Label:** A short piece of text that describes a nearby widget. Pango makes it easy to format labels. Labels aren't suitable for large amounts of text; see the text buffer and text view widgets in Section 3.12 for alternatives.

- **Image:** Displays a picture on the screen. These types of widgets work in conjunction with GdkPixbuf, a GDK interface that permits you to load and display image files in nearly every common format.

- **Progress bar:** Shows the user how far the application has progressed in a certain task. Progress bars can show the user exactly how far an application has gone. If the application doesn't quite know how long an operation will take, a progress bar can go into activity mode to show that something is happening (this looks a bit like the Cylon lights in *Battlestar Galactica*).

The rest of this section is a small demonstration of these widgets. The first part of the program consists of the usual GTK+ declarations and event handlers:

```
/* -*-coding: utf-8;-*- */
/* display.c -- demonstrate display widgets */

#include <gtk/gtk.h>
```

```
#include <math.h>
const gdouble PROGRESS_STEP = 0.05;

/* standard handlers */
gint delete_event(GtkWidget *widget, GdkEvent event, gpointer data) {
  return FALSE;
}

void end_program(GtkWidget *widget, gpointer data) {
  gtk_main_quit();
}
```

The function that follows is a handler for a progress bar. It is a very concrete example of how an event on a widget object causes a signal emission, eventually leading the handler to manipulate another object.

There are two **GtkProgressBar** properties in this handler: **fraction**, a number between 0 and 1 indicating how much of the progress bar is filled, and **text**, a text string to render on top of the progress bar. Section 3.3.3 contains more information about progress bars.

```
/* bump the display counter on the given
   GtkProgressBar one PROGRESS_STEP further */
void advance(GtkButton *button, gpointer progress_ptr)
{
  GtkProgressBar *progress_bar = GTK_PROGRESS_BAR(progress_ptr);
  gdouble current;
  gchar *embedded_text;

  g_object_get(progress_bar, "fraction", &current, NULL);
  current += PROGRESS_STEP;
  current = CLAMP(current, 0.0, 0.999);
  embedded_text = g_strdup_printf("%3.0f%% completed", current*100);
  g_object_set(progress_bar,
               "fraction", current,
               "text", embedded_text,
               NULL);
  g_free(embedded_text);
}
```

The main program comes next. Many normal declarations, gtk_init(), creation of the main window, and attachment of its **destroy** signal handlers, are here:

```
int main(int argc, char **argv)
{
  GtkWindow *window;
  GtkVBox *vbox;
  GtkLabel *label, *label_markup;
  GtkImage *image;
  GtkHBox *progress_bar_box;
```

```
GtkProgressBar *progress_bar;
GtkButton *pulse_button, *advance_button;

/* initialize GTK+, create a window, attach handlers */
gtk_init(&argc, &argv);
window = g_object_new(GTK_TYPE_WINDOW,
                        "title", "Display Widgets",
                        "border-width", 12,
                        NULL);

/* attach standard window event handlers */
g_signal_connect(window, "delete_event", G_CALLBACK(delete_event), NULL);
g_signal_connect(window, "destroy", G_CALLBACK(end_program), NULL);
```

This little piece creates a subcontainer widget called a VBox. The items in a VBox stack vertically:

```
/* create a vertical box and pack it into window  */
vbox = g_object_new(GTK_TYPE_VBOX, "spacing", 6, NULL);

gtk_container_add(GTK_CONTAINER(window), GTK_WIDGET(vbox));
```

You're ready to see the first **GtkLabel**. This one carries a small, unadorned message. This text goes in the `label` property.

```
/* a new label. */
label = g_object_new(GTK_TYPE_LABEL,
                        "label", "When lilacs last in the door-yard bloom'd.\n \
Fonts normally do not support all markup attributes:",
                        NULL);

gtk_box_pack_start_defaults(GTK_BOX(vbox), GTK_WIDGET(label));
```

Labels can be quite fancy, because Pango understands a type of markup language that you activate with the **use-markup** property. Notice that this (somewhat gaudy) example also sets the **wrap** property, telling Pango to wrap text lines if they get too long. These properties and others are in Section 3.3.1. (Yes, the program looks a little ugly.)

```
/* a label with extensive markup */
label_markup = g_object_new(GTK_TYPE_LABEL,
                              "wrap", TRUE,
                              "use-markup", TRUE,
                              "label", "\
<span font_desc=\"Courier New Bold 16\">Courier - </span>\
<span font_desc=\"Charter Bold 16\">Charter - </span>\
<span font_family=\"Times\">Times - </span>\
<span face=\"Verdana\">Verdana - </span>\
<span size=\"xx-small\">Tiny - </span>\
<span size=\"x-small\">Extra Small - </span>\
<span size=\"small\">Small - </span>\
```

```
<span size=\"medium\">Medium - </span>\
<span size=\"large\">Large - </span>\
<span size=\"x-large\">Extra Large - </span>\
<span size=\"xx-large\">Huge - </span>\
<span size=\"36000\">Gigantic - </span>\
<span face=\"Times\">\
<span style=\"oblique\">Oblique - </span>\
<span style=\"italic\">Italic - </span>\
</span>\
<span weight=\"ultrabold\">Ultra Bold - </span>\
<span face=\"Times New Roman\" variant=\"smallcaps\">\
Caps and Small Caps - </span>\
<span stretch=\"condensed\">Condensed - </span>\
H<span rise=\"-5000\">2</span>0 - \
<span background=\"black\" foreground=\"#FFFFFF\">Inverse</span> - \
<span underline=\"double\">Important - </span>\
<span strikethrough=\"true\">Strikethrough</span>\
\n\
The <tt>span</tt> tag appears to function \
well. However, it's <i>easier</i> to use \
<b>short forms</b><sup>*</sup>.\n\
\n\
<small><sup>*)</sup> short tags that work just\
 the same as <tt>span</tt> with corresponding \
attributes</small>");

  gtk_box_pack_start_defaults(GTK_BOX(vbox), GTK_WIDGET(label_markup));
```

The following statements create a **GtkImage** object to display a picture of an apple (*apple-green.png*). Section 3.3.2 goes into far more detail on images.

```
/* a GtkImage */
image = g_object_new(GTK_TYPE_IMAGE, "file", "apple-green.png", NULL);
gtk_box_pack_start_defaults(GTK_BOX(vbox), GTK_WIDGET(image));
```

This code creates the progress bar mentioned earlier:

```
/* a progress bar with buttons to advance the progress or pulse activity */
progress_bar_box = g_object_new(GTK_TYPE_HBOX, "spacing", 6, NULL);
gtk_box_pack_start_defaults(GTK_BOX(vbox), GTK_WIDGET(progress_bar_box));
```

These two buttons seem nearly identical at first, but notice that pulse_button gets a built-in signal handler, gtk_progress_bar_pulse(), described in Section 3.3.3.

```
advance_button = g_object_new(GTK_TYPE_BUTTON,
                             "label", "_Advance",
                             "use-underline", TRUE,
                             NULL);

pulse_button = g_object_new(GTK_TYPE_BUTTON,
                           "label", "_Pulse",
```

```
                        "use-underline", TRUE,
                        NULL);

  gtk_box_pack_start_defaults(GTK_BOX(progress_bar_box),
                        GTK_WIDGET(advance_button));
  gtk_box_pack_start_defaults(GTK_BOX(progress_bar_box),
                        GTK_WIDGET(pulse_button));

  progress_bar = g_object_new(GTK_TYPE_PROGRESS_BAR, NULL);
  gtk_box_pack_start_defaults(GTK_BOX(progress_bar_box),
                        GTK_WIDGET(progress_bar));

  g_signal_connect(advance_button,
                "clicked", G_CALLBACK(advance), progress_bar);

  /* attach a builtin GTK+ handler to pulse the progress bar */
  g_signal_connect_swapped(pulse_button,
        "clicked", G_CALLBACK(gtk_progress_bar_pulse), progress_bar);
```

We're finally ready to see the final window and start the main event loop.

```
  /* show window and begin GTK+ main loop */
  gtk_widget_show_all(GTK_WIDGET(window));
  gtk_main();
  return 0;
}
```

Figure 3.5 shows the final application. It's much easier to understand this program when you run it, so if you haven't retrieved the source code yet, this might be a good time to think about it (see the introduction for more information).

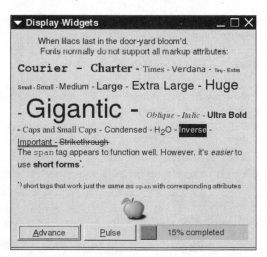

Figure 3.5: Display widgets.

3.3.1 Labels and Pango Markup

As you can see from the example in the previous section, it's not very hard to put a string into a label; just create a **GtkLabel** (GTK_TYPE_LABEL) object and set its `label` property.

A label with Pango formatting is only a little more complex. Set the label's **use-markup** property to TRUE so that you can use *markup language* directives.

Pango markup has few tags when compared to a cousin such as HTML. The most important tag pair is `<span>` ... `</span>`. You can put any text inside this pair and even nest other `<span>` tags. The `<span>` tag does nothing on its own; you must supply at least one of these attributes:

- `font_desc=string`: Sets the text with the full font description *string*. An example of such a description is `"Times Italic 12"`. Other attributes have precedence over `font_desc`. You can look up font descriptions with any number of GTK+ font chooser programs, including the one in Section 3.6.8.

- `font_family=font`: Selects a typeface family, such as `Times` or `Sans`.

- `face=font`: Identical to `font_family`.

- `size=value`: Controls the font size. There are three ways to do this:

    A **number** representing the actual size in thousandths of a point. For example, a 10-point type size translates to 10000.

    An **absolute description**: Pick one of `xx-small`, `x-small`, `small`, `medium`, `large`, `x-large`, and `xx-large`.

    A **relative description**: Use `smaller` to get text smaller than the current text, and `larger` for the other way around.

- `style=string`: Changes the style of the typeface; choose one of `normal`, `oblique` (leaning to the right), and `italic`. Most typeface families do not support both oblique and italic; one usually substitutes for the other.

- `weight=string`: Indicates how thick the typeface appears; possible values are `ultralight`, `light`, `normal`, `bold`, `ultrabold`, and `heavy`. You can specify a number instead (to serve as reference, ultralight is 200, normal is 400, ultrabold is 800, and heavy is 900). Keep in mind that very few typefaces actually support all of these weights.

- `variant=string`: Specifies `normal`, or `smallcaps` for caps and small caps. Few typefaces support small caps.

- `stretch=string`: Specifies the width of each character. Possible values, from narrow to wide, are `ultracondensed`, `extracondensed`, `condensed`, `semicondensed`, `normal`, `semiexpanded`, `expanded`, `extraexpanded`, and `ultraexpanded`. Again, typefaces with all of these are rare.

- `background=color`: Controls the text background color. This can be an RGB specification such as `#AACC40` or an X11 color name such as `midnightblue`. For a complete list of color names on a Unix system, consult */usr/X11R6/lib/X11/rgb.txt* (it's quite a poetic collection, including `honeydew`, `rosy brown`, and `medium spring green`).

- `foreground=`*`color`*: Controls the text color (the specification is as for `background=`*`color`*).

- `underline=`*`style`*: Draw lines underneath the text. The values are:

  > `single` for a single line.

  > `double` for two lines.

  > `low` to place a line underneath all descenders.

  > `none` for no underlining.

- `rise=`*`number`*: Shifts the text vertically, in thousandths of an *em*; *number* may be negative.

- `strikethrough=`*`value`*: If *value* is `true`, Pango renders the text with a horizontal line drawn straight through each character.

- `lang=`*`language`*: Selects the text's language. The value is a code as per RFC 3066/ISO 639: for example, `en` for English, `es` for Spanish, `de` for German, `fy` for Frisian, or `i-klingon` for Klingon.

There are some abbreviation tags that you can use for convenience. For example, `<b>` ... `</b>` is short for `<span weight="bold">` ... `</pan>`.

Abbreviation	Full Version
`<b>`	`<span weight="bold">`
`<big>`	`<span size="larger">`
`<i>`	`<span style="italic">`
`<s>`	`<span strikethrough="true">`
`<sub>`	`<span "rise=-5000" size="smaller">` (subscript)
`<sup>`	`<span "rise=5000" size="smaller">` (superscript)
`<small>`	`<span weight="smaller">`
`<u>`	`<span underline="single">`
`<tt>`	Use a monospaced (nonproportional) font

NOTE *Even though you have all of these formatting possibilities, try not to go too crazy. Use bold or italic fonts for emphasis and relative font sizes for superscripts or warnings (see the guidelines for dialog boxes in Section 3.10). Try to avoid absolute font sizes and don't arbitrarily mix and match typefaces.*

Other important **GtkLabel** properties include the following:

- **use-underline** (gboolean): If TRUE, you can put an underscore in front of a letter in the label to denote a keystroke.

- **mnemonic-widget** (**GtkWidget**): The widget to activate when the user presses the key mentioned in the preceding property.

- **justify** (GtkJustification): Determines the text justification. Possible values are:

  > `GTK_JUSTIFY_LEFT`

  > `GTK_JUSTIFY_RIGHT`

```
GTK_JUSTIFY_CENTER
```

GTK_JUSTIFY_FILL (fills in space between words; works only with multiline text)

- **wrap** (gboolean): If TRUE, Pango wraps long lines of text.
- **selectable** (gboolean): If TRUE, the user may select text inside the label with the mouse.
- **cursor-position** (gint, read-only): The position of the selection described in the preceding property; the number of characters between the beginning of the text and the start of the selection.
- **selection-bound** (gint, read-only): The number of characters in the selection.

When you create labels for your application, try to be as consistent and unambiguous as possible. Here are some tips:

- Left-justify your labels unless you have an important reason for doing otherwise.
- Make labels for user elements expressive enough for a sight-impaired user to know what the element does. A screen reader shouldn't need to need to read everything in a window before the user can take action. Dialog boxes, in particular, are something to watch out for.
- Place any labels for large icons and images underneath the picture, akin to a book's captions for illustrations.
- Put a label accompanying a small icon directly to the right of the icon. The icon serves as a visual point of entry.
- If a label describes a large area containing widgets, such as a list or group of buttons, place the label above the area.
- As was the case for small icons, labels for small widgets such as check boxes and radio buttons go to the right of these elements.
- When placing a label to the left of a widget because you want the user to read the whole as a sentence (such as a label next to a small text-entry box), end the label with a colon so that there is a clear connection between the label and widget.
- Don't use the same label text (or very similar text) in the same window.

3.3.2 Images and GDK Pixbufs

To represent an image, create a **GtkImage** (GTK_TYPE_IMAGE) widget and set its **file** property to the filename of an image.

GDK works behind the scenes with the **GdkPixbuf** class (GDK_TYPE_PIXBUF), GDK's fundamental class for image data. GDK understands many different graphics file formats, including JPEG, GIF, PNG, ICO, PNM, RAS, TGA, TIFF, Windows BMP, XPM, and even SVG. The image loader is modular, so GDK adds new format support from time to time.

In addition to loading your own files, you can select an image from a library of stock images. The fundamental **GtkImage** properties for loading and storing images are as follows:

- **pixbuf** (GdkPixbuf): The image data buffer.

- **pixbuf-animation** (GdkPixbufAnimation): The image data, if the image is animated.

- **file** (gchararray, write-only): An image file for GDK to load into the image buffer.

- **stock** (gchararray): The identifier for one of the GTK+ stock images, if you wish to display one.

- **icon-size** (gint): The desired size of the stock image (above).

- **storage-type** (GtkImageType, read-only): The representation type of the image in memory. Possible values include

    GTK_IMAGE_EMPTY: No image data present (yet).

    GTK_IMAGE_PIXBUF: The image came from a file or GdkPixbuf.

    GTK_IMAGE_STOCK: The image is part of a stock image library.

    GTK_IMAGE_ANIMATION: The image contains GDK Pixbuf animation.

GdkPixbuf

If you need to alter the image for display, or if you just want more control, you can create your own GdkPixbuf objects.

NOTE   *GtkImage stores its own data. Therefore, if you change a GdkPixbuf structure that you already have on the screen, you must tell the **GtkImage** object about this change, or nothing will happen on the screen. You'll see this in the render_image() function for the example program further on in this section.*

Here are the most important functions that operate on the GdkPixbuf type:

- GdkPixbuf *gdk_pixbuf_new_from_file(const gchar *filename, GError **error)
  Loads the image in *filename* into an image buffer and returns a pointer to the buffer. If some problem occurs in loading the image, this function returns NULL and sets *error* (the possible error classes are GDK_PIXBUF_ERROR and G_FILE_ERROR).

  Use g_object_unref() to free a pixbuf's memory.

- int gdk_pixbuf_get_width(GdkPixbuf *pixbuf)
  Returns the width of an image in pixels.

- int gdk_pixbuf_get_height(GdkPixbuf *pixbuf)
  Returns the height of an image in pixels.

- GdkPixbuf *gdk_pixbuf_copy(const GdkPixbuf *pixbuf)
  Returns a complete copy of *pixbuf* (not just a reference).

- void gdk_pixbuf_copy_area(const GdkPixbuf *source, int src_x, int src_y, int width, int height, GdkPixbuf *dest, int dest_x, int dest_y)
  Copies an area *width* by *height* pixels starting at the coordinates (*src_x, src_y*) in *source* to the coordinates (*dest_x, dest_y*) in *dest*. The origin (0,0) in a Pixbuf is at the upper left.

- GdkPixbuf *gdk_pixbuf_scale_simple(const GdkPixbuf *pixbuf, int width, int height, GdkInterpType interpolation)
  Returns a copy of *pixbuf* scaled to *width* by *height* pixels. You can choose the *interpolation* method from the following:

  > GDK_INTERP_NEAREST: Nearest neighbor approximation is the fastest algorithm, but it doesn't have very good results. It's unusable to scale down an image, but is acceptable for enlarging in certain circumstances.

  > GDK_INTERP_TILES: Tile interpolation is better than nearest neighbor; for example, PostScript uses this method. In particular, it delivers better results when you reduce an image's size.

  > GDK_INTERP_BILINEAR: If you're looking for good interpolation with moderate CPU time consumption, bilinear interpolation is usually a good choice.

  > GDK_INTERP_HYPER: Hyperbolic interpolation delivers excellent results, but consumes an enormous amount of processor time.

- void gdk_pixbuf_scale(const GdkPixbuf *source, GdkPixbuf *dest, int dest_x, int dest_y, int width, int height, double offset_x, double y_offset, double scale_x, double y_scale, GdkInterpType interpolation)
  This extremely verbose function gives you fine control over how to scale an image. Scales *source* by *scale_x* horizontally and *scale_y* vertically, shifts that result by *offset_x* (horizontally) and *offset_y* (vertically), and pastes this into *dest* at (*dest_x*, *dest_y*); *interpolation* method as described in the preceding function.

- void gdk_pixbuf_composite(const GdkPixbuf *source, GdkPixbuf *dest, int dest_x, int dest_y, int width, int height, double x_offset, double y_offset, double scale_x, double scale_y, GdkInterpType interpolation, int alpha)
  Works like the preceding function, but rather than replacing the target pixels, adds the newly scaled image as a transparent layer. This makes sense only if the source has transparent pixels or you specify a number smaller than 255 as the transparency value *alpha* (domain: 0 to 255).

- gboolean gdk_pixbuf_get_has_alpha(const GdkPixbuf *pixbuf)
  Returns TRUE if a Pixbuf contains an alpha channel (transparency information).

- GdkPixbuf *gdk_pixbuf_add_alpha(const GdkPixbuf *pixbuf, gboolean substitute, guchar r, guchar g, guchar b)
  Returns a copy of *pixbuf* with an alpha channel. If *substitute* is TRUE, this function makes all pixels that match the RGB color value given by *r*/*g*/*b* transparent. This function sets all other pixels to 255 (opaque) in the alpha channel.

- void gdk_pixbuf_saturate_and_pixelate(const GdkPixbuf *source, GdkPixbuf *dest, gfloat saturation, gboolean pixelate)
  Changes the saturation (color contrast) in *source*, pixelates the result (that is, if *pixelate* is TRUE), and copies the result to *dest*. *dest* must exist ahead of time and have the same dimensions as *source*; you might want to copy *source* or use the same Pixbuf as *source* and *target*. The *saturation* value is a floating-point

number greater than or equal to 0. At 0, the image becomes grayscale; 1.0 has no effect on the image, and any larger number exaggerates the colors (for example, to provide the GTK+ insensitive icon effect).

- void gdk_pixbuf_fill(const GdkPixbuf *pixbuf, guint32 color)
  Fills *pixbuf* with *color* pixels. The *color* value is a four-byte representation of red, green, blue, and alpha — for example, 0xcececeff for opaque gray, 0x00000000 for transparent black, and 0xffffff80 for half-transparent white.

A simple demonstration of **GdkPixbuf** that uses slider widgets for scaling and saturation operations follows. Figure 3.6 shows the end result.

Figure 3.6: Demonstration of saturation and scaling.

The first part of this program consists of signal handlers that you have already seen.

```
/* -*-coding: utf-8;-*- */
/* pixbufdemo.c -- GdkPixbuf demo */

#include <gtk/gtk.h>

/* standard handlers */
gint delete_event(GtkWidget *widget, GdkEvent event, gpointer data)
{
  return FALSE;
}

void end_program(GtkWidget *widget, gpointer data)
{
  gtk_main_quit();
}
```

The following function converts a number into a string, represented as a percent. You will see it in conjunction with the image's zoom value.

```
/* rounds a number to the nearest whole percentage and
   returns this (followed by %) in a newly allocated string */
gchar* percent(GtkScale *scale, gdouble number, gpointer data)
{
  gint percent;
  gchar *str;

  percent = (gint)(number * 100);
  str = g_strdup_printf("%d%%", percent);

  return str;
}
```

The render_image()handler that follows demonstrates the saturation and scaling
functions described earlier in this section. Notice that image comes through as
the handler's data pointer, and that render_image() retrieves several other parameters from image (you'll see where it all fits together later). The important
points to notice are how render_image() retrieves the original image, how it
manipulates the image, and how it must tell the image widget to display the
newly manipulated image.

```
/* (re-)render the image when it changes */
void render_image(GtkWidget *adjuster, gpointer data)
{
  GtkImage *image;
  GtkAdjustment *zoom, *saturation;
  GdkPixbuf *orig_pixbuf, *new_pixbuf;
  gint orig_width, orig_height;
  gint new_width, new_height;
  gdouble zoom_value, saturation_value;

  image = (GtkImage *) data;

  /* get the original pixbuf dimensions */
  orig_pixbuf = (GdkPixbuf *)g_object_get_data(G_OBJECT(image), "orig-pixbuf");
  orig_width = gdk_pixbuf_get_width(orig_pixbuf);
  orig_height = gdk_pixbuf_get_height(orig_pixbuf);

  /* get adjuster-induced changes */
  zoom = (GtkAdjustment *)g_object_get_data(G_OBJECT(image), "zoom");
  zoom_value = gtk_adjustment_get_value(zoom);
  saturation = (GtkAdjustment *)g_object_get_data(G_OBJECT(image), "saturation");
  saturation_value = gtk_adjustment_get_value(saturation);

  /* compute new size */
  new_width = (gint)(orig_width * zoom_value);
  new_height = (gint)(orig_height * zoom_value);

  /* prevent a height or width of 0 */
  new_width = MAX(1, new_width);
```

```
    new_height = MAX(1, new_height);

    /* scale the original pixbuf to the new dimensions
       (feel free to try other interpolation algorithms) */
    new_pixbuf = gdk_pixbuf_scale_simple(orig_pixbuf,
                                         new_width,
                                         new_height,
                                         GDK_INTERP_BILINEAR);

    /* modify the saturation on the newly scaled pixbuf
       note that args 1 and 2 are the same */
    gdk_pixbuf_saturate_and_pixelate(new_pixbuf,
                                     new_pixbuf,
                                     saturation_value,
                                     FALSE);

    /* display the new pixbuf in the image widget */
    g_object_set(image, "pixbuf", new_pixbuf, NULL);
    /* reference to new_pixbuf is no longer necessary,
       the system may dispose of it when convenient */
    g_object_unref(new_pixbuf);
}
```

WARNING *After passing* new_pixbuf *to the image widget,* render_image() *releases the Pixbuf reference. This is important because* render_image() *creates a new object for* new_pixbuf *upon every invocation (regardless of the old value). Therefore, there would be a big memory leak if GTK+ still thought that there was an active reference to the old Pixbuf. If you aren't careful, even a small program like this could quickly grow to 50MB in active memory and beyond after the user plays around a little.*

The main program starts with the usual mundane declarations and initializations.

```
int main(int argc, char **argv)
{
  GtkWindow *window;
  GtkHBox *hbox;

  GtkImage *image;

  GtkVBox       *zoom_box,    *saturation_box;
  GtkLabel      *zoom_label,  *saturation_label;
  GtkVScale     *zoom_slider, *saturation_slider;
  GtkAdjustment *zoom,        *saturation;

  GdkPixbuf *orig_pixbuf;

  /* initialize GTK+, create a window */
  gtk_init(&argc, &argv);
  window = g_object_new(GTK_TYPE_WINDOW,
                        "title", "GdkPixbuf Demo",
```

```
                        "default-width", 300,
                        "default-height", 300,
                        "border-width", 12,
                        NULL);

    /* attach standard event handlers */
    g_signal_connect(window, "delete_event", G_CALLBACK(delete_event), NULL);
    g_signal_connect(window, "destroy", G_CALLBACK(end_program), NULL);
```

The first order of business is to load the image from the disk. However, recall from earlier that render_image() needs the original pixmap. This program couples the original pixmap to image with the help of an object data extension named **orig-pixmap**.

```
    /* create image widget and load a file */
    image = g_object_new(GTK_TYPE_IMAGE, "file", "apple-green.png", NULL);

    /* store the original pixbuf in the image widget data */
    g_object_get(image, "pixbuf", &orig_pixbuf, NULL);
    g_object_set_data(G_OBJECT(image), "orig-pixbuf", (gpointer)orig_pixbuf);
```

The next part looks somewhat confusing because slider widgets come later in the book, in Section 3.6.5. This code creates a slider for scaling the image in the image widget; the values represented by the slider range from 0.01 to 7.5, and they will show up on the slider as 1% to 750%.

```
    /* define storage for zoom slider */
    zoom = GTK_ADJUSTMENT(gtk_adjustment_new(1.0,    /* default */
                                             0.01,   /* minimum */
                                             7.5,    /* maximum */
                                             0.01,   /* step increment */
                                             0.1,    /* page increment  */
                                             0.0));  /* page size */

    /* create zoom slider */
    zoom_slider = g_object_new(GTK_TYPE_VSCALE,
                               "draw_value", TRUE,
                               "value-pos", GTK_POS_BOTTOM,
                               "adjustment", zoom,
                               NULL);

    /* create label for zoom slider */
    zoom_label = g_object_new(GTK_TYPE_LABEL,
                              "label", "_Zoom:",
                              "use-underline", TRUE,
                              "mnemonic-widget", zoom_slider,
                              NULL);

    /* format the zoom slider's display as a percentage */
```

```
g_signal_connect(zoom_slider, "format-value", G_CALLBACK(percent), NULL);

/* put all of the zoom elements in a vbox */
zoom_box = g_object_new(GTK_TYPE_VBOX, NULL);
gtk_box_pack_start(GTK_BOX(zoom_box), GTK_WIDGET(zoom_label), FALSE, FALSE, 0);
gtk_box_pack_start_defaults(GTK_BOX(zoom_box), GTK_WIDGET(zoom_slider));
```

This code creates the saturation adjustment slider, with values from 0 to 5.0:

```
/* now do all of the above for a saturation slider */
saturation = GTK_ADJUSTMENT(gtk_adjustment_new(1.0, 0.0, 5.0, 0.01, 0.1, 0.0));

saturation_slider = g_object_new(GTK_TYPE_VSCALE,
                                 "draw-value", TRUE,
                                 "value-pos", GTK_POS_BOTTOM,
                                 "adjustment", saturation,
                                 "update-policy", GTK_UPDATE_DELAYED,
                                 NULL);

saturation_label = g_object_new(GTK_TYPE_LABEL,
                                "label", "_Saturation:",
                                "use-underline", TRUE,
                                "mnemonic-widget", saturation_slider,
                                NULL);

saturation_box = g_object_new(GTK_TYPE_VBOX, NULL);
gtk_box_pack_start(GTK_BOX(saturation_box),
                   GTK_WIDGET(saturation_label),
                   FALSE, FALSE, 0);

gtk_box_pack_start_defaults(GTK_BOX(saturation_box),
                            GTK_WIDGET(saturation_slider));
```

As was the case with the original pixmap, render_image() needs to access the values in zoom and saturation:

```
/* store the adjuster widgets in the image object */
g_object_set_data(G_OBJECT(image), "zoom", (gpointer)zoom);
g_object_set_data(G_OBJECT(image), "saturation", (gpointer)saturation);
```

Now the program must connect the render_image() handler that manipulates and redisplays the image when a user changes a slider. Remember that this handler needs the **GtkImage** object as its data pointer so that it can access the original pixmap dimensions and other object data extensions above:

```
/* install adjuster signal handlers */
g_signal_connect(zoom, "value-changed",
                 G_CALLBACK(render_image), (gpointer) image);
g_signal_connect(saturation, "value-changed",
                 G_CALLBACK(render_image), (gpointer) image);
```

Finally, the program can put all of the various containers together, show everything, and fall into the GTK+ main event loop:

```
/* create a new HBox, pack the image and vboxes above */
hbox = g_object_new(GTK_TYPE_HBOX, NULL);
gtk_box_pack_start_defaults(GTK_BOX(hbox), GTK_WIDGET(image));
gtk_box_pack_end(GTK_BOX(hbox), GTK_WIDGET(zoom_box), FALSE, FALSE, 3);

gtk_box_pack_end(GTK_BOX(hbox), GTK_WIDGET(saturation_box), FALSE, FALSE, 3);

/* pack everything into the window, show everything, start GTK+ main loop */
gtk_container_add(GTK_CONTAINER(window), GTK_WIDGET(hbox));
gtk_widget_show_all(GTK_WIDGET(window));
gtk_main();

return 0;
}
```

If you want to see some more operations with **GdkPixbuf**, take a look at Eye of GNOME, the GNOME image viewer. This application is easy to adapt for tests and demonstrations.

Stock Items and Images

GTK+ and GNOME include many prebuilt label strings for common tasks in GUI applications. A *stock item* is the label, its key combinations, and other data. Stock items are convenient — for example, you create a standard, full-featured **Cancel** or **OK** button without much fuss; as a bonus, the button appears in the user's native language.

There's another reason for using these stock items: They come with stock icons. Every icon is available in several standard sizes (usually in pairs, for example, one size for menu items and something slightly larger for toolbar buttons).

Each stock item has an identifier that you access with a macro (there is a string behind each macro in the current implementation). For example, for the GTK+ **Cancel** stock item, use GTK_STOCK_CANCEL. You'll find a list of the the GTK+ and GNOME stock items in Appendix A.

As mentioned in Section 3.3.2, a **GtkImage** object has a **stock** property for specifying a stock image and an **icon-size** property for choosing one of these standard sizes:

- GTK_ICON_SIZE_MENU for menu entries (16 x 16 pixels).

- GTK_ICON_SIZE_SMALL_TOOLBAR for small tool items (18 x 18 pixels).

- GTK_ICON_SIZE_LARGE_TOOLBAR for large tool items (24 x 24 pixels).

- GTK_ICON_SIZE_BUTTON for buttons (20 x 20 pixels).

- GTK_ICON_SIZE_DND icons that represent drag-and-drop objects (32 x 32 pixels).

- GTK_ICON_SIZE_DIALOG icons in a dialog box (48 x 48 pixels).

3.3.3 Progress Bars

The example in Section 3.3.2 introduced the progress bar, a widget that informs the user how far along a program is when it is busy at work. The progress bar class name is **GtkProgress**, and its type identifier is GTK_TYPE_PROGRESS_BAR. Progress bar objects contain the following properties:

- **fraction** (gdouble): The fraction of current progress; a floating-point number from 0 up to (but not including) 1.

- **pulse-step** (gdouble): The fraction of the progress bar width that the indicator should move at every pulse; applies to activity mode (discussed later).

- **orientation** (GtkProgressBarOrientation): The widget's orientation, including its direction of growth. Possible values are

    GTK_PROGRESS_LEFT_TO_RIGHT: Horizontal bar, growing left to right.

    GTK_PROGRESS_RIGHT_TO_LEFT: Horizontal bar, growing right to left.

    GTK_PROGRESS_BOTTOM_TO_TOP: Vertical bar, growing bottom to top.

    GTK_PROGRESS_TOP_TO_BOTTOM: Vertical bar, growing top to bottom.

- **text** (gchararray): Text to overlay on top of the progress bar.

NOTE   **fraction** *should never be greater or equal to 1.0, unless you enjoy ugly warnings on the console. The earlier example solves this problem with the* CLAMP() *macro.*

In activity mode, the progress bar does not display text. After entering activity mode, you can advance the indicator with

---

GtkProgressBar *progress_bar*;

gtk_progress_bar_pulse(*progress_bar*);

Activity mode works for situations where the program can't figure out how long its current task will take. For example, when traversing a directory tree, there is no terribly good way to tell how long the operation will take. Therefore, you could advance the indicator every time the program runs through 100 files.

Set **fraction** to leave activity mode.

The example also shows that you can switch between normal and activity mode without a problem — behavior that you might know from certain web browsers. (Of course, many people find this behavior to be very annoying.)

3.4 Container and Layout Widgets

It would be practically impossible to organize normal widgets without container widgets. Each container has a specific way of ordering its widgets based on parameters and packing order.

The principal container types are as follows:

- **Horizontal and vertical boxes.** These are the most important and fundamental containers. When you need to arrange several widgets in a row or column, you should use a box. The two classes here are **GtkHBox** for horizontal rows and **GtkVBox** for columns, both derived from the **GtkBox** parent class. This book will refer to the objects from these classes as HBoxes and VBoxes.

  There are special subclasses called **GtkHButtonBox** and **GtkVButtonBox** for groups of buttons. They work like any other box, except that all widgets packed into one of these boxes tend to receive consistent appearance and layout characteristics. Button boxes are good for buttons, as the name implies, but they aren't terribly good for anything else.

- **Horizontal and vertical panes.** A pane consists of two adjacent containers divided by a user-adjustable slider bar. A typical use of the horizontal paned container (**GtkHPaned**) is a window with a file manager in the primary pane and a list of items on the other side. A mail client could use a vertical paned container (**GtkVPaned**) to separate the message list and display. The abstract **GtkPaned** class is the parent of these two container classes.

- **Notebooks.** These organizer widgets (**GtkNotebook**) hold several pages with tabs along one of the edges for the user to select and view a page. Programs often use notebooks for property settings.

NOTE *Notebooks with too many pages are a plague of modern GUI development. Try to keep these things under control.*

- **Tables.** If you need to arrange several widgets in a grid, **GtkTable** is probably the best bet. Common uses of table containers include matrices of near-identical elements, such as a tic-tac-toe game or the Nautilus file permissions dialog box; you can also make certain widgets in the table span cells over a row and column. With the proper packing options, you can create good layouts for several kinds of applications. Cell coordinates can change when you add or delete a widget from the table; if you're doing this sort of thing, you probably want to get some help from Glade (see Chapter 5).

- **Alignment.** These simple containers (**GtkAlignment**) dictate the size and alignment of exactly one widget.

You already saw some examples of HBoxes and VBoxes in earlier examples. The following program demonstrates button boxes, panes, notebooks, and tables.

Notice that the widget declarations in the main program are grouped by container.

```
/* -*-coding: utf-8;-*- */
/* container.c -- container demo */

#include <gtk/gtk.h>

/* standard handlers */
gint delete_event(GtkWidget *widget, GdkEvent event, gpointer data)
```

```
{
  return FALSE;
}

void end_program(GtkWidget *widget, gpointer data)
{
  gtk_main_quit();
}

int main(int argc, char **argv)
{
  GtkWindow *window;
  GtkHPaned *h_pane;
  GtkVPaned *v_pane;
  GtkVButtonBox *button_column; /* button box elements */
  GtkButton *button[3];
  GtkTable *table;              /* table elements */
  GtkButton *tictac[3][3];
  gint i, j;
  GtkNotebook *notebook;        /* notebook elements */
  GtkLabel *page_1_content;
  GtkImage *page_2_apple;
  GtkButton *page_3_button;
  GtkLabel *page_1_title, *page_2_title, *page_3_title;

  /* initialize GTK+, create a window, attach handlers */
  gtk_init(&argc, &argv);
  window = g_object_new(GTK_TYPE_WINDOW,
                        "title", "Container Madness",
                        "default_height", 200,
                        "default_width", 300,
                        "border-width", 12,
                        NULL);

  /* attach standard event handlers */
  g_signal_connect(window, "delete_event", G_CALLBACK(delete_event), NULL);
  g_signal_connect(window, "destroy", G_CALLBACK(end_program), NULL);
```

The program initially divides the main window into two panes with a horizontal
pane widget that the user can slide left and right.

```
  /* Divide window horizontally with a pane */
  h_pane = g_object_new(GTK_TYPE_HPANED, NULL);
  gtk_container_add(GTK_CONTAINER(window), GTK_WIDGET(h_pane));
```

So far, there's been nothing terribly new about this application. Now let's put
another widget (a vertical paned container, to be specific) in the left pane
created by the preceding code:

```
/* create a vertical paned container and put it
   in the left side of the horizontal pane above */
v_pane = g_object_new(GTK_TYPE_VPANED, NULL);
gtk_paned_add1(GTK_PANED(h_pane), GTK_WIDGET(v_pane));
```

Notice that the packing function for paned containers here is `gtk_paned_add1()`, to put the widget into the left pane. If this were a vertical paned container, it would put the widget into the top pane. Refer to Section 3.4.3 for more information on paned containers.

The next three statements create three buttons; there is nothing unusual about them.

```
/* create three buttons */
button[0] = g_object_new(GTK_TYPE_BUTTON, "label", "Foo", NULL);
button[1] = g_object_new(GTK_TYPE_BUTTON, "label", "Bar", NULL);
button[2] = g_object_new(GTK_TYPE_BUTTON, "label", "Baz", NULL);
```

A vertical button box holds the buttons. Because a button box is a form of **GtkBox**, the packing functions are the same as for a regular box container (see Section 3.4.1).

```
/* put the buttons in a vertical button box */
button_column = g_object_new(GTK_TYPE_VBUTTON_BOX, NULL);
for (i=0; i<3; i++)
{
    gtk_box_pack_start_defaults(GTK_BOX(button_column), GTK_WIDGET(button[i]));
}
```

As the following comment indicates, this button box will go into the top pane of the vertically paned container (recall that this container is on the left side of the window).

```
/* put the vertical button box into the top pane of v_pane, from earlier */
gtk_paned_add1(GTK_PANED(v_pane), GTK_WIDGET(button_column));
```

The following code shows how to create a table container. Because the work of creating all of the widgets for the table can be mundane, a short loop will create a button for each cell in the table. See Section 3.4.2 for a description of a table container's properties and methods.

```
/* create a 3x3 table container */
table = g_object_new(GTK_TYPE_TABLE,
                     "n-rows", 3,
                     "n-columns", 3,
                     "homogeneous", TRUE,
                     NULL);

/* fill the table with some buttons */
for (i=0; i<3; i++)
```

```
{
   for (j=0; j<3; j++)
   {
      tictac[i][j] = g_object_new(GTK_TYPE_BUTTON, NULL);
      gtk_table_attach_defaults(table,
                                GTK_WIDGET(tictac[i][j]),
                                i, i+1, j, j+1);
   }
}
/* label the buttons in the table's diagonal */
g_object_set(tictac[0][0], "label", "Tic", NULL);
g_object_set(tictac[1][1], "label", "Tac", NULL);
g_object_set(tictac[2][2], "label", "Toe", NULL);

/* put the table in the lower pane of v_pane, from above */
gtk_paned_add2(GTK_PANED(v_pane), GTK_WIDGET(table));
```

The last container widget in this program is a notebook that occupies the right pane in the main window. The first of three pages in the notebook contains a "Page 1!" label. The page needs a title to put on its tab; the first page's title is "This."

```
/* create a notebook */
notebook = g_object_new(GTK_TYPE_NOTEBOOK, NULL);

/* put the notebook in the window's right pane */
gtk_paned_add2(GTK_PANED(h_pane), GTK_WIDGET(notebook));

/* create notebook's page 1, containing only a label */
page_1_content = g_object_new(GTK_TYPE_LABEL, "label", "Page 1!", NULL);

/* create page 1's title ("This") */
page_1_title = g_object_new(GTK_TYPE_LABEL, "label", "This", NULL);

/* add the page to the notebook */
gtk_notebook_append_page_menu(notebook,
                              GTK_WIDGET(page_1_content),
                              GTK_WIDGET(page_1_title),
                              NULL);
```

Section 3.4.4 describes notebook packing methods such as gtk_notebook_append_page_menu(), as well as the many properties that you can assign to notebooks.

The following fragment creates two more notebook pages: one with an image of an apple, and the other containing a single button. After all of the notebook pages are in place, we're also ready to display the window and start the main event loop. Figure 3.7 shows the final application.

```
/* add another page containing an apple image */
page_2_apple = g_object_new(GTK_TYPE_IMAGE, "file", "apple-green.png", NULL);
page_2_title = g_object_new(GTK_TYPE_LABEL, "label", "That", NULL);
gtk_notebook_append_page_menu(notebook,
                              GTK_WIDGET(page_2_apple),
                              GTK_WIDGET(page_2_title),
                              NULL);

/* page 3 contains a button */
page_3_button = g_object_new(GTK_TYPE_BUTTON, "label", "Click me", NULL);
page_3_title = g_object_new(GTK_TYPE_LABEL, "label", "The Other", NULL);
gtk_notebook_append_page_menu(notebook,
                              GTK_WIDGET(page_3_button),
                              GTK_WIDGET(page_3_title),
                              NULL);

/* show the whole thing and start GTK+ main loop */
gtk_widget_show_all(GTK_WIDGET(window));
gtk_main();

return 0;
}
```

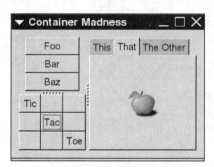

Figure 3.7: Container demonstration.

All container classes have **GtkContainer** as a superclass (class identifier: GTK_TYPE_CONTAINER). You have seen

gtk_container_add(*container*, *widget*)

from this class; all of the examples so far use it to pack a widget into the main window.

NOTE   *Use* gtk_container_add() *only with simple containers such as **GtkWindow** and **GtkFrame**. The more complex containers need more parameters and therefore have their own packing functions.*

To remove a widget from a container, use

gtk_container_remove(*container*, *widget*)

Taking a widget out of its container usually leads to the widget's destruction, because the container held the only (previously floating) reference to the widget object. Obtain a new reference for the widget object if you want to save it.

The gtk_container_add_with_properties() function is a convenience function that allows you to place a widget in a property like gtk_container_add(), but allows a NULL-terminated list of property and value pairs for the widget (the syntax for the list is the same as for g_object_set()).

If you need to run the same function on many widgets at once, one particularly useful utility is

gtk_container_foreach(*container*, *callback_function*, *data*)

This runs the GtkCallback function *callback_function* on all of the widgets inside *container*. The callback takes a widget and data as its parameters; the type definition is as follows:

typedef void (*GtkCallback) (GtkWidget *widget, gpointer data);

All objects derived from the **GtkContainer** class have these two properties:

- **border-width** (gint): The border width of the container, in pixels. If this value is zero, packed widgets extend to the very edge of the container.
- **child** (GtkWidget, write-only): Writing a widget to this property packs it into the container. Therefore,

g_object_set(*container*, "child", *widget*, NULL)

is identical to

gtk_container_add(*container*, *widget*)

3.4.1 Boxes

Whether a horizontal box (**GtkHBox**, GTK_TYPE_HBOX) or a vertical box (**GtkVBox**, GTK_TYPE_VBOX), all boxes has the same purpose: to arrange widgets in a line.

These two functions pack a widget into a box:

gtk_box_pack_start(*box*, *widget*, *expand*, *fill*, *padding*)
gtk_box_pack_end(*box*, *widget*, *expand*, *fill*, *padding*)

The parameters for both functions are

- *box* (GtkBox *): The container widget.
- *widget* (GtkWidget *): The widget to pack into *box*.
- *expand* (gboolean): Indicates whether the widget should try to center itself over any remaining free space in the box. This does not have any effect on the widget's size (see fill, described next). The box divides its free space among the widgets packed with this parameter set to TRUE.

- *fill* (gboolean): When TRUE, the widget actually grows to cover the free space, rather than float over it. This will not work unless you set expand to TRUE.

- *padding* (guint): The pixel count of free space to keep on each side of the widget.

The gtk_box_pack_start() function packs a widget at the front of the box. All widgets previously packed into the box with this function still appear in front of any new widget. gtk_box_pack_end() is a similar function for packing at the end of a container.

NOTE *In a VBox, the start of the container is the top. In an HBox, it's usually the left side, but don't always assume this. If a user's locale sets a language where the writing goes from right to left, the horizontal widgets are likely to be reversed.*

If you don't feel like typing all of the parameters for these two packing functions all of the time, use these two functions:

```
gtk_box_pack_start_defaults(box, widget)
gtk_box_pack_end_defaults(box, widget)
```

These are like their counterparts described earlier, but set *fill* and *expand* to TRUE, and *padding* to 0.

The **GtkBox** class has two properties:

- **spacing** (gint): The distance between packed widgets (in pixels). Keep in mind that this is in addition to any padding that you add when packing the widgets.

- **homogeneous** (gboolean): If TRUE, widgets inside the box become (and stay) the exact same size.

The button box classes (**GtkHButtonBox** and **GtkVButtonBox**, class type identifiers GTK_TYPE_HBUTTON_BOX and GTK_TYPE_VBUTTON_BOX) have the same methods and properties as normal boxes. There is one additional **GtkButtonBox** property that gives you finer control of how the box arranges the buttons: **layout-style**. Its value is one of the following:

- GTK_BUTTONBOX_DEFAULT_STYLE: The default layout; like a regular box.

- GTK_BUTTONBOX_SPREAD: The box spreads the buttons across its space at equal intervals. There is a half-interval at each end.

- GTK_BUTTONBOX_EDGE: Like the preceding, but with no space at each end.

- GTK_BUTTONBOX_START: The box groups the buttons at the beginning of its space.

- GTK_BUTTONBOX_END: The box groups the buttons at the end of its space.

Container Child Properties

When you pack a widget into a **GtkBox** container, the widget obtains some *child properties* that control how it appears in the box. However, these are not regular GObject properties; you need to use special functions to retrieve and set the values.

The child property access functions rely on the GValue system (see Section 2.4.2):

```
void gtk_container_child_get_property (GtkContainer *container,
                                       GtkWidget *child,
                                       const gchar *property_name,
                                       GValue *value);

void gtk_container_child_set_property (GtkContainer *container,
                                       GtkWidget *child,
                                       const gchar *property_name,
                                       const GValue *value);
```

The preceding child property functions require that *value* be an allocated and initialized GValue. This example with the **padding** child property should give you the idea:

```
GValue *value;

/* initialize value */
gv = g_new0(GValue, 1);
g_value_init(gv, G_TYPE_INT);

/* get current child property padding value */
gtk_container_child_get_property(container, widget, "padding", gv);

/* set padding value to a ludicrous value */
g_value_set_int(gv, 100);
gtk_container_child_set_property(container, widget, "padding", gv);

g_free(value);
```

Here are the **GtkBox** child properties:

- **expand** (gboolean): See the *expand* parameter described earlier.
- **fill** (gboolean): See the *fill* parameter described earlier.
- **padding** (guint): See the *padding* parameter described earlier.
- **pack-type** (GtkPackType): The side where the widget was packed; possible values are GTK_PACK_START and GTK_PACK_END.
- **position** (gint): The position of the widget in the box (positions start at 0).

A child of a **GtkButtonBox** widget receives an additional **secondary** child property (type: gboolean). When TRUE, the widget appears at the other side of the button box. Help buttons and the like often get this treatment.

3.4.2 Tables

An object of the **GtkTable** class is essentially a bounded two-dimensional box. The example in Section 3.4 showed that tables have **n-rows** and **n-columns** properties for the number of rows and columns in the table.

After you create a table, you can use it as a container. Naturally, it's not a good idea to arbitrarily pack widgets into the table. You can assign a widget to a specific table cell, and you can also tell it to span rows and columns. The function for inserting a widget into a table is

```
gtk_table_attach(table, widget,
              left_attach, right_attach,
              top_attach, bottom_attach,
              xoptions, yoptions,
              xpadding, ypadding)
```

The arguments are as follows:

- *table* (GtkTable *): The target **GtkTable** widget.
- *widget* (GtkWidget *): The widget to insert into *table*.
- *left_attach* (guint): The column index for the widget's left side. A table's first column and row index is 0.
- *right_attach* (guint): The column index for the widget's right side. If you don't want to span columns (that is, you want only one column), use *left_attach+1*.
- *top_attach* (guint): The row for the widget's top side.
- *bottom_attach* (guint): The row for the widget's right side. If you don't want to span rows, use *top_attach+1*.
- *xoptions* (GtkAttachOptions): Bitwise ORed options for layout in the horizontal direction. Choose from the following:

  GTK_EXPAND: Distribute widgets with this option evenly across the available space. This is similar to the *expand* parameter you saw for boxes in Section 3.4.1.

  GTK_FILL: In conjunction with the preceding option, the widget should grow to occupy the available space. This is also similar to the fill **GtkBox** parameter.

  GTK_SHRINK: If there isn't enough space for the widget, the table will attempt to shrink the widget.

- *yoptions* (GtkAttachOptions): Like **xoptions**, but for layout in the vertical direction.
- *xpadding* (guint): The number of pixels to reserve on the widget's left and right sides.
- *ypadding* (guint): The number of pixels to reserve on the widget's top and bottom sides.

After you insert a widget into a table, the widget gets most of the parameters just described as child properties. The property names are **left-attach**, **right-attach**, **top-attach**, **bottom-attach**, **x-options**, **y-options**, **x-padding**, and **y-padding**.

GtkTable containers also have these properties:

- `column-spacing`: The number of pixels between columns.

- `row-spacing`: The number of pixels between rows.

- `homogeneous`: If this gboolean property is TRUE, all columns should be of equal width, and all rows should have equal heights. In other words, all cells that don't span rows or columns should be the same size.

3.4.3   Paned Widgets

A paned widget is a container with two sides; each side holds a child widget. A user-adjustable slider bar divides the panes. On a **GtkHPaned** (GTK_TYPE_HPANED) widget, a vertical slider divides child widgets in the left and right panes, and a **GtkVPaned** (GTK_TYPE_VPANED) widget has a horizontal slider with child widgets above and below. If you have trouble associating the names with the correct orientation, forget about the sliders and think of them as boxes.

To place widgets into a paned container, use these functions:

```
gtk_paned_add1(paned, widget)
gtk_paned_add2(paned, widget)
```

gtk_paned_add1() places a widget into the left or top of the container, and gtk_paned_add2() packs widgets into the right or bottom. The only two arguments to these functions are the container and its new child widget, as you saw in Section 3.4's example program.

If you need some control over the size of the child widgets, use these two instead:

```
gtk_paned_pack1(paned, widget, resize, shrink)
gtk_paned_pack2(paned, widget, resize, shrink)
```

Here, resize and shrink are Boolean values. If resize is TRUE, the paned container may resize the widget. If you set shrink to TRUE, the user may shrink the widget as desired with the slider bar, but if it is FALSE, you cannot make the widget smaller than its requested minimum size.

The parent class of the two paned container types (**GtkPaned**) defines two properties:

- `position` (gint): The position of the slider bar, represented as the number of pixels from the left or top edge of the container.

- `position-set` (gboolean): Set this property to TRUE if you want to change the slider position with the `position` property.

3.4.4   Notebooks

A notebook container (**GtkNotebook**, GTK_TYPE_NOTEBOOK) consists of several pages with tabs. When you click a page's tab, the page comes to the foreground, and you can work with any widgets on the page. You can also assign a context menu to the tabs; when you right-click a tab, you get a menu of the tabs.

After you create a notebook, you can add pages with several functions. Among the most verbose of these is

---

gtk_notebook_append_page_menu(*notebook, widget, tab_label, menu_label*)

The parameters are

- *notebook* (GtkNotebook *): The container widget.
- *widget* (GtkWidget *): The widget to put in the main part of the new page.
- *tab_label* (GtkWidget *): The label for new page's tab.
- *menu_label* (GtkWidget *): A label for the notebook's context menu. If you set this to NULL and *tab_label* is a **GtkLabel** widget, GTK+ uses that latter label for the context menu. Keep in mind that context menus are off by default; set the container's **enable-popup** property to activate them (as described later in this chapter).

NOTE   *You can put just about any kind of widget in a page's tab, but the only one that really makes any sense is a label.*

If you don't care about the menu, use

---

gtk_notebook_append_page(*notebook, widget, tab_label*)

Here are some other ways to add pages:

- gtk_notebook_prepend_page_menu() is like its appending counterpart described earlier, but inserts the page at the front of the notebook rather than the end.
- gtk_notebook_prepend_page() works like the preceding function, but has no menu label parameter.
- gtk_notebook_insert_page_menu() has a fifth argument: where to insert the new page. The front of the notebook is at index 0.
- gtk_notebook_insert_page() works like the preceding function, but has no menu label parameter.

To remove a page from a notebook, use

---

gtk_notebook_remove_page(*notebook, page_number*)

Notebook properties include

- **tab-pos** (enumeration): The tab location; one of

    GTK_POS_LEFT

    GTK_POS_RIGHT

    GTK_POS_TOP

    GTK_POS_BOTTOM

- **show-tabs** (gboolean): If FALSE, the notebook has no tabs.
- **show-border** (gboolean): Enables or disables the border.

- **scrollable** (gboolean): If TRUE, the notebook creates a scrolling tab list when there are too many tabs to display.
- **tab-hborder** (guint): Controls the border thickness on the left and right sides of a tab's label.
- **tab-vborder** (guint): Controls the border thickness above and below a tab's label.
- **tab-border** (guint, write-only): Controls the border thickness around a tab's label.
- **page** (gint): Controls the current page index.
- **enable-popup** (gboolean): Enables or disables context menus that appear when you right-click a tab.
- **homogeneous** (gboolean): If TRUE, all tabs have the same width.

A widget packed into a notebook takes on these child properties:

- **tab-label** (gchararray): The text of the tab's label.
- **menu-label** (gchararray): The text of the widget's context menu label.
- **position** (gint): The widget's page position in the notebook.
- **tab-expand** (gboolean): If TRUE, the tab centers itself over open space.
- **tab-fill** (gboolean): In conjunction with **tab-expand**, if TRUE, the tab grows to fill the open space.
- **tab-pack** (enumeration): Indicates where you packed the page into the notebook; possible values are GTK_PACK_START and GTK_PACK_END.

3.4.5   Alignment Containers

If you want finer control of the placement and proportions of a widget, place it in a **GtkAlignment** (GTK_TYPE_ALIGNMENT) container. The container's properties are all gfloat values:

- **xalign**: The horizontal alignment of the child widget. The values 0.0, 0.5, and 1.0 specify left justification, centered, and right justification, respectively.
- **yalign**: The vertical alignment of the child widget. The values 0.0, 0.5, and 1.0 specify top, center, and bottom, respectively.
- **xscale**: The horizontal scale of the child widget if the container has more space than the child needs. The value 0.0 means that the child should not grow at all if space is available, and the value 1.0 means that the child should use all available space.
- **yscale**: Like the preceding, but for the vertical scale.

NOTE   *You will frequently encounter properties with names like* **xalign** *and* **yalign** *in other widget classes; they control alignment in the same manner as a **GtkWidget** container.*

3.4.6 Sensible Widget Arrangement

At this point, you should have a pretty good idea of how you can use containers to lay out your widgets. When it comes to how you *should* arrange them, the GNOME guidelines have some tips on how to achieve consistency, clarity, and legibility:

- Layouts should run top to bottom and right to left, starting at the top left corner, at least for applications in languages that write left to right.

- Use 3 as `border-width` in tables and boxes. In addition, set the distance between the elements inside (`spacing`) to 3 pixels.

- Specify other distances between widgets in multiples of 6:

    6 pixels between an icon and its label.

    12 pixels between other widgets and their labels.

    12 pixels of free space around the contents of a dialog box.

    18 pixels between vertically arranged widgets.

- If you align, indent, and group with distance, the result is usually a lot easier to look at and understand than something using visible frames, divider lines, and other fencelike elements.

3.5 Button Widgets

Buttons are among the most elementary user-operated widgets. There are three basic types of buttons:

- **GtkButton** (`GTK_TYPE_BUTTON`): A simple button; when you click the button, GTK+ emits a signal. The button goes back to its original state after the click and is therefore similar to a momentary electronic switch. If the button carries out a concrete action (as opposed to bringing up a list of preferences, for example), label it with the infinitive verb form of the action (without *to*; for example, "Do This" or "Apply"). You have seen buttons in several programs so far, including the very first program in this chapter.
This is also the parent class of the following two button classes.

- **GtkCheckButton** (`GTK_TYPE_CHECK_BUTTON`) is an on/off button. When you click the button, it changes state; another click reverts the button to its original state. Check buttons (sometimes called check boxes) look different than regular buttons. See Section 3.13 for more information on a practically identical widget class, **GtkToggleButton**.

- **GtkRadioButton** (`GTK_TYPE_RADIO_BUTTON`): These buttons typically come in sets; each set represents a single setting. You can select only one of the buttons at a time, and therefore, they resemble the buttons for preset stations on car radios.

The example program you're about to see demonstrates all three of these button types. It is supposed to be an interface for hot drinks. You select the temperature with a radio button, add some options with check buttons, and, finally, prepare your drink with one of three regular buttons.

Figure 3.8 shows the final application.

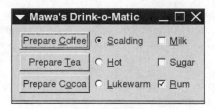

Figure 3.8: Button demonstration.

Like other examples, this program includes global variables for the radio and check button widgets along with the standard event handlers.

```
/* -*-coding: utf-8;-*- */
/* buttons.c -- button demo */

#include <gtk/gtk.h>

static GtkRadioButton *radio_temper[3];
static GtkCheckButton *check_option[3];

/* standard event handlers */
gint delete_event(GtkWidget *widget, GdkEvent event, gpointer data) {
  return FALSE;
}

void end_program(GtkWidget *widget, gpointer data) {
  gtk_main_quit();
}
```

When you click one of the three regular buttons, GTK+ runs the following signal handler to tell you how it will prepare your drink. This is mostly busy, repetitive work; however, the important thing to notice is the **active** property for the radio and check button objects. GTK+ sets these gboolean values according to the states of the widgets. Also, note that only one of the radio_temper widgets is active at any given time, but any combination of the check buttons is possible.

```
void prepare_drink(gpointer drink)
{
  gboolean scalding, hot, lukewarm = FALSE;
  gboolean milk, sugar, rum = FALSE;

  /* extract the temperature from radio buttons */
  g_object_get(radio_temper[0], "active", &scalding, NULL);
  g_object_get(radio_temper[1], "active", &hot, NULL);
  g_object_get(radio_temper[2], "active", &lukewarm, NULL);
  /* extract any options from check buttons */
  g_object_get(check_option[0], "active", &milk, NULL);
  g_object_get(check_option[1], "active", &sugar, NULL);
```

```
g_object_get(check_option[2], "active", &rum, NULL);

/* Piece together a little statement of drink to prepare. */
g_print("Preparing%s%s%s %s",
        scalding ? " scalding" : "",
        hot      ? " hot"      : "",
        lukewarm ? " lukewarm" : "",
        (gchar *) drink);

if (milk || sugar || rum)
{
    g_print(" with:%s%s%s",
            milk  ? " milk"  : "",
            sugar ? " sugar" : "",
            rum   ? " rum"   : "" );
}
g_print(".\n");
}
```

The application's layout consists of three columns (VBoxes) in a horizontal line
(HBox).

```
int main(int argc, char **argv)
{
  GtkWindow *window;
  GtkHBox *hbox;
  GtkVBox *vbox[3];
  GtkButton *button_prepare[3];
  gint i;

  /* initialize GTK+, create a window */
  gtk_init(&argc, &argv);

  window = g_object_new(GTK_TYPE_WINDOW,
                        "title", "Mawa's Drink-o-Matic",
                        "border-width", 12,
                        NULL);

  /* add standard signal handlers */
  g_signal_connect(window, "delete_event", G_CALLBACK(delete_event), NULL);
  g_signal_connect(window, "destroy", G_CALLBACK(end_program), NULL);

  /* create boxes and pack them */
  hbox = g_object_new(GTK_TYPE_HBOX, "spacing", 6, NULL);

  for (i=0; i<3; i++)
  {
     vbox[i] = g_object_new(GTK_TYPE_VBOX, "spacing", 6, NULL);
     gtk_box_pack_start_defaults(GTK_BOX(hbox), GTK_WIDGET(vbox[i]));
  }
  gtk_container_add(GTK_CONTAINER(window), GTK_WIDGET(hbox));
```

The regular buttons to prepare the drink are are in the following code. Look at the bindings to the prepare_drink() handler; you can now see the origin of its drink parameter.

(You could save a few lines of typing with a macro here, at the cost of a slightly more confusing program.)

```
/* create and pack regular buttons for preparing drinks */
/* they go in the leftmost VBox */
for (i=0; i<3; i++)
{
    button_prepare[i] = g_object_new(GTK_TYPE_BUTTON,
                                     "use-underline", TRUE,
                                     NULL);
    gtk_box_pack_start_defaults(GTK_BOX(vbox[0]), GTK_WIDGET(button_prepare[i]));
}

g_object_set(button_prepare[0], "label", "Prepare _Coffee", NULL);
g_signal_connect_swapped(button_prepare[0],
                         "clicked", G_CALLBACK(prepare_drink), "coffee");

g_object_set(button_prepare[1], "label", "Prepare _Tea", NULL);
g_signal_connect_swapped(button_prepare[1],
                         "clicked", G_CALLBACK(prepare_drink), "tea");

g_object_set(button_prepare[2], "label", "Prepare C_ocoa", NULL);
g_signal_connect_swapped(button_prepare[2],
                         "clicked", G_CALLBACK(prepare_drink), "cocoa");
```

Creating radio buttons and setting their labels isn't much different than creating regular buttons; all you need is the GTK_TYPE_RADIO_BUTTON class type identifier.

```
/* create temperature radio buttons, pack into center VBox */
for (i=0; i<3; i++)
{
    radio_temper[i] = g_object_new(GTK_TYPE_RADIO_BUTTON,
                                   "use-underline", TRUE,
                                   NULL);
    gtk_box_pack_start_defaults(GTK_BOX(vbox[1]), GTK_WIDGET(radio_temper[i]));
}
g_object_set(radio_temper[0], "label", "_Scalding", NULL);
```

After you create one radio button and are ready to initialize more, you need to group the radio buttons, so that only one in the group is allowed to be active at a time. To do this, set the **group** property in the remaining radio buttons to the first radio button.

```
g_object_set(radio_temper[1],
             "label", "_Hot",
             "group", radio_temper[0],
             NULL);
```

```
g_object_set(radio_temper[2],
            "label", "_Lukewarm",
            "group", radio_temper[0],
            NULL);
```

There aren't any special properties to worry about when you create the check buttons.

```
/* create check buttons for additives, pack into third VBox */
for (i=0; i<3; i++)
{
    check_option[i] = g_object_new(GTK_TYPE_CHECK_BUTTON,
                                   "use-underline", TRUE,
                                   NULL);
    gtk_box_pack_start_defaults(GTK_BOX(vbox[2]), GTK_WIDGET(check_option[i]));
}
g_object_set(check_option[0], "label", "_Milk", NULL);
g_object_set(check_option[1], "label", "S_ugar", NULL);
g_object_set(check_option[2], "label", "_Rum", NULL);

/* show window, start main event loop */
gtk_widget_show_all(GTK_WIDGET(window));
gtk_main();
return 0;
}
```

All **GtkButton** objects have these two gboolean properties that you can set only when you create the widget:

- **use-underline**: Enable a keyboard shortcut for this button. Set the key by placing an underscore (_) before the appropriate character in the **label** property.

- **use-stock**: This button should take on a stock item label with the **label** property.

Only **GtkRadioButton** objects have the **group** property; as you saw in the example, this is a radio button in the group. The easiest way to group radio buttons is to create the first button and then set the other buttons' **group** properties to the first button. **GtkRadioButton** and **GtkCheckButton** have these additional gboolean properties:

- **active** is TRUE if the button is the currently selected radio button or is otherwise checked.

- **inconsistent** is TRUE if the button is in some sort of transitional or disabled state; the widget will have a strikeout bar or be dimmed. For example, a check button could indicate an attribute in a text editor. If you mark out a large portion of the text with the mouse, the selection could contain text with and without the attribute, and therefore, the check button's **active** property doesn't make any sense, and therefore, the whole widget should be disabled. The program in Section 3.12 has a concrete example.

All **GtkButton** objects have signals with this handler prototype:

```
void handler(GtkButton *button, gpointer *data);
```

The signals and their emission circumstances are:

- **clicked**: When you click the button.
- **enter**: When you move the mouse pointer into the button.
- **leave**: When you move the pointer away from the button.
- **pressed**: When you click down *on* the button.
- **released**: When you let go of the button.
- **activate**: If you emit this signal with a button object, GTK+ clicks the button for you.

Normally, you should need to bother only with the **clicked** signal.

3.6 Data Entry Widgets

GTK+ has a number of basic data entry widgets:

- **GtkOptionMenu** (GTK_TYPE_OPTION): Functionally, an option menu is the same as a group of radio buttons, but you should use them only under certain circumstances:
  - When there just isn't enough space for radio buttons.
  - When the number of items and labels can change.
  - For a logical progression of items (such as days of the week).

  However, if there are more than ten items, you should use a list instead (see Section 3.11).

- **GtkEntry** (GTK_TYPE_ENTRY): An entry box is a single-line widget for entering a short bit of text. Use this type of entry box when you don't have any other way to represent data. If you need an entry box with history features, have a look at the derived class **GnomeEntry** in Section 4.3.4. If there are several sensible default options for the widget's state, consider the combo box; for numbers, use a slider or spin button.

- **GtkCombo** (GTK_TYPE_COMBO): is a cross between an entry box and an option menu. You can enter a short line of text into a box, but you can also place common items into an attached menu for quick access. Don't write-protect a combo box's entry box to create a menu — this is a popular tactic on other platforms, but GTK+ has option menus for this purpose.

- **GtkScale** (GTK_TYPE_SCALE): Slider widgets allow you to pick a value within a certain range. They work well for relative settings ("a little louder," for example) and other types of input where specifying a precise value isn't terribly important.

  GtkScale is an abstract class; you'll use **GtkHScale** (GTK_TYPE_HSCALE) and **GtkVScale** for horizontal and vertical sliders in your actual implementations.

- **GtkSpinButton** (GTK_TYPE_SPIN_BUTTON): Spin buttons allow the user to enter a precise numeric value that may or may not have particular bounds. The widget contains a box with a number and two buttons to increment and decrement the number by a certain amount.

The example you're about to see demonstrates all of these widgets. To make this interesting, the values of the two sliders and the spin button are linked; when you change one, the other two automatically change (the MVC lingo for this is that the widgets show different *views*; see Section 3.11 for more information). Figure 3.9 shows the application.

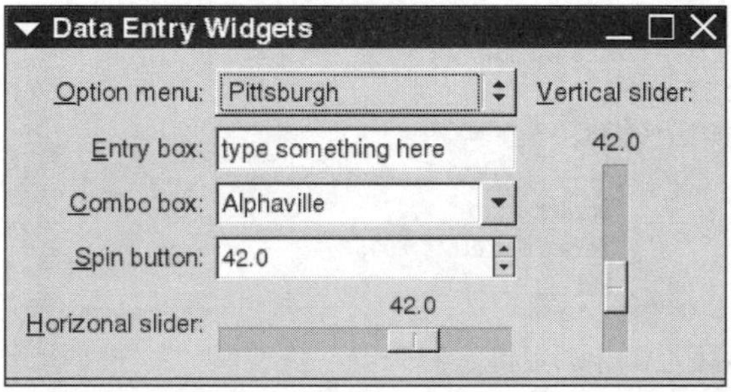

Figure 3.9: Option menu, entry box, combo box, spin button, and sliders.

The program starts with the standard event handlers for the main window. It also has a macro definition indicating the number of widgets in a table for the overall window layout:

```
/* -*-coding: utf-8;-*- */
/* dataentry.c -- basic data entry widgets */

#include <gtk/gtk.h>

/* usual event handlers */
gint delete_event(GtkWidget *widget, GdkEvent event, gpointer data) {
  return FALSE;
}

void end_program(GtkWidget *widget, gpointer data) {
  gtk_main_quit();
}

#define NUM_WIDGETS 5
```

The definitions for all of the entry widgets follow. The option menu, combo button, and slider require auxiliary data structures.

```
int main(int argc, char **argv)
{
  GtkWindow *window;
  GtkTable *table;
  GtkOptionMenu *option_menu;
```

```
GtkEntry *entry_box;
GtkCombo *combo_box;
GtkSpinButton *spin_button;
GtkHScale *h_slider;
GtkVScale *v_slider;

GtkMenu *names_menu;        /* for option menu */
GList *combo_list = NULL;    /* for combo button */
GtkAdjustment *adjust;       /* for sliders and spin button */

GtkWidget *mnemo;

/* initialize GTK+, create window */
gtk_init(&argc, &argv);
window = g_object_new(GTK_TYPE_WINDOW,
                      "title", "Data Entry Widgets",
                      "border-width", 12,
                      "default-width", 400,
                       NULL);

/* connect standard window handlers */
g_signal_connect(window, "delete_event", G_CALLBACK(delete_event), NULL);
g_signal_connect(window, "destroy", G_CALLBACK(end_program), NULL);
```

Sliders and spin buttons require a **GtkAdjustment** object so that they know the range of values that they may represent. This object also holds the value for the slider or spin button; see Section 3.6.4 for more information on these objects, including information on how to access the value.

```
/* define the range for the slider widgets, spin button */
adjust = GTK_ADJUSTMENT(gtk_adjustment_new(1.0,     /* initial value */
                                    -100.0, /* minimum */
                                    100.0,  /* maximum */
                                    0.5,    /* step */
                                    10.0,   /* page step*/
                                    0.0));  /* page size */
```

Now that you have adjust, it's easy to create the horizontal and vertical slider widgets. Because both sliders use adjust for their **adjustment** properties, when you change one of these widgets, the other will also react. Section 3.6.5 details the **GtkScale** properties.

```
/* create vertical slider */
v_slider = g_object_new(GTK_TYPE_VSCALE, "adjustment", adjust, NULL);

/* create horizontal slider */
h_slider = g_object_new(GTK_TYPE_HSCALE, "adjustment", adjust, NULL);
```

To create a **GtkOptionMenu** widget, you must create the menu that goes inside the widget. The following code creates names_menu with three items.

```
/* create and define a menu */
names_menu = g_object_new(GTK_TYPE_MENU, NULL);
gtk_menu_shell_append(GTK_MENU_SHELL(names_menu),
                    gtk_menu_item_new_with_label("Harrisburg"));
gtk_menu_shell_append(GTK_MENU_SHELL(names_menu),
                    gtk_menu_item_new_with_label("Pittsburgh"));
gtk_menu_shell_append(GTK_MENU_SHELL(names_menu),
                    gtk_menu_item_new_with_label("Hollidaysburg"));
```

With the menu in hand, you can create the **GtkOptionMenu** widget with a `menu` property. See Section 3.6.1 for more information on option menus.

```
/* create an options menu, using the menu above */
option_menu = g_object_new(GTK_TYPE_OPTION_MENU, "menu", names_menu, NULL);
```

You can set the current element in the option menu:

```
/* set index 1 as default */
gtk_option_menu_set_history(option_menu, 1);
```

Entry box widgets are simple; their **text** property is the current text inside the widget. Section 3.6.2 is dedicated to entry boxes.

```
/* create an entry box */
entry_box = g_object_new(GTK_TYPE_ENTRY, "text", "type something here", NULL);
```

A combo box (see also Section 3.6.3) is a little trickier than an option menu because you may frequently change its default entries. Combo boxes take a list of strings as default entries.

```
/* create a list of names */
combo_list = g_list_append(combo_list, "Townsville");
combo_list = g_list_append(combo_list, "Pleasantville");
combo_list = g_list_append(combo_list, "Springfield");
combo_list = g_list_append(combo_list, "Smallville");

/* create a combo box */
combo_box = g_object_new(GTK_TYPE_COMBO, NULL);

/* add the list of names to the combo box */
gtk_combo_set_popdown_strings(combo_box, combo_list);
```

There is actually an entry box inside each combo box; its **text** property represents the combo box's value.

```
/* set a default entry in combo box */
g_object_set(combo_box->entry, "text", "Alphaville", NULL);
```

After you feed the list of strings to the combo box, you no longer need the list data structure.

```
/* list structure no longer necessary */
g_list_free(combo_list);
```

When you create a spin button, you need a **GtkAdjustment** object for the
adjustment property, just as you did for sliders. More detail on spin buttons is in
Section 3.6.6.

```
/* spin button */
spin_button = g_object_new(GTK_TYPE_SPIN_BUTTON,
                           "adjustment", adjust,
                           "digits", 1,
                           "value", 42.0,
                           NULL);
```

Creating the table and putting the widgets into the table is primarily an exercise
in typing. However, you should take a look at the **mnemonic-widget** property in each
widget's label; it enables a hot key for the input focus to go straight to the label's
widget. Combo boxes are a little different in this respect. Typically, you don't
want the input focus on the combo box, but rather, the entry box inside.

NOTE *This code uses a macro to save some typing. If you were writing a real program, you would
probably make this into a function. Not only would a function offer more flexibility, but the
resulting object code would be smaller. Here, you can see the result of the macro expansion
alongside the macro calls.*

```
table = g_object_new(GTK_TYPE_TABLE,
                     "n-rows", NUM_WIDGETS,
                     "n-columns", 3,
                     "row-spacing", 6,
                     NULL);

/* this macro packs one of the data entry widgets into
   the table, along with a label */
/* if the widget is a combo box, set its mnemonic to
   the entry box inside the combo */
#define PACK_IN_TABLE(widget, label, row_num)                    \
    mnemo = GTK_WIDGET(widget);                                  \
    if (GTK_IS_COMBO(widget))                                    \
      { mnemo = GTK_COMBO(widget)->entry; }                      \
    gtk_table_attach(table,                                      \
                     g_object_new(GTK_TYPE_LABEL,                \
                                  "label", label,                \
                                  "use-underline", TRUE,         \
                                  "mnemonic-widget", mnemo,      \
                                  "xalign", 1.0,                 \
                                  "justify", GTK_JUSTIFY_RIGHT,\
                                  NULL),                         \
                     0, 1, row_num, row_num+1,                   \
                     GTK_EXPAND|GTK_FILL, 0, 0, 0);              \
                                                                 \
```

```
gtk_table_attach(table,                                       \
                g_object_new(GTK_TYPE_ALIGNMENT,              \
                            "xalign", 0.0,                    \
                            "child", widget,                  \
                            NULL),                            \
                1, 2, row_num, row_num+1,                     \
                GTK_EXPAND|GTK_FILL, 0, 6, 0);

/* pack the widgets and their labels into the table */
PACK_IN_TABLE(option_menu, "_Option menu:",        0)
PACK_IN_TABLE(entry_box,   "_Entry box:",          1)
PACK_IN_TABLE(combo_box,   "_Combo box:",          2)
PACK_IN_TABLE(spin_button, "_Spin button:",        3)
PACK_IN_TABLE(h_slider,    "_Horizonal slider:", 4)
```

The preceding code placed all of the widgets except the vertical slider into table rows. The vertical slider would look absurd inside a row, so it takes up an entire column instead.

```
/* pack the vertical slider and its label into the table */
gtk_table_attach(table,
                g_object_new(GTK_TYPE_LABEL,
                            "label", "_Vertical slider:",
                            "use_underline", TRUE,
                            "mnemonic-widget", v_slider,
                            NULL),
                2, 3, 0, 1,
                GTK_SHRINK, 0, 6, 0);

gtk_table_attach(table, GTK_WIDGET(v_slider),
                2, 3, 1, 5,
                GTK_SHRINK,
                GTK_EXPAND|GTK_FILL, 0, 0);

/* pack table into window, show everything, begin main loop */
gtk_container_add(GTK_CONTAINER(window), GTK_WIDGET(table));
gtk_widget_show_all(GTK_WIDGET(window));
gtk_main();
return 0;
}
```

There are three specialized data entry widgets that you may need from time to time:

- **Color picker:** This large, powerful widget lets the user choose a color with the help of a color wheel, sliders, and palette. **GtkColorSelection** is the base widget, but there is dialog box version: **GtkColorSelectionDialog**. See Section 3.6.7 for more information on these widgets.

- **Font chooser:** This is the font equivalent of the color picker. Section 3.6.8 covers **GtkFontSelection** and its dialog box cousin, **GtkFontSelectionDialog**.

- **File browser:** The average user frequently encounters this familiar list of directories and files. This widget comes only as a dialog box: **GtkFileSelection**. Section 3.6.9 shows you how to work with file browsers.

NOTE *GNOME offers additional interface widgets. If you need a small button of a current color that activates a color chooser on a mouse click, have a look at **GnomeColorPicker** in Section 4.3.7. For fonts and files, the equivalent classes are **GnomeFontPicker** (Section 4.3.6) and **GnomeFileEntry** (Section 4.3.5).*

3.6.1 Option Menus

An option menu (**GtkOptionMenu**, type identifier `GTK_TYPE_OPTION_MENU`) is a button that calls a true **GtkMenu** widget when clicked, and therefore, you need to know how to create menu objects. The example in the previous section should give you a fairly clear idea of how to do this; Section 4.3.1 details the complete workings of GTK+ menus.

NOTE *Use only regular menu items in an options menu. Separators, submenus, and key combinations are counterproductive.*

Normal menus typically call commands, but an option menu picks an element from a list. You can set the current element with

```
gtk_option_menu_set_history(menu, i)
```

where `menu` is the option menu object, and `i` is the index of the element (the first element is at index 0). To retrieve the menu's current element index, use

```
gtk_option_menu_get_history(menu)
```

The return value is gint; -1 means that there are no items in the option menu.

Option menus have a **changed** signal that GTK+ emits this when the user selects something in a menu. Use a prototype like this for your signal handler:

```
void handler(GtkOptionMenu *option_menu, gpointer data);
```

3.6.2 Entry Boxes

There are few widgets as easy to operate as an entry box (class **GtkEntry**, type `GTK_TYPE_ENTRY`). After you create and pack an entry widget, you can set and fetch the string with its **text** property.

Once you start to work with entry boxes, you'll quickly find that they can do a number of interesting things. For example, when you right-click the box, a small context menu appears with **Cut**/**Copy**/**Paste** and input mode items.

Other **GtkEntry** properties include the following:

- **cursor-position** (gint, read-only): The current position of the cursor in the box. A value of 0 means that the cursor is in front of the first character, 1 means that it is in front of the second character, and so on.

- **selection-bound** (gint, read-only): If the user has selected something in the entry box, this is the end of the selection.

- **editable** (gboolean): If FALSE, the user may not change the text inside the box.

- **max-length** (gint): Maximum length of the string inside the entry box; 0 specifies no limit.

- **visibility** (gboolean): If you set this property to FALSE, the real characters won't show up in the widget. There will be a substitute (see the next property). You can use this feature for password entry.

- **invisible-char** (guint): The character to substitute in conjunction with the **visibility** feature (the default is an asterisk).

- **has-frame** (gboolean): If TRUE, a relief frame appears around the box.

- **activates-default** (gboolean): If the entry box is part of a dialog, a TRUE value here means that pressing ENTER in the entry box also activates the default button in the dialog box.

- **width-chars** (gint): The width of the entry box in characters.

- **scroll-offset** (gint, read-only): If the user enters so much text into the box that scrolling is necessary, this property holds the number of pixels that the box scrolled.

Although the **cursor-position** and **selection-bound** properties are read-only, you can still manipulate the cursor position and selection though the **GtkEditable** (GTK_TYPE_EDITABLE) interface. Here are the methods in the interface:

- void gtk_editable_insert_text(GtkEditable *widget, const gchar *text, gint length, gint *position)
  Inserts *text* into *widget* at index *position*. The *length* value indicates the length of the text *in bytes*, not characters. Note that *position* is a pointer (or address); this function writes the new cursor position back into this location.

- void gtk_editable_delete_text(GtkEditable *widget, gint begin, gint end)
  Removes the characters from index *begin* up to (but not including) *end* from *widget*. If *end* is negative, this function removes all characters from *begin* to the end of the buffer.

- gchar *gtk_editable_get_chars(GtkEditable *widget, gint begin, gint end)
  Returns the string between *begin* and *end*.

- void gtk_editable_cut_clipboard(GtkEditable *widget)
  Removes the currently selected text in *widget* and places it in the clipboard.

- void gtk_editable_copy_clipboard(GtkEditable *widget)
  Copies the currently selected text in *widget* in the clipboard.

- void gtk_editable_paste_clipboard(GtkEditable *widget)
  Copies the clipboard's content into *widget* at its current cursor position.

- void gtk_editable_delete_clipboard(GtkEditable *widget)
  Removes the currently selected text in *widget* (does not save a copy).

The **GtkEditable** interface also defines these signals (and handler prototypes):

- **changed**
  `void handler(GtkEditable *widget, gpointer data)`
  Emitted when the user changes something inside the text.

- **insert-text**
  `void handler(GtkEditable *widget, gchar *text, gchar *length, gint *position, gpointer data)`
  Emitted when the user inserts text. The new text is at `text`, `length` *bytes* long. The `position` value is the new location of the cursor. You can attach a handler to this signal if you want to control if and when text is inserted.

- **delete-text**
  `void handler(GtkEditable *widget, gint begin, gint end, gpointer data)`
  Emitted when the user removes text between `begin` and `end`.

GtkEntry has one signal of its own: **activate**. GTK+ emits this when the user activates the entry box (for example, by pressing ENTER). Its prototype is

```
void handler(GtkEntry *widget, gpointer data)
```

3.6.3   Combo Boxes

GtkCombo class widgets (`GTK_TYPE_COMBO`) include an entry pointer in their instance structures, so they can also use all characteristics of the **GtkEntry** class. In the example in Section 3.6, you saw how to access this embedded object with `combo->entry`.

Combo boxes add the functionality of choosing from a number of default strings through lists. To set these defaults, create a `GList` of strings and call

```
gtk_combo_set_popdown_strings(combo, list)
```

where `combo` is the combo box, and `list` is the set of strings. The combo box sets the value in its entry box to the first string in the list. The example in the previous section also illustrates how you can get a different default: Set `combo->entry`'s **text** property *after* you initialize the defaults with the function described earlier.

gtk_combo_set_popdown_strings() writes the first list argument into the combo entry box.

Combo box widgets have these `gboolean` properties:

- **enable-arrow-keys**: If `TRUE`, the user can navigate through the default list with the up and down arrow keys.

- **enable-arrow-always**: If `FALSE`, the user can navigate through the default list with the arrow keys only when the current content of the box is one of the defaults.

- **case-sensitive**: If FALSE, the current content of the box can match a default even if it uses different case characters (this property works in conjunction with the preceding property).

- **allow-empty**: If FALSE, the user may not leave the box in an empty state.

NOTE *GtkCombo can do much more. For example, the item list can accept any kind of widget, and you can strictly control the text in the box. However, all of this detracts from its intended use. If you want a list, use a list box (see Section 3.11), and if you want an option menu, use an option menu (see Section 3.6.1).*

3.6.4 Adjustment Objects

A **GtkAdjustment** (class type GTK_TYPE_ADJUSTMENT) object works with a widget to help store the widget's represented value and give the widget some hints on appearance. Sliders, spin buttons, and scrollbars (see Section 3.9) typically work with **GtkAdjustment** objects.

To create an adjustment object, use

```
GtkAdjustment *adj;

adj = gtk_adjustment_new(initial,
                    lower, upper,
                    step_increment, page_increment,
                    page_size);
```

All of the parameters are gdouble floating-point numbers:

- *initial* is *adj*'s initial value.

- *lower* is the lower bound of *adj*'s value.

- *upper* is the upper bound of *adj*'s value.

- *step_increment* is a small step; when you drag a slider or click the spin button's arrow, *adj*'s value changes by at least this much.

- *page_increment* is a big step; a click in the trough of a slider changes *adj*'s value by this much.

- *page_size* is the currently visible size of the page. This parameter is useful only for scrollbars; set this to 0 for sliders and spin buttons.

To set and retrieve the value of an adjustment object, use

```
void gtk_adjustment_set_value(object)
```

and

```
gdouble gtk_adjustment_get_value(object)
```

This object is essentially a data structure, and you can directly access its fields as they appear above (for example, *adj*->upper). However, if you change something, you should tell the attached widgets about the change with gtk_adjustment_changed(*adj*).

GTK+ emits two signals for adjustment objects: **value-changed** when the value in the object changes, and **changed** when one of its parameters changes. The handler prototype for both signals is

```
void handler(GtkAdjustment *adjust, gpointer data)
```

3.6.5 Slider Widgets

Sliders can be horizontal (**GtkHScale**, GTK_TYPE_HSCALE) or vertical (**GtkVScale**, GTK_TYPE_VSCALE). Their parent class is **GtkScale**, and all scale widgets include these properties:

- **adjustment** (GtkAdjustment *): The range and value for the slider, as described in Section 3.6.4.

- **draw-value** (gboolean): If TRUE, GTK+ shows the slider's value next to the slider. See the **format-value** signal described later in this section if you want fine control over the displayed value's format.

- **digits** (gint): The number of digits to the right of the decimal point in the value display. The default is 1.

- **value-pos** (GtkPositionType): Determines where the slider value display appears relative to the slider. Possible values are

    GTK_POS_LEFT

    GTK_POS_RIGHT

    GTK_POS_TOP

    GTK_POS_BOTTOM

Sliders belong to the parent class **GtkRange** (not to be confused with **GtkAdjustment**); this is where **adjustment** comes from. There are two more properties:

- **update-policy** (enumeration): Specifies how often the slider should update its **GtkAdjustment** value. The possible values are

    GTK_UPDATE_CONTINUOUS: Update the value as soon as it changes; this is the default.

    GTK_UPDATE_DISCONTINUOUS: Update the value when the user lets go of the slider.

    GTK_UPDATE_DELAYED: If the user still has the mouse clicked down on the slider, update if there hasn't been any activity for a certain amount of time.

    The last two modes work well for sliders that require significant computation for a redisplay; one example is the saturation adjustment in Section 3.3.2's program.

- **inverted** (gboolean): If TRUE, the slider reverses its lower and upper bound ends.

Sliders come with a **format-value** signal, using this handler prototype:

```
gchar *handler(GtkScale *slider, gdouble number, gpointer data);
```

GTK+ emits **format-value** to get a string to display as the new value when the user adjusts the slider; the number parameter is the new value. In your handler, allocate a new string and fill it out as you prefer. GTK+ frees this new memory when it is no longer needed. The program in Section 3.3.2 contains an example of a custom handler.

NOTE   *If you have a slider with a large range (a large integral range, in particular), GNOME Usability Guidelines say that you should include a spin button with the same **GtkAdjustment** value/range object to allow for fine control. You can pack the spin button at one end of the slider and set the slider's **draw-value** property to FALSE.*

3.6.6   Spin Button Widgets

Spin buttons (**GtkSpinButton**, GTK_TYPE_SPIN_BUTTON) allow a user to adjust a value with arrow buttons; the user can also type a new value in the display, just as in an entry box. The programming interface resembles sliders in many respects. Spin button properties include the following:

- **adjustment** (GtkAdjustment *): The range and value for the spin button, as described in Section 3.6.4.

- **climb-rate** (gdouble): The rate at which the step increment grows when the user presses and holds the mouse button on the increment arrow. After every fifth increment with the mouse button down, the spin button adds this value to the step increment. The default is 0 (no acceleration).

- **digits** (gint): The number of digits to the right of the decimal point in the value display. The default is 0.

- **snap-to-ticks** (gboolean): If TRUE, the spin button rounds any typed-in value to the nearest increment. The default is FALSE.

- **wrap** (gboolean): If TRUE, the spin button's value cycles around when the user clicks past an upper or lower bound. The default is FALSE.

- **update-policy** (GtkSpinButtonUpdatePolicy): One of these two values:

    GTK_UPDATE_ALWAYS: Change the spin button's value whenever the user types something into the box.

    GTK_UPDATE_IF_VALID: Change the spin button's value if the user's input conforms to the range that the spin button can represent.

- **value** (gdouble): The current value of the spin button. You can also access this through the spin button's associated **GtkAdjustment** object.

- **numeric** (gboolean): If FALSE, you can enter nonnumeric characters into the spin button. This could be useful for hexadecimal values, but to do this, you will need to add handlers for the **input** and **output** signals (not covered in this book).

The spin button class is a subclass of **GtkEntry** (see Section 3.6.2) and therefore inherits all properties, methods, and signals from that class.

3.6.7   Color Chooser Widgets

GtkColorSelection (class type `GTK_TYPE_COLOR_SELECTION`) is a color selection, complete with red-green-blue controls, hue-saturation-value controls, and a color sampler (see Figure 3.12 on page 171 for an example). After you create a color picker, it can go anywhere in a window. The color chooser's properties are as follows:

- **has-palette** (gboolean): If `TRUE`, the chooser includes a palette alongside the other controls. The default is `FALSE`.
- **has-opacity-control** (gboolean): If `TRUE`, the chooser includes a slider for the opacity (alpha channel). The default is `FALSE`.
- **current-color** (GdkColor): The current color in the chooser. A GdkColor structure includes red, green, and blue fields, all guint16.
- **current-alpha** (guint): The current alpha channel value (0 is completely transparent; 65536 is opaque).

Every time the user changes the color in the chooser, GTK+ emits a **color-changed** signal. The prototype for the handler is

```
void handler(GtkColorSelection *widget, gpointer data);
```

Because this signal goes out even when the user drags a color across the color wheel, you need to think twice about doing serious computation based on the color. Use the function

```
gtk_color_selection_is_adjusting(chooser_widget)
```

in your signal handler to see if the user is still adjusting `chooser_widget`. If the return value is `TRUE`, you may want to wait for a later handler invocation to do any computation. The example in Section 3.6.10 does this.

   GtkColorSelectionDialog (`GTK_TYPE_COLOR_SELECTION_DIALOG`) is a complete color chooser inside a dialog box. However, because **GnomeColorPicker** (see Section 4.3.7) tends to handle these situations better, this book won't elaborate on the dialog box version of the color chooser.

3.6.8   Font Chooser Widgets

A **GtkFontSelection** (`GTK_TYPE_FONT_SELECTION`) widget, shown in Figure 3.10, allows the user to preview and choose fonts. There are two important properties, both gchararray strings:

- **font-name**: The name of the currently selected font.
- **preview-text**: The text at the bottom of the widget that demonstrates the currently selected font.

A font chooser doesn't have any important functions or signals. Therefore, you are responsible for creating the mechanism for determining what to do with the font selection. As with the color chooser, there is a dialog box version called

GtkFontSelectionDialog; however, because the **GnomeFontPicker** object in Section 4.3.6 is usually a better tool choice, there will be no further discussion of the font chooser dialog box in this book.

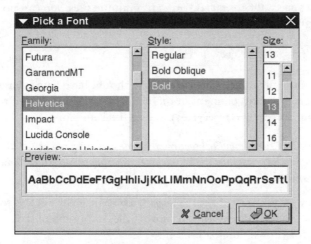

Figure 3.10: GTK+ font chooser.

3.6.9   File Browsers

Unlike the color and font widgets, **GtkFileSelection** (GTK_TYPE_FILE_SELECTION) is available only as a separate dialog box, shown in Figure 3.11. Normally, you create the dialog box with a button or menu item signal handler. You must also provide additional signal handlers to decide what to do when the user clicks the OK and Cancel buttons. These buttons are the ok_button and cancel_button fields of the file selection object, so when you attach a signal handler to *file_browser*'s OK button, you can access the button with *file_browser*->ok_button (an example of this appears in Section 3.6.10).

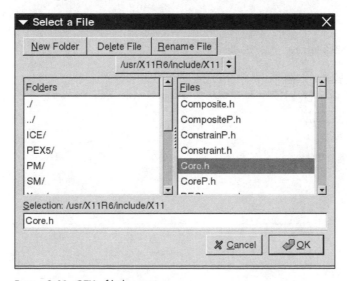

Figure 3.11: GTK+ file browser.

Normally, you can select only a single file from a file browser; the full pathname of the file is a gchararray string in the browser's **filename** property.

However, you can enable multiple-file selection with the gboolean **select-multiple** property. Of course, if you want multiple files, you can no longer get the file through the simple **filename** property. Use

```
files = gtk_file_selection_get_selections(file_browser);
```

to get all of the filenames. The *files* value should have type gchararray *; a NULL value indicates the last element in this array of strings. After you're finished with the filenames, use g_strfreev(*files*) to free their memory.

NOTE *All filenames that come from the browser are in the operating system's character encoding. If you want to put the name into a GTK+ widget, you should convert the name to UTF-8 with one of the functions in Section 1.4.4.*

A final browser property is **show-fileops** (gboolean). If you set this to TRUE, three buttons for creating directories, removing files, and renaming files appear at the top of the file browser dialog box.

If you need a filename with a file selection button, consider using **GnomeFileEntry**, described in Section 4.3.5.

3.6.10 Chooser Examples

This section presents a sample program for the color chooser, font chooser, and file browser; see Figure 3.12 for the final product. The demonstration starts with the usual window signal handlers as well as a global declaration for the file browser dialog box:

```
/* -*-coding: utf-8;-*- */
/* selections.c -- demonstrate selection widgets */

#include <gtk/gtk.h>

GtkFileSelection *file_browser;

/* standard handlers */
gint delete_event(GtkWidget *widget, GdkEvent event, gpointer data)
{
  return FALSE;
}

void end_program(GtkWidget *widget, gpointer data)
{
  gtk_main_quit();
}
```

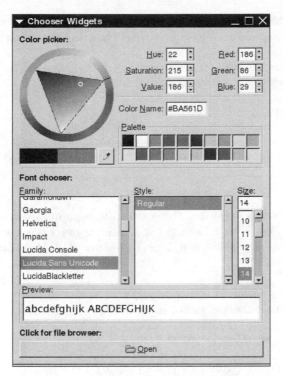

Figure 3.12: Color, font, and file selection application.

This handler function is meant for the color chooser's **color-changed** signal. Notice how it does nothing if the user is still dragging something around on the widget.

```
/* handler for "color-changed" signal, prints new color to console */
void print_color(GtkColorSelection *chooser, gpointer data)
{
  GdkColor color;
  guint red, green, blue;
  guint alpha;

  /* if user is still adjusting the widget, do nothing */
  if (!gtk_color_selection_is_adjusting(chooser))
  {
    g_object_get(chooser, "current-color", &color, NULL);
    red = color.red;
    green = color.green;
    blue = color.blue;

    g_object_get(chooser, "current-alpha", &alpha, NULL);

    g_print("color chosen: R=%d, G=%d, B=%d, A=%d\n",
            red, green, blue, alpha);
  }
}
```

This handler displays the selection from a file browser after the user clicks the OK button. Its signal attachment is discussed later in this section.

```
/* prints name file selected in file_browser */
void print_filename(GtkButton *button, gpointer data)
{
  gchar *filename;

  g_object_get(file_browser, "filename", &filename, NULL);
  g_print("file chosen: %s\n", filename);
  g_free(filename);
}
```

Creating the file browser dialog box is a fairly straightforward task. You can see how to connect the print_filename() handler in the preceding code to the browser's OK button, as well as how to remove the window after the user clicks OK or Cancel.

```
/* creates the file browser and attaches signals */
void make_file_dialog(GtkButton *button, gpointer data)
{
  file_browser = g_object_new(GTK_TYPE_FILE_SELECTION, NULL);

  gtk_window_set_title(GTK_WINDOW(file_browser), "Select a File");

  g_signal_connect(file_browser->ok_button,
                   "clicked", G_CALLBACK(print_filename), NULL);

  g_signal_connect_swapped(file_browser->ok_button,
                           "clicked", G_CALLBACK(gtk_widget_destroy),
                           file_browser);

  g_signal_connect_swapped(file_browser->cancel_button,
                           "clicked", G_CALLBACK(gtk_widget_destroy),
                           file_browser);

  gtk_widget_show(GTK_WIDGET(file_browser));
}
```

The main program window uses a simple layout: All widgets will go into a single column with a VBox.

```
int main(int argc, char **argv)
{
  GtkWindow *window;
  GtkColorSelection *color_chooser;
  GtkFontSelection *font_chooser;
  GtkButton *file_browser_button;
```

```
GtkVBox *vbox;
GtkLabel *color_label, *font_label, *file_label;

/* initialize GTK+, create window */
gtk_init(&argc, &argv);
window = g_object_new(GTK_TYPE_WINDOW, "title", "Chooser Widgets", NULL);

/* attach standard handlers */
g_signal_connect(window, "delete_event", G_CALLBACK(delete_event), NULL);
g_signal_connect(window, "destroy", G_CALLBACK(end_program), NULL);

/* create vbox for main display */
vbox = g_object_new(GTK_TYPE_VBOX, "spacing", 6, "border-width", 12, NULL);
```

Creating the color chooser is just like creating any simple widget. Every selection widget in this program has a label (for organization purposes).

```
/* create a color chooser and label, pack them into a VBox */
color_label = g_object_new(GTK_TYPE_LABEL,
                           "label", "<b>Color picker:</b>",
                           "use-markup", TRUE,
                           "xalign", 0.0,
                           NULL);

color_chooser = g_object_new(GTK_TYPE_COLOR_SELECTION,
                             "has-palette", TRUE,
                             NULL);
```

This code attaches the signal handler print_color() to print the selected color.

```
/* add an event handler for when user picks a color */
g_signal_connect(color_chooser,
                 "color-changed", G_CALLBACK(print_color), NULL);
```

You don't need to do anything special to pack the color chooser, either. The single horizontal separator implemented here is for organizational purposes; you'll see more detail on separators in Section 3.7.

```
gtk_box_pack_start_defaults(GTK_BOX(vbox), GTK_WIDGET(color_label));
gtk_box_pack_start_defaults(GTK_BOX(vbox), GTK_WIDGET(color_chooser));

gtk_box_pack_start_defaults(GTK_BOX(vbox),
                            g_object_new(GTK_TYPE_HSEPARATOR, NULL));
```

The font chooser setup is nearly identical to that of the color chooser, but it does not have an event handler.

```
/* create a font chooser and label, pack them into a VBox */
font_label = g_object_new(GTK_TYPE_LABEL,
                          "label", "<b>Font chooser:</b>",
                          "use-markup", TRUE,
```

```
                               "xalign", 0.0,
                               NULL);

    font_chooser = g_object_new(GTK_TYPE_FONT_SELECTION, NULL);

    gtk_box_pack_start_defaults(GTK_BOX(vbox), GTK_WIDGET(font_label));
    gtk_box_pack_start_defaults(GTK_BOX(vbox), GTK_WIDGET(font_chooser));
```

Because the file browser is available only as a dialog box, you can't pack it into the main window. This program packs a button into the window that calls the file browser dialog box when clicked.

```
    /* create a file browser button and label, pack them into a VBox */
    file_label = g_object_new(GTK_TYPE_LABEL,
                               "label", "<b>Click for file browser:</b>",
                               "use-markup", TRUE,
                               "xalign", 0.0,
                               NULL);

    /* use a stock label/image for the button */
    file_browser_button = g_object_new(GTK_TYPE_BUTTON,
                               "use-stock", TRUE,
                               "label", GTK_STOCK_OPEN,
                               NULL);

    /* handler for creating file browser */
    g_signal_connect(file_browser_button,
                     "clicked", G_CALLBACK(make_file_dialog), NULL);

    gtk_box_pack_start_defaults(GTK_BOX(vbox), GTK_WIDGET(file_label));
    gtk_box_pack_start_defaults(GTK_BOX(vbox), GTK_WIDGET(file_browser_button));

    /* pack VBox into window, show everything, start event loop */
    gtk_container_add(GTK_CONTAINER(window), GTK_WIDGET(vbox));
    gtk_widget_show_all(GTK_WIDGET(window));
    gtk_main();

    return 0;
}
```

3.7 Dividers and Decorations

If you need an occasional divider or decoration for widgets, GTK+ offers three:

- **GtkFrame** is a container that draws a line around one enclosed widget. You can add an optional label to the frame. Frames can be useful, but don't overdo it. See Section 3.7.1.

- **GtkSeparator** bars come in horizontal (**GtkHSeparator**) and vertical (**GtkVSeparator**) varieties. These typically divide two conceptually different parts of a window. See Section 3.7.2.

- **GtkArrow** widgets display . . . (drum roll) arrows. See Section 3.7.3.

The following program shows off all three kinds of decorations; Figure 3.13 shows the final application.

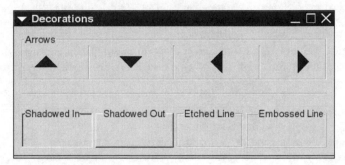

Figure 3.13: Decorations.

Because the widgets in this program don't actually do anything, there are no special signal handlers.

```
/* -*-coding: utf-8;-*- */
/* decorations.c -- various decoration widgets */

#include <gtk/gtk.h>

gint delete_event(GtkWidget *widget, GdkEvent event, gpointer data)
{
  return FALSE;
}

void end_program(GtkWidget *widget, gpointer data)
{
  gtk_main_quit();
}

int main(int argc, char **argv)
{
  GtkWindow *window;
  GtkHBox *hbox[2];
  GtkFrame *frame[5];
  GtkArrow *arrow[4];
  GtkVSeparator *v_sep[3];
  GtkHSeparator *h_sep;
  GtkVBox *vbox;
  gint i;

  /* initialize GTK+, create a window */
  gtk_init(&argc, &argv);
  window = g_object_new(GTK_TYPE_WINDOW,
                        "title", "Decorations",
                        "default-width", 500,
                        "default-height", 200,
```

```
                    "border-width", 12,
                    NULL);

/* attach standard event handlers */
g_signal_connect(window, "delete_event", G_CALLBACK(delete_event), NULL);
g_signal_connect(window, "destroy", G_CALLBACK(end_program), NULL);
```

Creating widgets for all four arrow directions is a typing exercise. At least you can pack them automatically. Notice how there are vertical separators between the arrows.

```
/* HBox with four arrows (different directions) */
hbox[0] = g_object_new(GTK_TYPE_HBOX, NULL);
arrow[0] = g_object_new(GTK_TYPE_ARROW, "arrow-type", GTK_ARROW_UP,    NULL);
arrow[1] = g_object_new(GTK_TYPE_ARROW, "arrow-type", GTK_ARROW_DOWN,  NULL);
arrow[2] = g_object_new(GTK_TYPE_ARROW, "arrow-type", GTK_ARROW_LEFT,  NULL);
arrow[3] = g_object_new(GTK_TYPE_ARROW, "arrow-type", GTK_ARROW_RIGHT, NULL);

/* pack the arrows into the hbox, put separators between */
for (i = 0; i < 4; i++)
{
   gtk_box_pack_start_defaults(GTK_BOX(hbox[0]), GTK_WIDGET(arrow[i]));
   if (i < 3)
   {
      v_sep[i] = g_object_new(GTK_TYPE_VSEPARATOR, NULL);
      gtk_box_pack_start_defaults(GTK_BOX(hbox[0]), GTK_WIDGET(v_sep[i]));
   }
}
```

Now it's time to show each frame style:

```
/* create a frame and put the hbox above inside */
frame[0] = g_object_new(GTK_TYPE_FRAME, "label", "Arrows", NULL);

gtk_container_add(GTK_CONTAINER(frame[0]), GTK_WIDGET(hbox[0]));

/* create another hbox and put four more frames inside */
hbox[1] = g_object_new(GTK_TYPE_HBOX, "spacing", 5, NULL);

frame[1] = g_object_new(GTK_TYPE_FRAME,
                    "shadow-type", GTK_SHADOW_IN,
                    "label", "Shadowed In",
                    "label-xalign", 0.0,
                    NULL);
frame[2] = g_object_new(GTK_TYPE_FRAME,
                    "shadow-type", GTK_SHADOW_OUT,
                    "label", "Shadowed Out",
                    "label-xalign", 0.5,
                    NULL);
frame[3] = g_object_new(GTK_TYPE_FRAME,
                    "shadow-type", GTK_SHADOW_ETCHED_IN,
                    "label", "Etched Line",
                    "label-xalign", 0.5,
                    NULL);
```

```
frame[4] = g_object_new(GTK_TYPE_FRAME,
                        "shadow-type", GTK_SHADOW_ETCHED_OUT,
                        "label", "Embossed Line",
                        "label-xalign", 1.0,
                        NULL);

/* pack the frames into the hbox */
for (i = 1; i < 5; i++)
{
    gtk_box_pack_start_defaults(GTK_BOX(hbox[1]), GTK_WIDGET(frame[i]));
}
```

With the frames out of the way, it's time to wrap things up by putting both HBoxes inside a VBox, with a **GtkHSeparator** object between:

```
/* create a vbox, put both hboxes inside with a separator */
vbox = g_object_new(GTK_TYPE_VBOX, NULL);
gtk_box_pack_start_defaults(GTK_BOX(vbox), GTK_WIDGET(frame[0]));

h_sep = g_object_new(GTK_TYPE_HSEPARATOR, NULL);
gtk_box_pack_start_defaults(GTK_BOX(vbox), GTK_WIDGET(h_sep));

/* put everything inside the window, show window, start loop */
gtk_box_pack_start_defaults(GTK_BOX(vbox), GTK_WIDGET(hbox[1]));
gtk_container_add(GTK_CONTAINER(window), GTK_WIDGET(vbox));
gtk_widget_show_all(GTK_WIDGET(window));
gtk_main();

return 0;
}
```

3.7.1 Frames

A frame (**GtkFrame**, GTK_TYPE_FRAME) is a decorated container for exactly one widget. When you create a frame, the following properties are at your disposal:

- **label** (gchararray): A label for the top of the frame.

- **label-widget** (GtkWidget): If you want to use an arbitrary widget instead of text for the label, assign this property to the widget. Don't put any user-adjustable widgets in the label — that sort of thing is likely to get you dragged off by the user interface police.

- **label-xalign** (gfloat): The label's relative position in the top of the frame; 0.0 tells the label to go all the way to the left, 0.5 to the center, and 1.0 to the right end.

- **shadow-type** (GtkShadowType): How GTK+ should draw the frame line. Possible values are

    GTK_SHADOW_IN: Draw so that the contents of the frame appear to be in a depression.

    GTK_SHADOW_OUT: Draw so that the contents of the frame appear elevated.

`GTK_SHADOW_ETCHED_IN`: Draw what appears to be a line etched around the contents.

`GTK_SHADOW_ETCHED_OUT`: Draw what appears to be an embossed (elevated) line around the contents.

`GTK_SHADOW_NONE`: Don't display a line.

NOTE *As mentioned many times before, try to exercise control when you employ frames. If you need to group widgets with frames, make sure that you do so with all of the widget groups, with a consistent frame style.*

If you want to annoy the user, put frames inside other frames. (Seriously, consider some other container, such as a notebook. You could also try to make all widget group sizes equal.)

3.7.2 Separators

The two separator subclasses, **GtkHSeparator** (`GTK_TYPE_HSEPARATOR`) and **GtkVSeparator** (`GTK_TYPE_VSEPARATOR`), do not have properties, methods, or signals of their own.

NOTE *Separators have an etched look and therefore fit best with frames using the* `GTK_SHADOW_ETCHED_IN` *style.*

3.7.3 Arrows

GtkArrow (`GTK_TYPE_ARROW`) widgets are almost as simple as separators, but they have an **arrow-type** property to indicate a direction. The possible values are `GTK_ARROW_UP`, `GTK_ARROW_DOWN`, `GTK_ARROW_LEFT`, and `GTK_ARROW_RIGHT`. You should set this property only when you create the widget.

3.8 Tooltips and Keyboard Control

This section covers tooltips and keyboard operation, two GTK+ features that can make your application more appealing to novices and experts. Although they are not necessary, they can have a subtle effect on your users (just don't expect the users to acknowledge it).

3.8.1 Tooltips

A *tooltip* is a short description of a widget's purpose that appears when the mouse pointer lingers over the widget for a short period of time. If used properly, tooltips can significantly reduce the amount of time that the user needs to become familiar with an application. A tooltip's exact appearance depends on the current GTK+ theme, but it is normally a small, borderless window with text on a light yellow background.

To outfit a group of widgets with tooltips, create one **GtkTooltips** (`GTK_TYPE_TOOLTIPS`) object for the group and call this for each widget in the group:

```
gtk_tooltips_set_tip(tip, widget, text, ext)
```

The arguments are:

- *tip* (GtkToolTips *): The tooltip object for the group.
- *widget* (GtkWidget *): The widget that text (next) describes.
- *text* (const gchar *): A string containing the tooltip text.
- *ext* (const gchar *): A more extensive description, meant for older help systems. Use an empty string here.

You should create *one* tooltip object for each group of widgets because of the way tooltips behave; the user must initially wait for a certain amount of time for the first tooltip to appear, but when the user drags the pointer over to some other widgets in the group afterward, the tooltips for those widgets immediately appear. After the user moves the mouse away from the widget group for a certain amount of time, the tooltips reset to their original delay times.

NOTE *You can attach a tooltip only to a widget that receives events. Therefore, you can't put a tooltip on something like a label, but that wouldn't make much sense anyhow.*

Here are the declarations and startup for a tooltip demonstration program:

```
/* -*-coding: utf-8;-*- */
/* tooltips.c -- demonstrate tooltips */

#include <gtk/gtk.h>

  << standard event handlers >>

int main(int argc, char **argv)
{
  GtkWindow *window;
  GtkButton *cut, *copy, *paste, *other_button;
  GtkVButtonBox *box;
  GtkTooltips *tips, *other_tips;

  /* start GTK+, create window, bind signal handlers */
  gtk_init(&argc, &argv);

  window = g_object_new(GTK_TYPE_WINDOW,
                        "title", "Tooltips Demonstration",
                        "default-width", 300,
                        "default-height", 100,
                        "border-width", 12,
                         NULL);

  << attach standard signal handlers to window >>
```

You need some widgets for tooltips, so here are three buttons with stock labels:

```
/* create three buttons using stock labels and images */
cut = g_object_new(GTK_TYPE_BUTTON,
                   "use-stock", TRUE,
```

```
                        "label", GTK_STOCK_CUT,
                        NULL);
    copy = g_object_new(GTK_TYPE_BUTTON,
                        "use-stock", TRUE,
                        "label", GTK_STOCK_COPY,
                        NULL);
    paste = g_object_new(GTK_TYPE_BUTTON,
                        "use-stock", TRUE,
                        "label", GTK_STOCK_PASTE,
                        NULL);

    /* pack buttons into VButtonBox */
    box = g_object_new(GTK_TYPE_VBUTTON_BOX, NULL);

    gtk_box_pack_end_defaults(GTK_BOX(box), GTK_WIDGET(cut));
    gtk_box_pack_end_defaults(GTK_BOX(box), GTK_WIDGET(copy));
    gtk_box_pack_end_defaults(GTK_BOX(box), GTK_WIDGET(paste));
```

Now you're ready to attach the tooltips to the buttons. Notice that there is only one **GtkTooltips** object for all three buttons.

```
    /* create tooltips object, assign to the buttons above */
    tips = g_object_new(GTK_TYPE_TOOLTIPS, NULL);

    gtk_tooltips_set_tip(tips, GTK_WIDGET(cut),
        "Cut selection and place it in clipboard", "");

    gtk_tooltips_set_tip(tips, GTK_WIDGET(copy),
        "Copy selection to the clipboard", "");

    gtk_tooltips_set_tip(tips, GTK_WIDGET(paste),
        "Paste clipboard into current location", "");
```

This program also creates a fourth button with its own tooltip object:

```
    /* create another button */
    other_button = g_object_new(GTK_TYPE_BUTTON,
                                "label", "_Other group",
                                "use-underline", TRUE,
                                NULL);

    gtk_box_pack_end_defaults(GTK_BOX(box), GTK_WIDGET(other_button));

    /* use a different tooltips object for this button */
    other_tips = g_object_new(GTK_TYPE_TOOLTIPS, NULL);

    gtk_tooltips_set_tip(other_tips, GTK_WIDGET(other_button),
        "This button uses a different Tooltips object", "");

    /* pack all boxes, show everything, start GTK+ loop */
```

```
gtk_container_add(GTK_CONTAINER(window), GTK_WIDGET(box));
gtk_widget_show_all(GTK_WIDGET(window));
gtk_main();

return 0;
}
```

Figure 3.14 shows a tooltip. When you run this program, see if you can tell the difference between the two tooltip objects. Hover over the Cut button until its tooltip appears; then move the mouse down across the other buttons. Tooltips will immediately pop up when the pointer reaches the Copy and Paste buttons. However, the last button has its own tooltip object and shows nothing until you wait for a while.

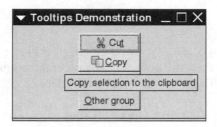

Figure 3.14: Tooltips.

There are functions for disabling and reenabling a **GtkTooltips** object:

```
gtk_tooltips_disable(tooltips_object)
gtk_tooltips_enable(tooltips_object)
```

You can use this in conjunction with a control panel check button so that the user can disable tooltips.

3.8.2 Keyboard Operation

Functional keyboard operation is important for a comfortable interface — not just for accessibility, but also for users who prefer keyboard operations for speed. GTK+ has two keyboard operation facilities:

- **Mnemonics** operate dialog boxes and menu items. You can discern them with an underlined character in a widget; when you press the character (possibly in conjunction with the ALT key), GTK+ activates the widget (in the case of buttons or menu items) or focuses on the widget (for anything else). The characters need only to be unique within the dialog or menu.

- **Accelerators** attach arbitrary actions to keystrokes. They are usually valid for the entire application and consist of a regular key and a modifier such as CONTROL, SHIFT, or ALT. Typical accelerators call menus, bring up dialogs, or have some other direct effect.

Mnemonics

You should bind a keystroke to every data entry widget in a window. If the widget has its own label (such as a button), do the following to bind the keystroke:

1. Place an underscore in front of the mnemonic character in the widget's `label` property.

2. Set the widget's `use-underline` property to `TRUE`.

However, if the widget requires its own **GtkLabel** object, perform these steps for that label object and, in addition, set the label's `mnemonic-widget` property to the target widget.

There are examples throughout this book; Section 3.6 includes a program with several mnemonic labels.

Accelerators

GtkAccelGroup (`GTK_TYPE_ACCEL_GROUP`) objects define global key combinations. This method uses signals; when you press a valid key combination, GTK+ emits a signal with a given object. Therefore, to install an accelerator, you must have an object and handler for the signal.

You really need to know only that **GtkAccelGroup** objects often represent menu items; as you will see in Section 4.3.1, the system typically makes the key binding for you. However, the following functions are at your disposal if you need to do the work by hand:

* `void gtk_window_add_accel_group(window, group)`
  Adds a **GtkAccelGroup** object *group* to the `GtkWindow` *window*, making the key combinations in the group valid for the window.

* `void gtk_window_remove_accel_group(window, group)`
  Removes the binding *group* from **window**.

* `GSList *gtk_accel_groups_from_object(object)`
  Returns a list containing all accelerator groups in *object* (this object is normally a window).

* `void *gtk_widget_add_accelerator(widget, signal, group, key, modifiers, options)`
  Adds a new key binding along with a signal to *group*. When you press the key combination defined by *key* and *modifiers*, GTK+ emits *signal* with *widget* (*signal* is the signal's string identifier). You may use an ASCII character such as *a* for *key* as well as one of the special keys listed at the end of this section.

    modifier is a bitwise OR of `GDK_SHIFT_MASK`, `GDK_CONTROL_MASK`, and/or `GDK_MOD1_MASK` (this last one is for the ALT key).

    options is a bitwise OR of `GTK_ACCEL_VISIBLE` (show it in the accelerator label) and `GTK_ACCEL_LOCKED` (if you don't want to be able to remove the binding from the group later).

* `gboolean gtk_accelerator_valid(key, modifiers)`
  Returns `TRUE` if *key* and *modifiers* form a valid key combination.

Some of the many special non-ASCII keys are listed in the following table (look in *gdk/gdkkeysyms.h* for a full-blown list). KP indicates the numeric keypad.

GDK_BackSpace	GDK_End	GDK_KP_Delete	GDK_KP_8
GDK_Tab	GDK_Print	GDK_KP_Equal	GDK_KP_9
GDK_Return	GDK_Insert	GDK_KP_Multiply	GDK_F1
GDK_Pause	GDK_Break	GDK_KP_Add	GDK_F2
GDK_Scroll_Lock	GDK_Num_Lock	GDK_KP_Subtract	GDK_F3
GDK_Sys_Req	GDK_KP_Enter	GDK_KP_Decimal	GDK_F4
GDK_Escape	GDK_KP_Home	GDK_KP_Divide	GDK_F5
GDK_Delete	GDK_KP_Left	GDK_KP_0	GDK_F6
GDK_Home	GDK_KP_Up	GDK_KP_1	GDK_F7
GDK_Left	GDK_KP_Right	GDK_KP_2	GDK_F8
GDK_Up	GDK_KP_Down	GDK_KP_3	GDK_F9
GDK_Right	GDK_KP_Page_Up	GDK_KP_4	GDK_F10
GDK_Down	GDK_KP_Page_Down	GDK_KP_5	GDK_F11
GDK_Page_Up	GDK_KP_End	GDK_KP_6	GDK_F12
GDK_Page_Down	GDK_KP_Insert	GDK_KP_7	

3.9 Scrolling

If you have a widget or collection of widgets that is too large to fit in a window, you can create a smaller viewport and navigate the large item by *scrolling*. A **GtkAdjustment** object (see Section 3.6.4) serves as the link between a scrollbar and the widget that you want to view. In MVC terminology, the adjustment object is the model, the viewable area is the view, and the scrollbar is the controller (see Section 3.11).

Horizontal scrollbars in GTK+ are **GtkHScrollbar** (GTK_TYPE_HSCROLLBAR) objects; their vertical counterparts use the class **GtkVScrollbar** (GTK_TYPE_VSCROLLBAR). Both are subclasses of **GtkScrollBar**.

These classes do not have any significant properties and methods, and furthermore, you should create objects with the generator function gtk_scrollbar_new(*adj*), where *adj* is an adjustment object (or NULL if you want the generator to create one for you).

Scrollbars are derived from the **GtkRange** class, so in principle, they can perform operations similar to those of a slider. However, scrollbars also have step increment buttons, and the slider bar itself is proportional to the widget that you're looking at through the viewport. (And, of course, users normally expect that a scrollbar scrolls something. If your users want a slider with a step increment feature, don't use a scrollbar; use a slider with a spin button.)

You normally won't have to deal with individual scrollbars. A special container widget called **GtkScrolledWindow** (GTK_TYPE_SCROLLED_WINDOW) holds exactly one widget. Furthermore, there are special scrolled widgets like **GtkTextView** (see Section 3.11) that you can pack into a scrolled window that automatically take on the required properties. Section 3.11.4 contains an example for **GtkTreeView**.

If you want to build an arbitrary scrolled window, you need to build up the content inside a **GtkViewport** (GTK_TYPE_VIEWPORT) object and then pack the viewport into a **GtkScrolledWindow** object. To do all of this in one step, call

```
gtk_scrolled_window_add_with_viewport(scrolled, widget)
```

The example you're about to see creates a large table of buttons and places it in a scrolled window. The declarations are as follows:

```
/* -*-coding: utf-8;-*- */
/* scroll.c -- demonstrate scrolled window */

#include <gtk/gtk.h>

  << standard window handlers >>

/* number of buttons to a side */
#define TABLE_SIZE 30

int main(int argc, char **argv)
{
  GtkWindow *window;
  GtkTable *table;
  GtkButton *button[TABLE_SIZE][TABLE_SIZE];
  GtkScrolledWindow *scr_window;
  gint i, j;
  gchar *string;

  /* initialize GTK+, create window */
  gtk_init(&argc, &argv);
  window = g_object_new(GTK_TYPE_WINDOW,
                        "title", "Scrolled Window",
                        "default-width", 600,
                        "default-height", 400,
                        NULL);

  << attach standard handlers to window >>
```

If you want to see how well your machine handles GTK+'s memory allocation for a *lot* of buttons, increase TABLE_SIZE.

Allocating and packing 900 buttons is a boring task suitable for a loop:

```
  /* create TABLE_SIZE**2 buttons inside the table */
  table = g_object_new(GTK_TYPE_TABLE,
                       "n-rows", TABLE_SIZE,
                       "n-columns", TABLE_SIZE,
                       "homogeneous", TRUE,
                       NULL);

  for (i=0; i < TABLE_SIZE; i++)
```

```
{
  for (j=0; j < TABLE_SIZE; j++)
  {
    string = g_strdup_printf("Button (%d, %d)", i, j);
    button[i][j] = g_object_new(GTK_TYPE_BUTTON, "label", string, NULL);
    g_free(string);
    gtk_table_attach_defaults(table, GTK_WIDGET(button[i][j]),
                              i, i+1, j, j+1);
  }
}
```

Finally, after all of the real work is out of the way, all you need to do is to put this big table into a scrolled window with the help of a viewport. Figure 3.15 shows the final application.

```
/* create scrolled window */
scr_window = g_object_new(GTK_TYPE_SCROLLED_WINDOW, NULL);

/* pack the table into the window with a viewport between */
gtk_scrolled_window_add_with_viewport(scr_window, GTK_WIDGET(table));

/* pack scrolled window and show everything */
gtk_container_add(GTK_CONTAINER(window), GTK_WIDGET(scr_window));

gtk_widget_show_all(GTK_WIDGET(window));
gtk_main();
return 0;
}
```

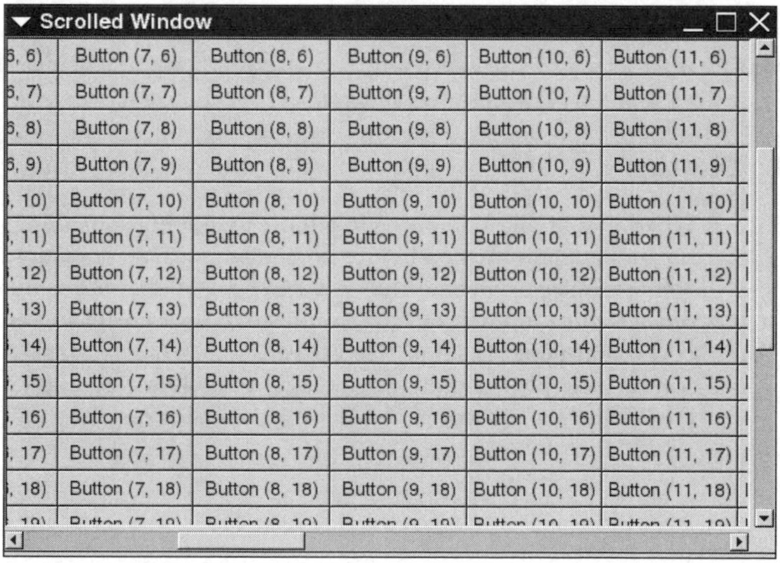

Figure 3.15: Scrolled window.

3.9.1 Scrolled Window Properties

The **GtkScrolledWindow** class has these properties:

- **hadjustment** (GtkAdjustment *): The **GtkAdjustment** object for the horizontal position of the child widget.

- **vadjustment** (GtkAdjustment *): The **GtkAdjustment** object for the vertical position of the child widget.

- **hscrollbar-policy** (GtkPolicyType): The policy for showing the horizontal scrollbar. Possible values are

    GTK_POLICY_ALWAYS: The scrollbar is always visible.

    GTK_POLICY_AUTOMATIC: The scrollbar is visible only when the viewable area of the child is larger than the viewport.

    GTK_POLICY_NEVER: The scrollbar is never visible. This is usually not a terribly good idea.

- **vscrollbar-policy** (GtkPolicyType): Like the preceding, but for vertical scrollbars.

- **window-placement** (GtkCornerType): Where the child widget goes relative to the scrollbars. Possible values are

    GTK_CORNER_TOP_LEFT: Scrollbars at the right and bottom. This is the default.

    GTK_CORNER_BOTTOM_LEFT: Scrollbars at the right and top.

    GTK_CORNER_TOP_RIGHT: Scrollbars at the left and bottom.

    GTK_CORNER_BOTTOM_RIGHT: Scrollbars at the left and top.

- **shadow-type** (enumeration): The shadow style of the child widget; values are the same as for **GtkFrame** (see Section 3.7.1).

NOTE   *If you have a window with a large quantity of vertically scrolled content (such as a text editor or terminal), put the scrollbar at the left, not the right.*

3.10 Dialogs

When your application needs to tell the user about something important or obtain some information before proceeding with an operation, you should create a *dialog* (sometimes called a *dialog box*). GTK+ has standard prepackaged dialogs with a uniform look; all you need to do is create and manipulate objects of the **GtkDialog** class (GTK_TYPE_DIALOG).

An example program with a dialog box follows, starting with the standard event handlers and then a handler for the dialog box:

```
/* -*-coding: utf-8;-*- */
/* dialog.c -- demonstrate a dialog box */

#include <gtk/gtk.h>

  << standard window handlers >>

/* handler for "response" signal from dialog */
```

```
void dialog_action(GtkDialog *dialog, gint response, gpointer data)
{
   g_assert(response == GTK_RESPONSE_ACCEPT || response == GTK_RESPONSE_REJECT);

   switch (response)
   {
      case GTK_RESPONSE_ACCEPT:
         g_print("Planet destroyed.\n");
         break;
      case GTK_RESPONSE_REJECT:
         g_print("Planet destruction aborted.\n");
         break;
      default:
         /* do nothing */
         break;
   }
}
```

As you might suspect from the comment earlier, GTK+ emits a **response** signal when the user does something with the dialog box. The handler's response parameter contains the details (you'll find more information later in this section).

There is nothing unusual about the start of the main program:

```
int main(int argc, char **argv)
{
   GtkWindow *window;
   GtkButton *button;
   GtkDialog *dialog;
   GtkHBox *dialog_hbox;
   GtkImage *dialog_icon;
   GtkLabel *dialog_text;

   /* initialize GTK, create window */
   gtk_init(&argc, &argv);

   window = g_object_new(GTK_TYPE_WINDOW,
                         "default_height", 200,
                         "default_width", 200,
                         "border-width", 12,
                         "title", "Dialog Demo",
                         NULL);

<< attach standard window handlers >>
```

The following code creates a standard dialog box with two buttons. Each button gets a label and a response code (this should be one of the standard responses listed on page 190). You can set a default response.

```
   /* create dialog box */
   dialog = GTK_DIALOG(gtk_dialog_new_with_buttons(
```

```
                "Destroy Planet?",              /* title */
                window,                         /* parent */
                GTK_DIALOG_DESTROY_WITH_PARENT, /* options */
                /* list of button labels and responses */
                "_Destroy",            GTK_RESPONSE_ACCEPT,
                "_Abort Destruction",  GTK_RESPONSE_REJECT,
                NULL));

    gtk_dialog_set_default_response(dialog, GTK_RESPONSE_REJECT);
```

The following handler attachment connects all of the buttons and responses in the preceding code to the signal handler defined earlier. You have probably noticed by now that creating the dialog boxes in this manner involves significantly less work (for starters, you do not have to create any individual button widgets or worry about their handlers).

```
    /* attach handler for dialog response */
    g_signal_connect(dialog, "response", G_CALLBACK(dialog_action), NULL);
```

Getting rid of the dialog box when the user clicks one of its buttons is just a matter of attaching a GTK+ widget destroy function to the **response** handler sequence:

```
    /* remove dialog box when it returns a response */
    g_signal_connect_swapped(dialog,
                        "response", G_CALLBACK(gtk_widget_destroy), window);
```

The only real work left to do is to create the dialog's actual contents (other than the buttons). The following creates an HBox with a custom message along with a stock image:

```
    /* fill dialog window: create HBox packed with icon and Text */
    dialog_hbox = g_object_new(GTK_TYPE_HBOX, "border-width", 8, NULL);

    dialog_icon = g_object_new(GTK_TYPE_IMAGE,
                        "stock", GTK_STOCK_DIALOG_WARNING,
                        "icon-size", GTK_ICON_SIZE_DIALOG,
                        "xalign", 0.5,
                        "yalign", 1.0,
                        NULL);

    gtk_box_pack_start(GTK_BOX(dialog_hbox), GTK_WIDGET(dialog_icon),
                    FALSE, FALSE, 0);

    dialog_text = g_object_new(GTK_TYPE_LABEL,
                        "wrap", TRUE,
                        "use-markup", TRUE,
                        "label", "\
<big><b>Do you really want to destroy the planet?</b></big>\
\n\
Please note that the annihilation of a planet is rarely \
```

```
regarded as a successful show of environmentally \
friendly behavior.");

gtk_box_pack_start(GTK_BOX(dialog_hbox), GTK_WIDGET(dialog_text),
                   TRUE, TRUE, 0);
```

You want to be able to put your new message in the dialog. Do this by packing it into the dialog's vbox field. This function call packs the message directly above the buttons:

```
/* pack HBox into dialog */
gtk_box_pack_start(GTK_BOX(dialog->vbox), GTK_WIDGET(dialog_hbox),
                   FALSE, FALSE, 0);
```

Normally, you don't bring up a dialog box as the main window. Therefore, the following creates a button for the main window. When you click the button, the dialog appears.

```
/* create button for main window */
button = g_object_new(GTK_TYPE_BUTTON,
                      "label", "_Show dialog",
                      "use-underline", TRUE,
                      NULL);

/* show the dialog when user clicks button */
g_signal_connect_swapped(button,
                         "clicked", G_CALLBACK(gtk_widget_show_all), dialog);

/* pack button, show everything, start main loop */
gtk_container_add(GTK_CONTAINER(window), GTK_WIDGET(button));
gtk_widget_show_all(GTK_WIDGET(window));
gtk_main();

return 0;
}
```

Figure 3.16 shows the dialog part of the application.

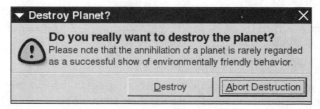

Figure 3.16: Dialog.

As you saw from this example, the generator function

```
gtk_dialog_new_with_buttons(title, parent, options, ...)
```

offers a good way to create a dialog box with buttons (there are more awkward ways, trust me). The *options* value is a bitwise OR of these constants:

- GTK_DIALOG_MODAL: For modal dialogs (these lock the input focus). Section 3.2 describes why you should be careful with these.

- GTK_DIALOG_DESTROY_WITH_PARENT: Removes the dialog window when the parent is destroyed.

WARNING *If you set this option, keep in mind that some outside action can remove the dialog. In any case, make sure that you write a clean* **destroy** *signal handler that adequately resolves the dialog's question.*

- GTK_DIALOG_NO_SEPARATOR: Don't place a horizontal separator between the dialog's lower buttons and the rest of the window.

The button list (. . . in the parameters) consists of label string/response code pairs. A NULL value terminates the list. You can use any positive integer for the response code, but you should always see whether one of the predefined GTK_RESPONSE_ codes (discussed in a moment) is appropriate first.

When the user clicks a button, GTK+ emits the **reponse** signal with the dialog box. The handler prototype should look like this:

---

void handler(GtkDialog *dialog*, gint *response*, gpointer *data*)

The *response* parameter is the response code from the button clicked. Here are some predefined codes:

- GTK_RESPONSE_NONE: The response when the application removes the dialog.
- GTK_RESPONSE_DELETE_EVENT: The user or window manager wants to delete the window.
- GTK_RESPONSE_ACCEPT
- GTK_RESPONSE_REJECT
- GTK_RESPONSE_OK
- GTK_RESPONSE_CANCEL
- GTK_RESPONSE_CLOSE
- GTK_RESPONSE_YES
- GTK_RESPONSE_NO
- GTK_RESPONSE_APPLY
- GTK_RESPONSE_HELP

As you can see from the example, creating dialogs in this manner is relatively easy because you need only create one handler. In that handler, you can use a switch statement to decipher the response code and carry out the appropriate action. You also saw that you can use the following

---

gtk_dialog_set_default_response(*dialog*, *code*)

---

to set a default button in the dialog (the one that gets the input focus).

To make your dialogs as consistent and clear as possible, follow these guidelines:

- *Use a short window title, not identical to the content title.*
- *Use a stock icon if possible, with the* GTK_ICON_SIZE_DIALOG *size.*
- *Use a short headline formatted with* <big><b> ... </b></big>.
- *Don't make the title too wordy.*
- *Avoid potentially ambiguous button labels such as Yes and No. Use verb phrases (see the example).*
- *When you set a default button (that is, you suggest to the user that this button is probably the correct thing to click), put that button at the lower right of the dialog.*

Finally, you should remember that you can pack any widgets into the vbox of a dialog box. Therefore, you can ask for some additional data in a dialog. This is usually preferable to doing everything by hand, because **GtkDialog** does a lot of behind-the-scenes work with the window manager and other pieces of the system to make dialogs *behave* like dialogs. Otherwise, you would need to do this by hand — an almost certain waste of time and energy.

3.11 Tree and List Widgets

GTK+ uses the notion of MVC for its largest and most powerful widgets. MVC stands for model, view, and controller; it means that the internal representation of the data (the model), the way the application shows the data (the view), and the means of manipulating the view and model (the controller) are separate objects that communicate with each other.

GTK+ does not strictly enforce these divisions. The model and view are certainly separate, but there aren't any special controller classes. You could rightly call the system for tree and list views a Swiss Army widget — it can display anything from a single-column list to a table in a complete tree structure. The only real disadvantage is that you have to disavow a few MVC purist ideals.

You have probably already seen lists and trees in user interfaces that represent hierarchies of items. Have a look at at Figure 3.18 on page 217 to see if it looks familiar. This book uses the following terminology:

- A *node* is a line in the display. Each node has a value.
- A *list* is a collection of a node's children.
- A *tree* is a list with each child's own children taken into account.
- A *drop arrow* expands (shows) and collapses a node's children in the display.

A tree can have several columns; each column corresponds to a value in a node. All values in a column are of the same type, and each node contains as many values as there are columns.

To use trees and lists in a program, you must start with a model that reflects this structure. Any class works, as long as it implements the **GtkTreeModel** (GTK_TYPE_TREE_MODEL) interface. You probably do not want to go so far as to come up with your own model and interface. For the most part, you should find one of

GTK+'s built-in model implementations more than adequate. These are
GtkListStore (`GTK_TYPE_LIST_STORE`) for lists and **GtkTreeStore**
(`GTK_TYPE_TREE_STORE`) for the fully blown trees.

You can process lists and trees with iterators of type `GtkTreeIter`. An iterator is
essentially a reference to one node in a tree. You manipulate iterators with utility
functions.

GtkTreeView (`GTK_TYPE_TREE_VIEW`) sits at the top level of the view component.
Every column requires its own **GtkTreeViewColumn** view object, and to draw
each value in the model, you need a *renderer* of the **GtkCellRenderer**
(`GTK_TYPE_CELL_RENDERER`).

To illustrate how these components fit together, here is an example that
creates a two-column list widget. The first column contains numerals, and the
second contains the spelled-out word corresponding to those numerals.

The initial declarations set the numeral spellings in an array and define
constant identifiers for the columns:

```
/* -*-coding: utf-8;-*- */
/* list.c -- demonstrate GtkTreeView */

#include <gtk/gtk.h>

const char *numbers[] = { "Zero", "One", "Two", "Three", "Four", "Five" };

enum {
   INT_COLUMN,
   STRING_COLUMN,
   N_COLUMNS
};

   << standard event handlers >>
```

You can see the declarations for the list, view, view columns, and cell renderer in
the following code:

```
int main(int argc, char **argv)
{
  GtkWindow *window;
  GtkListStore *list;
  GtkTreeIter iter;
  GtkTreeView *view;
  GtkTreeViewColumn *num_column, *word_column;
  GtkCellRenderer *text_renderer;
  gint i;

  /* initialize GTK+, create main window */
  gtk_init(&argc, &argv);
  window = g_object_new(GTK_TYPE_WINDOW,
                        "title", "Two Column List",
```

```
                    "default-width", 300,
                    NULL);
```

<< connect standard handlers to main window >>

The following code creates the list (model) structure; this is where you specify the number of columns and the type in each column.

```
/* create a two-column list */
list = gtk_list_store_new(N_COLUMNS, G_TYPE_INT, G_TYPE_STRING);
```

Loading data into the list is relatively easy. You can see the column identifiers from the beginning of the program here. Notice the iterator in the functions; use it first to get a handle to a new node in the list and then to set the values of the node.

```
/* put some data into the list */
for (i = 0; i < 5; i++)
{
    gtk_list_store_append(list, &iter);
    gtk_list_store_set(list, &iter,
                    INT_COLUMN, i,
                    STRING_COLUMN, numbers[i],
                    -1);
}
```

Now you're ready to create the overall view for the overall node display. The `model` property binds the preceding model into the view. There are several other properties; for example, `reorderable` allows the user to drag a node up and down in the list and drop it at a different location (try it yourself). A full list of properties and their descriptions is in Section 3.11.2.

```
/* create tree view for the list */
view = g_object_new(GTK_TYPE_TREE_VIEW,
                    "model", list,
                    "rules-hint", TRUE,
                    "headers-clickable", TRUE,
                    "reorderable", TRUE,
                    "enable-search", TRUE,
                    "search-column", STRING_COLUMN,
                    NULL);
```

This program's cell renderer doesn't have to be anything fancy. GTK+ comes with a few renderers; the text renderer here knows how to deal with numbers and strings.

```
/* create and initialize text renderer for cells */
text_renderer = gtk_cell_renderer_text_new();
```

Now you need to attend to the views for each column. The parameters for the column view generator include the title of the column and the renderer. In addition, you must tell the column what part of a node it should display. This program sets the column view's **text** property to the appropriate column identifier.

```
/* create column views */
num_column = gtk_tree_view_column_new_with_attributes("Numeral",
                                    text_renderer,
                                    "text", INT_COLUMN,
                                    NULL);
```

These column view properties are similar to those of the overall view. Setting the **reorderable** property, in particular, means that you can move an entire column around by dragging the title.

```
g_object_set(num_column,
             "resizable", TRUE,
             "clickable", TRUE,
             "reorderable", TRUE,
             NULL);
```

The column view for words is nearly the same as the preceding:

```
word_column = gtk_tree_view_column_new_with_attributes("Word",
                                    text_renderer,
                                    "text", STRING_COLUMN,
                                    NULL);

g_object_set(word_column,
             "resizable", TRUE,
             "clickable", TRUE,
             "reorderable", TRUE,
             NULL);
```

Finally, there's nothing left to do but place the column views into the overall views, pack all the widgets, and show the window.

```
/* insert columns into the view */
gtk_tree_view_append_column(view, num_column);
gtk_tree_view_append_column(view, word_column);

/* pack/show everything; start GTK+ main event loop */
gtk_container_add(GTK_CONTAINER(window), GTK_WIDGET(view));
gtk_widget_show_all(GTK_WIDGET(window));
gtk_main();

return 0;
}
```

Figure 3.17 shows the final application. You should definitely try this example to get a feel for how you can move nodes and columns around.

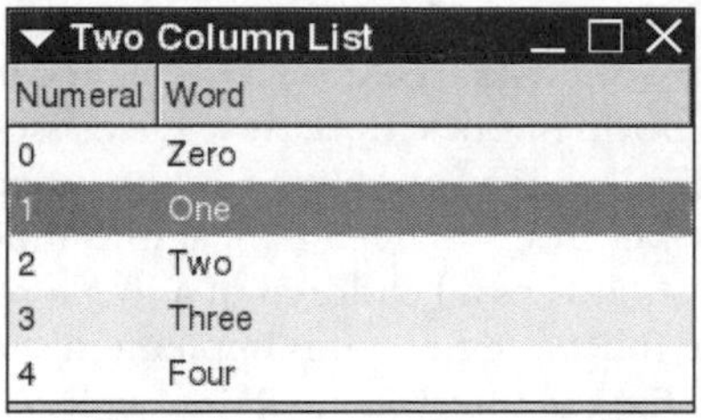

Figure 3.17: Two-column list.

For the specific arguments for the functions in this example, see Sections 3.11.1 and 3.11.2.

In general, if you want to create a list or tree widget, you should follow these steps.

1. Create a model object of the **GtkListStore** or **GtkTreeStore** class with gtk_list_store_new() or gtk_tree_store_new() as a generator function. The generator needs to know the number of columns and the type of each column.

2. Create a node in the list with gtk_list_store_append() (or any other appropriate function from Section 3.11.1). The second argument is a pointer to a GtkTreeIter structure. This function points the iterator at the new node as a side effect.

WARNING   *Iterators aren't objects; they're C structures. Most of the functions that take iterators as arguments have the ability to change the iterator. Therefore, if you want to use an iterator, declare one as a fully allocated structure like this:*

GtkTreeIter iterator;

Do not create a pointer by adding a *; use &iterator *to pass the iterator to functions.*

3. Set the contents of the new node with gtk_list_store_set() (or another function). Notice from the example that the contents are paired with their column identifiers, terminated by –1 (not NULL; this would evaluate to a column identifier).

4. Create the overall view, an object of the **GtkTreeView** class.

5. Create your cell rendering object(s). If you're just drawing text, gtk_cell_renderer_text_new() works fine.

6. Create a column view object for each column. Make sure that you include the appropriate cell renderer object and the column identifier. You normally create column views with gtk_tree_view_column_new_with_attributes().

7. Add the column views to the overall view with gtk_tree_view_append_column().

3.11.1   List and Tree API Reference

The **GtkTreeModel** interface defines a number of methods that work on any model that implements the interface — they're mostly for reading data from the model. However, **GtkListStore** and **GtkTreeStore** have many more functions of their own for writing and removing nodes. Because these classes are very similar, each function in one class usually has a counterpart in the other. The arguments are a little different, though, because you need to deal with the relationship between nodes; in a list, the nodes are all children of a single root.

You can tell whether the following functions implement the **GtkTreeModel** interface by looking at its prefix; the interface methods begin with gtk_tree_model, and the regular class methods start with gtk_tree_store and gtk_list_store.

- GtkTreeStore *gtk_tree_store_new(gint *num_columns*, ...)
  Creates a new **GtkTreeStore** object with *num_columns* columns. The remaining arguments are GValue type identifiers (see Section 2.4.2).

- GtkListStore *gtk_list_store_new(gint *num_columns*, ...)
  Like the preceding function, but creates a **GtkListStore** object.

- void gtk_tree_store_set_value(GtkTreeStore *tree*, GtkTreeIter *iterator*, gint *column*, GValue *value*)
  Stores a GValue *value* in *tree* at the node specified by *iterator*. The *column* value is an integral column identifier.

- void gtk_list_store_set_value(GtkListStore *list*, GtkTreeIter *iterator*, gint *column*, GValue *value*)
  Like the preceding function, but for lists.

- void gtk_tree_model_get_value(GtkTreeModel *model*, GtkTreeIter *iterator*, gint *column*, GValue *value*)
  Retrieves the value at node *iter* in *model* (column *column*), putting the result in the GValue pointed to by *value*. After you finish with *value*, free it with g_value_unset().

- void gtk_tree_model_get(GtkTreeModel *model*, GtkTreeIter *iterator*, ...)
  Like the preceding function, but retrieves all values from the current node. After *iterator*, place a list of GValue pointers; terminate the list with –1.

- void gtk_tree_store_set(GtkTreeStore *tree*, GtkTreeIter *iterator*, ...)
  Like the preceding function, but sets values in the current node instead of reading them. Note that the arguments are *not* GValues; they are pairs of column identifiers and data.

- void gtk_list_store_set(GtkListStore *list*, GtkTreeIter *iterator*, ...)
  Like the preceding function, but for lists.

- void gtk_tree_store_insert(GtkTreeStore *tree*, GtkTreeIter *iterator*, GtkTreeIter *parent*, gint *index*)
  Inserts a new node into *tree* with the index *index*. If *parent* is not NULL, the new node becomes a child of that node. This function points *iterator* to the new node.

- void gtk_list_store_insert(GtkListStore *list, GtkTreeIter *iterator,
  gint index)
  Like the preceding function, but for lists.

- void gtk_tree_store_insert_before(GtkTreeStore *tree, GtkTreeIter *iterator,
  GtkTreeIter *parent, GtkTreeIter *sibling)
  Inserts a new node into the tree as a child of parent in front of sibling (parent
  may be NULL). If sibling is NULL, the new node goes after the children of parent.
  If parent and sibling are NULL, the node goes into the top-level children. After
  invocation, iterator points to the new node.

- void gtk_list_store_insert_before(GtkListStore *list, GtkTreeIter *iterator,
  GtkTreeIter *sibling)
  Like the preceding function, but for lists.

- void gtk_tree_store_insert_after(GtkTreeStore *tree, GtkTreeIter *iterator,
  GtkTreeIter *parent, GtkTreeIter *sibling)
  Similar to gtk_tree_store_insert_before(), but inserts after sibling (or before all
  children if sibling is NULL).

- void gtk_list_store_insert_after(GtkListStore *list, GtkTreeIter *iterator,
  GtkTreeIter *sibling)
  Like the preceding function, but for lists.

- void gtk_tree_store_prepend(GtkTreeStore *tree, GtkTreeIter *iterator,
  GtkTreeIter *parent)
  Inserts a node into a tree as the first child of parent. This function works like
  gtk_tree_store_insert_before(), but without the sibling argument.

- void gtk_list_store_prepend(GtkListStore *list, GtkTreeIter *iterator,
  GtkTreeIter *parent)
  Like the preceding function, but for lists.

- void gtk_tree_store_append(GtkTreeStore *tree, GtkTreeIter *iterator,
  GtkTreeIter *parent)
  Like gtk_tree_store_prepend(), but the new node becomes the last child of
  parent instead of the first.

- void gtk_list_store_append(GtkListStore *list, GtkTreeIter *iterator)
  Like the preceding function, but for lists.

- void gtk_tree_store_remove(GtkTreeStore *tree, GtkTreeIter *iterator)
  Removes the tree node at iterator.

- void gtk_list_store_remove(GtkListStore *list, GtkTreeIter *iterator)
  Removes the list node at iterator.

- void gtk_tree_store_clear(GtkTreeStore *tree)
  Removes all nodes in tree.

- void gtk_list_store_clear(GtkListStore *list)
  Removes all nodes in list.

- gboolean gtk_tree_store_is_ancestor(GtkTreeStore *tree, GtkTreeIter *iterator,
  GtkTreeIter *child)
  Returns TRUE if child is in the tree rooted at iterator.

- gint gtk_tree_store_iter_depth(GtkTreeStore *tree, GtkTreeIter *iterator)
  Returns the depth of *iterator* in *tree* (0 is the top level, 1 is the next level, and so on).

- void gtk_tree_model_foreach(GtkTreeModel *model, GtkTreeModelForeachFunc *function, gpointer data)
  Runs *function* on all nodes of *tree*. See the following discussion.

This is the GtkTreeModelForeachFunc prototype:

```
typedef gboolean (*GtkTreeModelForeachFunc) (GtkTreeModel *model,
                                             GtkTreePath *path,
                                             GtkTreeIter *iter,
                                             gpointer data);
```

The model parameter here is the tree or list from the foreach function call, as is the data parameter. The current node is iter.

That leaves path to explain; it's the address of the node inside the tree. A path is essentially a list of numbers; if you follow the numbers in the list, you can reach a node from the parent. In a list, there is only one number in the path; 0 is the first element, and so 42 would represent the 43rd element in the list (remember that it eventually appears as a row in the view). For trees, you can string the numbers together with colons. 4:3 is the third child of the fourth node in the tree; another example is 0:6:2. Most tree paths begin with 0.

You could use a path to create a tree structure in a plain text file containing some data. When your program reads the file, it can read the tree structure directly and send it straight into a tree model object.

GtkTreePath is a data structure that you normally do not access directly. Use one of these access functions instead:

- GtkTreePath *gtk_tree_model_get_path(GtkTreeModel *model, GtkTreeIter *iter)
  Returns a newly allocated tree path containing *iter*'s path in *model*.

- GtkTreePath *gtk_tree_path_new(void)
  Returns a fresh, empty path.

- GtkTreePath *gtk_tree_path_new_first(void)
  Returns a new path containing the address 0.

- GtkTreePath *gtk_tree_path_new_from_string(const gchar *str)
  Converts the colon-delimited address in *str* to a new path.

- GtkTreePath *gtk_tree_path_copy(const GtkTreePath *path)
  Returns a new copy of *path*.

- void gtk_tree_path_free(GtkTreePath *path)
  Deallocates *path*'s memory.

- gchar *gtk_tree_path_to_string(GtkTreePath *path)
  Returns a colon-delimited string corresponding to *path*. You should deallocate this string with g_free() when you no longer need it.

- void gtk_tree_path_append_index(GtkTreePath *path, gint index)
  Appends *index* to the end of *path*.

- void gtk_tree_path_prepend_index(GtkTreePath *path, gint index)
  Inserts index at the beginning of path.

- gint gtk_tree_path_get_depth(GtkTreePath *path)
  Returns the depth of path.

- gint *gtk_tree_path_get_indices(GtkTreePath *path)
  Returns an array of gint. Each number corresponds to an index in path. This is a pointer to data inside path, so you should *not* free it when you are finished.

- gint gtk_tree_path_compare(const GtkTreePath *path1, const GtkTreePath *path2)
  Compares two GtkTreePath paths. If they are equal, this returns 0; if path1 is the lesser path, the result is –1; otherwise, the result is 1.

- void gtk_tree_path_next(GtkTreePath *path)
  Pushes path to the next node — that is, this function increments the last index by 1.

- gboolean gtk_tree_path_prev(GtkTreePath *path)
  Moves path to the previous node. In other words, this function decrements the last index by 1 and returns TRUE. If that isn't possible (that is, the last index is 0), this function returns FALSE and does not change path.

- gboolean gtk_tree_path_up(GtkTreePath *path)
  Changes path to its parent and returns TRUE. This is a matter of removing the last index in path; if there is only one index, this function returns FALSE.

- void gtk_tree_path_down(GtkTreePath *path)
  Adds a child to path by appending a 0 index to the end of path.

- gboolean gtk_tree_path_is_ancestor(GtkTreePath *parent, GtkTreePath *child)
  Returns TRUE if child is somewhere in the subtree of parent.

- gboolean gtk_tree_path_is_descendant(GtkTreePath *child, GtkTreePath *parent)
  Like the preceding function, but with the arguments reversed.

Keep in mind that a path is only an address; changing a path doesn't actually do anything to a tree. To modify trees, you need to use iterators (that you possibly obtained from a path). The most important iterator functions are

```
gtk_tree_model_get_iter(model, iter, path)
gtk_tree_model_get_iter_from_string(model, iter, path_string)
```

Both functions have gboolean return values, returning TRUE when they successfully point iter to the node in model corresponding to the path. The only difference is the path specification: path is a GtkTreePath structure, whereas path_string is a colon-delimited path string.

NOTE *Naturally, gtk_tree_model_get_iter_from_string() is a convenience function, but it can still save you three lines of code: a tree path structure declaration, its initialization, and its return to the free memory pool.*

Here are some more `GtkTreeIter` functions:

- `gboolean gtk_tree_model_get_iter_first(GtkTreeModel *model, GtkTreeIter *iter)`
  Sets iter to the first node in `model` (that would be the one with a path of 0). If the model is empty, this function returns `FALSE`.

- `gboolean gtk_tree_model_iter_next(GtkTreeModel *model, GtkTreeIter *iter)`
  Points `iter` to its next sibling in `model`. If this is the last sibling, this function returns `FALSE`.

- `gboolean gtk_tree_model_iter_children(GtkTreeModel *model, GtkTreeIter *iter, GtkTreeIter *parent)`
  Points `iter` to the first child of `parent`. If there are no children, this function returns `FALSE`.

- `gboolean gtk_tree_model_nth_child(GtkTreeModel *model, GtkTreeIter *iter, GtkTreeIter *parent, gint n)`
  Points `iter` to the `n`th child of `parent`. If `parent` is `NULL`, this function returns the `n`th child at the top level. If there are no children, this function returns `FALSE`.

- `gboolean gtk_tree_model_iter_has_child(GtkTreeModel *model, GtkTreeIter *iter)`
  Returns `TRUE` if the node at `iter` has children.

- `gint gtk_tree_model_iter_n_children(GtkTreeModel *model, GtkTreeIter *iter)`
  Returns the number of children of `iter`. If you specify `NULL` for the iterator, this function returns the number of nodes at the top level.

- `gboolean gtk_tree_model_iter_parent(GtkTreeModel *model, GtkTreeIter *iter)`
  Points `iter` to its parent. If this is impossible, this function returns `FALSE`.

Adding, removing, or otherwise modifying nodes in a model invalidates all of the model's iterators (for example, upon a signal emission). If you need a little more stability, there are pointer objects that use reference counts. Their class is **GtkTreeRowReference**, a type of weak reference that you can use regardless of signal emissions. One situation in which you might use these references is when you need to put marks on nodes that should be valid for as long as the nodes exist.

- `GtkTreeRowReference *gtk_tree_row_reference_new(GtkTreeModel *model, GtkTreePath *path)`
  Returns a new reference to the row (node) in `model` given by `path`. If there is no such node, this function returns `NULL`.

- `GtkTreePath *gtk_tree_row_reference_get_path(GtkTreeRowReference *ref)`
  Returns a new path corresponding to `ref`'s node in its tree, or `NULL` if the reference isn't valid.

- `gboolean gtk_tree_row_reference_valid(GtkTreeRowReference *ref)`
  Returns `TRUE` if `ref` is valid (that is, non-`NULL` and to an existing node).

- `void gtk_tree_row_reference_free(GtkTreeRowReference *ref)`
  Removes the row reference `ref`.

3.11.2 Tree Views

The **GtkTreeView** class implements the V part of MVC. You can have as many views for a single model as you like; an actual view display process is detached from the model and works by querying the model as a database.

The column and cell renderers do the actual work of querying and formatting the data. Therefore, the **GtkTreeView** functions and properties you're about to see pertain primarily to the view's outer appearance and user interface. (There are a few of exceptions, such as the **reorderable** property.)

- `void gtk_tree_view_scroll_to_cell(GtkTreeView *view, GtkTreePath *path, GtkTreeViewColumn *column, gboolean align, gfloat row_align, gfloat col_align)`
  Scroll to the cell in *view* given by *path* and/or *column*. One of these latter two parameters may be NULL if you need only horizontal or vertical scrolling. If you want finer control of where the cell appears in the view, set align to TRUE and *row_align* and *col_align* each to a number between 0.0 and 1.0 (as in the alignment settings for other widgets, 0.0 is the left or top, 0.5 is center, and 1.0 is right or bottom).

- `void gtk_tree_view_set_cursor(GtkTreeView *view, GtkTreePath *path, GtkTreeViewColumn *column, gboolean start_editing)`
  Moves the keyboard focus to the cell in *view* given by *path* (and *column* if non-NULL) and selects that cell or row. If you set *start_editing* to TRUE, GTK+ opens the cell for the user to modify.

- `void gtk_tree_view_get_cursor(GtkTreeView *view, GtkTreePath **path, GtkTreeViewColumn **column)`
  Retrieves the current *view* cursor position and sets the pointers behind the *path* and *column* addresses to the appropriate row and column. If there is no selected column, this function sets *column to NULL. If there is no current position, both pointers go to NULL.

- `void gtk_tree_view_row_activated(GtkTreeView *view, GtkTreePath *path, GtkTreeViewColumn *column)`
  Activates the row or cell in view specified by *path* and *column* (a double-click on a row or cell constitutes an activation, for example).

- `void gtk_tree_view_expand_all(GtkTreeView *view)`
  Completely expands *view*; in other words, this function opens all drop arrows in the display.

- `void gtk_tree_view_collapse_all(GtkTreeView *view)`
  Collapses all rows in *view* so that only the top level is visible.

- `gboolean gtk_tree_view_expand_row(GtkTreeView *view, GtkTreePath *path, gboolean recursive)`
  Expands the row in *view* corresponding to *path*. If recursive is TRUE, expand the entire subtree at *path*. This function returns TRUE if it successfully expands the row.

- `gboolean gtk_tree_view_collapse_row(GtkTreeView *view, GtkTreePath *path)`
  Collapses the row at *path* in *view* and returns TRUE if successful.

- `gboolean gtk_tree_view_row_expanded(GtkTreeView *view, GtkTreePath *path)`
  Returns TRUE if *path* in *view* is currently in an expanded state.

GtkTreeView has these properties:

- **model** (GtkTreeModel): The current model inside the view.
- **hadjustment** (GtkAdjustment): The adjustment object for the horizontal scroll direction (see Section 3.9).
- **vadjustment** (GtkAdjustment): The adjustment object for the vertical scroll direction.
- **headers-visible** (gboolean): If TRUE, column titles appear at the top of the columns.
- **headers-clickable** (gboolean): If TRUE, the user can click column titles (these events may reorder columns or change the sorting order).
- **expander-column** (GtkTreeViewColumn): The column where the drop arrow appears. The default is the first visible column.
- **reorderable** (gboolean): If TRUE, the user can reorder rows by dragging them to different places in the view.

NOTE *This works only with models that implement the **GtkDragSourceIface** and **GtkDragDestIface** interfaces, as **GtkListStore** and **GtkTreeStore** do. If you activate **reorderable**, you can arbitrarily manipulate rows. Otherwise, you will have to provide your own drag-and-drop mechanism (a relatively complicated task).*

- **rules-hint** (gboolean): If TRUE, the view takes on a table format and can benefit from predefined visual enhancements.

NOTE *This property doesn't directly influence the view's appearance; the current GTK+ theme decides what to do. Therefore, don't set this to TRUE if you desire a particular characteristic such as striped lists; the theme is not required to carry out any specific details.*

- **enable-search** (gboolean): If TRUE, the user can perform interactive searches (by pressing CONTROL-F) on one of the columns (see below).
- **search-column** (gint): The column on which the user can perform an interactive search.

GtkTreeView has an important signal, **row-activated**, that goes out when the user activates a cell with a double-click or keyboard action. It has this handler prototype, with path and column set to the corresponding row and cell:

```
void handler(GtkTreeView *view,
             GtkTreePath *path,
             GtkTreeViewColumn *column,
             gpointer *data);
```

Columns

GtkTreeViewColumn objects shuttle data between the model and cell renderer. You may have more than one renderer per column; for example, you can pack a person's name into a cell with a true/false check box next to the name indicating whether the person is left-handed.

You can create most view columns with

```
GtkTreeViewColumn *col;

col = gtk_tree_view_column_new_with_attributes(title, renderer, ...)
```

Here, *title* is a title string for the column header, and *renderer* draws the cells. A NULL-terminated list of cell renderer attributes follows (see the example in Section 3.11).

A cell renderer attribute usually consists of a rendering type as the key and a column identifier (or number) to render. The example in Section 3.11 maps the attribute "text" to one of the two column identifiers. Cell renderer attributes are not properties, so you can't set them with g_object_set(). Use these functions instead:

- void gtk_tree_view_column_set_attributes(GtkTreeViewColumn *column, GtkCellRenderer *renderer, ...)
  Completely replaces the attributes of *renderer* in *column* with a NULL-terminated list of attribute pairs.

- void gtk_tree_view_column_add_attribute(GtkTreeViewColumn *column, GtkCellRenderer *renderer, gchar *attribute, gint col_id)
  Adds a new attribute to *renderer* in *column*. The attribute string is the name of the attribute, and *col_id* is the column identifier for the attribute.

- void gtk_tree_view_column_clear_attributes(GtkTreeViewColumn *column, GtkCellRenderer *renderer)
  Removes all attributes for *renderer* in *column*.

- void gtk_tree_view_column_clear(GtkTreeViewColumn *column)
  Removes all attributes for all renderers in *column*.

If you want to put additional renderers in column, pack them with one of these two functions:

```
gtk_tree_view_column_pack_start(column, renderer, expand)
gtk_tree_view_column_pack_end(column, renderer, expand)
```

Here, *expand* is a gboolean value; TRUE means that the renderer should attempt to occupy any free space in a cell, much like its analog property for container widgets in Section 3.4.

The example showed

```
gtk_tree_view_append_column(view, column)
```

for appending *column* at the end of the *view* column list. This function returns the number of columns in the view, but programmers frequently ignore the return value.

Here are more functions for manipulating columns in a view:

- `gint gtk_tree_view_insert_column(GtkTreeView *view, GtkTreeViewColumn *column, gint index)`
  Inserts *column* into *view* in place *index*. Index 0 is the start of the column list; using –1 for index appends the element to the end of the view. This function returns the new number of columns in *view*.

- `gint gtk_tree_view_insert_column_with_attributes(GtkTreeView *view, GtkTreeViewColumn *column, gint index, GtkCellRenderer *renderer, ...)`
  Like the preceding function, but adds *renderer*, followed by a NULL-terminated list of cell renderer attributes.

- `GtkTreeViewColumn *gtk_tree_view_get_column(GtkTreeView *view, gint index)`
  Returns the column in *view* corresponding to *index*. The first column index in a view is 0. This function returns NULL upon failure.

- `GList *gtk_tree_view_get_columns(GtkTreeView *view)`
  Returns a freshly allocated GList of the columns in *view*. You should deallocate this list with g_list_free() when you are finished.

- `void gtk_tree_view_move_column_after(GtkTreeView *view, GtkTreeViewColumn *col1, GtkTreeViewColumn *col2)`
  Moves *col1* after *col2* in *view*. If *col2* is NULL, *col1* goes to the end of the view.

- `gint gtk_tree_view_remove_column(GtkTreeView *view, GtkTreeViewColumn *column)`
  Removes *column* from *view* and returns the new number of columns in the view.

There's a handy function for setting all column widths in a view to their optimal width:

`gtk_tree_view_columns_autosize(view)`

This function works only after you pack and realize *view*.

Data normally flows from the tree model to the renderer with the help of column associations that bind renderer attributes to column identifiers, but you can define your own column assignment functions:

```
gtk_tree_view_insert_column_with_data_func(view,
                                           position,
                                           title,
                                           renderer,
                                           func,
                                           func_data,
                                           destroy_notify)
```

As with gtk_tree_view_insert_column_with_attributes(), *view*, *position*, *title*, and *renderer* are the view, column position, title, and cell renderer for the new column, but func is your function for carrying data to the cell renderer; *func_data* is an untyped pointer that GTK+ passes to *func*, and destroy_notify is responsible for deallocating data.

The type definition of *func* is

```
typedef void (*GtkTreeCellDataFunc) (GtkTreeViewColumn *tree_column,
                                     GtkCellRenderer *cell,
                                     GtkTreeModel *tree_model,
                                     GtkTreeIter *iter,
                                     gpointer data);
```

To render a cell, GTK+ invokes this cell data function with the view column tree_column, cell renderer cell, and data model tree_model. The most important argument is perhaps iter, because it points to the target row to render. As usual, data is an optional data pointer.

This function should call the cell renderer cell with the appropriate (and perhaps slightly altered) data from tree_model. The program in Section 3.11.4 contains an example, room_convert(), for changing –1 into a dash.

If you wish to set a renderer data function after creating a column, call

```
gtk_tree_view_column_set_cell_data_func(tree_column,
                                        cell_renderer,
                                        func,
                                        func_data,
                                        destroy_notify)
```

NOTE   *To remove a renderer data function, call the preceding function with* NULL *for* func.

GtkTreeViewColumn objects have these properties:

- **visible** (gboolean): If FALSE, the column does not appear in the view.
- **resizable** (gboolean): If TRUE, the user may resize the column by dragging the column title's border.
- **widget** (gint, read-only): The current width of the column in pixels.
- **sizing** (GtkTreeViewColumnSizing): The column's width resize mode with respect to the model. Possible values are as follows:

   GTK_TREE_VIEW_COLUMN_GROW_ONLY: A change in the model can cause the column to expand, but not to contract.

   GTK_TREE_VIEW_COLUMN_FIXED: The column remains the same width according to the **fixed-width** property (described later in this section).

   GTK_TREE_VIEW_COLUMN_AUTOSIZE: The column may expand or contract to the optimal width as data enters or leaves the model. This can be inefficient with large models.

- **fixed-width** (gint): If you set **sizing** to the fixed setting, this property is the width of the column in pixels.
- **min-width** (gint): The minimum width of the column in pixels.
- **max-width** (gint): The maximum width of the column in pixels.
- **title** (gchararray): The column's title.
- **widget** (GtkWidget): A widget to put in the column heading instead of a text title.

NOTE *It doesn't make much sense to put arbitrary widgets in the title. Small icons work, but not many other widgets do.*

- **alignment** (gfloat): The horizontal alignment of the column title. As with other widgets, 0.0 left-justifies, 0.5 centers, and 1.0 right-justifies.
- **sort-indicator** (gboolean): If TRUE, the column contains a sort indicator (normally an arrow in the title).
- **sort-order** (enumeration): If the column view sorts its data, this property indicates the sort order; possible values are GTK_SORT_ASCENDING and GTK_SORT_DESCENDING.
- **clickable** (gboolean): If TRUE, the user may click the column header.
- **reorderable** (gboolean): If TRUE, the user may move the entire column to a different position in the view by dragging the header.

GtkTreeViewColumn has one signal, **clicked**, emitted when the user clicks the column header. The handler prototype is

```
void handler(GtkTreeViewColumn *column, gpointer data);
```

Cell Renderers

The final link between the model and view is the cell renderer (abstract class **GtkCellRenderer**). The renderer takes a cell's data as input and draws the cell in the view.

GTK+ has three prepackaged cell renderers, all subclasses of **GtkCellRenderer**:

- **GtkCellRendererText** (GTK_CELL_RENDERER_TEXT): Draws various data types as text.
- **GtkCellRendererPixbuf** (GTK_CELL_RENDERER_PIXBUF): Draws images.
- **GtkCellRendererToggle** (GTK_CELL_RENDERER_TOGGLE): Draws Boolean values as check boxes.

All renderers have these **GtkCellRenderer** properties:

- **mode** (GtkCellRendererMode): The activation mode for cells. Possible values are as follows:

    GTK_CELL_RENDERER_MODE_ACTIVATABLE: User may activate (click) cells.

    GTK_CELL_RENDERER_MODE_EDITABLE: User may edit cells.

    GTK_CELL_RENDERER_MODE_INTER: User may not activate or edit cells.
- **visible** (gboolean): If FALSE, the renderer does not draw cells.
- **xalign** (gfloat): Horizontal alignment for cell content. As usual, 0.0 left-justifies, 0.5 centers, and 1.0 right-justifies.
- **yalign** (gfloat): Vertical alignment for cells. As usual, 0.0 places the content at the top, 0.5 centers, and 1.0 places the content at the bottom of the cell.
- **xpad** (guint): The number of pixels to pad at the left and right of a cell.
- **ypad** (guint): The number of pixels to pad at the top and bottom of a cell.

- **width** (gint): Fixed width of cells, in pixels.
- **height** (gint): Fixed height of cells, in pixels.

GtkCellRendererText has several properties, including the following:

- **text** (gchararray): The cell text.
- **use-markup** (gchararray, write-only): Pango formats text written into this property.

In addition, the following properties have the same types and purpose as in **GtkTextTag: background, foreground, editable, font, family, style, variant, weight, stretch, size, size-points, scale, strikethrough, underline**, and **rise**. For each of these these, there is a gboolean **property-set** property; set it to FALSE if you don't want **property** to have any effect on the text.

GtkCellRendererText has one signal, **edited**, emitted when a cell's content is changed. Its handler prototype is

```
void handler(GtkCellRendererText *renderer,
             gchar *path,
             gchar *new_text,
             gpointer data);
```

Here, *path* represents the altered cell's path; *new_text* is the cell's new content.

GtkCellRendererPixbuf adds one property to its parent class:

- **pixbuf** (GdkPixBuf): The image to render in the cell.

GtkCellRendererToggle has these properties:

- **activatable** (gboolean): If TRUE, the user can click the cell to activate the toggle.
- **active** (gboolean): Represents the current state of the toggle. TRUE means that the cell is currently on.
- **radio** (gboolean): If TRUE, the cell is a radio button (grouped with the other cells drawn by the renderer object) rather than a toggle.

GtkCellRendererToggle has a **toggled** signal that goes out when the user clicks a cell. Its handler prototype is like the text renderer handler described earlier, but with no text field:

```
void handler(GtkCellRendererToggle *renderer, gchar *path, gpointer data);
```

You are responsible for writing any relevant data from a toggle cell back into your model; you would normally do this with a **toggled** handler. Keep in mind that you may have to change several rows in the model to enable the radio button feature.

3.11.3 Selecting Rows

After your application displays a list or tree in a view, the user can interact with the data. All **GtkTreeView** objects come with a **GtkTreeSelection** object (GTK_TYPE_TREE_SELECTION) that helps you manage rows that a user selects.

NOTE *A selection object belongs to a specific view. If you have several views of the same model, each view has its own selection object and therefore may show a different selection. In addition, you cannot use selections to permanently mark elements of all views.*

Because a selection is coupled to a view, you cannot create or destroy selection objects independent of their views. To get a handle on a view's selection object, use

```
GtkTreeSelection *selection;

selection = gtk_tree_view_get_selection(view);
```

You may also get a view from its selection with

```
view = gtk_tree_selection_get_view(selection);
```

After you obtain a **GtkTreeSelection** object, you should decide how the selection behaves with

```
gtk_tree_selection_set_mode(selection, mode)
```

where *mode* is one of the following:

- GTK_SELECTION_NONE: The user may not select anything in the view.
- GTK_SELECTION_SINGLE: The user may select at most one row in the view. This is the default.
- GTK_SELECTION_BROWSE: Exactly one row in the display shows up as the selection at any time. This is useful for lists of fonts, files, and the like, where there should always be only one selection.
- GTK_SELECTION_MULTIPLE: The user may select multiple rows.

In the GTK_SELECTION_SINGLE and GTK_SELECTION_BROWSE modes, you can get at the currently selected node with

```
gboolean gtk_tree_selection_get_selected(GtkTreeSelection *selection,
                                         GtkTreeModel **model,
                                         GtkTreeIter *iter)
```

If there is a current selection, this function returns TRUE, points *iter* at the current selection, and, if *model* is not NULL, sets that pointer to the selection's list or tree model. However, if there is no selection, this function returns NULL and does nothing else.

You can't use the preceding function if the selection mode is GTK_SELECTION_MULTIPLE. There are two ways to handle this; the easier is

```
gtk_tree_selection_selected_foreach(selection, func, data)
```

to call *func* on each row in *selection*, along with the *data* pointer. When you write *func*, you must follow this type definition:

```
typedef void (* GtkTreeSelectionForeachFunc) (GtkTreeModel *model,
                                              GtkTreePath *path,
                                              GtkTreeIter *iter,
                                              gpointer data);
```

Here, iter points to a selection's node in model; path is the node's address.

If you prefer to get multiple row selections as a GList (if you need to pass the selections to some other function, for example), use

gtk_tree_selection_get_selected_rows(*selection*, *model_ptr_addr*)

The return value is a GList of GtkTreePath structures. If you provide the address of a model pointer as *model_ptr_addr*, this function also sets the pointer to the current model. You are responsible for deallocating the return value's memory; you can do this with

g_list_foreach(*selected_rows*, gtk_tree_path_free, NULL);
g_list_free(*selected_rows*);

These additional functions query and manipulate selections:

- gboolean gtk_tree_selection_path_is_selected(GtkTreeSelection *selection*, GtkTreePath *path*)
  Returns TRUE if *path* is part of *selection*.

- gboolean gtk_tree_selection_iter_is_selected(GtkTreeSelection *selection*, GtkTreeIter *iter*)
  Returns TRUE if *iter* points to part of *selection*.

- void gtk_tree_selection_select_path(GtkTreeSelection *selection*, GtkTreePath *path*)
  Switches *selection* to the node addressed by *path*.

- void gtk_tree_selection_select_iter(GtkTreeSelection *selection*, GtkTreeIter *iter*)
  Switches *selection* to the node pointed to by *iter*.

- void gtk_tree_selection_select_all(GtkTreeSelection *selection*)
  Forces *selection* to select all nodes in its corresponding view.

- void gtk_tree_selection_unselect_path(GtkTreeSelection *selection*, GtkTreePath *path*)
  Removes the node addressed by *path* from *selection*.

- void gtk_tree_selection_unselect_iter(GtkTreeSelection *selection*, GtkTreeIter *iter*)
  Removes the node pointed to by *iter* from *selection*.

- void gtk_tree_selection_unselect_all(GtkTreeSelection *selection*)
  Deselects everything in *selection*.

- void gtk_tree_selection_select_range(GtkTreeSelection *selection*, GtkTreePath *begin*, GtkTreePath *end*)
  Switches *selection* to the nodes from *begin* to *end*.

The preceding functions work on paths and iterators, but you can also exert further control with a custom function. If your program calls

---
gtk_tree_selection_set_select_function(*selection*, *func*, *data*, *destroy*)
---

then the all selection functions run your own *func* on any candidate nodes to see if the nodes are valid. If *func* returns TRUE, the calling selection function selects or deselects the node as usual, but if the return value is FALSE, the selection function does nothing with the node. The *data* argument is an optional data pointer; *destroy* is *data*'s destroy function. As shown in the following, *func* uses the GtkTree-SelectionFunc type definition:

```
typedef gboolean (* GtkTreeSelectionFunc) (GtkTreeSelection *selection,
                                           GtkTreeModel *model,
                                           GtkTreePath *path,
                                           gboolean path_currently_selected,
                                           gpointer data);
```

The model and path parameters help you retrieve the model data; path_currently_selected is TRUE if the node is already a part of the current selection.

Your application can use GtkTreeSelectionFunc to determine whether a user can select rows, but you can also use it to select rows based on a search pattern.

NOTE   *Selection functions are powerful, but you should be careful where you apply them. Users with a list or tree in front of them generally expect that they can select anything in the view. If your application uses a GtkTreeSelectionFunc function to make it impossible to select certain rows, the reason should be obvious. For instance, if you outfit a view with subheadings, users should understand why they cannot click one of these subheadings.*

To understand the potential confusion, consider an opinion survey application with an extensive list of survey takers. If one particular survey were for potential voters, it would be logical to exclude anyone under 18 years old from the list of survey takers. However, if rows for people under 18 still appeared in the list, users would be confused if nothing happened upon a mouse click. It would be better to exclude the rows entirely.

3.11.4   An Extended Example

At this point, you have seen quite a bit of detail on tree views and models, but no real code. This section contains a larger example program that displays the personnel organization of Rixico, Inc. (Fine Flippers and Slop for Household and Industry — Since 1951.)

The first part of the program defines a small data set for the employee data. The structure includes a path component that conforms to GTK+ string path specification. In a real-life data set, this probably wouldn't be the case, so you would have to determine the path in some other way.

```
/* -*-coding: utf-8;-*- */
/* tree.c -- Rixico Inc. personnel */

#include <gtk/gtk.h>

/* employee data structure */
```

```
typedef struct _employee {
  gchar *path;
  gchar *last_name;
  gchar *first_name;
  gboolean on_site;
  gchar *job_title;
  gint room_no; /* -1 if employee is off-site */
} employee;

/* employee data */
employee staff[] = {
  { "0", "Ricshaw", "George", FALSE, "Majority Shareholder", -1 },
  { "1", "Kolakowski", "Edna", FALSE, "Shareholder", -1 },
  { "2", "Gainer", "Merideth", TRUE, "General Manager", 100 },
  { "2:0", "Zimmerman", "Walter", TRUE, "Administrative Assistant", 101 },
  { "2:1", "Fenner", "Harold", TRUE, "Accounting Director", 110 },
  { "2:1:0", "Kunkle", "Heather", TRUE, "Accountant", 111 },
  { "2:1:1", "Gasteiner", "Tom", TRUE, "Accountant", 111 },
  { "2:2", "Ardmore", "Henrietta", TRUE, "Production Director", 200 },
  { "2:2:0", "Lampoudi", "Fred", TRUE, "Flipper Lead", 210 },
  { "2:2:0:0", "Gray", "Anthony", TRUE, "Flipper Machinist", 211 },
  { "2:2:0:1", "de Vries", "Linda", TRUE, "Flipper Machinist", 211 },
  { "2:2:0:2", "Hawkins", "Drew", TRUE, "Flipper Machinist", 211 },
  { "2:2:0:3", "Wray", "Steven", TRUE, "Flipper Trainer", 212 },
  { "2:2:0:4", "Stein", "Martha", FALSE, "Flipper Trainee", 212 },
  { "2:2:1", "Sawyer", "Leonard", TRUE, "Slop Lead", 230 },
  { "2:2:1:0", "Nestroy", "Joan", TRUE, "Slop Assembler", 231 },
  { "2:2:1:1", "Parker", "Robin", FALSE, "Slop Assembler (Temp)", 232 },
  { "2:2:2", "Evering", "Tracy", TRUE, "Quality Control", 299 },
  { "2:2:3", "Zoidberg", "John", FALSE, "Company Doctor", -1 },
  { "2:3", "Stoner", "Martin", TRUE, "IT Director", 120 },
  { "2:3:0", "English", "Doug", FALSE, "Web Designer/Slacker", -1 },
  { "3", "Ledbetter", "Arthur", FALSE,
      "Research Partner, University of Cross Roads", -1},
  { NULL, NULL, NULL, FALSE, NULL, -1}
};
```

The view columns use the following column identifiers. The path (in the preceding code) is not in the column; the organization will appear under the title column.

```
/* column identifiers in tree view */
enum {
  LASTNAME_COL,
  FIRSTNAME_COL,
  ONSITE_COL,
  TITLE_COL,
  ROOMNO_COL,
  NUM_COLS
};
```

The following two functions help insert a node into the tree. Node insertion creates any parent and sibling nodes that precede the target path.

WARNING   *In this example, undefined parent and previous siblings show up as empty rows in the view; you must take care to define these nodes. In an industrial-strength application, you should avoid this kind of problem.*

```
/* verify that path is a valid node in tree */
gboolean node_exists(GtkTreeStore *tree, GtkTreePath *path)
{
  GtkTreeIter iter;

  return(gtk_tree_model_get_iter(GTK_TREE_MODEL(tree), &iter, path));
}

/* inserts a new node at path in tree */
void node_insert(GtkTreeStore *tree, GtkTreePath *path)
{
  gint depth;
  gint *indices;
  gint index;
  GtkTreeIter iter;

  /* determine depth and last index of path */
  depth = gtk_tree_path_get_depth(path);
  indices = gtk_tree_path_get_indices(path);
  index = indices[depth-1];

  if (!node_exists(tree, path))
  {
    if (depth == 1)
    { /* if this is a child of the root node, use NULL instead of iter */
      while (!(gtk_tree_model_iter_n_children( GTK_TREE_MODEL(tree), NULL)
             == (index+1)))
      {
        gtk_tree_store_append(tree, &iter, NULL);
      }
    } else {
      GtkTreePath *parent_path;
      GtkTreeIter parent;

      /* determine parent node, creating parent if it does not exist */
      parent_path = gtk_tree_path_copy(path);
      gtk_tree_path_up(parent_path);
      if (!node_exists(tree, parent_path))
      {
        node_insert(tree, parent_path);
      }
      /* append new nodes up to index-th child of parent */
      gtk_tree_model_get_iter(GTK_TREE_MODEL(tree), &parent, parent_path);
      while(!(gtk_tree_model_iter_n_children(
             GTK_TREE_MODEL(tree), &parent) == (index+1)))
```

```
        {
            gtk_tree_store_append(tree, &iter, &parent);
        }

        gtk_tree_path_free(parent_path);
    }
  }
}
```

Some of the employees do not have offices because they are off-site; the room number –1 denotes this situation. The table would look awkward if it had room numbers of –1, so this function converts a room number into a form appropriate for a text renderer.

```
/* read the room number column, and if the number is -1, send a dash (-)
   to the renderer instead */
void room_convert(GtkTreeViewColumn *column,
                  GtkCellRenderer *renderer,
                  GtkTreeModel *model,
                  GtkTreeIter *iter,
                  gpointer data)
{
  gint num;
  gchar *str;

  gtk_tree_model_get(model, iter, ROOMNO_COL, &num, -1);

  if (num == -1)
  {
     str = g_strdup(" - ");
  } else {
     str = g_strdup_printf("%d", num);
  }

  g_object_set(renderer, "text", str, NULL);
  g_free(str);
}
```

The main program's variable declarations are as you would expect for a view with several columns and renderers:

```
  << standard event handlers >>

int main(int argc, char **argv)
{
  GtkWindow *window;
  GtkTreeStore *company;
  employee *person;
  GtkTreePath *path;
  GtkTreeView *view;
```

```
   GtkScrolledWindow *scroller;

   GtkCellRenderer *room_no_renderer, *text_renderer,
                   *bold_renderer, *check_renderer;

   GtkTreeViewColumn *room_no_col, *title_col, *last_name_col,
                     *first_name_col, *on_site_col;

   /* initialize GTK+, create main window */
   gtk_init(&argc, &argv);
   window = g_object_new(GTK_TYPE_WINDOW,
                         "title", "Rixico Inc.",
                         "default-width", 600,
                         "default-height", 400,
                         NULL);

   << attach standard handlers for main window >>
```

The process for creating and populating the tree model is very similar to that in the previous example in Section 3.11, except that this has a tree structure. The node_insert() function creates the node. You can also see how this program converts the string path to an iterator using the functions in Section 3.11.1.

```
   /* create tree model */
   company = gtk_tree_store_new(NUM_COLS,
                                G_TYPE_STRING,
                                G_TYPE_STRING,
                                G_TYPE_BOOLEAN,
                                G_TYPE_STRING,
                                G_TYPE_INT);

   /* point at start of personnel data */
   person = staff;
   /* fill model with personnel data */
   while (person->path != NULL)
   {
      GtkTreeIter iter;

      path = gtk_tree_path_new_from_string(person->path);
      node_insert(company, path);
      gtk_tree_model_get_iter(GTK_TREE_MODEL(company), &iter, path);
      gtk_tree_path_free(path);
      gtk_tree_store_set(company, &iter,
                         LASTNAME_COL, person->last_name,
                         FIRSTNAME_COL, person->first_name,
                         ONSITE_COL, person->on_site,
                         TITLE_COL, person->job_title,
                         ROOMNO_COL, person->room_no,
                         -1);
      person++;
   }
```

Here are a few renderer variations.

```
/* create a right-justified renderer for room numbers */
room_no_renderer = gtk_cell_renderer_text_new();
g_object_set(room_no_renderer, "xalign", 1.0, NULL);

/* a normal text renderer */
text_renderer = gtk_cell_renderer_text_new();

/* a renderer for text in boldface (for last name column) */
bold_renderer = gtk_cell_renderer_text_new();
g_object_set(bold_renderer, "weight", 500, NULL);

/* a check box renderer */
check_renderer = gtk_cell_renderer_toggle_new();
```

Now it's time to create the view columns and put the renderers into the columns. The room number renderer gets a the special room_convert() data function from earlier:

```
/* create view columns */
room_no_col = gtk_tree_view_column_new_with_attributes(
                "Room", room_no_renderer,
                NULL);

gtk_tree_view_column_set_cell_data_func(room_no_col, room_no_renderer,
                                room_convert,
                                NULL, NULL);
```

The title is the only column that the user can move. The rest of the columns are relatively mundane:

```
title_col = gtk_tree_view_column_new_with_attributes("Title", text_renderer,
                                            "text", TITLE_COL,
                                            NULL);

/* allow user to move this column around */
g_object_set(title_col, "reorderable", TRUE, NULL);

last_name_col = gtk_tree_view_column_new_with_attributes(
                "Last name", bold_renderer,
                "text", LASTNAME_COL,
                NULL);

first_name_col = gtk_tree_view_column_new_with_attributes(
                "First name", text_renderer,
                "text", FIRSTNAME_COL,
                NULL);

on_site_col = gtk_tree_view_column_new_with_attributes(
                "On site?", check_renderer,
                "active", ONSITE_COL,
                NULL);
```

Creating the top-level tree view is nearly identical to creating a list view, as is packing the columns into the view.

```
/* create overall view */
view = g_object_new(GTK_TYPE_TREE_VIEW,
                    "model", company,
                    "rules-hint", TRUE,
                    "enable-search", TRUE,
                    "search-column", LASTNAME_COL,
                    NULL);

/* put all columns into the view */
gtk_tree_view_append_column(view, room_no_col);
gtk_tree_view_append_column(view, last_name_col);
gtk_tree_view_append_column(view, first_name_col);
gtk_tree_view_append_column(view, on_site_col);
gtk_tree_view_append_column(view, title_col);
```

This little bit puts the drop arrow in the title column instead of in the first column (the room number). It makes much more sense to view and interact with the hierarchy based on job title.

```
/* set drop arrow at front of the title column */
g_object_set(view, "expander-column", title_col, NULL);
```

Because the model can get relatively large, it should go into a scrolled container before going into the main window:

```
/* put everything into a scrolled window */
scroller = g_object_new(GTK_TYPE_SCROLLED_WINDOW, NULL);
gtk_container_add(GTK_CONTAINER(scroller), GTK_WIDGET(view));
gtk_container_add(GTK_CONTAINER(window), GTK_WIDGET(scroller));

/* show everything and start GTK+ main loop */
gtk_widget_show_all(GTK_WIDGET(window));
gtk_main();

return 0;
}
```

Figure 3.18 shows the completed application.

This concludes the discussion of the tree widget system. If you didn't quite understand everything, remember that you already have working code fragments. It is not difficult to adapt these small programs (or other code that you may find on the Net) to your own needs, learning new pieces of the system as you go.

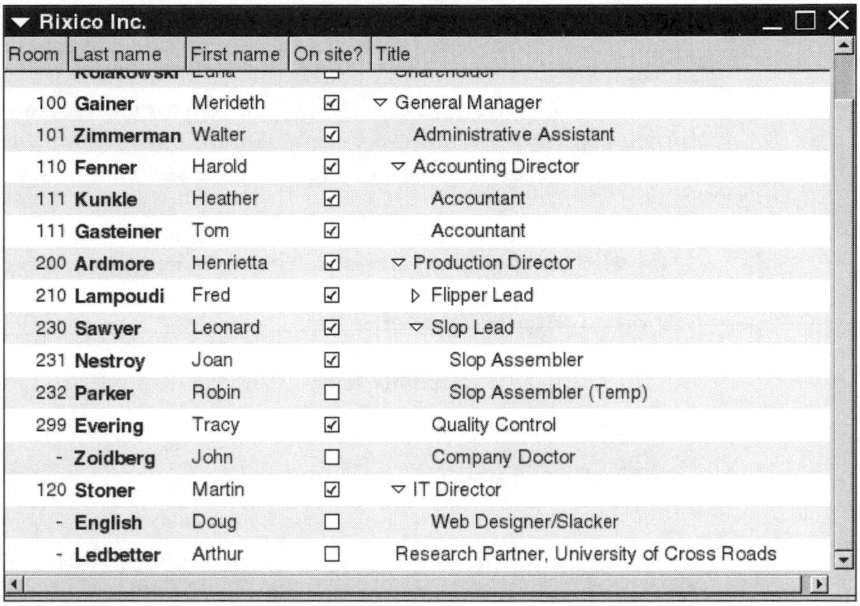

Room	Last name	First name	On site?	Title
	Kolakowski	Edna	☐	Shareholder
100	**Gainer**	Merideth	☑	▽ General Manager
101	**Zimmerman**	Walter	☑	Administrative Assistant
110	**Fenner**	Harold	☑	▽ Accounting Director
111	**Kunkle**	Heather	☑	Accountant
111	**Gasteiner**	Tom	☑	Accountant
200	**Ardmore**	Henrietta	☑	▽ Production Director
210	**Lampoudi**	Fred	☑	▷ Flipper Lead
230	**Sawyer**	Leonard	☑	▽ Slop Lead
231	**Nestroy**	Joan	☑	Slop Assembler
232	**Parker**	Robin	☐	Slop Assembler (Temp)
299	**Evering**	Tracy	☑	Quality Control
-	**Zoidberg**	John	☐	Company Doctor
120	**Stoner**	Martin	☑	▽ IT Director
-	**English**	Doug	☐	Web Designer/Slacker
-	**Ledbetter**	Arthur	☐	Research Partner, University of Cross Roads

Figure 3.18: Tree demonstration.

3.12 Text

Like the tree and list widgets, the GTK+ text widget system is very powerful if you understand its basic concepts. The separation between model and view is very important here.

The model class for text in GTK+ is **GtkTextBuffer** (GTK_TYPE_TEXT_BUFFER). To view the model, you must create a **GtkTextView** (GTK_TYPE_TEXT_VIEW) object. You can define and build these objects in any order.

Before diving into the details of the model and view classes, you should see the source code for a sample text editing application. This program supports different text formattings.

The first part of this program defines a few global variables for the model, view, and formatting buttons. In a real application, you could enclose all of this inside a data structure:

```
/* -*-coding: utf-8;-*- */
/* text.c -- demonstrate text widgets */

#include <gtk/gtk.h>

GtkTextBuffer *buffer;
GtkTextTag *bold, *italic, *underline;
GtkCheckButton *bold_button, *italic_button, *underline_button;
```

This small global variable indicates the state of the selection:

```
gboolean format_dirty = FALSE;
```

Two callback functions access format_dirty. The first is changed_selection(), below. Later, this program binds a signal handler that calls this function when the user moves the text buffer cursor or alters the selection. The idea is that the format buttons should change as the selection and cursor moves. However, verifying the format upon every event is very costly, visibly slowing down your machine. Therefore, this callback only changes a global state variable.

```
/* when someone moves the cursor or selects something in the view, mark
   the selection variable as "changed" so that verify_format() can change
   the format buttons accordingly */
void changed_selection(GtkTextBuffer *buf,
                       GtkTextIter i,
                       GtkTextMark *mark,   /* function does not use parms */
                       gpointer data)
{
  format_dirty = TRUE;
}
```

The callback function that follows does all of the real work of maintaining the formatting button states. Later, the main program binds a timeout so that the main loop runs this function every tenth of a second.

Notice how this callback returns TRUE (both when it has no work to do and at the very end). This is necessary to make the program continue generating timeouts in the main loop. Although this book does not cover timeouts in any detail, you can see that the return value and the function to set the timeout (near the end of the program) are nearly the only things you need to know to use timeouts in your own programs (if you need to know more, consult the GLib API reference).

```
/* check the selection and cursor position, set the format buttons to match */
gboolean verify_format(gpointer data) {
  GtkTextIter begin, end;
  gboolean bold_on, bold_off;
  gboolean italic_on, italic_off;
  gboolean underline_on, underline_off;

  /* if the cursor position or selection has not changed, do nothing */
  if (!format_dirty) {
    return(TRUE);
  }

  gtk_text_buffer_get_selection_bounds(buffer, &begin, &end);

  if (!gtk_text_iter_equal(&begin, &end))
  {
    GtkTextIter iter = begin;

    /* assume that all formatting styles are true at start */
    bold_on = bold_off = TRUE;
    italic_on = italic_off = TRUE;
```

```
underline_on = underline_off = TRUE;

/* run through the selection, setting format styles as necessary */
while (!gtk_text_iter_equal(&iter, &end))
{
   if (gtk_text_iter_has_tag(&iter, bold))
   {
      bold_off = FALSE;
   } else {
      bold_on = FALSE;
   }

   if (gtk_text_iter_has_tag(&iter, italic))
   {
      italic_off = FALSE;
   } else {
      italic_on = FALSE;
   }

   if (gtk_text_iter_has_tag(&iter, underline))
   {
      underline_off = FALSE;
   } else {
      underline_on = FALSE;
   }

   gtk_text_iter_forward_cursor_position(&iter);
}

/* set check buttons to inconsistent when the tags is both
   on and off in the selection */

if (!bold_on && !bold_off)
{
   g_object_set(bold_button, "inconsistent", TRUE, NULL);
} else {
   g_object_set(bold_button, "inconsistent", FALSE,
                             "active", bold_on,
                             NULL);
}

if (!italic_on && !italic_off)
{
   g_object_set(italic_button, "inconsistent", TRUE, NULL);
} else {
   g_object_set(italic_button, "inconsistent", FALSE,
                               "active", italic_on, NULL);
}

if (!underline_on && !underline_off)
{
   g_object_set(underline_button, "inconsistent", TRUE, NULL);
```

```
    } else {
       g_object_set(underline_button, "inconsistent", FALSE,
                                      "active", underline_on,
                                      NULL);
    }
  } else {
    /* if there isn't a selection, just show the tags at the
       current cursor position */
    bold_on = gtk_text_iter_has_tag(&begin, bold);
    italic_on = gtk_text_iter_has_tag(&begin, italic);
    underline_on = gtk_text_iter_has_tag(&begin, underline);

    g_object_set(bold_button, "inconsistent", FALSE,
                              "active", bold_on,
                              NULL);

    g_object_set(italic_button, "inconsistent", FALSE,
                                "active", italic_on,
                                NULL);

    g_object_set(underline_button, "inconsistent", FALSE,
                                   "active", underline_on,
                                   NULL);
  }
  /* reset state */
  format_dirty = FALSE;

  return(TRUE);
}
```

The format_text() function, shown next, adds or deletes a tag for the view's
current selection from the text buffer based on the tag button state.

A click on one of the formatting check buttons activates this function as
a handler.

```
/* when user clicks on a format check button, change tags */
void format_text(GtkCheckButton *tag_button, gpointer formatptr)
{
  gchar *format = (gchar *)formatptr;
  GtkTextIter begin, end;
  gboolean inconsistent;
  gboolean button_checked;

  gtk_text_buffer_get_selection_bounds(buffer, &begin, &end);
  if (!gtk_text_iter_equal(&begin, &end))
  {
    g_object_get(tag_button, "active", &button_checked,
                             "inconsistent", &inconsistent, NULL);
    if (button_checked || inconsistent)
```

```
      {
        gtk_text_buffer_apply_tag_by_name(buffer, format, &begin, &end);
        g_object_set(tag_button, "active", TRUE,
                                 "inconsistent", FALSE,
                                 NULL);
      } else {
        gtk_text_buffer_remove_tag_by_name(buffer, format, &begin, &end);
         g_object_set(tag_button, "active", FALSE,
                                  "inconsistent", FALSE,
                                  NULL);
      }
    }
}
```

There is nothing special about the main program or its declarations:

```
<< standard event handlers >>

int main(int argc, char **argv)
{
  GtkWindow *window;
  GtkTextTagTable *tags;
  GtkTextView *view;
  GtkScrolledWindow *scroller;
  GtkHButtonBox *buttons;
  GtkVBox *vbox;

  GtkTextChildAnchor *anchor;
  GtkTextIter embed_iter;
  GtkButton *text_button;
  GdkPixbuf *pixbuf;

  /* initialize GTK+, create main window */
  gtk_init(&argc, &argv);
  window = g_object_new(GTK_TYPE_WINDOW,
                        "title", "Text Demo",
                        "default-width", 400,
                        "default-height", 500,
                        NULL);

<< attach standard handlers >>
```

Now you're ready to create the text buffer (the model). This program creates the buffer's tag object and feeds it to the buffer generator function. However, you could also tell the generator to create a new tag table by passing NULL and then get a handle on the tag table with the buffer's **tag-table** property. You will see more text buffer functions in Section 3.12.1.

```
/* create new tag table and buffer objects */
tags = gtk_text_tag_table_new();
buffer = gtk_text_buffer_new(tags);
```

If you already have a text buffer on hand, you can create a text view widget and couple it to the buffer with one line. The `wrap-mode` property is one of many text view properties that you will see in Section 3.12.2.

```
/* create new text view using buffer */
view = GTK_TEXT_VIEW(gtk_text_view_new_with_buffer(buffer));

g_object_set(view, "wrap-mode", GTK_WRAP_WORD, NULL);
```

A text buffer's `mark-set` signal indicates that the cursor position and/or selection has changed:

```
/* add a handler to verify format buttons when the selection,
   cursor position, or mark otherwise changes */
g_signal_connect(buffer, "mark-set", G_CALLBACK(changed_selection), NULL);
```

The following statements give concrete formatting directives to tags in a buffer:

```
/* create tags for bold, italic, and underline */
bold = gtk_text_buffer_create_tag(buffer, "bold",
                                  "weight", 500,
                                  NULL);

italic = gtk_text_buffer_create_tag(buffer, "italic",
                                    "style", PANGO_STYLE_ITALIC,
                                    NULL);

underline = gtk_text_buffer_create_tag(buffer, "underline",
                                       "underline", PANGO_UNDERLINE_SINGLE,
                                       NULL);
```

Adding text to the buffer is easy, requiring only one function call:

```
/* add some default text to the buffer */
gtk_text_buffer_set_text(buffer, "\
The text you see in this window is currently stored in a \
GtkTextBuffer object; you see it with the help of a \
GtkTextView widget.\n
Feel free to type your own text anywhere in this window.\n\n\
If you click any of the buttons below, you will change the \
Widgets and images can appear in text widgets:\n", -1);
```

Just for fun, let's throw a button widget and an image into the text buffer:

```
/* add a button to the text */
text_button = g_object_new(GTK_TYPE_BUTTON, "label", "Button", NULL);
gtk_text_buffer_get_end_iter(buffer, &embed_iter);
anchor = gtk_text_buffer_create_child_anchor(buffer, &embed_iter);
gtk_text_view_add_child_at_anchor(view, GTK_WIDGET(text_button), anchor);

/* add an image to the text */
```

```
pixbuf = gdk_pixbuf_new_from_file("apple-green.png", NULL);
gtk_text_buffer_get_end_iter(buffer, &embed_iter);
gtk_text_buffer_insert_pixbuf(buffer, &embed_iter, pixbuf);
```

You have already seen how to create a scrolled container widget for the view and the formatting buttons:

```
/* put view into scrolling widget */
scroller = g_object_new(GTK_TYPE_SCROLLED_WINDOW, NULL);
gtk_container_add(GTK_CONTAINER(scroller), GTK_WIDGET(view));

/* create check buttons for text formatting */
bold_button = g_object_new(GTK_TYPE_CHECK_BUTTON,
                           "use-stock", TRUE,
                           "label", GTK_STOCK_BOLD,
                           NULL);

italic_button = g_object_new(GTK_TYPE_CHECK_BUTTON,
                             "use-stock", TRUE,
                             "label", GTK_STOCK_ITALIC,
                             NULL);

underline_button = g_object_new(GTK_TYPE_CHECK_BUTTON,
                                "use-stock", TRUE,
                                "label", GTK_STOCK_UNDERLINE,
                                NULL);
```

The following signal handler bindings exhibit an odd trait: The handler for these buttons does something only when there is a current selection. A click gives input focus to the button. If you want to continue typing, you must then focus back on the view. When you do this, the program resets the formatting buttons to the place where you focused.

```
/* bind format_text() to these check buttons so that the
   the selection's format changes when you click one */
g_signal_connect(bold_button, "clicked",
                 G_CALLBACK(format_text), "bold");
g_signal_connect(italic_button, "clicked",
                 G_CALLBACK(format_text), "italic");
g_signal_connect(underline_button, "clicked",
                 G_CALLBACK(format_text), "underline");
```

Packing and showing the widgets is a matter of routine:

```
/* pack the check buttons into a button box */
buttons = g_object_new(GTK_TYPE_HBUTTON_BOX, NULL);
gtk_box_pack_start_defaults(GTK_BOX(buttons), GTK_WIDGET(bold_button));
gtk_box_pack_start_defaults(GTK_BOX(buttons), GTK_WIDGET(italic_button));
gtk_box_pack_start_defaults(GTK_BOX(buttons), GTK_WIDGET(underline_button));

/* pack the text view into a scrolled container */
```

```
vbox = g_object_new(GTK_TYPE_VBOX, NULL);

/* put everything into a vbox, then into the main window*/
gtk_box_pack_start_defaults(GTK_BOX(vbox), GTK_WIDGET(scroller));
gtk_box_pack_end(GTK_BOX(vbox), GTK_WIDGET(buttons), FALSE, FALSE, 0);
gtk_container_add(GTK_CONTAINER(window), GTK_WIDGET(vbox));

/* show everything */
gtk_widget_show_all(GTK_WIDGET(window));
```

Just before starting the main loop, however, you need to set the periodic timeout to trigger the verify_format() callback that changes the format buttons if the selection or cursor has changed. The code below uses g_timeout_add() to run the callback every 100ms (a tenth of a second).

```
/* add a timeout for the format button update */
g_timeout_add(100, verify_format, NULL);

gtk_main();

return 0;
}
```

Figure 3.19 shows the final application. Notice that the Italic check button is on, but the Bold button has an inconsistent mark because the text selection contains text both with and without the bold tag.

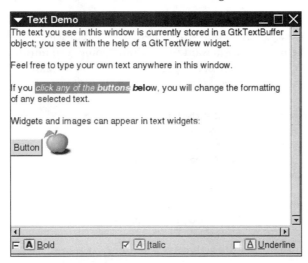

Figure 3.19: Text widget.

3.12.1 Text Buffers

To be proficient with text buffers, you must know the following:

- Text buffers use UTF-8 encoding, so byte counts (*indices*) and character counts (*offsets*) differ.

- A text buffer contains at least one (possibly empty) line. Every line but the last ends with a line separator, counted as a character. The separator can be a Unix newline, a CR-LF sequence, or another Unicode line separator. The last line in a text buffer never ends with a line separator.
- Use *iterators* (GtkTextIter) to represent a position in a text buffer. An iterator is a place between two characters. As with GtkTreeIter structures, you do not manipulate text iterators as pointers, but with special utility functions.

WARNING *Any change in a text buffer invalidates its current iterators.*

- To mark a place in a text buffer on a semi-permanent basis, use a *mark* (**Gtk-TextMark**, GTK_TYPE_TEXT_MARK). You can think of a mark as an invisible cursor.
- *Tags* hold formatting and other information for the text buffer. A tag holds an arbitrary description for a piece of the text; you may use the same description tag for many regions of the text at once.
- Each tag belongs to a tag table (**GtkTextTagTable**, GTK_TYPE_TEXT_TAG_TABLE). A text buffer can use tags only from its associated tag table. Tags have string identifiers for easy access.

As you saw in the example in Section 3.12, you can create a text buffer with

---

buffer = gtk_text_buffer_new(*tags*)

---

where *tags* is a text tag table. You can set this parameter to NULL if you would like the buffer to create a table for you. You can access this tag table with the buffer's **tag-table** property.

These functions manipulate the content of a **GtkTextBuffer**:

- void gtk_text_buffer_set_text(GtkTextBuffer *buffer*, const gchar *text*, gint *length*)
  Replaces *buffer*'s content with the UTF-8-encoded text. The *length* value should be the byte length of *text*, or –1 if the text is a NULL-terminated string.
- void gtk_text_buffer_insert(GtkTextBuffer *buffer*, GtkTextIter *iter*, const gchar *text*, gint *length*)
  Like the preceding function, but inserts *text* at *iter* rather than replacing *buffer*'s contents. This function results in an **insert-text** signal emission — the default handler does the actual work of inserting the text. In addition, the handler sets iter to the location just after the new text.
- gboolean gtk_text_buffer_insert_interactive(GtkTextBuffer *buffer*, GtkTextIter *iter*, const gchar *text*, gint *length*, gboolean *editable*)
  Like the preceding function, but refuses to insert text at a location marked as read-only. If *editable* is TRUE, this function inserts text at locations that are not explicitly marked read-only.

NOTE *Under most circumstances, you can determine* editable *by calling* gtk_text_view_get_editable(view) *to see the current status of the buffer's view.*

- void gtk_text_buffer_insert_at_cursor(GtkTextBuffer *buffer, const gchar *text, gint length)
  Like gtk_text_buffer_insert(), but inserts the new text at the cursor's location.

- gboolean gtk_text_buffer_insert_interactive_at_cursor(GtkTextBuffer *buffer, const gchar *text, gint length, gboolean editable)
  Like gtk_text_buffer_insert_interactive_at_cursor(), but inserts at the cursor position.

- void gtk_text_buffer_insert_range(GtkTextBuffer *buffer, const gchar *text, GtkTextIter *iter, const GtkTextIter *begin, GtkTextIter *end)
  Copies the text between *begin* and *end* to *iter* in *buffer*. If *begin* and *end* do not belong to *buffer*, their buffer must share a tag table with *buffer*. The **insert-text** and **apply-tag** signals carry out this function's work.

- gboolean gtk_text_buffer_insert_range_interactive(GtkTextBuffer *buffer, const gchar *text, GtkTextIter *iter, const GtkTextIter *begin, const GtkTextIter *end, gboolean editable)
  Like the preceding function, but reflects the behavior of the other _interactive functions.

- void gtk_text_buffer_delete(GtkTextBuffer *buffer, GtkTextIter *begin, GtkTextIter *end)
  Deletes the text between *begin* and *end* in *buffer*. As was the case with insertion, a signal carries out this function's work: **delete-range**.

- gboolean gtk_text_buffer_delete_interactive(GtkTextBuffer *buffer, GtkTextIter *begin, GtkTextIter *end, gboolean editable)
  Like the preceding function, but obeys read-only ranges like the other _interactive functions.

- gboolean gtk_text_buffer_delete_selection(GtkTextBuffer *buffer, gboolean interactive, gboolean editable)
  Removes the selection from *buffer*; that is, removes all text between the **insert** and **selection-bound** marks. If *interactive* is true, this function behaves like the _interactive functions described earlier, consulting *editable* for text marked neither as read-only nor read-write.

- void gtk_text_buffer_set_modified(GtkTextBuffer *buffer, gboolean modified)
  Alters the modified status of *buffer*. Setting *modified* to TRUE typically means that the buffer has changed since the last time it was saved; FALSE indicates that nothing has happened since the last save (GTK+ will set the modified status to TRUE upon the next modification).

- gboolean gtk_text_buffer_get_modified(GtkTextBuffer *buffer)
  Returns the modified status of *buffer*.

NOTE   *The preceding two functions can help you implement a file save feature in an editor. Every time the user saves the file, your application can set the modified status to* FALSE. *In addition, you can use the status to create an autosave feature.*

- void gtk_text_buffer_begin_user_action(GtkTextBuffer *buffer)
  Signals the start of a user action.

- void gtk_text_buffer_end_user_action(GtkTextBuffer *buffer)
  Signals the end of a user action.

  The user action functions emit **begin-user-action** and **end-user-action** signals. You can nest the signals. User actions can help you establish the history for an Undo feature.

  The _interactive functions from earlier call the user action functions. Therefore, if you stick to the _interactive functions, you do not need to manually call the user action functions.

These functions retrieve data from a text buffer:

- gchar *gtk_text_buffer_get_text(GtkTextBuffer *buffer, const GkTextIter *begin, const GtkTextIter *end, gboolean include_hidden)
  Returns the text in *buffer* between *begin* and *end*. If include_hidden is TRUE, the text will also contain any characters marked as hidden. Unlike the _get_slice() function, discussed next, this function does not replace embedded images and anchors with a special character. Therefore, the indices and offsets in the resulting text may not agree with those in *buffer*.

- gchar *gtk_text_buffer_get_slice(GtkTextBuffer *buffer, const GtkTextIter *begin, const GtkTextIter *end, gboolean include_hidden)
  Like the preceding function, but replaces embedded images and anchors with a special Unicode character, 0xFFFC. Indices and offsets in the slice reflect those in the original *buffer*.

- gunichar gtk_text_iter_get_char(const GtkTextIter *iter)
  Returns the character at *iter*; substitutes for images and anchors as described in the preceding function. If *iter* is at the end of its buffer, this function returns 0 and is thus suitable for use in a loop.

- gint gtk_text_buffer_get_line_count(GtkTextBuffer *buffer)
  Returns the number of lines in *buffer*. Because a **GtkTextBuffer** object maintains the line count internally, this function is quite fast.

- gint gtk_text_buffer_get_char_count(GtkTextBuffer *buffer)
  Returns the number of characters (*not* bytes) in *buffer*. Like the preceding function, this is an efficient function.

Iterators

GtkTextIter structures indicate locations in text buffers and therefore hold a central role in the entire **GtkTextBuffer** API.

NOTE *Functions that work with iterators want the address of a preexisting iterator structure; therefore, when you see* iter *in this chapter, you will probably use something like* &iter *as the function's argument. The example program in Section 3.12 shows how this works in practice.*

You can get an iterator in several ways. All of the following functions fill in a preexisting iterator structure:

- void gtk_text_buffer_iter_at_line(GtkTextBuffer *buffer, GtkTextIter *iter, gint line_number)
  Sets *iter* to the start of line *line_number* in *buffer*.

- `void gtk_text_buffer_iter_at_offset(GtkTextBuffer *buffer, GtkTextIter *iter, gint offset)`
  Sets *iter* to *offset* characters past the start of *buffer*.

- `void gtk_text_buffer_iter_at_line_offset(GtkTextBuffer *buffer, GtkTextIter *iter, gint line_number, gint offset)`
  Sets *iter* to *offset* characters past the start of line *line_number* in *buffer*.

- `void gtk_text_buffer_iter_at_line_index(GtkTextBuffer *buffer, GtkTextIter *iter, gint line_number, gint index)`
  Like the preceding function, but *index* indicates the number of *bytes* into *line_number*.

- `void gtk_text_buffer_iter_get_start_iter(GtkTextBuffer *buffer, GtkTextIter *iter)`
  Sets *iter* to the start of *buffer*.

- `void gtk_text_buffer_iter_get_end_iter(GtkTextBuffer *buffer, GtkTextIter *iter)`
  Sets *iter* to the end of *buffer*.

- `void gtk_text_buffer_iter_get_bounds(GtkTextBuffer *buffer, GtkTextIter *begin, GtkTextIter *end)`
  Sets *begin* and *end* to the start and end of *buffer*, respectively.

- `gboolean gtk_text_buffer_iter_get_selection_bounds(GtkTextBuffer *buffer, GtkTextIter *begin, GtkTextIter *end)`
  If there is a current selection in *buffer*, sets *begin* and *end* to the start and end of the selection and returns TRUE. Otherwise, returns FALSE and sets both iterators to the cursor position. If you're interested only in knowing whether or not there is a selection, you can set both iterators to NULL.

These functions return information about iterators:

- `GtkTextBuffer *gtk_text_iter_get_buffer(const GtkTextIter *iter)`
  Returns the buffer that *iter* describes.

- `gint gtk_text_iter_get_offset(const GtkTextIter *iter)`
  Returns the number of characters between *iter* and the start of its buffer.

- `gint gtk_text_iter_get_line(const GtkTextIter *iter)`
  Returns *iter*'s line number. The first line in a buffer is 0.

- `gint gtk_text_iter_get_line_offset(const GtkTextIter *iter)`
  Returns the number of characters between *iter* and the start of its line.

- `gint gtk_text_iter_get_visible_line_offset(const GtkTextIter *iter)`
  Like the preceding function, but counts only characters not marked as hidden.

- `gint gtk_text_iter_get_line_index(const GtkTextIter *iter)`
  Returns the number of *bytes* between *iter* and the start of its line.

- `gint gtk_text_iter_get_visible_line_index(const GtkTextIter *iter)`
  Like the preceding function, but counts only bytes in characters not marked as hidden.

- `gint gtk_text_iter_get_chars_in_line(const GtkTextIter *iter)`
  Returns the number of characters in *iter*'s line.

- `gint gtk_text_iter_get_bytes_in_line(const GtkTextIter *iter)`
  Returns the number of bytes in *iter*'s line.

- `gboolean gtk_text_iter_starts_word(const GtkTextIter *iter)`
  Returns TRUE if *iter* lies at the start of a word. Pango determines the start of a word based on language-specific algorithms.

- `gboolean gtk_text_iter_ends_word(const GtkTextIter *iter)`
  Returns TRUE if *iter* sits at the end of a word.

- `gboolean gtk_text_iter_inside_word(const GtkTextIter *iter)`
  Returns TRUE if *iter* sits inside of a word.

- `gboolean gtk_text_iter_starts_line(const GtkTextIter *iter)`
  Returns TRUE if *iter* sits at the start of a line.

- `gboolean gtk_text_iter_ends_line(const GtkTextIter *iter)`
  Returns TRUE if *iter* sits at the end of a line.

- `gboolean gtk_text_iter_starts_sentence(const GtkTextIter *iter)`
  Returns TRUE if *iter* sits at the start of a sentence.

- `gboolean gtk_text_iter_inside_sentence(const GtkTextIter *iter)`
  Returns TRUE if *iter* sits inside of a sentence.

- `gboolean gtk_text_iter_ends_sentence(const GtkTextIter *iter)`
  Returns TRUE if *iter* sits at the end of a sentence.

- `gboolean gtk_text_iter_is_start(const GtkTextIter *iter)`
  Returns TRUE if *iter* is at the start of its buffer.

- `gboolean gtk_text_iter_is_end(const GtkTextIter *iter)`
  Returns TRUE if *iter* is at the end of its buffer.

- `gboolean gtk_text_iter_is_cursor_position(const GtkTextIter *iter)`
  Returns TRUE if *iter* sits at its buffer's current cursor position.

- `gboolean gtk_text_iter_can_insert(const GtkTextIter *iter, gboolean default_editable)`
  Returns TRUE if *iter*'s current position is marked as read-write. If there is no such mark, this function returns *default_editable*. All of the _interactive functions from a few pages back call this to decide if they can insert something into or delete something from a buffer.

You can set the absolute position of an iterator with these functions (these functions assume that the iterator is already set to a place inside the appropriate buffer):

- `void gtk_text_iter_set_offset(GtkTextIter *iter, gint offset)`
  Moves *iter* to *offset* characters past the start of its buffer. If the offset is too large, *iter* goes to the last position in the buffer.

- `void gtk_text_iter_set_line(GtkTextIter *iter, gint line_number)`
  Places *iter* at the start of line *line_number*. A buffer starts at line 0. If the line number is too large, this function sets *iter* to the start of its buffer's last line.

- void gtk_text_iter_set_line_offset(GtkTextIter *iter, gint offset)
  Moves iter to offset characters past the start of its current line. The offset value must be between 0 and the number of characters in the line.

- void gtk_text_iter_set_visible_line_offset(GtkTextIter *iter, gint offset)
  Like the preceding function, but ignores characters marked as hidden.

- void gtk_text_iter_set_line_index(GtkTextIter *iter, gint index)
  Like gtk_text_iter_set_line_offset(), but skips bytes, not characters.

- void gtk_text_iter_set_visible_line_index(GtkTextIter *iter, gint index)
  Like the preceding function, but ignores characters marked as hidden.

The functions in the extensive list that follows move an iterator to a relative position inside a buffer. All return gboolean values — TRUE if it is possible to move the iterator as requested. If you ask one of these functions to move the iterator past the start or end of a buffer, the iterator goes as far as it can, and the function returns FALSE.

NOTE *A cursor position is any point in the buffer where the cursor can stand. This is not necessarily between every set of two adjacent characters, especially in languages that do not use a Latin or Greek alphabet. You can move the iterator in terms of cursor positions or characters; be sure that you pick the one that you need.*

- gboolean gtk_text_iter_forward_cursor_position(GtkTextIter *iter)
  Moves iter one cursor position ahead.

- gboolean gtk_text_iter_backward_cursor_position(GtkTextIter *iter)
  Moves iter one cursor position back.

- gboolean gtk_text_iter_forward_cursor_positions(GtkTextIter *iter, gint count)
  Moves iter count cursor positions ahead.

- gboolean gtk_text_iter_backward_cursor_positions(GtkTextIter *iter, gint count)
  Moves iter count cursor positions back.

- gboolean gtk_text_iter_forward_char(GtkTextIter *iter)
  Moves iter one character ahead.

- gboolean gtk_text_iter_backward_char(GtkTextIter *iter)
  Moves iter one character back.

- gboolean gtk_text_iter_forward_chars(GtkTextIter *iter, gint count)
  Moves iter count characters ahead.

- gboolean gtk_text_iter_backward_chars(GtkTextIter *iter, gint count)
  Moves iter count characters back.

- gboolean gtk_text_iter_forward_line(GtkTextIter *iter)
  Moves iter to the start of the next line.

- gboolean gtk_text_iter_backward_line(GtkTextIter *iter)
  Moves iter to the start of the previous line.

- gboolean gtk_text_iter_forward_lines(GtkTextIter *iter, gint count)
  Moves iter ahead count lines, to the start of the target line.

- gboolean gtk_text_iter_backward_lines(GtkTextIter *iter, gint count)
  Moves iter back count lines, to the start of the target line.

- `gboolean gtk_text_iter_forward_word_end(GtkTextIter *iter)`
  Moves *iter* to the next end of a word.

- `gboolean gtk_text_iter_backward_word_start(GtkTextIter *iter)`
  Moves *iter* to the previous start of a word.

- `gboolean gtk_text_iter_forward_word_ends(GtkTextIter *iter, gint count)`
  Moves *iter* ahead *count* word ends.

- `gboolean gtk_text_iter_backward_word_starts(GtkTextIter *iter, gint count)`
  Moves *iter* back *count* word starts.

- `gboolean gtk_text_iter_forward_sentence_end(GtkTextIter *iter)`
  Moves *iter* to the next end of sentence.

- `gboolean gtk_text_iter_backward_sentence_start(GtkTextIter *iter)`
  Moves *iter* to the previous start of sentence.

- `gboolean gtk_text_iter_forward_sentence_ends(GtkTextIter *iter, gint count)`
  Moves *iter* ahead *count* sentence ends.

- `gboolean gtk_text_iter_backward_sentence_starts(GtkTextIter *iter, gint count)`
  Moves *iter* back *count* sentence starts.

- `gboolean gtk_text_iter_forward_to_end(GtkTextIter *iter)`
  Moves *iter* to the position after the last character in its buffer.

- `gboolean gtk_text_iter_forward_to_line_end(GtkTextIter *iter)`
  Moves *iter* to the end of its current line.

- `gboolean gtk_text_iter_forward_to_tag_toggle(GtkTextIter *iter, GtkTextTag *tag)`
  Moves *iter* to the next place in the text where *tag* changes. If *tag* is NULL, this function moves the iterator to the next tag.

- `gboolean gtk_text_iter_backward_to_tag_toggle(GtkTextIter *iter, GtkTextTag *tag)`
  Like the preceding function, but searches backward.

- `gboolean gtk_text_iter_forward_find_char(GtkTextIter *iter, GtkTextCharPredicate func, gpointer data, const GtkTextIter *end)`
  Searches forward for characters until *end*, running *func* with *data* on each character until *func* returns TRUE (see the following GtkTextCharPredicate type definition discussion); at this point, this function sets *iter* to the matching character's position and returns. If *end* is NULL, this function searches until the end of the buffer.

- `gboolean gtk_text_iter_backward_find_char(GtkTextIter *iter, GtkTextCharPredicate func, gpointer data, const GtkTextIter *end)`
  Like the preceding function, but searches backward, and *end* must sit before *iter*.

GtkTextCharPredicate's type definition is

```
typedef gboolean (* GtkTextCharPredicate) (gunichar ch, gpointer user_data);
```

Your predicate functions should return TRUE if ch matches the search criteria (possibly determined in part by user_data).

Here are two more functions that search text buffers:

- gboolean gtk_text_iter_forward_search(const GtkTextIter *iter, const gchar *string, GtkTextSearchFlags flags, GtkTextIter *match_start, GtkTextIter *match_end, const GtkTextIter *end)

  Returns TRUE if *string* appears between *iter* and *end* (if *end* is NULL, search until the end of *iter*'s buffer). If *match_start* and *match_end* are not NULL, this function sets these to the bounds of the matching string in *iter*'s buffer.

  At the moment, *flags* may be one of the following (later GTK+ versions may implement a bitwise-OR version):

  > 0: The search string must match exactly.

  > GTK_TEXT_SEARCH_VISIBLE_ONLY: Search only text not marked as hidden.

  > GTK_TEXT_SEARCH_TEXT_ONLY: Search only the text portions of buffers that may contain images and anchors.

- gboolean gtk_text_iter_backward_search(const GtkTextIter *iter, const gchar *string, GtkTextSearchFlags flags, GtkTextIter *match_start, GtkTextIter *match_end, const GtkTextIter *end)

  Like the preceding function, but search backward from *iter*. The *end* value must come before *iter*, or you can set *end* to NULL to search back to the beginning of the buffer.

Marks

A mark represents a particular place in a text buffer. Unlike iterators, marks are true objects (**GtkTextMark**) and survive through any changes in the text buffer. Marks respond to changes in a text buffer by means of signals and adjust themselves if necessary. You can think of a mark as being similar to the cursor position, sitting between two characters in the buffer. In fact, the cursor *is* a mark — its name is **insert**. Furthermore, if you select something in the view, the end of the selection is the **selection_bound** mark.

WARNING   *When you want to move the cursor around in the text buffer, don't manipulate the* **insert** *and* **selection-bound** *marks directly. The two marks won't match after the change to* **insert** *and, therefore, a selection appears briefly in the text view. To change the cursor position, use*

---

gtk_text_buffer_place_cursor(*buffer*, *iter*)

---

to move buffer's cursor to GtkTextIter *iter*.

To create a mark object at the iterator *iter* in *buffer*, use

---

GtkTextMark *mark*;

---

mark = gtk_text_buffer_create_mark(*buffer*, *name*, *iter*, *left_gravity*);

Here, *name* is the new mark's name (a character string; you can specify NULL if you don't need a name), and *left_gravity* is a gboolean value indicating the new mark's *gravity*. TRUE means left gravity, meaning that the mark stays put if you insert some text into the buffer at the mark's position. However, FALSE asks for right gravity; if you insert some text at the mark in this case, the mark moves to the end of the inserted text. Most marks (including the cursor) use right gravity.

If a mark has a name, you can retrieve the mark at any time with

gtk_text_buffer_get_mark(*buffer*, *name*)

This function returns the desired GtkTextMark or NULL if no such mark exists.

There are two convenience functions to get the cursor and end-of-selection marks:

gtk_text_buffer_get_insert(*buffer*)
gtk_text_buffer_get_selection_bound(*buffer*)

WARNING   *Don't confuse* gtk_text_buffer_get_selection_bound() *with* gtk_text_buffer_get_selection_bounds().

Another important function is

gtk_text_buffer_get_iter_at_mark(*buffer*, *iter*, *mark*)

which sets the iterator at *iter* to the place in *buffer* corresponding to *mark*. You need this function whenever you want to process some text at a mark.

You cannot manipulate marks with properties. Use these access functions instead:

- void gtk_text_buffer_move_mark(GtkTextBuffer *buffer*, GtkTextMark *mark*, const GtkTextIter *iter*)
  Moves *mark* to *iter* in *buffer*.

- void gtk_text_buffer_move_mark_by_name(GtkTextBuffer *buffer*, const gchar *name*, const GtkTextIter *iter*)
  Like the preceding function, but uses the mark *name* string rather than the object handle.

- void gtk_text_buffer_delete_mark(GtkTextBuffer *buffer*, GtkTextMark *mark*)
  Removes *mark* from *buffer*. If there are no existing references to the mark, GTK+ frees the mark's memory.

- void gtk_text_buffer_delete_mark_by_name(GtkTextBuffer *buffer*, const gchar *name*)
  Like the preceding function, but uses the mark's *name* string instead of the object handle.

- gboolean gtk_text_mark_get_deleted(GtkTextMark *mark*)
  Returns TRUE if *mark* still exists due to outstanding references. You may want to call this function after a call to one of the preceding two functions.

- void gtk_text_mark_set_visible(GtkTextMark *mark*, gboolean *visible*)
  Makes *mark* visible if *visible* is TRUE, or invisible otherwise. GTK+ draws a visible mark as a line between two characters. Under normal circumstances, the cursor is the only visible mark in a buffer, but this feature can come in handy for debugging purposes.

- gboolean gtk_text_mark_get_visible(GtkTextMark *mark)
  Returns TRUE if mark is currently visible.

- const gchar *gtk_text_mark_get_name(GtkTextMark *mark)
  Returns the string identifier of mark, or NULL if there is none.

- GtkTextBuffer *gtk_text_mark_get_buffer(GtkTextMark *mark)
  Returns mark's buffer. If you remove the mark from its buffer, this function returns NULL.

- gboolean gtk_text_mark_get_left_gravity(GtkTextMark *mark)
  Returns TRUE if mark has left gravity or FALSE if mark has right gravity.

Tags

Whereas mark objects denote positions in a buffer, **GtkTextTag** objects represent portions of the text inside the buffer. Each buffer has a tag table containing all of the tags.

To create a tag for *buffer*, use

GtkTextTag *tag;

tag = gtk_text_buffer_create_tag(buffer, name, ..., NULL);

---

where *name* is a string identifier for the tag and ... is a list of properties and values.

WARNING   *You can't create more than one tag with the same name in a buffer's tag table.*

Tags have many properties (more than 60 at last count), often utilizing Pango markup features that the view recognizes (see Section 3.3.1). Here is a selection of the most important:

- **name** (gchararray, read-only): The tag's string identifier.
- **background** (gchararray): Background color.
- **foreground** (gchararray): Foreground color.
- **font** (gchararray): Complete font name.
- **family** (gchararray): Typeface family name.
- **style** (PangoStyle): Slant style of the typeface; possible values are

  PANGO_STYLE_NORMAL

  PANGO_STYLE_OBLIQUE

  PANGO_STYLE_ITALIC

- **variant** (PangoVariant): One of PANGO_VARIANT_NORMAL or PANGO_VARIANT_SMALL_CAPS, the latter for caps and small caps.
- **weight** (gint): Numeric weight of typeface (generally between 100 and 1000).
- **stretch** (PangoStretch): Character width; possible values include (from narrow to wide):

PANGO_STRETCH_ULTRA_CONDENSED (characters nearly joined)

PANGO_STRETCH_EXTRA_CONDENSED

PANGO_STRETCH_CONDENSED

PANGO_STRETCH_SEMI_CONDENSED

PANGO_STRETCH_NORMAL

PANGO_STRETCH_SEMI_EXPANDED

PANGO_STRETCH_EXPANDED

PANGO_STRETCH_EXTRA_EXPANDED

PANGO_STRETCH_ULTRA_EXPANDED

- **size** (gint): Font size in pixels.
- **size-points** (gdouble): Font size in points.
- **scale** (gdouble): Font scaling in relation to normal text; 1.0 represents the normal scale.
- **direction** (GtkTextDirection): Direction of the text on a line; possible values are

    GTK_TEXT_DIR_NONE: No particular preference.

    GTK_TEXT_DIR_LTR: Left to right.

    GTK_TEXT_DIR_RTL: Right to left.

- **strikethrough** (gboolean): If TRUE, the view renders the text with a horizontal line through the characters.
- **underline** (PangoUnderline): Text underlining; possible values are

    PANGO_UNDERLINE_NONE: No underlining.

    PANGO_UNDERLINE_SINGLE: Single-line underlining.

    PANGO_UNDERLINE_DOUBLE: Double-line underlining.

    PANGO_UNDERLINE_LOW: Single underlining below character descenders.

- **rise** (gint): How much to raise characters from the base line (may be negative to sink characters).
- **background-full-height** (gboolean): If TRUE, a line's text background gets the **background** color. Otherwise, the color applies only to the character height.
- **language** (gchararray): The language code (for example, en for English, es for Spanish, de for German, or fr for French; see ISO 639).

Further properties that reflect those in **GtkTextView** (see Section 3.12.2) include **pixels-above-lines**, **pixels-below-lines**, **pixels-inside-wrap**, **editable**, **justification**, **left-margin**, **right-margin**, **indent**, and **tabs**. You may want to set these properties in tags to give localized control of the text formatting.

Finally, there is a gboolean activation property ending in **-set** for each property that influences text formatting. For example, **foreground-set** corresponds to **foreground**; if you set **foreground-set** to FALSE, **foreground** has no effect on the formatted text.

To place tags into a buffer (and remove them), use the following functions (all return void):

- `gtk_text_buffer_apply_tag(GtkTextBuffer *buffer, GtkTextTag *tag, const GtkTextIter *begin, const GtkTextIter *end)`
  Applies *tag* to the text in *buffer* between *begin* and *end*. This function emits a **apply-tag** signal; the default handler does the actual work.

- `gtk_text_buffer_apply_tag_by_name(GtkTextBuffer *buffer, const gchar *name, const GtkTextIter *begin, const GtkTextIter *end)`
  Like the preceding function, but uses the tag's string identifier *name* instead of the tag object.

- `gtk_text_buffer_insert_with_tags(GtkTextBuffer *buffer, GtkTextIter *iter, const gchar *text, gint length, GtkTextTag *first_tag, ...)`
  Inserts text into *buffer* at *iter*, enclosing the new text with *first_tag* and any other tags that follow. The *length* value is the byte length of *text*, or −1 if *text* is NULL-terminated.

- `gtk_text_buffer_insert_with_tags_by_name(GtkTextBuffer *buffer, GtkTextIter *iter, const gchar *text, gint length, const gchar *first_tag_name, ...)`
  Like the preceding function, but uses tag string identifiers instead of **GtkTextTag** objects.

- `gtk_text_buffer_remove_tag(GtkTextBuffer *buffer, GtkTextTag *tag, const GtkTextIter *begin, const GtkTextIter *end)`
  Removes tag from all text in *buffer* between *begin* and *end*. Like the tag application, this function emits a **remove-tag** signal; the default handler does the actual work.

- `gtk_text_buffer_remove_tag_by_name(GtkTextBuffer *buffer, const gchar *name, const GtkTextIter *begin, const GtkTextIter *end)`
  Like the preceding function, but uses the tag's string identifier *name* instead of the tag object.

- `gtk_text_buffer_remove_all_tags(GtkTextBuffer *buffer, const GtkTextIter *begin, const GtkTextIter *end)`
  Removes all tags in *buffer* between *begin* and *end*.

WARNING   *Use this function only when you're sure that you know what all the tags in the target region are (and, of course, that it's harmless to remove them).*

If two tags influence the same formatting attribute in some text (for example, if one tag sets **point-size** to 36 and another sets it to 6), then the view has to make a decision on which value to use. Text buffers have a tag priority system for this purpose. Every tag has a gint priority. The lowest possible priority is zero; the highest is one less than the number of tags in the buffer's tag table. The tag with the highest priority determines the text formatting.

The newest tag in a buffer always receives its tag table's highest priority. To find the priority of a tag, use

gtk_text_tag_get_priority(*tag*)

To set a tag's priority, call

---

gtk_text_tag_set_priority(*tag*, *new_priority*)

After you set a tag's priority, the other tags in the table adjust their priorities accordingly.

These functions help you determine active tags in text buffers:

- GSList *gtk_text_iter_get_tags(const GtkTextIter *iter*)
  Returns all active tags at *iter*. You are responsible for freeing the resulting list with g_slist_free().

- GSList *gtk_text_iter_get_toggled_tags(const GtkTextIter *iter*, gboolean *on*)
  Like the preceding function, but returns tags that start or end at *iter*. If *on* is TRUE, this function returns the tags that start at *iter*; otherwise, it returns the tags that end at *iter*.

- gboolean gtk_text_iter_has_tag(const GtkTextIter *iter*, GtkTextTag *tag*)
  Returns TRUE if *iter* is inside *tag*.

- gboolean gtk_text_iter_begins_tag(const GtkTextIter *iter*, GtkTextTag *tag*)
  Returns TRUE if *iter* is at a position where *tag* starts.

- gboolean gtk_text_iter_ends_tag(const GtkTextIter *iter*, GtkTextTag *tag*)
  Returns TRUE if *iter* is at a position where *tag* ends.

- gboolean gtk_text_iter_toggles_tag(const GtkTextIter *iter*, GtkTextTag *tag*)
  Returns TRUE if *iter* is at a position where *tag* begins or ends.

Tag Tables

Tag tables are **GtkTextTagTable** objects. These functions manage tag tables:

- GtkTextTagTable *gtk_text_tag_table_new(void)
  Returns a new tag table object.

- GtkTextTagTable *gtk_text_buffer_get_tag_table(GtkTextBuffer *buffer*)
  Returns the tag table from *buffer*. You can use this function to get an implicitly created tag table from a buffer.

- void gtk_text_tag_table_add(GtkTextTagTable *table*, GtkTextTag *tag*)
  Inserts *tag* into *table*. This function fails if you try to insert a tag already in *table* or a tag with the same name as one already in *table*. The new tag gets the highest priority in the table.

- void gtk_text_tag_table_remove(GtkTextTagTable *table*, GtkTextTag *tag*)
  Removes *tag* from *table*. If you have no other references to *tag*, GTK+ destroys the tag.

- GtkTextTag *gtk_text_tag_table_lookup(GtkTextTagTable *table*,
  const gchar *name*)
  Returns any tag in *table* with the string identifier *name*. If there is no such tag, this function returns NULL.

- gint gtk_text_tag_table_get_size(GtkTextTagTable *table)
  Returns the number of tags in table.

- void gtk_text_tag_table_foreach(GtkTextTagTable *table, GtkTextTagTableForeach *func, gpointer data)
  Runs func on every tag in table, passing data as the second parameter to func. The type definition for func is

---

```
typedef void (* GtkTextTagTableForeach) (GtkTextTag *tag, gpointer data);
```

Images and Child Widgets

You can put a GDK Pixbuf image or an arbitrary widget inside a text buffer. With this capability, you can illuminate a text or include interactive elements. To put a **GdkPixbuf** object *pixbuf* into *buffer* at *iter*, use

---

```
gtk_text_buffer_insert_pixbuf(buffer, iter, pixbuf)
```

If *iter* points to a place in a buffer where an image resides, you can call

---

```
gtk_text_iter_get_pixbuf(iter)
```

---

to retrieve the GDK Pixbuf object. If there isn't an image at that spot, this function returns NULL.

To put a child widget into a buffer, you must put it into a child anchor container (**GtkTextChildAnchor**). To create an anchor at *iter* in *buffer*, use

---

```
GtkTextChildAnchor *anchor;

anchor = gtk_text_buffer_create_child_anchor(buffer, iter);
```

To pack *widget* into the text window at *anchor*, you need the **GtkTextView** object view that will eventually show *buffer*:

```
gtk_text_view_add_child_at_anchor(view, widget, anchor);
```

NOTE   *Always remember that the child anchors belong to the buffer, but their widgets belong to the view.*

To get a child anchor at a iterator *iter*, use

```
gtk_text_iter_get_child_anchor(iter)
```

If you want to put the position of a child anchor *anchor* in *buffer* into *iter*, use

---

```
gtk_text_buffer_get_iter_at_child_anchor(buffer, iter, anchor)
```

NOTE   *Text buffers represent images and child anchors as a special Unicode character, 0xFFFC (a crossed box with OBJ inside).*

Clipboards

Clipboards are temporary storage locations for copied or deleted text. You can create your own **GtkClipboard** (GTK_TYPE_CLIPBOARD) objects, but you'll probably find yourself using the system's standard clipboard more than your own; use

```
GtkClipboard *clipboard;

clipboard = gtk_clipboard_get(GDK_NONE);
```

to point *clipboard* at the default clipboard.

These functions perform the usual cut and and paste operations on text buffers (all have no return value):

- gtk_text_buffer_copy_clipboard(GtkTextBuffer *buffer, GtkClipboard *clipboard)
  Copies the current selection in *buffer* to *clipboard*.

- gtk_text_buffer_cut_clipboard(GtkTextBuffer *buffer, GtkClipboard *clipboard, gboolean *default_editable*)
  Attempts to remove the current selection from *buffer* and places it into *clipboard*. If *default_editable* is TRUE, this function will remove text not explicitly marked as read-write in the buffer.

- gtk_text_buffer_paste_clipboard(GtkTextBuffer *buffer, GtkClipboard *clipboard, GtkTextIter *iter, gboolean *default_editable*)
  Attempts to insert the contents of *clipboard* into *buffer* at *iter* (if *iter* is NULL, this function pastes at the current cursor position). See the preceding function for the read-only nuances of this function.

NOTE *Clipboard text insertion occurs asynchronously; that is, GTK+ performs the operation somewhere in its main loop when all of the data is in place. Therefore, don't expect newly inserted text from this function to be immediately available after this function call.*

GtkTextBuffer Signals

There are many signals that go along with **GtkTextBuffer** objects. Most have default handlers that do the actual work, but you can attach additional handlers if you want to add some special features:

- **apply-tag**
  void handler (GtkTextBuffer *buffer, GtkTextTag *tag, GtkTextIter *begin, GtkTextIter *end, gpointer *data*)
  Emitted when the application wants to put *tag* in *buffer* between *begin* and *end*.

- **remove-tag**
  void handler (GtkTextBuffer *buffer, GtkTextTag *tag, GtkTextIter *begin, GtkTextIter *end, gpointer *data*)
  Emitted when the application wants to remove all applications of *tag* in *buffer* between *begin* and *end*.

- **changed**
  void handler (GtkTextBuffer *buffer, gpointer *data*)
  Emitted when *buffer* changes in some way.

- **modified-changed**
  void handler (GtkTextBuffer *buffer*, gpointer *data*)
  Emitted when the program changes the modification status of *buffer* with
  gtk_text_buffer_set_modified(*buffer*).

- **mark-set**
  void handler (GtkTextBuffer *buffer*, GtkTextIter *iter*, GtkTextMark *mark*,
  gpointer *data*)
  Emitted when the program sets *mark* in *buffer* at *iter*. You can attach a handler to this signal to follow cursor or selection movement, because those are
  the marks named **insert** and **selection-bound**.

- **mark-deleted**
  void handler (GtkTextBuffer *buffer*, GtkTextMark *mark*, gpointer *data*)
  Emitted when the program removes *mark* from *buffer*.

- **begin-user-action**
  void handler (GtkTextBuffer *buffer*, gpointer *data*)
  Emitted when the program calls gtk_text_buffer_begin_user_action(*buffer*).

- **end-user-action**
  void handler (GtkTextBuffer *buffer*, gpointer *data*)
  Emitted when the program calls gtk_text_buffer_end_user_action(*buffer*).

3.12.2   Text View Widgets

A **GtkTextView** widget formats and displays a **GtkTextBuffer** object. The most
straightforward way to create a text view is with

```
GtkTextView *view;
GtkTextBuffer *buffer;

view = gtk_text_view_new_with_buffer(buffer);
```

(This assumes that you created the *buffer* object somewhere else in the
program.) However, if you have multiple buffers and you need to select one, you
can create the view with gtk_text_view_new() and display a buffer inside with

```
gtk_text_view_set_buffer(view, buffer)
```

NOTE   *The cursor and selection in text views are marks in the buffer, not a property in the view (as
was the case in tree views). Therefore, you cannot create several views with the same text
buffer that display separate cursor positions and selections.*

GtkTextView objects have several properties that primarily control the text
representation. Note that these are display options and do not deal with the
formatting of the individual characters; use text buffer tags for those features.

- **pixels-above-lines** (gint): The number of pixels to pad above paragraphs.
- **pixels-below-lines** (gint): The number of pixels to pad below paragraphs.
- **pixels-inside-wrap** (gint): The number of pixels between lines at a line break
  in a paragraph.

- **editable** (gboolean): If FALSE, the user may not change anything inside the view.
- **wrap-mode** (GtkWrapMode): The word wrap style. Possible values are

  GTK_WRAP_NONE: No word wrapping; the widget expands to fit any long lines.

  GTK_WRAP_CHAR: Per-character wrap (good for program code).

  GTK_WRAP_WORD: Per-word wrap (good for real language).
- **justification** (GtkJustification): The horizontal text alignment. Possible values are

  GTK_JUSTIFY_LEFT

  GTK_JUSTIFY_RIGHT

  GTK_JUSTIFY_CENTER

  GTK_JUSTIFY_FILL (Fill spaces between characters; this actually isn't implemented in the current version, but this may be all the better because it's ugly.)
- **left-margin** (gint): The number of pixels for the left margin.
- **right-margin** (gint): The number of pixels for the right margin.
- **indent** (gint): The number of pixels to indent paragraphs.
- **cursor-visible** (gboolean): If FALSE, the view hides the cursor.

One other interesting property is **tabs** (PangoTabArray); it controls tab stops. Consult the Pango documentation for more information.

Several functions operate on text views. Most of the interesting utilities involve scrolling to specific parts of the text.

- void gtk_text_view_scroll_to_mark(GtkTextView *view, GtkTextMark *mark, gdouble within_margin, gboolean align, gdouble xalign, gdouble yalign)
  Scrolls to view so that the mark position is visible. The text shows up at a minimum distance from the view border; within_margin is the percentage of the height or width to use as this distance (within_margin may lie between 0.0 and 0.5). If align is TRUE, align the target inside the window based on xalign and yalign instead. Here, 0.0 indicates the left and top, 0.5 indicates the center, and 1.0 indicates the right or bottom.
- void gtk_text_view_scroll_to_iter(GtkTextView *view, GtkTextIter *iter, gdouble within_margin, gboolean align, gdouble xalign, gdouble yalign)
  Like the preceding function, but scrolls to an iterator iter instead of a mark.
- void gtk_text_view_scroll_mark_onscreen(GtkTextView *view, GtkTextMark *mark)
  Scrolls view so that the position of mark is visible.
- gboolean gtk_text_view_move_mark_onscreen(GtkTextView *view, GtkTextMark *mark)
  Moves mark in its buffer to a position currently visible through view. This function returns TRUE if it actually moves the mark.
- gboolean gtk_text_view_place_cursor_onscreen(GtkTextView *view)
  Moves the cursor (and its mark) to a position currently visible through view. This function returns TRUE if it actually moves the cursor.

- `gboolean gtk_text_view_forward_display_line(GtkTextView *view, GtkTextIter *iter)`

  Moves an iterator *iter* forward to the position one line below the current location of *iter* in *view*. This function returns TRUE if it moves the iterator to the correct place (not the end position).

  This is not necessarily the current line offset into the next line in the buffer; it could be in the same text buffer line due to word wrapping.

- `gboolean gtk_text_view_backward_display_line(GtkTextView *view, GtkTextIter *iter)`

  Like the preceding function, but moves *iter* back one line.

- `gboolean gtk_text_view_move_visually(GtkTextView *view, GtkTextIter *iter, gint count)`

  Similar to the preceding functions, but moves *iter* by *count* lines (to move backward, use a negative number for *count*).

- `gboolean gtk_text_view_forward_display_line_end(GtkTextView *view, GtkTextIter *iter)`

  Like the preceding function, but moves *iter* to the end of its current line in *view*.

- `gboolean gtk_text_view_backward_display_line_start(GtkTextView *view, GtkTextIter *iter)`

  Like the preceding function, but moves *iter* to the start of its current line in *view*.

- `gboolean gtk_text_view_backward_starts_display_line(GtkTextView *view, const GtkTextIter *iter)`

  Returns TRUE if *iter* is at the beginning of its current line in *view*.

3.13   Further Topics

An entire book would be needed to describe all of the GTK+ widgets. By this point, though, you have seen the most important widgets and can now proceed to GNOME. Here is what awaits you if you want to delve deeper into GTK+.

- **Accessibility with ATK.** ATK offers many choices for presenting information in and around your widgets so that your application can provide full accessibility. If you do not build your own widgets, you do not have much work to do; the default GTK+ widgets offer built-in accessibility features.

- **GDK.** The link between GTK+ and its underlying windowing system (X11, for the most part) is GDK. All GTK+ widgets use the GDK library to draw to the screen and get input. However, if you don't need to create your own custom widgets, you will hardly ever use GDK.

- **GtkEventBox.** This container holds a single widget and does nothing other than capture events as an X window and send them to its child. This doesn't come up much; examples are context menus on labels, images, and any other widget that doesn't have its own event mechanism.

- **GtkFixed.** If you want to place widgets at fixed pixel positions, put them in a **GtkFixed** container. However, this usually isn't a good idea, because these containers don't respond well to resizing.

- **GdkPixbufAnimation.** This class offers a simple way to display animations.

- **GdkPixbufLoader.** If you have very large graphics, you can use this class to load images piece by piece rather than in one motion.

- **GtkAspectFrame.** This container's width and height always keep the same proportions.

- **GtkCalendar.** A monthly calendar that you can use for data entry. See Section 4.3.10 for **GnomeDataEdit**, a complete widget that provides date and time entry capability.

- **GtkCurve and GtkGammaCurve.** Two very specialized floating-point number mapping widgets that are important to image processing programs such as The GIMP.

- **GtkMessageDialog.** This class provides a quick and easy interface for common dialogs. It is limited in capability, and strangely enough, it's difficult to use for dialogs that conform to GUP guidelines (for example, it makes frowned-upon dialogs with Yes and No buttons). These limitations arise primarily because the class dates from before the guidelines. If you need a lot of dialog boxes, you can create your own utility functions and/or use Glade for the interface design (see Chapter 5).

- **GtkRuler, GtkHRuler, and GtkVRuler.** To precisely position certain elements inside your interface, you can put a ruler widget along one of the edges.

- **GtkSizeGroup.** This class can couple several arbitrary widgets so that they all remain the same size. This comes up very rarely in user applications, because other widgets such as **GtkTable** provide an easier interface.

- **GtkToggleButton.** These widgets are identical in function to **GtkCheckButton** widgets, but don't have a check box. Instead, they stay in a depressed state when turned on and snap up when turned off. You might use toggle buttons if you're really tight on space, but it's best to find a way around them because they look too much like regular buttons. If you absolutely must use them, group them in a place where it's obvious that they are not normal buttons.

- **Selected stock item topics.** The stock item system is expandable; if you find yourself using the same labels and images over and over, you can insert them as stock items so that you can call them by identifier rather than do everything by hand every time. The built-in stock items cover most of the bases, though.

- **Drag-and-drop and transparency in tree views.** Although you can set a tree view to reorder items with a property, you can exert more control by implementing your own system without *too* much trouble. In addition, you can enable interactive transparency in a tree view — for example, you can configure a keystroke to mark a matching row.

- **Pango.** This chapter covers only aspects of Pango relevant to GTK+. You normally do not need direct access to the Pango library.

- **Signals.** Only the most important signals have found their way into this chapter. Many signals come into play only when you develop your own widgets or other do something that is at a similarly lower level.

- **Themes, styles, and *gtkrc* files.** As mentioned earlier, you can significantly change the appearance of GTK+ widgets with themes. You can also alter widget settings on a global or per-class basis with configuration files such as *$HOME/.gtkrc*.

- **Widget development.** You can create your own widgets with GTK+. To do so, you need to derive a new class from some base class and then expand the class as shown in Chapter 2. If this doesn't suit your needs, you can employ GDK's drawing and event primitives to create an entirely new widget.

4

THE GNOME LIBRARIES

Previously, the GNOME libraries primarily contained GTK+ extensions. However, GTK+ 2 integrated several GNOME capabilities. GNOME still contains a few widgets that serve as replacements and enhancements to GTK+ widgets, and GNOME applications attempt to use these widgets as much as possible.

To build modern graphical user interfaces, you need additional tools not directly related to user operation and graphics. The GNOME system components that provide this functionality are the subjects of the remaining chapters.

4.1 What Characterizes a GNOME Application?

A GNOME application may use these libraries:

- **libgnome-2**: Graphics-independent GNOME core library (Section 4.2).
- **libgnomeui-2**: Graphics-dependent GNOME core library (Section 4.3).
- **libgnomecanvas-2**: GNOME canvas widget.
- **libgnomevfs-2**: GNOME file access abstraction layer (see Chapter 8).

- **libbonobo-2**: Graphics-independent component object model (not covered in this book).

- **libbonoboui-2**: Graphics-dependent component object model.

- **libbonobo-activation**: Bonobo's object activation system.

These libraries depend on a number of other libraries, but you won't normally need to directly access these extras.

GNOME developers use the functionality in these libraries whenever possible so that they don't have to reinvent the wheel and require even more memory or libraries. GNOME applications should behave well with each other and have a consistent look and feel. You can achieve this with the following:

- Adherence to the GNOME user interface guidelines (see Section 3.1).

- Stock items for uniform icon, label, and translation appearance in buttons, menus, and tool lists whenever possible.

- Help buttons and menus to activate documentation in the ScrollKeeper database (see Section 6.4.1).

- Smooth integration with the GNOME main menu (see Section 6.3).

- Interaction with the GNOME *Session Manager* (see Section 4.3.16).

- Configuration with GConf (see Chapter 7).

- File access with GnomeVFS (see Chapter 8).

4.1.1 *"Take This GNOME and Shove It"*

Among GTK+ developers is a small but vocal minority that wants no truck with the GNOME libraries. The reasons are somewhat unclear, but the most frequent argument is that linking with GNOME causes bloat in "lean" GTK+ programs.

On the surface, this sentiment appears to have some truth, because GNOME applications usually link against more than 30 libraries. However, many of these "pure" programs wander into GNOME territory anyway. One especially absurd situation can arise when it comes to viewing HTML. For example, the mail program CscMail comes with a modified version of the GNOME GtkHtml library named CscHtml. Only the name has changed; the functionality is identical.

This sort of situation can waste even more memory because the application does not link against a popular library, and there are other possible trouble spots. Therefore, it saves memory to link against GNOME — you should definitely think twice before coming up with your own solutions when GNOME already has one.

You may take some comfort in knowing that there aren't any plans to add more GNOME widgets. Instead, the new widgets go directly into GTK+ (and some of the old ones do, too).

4.2 libgnome

The *libgnome* library contains core GNOME code that has nothing to do with X11 (the graphical part is in *libgnomeui*). If you want to write command-line tools that use GNOME, you can do this if you use the features only in *libgnome*, not *libgnomeui*.

Other libraries reflect this separation between graphical and nongraphical modules. For example, Bonobo and Gnome-Print exhibit the same division. One of the consequences of the split in the core library, though, is that *libgnome* doesn't do a whole lot.

4.2.1 Initializing GNOME

Recall from Chapter 3 that all pure GTK+ programs share a common gtk_init() call and run gtk_main() to start the main event loop. GNOME applications also use gtk_main(), but their initialization is different because they must initialize every piece of the GNOME system.

To set up a GNOME application, create an object of the **GnomeProgram** (GNOME_TYPE_PROGRAM) class. You do this with a generator function:

```
#include <gnome.h>

GnomeProgram *app;

app = gnome_program_init(application_id,
                         application_version,
                         module_info,
                         argc,
                         argv,
                         [property list,]
                         NULL);
```

The parameters are as follows:

- *application_id* (char *): The *application identifier* string. The identifier is normally the name of the executable file. Later, this string serves as a directory name in the GNOME directory tree for any application-specific files.

- *application_version* (char *): The application's version number, as a string.

- *module_info* (GnomeModuleInfo *): The GNOME module identifier. The most useful values are LIBGNOMEUI_MODULE for graphical applications and LIBGNOME_MODULE for other programs.

- *argc* (int): Command-line argument count; normally argc from main().

- *argv* (char **): Command-line arguments; normally argc from main().

- *property list*: A list of key-value properties. The important keys and values are

  GNOME_PARAM_POPT_TABLE: A table of command-line parameters for the popt library (GNOME uses popt to parse parameters). If you have application-specific parameters, you can recognize them with the popt API. See [Johnson] for more information.

  GNOME_PARAM_POPT_FLAGS: Options for popt.

  GNOME_PARAM_POPT_CONTEXT: Context for popt.

  GNOME_PARAM_ENABLE_SOUND (gboolean): If TRUE, the application can make noise.

  GNOME_PARAM_HUMAN_READABLE_NAME (gchararray): The familiar name of the application, that is, something that humans might recognize. This string goes in menus and other locations. For example, "MiracleText" might be the human-readable name of miracletext.

  GNOME_PARAM_SM_CONNECT (gboolean): Set this to FALSE if you want this program to ignore the session manager. Normally, you want to be able to respond, so the default for this property is TRUE.

You should always specify GNOME_PARAM_STANDARD_PROPERTIES in the list in addition to the preceding properties. This isn't a true key; you do *not* supply a value with it. Instead, this is a macro that expands to the GNU-style directory identifiers and locations:

- PREFIX: Installation prefix (for example, */opt/gnome* or */usr/local*).
- SYSCONFDIR: Installation file directory (for example, *$(PREFIX)/etc*).
- DATADIR: Application data directory (for example, *$(PREFIX)/share*).
- LIBDIR: Library directory (for example, *$(PREFIX)/lib*).

The GNU autotools (see Section 6.2) can set these macros for you. Otherwise, you should define them in your Makefile.

Here is a simple program skeleton:

```
#include <gnome.h>

int main(int argc, char **argv)
{
  GnomeProgram *program;

  program = gnome_program_init("skeleton",
                               "0.1",
                               LIBGNOMEUI_MODULE,
                               argc, argv,
                               GNOME_PROGRAM_STANDARD_PROPERTIES,
                               GNOME_PARAM_HUMAN_READABLE_NAME, "Skeleton",
                               GNOME_PARAM_ENABLE_SOUND, FALSE,
                               NULL);

  /* rest of main program goes here */
```

```
  gtk_main();

  exit(0);
}
```

Without GNU autotools, the Makefile looks something like this:

```
PREFIX = /opt/gnome

CFLAGS = `pkg-config --cflags libgnomeui-2.0` -ansi -Wall \
            -DPREFIX=\""$(PREFIX)"\" \
            -DDATADIR=\""$(PREFIX)/share"\" \
            -DSYSCONFDIR=\""$(PREFIX)/etc"\" \
            -DLIBDIR=\""$(PREFIX)/lib"\"

LIBS = `pkg-config --libs libgnomeui-2.0`

skeleton: skeleton.c
        gcc -o skeleton skeleton.c $(CFLAGS) $(LIBS)
```

4.2.2   Utility Functions

One of the most important functions in the GNOME libraries locates a file:

```
char *path;

path = gnome_program_locate_file(program, domain, file_name, if_exists,
                                 ret_locations);
```

The return value is a newly allocated string pointer containing a file pathname if any file matched the criteria:

- *program* (GnomeProgram *): Your program object.
- *domain* (GnomeFileDomain): Determines the file type. Possible values include

    GNOME_FILE_DOMAIN_LIBDIR: GNOME libraries.

    GNOME_FILE_DOMAIN_DATADIR: GNOME data files.

    GNOME_FILE_DOMAIN_SOUND: GNOME sound files.

    GNOME_FILE_DOMAIN_PIXMAP: GNOME images.

    GNOME_FILE_DOMAIN_CONFIG: GNOME configuration files.

    GNOME_FILE_DOMAIN_HELP: GNOME help files.

    GNOME_FILE_DOMAIN_APP_LIBDIR: Application libraries.

    GNOME_FILE_DOMAIN_APP_DATADIR: Application data files.

    GNOME_FILE_DOMAIN_APP_SOUND: Application sound files.

    GNOME_FILE_DOMAIN_APP_PIXMAP: Application images.

    GNOME_FILE_DOMAIN_APP_CONFIG: Application configuration files.

    GNOME_FILE_DOMAIN_HELP: Application files.

Each of these names pertains to a directory with a standard path prefix. _APP_ domains refer to application-specific directories obtained from *program* (described earlier); they don't necessarily need to be anywhere near the GNOME core libraries, but they should at least have the same directory structure (lib for libraries, share for data, and so on).

- *file_name* (char *): The desired filename.

- *if_exists* (gboolean): If TRUE, GNOME returns the full pathname if there is actually a file in that location (and NULL otherwise). However, if you set *if_exists* to FALSE, a full pathname comes back even if the file doesn't exist.

- *ret_locations* (GSList **): If you need to know if there are multiple files matching *file_name*, pass the address of a GSList pointer here; GNOME creates a new list containing all matching pathnames at that pointer. You need to free the list when you're done. You can specify NULL here if you don't care.

The gnome_program_file_locate() function is the GNOME-approved method of finding application configuration and data files because it guarantees a correct pathname (at least with a properly installed system) and makes problems easier to track down.

Here is an example:

```
char *path;

/* find the green apple image; it should be in the standard
   GNOME pixmap directory */
path = gnome_program_locate_file(program,
                                 GNOME_FILE_DOMAIN_PIXMAP,
                                 "apple-green.png",
                                 TRUE,
                                 NULL);

g_print("Path for green apple: %s\n", path);
g_free(path);

/* look for an application-specific sound file --
   do not verify that it exists */
path = gnome_program_locate_file(program,
                                 GNOME_FILE_DOMAIN_APP_SOUND,
                                 "plop.wav",
                                 FALSE,
                                 NULL);

g_print("Alleged path for plop sound: %s\n", path);
g_free(path);

/* look for the same application-specific sound file --
   this time, return a path only if the file exists */
path = gnome_program_locate_file(program,
                                 GNOME_FILE_DOMAIN_APP_SOUND,
                                 "plop.wav",
```

```
                        TRUE,
                        NULL);

if (path)
{
   g_print(" ... the actual location is %s.\n", path);
   g_free(path);
} else {
   g_print(" ... however, plop.wav isn't there.\n");
}
```

Another useful function is

```
gnome_util_prepend_user_home(relative_path)
```

This returns a newly allocated string with the current user's home directory prepended to *relative_path*. If you want to go even further and specify a file in the user's personal GNOME directory (*.gnome2*), call

```
gnome_util_home_file(relative_path)
```

As usual, you have to free up the return value:

```
/* directory prepend functions */
path = gnome_util_prepend_user_home("pictures/house.png");
g_print("Path for house.png: %s\n", path);
g_free(path);

path = gnome_util_home_file("mega-app/config");
g_print("Path for mega-app configuration: %s\n", path);
g_free(path);
```

NOTE *You will likely call* gnome_util_home_file() *more than its counterpart, because it really isn't good style to clutter a user's home directory with nonstandard (and sometimes weird) configuration files and subdirectories. Furthermore, you should use GConf to store application configuration (see Chapter 7).*

If you need to find a file extension in a path, use the strangely named

```
g_extension_pointer(path)
```

If *path* ends with an extension, this function returns a pointer to that extension, after the period. This utility does not allocate new memory. If there is no extension, a pointer to the end of *path* comes back as the return value.

Executing Programs

The GNOME libraries include several functions for running external programs. Among these are asynchronous calls that fork off a program and let it run in the background.

These functions look somewhat similar to Unix system calls that use an array of command-line arguments (argv). The array's first element is a string containing the program name, followed by the program's parameters. You must provide the total count of program and parameters names separately with argc.

NOTE *Many of the following functions partially duplicate GLib GSpawn facilities (and are thus around for compatibility). You may want to look at the GLib reference documentation before using one of these.*

- int gnome_execute_async(const char *dir, int argc, char *const argv[])
  Runs the new process in *dir*. For the current directory, use NULL for *dir*. The return value is the process ID (PID) of the new program. If the program fails to start at all (that is, if it doesn't exist or some other problem occurs), the return value is –1.

- int gnome_execute_async_fds(const char *dir, int argc, char *const argv[], gboolean close_fds)
  Like the preceding function, but if *close_fds* is TRUE, the new process does not share any file descriptors with its parent other than the standard input, output, and error.

- int gnome_execute_async_with_env(const char *dir, int argc, char *const argv[], int envc, char *const envv[])
  Like gnome_execute_async(), but adds the environment variables in *envv* to the new child process. One entry in *envv* has the form VAR=*value*; *envc* is the number of elements in *envv*.

- int gnome_execute_async_with_env_fds(const char *dir, int argc, char *const argv[], int envc, char *const envv[], gboolean close_fds)
  Like the preceding function, but with the file description behavior in gnome_execute_async_fds().

If you want to run a process in a terminal window with one of the preceding functions, you can alter your *argc* and *argv* with this function:

---

int gnome_prepend_terminal_to_vector(int *argc, char ***argv)

This function writes a new argument vector containing a terminal program and sets the *argv* pointer to the new vector.

WARNING *You must create *argv with g_malloc(), and you must also individually create each of this array's component strings with g_malloc(). This function deallocates your original vector, so you can expect a core dump if you give it some nondynamic memory or try to use your original argument vector after the call.*

If you would rather start your new process with a shell, use one of these functions:

- int gnome_execute_shell(const char *dir, const char *command)
  Runs *command* in the directory *dir* with the user's default shell. Use NULL for the current directory. As with all other functions in this section, the command is forked off; the return value is the new process ID, or –1 if the command does not execute properly.

- int gnome_execute_terminal_shell(const char *dir, const char *command)
  Like the preceding function, but runs the command in a terminal window.
- int gnome_execute_shell_fds(const char *dir, const char *command, gboolean close_fds)
  Like gnome_execute_shell(), but does not pass any file descriptors other than standard input, output, and error if close_fds is TRUE.
- int gnome_execute_terminal_shell_fds(const char *dir, const char *command, gboolean close_fds)
  Like the preceding function, but runs the command in a terminal window.

WARNING *For any function in this section, be careful if some of your arguments come from the network. It's far too easy to open security holes this way. Be especially careful when starting things with the shell — it is a very powerful tool.*

Displaying URLs

You can make GNOME show a URL without worrying about the program responsible for viewing the content behind the URL. There is a central configuration mapping; if you want to show a website or FTP index to the user, you can do it with a single function:

```
gboolean gnome_url_show(const char *url, GError **error)
```

Here, *url* is a string containing the target URL, and *error* is a GError pointer (error class: GNOME_URL_ERROR). This function attempts to interpret the URL and send it to the appropriate helper program. Upon success, this function returns TRUE.

At the moment, the only error code you might get in *error* if there's a problem is GNOME_ERROR_URL_PARSE if a syntax error occurs in the URL.

Here is a short example:

```
GError *error;

gnome_url_show("http://www.gnome.org/" &error);
if (error != NULL)
{
  g_printerr("Can't open URL: %s\n", error->message);
  g_error_free(error);
}
```

NOTE *For the most part, your applications should display a URL in response to user input. In this case, you shouldn't use gnome_url_show(). **GnomeHRef** widgets work better. See Section 4.3.11 for more information.*

If you need to change the environment of the helper program (for example, to send to a different display), put the new environment variables in an array of strings *envp* (each string should be in the form VAR=value) and call this function:

```
gboolean gnome_url_show_with_env(const char *url, char **envp, GError **error)
```

Displaying Help

Help files use a special URI protocol (`ghelp:`), separate from other URL mechanisms. GNOME sends help data to a browser such as Yelp rather than a generic web browser.

To view a help file, use

```
gnome_help_display(filename, link_id, error)
```

If GNOME finds a help file matching *filename*, it displays the content, skipping to the section named `link_id` (this can be `NULL` if there is no section). Upon success, this function returns `TRUE`. The GError class for *error* is `GNOME_HELP_ERROR`, with one of these codes:

- `GNOME_HELP_ERROR_NOT_FOUND`: There is no such help file.
- `GNOME_HELP_ERROR_INTERNAL`: Unspecified help system error.

If you tell `gnome_help_display()` to look for *foo*, GNOME goes to the help directory for the current application to look for a matching file, including *foo.xml*, *foo.docbook*, *foo.sgml*, and *foo.html*. Therefore, if you install your help documents according to the conventions in Section 6.4.1, you do not need to worry about a subdirectory or extension.

Your program's help file (*filename*) should match the application identifier string because this makes it especially easy to jump to the main help index page. For example, assume that `miracletext` is your application ID and you choose *miracletext.xml* as the help filename.

Here are a few `gnome_help_display()` examples:

```
/* show main help page */
gnome_help_display("miracletext", NULL, NULL);

/* show main_window section of the same help page */
gnome_help_display("miracletext", "main_window", NULL);
```

4.2.3 Sound

GNOME has a primitive API for attaching sounds to events. On systems that do not support sound, these functions are harmless.

NOTE   *Although you can decorate events with sound in your application, don't expect miracles and do not make the usability of your programs depend on sounds. In addition, remember that some people find computer sounds annoying and therefore disable sound.*

If you just want to play a sound somewhere in your code, call

```
gnome_sound_play(sound_file)
```

where *sound_file* is the name of a sound file.

It's more likely that you want to attach a sound to an event in your application. Follow these steps:

1. Install the default sound file for the event in the GNOME sound directory (normally *$(PREFIX)/share/sounds*). You should try to put the file in a new directory that matches the name of your application (for example, */opt/gnome/share/sounds/miracletext*).

2. Create a file called *appname.soundlist* in *$(PREFIX)/etc/sound/events*, where *appname* is your program's application identifier string (see the following discussion for the format). For the continuing example, it would be */opt/gnome/etc/sound/events/miracletext.soundlist*.

3. Call gnome_triggers_do() in your event handlers to play the sound (more on this shortly).

NOTE *Use a .wav file for your sound, not an esoteric format. The user should find the sound comfortable — not too shrill, not too low, not too loud, not too quiet, and most important, not too long. Five seconds is the extreme maximum, but that can be an eternity when the user repeatedly encounters the sound.*

Here's a sample *.soundlist* file (encode this in UTF-8):

```
[__section_info__]
description=MiracleText

[miracle]
file=miracletext/miracle.wav
description=Miracle
description[de]=Wunder
description[es]=Milagro

[miracle_big]
file=miracletext/miracle_big.wav
description=Big Miracle
description[de]=Wunderbares Wunder
description[es]=Milagro Grande
```

This file breaks down into several sections, denoted with square brackets ([ ]). In the first section, __section_info__ is a special identifier; this section contains global definitions for the following sections. In the second and third sections, [miracle] and [miracle_big] define specific sound events.

The keys and settings in the sections are as follows:

- description describes the sound event. In __section_info__, this is the program description.

- file is the filename relative to *$(PREFIX)/share/sounds*.

NOTE *You can override a setting for a particular language by placing the language code within square brackets after the key.*

If all files are in the right locations, the user can also change the sound events with the **Sound** preference tool.

To connect the sounds to events, call

```
gnome_triggers_do(message, "program", app_id, event_id, NULL)
```

Here, *message* is an optional additional message, *app_id* is your application identifier, and *event_id* is the event identifier from the *.soundlist* file (gnome_triggers_do() does much more than this, so that is why the syntax looks a little strange). Here is an example:

```
/* event that tells you that a miracle happened */
gnome_triggers_do("A miracle occurred!",
                  "program", "miracletext", "miracle", NULL);

/* for really big miracles, you don't need to put it in writing */
gnome_triggers_do("", "program", "miracletext", "miracle_big", NULL);
```

4.2.4 Scores

If your GNOME application happens to be a game, you will inevitably run into the problem of how to maintain a high score table. Maintaining a high score table with fairly strict permissions is not terribly easy. The traditional Unix solution is to keep the scores in a directory accessible by the games group and make the game executables set-groupid games. However, GNOME offers a slightly easier way with three function calls that you will probably call in this order:

1. When you initialize your main program, call gint gnome_score_init(const char *game_name). Set *game_name* to your application identifier. This function returns 0 upon success and −1 if something goes wrong.

2. At the end of each game, call gint gnome_score_log(gfloat *score*, const gchar *score, gboolean *descending*) to enter *score* and *score* into the high score table. Set *descending* to TRUE if a lower score is better in your game (a golf game, for example). This function returns the new score's rank in the table (starting at 1), or 0 if an error occurs.

3. If you need to get the data in a high score table, use gint gnome_score_get_notable(const gchar *game_name, const gchar *level, gchar ***names, gfloat **scores, time_t **score_times) to fill arrays for the high scores, the player names, and times of the scores for *game_name* at *level*. This function returns the number of entries in the high score table. All of the the new information goes into newly allocated arrays; you must free everything inside with g_free().

NOTE   *It may ease your mind to know that you do not normally need to bother with the terrifying* gnome_score_get_notable(). *You can create a **GnomeScores** widget to display a high score list (see Section 4.3.12).*

4.3 libgnomeui

GNOME's *libgnomeui* includes several widgets and a support API to ensure that your programs are consistent and interact with other applications. In addition, they can keep your own code base small — you need worry about only what is important to your application; *libgnomeui* takes care of the boring parts such as menu bars and druid pages.

4.3.1 Application Windows

In Chapter 3, you placed widgets into otherwise empty **GtkWindow** objects. GNOME applications use a standardized window with these elements:

- **Menu bar**: At the top of the window.

- **Status bar**: At the bottom of the window.

- **Toolbars**: At least one, perhaps more; can be configured as movable and draggable.

- **Docked elements**: Any other draggable and/or detachable elements in the window.

GNOME has a single mechanism for creating these elements according to a global configuration. For example, your application will conform to the user's preference for icons in toolbars (**Applications > Desktop Preferences > Menus & Toolbars**).

Use the **GnomeApp** (`GNOME_TYPE_APP`) widget as the main window for all of your applications. When you create a **GnomeApp** object, always set its `app-id` property to the application identifier first mentioned in Section 4.2.1. **GnomeApp** is a subclass of **GtkWindow**, so you can also set its title and initial size as usual.

To set an application window title according to a document name, use

```
gnome_window_toplevel_set_title(window, document, app, extension)
```

Here, `window` is a top-level window casted as a **GtkWindow** object, `document` is a document filename, `app` is your application name, and `extension` is a filename extension. You can set `extension` to NULL to keep the document name intact in the window title.

You should outfit your window with an icon that appears in the window list and other places.

Here is how an application might set the title and icons:

```
GnomeApp *window, *apple_window;
gchar *icon;

  << ... >>

/* set title */
gnome_window_toplevel_set_title(GTK_WINDOW(window),
                                "order-2003-08.mtx",
```

```
                              "MiracleText",
                              ".mtx");

/* set icon for the apple window */
icon = gnome_program_locate_file(program, GNOME_FILE_DOMAIN_PIXMAP,
                                 "apple-green.png", TRUE, NULL);
gtk_window_icon_set_from_file(GTK_WINDOW(apple_window), icon);
g_free(icon);
```

This section concludes with a full working sample application that also provides your first real exposure to GTK+ menus.

Start with the normal GTK+ event handlers:

```
/* -*-coding: utf-8;-*- */
/* appdemo.c -- bare-bones GnomeApp */

#include <gnome.h>

/* standard event handlers */
gint delete_event(GtkWidget *widget, GdkEvent event, gpointer data)
{
  return FALSE;
}

void end_program(GtkWidget *widget, gpointer data)
{
  gtk_main_quit();
}
```

Here is the event handler for all items on the **Edit** menu:

```
void edit_handler(GtkWidget *item, gpointer data)
{
  g_print("`%s' called\n", (gchar *)data);
}
```

All GtkWidget declarations in the following main program are for menu items:

```
int main(int argc, char **argv)
{
  GnomeProgram *program;
  GnomeApp *window;
  GtkAccelGroup *accel_g;
  GtkMenuBar *menu_bar;
  GtkWidget *file, *edit, *help,
            *file_close,
            *edit_cut, *edit_copy, *edit_paste,
            *help_index, *help_about;
  GtkMenu *file_menu, *edit_menu, *help_menu;
  GtkToolbar *tools;
  GtkStatusbar *status;
  GtkLabel *label;
```

The application initialization includes the GNOME initialization from *libgnome,* the **GnomeApp** class from *libgnomeui,* and the usual event handlers from GTK+:

```
/* initialize GNOME */
program = gnome_program_init("appdemo",
                             "0.1",
                             LIBGNOMEUI_MODULE,
                             argc, argv,
                             GNOME_PROGRAM_STANDARD_PROPERTIES,
                             GNOME_PARAM_HUMAN_READABLE_NAME, "AppDemo",
                             GNOME_PARAM_ENABLE_SOUND, TRUE,
                             NULL);

/* create main window */
window = g_object_new(GNOME_TYPE_APP,
                      "title", "Application Window",
                      "app-id", "appdemo",
                      "default-width", 300,
                      "default-height", 300,
                      NULL);

/* attach standard event handlers */
g_signal_connect(window, "delete_event", G_CALLBACK(delete_event), NULL);
g_signal_connect(window, "destroy", G_CALLBACK(end_program), NULL);
```

Menu item generator functions want an accelerator group argument, so we'll create one here:

```
/* add accelerator group */
accel_g = g_object_new(GTK_TYPE_ACCEL_GROUP, NULL);
gtk_window_add_accel_group(GTK_WINDOW(window), accel_g);
```

Menu bars, toolbars, and status bars have their own GTK+ widgets.

```
/* create menu/tool/status bars */
menu_bar = g_object_new(GTK_TYPE_MENU_BAR, NULL);
tools = g_object_new(GTK_TYPE_TOOLBAR, NULL);
status = g_object_new(GTK_TYPE_STATUSBAR, NULL);
```

Now it's time to create the **File** menu. Start with the menu items and work your way up. Each menu item is an individual object. Because **Close** is a very common menu item, it is in the stock library. Notice the *activate* signal, emitted when the user chooses the menu item.

```
/* create file close item */
file_close = gtk_image_menu_item_new_from_stock(GTK_STOCK_CLOSE, accel_g);

/* attach the standard window destroy handler for the close item */
g_signal_connect(file_close, "activate", G_CALLBACK(end_program), NULL);
```

A menu is a container widget that holds menu items:

```
/* create file menu and attach the close item */
file_menu = g_object_new(GTK_TYPE_MENU, NULL);
gtk_menu_shell_append(GTK_MENU_SHELL(file_menu), file_close);
```

To see the menu, the user clicks yet another item. The following code creates an item labeled **File**, puts it into the menu bar, and attaches its menu (file_menu).

```
/* create the item for "File" in the menu bar and attach the menu */
file = gtk_menu_item_new_with_mnemonic("_File");
gtk_menu_shell_append(GTK_MENU_SHELL(menu_bar), file);
gtk_menu_item_set_submenu(GTK_MENU_ITEM(file), GTK_WIDGET(file_menu));
```

Edit and **Help** menus are nearly identical to those for **File**:

```
/* create edit menu items */
edit_cut = gtk_image_menu_item_new_from_stock(GTK_STOCK_CUT, accel_g);
/* use a custom handler */
g_signal_connect(edit_cut, "activate", G_CALLBACK(edit_handler), "Cut");

/* do the same for copy and paste items */
edit_copy = gtk_image_menu_item_new_from_stock(GTK_STOCK_COPY, accel_g);
g_signal_connect(edit_copy, "activate", G_CALLBACK(edit_handler), "Copy");

edit_paste = gtk_image_menu_item_new_from_stock(GTK_STOCK_PASTE, accel_g);
g_signal_connect(edit_paste, "activate", G_CALLBACK(edit_handler), "Paste");

/* create edit menu and put items inside */
edit_menu = g_object_new(GTK_TYPE_MENU, NULL);
gtk_menu_shell_append(GTK_MENU_SHELL(edit_menu), edit_cut);
gtk_menu_shell_append(GTK_MENU_SHELL(edit_menu), edit_copy);
gtk_menu_shell_append(GTK_MENU_SHELL(edit_menu), edit_paste);

/* create the item for "Edit" in the menu bar and attach the menu */
edit = gtk_menu_item_new_with_mnemonic( "_Edit");
gtk_menu_shell_append(GTK_MENU_SHELL(menu_bar), edit);
gtk_menu_item_set_submenu(GTK_MENU_ITEM(edit), GTK_WIDGET(edit_menu));

/* make a help menu */
help_index = gtk_image_menu_item_new_from_stock(GTK_STOCK_HELP, accel_g);
help_about = gtk_image_menu_item_new_from_stock(GNOME_STOCK_ABOUT, accel_g);

help_menu = g_object_new(GTK_TYPE_MENU, NULL);
gtk_menu_shell_append(GTK_MENU_SHELL(help_menu), help_index);
gtk_menu_shell_append(GTK_MENU_SHELL(help_menu), help_about);

help = gtk_menu_item_new_with_mnemonic("_Help");
gtk_menu_shell_append(GTK_MENU_SHELL(menu_bar), help);
gtk_menu_item_set_submenu(GTK_MENU_ITEM(help), GTK_WIDGET(help_menu));
```

Now you can declare the menu bar from earlier as the main application menu bar. Notice that you must show the menu bar separately from the rest of the application, because menus aren't normally visible (the menu bar is a special kind of menu).

```
/* place menus into application window and show everything */
gnome_app_set_menus(window, menu_bar);
gtk_widget_show_all(GTK_WIDGET(menu_bar));
```

Creating toolbar buttons and attaching handlers is simple:

```
/* put some buttons in the toolbar */
gtk_toolbar_insert_stock(tools, GTK_STOCK_CUT,
                         "Delete selection and place into clipboard",
                         NULL, G_CALLBACK(edit_handler), "Cut", -1);

gtk_toolbar_insert_stock(tools, GTK_STOCK_COPY,
                         "Copy selection to clipboard",
                         NULL, G_CALLBACK(edit_handler), "Copy", -1);

gtk_toolbar_insert_stock(tools, GTK_STOCK_PASTE,
                         "Paste clipboard",
                         NULL, G_CALLBACK(edit_handler), "Paste", -1);

/* put toolbar in main application window */
gnome_app_set_toolbar(window, tools);
```

This application has a status bar, but does nothing with it.

```
/* add the status bar */
gnome_app_set_statusbar(window, GTK_WIDGET(status));
```

The main window in this application contains a single label:

```
/* a simple placeholder label as the content */
label = g_object_new(GTK_TYPE_LABEL, "label", "Your idea goes here.", NULL);

/* set the label as the application content */
gnome_app_set_contents(window, GTK_WIDGET(label));
```

Show the window and everything inside (except the menus) just as you did with GTK+. Figure 4.1 on the next page shows this application.

```
/* show everything and start GTK+ main event loop */
gtk_widget_show_all(GTK_WIDGET(window));
gtk_main();

return 0;
}
```

Figure 4.1: Basic GNOME application: menu bar, toolbar, contents, and status bar.

The big picture that you should take away from this example is that after you create a **GnomeApp**, you need to put things into its menu bar, toolbar, main content window, and status bar. Otherwise, a GNOME application's widget setup is not significantly different from a GTK+ application.

Menus

There are two menu container widgets: **GtkMenu** (GTK_TYPE_MENU) to hold menu items, and **GtkMenuBar** to hold several menus. Technically, these two classes are the same — menus are vertical containers and menu bars are horizontal containers. They are both subclasses of **GtkMenuShell**, so you frequently see menu_shell API when placing widgets into menus.

NOTE *You can have more than one menu bar in your application, but it would violate nearly every axiom of user-friendly GUI development. **GnomeApp** defines only one built-in menu bar.*

To get started with menus, you need to create a number of *items*. Each item in a menu container is an object of the **GtkMenuItem** (GTK_TYPE_MENU_ITEM) class or its subclasses.

GtkMenuItem displays only text. Its subclasses can do more:

- **GtkImageMenuItem** (GTK_TYPE_IMAGE_MENU_ITEM): Icons and other images.
- **GtkCheckMenuItem** (GTK_TYPE_CHECK_MENU_ITEM): Check (toggled) items.
- **GtkRadioMenuItem** (GTK_TYPE_RADIO_MENU_ITEM): Radio items.
- **GtkSeparatorMenuItem** (GTK_TYPE_CHECK_MENU_ITEM): Menu separators.

You can create menu items with generator functions. For normal **GtkMenuItem** objects, call

```
GtkWidget *item;

item = gtk_menu_item_new_with_mnemonic(label);
```

where *label* is the item text. You can put an underscore (_) in front of the character that you want as a keyboard shortcut.

NOTE *All menu item generator functions return objects of the* GTK_TYPE_WIDGET *type, and menu API functions expect this type. Therefore, it's much easier to declare menu item variables as* GtkWidget * *rather than* GtkMenuItem *. In theory, this looks somewhat unclean, but in practice, you will save a lot of space and development time because you won't need to cast the object every time you want to use it.*

To create a menu entry containing an image, use

```
gtk_image_menu_item_new_with_mnemonic(label)
```

After you get the item object, set its **image** property to a **GtkImage** widget (see Section 3.3.2). Although you can put any widget into the item, you should stick to images that are 16×16 pixels.

For the most part, you can choose stock images and labels for menu items. There is a special function for creating an image widget from the stock item library:

```
gtk_image_menu_item_new_from_stock(stock_id, accel_group)
```

Here, *stock_id* is an identifier as described in Section 3.3.2. If you want the item's keyboard operation defined by the stock item library, supply a **GtkAccelGroup** object as *accel_group* (see Section 3.8.2). If you don't care, use NULL.

GTK+ emits the **activate** signal when the user selects a menu item. The signal handler prototype looks like this:

```
void handler(GtkWidget *item, gpointer data);
```

NOTE *This signal and handler work with the more complex menu items described in a moment, but aren't terribly useful with those items.*

To create a check (box) menu item, use

```
gtk_check_menu_item_new_with_mnemonic(label)
```

Like regular check buttons, these items have the gboolean properties **active** and **inconsistent** for the items' current state. You can detect state changes by attaching a handler to the **toggled** signal. The prototype here is

```
void handler(GtkCheckMenuItem *item, gpointer data);
```

Radio button menu items are somewhat more complex because you must group them with a GSList parameter:

```
gtk_radio_menu_item_new_with_mnemonic(group, label)
```

You can build group as you create a set of radio menu items. Start with NULL, and after you create each item, call

```
group = gtk_radio_menu_item_get_group(item);
```

With this method, you rarely need to deal with the actual elements of the radio group. Here is an example:

```
GSList *group = NULL;
GtkWidget *radio[4];
gint i;

gchar *text[] = {
  "_CD",
  "_Phono",
  "_Tape",
  "Tune_r"
};

for (i = 0; i < 4; i++)
{
  radio[i] = gtk_radio_menu_item_new_with_mnemonic(group, text[i]);
  group = gtk_radio_menu_item_get_group(GTK_RADIO_MENU_ITEM(radio[i]));
}

g_object_set(radio[1], "active", TRUE, NULL);
```

NOTE   *Make sure that you set the default item's* **active** *property to* TRUE *after you create a group of radio items.*

GtkRadioMenuItem is a subclass of **GtkCheckMenuItem**, so it inherits the **toggled** signal in addition to the **active** property.

If you do not want to allow keyboard operation with your menu items, use one of these functions (they operate just like their _with_mnemonic() counterparts, but without the underscore in the label):

```
gtk_menu_item_new_with_label(label)
gtk_image_menu_item_new_with_label(label)
gtk_check_menu_item_new_with_label(label)
gtk_radio_menu_item_new_with_label(group, label)
```

To create a line in your menu (for example, to separate a group of radio items from other items), use

```
gtk_separator_menu_item_new()
```

Now that you have your menu items, you must add them to a menu. The **GtkMenuShell** API performs these operations:

- void gtk_menu_shell_append(GtkMenuShell *menu, GtkWidget *child)
  Adds *child* to the bottom (or right) of *menu*.

- void gtk_menu_shell_prepend(GtkMenuShell *menu, GtkWidget *child)
  Adds *child* to the top (or left) of *menu*.

- void gtk_menu_shell_insert(GtkMenuShell *menu, GtkWidget *child, gint *position*)
  Inserts *child* at slot *position* in *menu*. The first position in a menu is 0.

After all of your items are in a menu, you need some way to activate the menu. Build a **GtkMenuBar** container filled with menu heading items (for example, **File** and **Edit**). The idea is that the user clicks one of these to activate the regular vertical menu, and therefore, what you're really trying to do is attach a submenu to an item in the menu bar (if this sounds confusing, refer back to the example program to see how this works in practice). To attach a submenu to a menu item, use

---

gtk_menu_item_set_submenu(*menu_item*, *submenu*)

NOTE *For this function,* menu_item *is a **GtkMenuItem** object, and* submenu *is a **GtkWidget**. If you declared your menu items as* GtkWidget, *you need to do some casting for this function.*

To remove an item's submenu, use

---

gtk_menu_item_remove_submenu(*menu_item*)

In summary, to build a menu hierarchy with a menu bar, follow these steps:

1. Create the menu items according to these guidelines:

    In general, use the _with_mnemonic generator functions to create labels with unique keyboard shortcuts.

    If a plain **GtkMenuItem** object does not contain a submenu, set its **activate** signal handler.

    For **GtkImageMenuItem** objects, set the image property to specify a custom image. When using stock items, you need a **GtkAccelGroup** object to make the keyboard operation work.

    For **GtkCheckMenuItem** objects, you might want to attach a handler to the **toggled** signal.

    For **GtkRadioMenuItem** objects, you need a GSList for the radio button group. You should also set one of the radio items in a group to active (meaning that it is the default button).

2. Create a menu bar and fill it with items to activate each of your menus. As before, assign unique keyboard operators.

3. Create submenu objects for the menu bar and fill them with the items in Step 1. You can do this before (or alongside) Step 2 if you like.

4. Attach each of the submenus to its corresponding items in the menu bar.

Once you have your menu bar, place it into your GNOME application window with

```
gnome_app_set_menus(window, menu_bar)
```

Finally, show the menu bar with

```
gtk_widget_show_all(menu_bar)
```

WARNING *You must perform this final step. As mentioned in the example, GTK+ ignores menus when it shows an entire widget tree because a menu normally appears only when the user activates the menu. However, you want to see the menu bar all of the time.*

Toolbars

Your application should provide toolbar buttons for frequent actions such as **Save** (this is in addition to menu items and keyboard combinations). You can also place other compact widgets into the toolbar. For example, a zoom (scaling) widget works here.

The GTK+ toolbar widget class is **GtkToolbar** (GTK_TYPE_TOOLBAR), with these two properties:

- **orientation**: The current orientation of the toolbar; one of

    GTK_ORIENTATION_HORIZONTAL

    GTK_ORIENTATION_VERTICAL

- **toolbar-style**: The current orientation of the toolbar; one of

    GTK_TOOLBAR_ICONS: Toolbar contains images only.

    GTK_TOOLBAR_TEXT: Toolbar contains text only.

    GTK_TOOLBAR_BOTH: Toolbar contains images and text.

    GTK_TOOLBAR_BOTH_HORIZ: Like the preceding choice, but labels are next to (rather than under) images.

NOTE *GNOME applications should not alter these properties. With the exception of some toolbar orientations, the user should be able to choose the style with the GNOME **Menus & Toolbars** control panel. If you want to give your users the opportunity to override the toolbar style in an application, make sure that you also provide a "Use GNOME defaults" option. To set your toolbar's properties back to the GNOME defaults, call:*

```
gtk_toolbar_unset_style(toolbar)
```

Toolbars aren't as complicated to operate or program as menu bars. There is no separate "toolbar entry" widget — only a number of functions to insert toolbar items. Each of these functions returns a new toolbar item widget; to remove the item, destroy the widget.

A toolbar can contain four kinds of objects:

- Buttons that contain an icon and label of your specification.
- Buttons that contain stock items and images.
- Arbitrary widgets.
- Empty space (not a true item).

Here are the toolbar API functions:

- `GtkWidget *gtk_toolbar_append_item(GtkToolbar *toolbar, const char *text, const char *tooltip, "", GtkWidget *icon, GtkSignalFunc func, gpointer data)`
  Appends a new item to *toolbar* with the label *text* and image *icon*. This function attaches the tooltip text *tooltip* to the item and returns a new item widget. When the user clicks the item, GTK+ calls *func* with the item widget and *data* as arguments.

  The prototype for *func* should resemble

```
void handler(GtkWidget *item, gpointer data);
```

- `GtkWidget *gtk_toolbar_prepend_item(GtkToolbar *toolbar, const char *text, const char *tooltip, "", GtkWidget *icon, GtkSignalFunc func, gpointer data)`
  Like the preceding function, but places the new item at the start of the toolbar.

- `GtkWidget *gtk_toolbar_insert_item(GtkToolbar *toolbar, const char *text, const char *tooltip, "", GtkWidget *icon, GtkSignalFunc func, gpointer data, gint position)`
  Like the preceding function, but inserts the new item at *position* in *toolbar*. The first position is 0.

- `GtkWidget *gtk_toolbar_insert_stock(GtkToolbar *toolbar, const char *stock_id, const char *tooltip, "", GtkWidget *icon, GtkSignalFunc func, gpointer data, gint position)`
  Like the preceding function, but inserts a stock item *stock_item*. If *position* is −1, the item goes to the end of the toolbar.

- `GtkWidget *gtk_toolbar_append_widget(GtkToolbar *toolbar, GtkWidget *widget, const char *tooltip, "")`
  Like gtk_toolbar_append_item(), but appends an arbitrary *widget* to the toolbar.

- `GtkWidget *gtk_toolbar_prepend_widget(GtkToolbar *toolbar, GtkWidget *widget, const char *tooltip, "")`
  Like the preceding function, but inserts *widget* at the front of the toolbar.

- `GtkWidget *gtk_toolbar_insert_widget(GtkToolbar *toolbar, GtkWidget *widget, const char *tooltip, "", gint position)`
  Like the preceding function, but inserts *widget* at *position*.

- `void gtk_toolbar_append_space(GtkToolbar *toolbar)`
  Appends an empty space to the end of *toolbar*.

- `void gtk_toolbar_prepend_space(GtkToolbar *toolbar)`
  Inserts an empty space at the start of *toolbar*.

- void gtk_toolbar_insert_space(GtkToolbar *toolbar, gint position)
Inserts an empty space at position in toolbar.

- void gtk_toolbar_remove_space(GtkToolbar *toolbar, gint position)
Removes the empty space at position in toolbar. (This little utility is necessary because spaces in toolbars are not objects.)

Section 3.8.1 covers the significance of the "" argument in some of these functions.

To pack a toolbar widget into a main GNOME application window, use

```
gnome_app_set_toolbar(window, toolbar)
```

Status Bars

Many applications display their current state in a short strip at the bottom of the window. You can also put descriptions of menu items into a status bar.

In GTK+, the status bar widget class is **GtkStatusbar** (GTK_TYPE_STATUSBAR). You do not need a special generator function to create a status bar. To link a status bar to a GNOME application window, use

```
gnome_app_set_statusbar(window, status_bar)
```

NOTE *You must cast* status_bar *to a **GtkWidget** in this function call. Any other widget can go into the GNOME status bar location, but there are few reasonable alternatives to **GtkStatusBar**; a horizontal box containing a progress bar is one.*

In some applications, the status bar may have a secondary purpose: to resize the window through a small grip in one corner.

The status bar works like a stack with push and pop operations for messages. The message at the top of the stack shows up in the status bar display. Here are the stack manipulation functions:

- guint gtk_statusbar_push(GtkStatusBar *status_bar, guint context, const gchar *message)
Places message on top of the stack for status_bar and returns a numeric identifier for the new message.

  Here, context is an identifier for the part of the application that sent the message. Very few applications use this, and you should enter 0 if you don't want to bother with it. (If you *really* want to know, look in the API documentation for gtk_statusbar_get_context_id().)

- void gtk_statusbar_pop(GtkStatusBar *status_bar, guint context)
Removes the message at the top of a status bar's stack.

- void gtk_statusbar_remove(GtkStatusBar *status_bar, guint context, guint message_id)
Removes message_id from a status bar's stack.

NOTE *To remove the status bar grip, use*

```
gtk_statusbar_set_has_resize_grip(status_bar, FALSE)
```

Do this only when there's a really good reason (for example, if the status bar is not at the bottom of the window).

4.3.2 Context Menus

You may recall that you can define a menu at any spot in the application with a GTK+ context menu; they need a little help with signal handlers for the window focus.

It's much easier with GNOME. To put a context menu in your application, follow these steps:

1. Create a popup widget.

```
GtkWidget *popup, *widget;

popup = gnome_popup_menu_new(uiinfo);
```

This function creates a new menu from the GnomeUIInfo items in *uiinfo* and returns a new **GtkWidget** for the popup menu.

2. Call

```
gnome_popup_menu_attach(popup, widget, data);
```

where *widget* is the target widget in your application (users will right-click this widget to get the popup menu).

WARNING *You can attach a content menu only to a widget that accepts events — don't try it with a label or a plain image.*

Here are some other GNOME functions for manipulating context menus:

- GtkWidget *gnome_popup_menu_new_with_accelgroup(GnomeUIInfo *uiinfo, GtkAccelGroup *accelgroup)
  Like gnome_popup_menu_new(), but with keyboard operation defined by *accelgroup*.

- GtkAccelGroup *gnome_popup_menu_get_accel_group(GtkWidget *menu)
  Returns the accelerator group for *menu*.

- void gnome_popup_menu_append(GtkWidget *popup, GnomeUIInfo *uiinfo)
  Adds the items in *uiinfo* to *popup*.

- void gnome_gtk_widget_add_popup_items(GtkWidget *widget, GnomeUIInfo *uiinfo, gpointer data)
  Adds the items in *uiinfo* to the popup menu for *widget*. If *widget* doesn't have a context menu, this function creates a popup menu for it and uses *data* as the callback data pointer.

4.3.3 Enhanced Data Entry Widgets

The *libgnomeui* library offers a number of extensions to GTK+ data entry widgets such as **GtkEntry**. These tend to be far more capable than their bare GTK+ counterparts. This section's example program demonstrates enhanced text entry boxes, file choosers, font pickers, color pickers, icon pickers, image pickers, and date entry widgets. Each widget type has a detailed explanation in subsequent sections.

The only new concept in this program is the history feature. As you read this program, take a look at the **history-id** property for widgets such as **GnomeEntry**. GNOME stores the history for one of these widgets based on the application and history identifier.

Otherwise, you should be able to tell how these widgets work by reading the code and comments, so there is no inline explanation for this program as there has been in previous examples in this book. Figure 4.2 shows the results of this program.

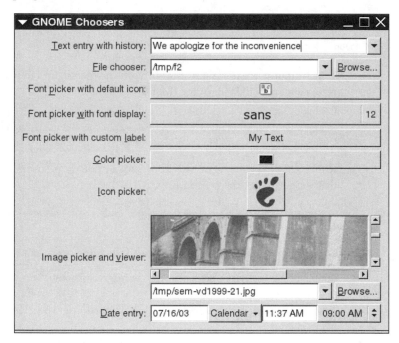

Figure 4.2: GNOME data entry widgets.

```
/* -*-coding: utf-8;-*- */
/* choosers.c -- demonstrate GNOME choosers */

#include <gnome.h>

#define NUM_WIDGETS 9

gchar *widget_label[NUM_WIDGETS] = {
  "_Text entry with history:",
  "_File chooser:",
  "Font _picker with default icon:",
```

```c
    "Font picker _with font display:",
    "Font picker with custom _label:",
    "_Color picker:",
    "_Icon picker:",
    "Image picker and _viewer:",
    "_Date entry:" };

/* handler for GnomeEntry::activate */
void textentry_activated(GnomeEntry *text_widget, gpointer data)
{
  GtkEntry *gtk_entry;
  gchar *contents;

  g_object_get(text_widget, "gtk-entry", &gtk_entry, NULL);
  g_object_get(gtk_entry, "text", &contents, NULL);

  g_object_unref(gtk_entry);

  g_print("Text entry box activated; new contents: %s\n", contents);
  g_free(contents);
}

/* handler for GnomeFileEntry::activate */
void fileentry_activated(GnomeFileEntry *file_widget, gpointer data)
{
  gchar *path;

  path = gnome_file_entry_get_full_path(file_widget, FALSE);

  g_print("File chooser activated; new File: %s\n", path);
  g_free(path);
}

/* handler for GnomeFontPicker::font-set
   gets a picker id through the data pointer
   so that you know what picker changed */
void fontpicker_changed(GnomeFontPicker *picker, gchar *font_name, gpointer id)
{
  g_print("Font picker %d changed; new font: %s\n", (gint)id, font_name);
}

/* handler for GnomeColorPicker::color-set */
void colorpicker_changed(GnomeColorPicker *picker,
                         guint red, guint green, guint blue, guint alpha,
                         gpointer data)
{
  g_print("Color picker changed; new color: R=%d; G=%d; B=%d; A=%d\n",
          red, green, blue, alpha);
}

/* handler for GnomeIconEntry::changed */
void iconpicker_changed(GnomeIconEntry *picker, gpointer data)
{
  gchar *path;

  g_object_get(picker, "filename", &path, NULL);

  g_print("Icon picker changed; new icon: %s\n", path);
```

```c
    g_free(path);
  }

/* handler for GnomePixmapEntry::activate */
void pixmap_changed(GnomePixmapEntry *picker, gpointer data)
{
  gchar *path;

  g_print("Pixmap changed; ");

  path = gnome_pixmap_entry_get_filename(picker);
  if (path == NULL)
  {
    g_print("selection invalid.\n");
  } else {
    g_print("new image file: %s\n", path);
    g_free(path);
  }
}

/* handler for GnomeDateEdit::date-changed and GnomeDateEdit::time-changed
   If this is a date, is_date_ptr is TRUE */
void date_or_time_changed(GnomeDateEdit *widget, gpointer is_date_ptr)
{
  gboolean is_date = (gboolean)is_date_ptr;
  time_t time;
  gchar *date_or_time;

  date_or_time = is_date? "date" : "time";
  g_print("%s changed; ", date_or_time);

  g_object_get(widget, "time", (gulong*)(&time), NULL);
  g_print("new %s: %s", date_or_time, ctime(&time));
}

/* standard event handlers */
gint delete_event(GtkWidget *widget, GdkEvent event, gpointer data)
{
  return FALSE;
}

void end_program(GtkWidget *widget, gpointer data)
{
  gtk_main_quit();
}

int main(int argc, char **argv)
{
  GnomeProgram *program;
  GtkWindow *window;
  GtkTable *table;
  GtkWidget *widgets[NUM_WIDGETS];
  gint i;

  program = gnome_program_init("choosers",
                               "0.1", LIBGNOMEUI_MODULE,
                               argc, argv,
```

```
                              GNOME_PROGRAM_STANDARD_PROPERTIES,
                              GNOME_PARAM_HUMAN_READABLE_NAME,
                              "GNOME Choosers Demo",
                              GNOME_PARAM_ENABLE_SOUND, TRUE,
                              NULL);

     window = g_object_new(GTK_TYPE_WINDOW,
                              "title", "GNOME Choosers",
                              "default-height", 300,
                              "default-width", 300,
                              "border-width", 12,
                              NULL);

     /* attach standard event handlers */
     g_signal_connect(window, "delete_event", G_CALLBACK(delete_event), NULL);
     g_signal_connect(window, "destroy", G_CALLBACK(end_program), NULL);

     /* create entry/chooser widgets and bind handlers */

     /* text widget with history */
     widgets[0] = g_object_new(GNOME_TYPE_ENTRY, "history-id", "textentry", NULL);

     g_signal_connect(widgets[0], "activate", G_CALLBACK(textentry_activated),
                      NULL);

     /* file chooser */
     widgets[1] = g_object_new(GNOME_TYPE_FILE_ENTRY, "history-id", "fileentry",
                              NULL);

     g_signal_connect(widgets[1], "activate", G_CALLBACK(fileentry_activated),
                      NULL);

     /* font picker with default font picker image */
     widgets[2] = g_object_new(GNOME_TYPE_FONT_PICKER,
                              "mode", GNOME_FONT_PICKER_MODE_PIXMAP,
                              NULL);

     /* font picker with selected font on label */
     widgets[3] = g_object_new(GNOME_TYPE_FONT_PICKER,
                              "mode", GNOME_FONT_PICKER_MODE_FONT_INFO,
                              "use-font-in-label", TRUE,
                              NULL);

     /* font picker with custom label */
     widgets[4] = g_object_new(GNOME_TYPE_FONT_PICKER,
                              "mode", GNOME_FONT_PICKER_MODE_USER_WIDGET,
                              NULL);

     gnome_font_picker_uw_set_widget(
        GNOME_FONT_PICKER(widgets[4]),
        GTK_WIDGET(g_object_new(GTK_TYPE_LABEL, "label", "My Text", NULL)));

     /* attach signal handlers for all three font pickers */
     for (i=2; i<=4; i++)
     {
        g_signal_connect(widgets[i],
```

```
                    "font-set", G_CALLBACK(fontpicker_changed), (gpointer)(i-1));
}

/* color picker */
widgets[5] = g_object_new(GNOME_TYPE_COLOR_PICKER,
                          "dither", TRUE,
                          "use-alpha", TRUE,
                          NULL);

g_signal_connect(widgets[5], "color-set", G_CALLBACK(colorpicker_changed),
                 NULL);

/* icon picker */
widgets[6] = g_object_new(GNOME_TYPE_ICON_ENTRY,
                          "history-id", "iconpicker",
                          "browse-dialog-title", "Select icon",
                          NULL);

g_signal_connect(widgets[6], "changed", G_CALLBACK(iconpicker_changed),
                 NULL);

/* image picker/viewer */
widgets[7] = gnome_pixmap_entry_new("pixmapentry", "Select image", TRUE);

g_signal_connect(widgets[7], "activate", G_CALLBACK(pixmap_changed),
                 NULL);

/* date/time entry: workday from 9 'til 5 */
widgets[8] = g_object_new(GNOME_TYPE_DATE_EDIT,
                          "time", (gulong)time(NULL),
                          "lower-hour", 9,
                          "upper-hour", 17,
                          NULL);

/* distinguish date and time to event handler with gboolean */
g_signal_connect(widgets[8],
                 "date-changed", G_CALLBACK(date_or_time_changed),
                 (gpointer)TRUE);

g_signal_connect(widgets[8],
                 "time-changed", G_CALLBACK(date_or_time_changed),
                 (gpointer)FALSE);

/* create a two-column table for all of the widgets */
table = g_object_new(GTK_TYPE_TABLE,
                     "n-rows", 9,
                     "n-columns", 2,
                     "column-spacing", 6,
                     "row-spacing", 6,
                     NULL);

/* pack a widget with its label in each row */
for (i = 0; i < NUM_WIDGETS; i++)
{
   gtk_table_attach(table, g_object_new(GTK_TYPE_LABEL,
```

```
                                      "label", widget_label[i],
                                      "use-underline", TRUE,
                                      "mnemonic-widget", widgets[i],
                                      "xalign", 1.0,
                                      "justify", GTK_JUSTIFY_RIGHT,
                                      NULL),
                     0, 1, i, i+1, GTK_EXPAND|GTK_FILL, 0, 0, 0);

    gtk_table_attach(table, g_object_new(GTK_TYPE_ALIGNMENT,
                                      "xalign", 0.0,
                                      "child", widgets[i],
                                      NULL),
                     1, 2, i, i+1, GTK_EXPAND|GTK_FILL, 0, 0, 0);
  }

  /* pack table, show all widgets, and start GTK+ main event loop */
  gtk_container_add(GTK_CONTAINER(window), GTK_WIDGET(table));
  gtk_widget_show_all(GTK_WIDGET(window));

  gtk_main();

  return 0;
}
```

4.3.4 Text Entry Widgets with History

GnomeEntry (`GNOME_TYPE_ENTRY`) widgets are slightly enhanced **GtkEntry** text entry widgets. The GNOME variant has a built-in history feature that allows the users to select a previous entry from a drop-down list. Therefore, it is a subclass of **GtkCombo**. You can access the entry box in a **GnomeEntry** object as a **GtkEntry** object through the **gtk-entry** property.

To take advantage of the history feature, set the **history-id** property to a string identifier unique to your application. The GNOME libraries store the history based on this identifier. The widget's history persists if you quit and restart the application.

The entry widget records a new history item in the widget when the user activates the widget. However, if you need to insert a few default suggestions or do some housekeeping, you can manipulate the history independently with these functions:

- void gnome_entry_prepend_history(GnomeEntry *entry, gboolean save, const gchar *text)
  Places text at the start of the history for entry. If you set save to TRUE, the GNOME libraries store this entry for later use.

- void gnome_entry_append_history(GnomeEntry *entry, gboolean save, const gchar *text)
  Like the preceding function, but places text at the end of the history list.

- void gnome_entry_clear_history(GnomeEntry *entry)
  Clears the history for entry.

- `void gnome_entry_set_max_saved(GnomeEntry *entry, guint max)`
  Sets the maximum number of items in *entry* to *max*.

- `guint gnome_entry_get_max_saved(GnomeEntry *entry)`
  Returns the maximum number of items in *entry*.

GnomeEntry has an **activate** signal that works like **GtkEntry**; its handler is

```
void handler(GnomeEntry *entry, gpointer data);
```

NOTE *Use **GnomeEntry** instead of **GtkEntry** when you feel that the user will frequently retrieve previously entered items, and keep in mind that there is a limit on the number of items in the history.*

If you feel that the user will not (or should not) want to change any of the entries in the list, try a **GtkCombo** widget instead.

If the user won't likely repeat anything in the entry box (for example, in an installation dialog), use **GtkEntry**.

4.3.5 File Choosers

File entry boxes are GNOME text entry boxes for filenames, incorporating a history feature and a **Browse...** button nearby to summon a file browser. After the user selects a file in the file browser, GNOME places the filename in the entry box and then activates the entry box. These file choosers combine the convenience of file browsing with the speed of typing the filename directly without additional dialogs. File choosers can also verify that a file exists.

This widget's implementation is the **GnomeFileEntry** class (`GNOME_TYPE_FILE_ENTRY`). Its properties are as follows:

- **history-id** (gchararray): The history identifier (you *must* supply this property).
- **browse-dialog-title** (gchararray): The file browser dialog title (for when the user clicks the **Browse...** button).
- **directory-entry** (gboolean): Set this to TRUE if the widget should choose a directory.
- **modal** (gboolean): If TRUE, the browser dialog is modal (monopolizes the input focus). Set this only if absolutely necessary.
- **filename** (gchararray): The name currently in the entry box.
- **default-path** (gchararray): The default path in for the file chooser (for when the user types a relative pathname into the box).
- **gnome-entry** (GnomeEntry *, read-only): The **GnomeEntry** widget in the file chooser.
- **gtk-entry** (GtkEntry *, read-only): The **GtkEntry** widget in the file chooser.

To read a full file path from a **GnomeEntry** widget, use

```
char *filename;

filename = gnome_file_entry_get_full_path(widget, verify);
```

Set *verify* to TRUE if you want GNOME to make sure that the file actually exists (in that case, this function returns NULL if the file does not exist).

Like **GnomeEntry** and **GtkEntry**, file chooser widgets have an **activate** signal with this handler prototype:

```
void handler(GnomeFileEntry *entry, gpointer data);
```

4.3.6 Font Pickers

Picking fonts with the **GnomeFontPicker** (GNOME_TYPE_FONT_PICKER) widget is similar to choosing files, except that there is no entry box (it doesn't make much sense to type the font name). Therefore, a font picker widget is just a button that the user clicks to get the font selection dialog from Section 3.6.8.

A font picker's configuration primarily consists of a button's appearance, reflected in several of the following properties:

- **mode** (enumeration): The button's appearance. Possible values are as follows:

    GNOME_FONT_PICKER_MODE_PIXMAP: The button has an icon label.

    GNOME_FONT_PICKER_MODE_FONT_INFO: The button displays the selected font name.

    GNOME_FONT_PICKER_MODE_USER_WIDGET: The button displays an arbitrary widget.

- **use-font-in-label** (gboolean): Set the button's label in the selected font. This is useful in conjunction with GNOME_FONT_PICKER_MODE_FONT_INFO (see the preceding property).

- **show-size** (gboolean): When displaying the font name in the label with GNOME_FONT_PICKER_MODE_FONT_INFO, include the font size. The default is TRUE.

- **label-font-size** (gint): The font size in the label. Even when using GNOME_FONT_PICKER_MODE_FONT_INFO, GNOME sets the label in this size.

- **font-name** (gchararray): The current font.

- **title** (gchararray): The title for the font picker dialog window.

- **preview-text** (gchararray): The dialog preview text. The default for font choosers is the alphabet set in uppercase and lowercase, but you can use something like "The quick brown fox jumped over the lazy dogs" if you feel the need for variety.

If you set **mode** to GNOME_FONT_PICKER_MODE_USER_WIDGET, you can put any widget that you like inside the picker button with this function:

```
gnome_font_picker_uw_set_widget(picker, widget)
```

NOTE *Like regular buttons and other similar elements, the only two widgets that make much sense here are **GtkLabel** and **GtkImage**.*

GnomeFontPicker has a `font-set` signal, emitted when the user chooses a font from the dialog. Its handler prototype looks like this:

```
void handler(GnomeFontPicker *picker, gchar *font_name, gpointer data);
```

4.3.7   Color Pickers

The **GnomeColorPicker** (`GNOME_TYPE_COLOR_PICKER`) widget is like the GNOME font picker, but simpler, because the button in the color picker displays only a sample of the current color. When you click the button, a **GtkColorSelection** dialog appears.

A GNOME color picker's properties are as follows:

- `red` (guint): The current color's red component.
- `green` (guint): The current color's green component.
- `blue` (guint): The current color's blue component.
- `use-alpha` (gboolean): If TRUE, the color has an alpha channel (transparency factor).
- `alpha` (guint): The alpha channel value.
- `title` (gchararray): The **GtkColorSelection** dialog title.
- `dither` (gboolean): If TRUE, GNOME dithers the color sample in the button if it cannot display the color precisely.

By default, color components are 16 bits wide; that is, they are between 0 and 65535.

GnomeColorPicker has one significant signal, `color-set`, emitted when the user chooses a color. Its handler prototype is

```
void handler(GnomeColorPicker *picker,
             guint red, guint green, guint blue, guint alpha);
```

4.3.8   Icon Pickers

The **GnomeIconEntry** `GNOME_TYPE_ICON_ENTRY` widget is a small square button that displays an icon. When the user clicks the button, a dialog appears with a choice of icons (see Figure 4.3).

GnomeIconEntry properties include the following:

- `filename` (gchararray): The selected icon's filename.
- `pixmap-subdir` (gchararray): The icon directory that the dialog searches (relative to *$(PREFIX)/share/pixmaps*).
- `history-id` (gchararray): The icon picker's history identifier.
- `browse-dialog-title` (gchararray): The icon selection dialog title.
- `pick-dialog` (GtkDialog *, read-only): The dialog widget (for changing its properties).

Figure 4.3: GNOME icon selection dialog.

When the user selects an icon, GNOME emits a **changed** signal. The handler prototype is

```
void handler(GnomeIconEntry *entry, gpointer data);
```

4.3.9 Image Pickers

To allow the user to choose an arbitrary image instead of an icon, you can put a **GnomePixmapEntry** (`GNOME_PIXMAP_ENTRY`) widget in your application. This subclass of **GnomeFileEntry** displays the selected image in addition to the filename.

To create a **GnomePixmapEntry** widget, use this generator function:

```
GtkWidget *image_entry;

image_entry = gnome_pixmap_entry_new(history_id, dialog_title, TRUE);
```

Here, `history_id` is a GNOME history identifier for previous images, and `dialog_title` is the picker's dialog box title.

NOTE   *The third parameter in the preceding function enables the view of the image in the picker widget. Under most circumstances, you should set this parameter to* TRUE. *Otherwise, this widget does not verify that the file is an image and is therefore nearly identical to* **GnomeFileEntry** — *the only difference is that there is a small thumbnail in the image picker dialog.*

These functions operate on **GnomePixmapEntry** widget objects:

- `void gnome_pixmap_entry_set_pixmap_subdir(GnomePixmapEntry *entry, const char *subdir)`
  Sets a default directory for the *entry* file browser; *subdir* should be relative to *$(PREFIX)/share/pixmaps*.

- `void gnome_pixmap_entry_set_preview_size(GnomePixmapEntry *entry, gint width, gint height)`
  Sets the image picker *entry* view size to *width* by *height* pixels.

- `gchar *gnome_pixmap_entry_get_filename(GnomePixmapEntry *entry)`
  Returns the current image in the picker as a newly allocated string. When the preview is active, this function verifies that the selected file is an image and returns NULL if the file is not an image.

GnomePixmapEntry inherits the **activate** signal from its **GnomeFileEntry** parent class (see Section 4.3.5).

4.3.10   Date/Time Widgets

For your application's date and time entry needs, you could try to come up with a collection of spin buttons and entry widgets, or you could make your life a lot easier with **GnomeDateEdit** (GNOME_TYPE_DATE_EDIT) widgets. These consist of text entry boxes for the date and time. The date box comes with a drop-down calendar, and the time box has an option menu. (If you run the example in Section 4.3.3, you'll get the idea.)

These **GnomeDateEdit** properties are available:

- **dateedit-flags**: A bitwise OR of the following options:

  GNOME_DATE_EDIT_SHOW_TIME: Shows the time in addition to the date. In the current implementation, omitting this option appears to have no effect.

  GNOME_DATE_EDIT_24_HR: Shows the time in 24-hour format (military and continental European formats).

  GNOME_DATE_EDIT_WEEK_STARTS_ON_MONDAY: Weeks will start on Monday in the drop-down calendar. Many continental European calendars use this format.

  The default is GNOME_DATE_EDIT_SHOW_TIME.

- **lower-hour** (gint): The first hour to show in the time entry option menu. Note that this is in 24-hour format.

- **upper-hour** (gint): The last hour to show in the time entry option menu.

- **time** (gulong): The current time and date. Use a time_t cast for this property.

WARNING   *Make sure that you set the* **time** *property when you create the widget; otherwise, you'll get a few critical log messages when you first try to access the widget. To get the current time and date from the system, use* (gulong)time(NULL).

GnomeDateEdit has two signals, **date-changed** and **time-changed**, emitted when the user changes the date or time. The handler prototype is the same for both:

```
void handler(GnomeDateEdit *entry, gpointer data);
```

4.3.11 Hyperlinks

Your application may occasionally need to provide a link to information available on the Internet. The **GnomeHRef** (GNOME_TYPE_HREF) widget is a subclass of **GtkButton** that looks like a link in a web browser. When the user clicks the link, GNOME opens the URL.

When you create a **GnomeHRef** object, use its **text** property to supply a label, and set the **url** property to the target URL (both of these properties are strings).

Here is a short example; see Figure 4.4 on the next page for the final result. Although a link usually shows up as underlined, blue text, its ultimate appearance depends on the user's GTK+ theme.

```
/* -*-coding: utf-8;-*- */
/* href.c -- demonstrate GNOME hyperlinks */

#include <gnome.h>

  << standard event handlers >>

int main(int argc, char **argv)
{
  GnomeProgram *program;
  GtkWindow *window;
  GtkVBox *vbox;
  GnomeHRef *link[5];
  gint i;

  /* initialize application */
  program = gnome_program_init("href", "0.1", LIBGNOMEUI_MODULE,
                               argc, argv,
                               GNOME_PROGRAM_STANDARD_PROPERTIES,
                               GNOME_PARAM_HUMAN_READABLE_NAME, "HRef",
                               GNOME_PARAM_ENABLE_SOUND, TRUE,
                               NULL);

  /* create main window */
  window = g_object_new(GTK_TYPE_WINDOW,
                        "title", "GNOME Links",
                        "border-width", 12,
                        NULL);

  << attach standard event handlers >>

  /* create five hyperlink objects */
  link[0] = g_object_new(GNOME_TYPE_HREF,
                         "url", "http://www.gnome.org",
```

```
                              "text", "www.gnome.org",
                              NULL);

    link[1] = g_object_new(GNOME_TYPE_HREF,
                              "url", "http://news.gnome.org/gnome-news/",
                              "text", "Gnotices",
                              NULL);

    link[2] = g_object_new(GNOME_TYPE_HREF,
                              "url", "http://www.gnomedesktop.org",
                              "text", "FootNotes",
                              NULL);

    link[3] = g_object_new(GNOME_TYPE_HREF,
                              "url", "http://download.gnome.org",
                              "text", "download.gnome.org",
                              NULL);

    link[4] = g_object_new(GNOME_TYPE_HREF,
                              "url", "http://developer.gnome.org",
                              "text", "developer.gnome.org",
                              NULL);

    /* pack all of these into a VBox */
    vbox = g_object_new(GTK_TYPE_VBOX, "spacing", 6, NULL);
    for (i=0; i<5; i++)
    {
        gtk_box_pack_start_defaults(GTK_BOX(vbox), GTK_WIDGET(link[i]));
    }

    /* pack VBox, show everything, start GTK+ main event loop */
    gtk_container_add(GTK_CONTAINER(window), GTK_WIDGET(vbox));
    gtk_widget_show_all(GTK_WIDGET(window));
    gtk_main();

    return 0;
}
```

Figure 4.4: GNOME hyperlinks.

4.3.12 High Scores

As mentioned in Section 4.2.4, *libgnome* has a facility for video game scores. The *libgnomeui* library has a special widget (**GnomeScores**) to display the top ten scores. To create one of these special dialog windows, call

```
gnome_scores_display_with_pixmap(image_file, game_name, level, rank)
```

Here, *image_file* is the filename of a representative image, *game_name* is the game's name (from gnome_score_init()), *level* is the game level (a string), and *rank* is the last game's rank in the high score list (obtained from gnome_score_log()). If you don't have a rank, use 0.

You'll get a new **GnomeScores** object for the new dialog window; see Figure 4.5. **GnomeScores** is a subclass of **GtkDialog** with an **OK** button to close the window.

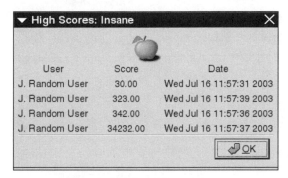

Figure 4.5: A GnomeScores high score list.

Although this book does not show any actual high score code, the accompanying code available on the Web contains a sample program called high-scores.

4.3.13   About (Credits) Windows

Nearly all applications have a window to give some credit to the developers. This is the About window that lists the application name, version, and developers' names. All GNOME applications should have such a window attached to the **Help > About** menu. As you might expect, GNOME offers a **GnomeAbout** (GNOME_TYPE_ABOUT) widget, and you can create one with a single function call:

```
gnome_about_new(name, version, copyright, comments,
                programmers, documenters, translator, logo)
```

These parameters are

- *name* (gchar *): The application name.

- *version* (gchar *): The application version.

- *copyright* (gchar *): A copyright statement.

- *comments* (gchar *): Other comments.

- *programmers* (gchar **): The people who wrote the code (a NULL-terminated array).

- *documenters* (gchar **): The people who wrote the documentation (a NULL-terminated array).

- *translator* (gchar *): The translator name for the current locale (or NULL if there wasn't any).

- *logo* (GdkPixbuf *): The application's logo image file.

Here is an example that should give you the idea. Figure 4.6 shows the window in action; you can click the **Credits** button to see who wrote the program. The **OK** button closes the window.

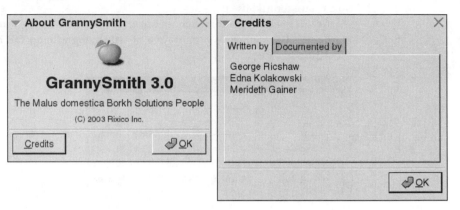

Figure 4.6: About dialog.

```c
/* -*-coding: utf-8;-*- */
/* about.c -- demonstrate gnome "about" windows */

#include <gnome.h>

/* standard event handlers */
gint delete_event(GtkWidget *widget, GdkEvent event, gpointer data)
{
  return FALSE;
}

void end_program(GtkWidget *widget, gpointer data)
{
  gtk_main_quit();
}

int main(int argc, char **argv)
{
  GnomeProgram *program;
  GnomeAbout *info;
  gchar *translator;
  gchar *apple;
  GdkPixbuf *logo;

  const gchar *programmers[] = {
      "George Ricshaw",
      "Edna Kolakowski",
      "Merideth Gainer",
      NULL
  };

  const gchar *documenters[] = {
      "Walter Zimmerman",
      "Harold Fenner",
```

```
    "Heather Kunkle",
    NULL
};

/* Initialize GNOME */
program = gnome_program_init(
            "about", "3.0",
            LIBGNOMEUI_MODULE,
            argc, argv,
            GNOME_PROGRAM_STANDARD_PROPERTIES,
            GNOME_PARAM_HUMAN_READABLE_NAME, "AboutDemo(GrannySmith)",
            GNOME_PARAM_ENABLE_SOUND, TRUE,
            NULL);

/* determine if the program is running in a translated environment;
   if no, set translator to NULL */
if (_("Translator") == "Translator")
{
    translator = NULL;
} else {
    translator = g_strdup(_("Put your translator here."));
}

/* find the green apple image; it should be in the standard
   GNOME pixmap directory */
apple = gnome_program_locate_file(program,
                                  GNOME_FILE_DOMAIN_PIXMAP,
                                  "apple-green.png",
                                  TRUE,
                                  NULL);

/* allocate logo pixmap */
logo = gdk_pixbuf_new_from_file(apple, NULL);
g_free(apple);

/* create "about" window */
info = GNOME_ABOUT(
        gnome_about_new("GrannySmith", "3.0",
                        "(C) 2003 Rixico Inc.",
                        "The Malus domestica Borkh Solutions People",
                        programmers, documenters, translator, logo));

/* because this data was copied, it should be freed */
g_free(translator);
g_object_unref(logo);

/* attach standard event handlers to info window */
g_signal_connect(info, "delete-event", G_CALLBACK(delete_event), NULL);
g_signal_connect(info, "destroy", G_CALLBACK(end_program), NULL);

/* show widget, start GTK+ main loop */
gtk_widget_show(GTK_WIDGET(info));
gtk_main();

return 0;
}
```

4.3.14 GNOME Stock Item Additions

The GTK+ stock item library originated in GNOME. Some of the GNOME 1 stock items are somewhat too specialized for GTK+, so *libgnomeui* offers these as extensions as soon as you initialize a GNOME program. See Appendix A for the list.

4.3.15 Druids

Druid is the GNOME name for what other systems call wizards or assistants: a means of stepping users through a somewhat complicated process that doesn't come up often. A druid displays a series of pages with input widgets and with detailed explanations.

NOTE *Among typical druid tasks are an application's first-time setup and new-profile configuration (for example, a new email account or application project environment). Never use druids for frequent tasks such as sending email or adding a new source code file.*

Here is a complete druid example that illustrates the GNOME druid classes. The first part contains some declarations, global constants, and an event handler to finish the program:

```
/* -*-coding: utf-8;-*- */
/* druid.c -- sample GNOME druid */

#include <gnome.h>

GtkEntry *last_name_entry;
GtkEntry *first_name_entry;
GtkWindow *window;

gchar *flavors[] = {
  "Vanilla", "Chocolate", "Strawberry", "Pistachio", "Mustard onion"
};
#define NUM_FLAVORS 5
#define NUM_MUSTARD NUM_FLAVORS - 1
GtkRadioButton *ice_cream[NUM_FLAVORS];

/* standard handler to terminate event loop */
void end_program(GtkWidget *widget, gpointer data)
{
  gtk_main_quit();
}
```

The auxiliary following function creates a warning dialog in case one of the pages in the druid isn't filled out correctly.

```
/* warning dialog using GNOME guidelines, as in dialog.c */
void warn_dialog(gchar *message)
{
  gchar *markup;
  GtkDialog *dialog;
  GtkHBox *hbox;
```

```
  GtkImage *icon;
  GtkLabel *text;

  markup = g_strdup_printf("<big><b>Druid configuration</b></big>\n\n%s",
                            message);

  dialog = GTK_DIALOG(gtk_dialog_new_with_buttons(
                      "Warning", window, GTK_DIALOG_MODAL,
                      "OK", GTK_RESPONSE_OK, NULL));

  gtk_dialog_set_default_response(dialog, GTK_RESPONSE_OK);
  g_signal_connect_swapped(dialog, "response", G_CALLBACK(gtk_widget_destroy),
                            GTK_WIDGET(dialog));

  hbox = g_object_new(GTK_TYPE_HBOX, "border-width", 8, NULL);
  icon = g_object_new(GTK_TYPE_IMAGE,
                      "stock", GTK_STOCK_DIALOG_WARNING,
                      "icon-size", GTK_ICON_SIZE_DIALOG,
                      "xalign", 0.5, "yalign", 0.5, NULL);

  gtk_box_pack_start(GTK_BOX(hbox), GTK_WIDGET(icon), FALSE, FALSE, 0);
  text = g_object_new(GTK_TYPE_LABEL,
                      "wrap", TRUE,
                      "label", markup,
                      "use-markup", TRUE, NULL);
  g_free(markup);

  gtk_box_pack_start(GTK_BOX(hbox), GTK_WIDGET(text), TRUE, TRUE, 0);
  gtk_box_pack_start(GTK_BOX(dialog->vbox), GTK_WIDGET(hbox),
                    FALSE, FALSE, 0);
  gtk_widget_show_all(GTK_WIDGET(dialog));
}
```

The following signal handler makes sure that the user entered their first and last names on the page. Notice the return value; if a handler that is supposed to verify a page returns TRUE, the druid does not allow the user to proceed to the next page.

```
/* verify the first and last name (page 1) */
gboolean check_page1(GnomeDruidPage *page, GtkWidget *druid, gpointer data)
{
  gchar *last_name = NULL;
  gchar *first_name = NULL;
  gboolean return_val;

  g_object_get(last_name_entry, "text", &last_name, NULL);
  g_object_get(first_name_entry, "text", &first_name, NULL);
  if ((!*last_name) || (!*first_name))
  {
     warn_dialog("You must supply your first and last names.");
     return_val = TRUE;
  } else {
     return_val = FALSE;
  }

  g_free(last_name);
```

```
    g_free(first_name);
    return return_val;
}
```

Here is a slight variation on the preceding handler. This time, the handler asks the user to double-check a certain input value, but will not complain if it gets the same value again.

```
/* check the favorite ice cream flavor (page 2) */
/* if someone picks "mustard onion" as their favorite ice cream
    flavor, show a warning, but only once. If the user insists, they
    get it the second time. */
gboolean check_page2(GnomeDruidPage *page, GtkWidget *druid, gpointer data)
{
    static gboolean already_warned = FALSE;
    gboolean mustard_onion;

    if (!already_warned)
    {
        g_object_get(ice_cream[NUM_MUSTARD], "active", &mustard_onion, NULL);
        if (mustard_onion)
        {
            warn_dialog("Do you really want mustard onion? If you're\
 sure about this, click Forward again.");
            already_warned = TRUE;
            return TRUE;
        }
    }
    return FALSE;
}
```

The finish_config() function prints the final configuration. The druid emits a signal to call this handler when the user is done.

```
/* signal handler to finish configuration */
void finish_config(GnomeDruidPage *page, GtkWidget *druid, gpointer data)
{
    gboolean active;
    gchar *first, *last;
    gint i;

    for (i = 0; i < NUM_FLAVORS; i++)
    {
        g_object_get(ice_cream[i], "active", &active, NULL);
        if (active)
        {
            break;
        }
    }
    g_object_get(first_name_entry, "text", &first, NULL);
    g_object_get(last_name_entry, "text", &last, NULL);

    g_print("Druid finished. Configuration:\n");
    g_print("First name: %s\nLast name: %s\nFavorite flavor: %s\n",
            first, last, flavors[i]);
    g_free(first);   g_free(last);
```

```
  /* end the program */
  g_signal_emit_by_name(window, "destroy", NULL);
}
```

NOTE *The last line in the preceding code terminates the application because there is nothing more to this example. However, in a real program, you would want to destroy* druid *instead of* window, *to let the main program run as usual.*

The first part of the main program contains the usual declarations, as well as some image loading:

```
int main(int argc, char **argv)
{
  GnomeProgram *program;
  GdkColor color;
  GnomeDruid *druid;
  GdkPixbuf *logo, *watermark, *watermark_top;
  GnomeDruidPageEdge *title_page, *finish_page;
  GnomeDruidPageStandard *page_1, *page_2;
  GtkVBox *ice_vbox;
  gint i;

  /* initialize GNOME */
  program = gnome_program_init("druid", "0.1",
                               LIBGNOMEUI_MODULE,
                               argc, argv,
                               GNOME_PARAM_HUMAN_READABLE_NAME, "Druid",
                               NULL);

  /* load images */
  logo = gdk_pixbuf_new_from_file("settings.png", NULL);
  watermark = gdk_pixbuf_new_from_file("watermark.png", NULL);
  watermark_top = gdk_pixbuf_new_from_file( "watermark-top.png", NULL);
```

Now you're ready to create the first page in the druid with a special generator function (see Figure 4.7 on page 293):

```
  /* create title page */
  title_page = GNOME_DRUID_PAGE_EDGE(
      gnome_druid_page_edge_new_with_vals(
          GNOME_EDGE_START, TRUE,
          "Welcome to the Sample Druid!",
          "This is the explanation on the title page.\n\
Like other druid pages, this page has a title and images: \n\
 - A logo in the upper right corner,\n\
 - A watermark at the top (empty in this druid), and\n\
 - A watermark along the left edge.",
          logo, watermark, watermark_top));

  /* title page uses black text on a white background */
  gdk_color_parse("white", &color);
  gnome_druid_page_edge_set_bg_color(title_page, &color);
  gdk_color_parse("black", &color);
  gnome_druid_page_edge_set_title_color(title_page, &color);
```

Notice, however, that page 2 does not use the generator function — in fact, it has a different type.

```
/* create page 1 (the one after the title) */
page_1 = g_object_new(GNOME_TYPE_DRUID_PAGE_STANDARD,
                      "title", "Your Name",
                      "logo", logo,
                      "top-watermark", watermark_top,
                       NULL);
```

There are some entry widgets in this page. Figure 4.8 on page 294 shows the final page.

```
/* fill page 1 main content */
first_name_entry = g_object_new(GTK_TYPE_ENTRY, NULL);

gnome_druid_page_standard_append_item(
    page_1,
    "This is page 1.\nThere are no graphics to the left, but \
the bar at the top remains.\n\n
What is your first name?",
    GTK_WIDGET(first_name_entry),
    "Your parents probably supplied your first name. Ask them \
if you can't remember what it is.");

last_name_entry = g_object_new(GTK_TYPE_ENTRY, NULL);
gnome_druid_page_standard_append_item(
    page_1,
    "What is your last name?",
    GTK_WIDGET(last_name_entry),
    "If you don't know, open a telephone book and pick one that looks nice.");
```

You can also see that the **next** signal is for when the user clicks the **Next** button:

```
/* attach handler for verifying the information on this page */
g_signal_connect(page_1, "next", G_CALLBACK(check_page1), NULL);
```

The next page is similar (see Figure 4.10 on page 295):

```
/* create page 2 */
page_2 = g_object_new(GNOME_TYPE_DRUID_PAGE_STANDARD,
                      "title", "Favorite Ice Cream",
                      "logo", logo,
                      "top-watermark", watermark_top,
                      NULL);

/* fill second page */
ice_vbox = g_object_new(GTK_TYPE_VBOX, NULL);
for (i = 0; i < NUM_FLAVORS; i++)                    /* ice cream widgets */
{
    ice_cream[i] = g_object_new(GTK_TYPE_RADIO_BUTTON, NULL);
    gtk_box_pack_start_defaults(GTK_BOX(ice_vbox), GTK_WIDGET(ice_cream[i]));
    g_object_set(ice_cream[i], "label", flavors[i], NULL);
    if (i != 0)
    {
```

```
            g_object_set(ice_cream[i], "group", ice_cream[0], NULL);
        }
    }

    gnome_druid_page_standard_append_item(
        page_2,
        "Choose your favorite ice cream flavor.",
        GTK_WIDGET(ice_vbox),
        "Please note that mustard onion is an acquired taste.");

    /* attach signal to check the page input */
    g_signal_connect(page_2, "next", G_CALLBACK(check_page2), NULL);
```

However, for the final page (Figure 4.8 on page 294), you need the same type and generator function as the first page.

```
    /* create final page */
    finish_page = GNOME_DRUID_PAGE_EDGE(
        gnome_druid_page_edge_new_with_vals(
            GNOME_EDGE_FINISH,
            TRUE,
            "Configuration Finished",
            "Thanks for using this sample druid!",
            logo, watermark, watermark_top));

    /* text and title black on white */
    gdk_color_parse("white", &color);
    gnome_druid_page_edge_set_bg_color(finish_page, &color);
    gnome_druid_page_edge_set_textbox_color(finish_page, &color);
    gdk_color_parse("black", &color);
    gnome_druid_page_edge_set_text_color(finish_page, &color);
    gnome_druid_page_edge_set_title_color(finish_page, &color);
```

To define an action for when the user finishes with the druid, attach a handler to the **finish** signal with this page:

```
    /* connect signal for the finish button */
    g_signal_connect(finish_page, "finish", G_CALLBACK(finish_config), NULL);
```

Now that you have all of the pages, you can create and show the druid and get on with the rest of the program:

```
    /* create main druid widget */
    druid = GNOME_DRUID(gnome_druid_new_with_window(
            "Druid Demonstration", NULL, TRUE, (GtkWidget**)(&window)));

    /* add all of the pages to the druid and show the widget */
    gnome_druid_append_page(druid, GNOME_DRUID_PAGE(title_page));
    gtk_widget_show_all(GTK_WIDGET(title_page));
    gnome_druid_append_page(druid, GNOME_DRUID_PAGE(page_1));
    gtk_widget_show_all(GTK_WIDGET(page_1));
    gnome_druid_append_page(druid, GNOME_DRUID_PAGE(page_2));
    gtk_widget_show_all(GTK_WIDGET(page_2));
    gnome_druid_append_page(druid, GNOME_DRUID_PAGE(finish_page));
```

```
    gtk_widget_show_all(GTK_WIDGET(finish_page));

    /* attach destroy handler (end program when druid cancels) */
    g_signal_connect(druid, "destroy", G_CALLBACK(end_program), NULL);

    /* no longer need references to these images */
    g_object_unref(logo);
    g_object_unref(watermark);
    g_object_unref(watermark_top);

    /* start GTK+ main event loop */
    gtk_main();

    return 0;
}
```

On to the details of the druid components.

Druid Pages

A druid is a digital workbook for the user to fill out. Druid widgets are
GnomeDruid objects filled with page objects. All of the page classes described
here inherit characteristics from the abstract **GnomeDruidPage** parent class:

- A title page explaining the druid's purpose. This page belongs to the
  GnomeDruidPageEdge class.
- Two or more normal pages, usually containing input widgets. These pages
  are **GnomeDruidPageStandard** objects.
- A final page explaining that the user is finished with the druid. Like the title,
  this is a **GnomeDruidPageEdge** object.

All druid pages have three buttons at the bottom: **Cancel** to abort the druid, **Back**
to move back a page, and **Forward** to go to the next page. On the final page, the
Forward button becomes an **Apply** button to complete the process.

NOTE   *All druids should have at least four pages (counting the title and finish pages). There is no
real difference between a druid with one normal page and a simple dialog box, other than
that the druid version is annoying.*

Title and Final Pages

Title and final pages contain only text and graphics; their appearance should
differ slightly from normal pages. If you have a lot of fancy graphics that you
need to get out of your system, consider using them in these pages instead of
the normal pages. Figure 4.7 shows a title page; Figure 4.8 on page 294 shows a
final page.

    To create a **GnomeDruidPageEdge** (GNOME_TYPE_DRUID_PAGE_EDGE) object, use
this generator function:

```
GtkWidget *page;

page = gnome_druid_page_edge_new_with_vals(position,
                                           antialiased,
                                           title,
```

```
                                    text,
                                    logo,
                                    watermark,
                                    top_watermark);
```

- *position* (GnomeEdgePosition): The type of page. Possible values are

  GNOME_EDGE_START: Title page.

  GNOME_EDGE_FINISH: Final page.

  GNOME_EDGE_OTHER: An internal page (for long druids).

- *antialiased* (gboolean): Set this to TRUE if you want GNOME to smooth edges in the druid.

- *title* (gchar *): The title to appear at the top of the page.

- *text* (gchar *): The text inside the page.

- *logo* (GdkPixbuf *): A pixbuf for the top-right corner of the druid (next to the title).

- *watermark* (GdkPixbuf *): A pixbuf for the druid's left side. This image should be tall and narrow.

- *top_watermark* (GdkPixbuf *): A pixbuf to place underneath the title. If you feel that this is absolutely necessary, make sure that the image is wide, thin, and as transparent as possible.

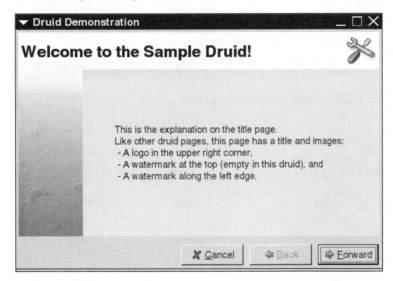

Figure 4.7: Druid title page.

The return value is a **GtkWidget**, but you may want to cast it to **GnomeDruidPageEdge** so that you can use it with these API functions to set the colors:

- void gnome_druid_page_edge_set_bg_color(GnomeDruidPageEdge *page, GdkColor *color)

  Sets the edge and top background color of a title/final *page* to *color*. By default, this is a shade of blue.

- void gnome_druid_page_edge_set_textbox_color(GnomeDruidPageEdge *page, GdkColor *color)
  Sets the text background color of *page* to *color*.

- void gnome_druid_page_edge_set_logo_bg_color(GnomeDruidPageEdge *page, GdkColor *color)
  Sets the background color behind the logo in *page* to *color*.

- void gnome_druid_page_edge_set_title_color(GnomeDruidPageEdge *page, GdkColor *color)
  Sets the title text color in *page* to *color*.

- void gnome_druid_page_edge_set_text_color(GnomeDruidPageEdge *page, GdkColor *color)
  Sets the body text color in *page* to *color*.

Remember that these are for title and final pages only; for normal pages, use the properties in the next section.

To define a color for use in one of the preceding functions, fill a GdkColor structure like this:

```
GdkColor color;

gdk_color_parse("color_name", &color);
```

Here, *color_name* is an X11 name such as white, honeydew, or #000050. After you call gdk_color_parse(), you can use *&color* as a color parameter in the **GnomeDruidPageEdge** functions.

Figure 4.8: Final druid page.

To attach a handler to the **Apply** button in a final page, refer to the **next** signal, described on page 297.

Normal Druid Pages

GnomeDruidPageStandard (`GNOME_TYPE_DRUID_PAGE_STANDARD`) objects do not have side images. Normal pages may contain any kind of widget and explanatory text, as you can see from Figures 4.9 and 4.10.

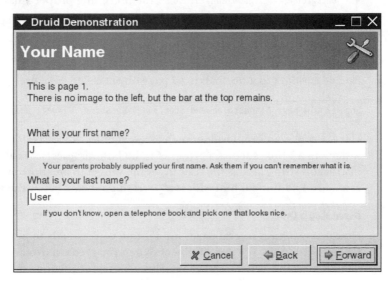

Figure 4.9: A normal druid page.

You do not need a special generator function for normal druid pages. To manipulate the page, these properties are at your disposal:

- **title** (gchararray): The page title.
- **logo** (GdkPixBuf *): The logo at the top right.
- **top-watermark** (GdkPixBuf *): A watermark image to place under the title.

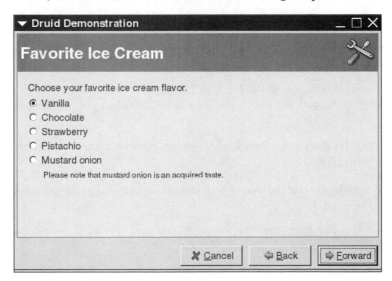

Figure 4.10: Another normal druid page.

- **title-foreground** (gchararray): The title text color.

- **title-foreground-set** (gboolean): If FALSE, the preceding property has no effect.

- **background** (gchararray): The title and border background color.

- **background-set** (gboolean): If FALSE, the preceding property has no effect.

- **logo-background** (gchararray): The background color for the logo in the upper right corner.

- **logo-background-set** (gboolean): If FALSE, the preceding property has no effect.

To add a widget to a normal druid page object called *page*, use

```
gnome_druid_page_standard_append_item(page, question, widget, more_info)
```

Here, *widget* is an input widget such as a text entry box or collection of input widgets in a VBox, such as a group of radio buttons; *question* is a question or instruction string asking the user to set the widget to an appropriate value. You can add an additional hint with *more_info*; this appears below the widget.

Assembling a Druid

Now that you have several pages for a druid, you're ready to put them into a **GnomeDruid** (GTK_TYPE_DRUID) object. When you create a druid widget, you likely want it in a separate window. This generator function comes in handy for just that:

```
GtkWidget *druid;

druid = gnome_druid_new_with_window(title, window, close_on_cancel, window_ptr);
```

- *title* (char *): The title of the new druid window. You can set this to NULL if you want to use the application identifier.

- *window* (GtkWindow *): The parent window that owns the druid. This can be NULL if this druid is a stand-alone application.

- *close_on_cancel* (gboolean): If TRUE, GNOME destroys the druid window when the user clicks the **Cancel** button.

- *window_ptr* (GtkWidget **): If you need to store the window container that holds druid, pass an address of a **GtkWidget** pointer here. If you don't care, use NULL.

After you get the new druid, you can fill it with pages using the following functions.

WARNING   *Make sure that you show a page with* gtk_widget_show_all(page) *when adding it to a druid.*

- void gnome_druid_append_page(GnomeDruid *druid, GnomeDruidPage *page)
  Adds *page* to the end of *druid*.

- void gnome_druid_prepend_page(GnomeDruid *druid, GnomeDruidPage *page)
  Places page at the start of druid.
- void gnome_druid_insert_page(GnomeDruid *druid, GnomeDruidPage *prev_page, GnomeDruidPage *page)
  Inserts page after prev_page in druid.

NOTE *After calling* gnome_druid_new_with_window(), *you do not need to show the new druid window; GNOME does that for you. However, you still need to show each page (see the preceding discussion).*

The GNOME druid API lets you reconfigure and redisplay druid pages at run time. This can be handy for several tasks, including showing a summary of the user's choices on the final page.

Interacting with Druids

A **GnomeDruidPage** widget has several signals:

- next
  gboolean handler(GnomeDruidPage *page, GtkWidget *druid, gpointer data)
  GNOME emits this signal when the user clicks the **Next** button in the page belonging to druid. If handler returns TRUE, the signal emission stops, and therefore druid does not proceed to the next page. Use this signal to check for valid input on a page or to skip to a different page in the druid (see the following discussion).

- back
  gboolean handler(GnomeDruidPage *page, GtkWidget *druid, gpointer data)
  Like the preceding signal, but for the **Back** button.

- cancel
  gboolean handler(GnomeDruidPage *page, GtkWidget *druid, gpointer data)
  Like the preceding signal, but for the **Cancel** button. If you don't want the default handler to run (possibly destroying the druid), install an appropriate handler here that returns TRUE.

- finish
  void handler(GnomeDruidPage *page, GtkWidget *druid, gpointer data)
  Like the preceding signal, but for a finish page's **Apply** button. Note than you cannot stop the signal emission because there is no return value.

WARNING *Don't use* finish *to check for valid input. You should do that with the previous pages'* next *handlers.*

To skip to a different page in a signal handler, use

gnome_druid_set_page(druid, page)

Make sure that you return TRUE in your signal handler after you make this call, or the default handler will try to advance the page.

The example program does not skip pages, but does check for valid input.

4.3.16 Session Management

Session management saves an application's state in a user's session. The state is normally the set of document names in all of the application's windows. As a general rule of thumb, an application should be able to go back to its previous state with command-line arguments.

Therefore, a session manager's task is to ask an application for a command that restarts the application, going back to the current state. This session manager request is known as "SaveYourself." For example, if the MiracleText application presented earlier had open windows containing *letter.mtx*, *omissions.mtx*, and *diary.mtx*, the response to the session manager's SaveYourself command might look something like this:

```
miracletext -f letter.mtx -f omissions.mtx -f diary.mtx
```

NOTE *It's important that the application start with the same number of windows as earlier. Otherwise, the window manager won't put the windows back in their previous positions and sizes.*

The session manager allows for parallel sessions, where each session has a unique identifier. To use a certain session identifier when starting an application, use the command-line parameter --sm-client-id=id. The GNOME session manager API creates and processes this parameter for you.

NOTE *It's also possible to save more complicated information than that mentioned here. For example, an application can save its state with GConf under a unique key (perhaps made from the process ID, time, and other information) at every* **Save** *operation and then pass the key and an appropriate parameter to the session manager.*

However, this makes session management much more complicated because the program also needs to keep track of its own configuration somewhere else on the system. Therefore, you should always try to put *all* states in the command line, so that you don't have to deal with auxiliary files or other pieces that can disappear without notice. This book explains only the parts of the session manager dealing with command-line arguments.

Working with the Session Manager

To make your application aware of the session manager, create a **GnomeClient** object:

```
GnomeClient *client;

client = gnome_master_client();
```

If you decide that you need to verify that your application can talk to the session manager through client, use this macro:

```
GNOME_CLIENT_CONNECTED(client)
```

The code behind this macro expansion returns TRUE when the client is connected.

GnomeClient objects come with these signals:

- **connect**
  void handler(GnomeClient *client, gboolean restart, gpointer data);
  Emitted when the session manager wants to talk to the application. If restart is TRUE, the session manager is trying to start the application using the state from the previous session.

- **save-yourself**
  gboolean handler(GnomeClient *client, gint phase, GnomeSaveStyle what, gboolean end, GnomeInteractStyle interaction, gboolean fast, gpointer data);
  Emitted when the session manager wants the application to save its state. Here, phase is the save phase (either 1 or 2), but is essentially irrelevant; end is TRUE if the end of the session is close at hand; and fast is true if the program should try to save its state quickly.

  what indicates the program data to save:

  > GNOME_SAVE_GLOBAL: Saves general configuration data. If you use GConf to store your configuration data, you can ignore this (see Chapter 7).

  > GNOME_SAVE_LOCAL: Saves open document names and similar data.

  > GNOME_SAVE_BOTH: Saves global and local data.

  The interaction parameter tells the application if it should tell the user about any problems in saving the state:

  > GNOME_INTERACT_NONE: The user doesn't need to know anything.

  > GNOME_INTERACT_ERRORS: Tells the user if any problems occur.

  > GNOME_INTERACT_ANY: Tells the user whatever you want it to.

  The signal handler must return TRUE if it successfully saves the state and FALSE if an error occurs.

- **save-complete**
  void handler(GnomeClient *client, gpointer data);
  Emitted when the session manager completes a round of SaveYourself commands to its clients.

- **disconnect**
  void handler(GnomeClient *client, gpointer data);
  Emitted when the session manager is about to disconnect from the client.

- **die**
  void handler(GnomeClient *client, gpointer data);
  Emitted when the session manager wants the application to terminate.

The handlers for these signals are at the heart of an application's session management code. The most important are **save-yourself** and **die**. Because it wouldn't be right to ask the program to terminate before saving its state, a SaveYourself command arrives before every Die command.

If your application needs only to save a command line in response to a SaveYourself command, implementing the handler for **save-yourself** is easy. Use these functions on your *client* object:

- void gnome_client_set_clone_command(GnomeClient *client, gint *argc, gchar *argv[])
  Gives the session manager the command line for a completely new instance of the application by way of *argc* and *argv*. Normally, you can just supply the command without any options.

- void gnome_client_set_restart_command(GnomeClient *client, gint *argc, gchar *argv[])
  Like the preceding function, but the command line should reflect the *current* state of the application.

- void gnome_client_set_discard_command(GnomeClient *client, gint *argc, gchar *argv[])
  Gives the session manager a command to run when the application leaves the management session. If you store the application state with command lines only, you do not need to use this function.

- void gnome_client_set_current_directory(GnomeClient *client, const gchar *dir)
  Tells the session manager that it should run the commands in *dir*.

- void gnome_client_set_environment(GnomeClient *client, const gchar *varname, const gchar *value)
  Tells the session manager that it should set the environment variable *varname* to *value* before running any commands.

If you have to interact with the user by way of a dialog in your **save-yourself** signal handlers, do it with these functions:

- void gnome_client_save_any_dialog(GnomeClient *client, GtkDialog *dialog)
  Ask the session manager to show *dialog* if the interaction mode is GNOME_INTERACT_ANY. The session manager adds **Cancel** and **Log out** buttons to *dialog* if the session is at an end.

- void gnome_client_save_error_dialog(GnomeClient *client, GtkDialog *dialog)
  Like the preceding function, but operates when an error occurs while saving the state.

WARNING *It's pointless to use these outside a **save-yourself** signal handler. They do not guarantee that the session manager will actually show the dialog box.*

The Async example in Section 8.5.5 contains minimal session management. Here is a template for how you might use session management in your program:

```
gboolean save_yourself(GnomeClient *client, int phase,
                       GnomeSaveStyle what,
                       gboolean end,
                       GnomeInteractStyle interaction,
                       gboolean fast,
                       gpointer user_data)
```

```
{
  << other declarations >>
  gint save_argc;
  gchar *save_argv[];
  gchar *working_dir;

  << set working_dir >>
  << build save_argv >>
  << set save_argc to the length of save_argv >>

  gnome_client_set_current_directory(client, working_dir);

  gnome_client_set_clone_command(client, 1, save_argv);
  gnome_client_set_restart_command(client, save_argc, save_argv);

  return TRUE;
}

void die(GnomeClient *client, gpointer data)
{
  gtk_main_quit();
}

int main(int argc, char **argv)
{
  GnomeProgram *program;
  GnomeClient *client;
  << other declarations >>

  program = gnome_program_init(<< ... >>);

  /* initialize session management */
  client = gnome_master_client();

  /* bind session management handlers */
  g_signal_connect(client, "save_yourself", G_CALLBACK(save_yourself), NULL);
  g_signal_connect(client, "die", G_CALLBACK(die), NULL);

  << build application >>

  << parse command line >>

  gtk_main();

  << ... >>
}
```

If you want to know more about session management (though few applications use many of its features), have a look at the X11 API [Mor] and the protocol specification [Wexler]. For something a little specific to GNOME, have a look at the session management chapter in [Tredinnick].

4.4 Further Topics

This book covers nearly everything in *libgnome* and *libgnomeui*, but a few things in the API remain:

- **gnome-i18n**. The *libgnomeui* library has several functions for manipulating the gettext program (see Section 6.5). There aren't many real-life examples, so this book will not cover the API.

- **GnomeAppBar**, a status bar with built-in progress meter and other accessories. Although the GNOME API does not mark this class as obsolete and notes that it "mostly" works, the documentation still discourages you from using any interactive features.

- **GnomeThumbnail**, a system for getting thumbnail representations of image files.

- **GnomeIconList and GnomeIconSelection** help the user select and manipulate groups of icons. Not only do these widgets seldom come up in practice, but there are also plans to replace them.

- **gnome-app-helper** is an old, deprecated system for semi-automated graphical interface generation. You should use Glade instead; see Chapter 5.

- **Loading Pixbufs from URIs**. With the help of various gdk_pixbuf_new_from_uri functions, *libgnomeui* allows you to load a **GdkPixbuf** synchronously or asynchronously via GnomeVFS.

- **GnomeCanvas** is perhaps the most powerful GNOME widget. It is a scrollable, scalable surface where you can stack, manage, group, and otherwise manipulate graphical objects. It would take an entire book to cover this widget.

The canvas provides custom graphical elements that can either expand existing tools or build entirely new widget systems. The material here is meant as a guide for the existing widgets, not for building your own, so like GDK, the canvas does not fit in with the material in this book. If you want to know more about the canvas, have a look at [Pennington]. Although these documents cover the GNOME 1 API, they also mostly hold for GNOME 2.

5

GLADE AND LIBGLADE

In the previous chapters, you saw how graphical user interface development usually works: You define a system of containers, pack widgets into the containers, and configure the widget properties. If the final result is not quite what you had in mind, you have to go back and forth between your source code and testing environment when tweaking parameters.

However, you can also interactively create and customize your interface with Glade. This chapter shows you how to use Glade by way of a small example. In Section 5.1, you will create a temperature converter interface with Glade. In Section 5.2, you'll see how to attach your new interface to a program.

5.1 Glade

To start Glade, select its entry in GNOME's **Applications > Programming** menu, or run glade-2 from the command line. The windows in Figure 5.1 on the next page should appear.

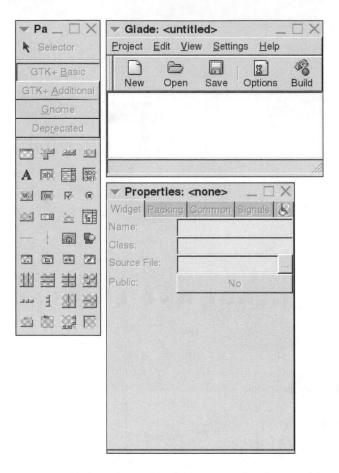

Figure 5.1: Glade: widget palette (left), main window (upper right), and property editor
(lower right).

5.1.1 Create a Project

Aside from a toolbar, menu bar, and status bar, the main Glade window contains
a list, initially empty. Every window that you create has an entry here. To create a
new interface, follow these steps:

1. Choose **Project > New** in the main window. A New dialog appears.
2. Click the **New GNOME Project** button.
3. Check the status bar. "New project created" should appear.

NOTE   *If you choose **New GTK+ Project** instead, you can use only GTK+ widgets. Furthermore,
you cannot convert a GTK+ project into a GNOME project.*

5.1.2 The Widget Palette

To create widgets, use the widget palette. The top of the palette has a selector tool, the center contains widget category buttons, and the lower part holds symbols representing the widgets in the current category. Figure 5.2 illustrates the three most important categories: **GTK+ Basic**, **GTK+ Additional**, and **Gnome**.

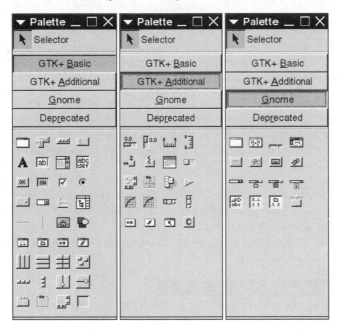

Figure 5.2: Glade widget palette with GTK+ Basic, GTK+ Additional, and GNOME widgets.

To get started with the temperature scale converter, you need a main window. In this case, a dialog window will do:

1. Choose the **GTK+ Basic** widget category.
2. Click the symbol for dialog (leftmost column, fourth from bottom). A **New dialog** window appears.
3. Leave the settings on **Standard Button Layout**, but choose **Close** from the options on the right; then click **OK**.

A new window named **dialog1** appears; this is a preview window. It looks like a regular dialog box with a **Close** button, but the top portion has a gray, crosshatched texture. In addition, the new dialog shows up inside the main window. If you accidentally lose track of where the dialog window is, double-click this entry; Glade brings the window to the top.

NOTE   *Feel free to explore the widgets for other window types (all three categories contain window widgets). If you don't recognize the symbols, use the tooltips to figure them out: Let the mouse hover for a short time.*

5.1.3 Property Editor

When you click a widget or free space inside the preview, a frame pops up around the widget, and the property editor window displays the widget settings.

NOTE *To select a container that you can't see because its widgets fill all of its space, right-click one of these widgets. A context menu appears, and you should see submenus for the widget's containers below the **Delete** button. Choose **Select** inside one of those submenus to select a container.*

You will work with the property editor more than any other part of Glade. It consists of five notebook pages (from left to right):

- **Widget** (Figure 5.3). You can edit all of the widget's specific properties here. Because each widget class has different properties, the elements on this page change accordingly when you switch to a different class. The **Name** property is important; this is the name to use inside your program to talk to the widget.

NOTE *Even though Glade picks a unique name for every widget, you should try to select your own names so that you don't have to spend time trying to figure out what widgets correspond to names such as* button1 *and* dialog5*. Naming isn't a big deal for widgets that you never access in your program code (labels, in particular), but it can be important with certain containers.*

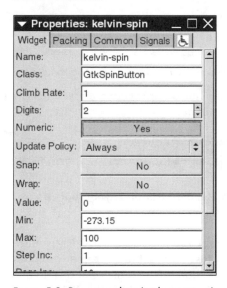

Figure 5.3: Property editor (widget settings).

- **Packing** (Figure 5.4). If a widget has any packing options, they appear here. Remember that these settings depend on the widget's container; if there are are no applicable packing options, this page is empty.

NOTE *Experimenting with these options is a great way to figure out how GTK+ packing options work.*

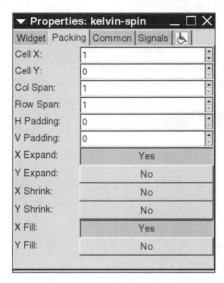

Figure 5.4: Property editor (packing settings).

- **Common** (Figure 5.5). Properties that all widgets have (that is, the **GtkWidget** superclass properties).

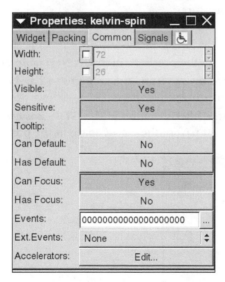

Figure 5.5: Property editor (common settings).

- **Signals** (see Section 5.2.3). You can add signal handlers to a widget here.
- **Accessibility**. These settings are not covered in this book.

Continuing with the temperature converter:

1. Select the main dialog window.
2. Click the **Widget** tab in the property editor.
3. Change the widget name to "window."
4. Change the title to "Temperature Converter."
5. Increase the border width so that the window looks like Figure 5.6.

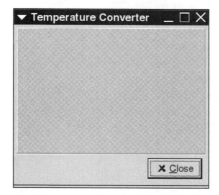

Figure 5.6: The empty dialog window.

Now you're ready fill in the empty space in the window with five spin buttons (and labels) for the temperatures:

1. Click the table symbol in the **GTK+ Basic** widget palette category.
2. Click the empty space in the preview window. A **New table** window appears.
3. Change the number of rows to 5 and the columns to 2 and click **OK**. Several lines should now divide the empty space.
4. Create a label: Click the big "A" button in the **GTK+ Basic** widget palette; then click the upper-left part of the empty space in the preview window.

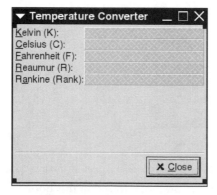

Figure 5.7: Preview with table and labels.

5. In the property editor, change the **Label** property to "_Kelvin (K):" and change the use underline setting to **Yes**.

6. Repeat the previous two steps for the rest of the rows so that the preview looks like Figure 5.7.

Now create five spin buttons for each label:

1. Select the spin button symbol in the **GTK+ Basic** widget palette; then click a free space in the preview window.

2. In the property editor, change the name as appropriate (for example, enter "kelvin-spin" for the spin button next to the Kelvin label).

3. Set **Digits** to 2.

4. Set **Numeric** to Yes.

5. Set **Value** to 0.

6. Pick an appropriate minimum value for the button (Kelvin and Rankine, 0; Celsius, –273.15; Fahrenheit, –459.67; Reaumur, –341.44). Set the maximum value to a fairly high number.

The interface now looks reasonable, but there are still some loose ends to tie up:

1. Select the table.

2. In the property editor, set the column and row spacings to 6 so that the cells aren't mashed against one another.

3. For each label, change the **X Align** property setting to 1.0. After performing this step for each label, the preview should look like Figure 5.8.

4. For each label, change the **Focus Target** property setting to the spin button next to the label. This makes the accelerator keys work properly.

Figure 5.8: Preview with spin buttons.

This looks nice, but something's still missing. You forgot to tell the user how to use the application. Now you have a problem: Where do you put that message? It would be nice to put it above the table, but there is no empty space left.

As it turns out, a **GtkDialog** widget uses a **GtkVBox** container to store its main contents. Right now, that box (the table) appears full, but you can insert another slot to fill with a label:

1. Right-click the table. A context menu appears; one of the items should be a **dialog-vbox1** submenu for the dialog's VBox.

2. Choose **dialog-vbox1 > Insert Before** from that menu. A new empty slot appears above the table, as shown in Figure 5.9.

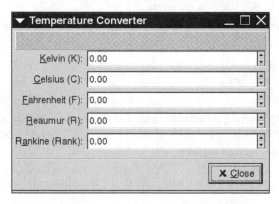

Figure 5.9: Preview with empty slot above table.

3. Enter a label in the empty slot. You will fill this with left-justified text in the next few steps.

4. Change the label's **Wrap Text** property to Yes.

5. Set the X alignment to 0.

6. Change the label text to a descriptive message, such as the one in Figure 5.10.

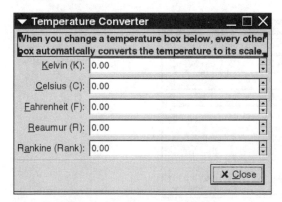

Figure 5.10: Preview with instruction label.

7. Set **Use Markup** to Yes; then add <b> </b> around your message.

8. As a final step, select the **Close** button widget and change its name to "closebutton."

5.1.4 The Widget Tree

So you're finished with the interface definition. Now choose **View > Show Widget Tree** in the main window to see the entire widget hierarchy as a tree. A fully expanded tree resembles Figure 5.11.

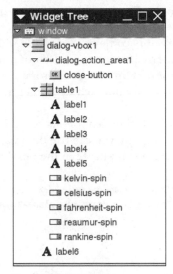

Figure 5.11: Temperature converter widget tree.

NOTE *When you click a widget in the tree, Glade selects the widget in the preview window.*

5.1.5 Clipboard

Another handy window is the clipboard, shown in Figure 5.12, accessed with the **View > Show Clipboard** main menu item.

Figure 5.12: Glade clipboard.

Cutting or copying a widget with an **Edit** or context menu item causes the widget to appear in the clipboard list. You can copy a clipboard widget back to the preview by right-clicking a slot and selecting **Paste** from the context menu. The clipboard is handy for making several copies of the same widget, because Glade duplicates initial widget property values (except for the name).

WARNING *There is no undo feature, so be careful where you paste widgets. Glade unscrupulously writes over anything in the paste target slot.*

5.2 Using the Interface

When you're happy with an interface (or are paranoid about losing data), save it with **Project > Save**. The first time you save a project, the **Project Options** dialog appears; you must supply a new directory and name here. Make sure that you deselect all of the check buttons under **File Output Options** on the **C Options** tab *except* **Set Widget Names**.

After the save, your project directory contains a *.glade* file with widget definitions and a *.gladep* file with internal information. Do not remove the *.gladep* file; it contains the Glade settings for that project. Your program does not need a *.gladep* file to run, though, and you should not include it when you distribute your program.

As you can see from the extensive listing that follows, a *.glade* file is an XML document. To use this file in your program, you can use the small, frequently overlooked library called *libglade*, which you will see in the next section.

```
<?xml version="1.0" standalone="no"?> <!--*- mode: xml -*-->
<!DOCTYPE glade-interface SYSTEM "http://glade.gnome.org/glade-2.0.dtd">

<glade-interface>
<requires lib="gnome"/>

<widget class="GtkDialog" id="window">
  <property name="border_width">3</property>
  <property name="visible">True</property>
  <property name="title" translatable="yes">Temperature Converter</property>
  <property name="type">GTK_WINDOW_TOPLEVEL</property>
  <property name="window_position">GTK_WIN_POS_NONE</property>
  <property name="modal">False</property>
  <property name="resizable">True</property>
  <property name="destroy_with_parent">False</property>
  <property name="has_separator">True</property>

  <child internal-child="vbox">
    <widget class="GtkVBox" id="dialog-vbox1">
      <property name="visible">True</property>
      <property name="homogeneous">False</property>
      <property name="spacing">0</property>

      <child internal-child="action_area">
        <widget class="GtkHButtonBox" id="dialog-action_area1">
          <property name="visible">True</property>
          <property name="layout_style">GTK_BUTTONBOX_END</property>

          <child>
            <widget class="GtkButton" id="close-button">
              <property name="visible">True</property>
              <property name="can_default">True</property>
              <property name="can_focus">True</property>
```

```
                <property name="label">gtk-close</property>
                <property name="use_stock">True</property>
                <property name="relief">GTK_RELIEF_NORMAL</property>
                <property name="response_id">-7</property>
              </widget>
            </child>
          </widget>
          <packing>
            <property name="padding">0</property>
            <property name="expand">False</property>
            <property name="fill">True</property>
            <property name="pack_type">GTK_PACK_END</property>
          </packing>
        </child>

        <child>
          <widget class="GtkLabel" id="label6">
            <property name="visible">True</property>
            <property name="label" translatable="yes">&lt;b&gt;When you change a \
temperature box below, every other box automatically converts the \
temperature to its scale.&lt;/b&gt;</property>
            <property name="use_underline">False</property>
            <property name="use_markup">True</property>
            <property name="justify">GTK_JUSTIFY_LEFT</property>
            <property name="wrap">True</property>
            <property name="selectable">False</property>
            <property name="xalign">0</property>
            <property name="yalign">0.5</property>
            <property name="xpad">0</property>
            <property name="ypad">0</property>
          </widget>
          <packing>
            <property name="padding">0</property>
            <property name="expand">False</property>
            <property name="fill">False</property>
          </packing>
        </child>

        <child>
          <widget class="GtkTable" id="table1">
            <property name="visible">True</property>
            <property name="n_rows">5</property>
            <property name="n_columns">2</property>
            <property name="homogeneous">False</property>
            <property name="row_spacing">6</property>
            <property name="column_spacing">6</property>

            <child>
              <widget class="GtkLabel" id="label1">
```

```
            <property name="visible">True</property>
            <property name="label" translatable="yes">_Kelvin (K):</property>
            <property name="use_underline">True</property>
            <property name="use_markup">False</property>
            <property name="justify">GTK_JUSTIFY_RIGHT</property>
            <property name="wrap">False</property>
            <property name="selectable">False</property>
            <property name="xalign">1</property>
            <property name="yalign">0.5</property>
            <property name="xpad">0</property>
            <property name="ypad">0</property>
            <property name="mnemonic_widget">kelvin-spin</property>
          </widget>
          <packing>
            <property name="left_attach">0</property>
            <property name="right_attach">1</property>
            <property name="top_attach">0</property>
            <property name="bottom_attach">1</property>
            <property name="x_options">fill</property>
            <property name="y_options"></property>
          </packing>
        </child>

        << more GtkLabel widget definitions >>

        <child>
          <widget class="GtkSpinButton" id="kelvin-spin">
            <property name="visible">True</property>
            <property name="can_focus">True</property>
            <property name="climb_rate">1</property>
            <property name="digits">2</property>
            <property name="numeric">True</property>
            <property name="update_policy">GTK_UPDATE_ALWAYS</property>
            <property name="snap_to_ticks">False</property>
            <property name="wrap">False</property>
            <property name="adjustment">1 0 10000 1 10 10</property>
          </widget>
          <packing>
            <property name="left_attach">1</property>
            <property name="right_attach">2</property>
            <property name="top_attach">0</property>
            <property name="bottom_attach">1</property>
            <property name="y_options"></property>
          </packing>
        </child>

        << more GtkSpinButton widget definitions >>

      </widget>
```

```
      <packing>
        <property name="padding">0</property>
        <property name="expand">True</property>
        <property name="fill">True</property>
      </packing>
    </child>
  </widget>
 </child>
</widget>

</glade-interface>
```

5.2.1 Reading Glade Files

To read the *file.glade* file into your program, include the Glade header files and call glade_xml_new().

```
#include <glade/glade.h>
GladeXML *ui_defs;

ui_defs = glade_xml_new("file.glade", root, domain);
```

Here, *root* is a widget root (use NULL if the file contains only one top-level widget), and *domain* is a translation environment (it can be NULL). After the function call, the *ui_defs* **GladeXML** object contains the interface definitions. The **GladeXML** object is not a widget — it's just an internal representation.

You should copy your application's *.glade* files along with any other program data to *$(PREFIX)/share/app_id* (*app_id* is your program's application identifier). Use a *glade* subdirectory if you feel that this is necessary. Use gnome_program_locate_file() with the GNOME_FILE_DOMAIN_APP_DATADIR category to return a path for the *.glade* file.

Here is how you might include a *.glade* file in a real program:

```
GnomeProgram *program;
gchar *filename;

GladeXML *all_defs, *window1_defs;

  << ... >>

filename = gnome_program_locate_file(program, GNOME_FILE_DOMAIN_APP_DATADIR,
                                     "interface.glade", TRUE, NULL);

/* read all definitions from the file */
all_defs = glade_xml_new(filename, NULL, NULL);

/* read only the widget tree starting at window1 */
window1_defs = glade_xml_new(filename, "window1", NULL);

g_free(filename);
```

5.2.2 Accessing Widgets

After reading one or more windows into a **GladeXML** object, you can get a
GtkWidget * pointer to access the widgets with these functions:

- GtkWidget *glade_xml_get_widget(GladeXml *ui_defs, const char *name)
  Returns a widget matching *name* in *ui_defs*, or NULL if there is no such widget.
  In many cases, you probably want to cast the return value to a more convenient form.

- GList *glade_xml_get_widget_prefix(GladeXml *ui_defs, const char *prefix)
  Returns a list of all widgets in *ui_defs* that begin with *prefix*. This function
  can be useful for iterating through several widgets with g_list_foreach().

5.2.3 Automatically Attaching Signals

You could call glade_xml_get_widget() to get a widget pointer and bind the
widget's signals by hand, but there's an even easier way: Add a handler identifier
with Glade.

In the Glade property editor for a widget, click the **Signals** tab. To add a
handler identifier, follow these steps:

1. Pick a signal from the **Signal** list.
2. Enter a handler identifier in the **Handler** box.
3. Click **Add**.

Figure 5.13 shows the signal display for the temperature converter's **Close**
button; the **clicked** signal carries the close-button-clicked identifier.

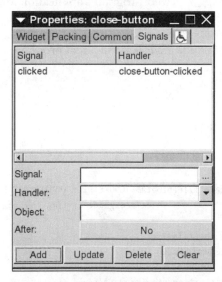

Figure 5.13: Glade signal editor display.

To connect the signal handler function in your program, use

```
glade_xml_signal_connect(ui_defs, handler_id, func)
```

Here, *ui_defs* is a **GladeXML** object, *handler_id* is the new handler identifier, and *func* is the handler callback function. Widgets may share handler identifiers; glade_xml_signal_connect() binds the signal to all applicable widgets. If you want to include a data pointer with the signal, use

```
glade_xml_signal_connect_data(ui_defs, handler_id, func, data)
```

You can make *libglade* attempt to automatically connect signal handlers with

```
glade_xml_signal_autoconnect(ui_defs)
```

Here, *libglade* attaches a handler to the function's widget if the handler identifier matches a function name. However, a couple of things can go wrong:

- You need to compile with a special option like -export-dynamic.
- GModule must work properly; that is, it must understand how to grovel around in a binary's symbol table.
- You can't pass much for a data pointer.
- You can't use g_signal_connect_swapped().
- You can't use dashes and other restricted characters in your handler identifiers.

The temperature conversion example uses glade_xml_signal_connect_data(); see Section 5.2.5.

5.2.4 Associative Functions

There are two functions that can help you go back and forth between Glade identifiers and widgets:

- const char *glade_get_widget_name(GtkWidget *widget)
  Returns the Glade widget name corresponding to *widget*. Do not change or deallocate this string.
- GladeXML *glade_get_widget_tree(GtkWidget *widget)
  Returns the **GladeXML** object that defines *widget*.

5.2.5 The Complete Temperature Converter

This section contains the entire temperature conversion program that goes with *temperature.glade*. Notice that there are no big pieces dealing with widget creation and packing — one glade_xml_new() call does the work. Not only do a dozen lines or so replace what would otherwise be a huge portion of a conventional program, but you should also remember that you can tweak small parts of the interface at any time with Glade, eliminating the need to recompile the code.

Notice that the global definitions reflect only some of the widgets:

```
/* -*-coding: utf-8;-*- */
/* temperature.c -- temperature converter using libglade */

#include <gnome.h>
#include <glade/glade.h>

typedef enum {
  KELVIN,
  CELSIUS,
  FAHRENHEIT,
  REAUMUR,
  RANKINE,
  NUM_TEMPERATURE_SCALES
} TemperatureScale;

const gchar *widget_name[] = {
  "kelvin-spin",
  "celsius-spin",
  "fahrenheit-spin",
  "reaumur-spin",
  "rankine-spin"
};

GtkSpinButton *temp_spin[NUM_TEMPERATURE_SCALES];
gulong handler[NUM_TEMPERATURE_SCALES];
gdouble temp_value[NUM_TEMPERATURE_SCALES];
```

This handler function is the meat of the program. Notice how this callback blocks signals at the very end, where the values go back to the spin buttons.

```
void changed(GtkSpinButton *spin_button, gpointer id_ptr)
{
  TemperatureScale scale_id = (TemperatureScale)id_ptr;
  TemperatureScale i;

  g_assert(scale_id >= KELVIN && scale_id < NUM_TEMPERATURE_SCALES);

  /* read the temperature from the spin button */
  g_object_get(temp_spin[scale_id], "value", &temp_value[scale_id], NULL);

  /* determine the Kelvin equivalent of that temperature */
  switch (scale_id)
  {
    case CELSIUS:
```

```
            temp_value[KELVIN] = temp_value[CELSIUS] + 273.15;
            break;

      case FAHRENHEIT:
            temp_value[KELVIN] = (5.0/9.0)*(temp_value[FAHRENHEIT]-32.0) + 273.15;
            break;

      case REAUMUR:
            temp_value[KELVIN] = (5.0/4.0)*temp_value[REAUMUR] + 273.15;
            break;

      case RANKINE:
            temp_value[KELVIN] = (5.0/9.0)*temp_value[RANKINE];
            break;

      default:
            break;
   }

   /* determine the rest of the values based on the Kelvin temperature */
   if (scale_id != CELSIUS)
      temp_value[CELSIUS] = temp_value[KELVIN] - 273.15;

   if (scale_id != FAHRENHEIT)
      temp_value[FAHRENHEIT] = (9.0/5.0)*(temp_value[KELVIN]-273.15) + 32.0;

   if (scale_id != REAUMUR)
      temp_value[REAUMUR] = (4.0/5.0)*(temp_value[KELVIN]-273.15);

   if (scale_id != RANKINE)
      temp_value[RANKINE] = (9.0/5.0)*temp_value[KELVIN];

   /* write the new values back into the spin buttons;
      disable signal handlers when doing this so that this
      handler function doesn't get called again and again and.. */
   for (i=KELVIN; i < NUM_TEMPERATURE_SCALES; i++)
   {
      if (scale_id != i)
      {
         g_signal_handler_block(temp_spin[i], handler[i]);
         g_object_set(temp_spin[i], "value", temp_value[i], NULL);
         g_signal_handler_unblock(temp_spin[i], handler[i]);
      }
   }
}

/* standard event handlers */
gint delete_event(GtkWidget *widget, GdkEvent event, gpointer data)
```

```
{
  return FALSE;
}

void end_program(GtkWidget *widget, gpointer data)
{
  gtk_main_quit();
}
```

This event handler is for the **Close** button on the main dialog window.

```
void close_clicked(GtkButton *button, gpointer window_ptr)
{
  GtkDialog *window = GTK_DIALOG(window_ptr);
  gtk_widget_destroy(GTK_WIDGET(window));
}
```

Here is the main program — just about 50 lines of code. The *libglade* library assists in attaching the handler near the end of the program.

```
int main(int argc, char **argv)
{
  GladeXML *ui;
  GnomeProgram *program;
  GtkDialog *window;
  TemperatureScale i;

  /* initialize GNOME */
  program = gnome_program_init("temperature", "0.1",
                               LIBGNOMEUI_MODULE,
                               argc, argv,
                               GNOME_PROGRAM_STANDARD_PROPERTIES,
                               GNOME_PARAM_HUMAN_READABLE_NAME, "Temperature",
                               NULL);

  /* read the definitions with libglade */
  ui = glade_xml_new("temperature.glade", NULL, NULL);

  /* get a handle on each of the spin button widgets */
  for (i=KELVIN; i < NUM_TEMPERATURE_SCALES; i++)
  {
     temp_spin[i] = GTK_SPIN_BUTTON(glade_xml_get_widget(ui, widget_name[i]));
  }
  window = GTK_DIALOG(glade_xml_get_widget(ui, "window"));

  /* bind "value-changed" signal handler for each spin button,
     use an identifier as the the user data pointer */
  for (i = KELVIN; i < NUM_TEMPERATURE_SCALES; i++)
```

```
{
   handler[i] = g_signal_connect(temp_spin[i],
                              "value-changed", G_CALLBACK(changed),
                              GUINT_TO_POINTER(i));
}

/* set the starting value to the boiling point of water */
g_object_set(temp_spin[CELSIUS], "value", 100.0, NULL);

/* attach standard handlers */
g_signal_connect(window, "delete_event", G_CALLBACK(delete_event), NULL);
g_signal_connect(window, "destroy", G_CALLBACK(end_program), NULL);

/* attach the close button handler with the help of libglade */
glade_xml_signal_connect_data(ui,
                           "close-button-clicked",
                           G_CALLBACK(close_clicked),
                           GUINT_TO_POINTER(window));

gtk_main();          /* start GTK+ main event loop */
return 0;
}
```

5.3 Further Topics

Glade is not hard to learn, and for programmers, there isn't much to see beyond the few API functions. However, this book has left out a few things:

- **Generating code**. As you might guess from terminology such as "Project," Glade can generate more than a little *.glade* file. If you check more options in the **Project Options** window, then Glade constructs an entire Autotools-configurable source tree when you select **Project > Build** from the main menu bar. You need only fill in your own code.

    Here's the catch: It's a one-way street. You can't go from a source tree back to a *.glade* file, and therefore, it's hard to go back and change something in the interface. This feature may be good for generating quick one-off bits of code, but that's about all.

- **Multilanguage support**. Glade can generate code for languages other than C, such as Python, Perl, C++, Eiffel, and Ada.

- **Accessibility**. Glade's property editor has a tab for ATK settings. Most of these settings supply additional information about a widget so that they can better interface with screen readers, voice recognition systems, and other such tools. This book does not cover ATK, so a description of the ATK settings in Glade would not be particularly enlightening here, either.

6

ADDITIONAL SOFTWARE DEVELOPMENT TOOLS

The sections in this chapter cover several utilities that do not quite fit anywhere else. These tools come with GNOME and can save a significant amount of time and energy when building a GNOME application.

6.1 pkg-config

If you try any of the programming examples in this book, you need to compile the code with options for the libraries, include paths, and library paths. Let's say that your GNOME installation prefix is */opt/gnome*. To compile a program that requires only GLib, you need to enter something like this:

```
$ gcc -I/opt/gnome/include/glib-2.0 -I/opt/gnome/lib/glib-2.0/include \
    -o program program.c -L/opt/gnome/lib -lglib-2.0
```

This requires quite a bit of typing — but things really get out of control when you try to compile one of the GTK+ examples from Chapter 3:

```
$ gcc -I/opt/gnome/include/gtk-2.0 -I/opt/gnome/lib/gtk-2.0/include \
    -I/opt/gnome/include/atk-1.0 -I/opt/gnome/include/pango-1.0 \
    -I/usr/X11R6/include -I/usr/include/freetype2 \
    -I/opt/gnome/include/glib-2.0 -I/opt/gnome/lib/glib-2.0/include \
    -o program program.c \
    -L/opt/gnome/lib -L/usr/X11R6/lib -lgtk-x11-2.0 -lgdk-x11-2.0 \
    -latk-1.0 -lgdk_pixbuf-2.0 -lm -lpangoxft-1.0 -lpangox-1.0 \
    -lpango-1.0 -lgobject-2.0 -lgmodule-2.0 -ldl -lglib-2.0
```

And if you think this is bad, just think of what the GNOME examples in Chapter 4 require. Even entering this information into a Makefile is too much to ask. Not only is it nearly impossible to remember the exact paths and version numbers, but the specifics vary wildly between systems and releases.

Older releases of GNOME addressed this problem with configuration shell scripts for each component. When you wanted to include a certain path in your compiler's options, you could use command substitution to send the shell script's output to your compiler command line. However, this had its own share of glitches, especially with dependencies.

In GNOME 2.0, one program named pkg-config replaces each shell script. One directory (typically *$(PREFIX)/lib/pkgconfig*) contains configuration files with *.pc* extensions for each GNOME package. You should take a look at one of them; for example, here is *gtk+-2.0.pc*:

```
prefix=/opt/gnome
exec_prefix=${prefix}
libdir=${exec_prefix}/lib
includedir=${prefix}/include
target=x11

gtk_binary_version=2.2.0
gtk_host=i586-pc-linux-gnu

Name: GTK+
Description: GIMP Tool Kit (${target} target)
Version: 2.2.1
Requires: gdk-${target}-2.0 atk
Libs: -L${libdir} -lgtk-${target}-2.0
Cflags: -I${includedir}/gtk-2.0
```

Everything is there: The name, version, installation path, dependencies, compiler options, and more are all available with a single pkg-config command.

Make sure that your PKG_CONFIG_PATH contains all of the directories on your system that have *.pc* files. Like PATH and MANPATH, this is a colon-delimited set of directory names:

```
$ echo PKG_CONFIG_PATH
/usr/local/lib/pkgconfig:/usr/lib/pkgconfig:/opt/gnome/lib/pkgconfig
```

6.1.1   Package Lists, Versions, and Descriptions

If your system and environment are working correctly, you can run the following command to print a catalog of all known packages with descriptions:

```
pkg-config --list-all
```

All other `pkg-config` options require a package name. Run this to see if *package* exists on your system:

```
$ pkg-config --exists package
```

The `pkg-config` command exits with status 0 if the package exists (useful for shell programming). If you want to know the exact version number, type

```
$ pkg-config --modversion package
```

Here are some examples of how you might use `pkg-config` to check on GLib and a nonexistent package:

```
$ pkg-config --exists glib-2.0
$ echo $?
0

$ pkg-config --exists glont-5.9
$ echo $?
1

$ pkg-config --modversion glib-2.0
2.2.1

$ pkg-config --modversion glont-5.9
Package glont-5.9 was not found in the pkg-config search path.
Perhaps you should add the directory containing `glont-5.9.pc'
to the PKG_CONFIG_PATH environment variable
No package 'glont-5.9' found
```

NOTE   *Don't confuse* --modversion *with* --version. *The* --version *option always returns the* pkg-config *version.*

6.1.2   Determining Compiler and Linker Options

Although it's nice to know a package version, the real purpose of `pkg-config` is to determine compiler options with `--cflags` and linker options with `--libs`.

You can combine options and packages; here are some examples:

```
$ pkg-config --cflags glib-2.0
-I/opt/gnome/include/glib-2.0 -I/opt/gnome/lib/glib-2.0/include

$ pkg-config --libs glib-2.0
-L/opt/gnome/lib -lglib-2.0

$ pkg-config --cflags --libs glib-2.0
-I/opt/gnome/include/glib-2.0 -I/opt/gnome/lib/glib-2.0/include \
-L/opt/gnome/lib -lglib-2.0

$ pkg-config --cflags --libs glib-2.0 libxml-2.0
-I/opt/gnome/include/glib-2.0 -I/opt/gnome/lib/glib-2.0/include \
-I/opt/gnome/include/libxml2 \
-L/opt/gnome/lib -L/opt/gnome/lib -lglib-2.0 -lxml2 -lz -lm
```

Use shell command substitution to compile a single source file `glib_program.c` into an executable:

```
gcc -o glib_program glib_program.c `pkg-config glib-2.0 --cflags --libs`
```

6.1.3 Using pkg-config in a Makefile

Most software packages are too large for a single command line. Here is how you might use `pkg-config` in a Makefile:

```
CFLAGS=-ansi -Wall `pkg-config glib-2.0 --cflags`
LDFLAGS=`pkg-config glib-2.0 --libs`

glib_program: glib_program.c
        gcc $(CFLAGS) -o glib_program glib_program.c $(LDFLAGS)
```

6.2 The GNU Autotools

Although Makefiles are very powerful (especially when using `pkg-config`), they run against limitations in the following situations:

- The source code distribution has several subdirectories, most requiring their own Makefiles.
- Several Makefiles share common components.
- The installation process copies files into several user-configured places on your system.
- Target platforms have slight incompatibilities requiring preprocessor directives or other circumvention methods.

Free software usually has all of the above traits, so managing compiles can get to be a problem. Perhaps you've already seen one popular solution to this problem when issuing these three commands to build a package:

```
$ ./configure
$ make
$ make install
```

The tools behind the `configure` program are collectively known as the GNU autotools. This book provides only a survey of this powerful configuration/ compilation system. For more detailed information, see [Vaughan].

6.2.1 Overview

The general procedure for outfitting your source code with the GNU autotools is as follows:

1. Create a *configure.ac* file in your top-level source distribution directory. This file not only defines GNU autotool behavior, but later, a macro expansion creates the `configure` script. (At one time, *configure.ac* carried the name *configure.in*.)
2. Create a *Makefile.am* file in each subdirectory where the compiler or installer runs.
3. Run `gettexttize` for localization, `intltoolize` for additional translation support, and/or `libtoolize` to build your own libraries.
4. Run `aclocal` to gather all necessary macros from the macro library into the *aclocal.m4* file.
5. Run `autoheader` to create a *config.h.in* file — a template for the preprocessor macros necessary for your package.
6. Run `automake` to build a *Makefile.in* template from each of your *Makefile.am* files.
7. Use `autoconf` to run the `m4` macro processor on *configure.ac* with the macros in *aclocal.m4* to create the `configure` script.

You do not need to perform any of these steps with most public source code distributions because the developers do everything for you. However, if you get your hands on developer code (with **CVS**, for instance), things look quite different, because you may need several other current software packages and a complete set of GNU autotools just to get to the point where you can run `./configure`.

The `configure` script checks your system for necessary prerequisites to build the package. If successful, `configure` creates a number of files from *.in* templates (for example, *config.h* from *config.h.in*).

NOTE   *Makefiles also come from Makefile.in templates in the GNU autotools system and are therefore disposable. Furthermore, a program called* automake *sometimes generates Makefile.in templates from Makefile.am files.*

If everything goes well, configure leaves you with Makefiles in all of the relevant subdirectories. The top-level Makefile contains targets like all, install, clean, and distclean; a make command to build one of these targets also runs make on the Makefile in the each subdirectory.

Even given the simplified description of the autotools so far, you can see that the process is far from trivial. The tools (and the files that they generate) work together to form one complex, powerful system, sort of like the gears in a clock. Rather than go into hundreds of pages of explanation, this book contains a recipe for everyday autotool use.

The example you're about to see is a fictitious GNOME package named example. Its distribution tree contains the subdirectories *src* for the source code and *pixmaps* for image data.

6.2.2   configure.ac

The centerpiece of the configuration process is *configure.ac*, located in your software distribution's top-level directory. Several tools read and process the macro invocations inside *configure.ac*, including autoconf (to create the configure script).

NOTE   *The name configure.ac has not been around for very long — you may see configure.in instead.*

You may find the m4 macro syntax somewhat unusual. You should always remember that *configure.ac* contains no real instructions, but rather, macro invocations that m4 expands into shell script fragments.

As you look at *configure.ac*, remember the following rules:

- Do not leave whitespace between the macro name and its opening parenthesis.

- Do not leave whitespace between a macro argument and its comma separator, and do not leave whitespace between the last argument and the closing parenthesis.

- m4 normally processes its input until there is nothing left to expand.

- m4 does not process anything inside square brackets ([ ]).

- Comments start with a hash mark (#).

```
# ============== initialization =====================
AC_INIT([Example], [0.1], [example-bugs@example.com], [example])

AC_CONFIG_SRCDIR([src/main.c])
AC_CONFIG_HEADER(config.h)
AM_INIT_AUTOMAKE
AM_MAINTAINER_MODE

# ============== basic compiler settings =============
AC_PROG_CC
AC_HEADER_STDC

# ============== take care of some localization ======
```

```
AH_TEMPLATE([GETTEXT_PACKAGE], [Package name for gettext])
GETTEXT_PACKAGE=example # note that this is a command
AC_DEFINE_UNQUOTED(GETTEXT_PACKAGE, "$GETTEXT_PACKAGE")
AC_SUBST(GETTEXT_PACKAGE)
ALL_LINGUAS="de es"
AM_GLIB_GNU_GETTEXT
AC_PROG_INTLTOOL


# ============== export compiler/linker options ======
AC_SUBST(CFLAGS)
AC_SUBST(CPPFLAGS)
AC_SUBST(LDFLAGS)


# ============== look for GNOME =====================
GNOME_MODULES="libgnomeui-2.0 >= 2.0.0"
PKG_CHECK_MODULES(GNOME, $GNOME_MODULES)
AC_SUBST(GNOME_CFLAGS)
AC_SUBST(GNOME_LIBS)


# ============== generate files ====================
AC_CONFIG_FILES([
Makefile
src/Makefile
pixmaps/Makefile
po/Makefile.in
])
AC_OUTPUT
```

The *configure.ac* file starts with this expansion:

```
AC_INIT(name, version, email, short_name)
```

where *name* is the package's full name, *version* is the version number, *email* is a
contact address, and *short_name* is the package's main program. Put each of these
in square brackets to disable further expansion. For GNOME applications, use
the parameters that you gave to gnome_program_init().

AC_CONFIG_SRCDIR(*path*) configures the source directory; path defines the
relative path to a file in the actual source code directory.

AC_CONFIG_HEADER(*header_file*) specifies the main C preprocessor target file
that configure generates. Normally, *header_file* is *config.h*.

The next part of the file is AM_INIT_AUTOMAKE to initialize automake, and then
AM_MAINTAINER_MODE to enable certain developer targets in the Makefiles when you
run configure with the --enable-maintainer-mode option.

Now you're ready for compiler settings. Make sure that the compiler works
and has standard C headers with

```
AC_PROG_CC
AC_HEADER_STDC
```

The next section in the *configure.ac* file deals with gettext, to make sure that the program can match different locales. The expansion of

---
AH_TEMPLATE(*var_name, description*)

---

causes autoheader to define *var_name* in the preprocessor template file. If you want GETTEXT_PACKAGE in *config.h.in*, you should specify it with AH_TEMPLATE, because you'll get error messages from autoheader otherwise.

To set GETTEXT_PACKAGE to a program name that should be localized, assign it as you would a shell variable. Then use

---
AC_DEFINE_UNQUOTED(*var_name*, "$*var_name*")

---

to make sure that *var_name* and its value make it into *config.h*. In addition, use

---
AC_SUBST(*var_name*)

---

to export *var_name* to *Makefile.am*.

ALL_LINGUAS defines additional locales (here, "de es" for German and Spanish). Finally, activate gettext and intltool with

---
AM_GLIB_GNU_GETTEXT
AC_PROG_INTLTOOL

You're finished with localization; it's time to export some more variables for the compiler. Use AC_SUBST on CFLAGS (compiler options), CPPFLAGS (C preprocessor options, such as include paths), and LDFLAGS (linker options).

The next part uses pkg-config to see if the GNOME version number is high enough:

GNOME_MODULES="libgnomeui-2.0 >= 2.0.0"
PKG_CHECK_MODULES(GNOME, $GNOME_MODULES)

That first parameter to PKG_CHECK_MODULES is very important; the expansion of PKG_CHECK_MODULES(*name*, "*package ..*")) sets *name*_CFLAGS to the output of pkg-config --cflags *package* (*name*_LDFLAGS is similar). Therefore, the next two lines export the GNOME compiler and linker options:

AC_SUBST(GNOME_CFLAGS)
AC_SUBST(GNOME_LIBS)

Now you're ready to tell the autotools what files configure should generate with

---
AC_CONFIG_FILES([*file1*
file2
...
])

To generate the files, use

```
AC_OUTPUT
```

Every file that `configure` generates needs a *.in* template. You do not need to create all of these by yourself; in particular, you can tell `automake` to create *Makefile.in* files for you.

6.2.3   Makefile Templates

The `automake` utility builds *Makefile.in* from *Makefile.am*, a file that consists of these definitions:

- The programs to compile.
- The header and library requirements.
- The files that in the current directory need to be installed upon a `make` `install`, and where to install them.
- Any subdirectories that need `make`.

Top-Level Makefile.am

Here is the top-level *Makefile.am* for the example program:

```
## Process this file with automake to produce Makefile.in
SUBDIRS = src pixmaps po

desktopdir = $(datadir)/applications
desktop_in_files = example.desktop.in
desktop_DATA = $(desktop_in_files:.desktop.in=.desktop)
@INTLTOOL_DESKTOP_RULE@

EXTRA_DIST = example.desktop.in \
             intltool-extract.in \
             intltool-merge.in \
             intltool-update.in

DISTCLEANFILES = intltool-extract \
                 intltool-merge \
                 intltool-update

clean-local:
        rm -f example.desktop
        rm -f po/.intltool-merge-cache
```

At the very top is `SUBDIRS`, the other subdirectories that `make` should enter. Notice that if you add a directory to your source distribution, you need to add it in *configure.ac* and the top-level *Makefile.am*.

The menu item definitions in *example.desktop* (see Section 6.3) comes from *example.desktop.in*. You need some more definitions to tell automake how to build an appropriate Makefile rule:

1. Set `desktopdir` to the installation directory. automake knows that variables ending in `dir` are installation directories.
2. The `desktop_in_files` line sets the input file to *example.desktop.in*.
3. A `_DATA` suffix tells automake that the given file needs no further compilation or processing. However, you may be confused by this part:

```
$(desktop_in_files:.desktop.in=.desktop)
```

This means "expand the $desktop_in_files variable, but substitute .desktop.in with .desktop."

4. `@INTLTOOL_DESKTOP_RULE@` tells automake to insert an intltool Makefile rule to convert *.desktop.in* to *.desktop*. See Section 6.5 for more information on gettext and intltool.

Next up in this *Makefile.am* is `EXTRA_DIST`, a list of extra files to include in when packing the source code for distribution (see Section 6.2.7 for a list of the standard files).

The `DISTCLEANFILES` variable is a list of files to remove when running make distclean.

Finally, there is a normal make target, `clean-local`, to remove files generated from *.in* templates; automake and autoconf support `-local` as dependencies of standard targets (see Section 6.2.10 for a list), and therefore, a make `clean` runs the rule for `clean-local`.

NOTE *In all honesty, you should use* `CLEANFILES` *to add files to the* make `clean` *sequence, just as was the case with* `DISTCLEANFILES`. *This slightly unconventional approach is here only for didactic purposes.*

Source Directory Makefile.am

This is *src/Makefile.am* in the example package:

```
## Process this file with automake to produce Makefile.in
INCLUDES = -DGNOMELOCALEDIR=\""$(datadir)/locale/"\" \
            -DG_LOG_DOMAIN=\"Example\" \
            -I$(top_srcdir) \
            $(GNOME_CFLAGS)

LIBS = $(GNOME_LIBS)

bin_PROGRAMS = example
example_SOURCES = main.c
```

The standard variable `INCLUDES` contains preprocessor options such as include paths and macro definitions:

- GNOMELOCALEDIR is the end target for localization files (note the backslash before the first and last quotation marks).

- You saw G_LOG_DOMAIN (for message logging) in Section 1.4.6.

- -I$(top_srcdir) includes the top-level distribution directory, so that your program can include *config.h*.

- $(GNOME_CFLAGS) includes the configure options for GNOME. Recall that *configure.ac* exported GNOME_CFLAGS as the output of a pkg-config --cflags command.

LIBS is the standard variable for linker options. GNOME_LIBS comes from configure, much like the C flags just mentioned.

With the options out of the way, you must now specify the programs to build, where to install them, and the source code to compile. Set the special variable bin_PROGRAMS to the names of the programs to build. The bin component means that a make install should put the executables in the user-configured binary directory, and _PROGRAMS says that the linker must create the given program from object files.

The example_SOURCES setting tells automake how to form a target for a program from a collection of source code files. example is a program name; _SOURCES, another special suffix, indicates that the following source files are the basis for example. The automake utility defines rules for creating object files from these source files.

Pixmap Directory Makefile.am

The *pixmaps/Makefile.am* file demonstrates how easy it is to create a Makefile to copy files into a user-configured directory:

```
## Process this file with automake to produce Makefile.in

pixmapsdir = $(datadir)/pixmaps
pixmaps_DATA = example.png
```

6.2.4   Extra Tools

If you want to support locale with GNU gettext, run gettextize to set up the infrastructure in your distribution. Among other things, this program initializes the *po* directory for translation files.

You can add support for the intltool- utilities with intltoolize. This setup program is necessary to convert GConf *.schemas* files, menu items (*.desktop*), and GnomeVFS *.keys* files. Refer to Section 6.5 for information on how to use gettext and intltool.

To build your own dynamic libraries, run libtoolize to add libtool to your distribution. Refer to the libtool info page for information on how to tie it into your source code.

6.2.5 aclocal and m4 Libraries

Before you can process the macros in *Makefile.am* and *configure.ac*, you must run aclocal to gather the macro definitions from the system libraries and place them into *aclocal.m4*. On an ideal system, you would not need to supply any arguments, but for GNOME programs, you often need to grab macros from your GNOME installation. For example, if GNOME lives in */opt/gnome*, run

```
aclocal -I /opt/gnome/share/aclocal
```

WARNING *Don't forget the space between* -I *and the path. It's easy to confuse this with a compiler option.*

6.2.6 autoheader

You're almost ready to run automake, but first, you need to run autoheader to create *config.h.in*. If you want to create your own macro templates for the *config.h.in* macro, see the GETTEXT_PACKAGE example in Section 6.2.2.

6.2.7 automake and Standard Package Files

To build a *Makefile.in* from each of your *Makefile.am* files, run automake. Normally, you should run

```
automake --add-missing --gnu
```

to add any of these standard files:

- *AUTHORS:* A list of the authors. Email addresses are optional (you may want to use disguises, so that spam address harvesters can't collect anything).
- *ChangeLog:* A detailed list of all changes in the code in GNU Emacs change-log-mode format. Have a look at the *ChangeLog* file in any GNOME component package if you don't know what this is. CVS servers require a *ChangeLog* entry for each change in a source tree.
- *COPYING:* Your package's license. By default, this is the newest version of the GNU GPL [FSF 1991].
- *INSTALL:* Installation instructions. A generic configure-based document is the default.
- *NEWS:* A small summary of your package's changes and new features, indexed by version.
- *README:* A description of your package, along with any other notes.

NOTE *The* automake *program creates empty files for AUTHORS, ChangeLog, NEWS, and README if they do not exist. For the remaining files,* automake *normally creates symbolic links to files in your automake installation directory. However, if you are assembling a package for distribution, add* -c *to actually copy the missing files. If you want to make sure that the files (the license, for example) are up-to-date, use* -f.

6.2.8   autoconf

Run autoconf in your package's top-level directory to create configure. A by-product is *autom4te.cache*, containing macro cache data. Deleting this directory has no ill effects.

6.2.9   configure

Most people run ./configure alone on the command line. However, there are several important options:

- --prefix=*dir* sets the package installation prefix to *dir*. The default is */usr/ local*. Many systems put GNOME in */opt/gnome*, with binaries in */opt/gnome*, header files in */opt/gnome/include*, and so on.

- --help displays an extensive help message for all of the configure options.

- --version displays the version of the software package and the autoconf used to generate configure.

- --enable-maintainer-mode adds Makefile targets to ensure that the tree stays current when someone updates a *Makefile.am* or *configure.ac* file.

The configure script performs a number of tests on your system, printing messages as it progresses. The *config.log* file contains more specific information and is the place to look if configure aborts with an error.

Finally, configure runs config.status to create all Makefiles and anything else in AC_CONFIG_FILES.

6.2.10   Standard Targets

After you configure your source tree, you have the following make targets at your disposal:

- make all: Compiles all code in the tree. This is usually the default target.

- make clean: Removes all executables and object files.

- make distclean: Cleans the source tree to a state suitable for redistribution. In particular, this removes all files generated by configure.

- make maintainer-clean: Like make distclean, but removes everything automatically generated by the GNU autotools.

- make install: Installs the package.

- make install-strip: Installs the package, removing the symbol table from executables and libraries as it goes. This saves some space.

- make dist: Creates a *.tar.gz* distribution file for the source tree based on the application identifier and version number.

- make distcheck: Verifies that a package compiles and makes sure that it is ready to distribute (for example, it checks whether make distclean really does what it is supposed to do).

- make uninstall: Removes the package from your system. This works only in a configured source tree.

6.2.11   autogen.sh

Most packages include a `autogen.sh` script to run everything from gettextize to configure for you, so that you don't have to worry about getting all of the steps in the right order.

You must come up with your own `autogen.sh` script. In other words, you're probably going to steal one from some other place. You have two options here:

1.   Glade comes with an `autogen.sh` script to copy into new projects. You may have to make some changes (for example, the script may refer to *configure.in* instead of *configure.ac*), but it's better than nothing.

2.   Adapt the `autogen.sh` script from the gnome-common package from cvs.gnome.org.

6.3   Menu Items

If you have a graphical application, you should put it into your GNOME application menu. All you have to do is create *appname.desktop*, where *appname* is your application's name, and install this file into *$(PREFIX)/share/applications*. Here is an example, *miracletext.desktop*:

```
[Desktop Entry]
Name=Example
Comment=MiracleText Word Processor
Comment[de]=MiracleText Textverarbeitung
Comment[es]=MiracleText procesador de textos
Name=Edit documents with MiracleText
Name[de]=Dokumente bearbeiten mit MiracleText
Name[es]=Edita documentos con MiracleText
TryExec=example
Exec=example %U
Icon=example.png
Terminal=0
Type=Application
Categories=Application
```

Like many other files that you have seen so far, there are keys and values here, and you can specify a locale with square brackets ([ ]). You must use UTF-8 for all values with a locale identifier and ASCII for the rest. The key meanings are as follows:

- `Version`: The *.desktop* file format, currently 1.0.

- `Type`: For applications, this is always `Application`.

- `Encoding`: Character encoding; set this to `UTF-8`.

- `Name`: The name of the application that should show up in the menu item. If there's enough space, include a very short blurb indicating the application's purpose.

- **Comment**: A fairly detailed description of what the user can do with the application. Use a verb's imperative form in the phrase: for example, "Set the system clock" or "Automatically upload to websites."

- **TryExec**: The name of the application's executable without options.

- **Exec**: The executable's syntax. You may use any of the following placeholders:

  %f A filename.

  %F A set of filenames.

  %u A URI.

  %U A set of URIs.

  %d A directory.

  %D A set of directories.

  %n A filename without a path.

  %N A set of filenames without paths.

  As you can see, MiracleText is a fairly modern application, accepting URIs on the command line.

- **Icon**: The icon for the menu; the path should be relative to *$(PREFIX)/share/pixmaps*.

- **Terminal**: Set this to true if the application must run in a terminal emulator window, and false otherwise.

- **Categories**: A semicolon-delimited category path for the application. Use one of the following:

  GNOME;Application;AudioVideo;

  GNOME;Application;Development;

  GNOME;Application;Game;

  GNOME;Application;Graphics;

  GNOME;Application;Network;

  GNOME;Application;Office;

  GNOME;Application;Settings;

  GNOME;Application;Utility;

A new menu item should appear as soon as you copy its *.desktop* file into *$(PREFIX)/share/applications*.

For more information on the file format, see [Brown]. You can also edit a *.desktop* graphically with gnome-desktop-item-edit.

6.4 Help Documents

Good applications not only have a well-designed interface, but also provide extensive online documentation. GNOME uses the widely known DocBook standard. The preferred format is DocBook XML, and you may use DocBook SGML or plain HTML if you prefer. However, you should stick with DocBook, because it has organizational advantages over plain old HTML.

The easiest way to learn DocBook is to look through the help files that come with GNOME. The specifics on GNOME style and structure are in [GDSG]; the official GNOME Documentation Project manual is in [Mason]. [Walsh] is a good reference to DocBook in general.

6.4.1 Installing Documentation

An application's help files go in *$(DATADIR)/gnome/help/appname/locale*, where *appname* is the application name and *locale* is the locale identifier. Files with no locale go in *C*. Any images go in *figures*, under the locale directory.

For example, if your installation prefix is */opt/gnome*, you'll find the original documentation for the GNOME terminal in */opt/gnome/share/gnome/help/terminal/C* and the images for the German documentation for Gnumeric in */opt/gnome/share/gnome/help/gnumeric/de/figures*.

If you put everything in the right place, you can use the URI functions described in Section 4.2.2 to access the help files from your application.

There's only one task left to do: Write a description file so that you can register your documentation with *ScrollKeeper*. Description files are in **OMF** format and carry a *.omf* extension. Here is an example:

```
<?xml version="1.0" encoding="UTF-8"?>
<!DOCTYPE omf PUBLIC "-//OMF//DTD Scrollkeeper OMF Variant V1.0//EN"
"http://scrollkeeper.sourceforge.net/dtds/scrollkeeper-omf-1.0/scrollkeeper-omf.dtd">
<omf>
  <resource>
    <creator>
     gric@example.com (George Ricshaw)
    </creator>
    <maintainer>
     gric@example.com (George Ricshaw)
    </maintainer>
    <title>
      MiracleText Manual
    </title>
    <date>
    2003-06-24
    </date>
    <subject category="GNOME|Applications|Office"/>
    <format mime="text/xml"/>
    <identifier url="file:///opt/gnome/share/gnome/help/miracletext/C/miracletext.xml"/>
    <language code="C"/>
    <relation seriesid="2619c82a-a636-11d6-8522-d29c286dcc64"/>
  </resource>
</omf>
```

For more information on writing and installing OMF files, open a GNOME help browser and look at **System > Other > Writing ScrollKeeper OMF Files** [Mueth] (it's under the **Additional documents** header).

You can install an OMF file with

```
scrollkeeper-install file.omf
```

6.5 Supporting Locale Options with gettext and intltool

GNOME uses GNU gettext to support locale. Here is how to use gettext in your program:

1. Set the *configure.ac* macros for gettext as described in Section 6.2.2.
2. Run gettextize and intltoolize in your source tree.
3. In your source code, enclose all target strings with _( ), and all target string constants with N_( ):

```
const gchar *str_array[] =
{
  N_("egg"),
  N_("miracle"),
  N_("drill"),
};

g_print("%s\n", _(str_array[i]));
```

4. Change to your *po* directory and create *POTFILES.in*, a list of all of the source file names that you changed (relative to your source tree root):

```
src/main.c
src/aux.c
```

5. Run make prog.pot in your *po* directory to create a translation template that looks something like this:

```
# SOME DESCRIPTIVE TITLE.
# Copyright (C) YEAR THE PACKAGE'S COPYRIGHT HOLDER
# This file is distributed under the same license as the PACKAGE package.
# FIRST AUTHOR <EMAIL@ADDRESS>, YEAR.
#
#, fuzzy
msgid ""
msgstr ""
"Project-Id-Version: PACKAGE VERSION\n"
"Report-Msgid-Bugs-To: \n"
"POT-Creation-Date: 2003-07-03 16:51-0700\n"
"PO-Revision-Date: YEAR-MO-DA HO:MI+ZONE\n"
"Last-Translator: FULL NAME <EMAIL@ADDRESS>\n"
"Language-Team: LANGUAGE <LL@li.org>\n"
"MIME-Version: 1.0\n"
```

```
"Content-Type: text/plain; charset=CHARSET\n"
"Content-Transfer-Encoding: 8bit\n"

#: src/main.c:7
msgid "egg"
msgstr ""

#: src/main.c:8
msgid "miracle"
msgstr ""

#: src/main.c:9
msgid "drill"
msgstr ""

#: src/main.c:15
msgid "strings:\n"
msgstr ""
```

6. Edit *prog.pot*, changing the header lines. Do not change `PO-Revision-Date` and `Last-Translator`; the translator should do this.

7. Copy *prog.pot* to *locale.po*, where *locale* is the target locale, and fill in the blanks. Here is *de.po* for the preceding example:

```
# Example package.
# Copyright (C) 2003 J. Random Developer
# This file is distributed under the same license as the example package.
# J. Random Developer <jrd@example.com>, 2003.
#
#, fuzzy
msgid ""
msgstr ""
"Project-Id-Version: Example 0.1\n"
"Report-Msgid-Bugs-To: \n"
"POT-Creation-Date: 2003-07-03 16:51-0700\n"
"PO-Revision-Date: 2003-07-08 13:32+0100\n"
"Last-Translator: J. Zufaelliger Uebersetzer <jzu@example.com>\n"
"Language-Team: Example Translator Team <ett@example.com>\n"
"MIME-Version: 1.0\n"
"Content-Type: text/plain; charset=UTF-8\n"
"Content-Transfer-Encoding: 8bit\n"

#: src/main.c:7
msgid "egg"
msgstr "Ei"

#: src/main.c:8
msgid "miracle"
msgstr "Wunder"

#: src/main.c:9
```

```
msgid "drill"
msgstr "Bohrmaschine"

#: src/main.c:15
msgid "strings:\n"
msgstr "Zeichenketten:\n"
```

8. Make sure that you define the character set as UTF-8.
9. Rebuild your source tree; `make install` checks the available translations and puts them in their proper system directory, and the program is ready to use.

As a programmer, you only need to put `_( ... )` and `N_( ... )` into the strings in your code. If your package is popular enough, someone else will probably volunteer to maintain translations.

6.5.1   intltool

gettext supports only C source files, but you can use the same *.po* files for auxiliary data; for instance, you can use *prog.desktop* with intltool. Let's say that you want to create *miracletext.desktop* from Section 6.3:

1. Rename your *miracletext.desktop* file to *miracletext.desktop.in*.
2. Edit *miracletext.desktop.in*, adding an underscore to the beginning of each line that you want translated:

```
[Desktop Entry]
Name=Example
_Comment=MiracleText Word Processor
_Name=Edit documents with MiracleText
TryExec=example

<< ... >>
```

3. Add *miracletext.desktop.in* to your *po/POTFILES.in* file.
4. Add a set of intltool directives to your top-level *Makefile.am*. Section 7.3.6 contains an example for a schemas file, and a MIME keys example appears in Section 8.7.2.
5. Add a rule to remove *miracletext.desktop* for `clean-local` in *Makefile.am*.
6. Rebuild your source tree.

7

GCONF

Most applications allow the user to customize their appearance and behavior, saving a list of configuration values somewhere on the system. Certain programs require very few parameters (Gnomine's field and square size, for example), and some applications, like the Epiphany web browser, have a tremendous number of possibilities in their menus and settings windows. The number of configuration values doesn't matter — somewhere or other, you still have to code the system.

Conventional user configuration support proceeds roughly as follows:

1. Define data structures or simple variables for the values.
2. Export these values to all parts of the application.
3. Create a configuration dialog for the user to alter the values.
4. Make sure that the application writes the values to a file when the user quits the application.
5. Have the application read values from this file at startup.

Several problems can crop up. How does the application know when a configuration value changes? What file format should you use, and where should you put the file? How do you deal with concurrent access to the configuration file? And do you have to reinvent the wheel for every new application?

7.1 Overview

GConf solves the problems described in the preceding section with a central database containing a directory hierarchy of keys attached to configuration values. You need only do the following to add GConf support to your application:

1. Break your configuration data into GConf values, assigning keys to the values.
2. Attach signal handlers to the pieces of your application that use the configuration values.
3. Write your settings dialog so that it modifies the values behind the GConf keys.

When your configuration signal handlers work properly, your application reacts to changes in values regardless of when and where the change happened. You don't need to export any variables or worry about other application-specific infrastructure; all access to the values goes through the configuration database. Furthermore, you don't need to worry about how to store the keys and values. A pleasant side effect is that you can also configure the application with an external tool (systems administrators take heart in hearing this).

The application-side implementation is in the *libgconf-2* library, with a gconfd-2 daemon to handle database-application communication. Each user on the system has exactly one gconfd-2 process when logged in.

User database files are in XML format, located in a directory hierarchy. Take a look at your *.gconf* directory if you want to see the format for keys and values.

There is more to the database than *.gconf*. For the full story, look at the GConf path file, normally *$(PREFIX)/etc/gconf/2/path*.

```
# Look first in systemwide mandatory settings directory
xml:readonly:/opt/gnome/etc/gconf/gconf.xml.mandatory

# Add any user sources
include "$(HOME)/.gconf.path"

# Default user storage location
xml:readwrite:$(HOME)/.gconf

# System default values, in case none of the above exist
xml:readonly:/opt/gnome/etc/gconf/gconf.xml.defaults
```

Each line defines a configuration source with a back-end type (xml at the moment), permissions (readonly or readwrite), and a location (directory name). Every time the application accesses a configuration value, GConf reads *path* from top to bottom, looking for the configuration value in each source. You can force certain configuration values by placing them in a read-only source at the top of *path*. In addition, you can provide defaults with an all-inclusive source at the bottom. Finally, users can define their own source path files with the include directive.

NOTE   *GConf does not guarantee read-write access to its database. GConf-aware applications should work properly if they cannot write to the database. You might encounter this in public X terminals, Internet kiosk systems, and other such installations where complete read-only access is necessary.*

7.2   The User End

The following sections describe the user's GConf database and how to view and manipulate keys and values independent of an application. Although most users never see any of this, the tools described here can be quite useful when you debug your applications.

7.2.1   Configuration Database Keys and Values

The GConf database looks like a Unix file system. The root and directory separator is the / character. Path components may include letters, numbers, and underscores; a full path is a GConf key. A key may not start with a dot.

The value behind a key can use the following types:

- Integer: A 32-bit signed integer, like the C int.

- Floating-point number: Similar to C double, but with no defined precision (for portability).

- String: A C string encoded in UTF-8. You cannot store binary data in a GConf string because it may not contain NULL bytes.

- Boolean: True or false.

- List: A set of elements with the preceding basic value types. You may not have a list of lists, a list of pairs (described next), or a list with differently typed elements.

- Pair: Two values of any two basic types.

- Schema: Describes a key. You probably will not need to work with schemas directly because GConf automatically installs them; see Section 7.3.6.

To get a clearer picture, you should run a GConf configuration editor.

7.2.2   The GConf Configuration Editor

To start a graphical, interactive GConf configuration editor, run gconf-editor from the command line. You should get a window similar to Figure 7.1 on the next page.

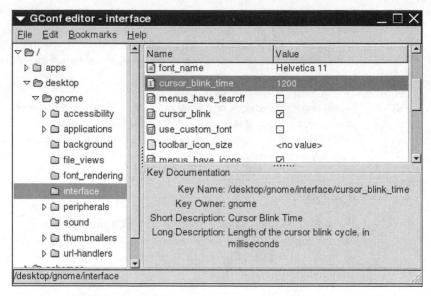

Figure 7.1: GConf configuration editor.

The left side of the window contains the GConf database's tree structure with these primary directories:

- */apps:* Application-specific settings. Each GConf-enabled application has a subdirectory named after its application identifier here. The */apps/gnome-settings* subdirectory is the lone exception; it contains certain GNOME internal values, such as **GnomeEntry** history items.

- */desktop:* Environment-wide settings that apply to more than one application. GNOME-specific settings are in */desktop/gnome.* There is room for other environments (for example, */desktop/kde* for KDE), and any keys that apply to all environments go in */desktop/standard.*

- */system:* Settings that apply to the entire GNOME system, not just applications. For example, the HTTP proxy settings are in */system/http_proxy.*

- */schemas:* Key descriptions. This category contains only metadata, so it isn't terribly interesting.

When you navigate through the GConf database tree and choose a directory, a list of the directory's keys and values appears in the upper-right part of the window. You can change values here and see how an application reacts. Try it yourself — start Gnomine and then alter some of the values in */apps/gnomine/geometry.* This process works the other way around, too; the GConf editor values change when you set them in the application.

When you select a key in the list, the key description appears below the list if the key has a schema.

7.2.3 gconftool-2

You can manipulate and view GConf values on the command line with gconftool-2. There are several things that gconftool-2 can do that its graphical counterpart in the previous section cannot, and a command-line tool can go in a Makefile rule.

Retrieving Information

To see the value for a GConf key, use

```
$ gconftool-2 --get key
```

Make sure that *key* is a full pathname. Note that -g is an abbreviation for --get.
  If the key has a schema, you can see its short and long descriptions with

```
$ gconftool-2 --short-docs key
$ gconftool-2 --long-docs key
```

To list the keys and values in a directory, run

```
$ gconftool-2 --all-entries dir
```

You may substitute -a for --all-entries. To see the directories in a path component, you can use the --all-dirs option:

```
$ gconftool-2 --all-dirs dir
```

If you just want to list everything in a directory and all of its subdirectories, use

```
$ gconftool-2 -R dir
```

(Here, -R is short for --recursive-list.) To see a lot of output, try gconftool-2 -R /.
  You can test that a directory exists with

```
$ gconftool-2 --dir-exists dir
```

If *dir* exists, the return value is 0, and 2 otherwise, as this example shows:

```
$ gconftool-2 --dir-exists=/desktop/gnork
$ echo $?
2
$ gconftool-2 --dir-exists=/desktop/gnome
$ echo $?
0
```

Here is more of what you can expect from gconftool-2:

```
$ gconftool-2 --all-dirs /desktop/gnome
 /desktop/gnome/file_views
 /desktop/gnome/applications
 /desktop/gnome/sound
 /desktop/gnome/interface
 /desktop/gnome/url-handlers
 /desktop/gnome/accessibility
 /desktop/gnome/background
 /desktop/gnome/thumbnailers
 /desktop/gnome/peripherals
 /desktop/gnome/font_rendering

$ gconftool-2 -R /desktop/gnome/applications
 /desktop/gnome/applications/help_viewer:
  needs_term = false
  accepts_urls = true
  exec = nautilus
 /desktop/gnome/applications/window_manager:
  workspace_names = (no value set)
  current = (no value set)
  default = /usr/local/bin/metacity
  number_of_workspaces = (no value set)
 /desktop/gnome/applications/browser:
  nremote = true
  needs_term = false
  exec = mozilla
 /desktop/gnome/applications/terminal:
  exec_arg = -x
  exec = gnome-terminal

$ gconftool-2 -a /desktop/gnome/interface
 gtk-im-status-style = callback
 toolbar_style = both
 gtk_key_theme = Default
 enable_animations = true
 font_name = Sans 10
 cursor_blink_time = 1200
 menus_have_tearoff = false
 cursor_blink = true
 use_custom_font = false
 toolbar_icon_size = (no value set)
 menus_have_icons = true
 can_change_accels = false
 accessibility = false
 gtk_theme = Default
 status_bar_meter_on_right = false
 gtk-im-preedit-style = callback
```

```
 menubar_detachable = false
 icon_theme = gnome
 toolbar_detachable = true

$ gconftool-2 -g /desktop/gnome/interface/gtk_theme
Default

$ gconftool-2 --short-docs /desktop/gnome/interface/gtk_theme
Gtk+ Theme

$ gconftool-2 --long-docs /desktop/gnome/interface/gtk_theme
Basename of the default theme used by gtk+.
```

Editing Keys

To set a key's value with a basic type, use --set (or -s) with the --type (-t) qualifier:

```
$ gconftool-2 --set key --type=type value
```

The basic *type* identifiers are int, float, bool, and string.

Set a list with

```
$ gconftool-2 --set key --type=list --list-type=type [value1,value2, ...]
```

Here, *type* is the list element type. Pairs are similar:

```
$ gconftool-2 --set key --type=pair --car-type=type1 --cdr-type=type2 '(value1,value2)'
```

Here, *type1* and *type2* are the types of the elements inside the pair.

NOTE *When setting a list or pair, do not leave any whitespace between brackets, parentheses, commas, and values.*

You can remove a key (and its value) by running

```
$ gconftool-2 --unset key
```

This works only when *key* is not a directory; -u is the short form of this option. If *key* is a directory and you want to remove everything inside, use

```
$ gconftool-2 --recursive-unset dir
```

Here a few examples that set and remove keys and values:

```
$ gconftool-2 --set /example/number --type=int 42
$ gconftool-2 --set /example/floatnumber --type=float 42.37e-13
$ gconftool-2 --set /example/state --type=bool true
$ gconftool-2 --set /example/name --type=string "J. Random"
$ gconftool-2 -s /example/animals --type=list --list-type=string [dog,cat,mouse]
```

```
$ gconftool-2 -s /example/assoc --type=pair --car-type=int --cdr-type=string \
(534,"num"\)
$ gconftool-2 -a /example/assoc
$ gconftool-2 -a /example
 assoc = (534,num)
 floatnumber = 4.2370000737090852e-12
 state = true
 number = 42
 animals = [dog,cat,mouse]
 name = J. Random
$ gconftool-2 --unset /example/assoc
$ gconftool-2 -g /example/assoc
No value set for `/example/assoc'
$ gconftool-2 --recursive-unset /example
$ gconftool-2 -R /example
$
```

Two of the most useful gconftool-2 commands for debugging a program are

```
$ gconftool-2 --break-key key
$ gconftool-2 --break-directory dir
```

The --break-key command cycles a key's value through many different types in an attempt to break an application. Your application should be able to survive this test, possibly giving some warning messages. The --break-directory command does the same thing for all keys in a directory. You can specify more than one key or directory with each option; in addition, these two options restore the keys' original values when they finish.

Now that you've seen the how to view and manipulate GConf values, you're ready to use them in your applications.

7.3 Programming with GConf

To use GConf in your application, add the client include file to your application header:

```
#include <gconf/gconf-client.h>
```

You can get the header and library paths with pkg-config (package name: gconf-2.0), but this is not necessary if your program is a GNOME application, because the GNOME libraries depend on GConf.

7.3.1 Initializing and Finalizing GConf

To use GConf, you must create a **GConfClient** object that represents the connection between your application and gconfd-2 and holds a data cache. Use this generator function to get a connection:

```
GConfClient *client;

client = gconf_client_get_default();
```

To initialize a **GConfClient** cache, you must inform the object of the directories that you plan to use:

```
GError *error;
gchar *path;

gconf_client_add_dir(client, path, preload, error);
```

Here, *path* is a GConf path, *error* follows the usual error-reporting rules through the GCONF_ERROR domain (see Section 7.3.5 for the error codes), and *preload* determines the keys and values that client adds to its cache. Possible *preload* values are as follows:

- GCONF_CLIENT_PRELOAD_NONE: Do not cache any keys and values.
- GCONF_CLIENT_PRELOAD_ONELEVEL: Cache the keys and values in the path.
- GCONF_CLIENT_PRELOAD_RECURSIVE: Cache all keys and values in this directory and all subdirectories. This can take some time for extensive directory hierarchies, but it does substantially speed up subsequent access.

You can find *path* for your application with

```
GnomeProgram *program;
gchar *relative_path;

path = gnome_gconf_get_app_settings_relative(program, relative_path);
```

This function returns */apps/app_id/relative_path*, where *app_id* is the application identifier in *program*, and *relative_path* is the string behind *relative_path*. Most applications aren't so extensive that they need configuration subdivisions; you will probably stick with "" as the relative path.

You can remove a directory from a client with

```
gconf_client_remove_dir(client, path, error)
```

NOTE *You may add a directory to a client as many times as you like, as long as you remove it that many times.*

Here is how a GConf-aware application skeleton might look:

```
#include <gnome.h>
#include <gconf/gconf-client.h>

  << ... >>

int main(int argc, char **argv)
```

```
{
  GnomeProgram *program;
  GConfClient *client;
  gchar *path;

  << initialize program >>

  /* create GConf client object */
  client = gconf_client_get_default();
  gconf_client_set_error_handling(client, GCONF_CLIENT_HANDLE_UNRETURNED);

  /* add this application's recommended path */
  path = gnome_gconf_get_app_settings_relative(program, "");
  gconf_client_add_dir(client, path, GCONF_CLIENT_PRELOAD_RECURSIVE, NULL);

  << ... >>

  gtk_main();

  << ... >>

  /* remove path */
  gconf_client_remove_dir(client, path, NULL);
  g_free(path);

  /* destroy client object */
  g_object_unref(client);

  << ... >>
}
```

NOTE   *You cannot add a subdirectory to a GConf client after you add a parent. For example, adding /*apps/my_app/this/that *after /*apps/my_app/this *will not work.*

7.3.2   *Reading and Writing GConf Values*

After you create your client and add a directory, you're ready to get down to the real business of reading and writing the values behind keys. These functions retrieve values:

- gint gconf_client_get_int(GConfClient *client*, const gchar *key*,
  GError **error*)
  Returns the integer at *key* in the **GConfClient** object *client*. If no such key exists or an error occurs, this function returns 0 as a default. As before, errors show up in *error*.

- gdouble gconf_client_get_float(GConfClient *client*, const gchar *key*,
  GError **error*)
  Like the preceding function, but for a floating-point value. The default is 0.0.

- gboolean gconf_client_get_bool(GConfClient *client, const gchar *key, GError **error)

  Like the preceding function, but for a Boolean value. The default is FALSE.

- gchar *gconf_client_get_string(GConfClient *client, const gchar *key, GError **error)

  Like the preceding function, but for a string; the return value is a newly allocated string, or NULL if no such key exists or some other error occurs.

- GSList *gconf_client_get_list(GConfClient *client, const gchar *key, GConfValueType type, GError **error)

  Returns a list at *key*, but only if the list elements match *type*. Types include:

  GCONF_VALUE_INT

  GCONF_VALUE_FLOAT

  GCONF_VALUE_BOOL

  GCONF_VALUE_STRING

  The elements of the newly allocated list are untyped pointers (gpointer). To get at integers and Boolean values, you need only cast an element with GPOINTER_TO_INT(). However, floating-point and string elements use new memory. You must dereference a node's data pointer to get at a floating-point number and free the memory for each node when you're through.

- gboolean *gconf_client_get_pair(GConfClient *client, const gchar *key, GConfValueType type1, GConfValueType type2, gpointer val1_target, gpointer val2_target, GError **error)

  Like the preceding function, but for pairs: *type1* and *type2* indicated the types in the pair; *val1_target* and *val2_target* point to some memory for the values in the pair (for strings, you must supply the address of a pointer). Upon success, this function returns TRUE.

Similar functions set a key's value. All of the following return TRUE upon success. When a problem arises, the return value is FALSE, and an error condition shows up at *error*.

- gboolean gconf_client_set_int(GConfClient *client, const gchar *key, gint value, GError **error)

  Sets the value for *key* to the integer *value*.

- gboolean gconf_client_set_float(GConfClient *client, const gchar *key, gdouble value, GError **error)

  Sets the value for *key* to the floating-point number *value*.

- gboolean gconf_client_set_bool(GConfClient *client, const gchar *key, gboolean value, GError **error)

  Sets the value for *key* to the Boolean *value*.

- gboolean gconf_client_set_string(GConfClient *client, const gchar *key, gchar *value, GError **error)

  Sets the value for *key* to the string *value*.

- gboolean gconf_client_set_list(GConfClient *client, const gchar *key, GConfValueType type, GSList *list, GError **error)
  Sets the value for key to a list; the elements in list have type type.

- gboolean gconf_client_set_pair(GConfClient *client, const gchar *key, GConfValueType type1, GConfValueType type2, gconstpointer *value1, gconstpointer *value2, GError **error)
  Sets the value for key to a pair; the first element is behind value1 and has type type1; the second element is behind value2 and has type type2.

WARNING *All GConf database transactions are asynchronous. After you call one of the* gconf_client_set_*() *functions, the new value may not be immediately available to other processes;* gconfd-2 *waits until it has the time to set the value. Therefore, you should not use GConf values for critical interprocess communication.*

Before you try to write a value, you can see if its key is read-only with

```
gconf_client_key_is_writable(client, path, error)
```

This function returns FALSE if the key is read-only and TRUE if you can write to its value.

Here is some example code that reads and writes values:

```
GConfClient *client;
GSList *list, *l_ptr;
gchar *name;
gint n;

  << ... >>

/* read some values */
g_print("Your desktop has %d workspace(s).\n",
        gconf_client_get_int(client,
           "/desktop/gnome/applications/window_manager/number_of_workspaces",
           NULL));

g_print("The desktop names are:\n");
list = gconf_client_get_list(client,
        "/desktop/gnome/applications/window_manager/workspace_names",
        GCONF_VALUE_STRING,
        NULL);

for (l_ptr = list; l_ptr != NULL; l_ptr = g_slist_next(l_ptr))
{
   g_print(" %s", (gchar *)l_ptr->data);
   g_free(l_ptr->data);
}
g_slist_free(list);
```

```
g_print("\n");

if (gconf_client_get_bool
    (client, "/desktop/gnome/applications/cursor_blink", NULL))
{
  g_print("Your cursor blinks.\n");
} else {
  g_print("Your cursor does not blink.\n");
}

name = gconf_client_get_string(client,
                               "/desktop/gnome/interface/gtk_theme",
                               NULL);

g_print("Your GTK+ theme is: %s\n", name);
g_free(name);

/* write some values */
gconf_client_set_int(client, "/example/number", 42, NULL);
gconf_client_set_float(client, "/example/pi", 3.14159, NULL);
gconf_client_set_bool(client, "/example/state", FALSE, NULL);
gconf_client_set_string(client, "/example/message", "Hello, World.", NULL);

/* put a list of integers into conf value */
list = NULL;
list = g_slist_append(list, GINT_TO_POINTER(42));
list = g_slist_append(list, GINT_TO_POINTER(37));
list = g_slist_append(list, GINT_TO_POINTER(11217));
gconf_client_set_list(client, "/example/nums", GCONF_VALUE_INT, list, NULL);
g_slist_free(list);

/* set a pair; a number and a string */
n = 52;
name = g_strdup("fifty-two");
gconf_client_set_pair(client,
                      "/example/number_name",
                      GCONF_VALUE_INT,
                      GCONF_VALUE_STRING,
                      &n,
                      &name,
                      NULL);
g_free(name);
```

GConfValue

The preceding functions assume that you know the key type; if you try to read or write a value with the wrong type, you get an error. However, you can read a value if you do not know its type by creating a GConfValue data structure with the GConfValueType identifier field (type). You saw this earlier when reading and writing lists, but did not encounter the full list of identifiers:

- GCONF_VALUE_INVALID
- GCONF_VALUE_STRING
- GCONF_VALUE_INT
- GCONF_VALUE_FLOAT
- GCONF_VALUE_BOOL
- GCONF_VALUE_LIST
- GCONF_VALUE_PAIR
- GCONF_VALUE_SCHEMA

You can create a new GConfValue structure as follows:

```
GConfValue *conf_value;

conf_value = gconf_value_new(type_identifier);
```

Here, `type_identifier` is one of the identifiers in the preceding list. To deallocate the structure memory, use

```
gconf_value_free(conf_value)
```

WARNING *Do not try to free a* GConfValue *structure by any other means.*

You can also get a newly allocated GConfValue from a key at the GConf database *client*:

```
conf_value = gconf_client_get(client, key, error);
```

To write an entry in the database, use

```
gconf_client_set(client, key, conf_value, error);
```

Once you have a GConfValue structure, you can look at its type field (for example, *conf_value*->type). Then you can set a basic type with one of these functions:

```
void gconf_value_set_int(GConfValue *conf_value, gint number)
void gconf_value_set_float(GConfValue *conf_value, gdouble number)
void gconf_value_set_bool(GConfValue *conf_value, gboolean state)
void gconf_value_set_string(GConfValue *conf_value, gchar *string)
```

To return a value from a GConfValue, call one of the following:

```
int gconf_value_get_int(const GConfValue *conf_value)
double gconf_value_get_float(const GConfValue *conf_value)
gboolean gconf_value_get_bool(const GConfValue *conf_value)
const char *gconf_value_get_string(const GConfValue *conf_value)
```

WARNING *A string return value is a constant; you may not alter or deallocate it.*

Setting lists is a little trickier. First set the list type; then pass a GSList of GConfValue structures:

```
void gconf_value_set_list_type(GConfValue *conf_value, GConfValueType type)
void gconf_value_set_list(GConfValue *conf_value, GSList *list)
void gconf_value_set_list_nocopy(GConfValue *conf_value, GSList *list)
```

The _nocopy variant does not make copies of the GConfValue structures in list when writing to conf_value. If you create your own structures just for the list, you can save a little time with this.

To get a GSList of GConfValue structures in a GConf list conf_value, use

```
GSList *gconf_value_get_list(const GConfValue *conf_value)
```

WARNING *The strings in lists of strings are not copies. Do not try to alter or deallocate any string data inside the* GConfValue *structures.*

Setting and retrieving GConfValue pair structures is similar, except that there are separate functions for the first and second elements in the pair:

```
void gconf_value_set_car(GConfValue *conf_value, const GConfValue *first)
void gconf_value_set_cdr(GConfValue *conf_value, const GConfValue *second)
void gconf_value_set_car_nocopy(GConfValue *conf_value, const GConfValue *first)
void gconf_value_set_cdr_nocopy(GConfValue *conf_value, const GConfValue *second)
GConfValue *gconf_value_get_car(const GConfValue *conf_value)
GConfValue *gconf_value_get_cdr(const GConfValue *conf_value)
```

There are two interesting GConfValue utility functions:

- GConfValue *gconf_value_copy(const GConfValue *conf_value)
  Returns a complete copy of conf_value, including all list and pair elements.
- gchar *gconf_value_to_string(const GConfValue *conf_value)
  Returns a newly allocated string representation of conf_value. This function is good for diagnostic purposes, but it does not have a specific format.

Here are some GConfValue structures in action:

```
GConfValue *conf_value;
GSList *list;
gchar *string;

/* create a value */
conf_value = gconf_value_new(GCONF_VALUE_INT);

/* set a value */
gconf_value_set_int(conf_value, 42);

/* check the value's type */
switch (conf_value->type)
```

```
  {
    case GCONF_VALUE_INT:
      g_print("conf_value is an integer.\n");
      break;
    case GCONF_VALUE_STRING:
      g_print("conf_value is a string.\n");
      break;
    default:
      g_print("conf_value is not an integer or a string.\n");
      break;
  }

  /* print the value (by means of access function) */
  g_print("conf_value = %d\n", gconf_value_get_int(conf_value));

  /* print with diagnostic function */
  string = gconf_value_to_string(conf_value);
  g_print("conf_value = %s\n", string);
  g_free(string);

  /* deallocate */
  gconf_value_free(conf_value);

  /* create a list */
  list = NULL;
  conf_value = gconf_value_new(GCONF_VALUE_STRING);
  gconf_value_set_string(conf_value, "yesterday");
  list = g_slist_append(list, conf_value);

  conf_value = gconf_value_new(GCONF_VALUE_STRING);
  gconf_value_set_string(conf_value, "today");
  list = g_slist_append(list, conf_value);

  conf_value = gconf_value_new(GCONF_VALUE_STRING);
  gconf_value_set_string(conf_value, "tomorrow");
  list = g_slist_append(list, conf_value);

  /* put the list into a GConfValue (conf_list_value) */
  conf_value = gconf_value_new(GCONF_VALUE_LIST);
  gconf_value_set_list_type(conf_value, GCONF_VALUE_STRING);
  gconf_value_set_list_nocopy(conf_value, list);

  /* print string with diagnostic function */
  string = gconf_value_to_string(conf_value);
  g_print("conf_value = %s\n", string);
  g_free(string);

  gconf_value_free(conf_value);
```

GConfEntry

You can go one step beyond GConfValue with GConfEntry, a data structure that contains the key along with its value. To create a GConfEntry data structure, call this function:

```
GConfEntry *entry;

entry = gconf_client_get_entry(client, key, NULL, use_default, error);
```

Here, *client*, *key*, and *error* are the **GConfClient** object, key string, and error structure pointer, as in the access functions that you saw earlier. Set the Boolean *use_default* parameter to TRUE if you want to get the schema default values. The third parameter is supposed to be the locale, but is not supported at the moment. Use NULL for the default locale.

You can get the key or GConfValue inside a GConfEntry structure with these two functions:

```
const char *gconf_entry_get_key(const GConfEntry *entry)
GConfValue *gconf_entry_get_value(const GConfEntry *entry)
```

WARNING   *The* gconf_entry_get_value() *function can return* NULL *if its key has no value. You should always check this by hand.*

To deallocate a GConfEntry structure, call

```
gconf_entry_free(entry)
```

If you want to retain the GConfValue structure inside an entry before you free an entry, call this function first:

```
conf_value = gconf_entry_steal_value(entry);
```

Remember that you are responsible for deallocating *conf_value*.

Here are a few other GConf API functions that can help you replicate some gconftool-2 navigation functionality:

- gboolean gconf_client_dir_exists(GConfClient *client, const gchar *dir, GError **error)
  Returns TRUE if *dir* exists in the GConf database.
- GSList *gconf_client_all_entries(GConfClient *client, const gchar *dir, GError **error)
  Returns a list of GConfEntry structures for all keys and values in *dir*.
- GSList *gconf_client_all_dirs(GConfClient *client, const gchar *dir, GError **error)
  Returns a list of all subdirectories in *dir*. The list elements are newly allocated strings containing the absolute paths of each subdirectory. Make sure that you free the strings before the list when you are finished with the list.

- gboolean gconf_client_unset(GConfClient *client, const gchar *path, GError **error)

  Removes the directory or key at *path* and returns TRUE. If no such item exists or the path is read-only, this function returns FALSE and sets *error*.

Now it's time for an example: a program that searches and prints all entries in an entire directory and its subdirectories, similar to gconftool-2 -R. Notice that you do not need the entire GNOME include paths:

```
/* -*-coding: utf-8;-*- */
/* gconflister.c -- lists contents in a GConf database */

#include <gnome.h>
#include <gconf/gconf-client.h>

/* the path to list */
#define PATH "/"
```

The list_contents procedure that follows does all of the work. The parameters are a GConf client, a path, and a current depth. This function calls itself with depth+1 to update the depth.

```
/* recursively list the entries in the GConf database under path */
void list_contents(GConfClient *client, gchar *path, gint depth)
{
  GSList *subdirs = NULL, *entries = NULL, *p;
  gint i;
  gchar *value_str;
```

The preparatory work includes error checking, extraction of the directory contents, and printing of the directory name:

```
  /* make sure that this is a directory */
  if (!gconf_client_dir_exists(client, path, NULL))
  {
    g_printerr("%s: No such GConf directory in database\n", path);
    return;
  }

  /* extract all subdirectories in path */
  subdirs = gconf_client_all_dirs(client, path, NULL);

  /* extract all entries in path */
  entries = gconf_client_all_entries(client, path, NULL);

  /* depth is the current directory depth; print spaces before the output */
  if (depth)
  {
    for (i=0; i < depth; i++)
```

```
    {
        g_print(" ");
    }
}

/* print directory name */
g_print("%s:\n", path);
```

To print the contents of each subdirectory, this function traverses the subdirectory list and calls itself on each subdirectory.

```
/* print the subdirectory contents */
if (subdirs)
{
    for (p = subdirs; p != NULL; p = g_slist_next(p))
    {
        list_contents(client, p->data, depth+1);
        g_free(p->data);
    }
    g_slist_free(subdirs);
}
```

The last order of business is to print the values of any keys that might be in the current directory:

```
/* print all entries in the directory */
if (entries)
{
    for (p = entries; p != NULL; p = g_slist_next(p))
    {
        /* if there is no value behind a key, print the value as NULL,
           otherwise, format the value a diagnostic function */
        if (!gconf_entry_get_value(p->data))
        {
            value_str = g_strdup("NULL");
        } else {
            value_str =
                gconf_value_to_string(gconf_entry_get_value((GConfEntry*)(p->data)));
        }

        /* indent the output */
        for (i=0; i < (depth+1); i++)
        {
            g_print(" ");
        }

        /* print the key and formatted value */
        g_print("%s = %s\n",
```

```
            gconf_entry_get_key((GConfEntry*)(p->data)), value_str);

        g_free(value_str);
        gconf_entry_free(p->data);
      }
      g_print("\n");
      g_slist_free(entries);
    }
}
```

The main program creates a client and starts printing at PATH.

```
int main(int argc, char **argv)
{
  GnomeProgram *program;
  GConfClient *client;

  program = gnome_program_init("gconflister", "0.1",
                               LIBGNOMEUI_MODULE,
                               argc, argv,
                               GNOME_PROGRAM_STANDARD_PROPERTIES,
                               GNOME_PARAM_HUMAN_READABLE_NAME, "GConfLister",
                               GNOME_PARAM_ENABLE_SOUND, TRUE,
                               NULL);

  /* create client object */
  client = gconf_client_get_default();
  gconf_client_set_error_handling(client, GCONF_CLIENT_HANDLE_UNRETURNED);

  /* list everything in PATH */
  list_contents(client, PATH, 0);

  /* finalize client object */
  g_object_unref(client);

  return 0;
}
```

Now it's time to see how your application should recognize changes in
GConf keys.

7.3.3 GConf Value Change Notification

To detect a change in a GConf value, bind a callback function to the value's key.
If any application changes the value, GConf calls the callback function so that
your application can react appropriately.

The callback function prototype follows the GConfClientNotifyFunc
type definition:

```
typedef void (*GConfClientNotifyFunc)(GConfClient *client,
                                      guint cnxn_id,
                                      GConfEntry *entry,
                                      gpointer user_data);
```

Here, client and entry are the GConf client and applicable GConf entry; user_data is the auxiliary data pointer that you have already seen many times in this book in connection with signals.

The cnxn_id identifier is a connection identifier; it is the return value when you bind the handler *callback_func* to the *path* in *client* with this function:

```
guint gconf_client_notify_add(GConfClient client,
                              const gchar *path,
                              GConfClientNotifyFunc callback_func,
                              gpointer user_data,
                              GFreeFunc destroy_notify,
                              GError **error)
```

Here, *path* can be a key or a directory (for directories, GConf calls *callback_func* when anything in or below the directory changes), and *destroy_notify* is a destructor function for *user_data*.

To remove a callback function from GConf's watchlist, use

```
gconf_client_notify_remove(client, connection_id)
```

where *connection_id* is the connection identifier described earlier.

Here is a callback function that prints only a changed value:

```
void print_changes(GConfClient *client, guint id,
                   GConfEntry *entry, gpointer data)
{
  gchar *key, *value_str;
  key = (gchar *)gconf_entry_get_key(entry);
  value_str = gconf_value_to_string(gconf_entry_get_value(entry));
  g_print("%s: value changed to: %s\n", key, value_str);
  g_free(value_str);
}
```

You can attach and remove the callback as follows:

```
gchar *path;
GnomeProgram *program;
guint print_cxnid;

  << ... >>

path = gnome_gconf_get_app_settings_relative(program, "some/path")
gconf_client_notify_remove(client, print_cxnid);
```

```
g_free(path);

<< ... >>

gconf_client_notify_remove(client, print_cxnid);
```

An application's GConf callback function normally alters its widget properties, and that, in turn, alters the appearance of the application. If you keep all of your important settings in widget and object properties, your GConf callback functions will not be hard to implement.

7.3.4 The GConf Cache

You can manipulate the cache in a **GConfClient** object, for example, if you need GConf to take action immediately (remember that the database transactions are asynchronous).

- void gconf_client_clear_cache(GConfClient *client)
  Clear the cache for client so that the next read comes directly from the database. This can save a little bit of memory.

- void gconf_client_preload(GConfClient *client, const gchar *dir, GConfClientPreloadType type, GError **error)
  If you think that you're going to use several components in dir at once, you can call this function to load some entries into the cache. The domain for type is the same as for gconf_client_add_dir(); the useful values are GCONF_CLIENT_PRELOAD_ONELEVEL and GCONF_CLIENT_PRELOAD_RECURSIVE.

- void gconf_client_suggest_sync(GConfClient *client, GError **error)
  Tells client and gconfd-2 that they should bring all of their cache data up-to-date. Normally, gconfd-2 decides when to write its configuration cache.

7.3.5 Error Handling

You have probably noticed that a large portion of the **GConfClient** functions has a GError argument. Normally, you can put NULL into this place because **GConfClient** does extensive error checking on its own. If you need some extra information, here are the error codes for the GCONF_ERROR domain:

- GCONF_ERROR_SUCCESS: No error.

- GCONF_ERROR_FAILED: Unknown error. You may be able to determine the problem from an auxiliary message.

- GCONF_ERROR_NO_SERVER: The client cannot make contact with gconfd-2; this could be a configuration or installation error.

- GCONF_ERROR_NO_PERMISSION: Database access denied. This could be as minor as a permissions problem.

- GCONF_ERROR_BAD_ADDRESS: There is a problem with a configuration source in GConf path (see Section 7.1).

- GCONF_ERROR_BAD_KEY: Invalid key name.

- `GCONF_ERROR_PARSE_ERROR`: GConf could not parse the string representation of one of its data structures; see the message log. **GConfClient** objects should not get this error because they do not use the string representation.

- `GCONF_ERROR_CORRUPT`: The GConf database has a defect (probably a problem with an XML file).

- `GCONF_ERROR_TYPE_MISMATCH`: You asked for a value with a certain type, but the value in the database does not match that type.

- `GCONF_ERROR_IS_DIR`: You tried to access a directory as a key.

- `GCONF_ERROR_IS_KEY`: You tried to access a key as a directory.

- `GCONF_ERROR_OVERRIDDEN`: You tried to change a value for a key that has a read-only value GConf path.

As mentioned earlier, **GConfClient** performs its own error handling. If you link against the GNOME libraries, a dialog such as Figure 7.2 appears when a problem crops up.

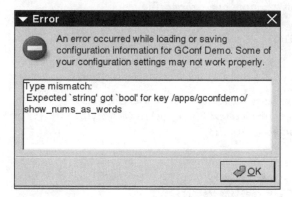

Figure 7.2: Built-in GConf error dialog.

You can control these error dialogs with

```
gconf_client_set_error_handling(client, mode)
```

where *mode* is one of the following:

- `GCONF_CLIENT_HANDLE_NONE`: No dialogs.

- `GCONF_CLIENT_HANDLE_UNRETURNED`: Dialogs appear only when the error does not go into a `GError` structure.

- `GCONF_CLIENT_HANDLE_ALL`: Shows dialogs for every error.

You can set your own error handler with the **GConfClient error** signal. The handler prototype is

```
void handler(GConfClient *client, gpointer *error, gpointer data);
```

Here, error is a pointer to a `GError` structure. You can also set the **unreturned-error** signal handler to catch any errors where you passed `NULL` as the `GError` parameter in a gconf_client_*() function.

With all of this infrastructure, you can define complex layers of error handling, but for the most part, the warning dialogs suffice.

7.3.6 Schemas

You have not seen much about the GConf schema key type so far, because schemas are not normal configuration values that you can use in your application — they serve only to document other keys. For example, the GConf configuration editor displays the schema data for an entry that you click.

Schemas go in */schemas*; if you have a key named */apps/example/setting1*, the corresponding schema is */schemas/apps/example/setting1*.

NOTE   *A schema can describe several keys with identical properties.*

GConf has an entire API to read and write schemas, but this really isn't necessary. All you need to do is supply your schemas in a *.schemas* XML file and then install the file with gconftool-2.

Here is an example of a *.schemas* file:

```
<gconfschemafile>
 <schemalist>

  <schema>
  <key>/schemas/apps/miracletext/check_spelling</key>
  <applyto>/apps/miracletext/check_spelling</applyto>
  <owner>miracletext</owner>
  <type>bool</type>
  <locale name="C">
     <default>true</default>
     <short>Check spelling</short>
     <long>Automatically check spelling in documents</long>
  </locale>
  <locale name="de">
     <default>true</default>
     <short>Rechtschreibung pruefen</short>
     <long>Rechtschreibung in Dokumenten automatisch prüfen</long>
  </locale>
  </schema>

  <schema>
  <key>/schemas/apps/miracletext/signature</key>
  <applyto>/apps/miracletext/signature</applyto>
  <owner>miracletext</owner>
  <type>string</type>
  <locale name="C">
     <short>Signature</short>
     <long>Signature for the bottom of letters</long>
  </locale>
  <locale name="de">
     <short>Signatur</short>
```

```
      <long>Signatur under Briefen</long>
    </locale>
   </schema>


 </schemalist>
</gconfschemafile>
```

Enclose the entire file with `<gconfschemafile>` tags, with `<schemalist>` just inside. Then you can add as many schemas as you like with `<schema>` tags.

The internal schema tags are as follows:

- `<key>`: The schema key path: for example, */schemas/apps/example/setting1*.

- `<applyto>`: The key that the schema describes: for example, */apps/example/setting1*. You may have more than one applyto element in a schema.

- `<owner>`: The application that owns the schema; this should be the application identifier.

- `<type>`: The key type; one of `int`, `float`, `bool`, `string`, `pair`, `list`.

- `<default>`: The key's default value. This should permit the application to function normally if the user has not set the value. The format is identical to the output of `gconftool-2`.

- `<list_type>`: If the key is a list, this is the type of the list elements.

- `<car_type>`: If the key is a pair, this is the first element's type.

- `<cdr_type>`: If the key is a pair, this is the second element's type.

- `<locale>`: Key descriptions for a locale; specify the locale with the `name=locale` attribute. You should always set a `C` locale. Each locale section should have these two elements:

  `<short>` A label for the key; this label should not be more than 40 characters long.

  `<long>` A more drawn-out description that says what the key's value actually does.

You can place a default values inside or outside of the locale section; if it is outside, the default applies to all locales. If you opt to put the default value inside the locale, make sure that you define a default for all locales. The default locale is C.

Installing Schemas

If you decide to use `intltool` in conjunction with the GNU autotools, do the following to install your schemas:

1. Create a schemas file with a single locale, C; store this as a *.schemas.in* file.

2. Add something like this to your top-level *Makefile.am*:

```
schemasdir = $(sysconfdir)/gconf/schemas
schemas_in_files = prog.schemas.in
```

```
schemas_DATA = $(schemas_in_files:.schemas.in=.schemas)
@INTLTOOL_SCHEMAS_RULE@
```

3. Add an install-data-local target to your *Makefile.am* that looks something like this:

```
install-data-local:
        GCONF_CONFIG_SOURCE=$(GCONF_CONFIG_SOURCE) \
        $(GCONFTOOL) --makefile-install-rule $(top_src_dir)/miracletext.schemas
```

4. Enter translations for the schema in your po/*.po files. When you build the package, intltool creates a *.schemas* file with appropriate <locale> sections.

GCONF_CONFIG_SOURCE tells gconftool-2 where to install the schemas. This is a source (for example, xml:readwrite:*/some/path*).

If you just want to install a *.schemas* file by hand, use

```
$ gconftool-2 --makefile-install-rule name.schemas
```

7.3.7 A Complete Example

You're ready to see a complete example that includes a schema. The application has a single Boolean GConf value (*/apps/gconfdemo/show_nums_as_words*) and three labels that display numbers. When the configuration value is TRUE, the labels spell their numbers in words. Figure 7.3 shows the final application.

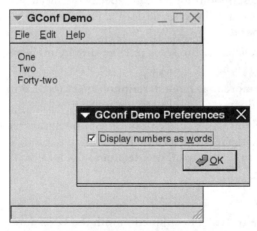

Figure 7.3: GConf demonstration application.

The global declarations include the label widgets and the top-level window. In addition, the WORDS_KEY macro defines the relative GConf key pathname. The application always combines WORDS_KEY with the application GConf path (*/apps/gconfdemo*).

```
/* -*-coding: utf-8;-*- */
/* gconfdemo.c -- GConf demo application */

#include <gnome.h>
#include <gconf/gconf-client.h>

GnomeProgram *program;
GConfClient *client;
GtkLabel *label[3];
GnomeApp *window;

/* the relative path of the key */
#define WORDS_KEY "show_nums_as_words"

/* standard window event handlers */
gint delete_event(GtkWidget *widget, GdkEvent event, gpointer data)
{
  return FALSE;
}

void end_program(GtkWidget *widget, gpointer data)
{
  gtk_main_quit();
}
```

The application includes a **Preferences** dialog with a check box for turning
WORDS_KEY on and off. The button_changed handler is a signal handler for the check
box and does the work of changing the GConf value in the database. Notice that
WORDS_KEY does not appear in the function. The key name goes through the
key_ptr data pointer. Therefore, you can use this handler for any number of
check boxes attached to GConf keys.

```
void button_changed(GtkCheckButton *button, gpointer key_ptr)
{
  gboolean value;
  gchar *path;
  gchar *key = (gchar *)key_ptr;

  g_object_get(button, "active", &value, NULL);

  path  = gnome_gconf_get_app_settings_relative(program, key),
  gconf_client_set_bool(client, path, value, NULL);
  g_free(path);
}
```

You have seen the setup for dialogs like **Preferences** before:

```
void preferences(void)
{
  static GtkDialog *dialog;
  static GtkCheckButton *word_button;
  gboolean show_words_init;
  gboolean words_key_writable;
  GError *error = NULL;
  gchar *path;

  dialog = GTK_DIALOG(gtk_dialog_new_with_buttons(
                      "GConf Demo Preferences",
                      GTK_WINDOW(window),
                      GTK_DIALOG_DESTROY_WITH_PARENT,
                      GTK_STOCK_OK, GTK_RESPONSE_ACCEPT,
                      NULL));
  g_object_set(dialog, "border-width", 12, NULL);
  gtk_dialog_set_default_response(dialog, GTK_RESPONSE_ACCEPT);
  g_signal_connect_swapped(dialog,
                      "response", G_CALLBACK(gtk_widget_destroy), dialog);

  word_button = g_object_new(GTK_TYPE_CHECK_BUTTON,
                      "label", "Display numbers as _words",
                      "use-underline", TRUE,
                      NULL);
```

To set up the word_button check button correctly, you need to know the current WORDS_KEY configuration value. If there is no such value, use a default of TRUE.

```
  path = gnome_gconf_get_app_settings_relative(program, WORDS_KEY);

  show_words_init = gconf_client_get_bool(client, path, &error);

  if (error)
  {
    show_words_init = TRUE;
    g_error_free(error);
  }

  words_key_writable = gconf_client_key_is_writable(client, path, NULL);

  g_free(path);

  g_object_set(word_button,
              "active", show_words_init,
              "sensitive", words_key_writable,
              NULL);
```

Now you attach the check button's **toggled** signal to the function in the preceding code. Note that the data pointer is WORDS_KEY.

```
g_signal_connect(word_button,
                 "toggled", G_CALLBACK(button_changed), WORDS_KEY);

gtk_box_pack_start_defaults(GTK_BOX(dialog->vbox), GTK_WIDGET(word_button));

gtk_widget_show_all(GTK_WIDGET(dialog));
}
```

This program uses gnome-app-helper to create a menu bar. The application runs preferences (in the preceding code) when the user selects **Edit > Preferences**.

```
GnomeUIInfo file_items[] = {
  GNOMEUIINFO_MENU_QUIT_ITEM(end_program, NULL),
  GNOMEUIINFO_END
};

GnomeUIInfo edit_items[] = {
  GNOMEUIINFO_MENU_PREFERENCES_ITEM(preferences, NULL),
  GNOMEUIINFO_END
};

GnomeUIInfo menu_bar_items[] = {
  GNOMEUIINFO_MENU_FILE_TREE(file_items),
  GNOMEUIINFO_MENU_EDIT_TREE(edit_items),
  GNOMEUIINFO_END
};
```

Although you do not yet know the origin of label, it's easy to see that the following function changes label text based on the value of WORDS_KEY.

```
void set_labels(void)
{
  gboolean show_as_words;
  GError *error = NULL;
  gchar *path;

  path = gnome_gconf_get_app_settings_relative(program, WORDS_KEY);
  show_as_words = gconf_client_get_bool(client, path, &error);
  g_free(path);

  if (error)
  {
    show_as_words = TRUE;
    g_error_free(error);
  }

  if (show_as_words)
```

```
{
    g_object_set(label[0], "label", "One", NULL);
    g_object_set(label[1], "label", "Two", NULL);
    g_object_set(label[2], "label", "Forty-two", NULL);
} else {
    g_object_set(label[0], "label", "1", NULL);
    g_object_set(label[1], "label", "2", NULL);
    g_object_set(label[2], "label", "42", NULL);
    }
}
```

Next is a callback function for changing a GConf configuration value. The main program attaches this callback to changes to WORDS_KEY.

NOTE   *The pedants among us might note that this does not change the check button in **Preferences** (if this dialog exists). Therefore, if some external application changed WORDS_KEY, that check button would hold invalid data. To make the button widget update, you should block its signal handlers when you set its **active** property, because you risk infinite signal recursion otherwise.*

```
void display_type_changed(GConfClient *client, guint cxnid,
                          GConfEntry *entry, gpointer data)
{
    set_labels();
}
```

The bulk of the main program defines the main window and label widgets, as well as the GConf initialization.

```
int main(int argc, char **argv)
{
    gchar *gconf_path;
    GtkStatusbar *status;
    GtkVBox *vbox;
    gint i;
    guint words_cxnid;
    gchar *path;

    program = gnome_program_init("gconfdemo", "0.1",
                                 LIBGNOMEUI_MODULE,
                                 argc, argv,
                                 GNOME_PROGRAM_STANDARD_PROPERTIES,
                                 GNOME_PARAM_HUMAN_READABLE_NAME, "GConf Demo",
                                 GNOME_PARAM_ENABLE_SOUND, TRUE,
                                 NULL);

    /* create GConf client object */
```

```
client = gconf_client_get_default();
gconf_client_set_error_handling(client, GCONF_CLIENT_HANDLE_UNRETURNED);

/* add this application's recommended path */
gconf_path = gnome_gconf_get_app_settings_relative(program, "");
gconf_client_add_dir(client, gconf_path, GCONF_CLIENT_PRELOAD_ONELEVEL, NULL);

/* create window */
window = g_object_new(GNOME_TYPE_APP,
                      "title", "GConf Demo",
                      "app-id", "gconfdemo",
                      "default-width", 300,
                      "default-height", 300,
                       NULL);

/* attach standard signal handlers */
g_signal_connect(window, "delete_event", G_CALLBACK(delete_event), NULL);
g_signal_connect(window, "destroy", G_CALLBACK(end_program), NULL);

/* add menu and status bar */
gnome_app_create_menus(window, menu_bar_items);
status = g_object_new(GTK_TYPE_STATUSBAR, NULL);
gnome_app_set_statusbar(window, GTK_WIDGET(status));

/* create some labels for the main window */
vbox = g_object_new(GTK_TYPE_VBOX, "border-width", 12, NULL);
for (i=0; i<3; i++)
{
    label[i] = g_object_new(GTK_TYPE_LABEL, "xalign", 0.0, NULL);
    gtk_box_pack_start(GTK_BOX(vbox), GTK_WIDGET(label[i]), FALSE, FALSE, 0);
}
/* set the label text */
set_labels();

/* add label vbox to main window */
gnome_app_set_contents(window, GTK_WIDGET(vbox));
```
Now you're ready to attach the GConf callback functions.
```
/* attach callback functions for when value behind WORDS_KEY changes */
path = gnome_gconf_get_app_settings_relative(program, WORDS_KEY),
words_cxnid = gconf_client_notify_add(client, path, display_type_changed,
                                      NULL, NULL, NULL);
g_free(path);

/* show window, start main event loop */
gtk_widget_show_all(GTK_WIDGET(window));

gtk_main();
```

After the user leaves the main event loop, you can clean and finalize GConf.

```
/* remove callback functions */
gconf_client_notify_remove(client, words_cxnid);

/* remove path */
gconf_client_remove_dir(client, gconf_path, NULL);
g_free(gconf_path);

/* let go of reference to GConf client object */
g_object_unref(client);

return 0;
}
```

The GConf error reporting mode is `GCONF_CLIENT_HANDLE_UNRETURNED` (see the preceding code). Therefore, you can safely run a stress test:

```
gconftool-2 --break-key /apps/gconfdemo/show_nums_as_words
```

The gconfdemo program handles errors silently because it checks error codes by hand when trying to retrieve a value. Otherwise, there is no reason to bother with errors.

Schemas

Here is the *.schemas* file for gconfdemo:

```
<gconfschemafile>
 <schemalist>
  <schema>
   <key>/schemas/apps/gconfdemo/show_nums_as_words</key>
   <applyto>/apps/gconfdemo/show_nums_as_words</applyto>
   <owner>gconfdemo</owner>
   <type>bool</type>
   <locale name="C">
      <default>true</default>
      <short>Numbers as words</short>
      <long>Display numbers as words?</long>
   </locale>
  </schema>
 </schemalist>
</gconfschemafile>
```

7.3.8   Preferences Guidelines

When you build a **Preferences** dialog, try to follow these rules:

- Don't use **Cancel**, **Apply**, or **OK** buttons in GNOME 2 applications. It is difficult to build such dialogs with GConf, and applications are easier to use when you see the changes immediately.

- Use a window title such as *Application* **Preferences**, where *Application* is your application's name.

- If you have a lot of preferences, use **GtkNotebook** pages to display all of the widgets. However, if there is a tremendous number, you may want to consider icon hierarchies (like Nautilus) or a tree representation (for infrequently used settings).

- Don't stuff a lot of unrelated preferences into one dialog. Use **GtkNotebook** or a frame container to group related settings.

7.4   Further Topics

Under the **GConfClient** API are several low-level GConf subsystems. Because all *libgnome* and *libgnomeui* applications are supposed to interface with GConf through **GConfClient** objects, there is no point in discussing the implementation layer.

Although the material in this chapter covers **GConfClient** components, you should look at some large applications such as Nautilus — they can show you how to manage large groups of GConf entries in their **Preferences** windows. And of course, it's always interesting to explore a large application's GConf entries with the configuration editor.

8

GNOMEVFS

GnomeVFS is a library and module set that provides virtual file systems for GNOME applications. Why you should use a virtual, abstract file system and not your system's native file system? In addition to the usual justification of abstraction (portability), GnomeVFS extends the file system beyond your local disk. For example, you can access archives and web servers with the same interface as your local file system.

GnomeVFS also offers a number of practical utility functions, including an entire subsystem for asynchronous access (see Section 8.5).

8.1 Transparency with URIs

The two governing principles behind GnomeVFS are

- A *URI* identifies directories and files.
- Access is transparent; all API functions use the same URI-based format regardless of what and where the files are.

Modules support underlying media types, so you can easily outfit GnomeVFS with new access capabilities. A system with gnome-vfs and gnome-vfs-extras already contains modules for these formats:

- a: Static C library archives.
- all-applications: The GNOME application menu (single directory).
- all-preferences: GNOME application preferences (single directory).
- applications: The GNOME applications menu (directory hierarchy).
- ar: Generic ar archives.
- arj: arj archives.
- bzip2: bzip2 archives.
- cdda: Audio compact disc information database.
- cdemenu: CDE applications menu (for example, a Solaris menu).
- cpio: CPIO archives.
- deb: Debian packages.
- favorites: GNOME favorites menu.
- file: Local file system.
- ftp: FTP sites.
- gzip, ugzip: GNU Zip archives.
- hp48: Hewlett-Packard model HP48 calculators.
- http: Websites.
- lha: LHA archives.
- mailfs: Berkeley mbox format (may be compressed).
- nttp: Usenet news service.
- patchfs: Patches.
- pipe: Command I/O.
- preferences: GNOME application preferences (directory hierarchy).
- rar: RAR archives.
- rio500: Diamond Rio 500 MP3 player.
- rpm, rpms, trpm: Red Hat Package Manager archives.
- tar: tar archives.
- smb: CIFS (Windows) shares.
- ssh: Remote systems with SSH.
- start-here: The GNOME **Start Here** directory.
- system-settings: GNOME system settings.
- zip: PKZIP archives.
- zoo: ZOO archives.

To construct a URI, start with one of the preceding identifiers followed by a colon (:). If you need a remote machine name, username, and/or password, add two slashes (//) and the appropriate information (for a local file, just use two slashes). Then, to specify the filename, add the absolute path.

GnomeVFS allows nested access types. To specify an additional access type *type* on a file, add *#type* to the URI. If your target happens to be an archive (or similar), you can append another path component. Here are some examples:

- *file:///home/walter/stairway.crd*

  A local file.

- *file:///home/walter/stairway.ps.gz#gzip*

  A local file compressed with GNU Zip. Adding the *#gzip* applies decompression and compression so that the file appears uncompressed on the user side.

- *file:///home/walter/dublin78.tar.gz#gzip#tar/dublin78/highwaystar.tab*

  A file inside a compressed tar archive.

- *http://www.example.com/mosh-1.tar.gz#gzip#tar/mosh-1/README*

  A file inside an archive on a web server.

- *ftp://headbanger:daanimal37@ftp.example.com/people/headbanger/fest2-setlist*

  A file on an FTP site (including username and password).

8.2 Initializing and Shutting Down GnomeVFS

To use GnomeVFS, include *libgnomevfs/gnome-vfs.h* in your source code. Compile and link with the flags you get with `pkg-config` (package name `gnome-vfs-2.0`).

The `gnome_program_init()` function initializes GnomeVFS for you, so if you're writing a GNOME application, you need only worry about shutting down the system. However, if you don't have a GNOME program, call

```
gnome_vfs_init()
```

to set up GnomeVFS. This call returns `FALSE` when it cannot get GnomeVFS working.

At the end of your program, you should shut down the GnomeVFS subsystem to force all pending cache operations and free the resources:

```
gnome_vfs_shutdown()
```

For example, a GTK+ (non-GNOME) application that uses GnomeVFS might have this structure:

```
#include <libgnomevfs/gnome-vfs.h>
#include <gtk/gtk.h>

int main(int argc, char **argv)
{
  << miscellaneous initialization >>

  if (!gnome_vfs_init())
  {
    g_error("could not initialize GnomeVFS");
```

```
    << ... >>
}

<< build application >>

gtk_main();

<< miscellaneous shutdown >>

gnome_vfs_shutdown();

return(0);
}
```

If some other library is supposed to initialize GnomeVFS, you can check the
status of GnomeVFS with

```
if (!gnome_vfs_initialized())
{
  if (!gnome_vfs_init())
  {
      g_error("could not initialize GnomeVFS");
      << ... >>
  }
}
```

8.3 Synchronous Access

The easiest way to interact with GnomeVFS is with synchronous access. After
obtaining a file descriptor by opening a file, you can read, write, and seek.
During synchronous access, read and write data is passed in an allocated buffer,
and function calls return only when they have finished their work, blocking the
rest of the program.

The Unix stream system is the model for synchronous mode in GnomeVFS,
and the function calls are similar, as shown here.

Unix Function	GnomeVFS Equivalent
open()	gnome_vfs_open*()
creat()	gnome_vfs_create*()
close()	gnome_vfs_close()
read()	gnome_vfs_read()
write()	gnome_vfs_write()
lseek()	gnome_vfs_seek()
ftell()	gnome_vfs_tell()
truncate()	gnome_vfs_truncate*()
unlink()	gnome_vfs_unlink*()
symlink()	gnome_vfs_create_symbolic_link()

Unix Function	GnomeVFS Equivalent
stat(), lstat()	gnome_vfs_get_file_info*()
rename(), chown(), chmod()	gnome_vfs_set_file_info()
mkdir()	gnome_vfs_make_directory*()
rmdir()	gnome_vfs_remove_directory*()

Before you see the long, drawn-out description of these GnomeVFS functions, you should see them in use. The program's initial section includes a small utility function to print an appropriate error message when there is a problem with file access:

```c
/* -*-coding: utf-8;-*- */
/* vfsdemo.c -- synchronous operations */

#include <string.h>
#include <libgnome/libgnome.h>
#include <libgnomevfs/gnome-vfs.h>

/* print a VFS error code, its description, and the problem URI */
int print_error(GnomeVFSResult code, const gchar *uri)
{
  const gchar *error_desc;

  error_desc = gnome_vfs_result_to_string(code);
  g_printerr("error %d when accessing %s: %s\n", code, uri, error_desc);

  return (code);
}
```

The main program creates or opens a file and writes a test string:

```c
const gchar filename[] = "gnome-vfsdemo-testfile";
const gchar test_text[] = "This is a test.";

int main(int argc, char **argv)
{
  gchar *file_path;
  gchar *uri;
  guint permissions;
  GnomeVFSHandle *fd;
  GnomeVFSResult result;
  GnomeVFSFileSize bytes_written;

  /* initialize GnomeVFS */
  if (!gnome_vfs_init())
  {
```

```
        g_error("could not initialize GnomeVFS\n");
    }

    /* get full pathname and URI */
    file_path = gnome_util_prepend_user_home(filename);
    g_print("filename is %s\n", file_path);

    uri = gnome_vfs_get_uri_from_local_path(file_path);
    g_print("URI is %s\n", uri);

    g_free(file_path);

    /* permissions: user has read-write access, group, and other read-only */
    permissions = GNOME_VFS_PERM_USER_READ | GNOME_VFS_PERM_USER_WRITE |
                  GNOME_VFS_PERM_GROUP_READ | GNOME_VFS_PERM_OTHER_READ;

    /* create and open URI */
    g_print("creating/opening URI...\n");
    result = gnome_vfs_create(&fd, uri, GNOME_VFS_OPEN_WRITE, FALSE, permissions);
    if (result != GNOME_VFS_OK)
    {
        return (print_error(result, uri));
    }
    g_print(" success.\n");

    /* write test_text into file descriptor */
    g_print("writing \"%s\" into file descriptor...\n", test_text);
    result = gnome_vfs_write(fd, test_text, strlen(test_text), &bytes_written);
    if (result != GNOME_VFS_OK)
    {
        return (print_error(result, uri));
    }
    g_print(" success. %d bytes written.\n", (guint) bytes_written);

    /* close file */
    g_print("closing file descriptor...\n");
    result = gnome_vfs_close(fd);
    if (result != GNOME_VFS_OK)
    {
        return (print_error(result, uri));
    }
    g_print(" success.\n");

    g_free(uri);

    /* shut down GnomeVFS */
    gnome_vfs_shutdown();

    return (0);
}
```

If you'd like to see an error message, run this program, run `chmod 000 gnome-vfsdemo-testfile` in your home directory, and then run the program again.

As you can see from this example, synchronous GnomeVFS operations are similar to those of traditional Unix utilities, but the implementation is slightly different. A URI as a string or a `GnomeVFSURI` structure takes the place of a filename (see Section 8.8 for more information on `GnomeVFSURI`). Because there are two ways to specify URIs, there are two versions of many functions (for example, `gnome_vfs_open()` and `gnome_vfs_open_uri()`).

GnomeVFS does *not* use GError, opting instead for a system very similar to `errno`/`strerror()` in Unix. All access functions return a `GnomeVFSResult` code. The preceding example illustrates how you might work with this error code; see Section 8.10 for a full description of the error codes.

`GnomeVFSFileHandle` is a full data structure. Because functions such as `gnome_vfs_open()` return `GnomeVFSResult`, they take the addresses of pointers to a `GnomeVFSFileHandle` as parameters. Addresses of pointers and memory pervade the GnomeVFS API.

NOTE   `GnomeVFSFileHandle` *structures are not GObject objects. There are special management functions for file descriptors.*

The next few subsections form a reference to synchronous GnomeVFS file operations.

8.3.1 Opening, Creating, and Closing Files

The functions in this section use these parameters:

- *handle* (`GnomeVFSHandle *`) is a file descriptor pointer.
- *handle_addr* (`GnomeVFSHandle **`) is the address of a file descriptor pointer.
- *uri_string* (`gchar *`) is a string containing a URI.
- *uri* (`GnomeVFSURI *`) is a URI structure (see Section 8.8).
- *mode* (`guint`) is the access mode, described later in this section.

All of these functions return `GnomeVFSResult`:

- `gnome_vfs_open(`*handle_addr*`, `*uri_string*`, `*mode*`)`
  Opens *uri_string* and sets the pointer at *handle_addr* to point to the new file descriptor.
- `gnome_vfs_open_uri(`*handle_addr*`, `*uri*`, `*mode*`)`
  Same as the preceding function, but with the `GnomeVFSURI` *uri*.
- `gnome_vfs_create(`*handle_addr*`, `*uri_string*`, `*mode*`, `*exclusive*`, `*permissions*`)`
  Creates and opens a file at *uri_string*, setting the pointer at *handle_addr* to point to the new file descriptor. The *exclusive* parameter is a Boolean value; if this is `TRUE`, this function returns an error if the file already exists. See the discussion that follows for a description of *permissions*.

- gnome_vfs_create_uri(*handle_addr, uri, mode, exclusive, permissions*)
  Same as the preceding function, but with a URI structure instead of a
  URI string.

- gnome_vfs_close(*handle*)
  Closes the file descriptor at *handle*.

Specify the GnomeVFSOpenMode *mode* parameter as a bitwise OR of any of the
following values:

- GNOME_VFS_OPEN_READ: Read access.

- GNOME_VFS_OPEN_WRITE: Write access.

- GNOME_VFS_OPEN_RANDOM: Random access (allows seek operations).

Make sure that you set the options that you need; GNOME_VFS_OPEN_WRITE *does* not *imply*
GNOME_VFS_OPEN_READ.

The permissions *mode* parameter is a Unix-style unsigned integer. Set it to a
bitwise OR of these values:

- GNOME_VFS_PERM_USER_READ: User has read permission.

- GNOME_VFS_PERM_USER_WRITE: User has write permission.

- GNOME_VFS_PERM_USER_EXEC: User has execute permission.

- GNOME_VFS_PERM_USER_ALL: A bitwise OR of the three preceding permissions.

- GNOME_VFS_PERM_GROUP_READ: Group has read permission.

- GNOME_VFS_PERM_GROUP_WRITE: Group has write permission.

- GNOME_VFS_PERM_GROUP_EXEC: Group has execute permission.

- GNOME_VFS_PERM_GROUP_ALL: A bitwise OR of the three preceding permissions.

- GNOME_VFS_PERM_OTHER_READ: Everyone has read permission.

- GNOME_VFS_PERM_OTHER_WRITE: Everyone has write permission.

- GNOME_VFS_PERM_OTHER_EXEC: Everyone has execute permission.

- GNOME_VFS_PERM_OTHER_ALL: A bitwise OR of the three preceding permissions.

- GNOME_VFS_PERM_SUID: An executable with this bit set runs as the file's owner.

- GNOME_VFS_PERM_SGID: An executable with this bit set runs with the file's group.

- GNOME_VFS_PERM_STICKY: You can delete a a file in a directory with this
  permission, but only if you are the file owner.

8.3.2 Reading, Writing, and Seeking

The functions in this section use these parameters:

- *handle* (GnomeVFSHandle *) is a file descriptor.

- *buffer* (gpointer) points to a buffer.

- *bytes* (GnomeVFSFileSize) is a byte count, *buffer*.

- *byte_count_addr* (GnomeVFSFileSize *) indicates where to write a byte count.

All of these functions return GnomeVFSResult:

- gnome_vfs_read(*handle, buffer, n_bytes, byte_count_addr*)
  Reads at most *bytes* from *handle* into *buffer* and writes the number of bytes read into the location at *byte_count_addr*. Usually, *bytes* is the size of *buffer*.

- gnome_vfs_write(*handle, buffer, n_bytes, byte_count_addr*)
  Same as the preceding function, but writes from *buffer* to *handle*.

- gnome_vfs_tell(*handle, offset_addr*)
  Writes the current file position in *handle* to *offset_addr* (GnomeVFSFileSize *).

- gnome_vfs_seek(*handle, start_pos, offset*)
  Sets the file position in *handle* to *offset* bytes from *start_pos*. The *offset* parameter has type GnomeVFSFileSize, and *start_pos* is one of the following:

  > GNOME_VFS_SEEK_START: Beginning of file.

  > GNOME_VFS_SEEK_END: End of file.

  > GNOME_VFS_SEEK_CURRENT: Current file position in *handle*.

8.3.3 Extracting and Changing File Information

The most important function to retrieving information on a file is

```
GnomeVFSResult result;
result = gnome_vfs_get_file_info(uri_string, info, options);
```

Here, *uri_string* is the URI to query, *info* is a GnomeVFSFileInfo structure to fill, and *options* is a bitwise OR of any of the following:

- GNOME_VFS_FILE_INFO_DEFAULT

- GNOME_VFS_FILE_INFO_GET_MIME_TYPE: Retrieve the MIME type of the file.

- GNOME_VFS_FILE_INFO_FORCE_FAST_MIME_TYPE: Try to determine the MIME type without looking inside the file; that is, look at the file extension.

- GNOME_VFS_FILE_INFO_FORCE_SLOW_MIME_TYPE: Use every available means to detect the MIME type. This can take some time.

- GNOME_VFS_FILE_INFO_FOLLOW_LINKS: Automatically follow symbolic links.

- GNOME_VFS_FILE_INFO_GET_ACCESS_RIGHTS: Extract permissions. This can take some time on remote systems.

A GnomeVFSFileInfo result usually has invalid fields because not all files exhibit every characteristic in the structure (for example, a file from the Web does not have a hard link count). Furthermore, you can turn off permissions fields. At the very least, though, you can count on this field being valid:

- name (char *): The file's base name (without a path).

Admittedly, the name alone isn't much to go on. These three fields are usually also available:

- uid (guint): The file owner.
- gid (guint): The file group.
- valid_fields (GnomeVFSFileInfoFields): Valid fields in the rest of the GnomeVFSFileInfo structure. This is a bit field; GNOME_VFS_FILE_INFO_FIELDS_NONE means that no other fields are valid. See the discussion that follows for the other bit settings.

Here are the other fields along with their validity bits:

- type (GnomeVFSFileType)
  Validity bit: GNOME_VFS_FILE_INFO_FIELDS_TYPE
  The file type. Possible values include

  > GNOME_VFS_FILE_TYPE_UNKNOWN
  >
  > GNOME_VFS_FILE_TYPE_REGULAR
  >
  > GNOME_VFS_FILE_TYPE_DIRECTORY
  >
  > GNOME_VFS_FILE_TYPE_FIFO (named pipe)
  >
  > GNOME_VFS_FILE_TYPE_SOCKET
  >
  > GNOME_VFS_FILE_TYPE_CHARACTER_DEVICE
  >
  > GNOME_VFS_FILE_TYPE_BLOCK_DEVICE
  >
  > GNOME_VFS_FILE_TYPE_SYMBOLIC_LINK

- permissions (GnomeVFSFilePermissions)
  Validity bit: GNOME_VFS_FILE_INFO_FIELDS_PERMISSIONS
  Access permissions.

- flags (GnomeVFSFileFlags; bit mask)
  Validity bit: GNOME_VFS_FILE_INFO_FIELDS_FLAGS
  A bitwise OR of the following miscellaneous options:

  > GNOME_VFS_FILE_FLAGS_NONE
  >
  > GNOME_VFS_FILE_FLAGS_SYMLINK (symbolic link)
  >
  > GNOME_VFS_FILE_FLAGS_LOCAL (resides on the local file system)

- device (dev_t)
  Validity bit: GNOME_VFS_FILE_INFO_FIELDS_DEVICE
  The device number, if this is a local file and a device. Depending on your operating system, you may be able extract the major and minor device numbers with MAJOR() and MINOR().

- inode (GnomeVFSInodeNumber)
  Validity bit: GNOME_VFS_FILE_INFO_FIELDS_INODE
  The file system *inode* number.

- link_count (guint)
  Validity bit: GNOME_VFS_FILE_INFO_FIELDS_LINK_COUNT
  The file system **hard link** count.

- size (GnomeVFSFileSize)
  Validity bit: GNOME_VFS_FILE_INFO_FIELDS_SIZE
  The file size, in bytes.

- block_count (GnomeVFSFileSize)
  Validity bit: GNOME_VFS_FILE_INFO_FIELDS_BLOCK_COUNT
  The number of 512-byte blocks that the file occupies.

- io_block_size (guint)
  Validity bit: GNOME_VFS_FILE_INFO_FIELDS_IO_BLOCK_SIZE
  Optimal buffer size for reading to or from the file.

- atime (time_t)
  Validity bit: GNOME_VFS_FILE_INFO_FIELDS_ATIME
  The file's last access (read or write) time; time_t is not completely platform independent.

- mtime (time_t)
  Validity bit: GNOME_VFS_FILE_INFO_FIELDS_MTIME
  The file's last modification time (creation or alteration of the file content).

- ctime (time_t)
  Validity bit: GNOME_VFS_FILE_INFO_FIELDS_CTIME
  The file's last change time. A change is anything that alters the file's inode structure.

- symlink_name (char *)
  Validity bit: GNOME_VFS_FILE_INFO_FIELDS_SYMLINK_NAME
  If the file is a symbolic link, this is the link target.

- mime_type (char *)
  Validity bit: GNOME_VFS_FILE_INFO_FIELDS_MIME_TYPE
  The file's MIME type.

You can change some of a file's information with

```
result = gnome_vfs_set_file_info(uri_string, info, fields);
```

Here, uri_string is the target URI, info is the GnomeVFSFileInfo structure containing the information, and fields is a bitwise OR for the fields to change:

- GNOME_VFS_SET_FILE_INFO_NAME (filename)
- GNOME_VFS_SET_FILE_INFO_PERMISSIONS
- GNOME_VFS_SET_FILE_INFO_OWNER
- GNOME_VFS_SET_FILE_INFO_TIME (access and modification times)

The following functions are similar to the preceding basic functions and return GnomeVFSResult:

- gnome_vfs_get_file_info_uri(GnomeVFSURI *uri, GnomeVFSFileInfo *info, GnomeVFSFileInfoOptions options)
  Like gnome_vfs_get_file_info(), but uses a URI structure rather than a string.

- gnome_vfs_get_file_info_from_handle(GnomeVFSHandle *handle*, GnomeVFSFileInfo *info*, GnomeVFSFileInfoOptions *options*)
  Like gnome_vfs_get_file_info(), but operates on an the open file descriptor *handle*.

- gnome_vfs_set_file_info_uri(GnomeVFSURI *uri*, GnomeVFSFileInfo *info*, GnomeVFSSetFileInfoMask *fields*)
  Like gnome_vfs_set_file_info(), but uses a URI structure rather than a string.

- gnome_vfs_check_same_fs(const gchar *uri_str1*, const gchar *uri_str2*, gboolean *same_fs*)
  Writes TRUE into *same_fs* if *uri_str1* and *uri_str2* are on the same file system.

You can manage GnomeVFSFileInfo structures with these functions:

- GnomeVFSFileInfo *gnome_vfs_file_info_new(void)
  Returns a freshly allocated and initialized GnomeVFSFileInfo structure. This structure will have one reference count.

- void gnome_vfs_file_info_ref(GnomeVFSFileInfo *info*)
  Increases the reference count for *info* by one.

- void gnome_vfs_file_info_unref(GnomeVFSFileInfo *info*)
  Decreases the reference count for *info* by one; deallocates the structure if that was the last reference count.

- void gnome_vfs_file_info_clear(GnomeVFSFileInfo *info*)
  Clears the fields in *info* so that you can start filling it with information.

- void gnome_vfs_file_info_copy(GnomeVFSFileInfo *dest*, const GnomeVFSFileInfo *src*)
  Copies the fields in *src* to *dest*.

- GnomeVFSFileInfo *gnome_vfs_file_info_dup(const GnomeVFSFileInfo *info*)
  Returns a freshly allocated copy of *info*.

- gboolean gnome_vfs_file_info_matches(const GnomeVFSFileInfo *a*, const GnomeVFSFileInfo *b*)
  Returns TRUE if the fields in *a* and *b* are equal.

8.3.4 File Management

Functions in this section manage existing files and return GnomeVFSResult:

- gnome_vfs_unlink(const gchar *uri_string*)
  Removes (a hard link to) the file at *uri_string*.

- gnome_vfs_unlink_from_uri(GnomeVFSURI *uri*)
  Same as the preceding function, but with a URI structure *uri*.

- gnome_vfs_move(const gchar *old_name*, const gchar *new_name*, gboolean *force*)
  Moves the file from URI *old_name* to *new_name*. If *force* is TRUE, this function overwrites any file already at *new_name*.

- gnome_vfs_move_uri(GnomeVFSURI *old_uri*, GnomeVFSURI *new_uri*, gboolean *force*)
  Same as the preceding function, but with URI structure arguments.

- `gnome_vfs_create_symbolic_link(GnomeVFSURI *uri, const gchar *target)`
  Creates a symbolic link at *uri* that points to *target*; you can supply relative paths for *target* such as *../../example*. Remember that *target* is just a name; it doesn't need to exist.

- `gnome_vfs_truncate(const gchar *uri_string, GnomeVFSFileSize length)`
  Truncates the file at *uri_string* to *length* bytes.

- `gnome_vfs_truncate_uri(GnomeVFSFileSize *uri, GnomeVFSFileSize length)`
  Same as the preceding function, but with the URI structure *uri*.

- `gnome_vfs_truncate_handle(GnomeVFSHandle *handle, GnomeVFSFileSize length)`
  Same as the preceding function, but with the open file descriptor *handle*.

Now that you can work with files, you are ready to navigate and operate on GnomeVFS directories.

8.4 Directory Operations

These functions create and remove directories (as usual, all return values are `GnomeVFSResult`):

- `gnome_vfs_make_directory(const gchar *uri_string, guint permissions)`
  Creates a directory at *uri_string* with permissions *permissions* (see Section 8.3.1). Remember that you need to have execute permission for a directory to access any file inside.

- `gnome_vfs_make_directory_for_uri(GnomeVFSURI *uri, guint permissions)`
  Same as the preceding function, but for a URI structure at *uri*.

- `gnome_vfs_remove_directory(const gchar *uri_string)`
  Removes the directory at *uri_string*; fails if the directory is not empty.

- `gnome_vfs_remove_directory_from_uri(GnomeVFSURI *uri)`
  Same as the preceding function, but for a URI structure at *uri*.

8.4.1 Directory Navigation

GnomeVFS directory functions are very similar to Unix counterparts. If you are familiar with `opendir()`, `readdir()`, and `closedir()`, you won't have any trouble with the GNOME API.

To access a directory, you need a special `GnomeVFSDirectoryHandle` descriptor. These functions operate on directory descriptors and return `GnomeVFSResult`:

- `gnome_vfs_directory_open(GnomeVFSDirectoryHandle **handle_addr,`
  `const gchar *uri_string, GnomeVFSFileInfoOptions options)`
  Opens the directory at *uri_string* and writes the directory descriptor into **handle_addr*. See Section 8.3.3 for *options*; these apply to each item that you read from the directory.

- `gnome_vfs_directory_open_from_uri(GnomeVFSDirectoryHandle **handle_addr,`
  `GnomeVFSURI *uri, GnomeVFSFileInfoOptions options)`
  Same as the preceding function, but uses the URI structure *uri*.

- gnome_vfs_directory_read_next(GnomeVFSDirectoryHandle *handle, GnomeVFSFileInfo *info)
  Reads the next item from *handle* into *info*.

- gnome_vfs_directory_close(GnomeVFSDirectoryHandle *handle)
  Closes the directory descriptor *handle*.

You might find it more convenient to operate on a directory's entire contents at once:

- gnome_vfs_directory_list_load(GList **list, const gchar *uri_string, GnomeVFSFileInfoOptions options)
  Loads all entries in *uri_string* into a newly allocated list at **list*. List nodes have GnomeVFSFileInfo structures that follow *options*.

- gnome_vfs_file_info_list_free(GList *list)
  Deallocates a list of GnomeVFSFileInfo structures. This function has no return value.

- gnome_vfs_directory_visit(const gchar *uri_string, GnomeVFSFileInfoOptions info_options, GnomeVFSDirectoryVisitOptions visit_options, GnomeVFSDirectoryVisitFunc function, gpointer data)
  Recursively traverses the directory at *uri_string*, running *function* on each item in the directory (see the discussion that follows for the type definition). Use *info_options* for extracting file information for *function*.

  The *visit_options* parameter is a bitwise OR of any of these options:

  > GNOME_VFS_DIRECTORY_VISIT_DEFAULT
  >
  > GNOME_VFS_DIRECTORY_VISIT_SAMEFS (does not leave the current file system)
  >
  > GNOME_VFS_DIRECTORY_VISIT_LOOPCHECK (avoids infinite loops)

- gnome_vfs_directory_visit_uri(GnomeVFSURI *uri, GnomeVFSFileInfoOptions info_options, GnomeVFSDirectoryVisitOptions visit_options, GnomeVFSDirectoryVisitFunc function, gpointer data)
  Same as the preceding function, but uses the URI structure *uri*.

- gnome_vfs_directory_visit_files(const gchar *uri_string, GList *files, GnomeVFSDirectoryVisitOptions visit_options, GnomeVFSDirectoryVisitFunc function, gpointer data)
  Like gnome_vfs_directory_visit(), but visits only the files in *files* (a list of gchar * relative pathnames).

- gnome_vfs_directory_visit_files_at_uri(GnomeVFSURI *uri, GList *files, GnomeVFSDirectoryVisitOptions visit_options, GnomeVFSDirectoryVisitFunc function, gpointer data)
  Same as the preceding function, but uses the URI structure *uri*.

Here is the GnomeVFSDirectoryVisitFunc type definition:

```
typedef gboolean (*GnomeVFSDirectoryVisitFunc) (const gchar *rel_path,
                                                GnomeVFSFileInfo *info,
                                                gboolean recursing_will_loop,
                                                gpointer data,
                                                gboolean *recurse);
```

The preceding functions call a GnomeVFSDirectoryVisitFunc with rel_path set to the item path relative to the directory URI, and info filled with the directory entry information. If the item is a subdirectory, you can set *recurse to FALSE if you don't want to visit the subdirectory. If you activate loop detection, GnomeVFS initially sets *recurse to FALSE when it detects a possible loop.

To halt the directory traversal, have your visiting function return FALSE rather than TRUE.

There is one special utility for creating and finding GNOME-specific directories:

```
gnome_vfs_find_directory(GnomeVFSURI *near_uri,
                         GnomeVFSFindDirectoryKind type,
                         GnomeVFSURI **result,
                         gboolean create,
                         gboolean find,
                         guint permissions)
```

This function searches *near_uri*'s volume for *type*:

- GNOME_VFS_DIRECTORY_KIND_DESKTOP (GNOME desktop directory)
- GNOME_VFS_DIRECTORY_KIND_TRASH (GNOME trash directory)

A successful result goes into *result. If *search* is TRUE, this function looks around if the location isn't obvious (this can take some time). If the directory does not exist and *create* is TRUE, this function creates the directory according to *permissions*.

8.5 Asynchronous I/O

The synchronous access functions that you just saw are optimal for traditional command-line programs and similar situations. However, synchronous I/O doesn't work very well for interactive, graphical applications. During synchronous file operations, an application does absolutely nothing — it does not accept user input and does not update the display. The application's window may freeze, blank out, or become garbled, returning to life only when the file operation completes. Users tend to find this sort of behavior annoying and unsatisfactory.

Asynchronous I/O fixes these problems by placing the file operations into the background, where GnomeVFS can signal the application when an operation completes. The asynchronous callback functions that you will see in this section run during the main GTK+ loop. Therefore, in multithreaded applications, callbacks run in the main thread.

To use asynchronous I/O in GnomeVFS, call gnome_vfs_async_ functions with GnomeVFSAsyncHandle file descriptors. If you have a file handle, you can cancel an asynchronous operation at any time with

```
gnome_vfs_async_cancel(handle)
```

GnomeVFS sets a limit to the number of simultaneous file operations; if you run past this limit, GnomeVFS puts your request into a priority queue, where –10 is the highest priority and 10 is the lowest. Use higher priorities for short, critical operations.

After an asynchronous operation completes, GnomeVFS invokes a callback function that you must define. Your callback function should perform any tasks that depend on the operation's completion, because you do not know if the operation was successful until the callback runs. GnomeVFS passes any processed data and return code as parameters to the callback, and all callback functions take the usual additional data pointer that you have seen throughout this book.

NOTE *GnomeVFS allocates the memory for certain callback data parameters and frees the memory after the callback completes. Do not try to deallocate this data by hand.*

8.5.1 Opening and Closing Files

These parameters are used in the descriptions that follow and throughout the subsequent subsections:

- *handle_addr* (GnomeVFSAsyncHandle **) is the address of an asynchronous file descriptor.
- *handle* (GnomeVFSAsyncHandle *) is an asynchronous file descriptor.
- *uri_string* (const gchar *) is a string containing a URI.
- *uri* (GnomeVFSURI *) is a URI structure.
- *mode* (GnomeVFSOpenMode) is the open mode (see Section 8.3.1).
- *priority* (int) is the operation priority.
- *callback* (GnomeVFSAsyncOpenCallback) an open or close operation callback (see the following discussion).
- *data* (gpointer) is an untyped data pointer.
- *result* (GnomeVFSResult) is the result code of the operation.

These functions return nothing:

- gnome_vfs_async_open(*handle_addr, uri_string, mode, priority, callback, data*)
  Opens a file at *uri_string*. When this operation completes, GnomeVFS invokes *callback(*handle_addr, result, data*)
  Note that immediately after gnome_vfs_async_open() returns, *handle_addr* is valid, so you can use it to interrupt the operation.
- gnome_vfs_async_open_uri(*handle_addr, uri, mode, priority, callback, data*)
  Same as the preceding function, but uses the URI structure *uri*.
- gnome_vfs_async_create(*handle_addr, uri_string, mode, exclusive, priority, callback, data*)
  Creates a file at *uri_string* and opens the new file as gnome_vfs_async_open() would. If *exclusive* is TRUE and the file already exists, the operation fails.

- gnome_vfs_async_create_uri(*handle_addr, uri, mode, exclusive, priority, callback, data*)
  Same as the preceding function, but uses the URI structure *uri*.

- gnome_vfs_async_close(*handle, callback, data*)
  Closes *handle*. Upon completion, GnomeVFS invokes *callback(handle, result, data)*.

The open and close callback type definitions are as follows:

```
typedef void (* GnomeVFSAsyncCallback) (GnomeVFSAsyncHandle *handle,
                                        GnomeVFSResult result,
                                        gpointer callback_data);

typedef GnomeVFSAsyncCallback GnomeVFSAsyncOpenCallback;
typedef GnomeVFSAsyncCallback GnomeVFSAsyncCloseCallback;
```

As you can see, GnomeVFSAsyncCallback is a basic callback definition with no special data parameters.

8.5.2 Reading and Writing

In addition to the parameters in the previous section, these functions take gpointer for *buffer* and guint for *n_bytes*:

- gnome_vfs_async_read(*handle, buffer, n_bytes, rcallback, data*)
  Attempts to read *n_bytes* from *handle* into *buffer*. When this operation completes, GnomeVFS invokes *rcallback(handle, result, buffer, n_bytes, actual, data)*, where *actual* is the actual number of bytes read. See the discussion that follows for the type definition of *rcallback*.

- gnome_vfs_async_write(*handle, buffer, n_bytes, wcallback, data*)
  Same as the preceding function, but writes the data from *buffer* to *handle* and invokes *wcallback*.

The callback type definitions for reading and writing are nearly identical:

```
typedef void (* GnomeVFSAsyncReadCallback) (GnomeVFSAsyncHandle *handle,
                                            GnomeVFSResult result,
                                            gpointer buffer,
                                            GnomeVFSFileSize bytes_requested,
                                            GnomeVFSFileSize bytes_read,
                                            gpointer callback_data);

typedef void (* GnomeVFSAsyncWriteCallback) (GnomeVFSAsyncHandle *handle,
                                             GnomeVFSResult result,
                                             gconstpointer buffer,
                                             GnomeVFSFileSize bytes_requested,
                                             GnomeVFSFileSize bytes_written,
                                             gpointer callback_data);
```

8.5.3 Retrieving and Setting File Information

The parameters for the two functions in this section include the following:

- *uri_list* (GList *): A list of GnomeVFSURI structures.
- *options* (GnomeVFSFileInfoOptions): See Section 8.3.3.
- *info* (GnomeVFSFileInfo *): A file information structure.
- *mask* (GnomeVFSSetFileInfoMask): File information to set.
- *callback*: Callback functions.

All of these functions return nothing:

- gnome_vfs_async_get_file_info(*handle_addr*, *uri_list*, *options*, *priority*, *callback*, *data*)
  Retrieves information about the URIs in *uri_list* according to *options*.
  handle_addr* is immediately available for canceling the operation. Upon completion, GnomeVFS invokes *callback*(handle_addr*, *results*, *data*), where *results* is a GList of GnomeVFSGetFileInfoResult * structures:

```
typedef struct {
    GnomeVFSURI *uri;
    GnomeVFSResult result;
    GnomeVFSFileInfo *file_info;
} GnomeVFSGetFileInfoResult;
```

- gnome_vfs_async_set_file_info(*handle_addr*, *uri*, *info*, *mask*, *options*, *priority*, *callback*, *data*)
  Sets the *uri* information to the fields in *info*. Upon completion, GnomeVFS invokes *callback*(**handle_addr*, *result*, *info*, *data*).

The callback type definitions are as follows:

```
typedef void (* GnomeVFSAsyncGetFileInfoCallback) (GnomeVFSAsyncHandle *handle,
                                                   GList *results,
                                                   gpointer callback_data);

typedef void (* GnomeVFSAsyncSetFileInfoCallback) (GnomeVFSAsyncHandle *handle,
                                                   GnomeVFSResult result,
                                                   GnomeVFSFileInfo *file_info,
                                                   gpointer callback_data);
```

8.5.4 Miscellaneous Operations

These asynchronous functions don't quite fit anywhere else.

- gnome_vfs_async_load_directory(GnomeVFSAsyncHandle **handle_addr*,
                                const gchar **uri_string*,
                                GnomeVFSFileInfoOptions *options*,
                                guint *items_per_notification*,

```
                              int priority,
                              GnomeVFSAsyncSetFileInfoCallback callback,
                              gpointer data)
```

Loads the items in *uri_string* with file information according to *options*.
Upon completion, GnomeVFS invokes

```
callback(*handle_addr, list, num_read, data)
```

Here, *list* is a list of GnomeVFSFileInfo structures, and *num_read* is the number
of items in the list. The value of *num_read* is never greater than
items_per_notification; if the directory contains more items, GnomeVFS
invokes *callback* as many times as necessary.

- gnome_vfs_async_load_directory_uri(GnomeVFSAsyncHandle **handle_addr,
                              GnomeVFSURI *uri,
                              GnomeVFSFileInfoOptions options,
                              guint items_per_notification,
                              int priority,
                              GnomeVFSAsyncSetFileInfoCallback callback,
                              gpointer data)

Same as the preceding function, but uses the URI structure *uri*.

- gnome_vfs_async_find_directory(GnomeVFSAsyncHandle **handle_addr,
                              GList *near_uris,
                              GnomeVFSFindDirectoryKind type,
                              gboolean create_if_needed,
                              gboolean find_if_needed,
                              guint permissions,
                              int priority,
                              GnomeVFSAsyncFindDirectoryCallback callback,
                              gpointer data)

Like gnome_vfs_find_directory() in Section 8.4, but asynchronous. This function takes a list of GnomeVFSURI structures in *near_uris*. Upon completion,
GnomeVFS invokes

```
callback(*handle_addr, results, data)
```

The *results* parameter is a GList of this structure:

```
typedef struct {
    GnomeVFSURI *uri;
    GnomeVFSResult result;
    << ... >>
} GnomeVFSFindDirectoryResult;
```

- gnome_vfs_async_create_symbolic_link(GnomeVFSAsyncHandle **handle_addr,
                              GnomeVFSURI *uri,
                              const gchar *target,
                              int priority,
                              GnomeVFSAsyncOpenCallback callback,
                              gpointer data)

Creates a symbolic link at *uri* pointing to *target*. Upon completion, GnomeVFS invokes

---

callback(*handle_addr, result, data)

See Section 8.5.1 for the GnomeVFSAsyncOpenCallback type definition.

- gnome_vfs_async_cancel(GnomeVFSAsyncHandle *handle)
  Cancels any GnomeVFS asynchronous operations on handle. You can cancel an operation from any function that uses a handle_addr argument with

---

gnome_vfs_async_cancel(*handle_addr)

The exact type definitions for the load and find callbacks are as follows:

```
typedef void (* GnomeVFSAsyncDirectoryLoadCallback)
                         (GnomeVFSAsyncHandle *handle,
                          GnomeVFSResult result,
                          GList *list,
                          guint entries_read,
                          gpointer callback_data);
typedef void (* GnomeVFSAsyncFindDirectoryCallback)
                         (GnomeVFSAsyncHandle *handle,
                          GList *results,
                          gpointer data);
```

8.5.5 An Example

The file viewer application you're about to see loads a file's text asynchronously. You do not have to wait for the entire file to load before seeing some of it; this is especially handy for looking at large files. If the file isn't interesting (or too large), you can click a **Stop** button to stop the load. Figure 8.1 shows the results.

The extra usability comes at a higher programming cost. For example, you must make sure that the user does not attempt to load a file if the viewer is already loading a file, and that the **Stop** button is active only when a file load operation is in progress.

The declarations include a LoadInfo structure that the application's various callbacks use to manipulate widgets and other configuration data. Therefore, the program needs no global variables.

```
/* -*-coding: utf-8;-*- */
/* asyncviewer.c -- asynchronous GNOME VFS file viewer */

#include <gnome.h>
#include <libgnomeui/gnome-window.h>
#include <libgnomevfs/gnome-vfs.h>

#define MAX_BLOCKSIZE (8 * 1024)
#define MAX_PATHLEN (8 * 1024)
```

```
#define PRIORITY GNOME_VFS_PRIORITY_DEFAULT

/* information about a (current) file load operation */
typedef struct _LoadInfo {
  gchar *prog_name;
  gchar current_dir[MAX_PATHLEN];    /* current working directory */
  gchar *uri_string;
  GnomeVFSAsyncHandle *fd;
  guint block_size;
  GnomeVFSFileSize total_size;
  GnomeVFSFileSize bytes_read;
  GtkWindow *window;
  GtkTextBuffer *text_buffer;
  GtkProgressBar *progress_bar;
  GnomeFileEntry *file_entrybox;
  GtkButton *open_button;
  GtkButton *close_button;
  GtkButton *stop_button;

  /* initially TRUE; error detection changes this to FALSE */
  gboolean status_normal;
} LoadInfo;
```

Figure 8-1: Asynchronous file viewer.

The following is a very basic error-reporting function with a dialog. You should provide something a little more extensive in your program, perhaps using Glade to create a dialog that conforms to the GUP guidelines.

```c
/* Report an error with string (can be a URI or otherwise). If result is a
   valid GnomeVFSResult, display the string error representation; otherwise,
   show a custom message. */
void report_error(gchar *name, gchar *desc, GnomeVFSResult result, GtkWindow *win)
{
  GtkDialog *dialog;
  gchar *err_title, *err_message;

  if (name)
  {
    err_title = g_strdup_printf("File access error:\n %s: ", name);
  } else {
    err_title = g_strdup_printf("File access error:\n");
  }

  if (result < GNOME_VFS_NUM_ERRORS)
  {
    err_message = g_strdup(gnome_vfs_result_to_string(result));
  } else {
    err_message = g_strdup_printf("%s\n", desc ? desc : "");
  }
  dialog = GTK_DIALOG(gtk_message_dialog_new(win,
                                             GTK_DIALOG_DESTROY_WITH_PARENT,
                                             GTK_MESSAGE_ERROR,
                                             GTK_BUTTONS_CLOSE,
                                             "%s %s", err_title, err_message));
  g_signal_connect_swapped(dialog,
                           "response", G_CALLBACK (gtk_widget_destroy), dialog);
  g_object_set(dialog, "title", "", NULL);
  gtk_widget_show_all(GTK_WIDGET(dialog));
  g_free(err_title);
  g_free(err_message);
}
```

The small procedure that follows resets the application's various widgets when a file read operation completes.

```c
/* reset widgets after a file load */
void finish_file_load(LoadInfo *load_info)
{
  /* update progress bar; clear if the load was completely successful,
     clear the status bar. Otherwise, show a warning message. */
  if (load_info->status_normal)
  {
    g_object_set(load_info->progress_bar,
                 "text", "",
                 "fraction", 0.0,  NULL);
```

```
  } else {
    g_object_set(load_info->progress_bar,
                  "text", "Warning: File view incomplete",
                  "fraction", 0.0,  NULL);
  }

  /* disable the stop button, enable close and open buttons */
  g_object_set(load_info->stop_button,   "sensitive", FALSE, NULL);
  g_object_set(load_info->close_button,  "sensitive", TRUE,  NULL);
  g_object_set(load_info->open_button,   "sensitive", TRUE,  NULL);
  g_object_set(load_info->file_entrybox, "sensitive", TRUE,  NULL);
}
```

The file close callback checks for errors and resets the widgets with the preceding function:

```
/* callback (GnomeVFSAsyncCloseCallback) for a file close operation */
void file_closed(GnomeVFSAsyncHandle *fd, GnomeVFSResult result, gpointer li_ptr)
{
  LoadInfo *load_info = (LoadInfo*)li_ptr;

  if (result != GNOME_VFS_OK)
  {
     report_error(load_info->uri_string, NULL, result, load_info->window);
  }

  finish_file_load(load_info);
}
```

The **Stop** button handler sets off the preceding chain of functions when closing a file.

```
/* handler for when the user clicks the "stop" button */
void stop_load(GtkButton *knopf, gpointer li_ptr)
{
  LoadInfo *load_info = (LoadInfo*)li_ptr;

  gnome_vfs_async_cancel(load_info->fd);
  load_info->status_normal = FALSE;
  gnome_vfs_async_close(load_info->fd, file_closed, li_ptr);
}
```

The read block callback performs most of the program's actual work. In addition to copying the block buffer into the application's main text buffer, it must update the progress bar and check for several kinds of errors.

This callback keeps itself going by requesting another read operation at the very end of a successful read.

```
/* callback (GnomeVFSAsyncReadCallback) to move the bytes in a buffer to
   the text buffer inside the application window; reports the progress. */
void block_to_text_buffer(GnomeVFSAsyncHandle *fd,
                          GnomeVFSResult result,
                          gpointer buffer,
                          GnomeVFSFileSize bytes_requested,
                          GnomeVFSFileSize bytes_received,
                          gpointer load_info_ptr)
{
  LoadInfo *load_info = (LoadInfo*)load_info_ptr;
  GtkTextIter buffer_end;
  gdouble fraction_complete;
  gchar *progress_text;

  /* if there's an error, report the error, set the error flag, close file,
     and deallocate buffer */
  if ((result != GNOME_VFS_OK) && (result != GNOME_VFS_ERROR_EOF))
  {
    report_error(load_info->uri_string, NULL, result, load_info->window);
    load_info->status_normal = FALSE;
    gnome_vfs_async_close(load_info->fd, file_closed, load_info_ptr);
    g_free(buffer);
    return;
  }

  /* insert read operation buffer contents into text buffer */
  gtk_text_buffer_get_end_iter(load_info->text_buffer, &buffer_end);
  gtk_text_buffer_insert_with_tags_by_name(
    load_info->text_buffer, &buffer_end, buffer, bytes_received, "mono", NULL);

  /* update the fraction complete and progress bar */
  load_info->bytes_read += bytes_received;
  if (load_info->total_size != 0)
  {
    fraction_complete = (gdouble)(load_info->bytes_read) /
                        (gdouble)(load_info->total_size);
    fraction_complete = CLAMP(fraction_complete, 0.0, 0.999);
    progress_text = g_strdup_printf("%3.0f%% complete",
                                    fraction_complete * 100);
    g_object_set(load_info->progress_bar,
                 "fraction", fraction_complete,
                 "text", progress_text,
                 NULL);
    g_free(progress_text);
  }

  /* if this isn't the end of the file, read another block */
```

```
  if (result != GNOME_VFS_ERROR_EOF)
  {
    gnome_vfs_async_read(
        fd, buffer, bytes_requested, block_to_text_buffer, load_info_ptr);
  } else {
    g_free(buffer);
    gnome_vfs_async_close(fd, file_closed, load_info_ptr);
    load_info->status_normal = TRUE;
  }
}
```

The most important thing to notice about the file open operation's callback is
that it sets the read process in motion — look at the very end of the function.

```
/* callback (GnomeVFSAsyncOpenCallback) for completion of file open;
   initiates the first block read from the file */
void file_opened(GnomeVFSAsyncHandle *fd, GnomeVFSResult result, gpointer li_ptr)
{
  LoadInfo *load_info = (LoadInfo*)li_ptr;
  GnomeVFSURI *uri_tmp;
  gchar *short_name;
  gpointer buffer;

  /* report error and reset buttons when GnomeVFS can't open file  */
  if (result != GNOME_VFS_OK)
  {
    report_error(load_info->uri_string, NULL, result, load_info->window);
    load_info->status_normal = FALSE;
    finish_file_load(load_info);
    return;
  }

  /* extract file's short name and include this in window's title */
  uri_tmp = gnome_vfs_uri_new(load_info->uri_string);
  short_name = gnome_vfs_uri_extract_short_name(uri_tmp);
  gnome_vfs_uri_unref(uri_tmp);
  gnome_window_toplevel_set_title(load_info->window, short_name, "AsyncViewer",
                                  NULL);
  g_free(short_name);

  /* create a buffer and read a block from the file */
  buffer = g_malloc(load_info->block_size);
  gnome_vfs_async_read(
      fd, buffer, load_info->block_size, block_to_text_buffer, li_ptr);
}
```

To get to the preceding callback, the user must click the **Open** button or otherwise activate the file entry widget. This is the handler for the button, consisting of error checking and filling a LoadInfo structure with information that the callbacks use. Note that open_file does not fill *all* of the LoadInfo structure; the main program records the widgets.

This is the next link for the chain of functions; near the end of open_file is an asynchronous open file request using the preceding callback.

```
/* handler for "Open" button - try to open the file */
void open_file(GtkButton *button, gpointer li_ptr)
{
  LoadInfo *load_info = (LoadInfo*)li_ptr;
  gchar *path;
  GtkTextIter text_begin, text_end;
  GnomeVFSResult result;
  GnomeVFSFileInfo *file_stats;
  GnomeVFSAsyncHandle *fd;

  /* clear text buffer */
  gtk_text_buffer_get_bounds(load_info->text_buffer, &text_begin, &text_end);
  gtk_text_buffer_delete(load_info->text_buffer, &text_begin, &text_end);

  /* free any pre-existing URI string */
  if (load_info->uri_string)
  {
    g_free(load_info->uri_string);
    load_info->uri_string = NULL;
  }

  /* extract URI from file entry box; return error when file does not exist */
  path = gnome_file_entry_get_full_path(load_info->file_entrybox, TRUE);
  load_info->uri_string = gnome_vfs_get_uri_from_local_path(path);
  if (path)
  {
    g_free(path);
  }
  if (!load_info->uri_string)
  {
    g_object_get(load_info->file_entrybox, "filename", &path, NULL);
    report_error(path, "File not found", GNOME_VFS_NUM_ERRORS,
                 load_info->window);
    g_free(path);
    return;
  }

  /* get the file information */
  file_stats = gnome_vfs_file_info_new();
  result = gnome_vfs_get_file_info(load_info->uri_string,
                           file_stats, GNOME_VFS_FILE_INFO_FOLLOW_LINKS);
```

```
if (result != GNOME_VFS_OK)
{
    report_error(load_info->uri_string, NULL, result, load_info->window);
    return;
}

/* determine buffer block size: optimal block size or MAX_BLOCKSIZE */
if (file_stats->valid_fields & GNOME_VFS_FILE_INFO_FIELDS_IO_BLOCK_SIZE)
{
    load_info->block_size = file_stats->io_block_size;
} else {
    load_info->block_size = MAX_BLOCKSIZE;
}

/* determine file size */
if (file_stats->valid_fields & GNOME_VFS_FILE_INFO_FIELDS_SIZE)
{
    load_info->total_size = file_stats->size;
} else {
    load_info->total_size = 0;
}

gnome_vfs_file_info_unref(file_stats);

/* reset the number of bytes already read */
load_info->bytes_read = 0;

/* open file and set file descriptor in load_info */
gnome_vfs_async_open(&fd, load_info->uri_string, GNOME_VFS_OPEN_READ,
                     PRIORITY, file_opened, load_info);
load_info->fd = fd;

/* enable cancel; disable open and close */
g_object_set(load_info->stop_button,   "sensitive", TRUE,  NULL);
g_object_set(load_info->close_button,  "sensitive", FALSE, NULL);
g_object_set(load_info->open_button,   "sensitive", FALSE, NULL);
g_object_set(load_info->file_entrybox, "sensitive", FALSE, NULL);
}
```

This is just a "glue" handler to link the file entry box with the **Open** button handler:

```
/* the handler for the file entry box; "clicks" the Open button */
void file_entered(GnomeFileEntry *entry, gpointer li_ptr)
{
    LoadInfo *load_info = (LoadInfo*)li_ptr;
    g_signal_emit_by_name(load_info->open_button, "activate");
}
```

The standard end_program() event handler is slightly different for this program; it interrupts and cleans a file read operation if one is active.

```
/* standard window event handlers */
gint delete_event(GtkWidget *widget, GdkEvent event, gpointer data)
{
  return FALSE;
}

void end_program(GtkWidget *widget, gpointer li_ptr)
{
  LoadInfo *load_info = (LoadInfo*)li_ptr;
  gboolean still_loading_file;

  /* the application is still reading if the Cancel button is enabled;
     stop the load if that's the case */
  g_object_get(load_info->stop_button, "sensitive", &still_loading_file, NULL);
  if (still_loading_file)
  {
    stop_load(load_info->stop_button, li_ptr);
  }

  /* quit the main loop */
  gtk_main_quit();
}
```

Section 4.3.16 mentioned that this program has session manager support. Here it is:

```
/* handler for session manager's "save-yourself" request */
gboolean save_yourself(GnomeClient *client, int phase,
                       GnomeSaveStyle what,
                       gboolean end,
                       GnomeInteractStyle interaction,
                       gboolean fast,
                       gpointer li_ptr)
{
  LoadInfo *load_info = (LoadInfo*)li_ptr;
  gchar *argv[3];
  gchar *filename;

  /* determine the current directory */
  gnome_client_set_current_directory(client, load_info->current_dir);

  /* transmit a command for a new instance */
  argv[0] = g_strdup(load_info->prog_name);
  gnome_client_set_clone_command(client, 1, argv);

  /* transmit command for restarting this command with the current file */
```

```
  if (load_info->uri_string != NULL)
  {
      filename = gnome_vfs_get_local_path_from_uri(load_info->uri_string);
  }
  if (filename != NULL)
  {
      argv[1] = "-f";
      argv[2] = filename;
      gnome_client_set_restart_command(client, 3, argv);
  } else {
      gnome_client_set_restart_command(client, 1, argv);
  }
  return TRUE;
}


/* signal handler for termination via session manager */
void die(GnomeClient *client, gpointer data)
{
  end_program(NULL, data);
}
```

Most of the main program deals with initialization and widget setup. See if you can pick out the session management in the following code:

```
int main(int argc, char **argv)
{
  GnomeProgram *program;
  GnomeClient *client;
  GnomeFileEntry *file_entrybox;
  GtkLabel *file_label;
  LoadInfo load_info;
  GtkTextBuffer *text_buffer;
  GtkTextView *text_view;
  GtkScrolledWindow *text_window;
  GtkProgressBar *progress_bar;
  GtkButton *stop_button, *close_button, *open_button;
  GtkHBox *hbox, *hbox1;
  GtkVBox *vbox;
  GtkWindow *window;
  gint i;

  program = gnome_program_init("asyncviewer", "0.1", LIBGNOMEUI_MODULE,
                      argc, argv,
                      GNOME_PROGRAM_STANDARD_PROPERTIES,
                      GNOME_PARAM_HUMAN_READABLE_NAME, "AsyncViewer",
                      GNOME_PARAM_ENABLE_SOUND, TRUE,
                      NULL);

  /* initialize session management */
```

```
client = gnome_master_client();

/* bind session management handlers */
g_signal_connect(client,
                 "save_yourself", G_CALLBACK(save_yourself), &load_info);
g_signal_connect(client, "die", G_CALLBACK(die), &load_info);

/* create text view and buffer; put view into a scrolled window */
text_buffer = gtk_text_buffer_new(NULL);
gtk_text_buffer_create_tag(text_buffer, "mono", "family", "Courier", NULL);
text_view = GTK_TEXT_VIEW(gtk_text_view_new_with_buffer(text_buffer));

g_object_set(text_view,
             "wrap-mode", GTK_WRAP_CHAR,
             "editable", FALSE,
             "cursor-visible", FALSE,
             NULL);

text_window = g_object_new(GTK_TYPE_SCROLLED_WINDOW,
                           "hscrollbar-policy", GTK_POLICY_AUTOMATIC,
                           "vscrollbar-policy", GTK_POLICY_ALWAYS,
                           NULL);

gtk_container_add(GTK_CONTAINER(text_window), GTK_WIDGET(text_view));

/* create progress bar, stop/close buttons */
progress_bar = g_object_new(GTK_TYPE_PROGRESS_BAR,
                            "text", "Choose a file and click Open",
                            NULL);

stop_button = g_object_new(GTK_TYPE_BUTTON,
                           "label", GTK_STOCK_STOP,
                           "use-stock", TRUE,
                           "sensitive", FALSE,
                           NULL);

close_button = g_object_new(GTK_TYPE_BUTTON,
                            "label", GTK_STOCK_CLOSE,
                            "use-stock", TRUE,
                            NULL);

hbox = g_object_new(GTK_TYPE_HBOX, "border-width", 6,  "spacing", 6,  NULL);
gtk_box_pack_start_defaults(GTK_BOX(hbox), GTK_WIDGET(progress_bar));
gtk_box_pack_start(GTK_BOX(hbox), GTK_WIDGET(stop_button), FALSE, FALSE, 0);
gtk_box_pack_start(GTK_BOX(hbox), GTK_WIDGET(close_button), FALSE, FALSE, 0);

/* file entry box with Open button */
```

```
file_entrybox = g_object_new(GNOME_TYPE_FILE_ENTRY,
                             "history-id", "filename",
                             "browse-dialog-title", "Choose a File",
                             NULL);

file_label = g_object_new(GTK_TYPE_LABEL,
                          "label", "_File:",
                          "use-underline", TRUE,
                          "mnemonic-widget", file_entrybox,
                          NULL);

open_button = g_object_new(GTK_TYPE_BUTTON,
                           "label", GTK_STOCK_OPEN,
                           "use-stock", TRUE,
                           NULL);

hbox1 = g_object_new(GTK_TYPE_HBOX, "border-width", 6,  "spacing", 6,  NULL);
gtk_box_pack_start(GTK_BOX(hbox1), GTK_WIDGET(file_label), FALSE, FALSE, 0);
gtk_box_pack_start_defaults(GTK_BOX(hbox1), GTK_WIDGET(file_entrybox));
gtk_box_pack_start(GTK_BOX(hbox1), GTK_WIDGET(open_button), FALSE, FALSE, 0);

vbox = g_object_new(GTK_TYPE_VBOX, NULL);
gtk_box_pack_start(GTK_BOX(vbox), GTK_WIDGET(hbox1), FALSE, FALSE, 0);
gtk_box_pack_start(GTK_BOX(vbox), GTK_WIDGET(text_window), TRUE, TRUE, 0);
gtk_box_pack_start(GTK_BOX(vbox), GTK_WIDGET(hbox), FALSE, FALSE, 0);

/* create and fill window */
window = g_object_new(GTK_TYPE_WINDOW,
                      "default-height", 500,
                      "default-width", 400,
                      "title", "AsyncViewer",
                      NULL);

gtk_container_add(GTK_CONTAINER(window), GTK_WIDGET(vbox));
```

The main program fills the rest of the LoadInfo structure below (recall that open_file() does the rest). Notice that this load_info structure is not a pointer.

```
/* write widgets into LoadInfo structure so that the callbacks can
   access the widgets */
load_info.window       = window;
load_info.text_buffer  = text_buffer;
load_info.progress_bar = progress_bar;
load_info.open_button  = open_button;
load_info.close_button = close_button;
load_info.stop_button  = stop_button;
load_info.file_entrybox = file_entrybox;

/* record command for the saveyourself signal */
```

```
load_info.prog_name = argv[0];

if (!getcwd(load_info.current_dir, MAX_PATHLEN))
{
    g_error("could not determine current working directory\n");
}
load_info.uri_string = NULL;
```

After the LoadInfo information is in place, you can set up the signal handlers, using &load_info as the data pointer:

```
/* attach all signal handlers */
g_signal_connect(open_button, "clicked", G_CALLBACK(open_file), &load_info);
g_signal_connect(file_entrybox,
                 "activate", G_CALLBACK(file_entered), &load_info);

g_signal_connect(stop_button, "clicked", G_CALLBACK(stop_load), &load_info);
g_signal_connect_swapped(close_button,
                         "clicked", G_CALLBACK(gtk_widget_destroy), window);

g_signal_connect(window, "delete-event", G_CALLBACK(delete_event), NULL);
g_signal_connect(window, "destroy", G_CALLBACK(end_program), &load_info);
```

The command-line parsing works in conjunction with the session manager code from earlier.

```
/* rudimentary command line parsing (use popt if you want better handling) */
for (i=1; i < (argc-1); i++)
{
    if (!strcmp("-f", argv[i]))
    {
        g_object_set(file_entrybox, "filename", argv[i+1], NULL);
        open_file(NULL, &load_info);
        break;
    }
}

/* show everything, start GTK+ main event loop */
gtk_widget_show_all(GTK_WIDGET(window));
gtk_main();

gnome_vfs_shutdown();
return 0;
}
```

8.6 Transfers

Transfers are powerful utilities for transferring files from one place to another. You can copy anything from a single file to an entire directory tree with just a single statement, regardless of the file system type.

The API and mechanism is somewhat complicated. After you start a transfer, GnomeVFS periodically runs one of your callback functions. Your callback may need to answer a query, and that's the tricky part; you need to take a very close look at the callback parameters so that you know what kind of answer is appropriate.

The basic URI transfer function is

```
GnomeVFSResult gnome_vfs_xfer_uri(const GnomeVFSURI *src_uri,
                                   const GnomeVFSURI *target_uri,
                                   GnomeVFSXferOptions options,
                                   GnomeVFSXferErrorMode error_mode,
                                   GnomeVFSXferOverwriteMode overwrite_mode,
                                   GnomeVFSXferProgressCallback callback,
                                   gpointer data)
```

This function transfers *src_uri* to its corresponding location in *target_uri*.

Specify *options* as a bitwise OR of these constants:

- GNOME_VFS_XFER_DEFAULT
- GNOME_VFS_XFER_REMOVESOURCE: Moves the files; doesn't just copy.
- GNOME_VFS_XFER_LINK_ITEMS: Does not copy; creates symbolic links.
- GNOME_VFS_XFER_FOLLOW_LINKS: Follows symbolic links in the source.
- GNOME_VFS_XFER_RECURSIVE: If the source is a directory, copies the entire contents.
- GNOME_VFS_XFER_SAMEFS: Limits transfer to the same (local) file system.
- GNOME_VFS_XFER_USE_UNIQUE_NAMES: Makes sure that the transfer does not overwrite files at the target by giving new names to the source files that already exist in the target.
- GNOME_VFS_XFER_DELETE_ITEMS: Does not copy; removes the source (set *target_uri* to NULL).
- GNOME_VFS_XFER_EMPTY_DIRECTORIES: Does not copy; removes the contents of the source (set *target_uri* to NULL).
- GNOME_VFS_XFER_NEW_UNIQUE_DIRECTORY: Does not copy; creates a new directory at the target. If the target already exists, the callback function will have the name of another new, unique directory.

Specify *error_mode* as one of the following:

- GNOME_VFS_XFER_ERROR_MODE_ABORT: Terminates the transfer if errors occur.
- GNOME_VFS_XFER_ERROR_MODE_QUERY: Stops transfer and asks the callback for advice.

The *overwrite_mode* parameter determines what GnomeVFS does when a transfer can overwrite a file:

- GNOME_VFS_XFER_OVERWRITE_MODE_ABORT: Terminates the transfer.
- GNOME_VFS_XFER_OVERWRITE_MODE_QUERY: Asks the callback function for advice.
- GNOME_VFS_XFER_OVERWRITE_MODE_REPLACE: Replaces the file (silently).
- GNOME_VFS_XFER_OVERWRITE_MODE_SKIP: Skips the file.

Every few hundred milliseconds, or whenever interaction is necessary as noted in the preceding discussion, GnomeVFS invokes

---

callback(info, data)

The full type definition for *callback* is

```
typedef gint (* GnomeVFSXferProgressCallback) (GnomeVFSXferProgressInfo *info,
                                               gpointer data);
```

Note that *callback* must be able to answer queries from GnomeVFS. To determine the answer, use the following general procedure:

1. Look at *info->*status to see what GnomeVFS wants.
2. Figure out what return codes work for the status.
3. Look at any other fields in *info* to make a final decision.

Detailed descriptions of each step follow.

Step 1:

The value of *info->*status can be any of the following:

- GNOME_VFS_XFER_PROGRESS_STATUS_OK: No errors; a normal status report.
- GNOME_VFS_XFER_PROGRESS_STATUS_VFSERROR: The callback must react to an error.
- GNOME_VFS_XFER_PROGRESS_STATUS_OVERWRITE: The callback must determine whether GnomeVFS should overwrite a file.
- GNOME_VFS_XFER_PROGRESS_STATUS_DUPLICATE: The callback must determine what to do about a duplicate filename.

Step 2:

If *info->*status says that everything is going well, return 1 to continue or 0 to terminate the transfer. For an error, your callback can return one of the following:

- GNOME_VFS_XFER_ERROR_ACTION_ABORT: Terminate the transfer.
- GNOME_VFS_XFER_ERROR_ACTION_RETRY: Try again.
- GNOME_VFS_XFER_ERROR_ACTION_SKIP: Skip this operation and continue.

For overwrite questions, the return codes are

- GNOME_VFS_XFER_OVERWRITE_ACTION_ABORT: Terminate the transfer.
- GNOME_VFS_XFER_OVERWRITE_ACTION_REPLACE: Replace the file.
- GNOME_VFS_XFER_OVERWRITE_ACTION_REPLACE_ALL: Replace this and any other files with duplicate names in the future.
- GNOME_VFS_XFER_OVERWRITE_ACTION_SKIP: Skip this file.
- GNOME_VFS_XFER_OVERWRITE_ACTION_SKIP_ALL: Skip this and any other files with duplicate names in the future.

For duplicate filenames, set *info->duplicate_name* (see the discussion that follows) and return 1 to continue or 0 to stop.

Step 3:

GnomeVFSXferProgressInfo is a large structure with these fields:

- status (GnomeVFSXferProgressStatus): See the preceding discussion.
- vfs_status (GnomeVFSResult): Error code from VFS operation (see Section 8.10).
- phase (GnomeVFSXferPhase): Current transfer phase; one of

    GNOME_VFS_XFER_PHASE_INITIAL

    GNOME_VFS_XFER_CHECKING_DESTINATION

    GNOME_VFS_XFER_PHASE_COLLECTING (collecting source files)

    GNOME_VFS_XFER_PHASE_READYTOGO

    GNOME_VFS_XFER_PHASE_OPENSOURCE (opening the source file)

    GNOME_VFS_XFER_PHASE_OPENTARGET (opening the target file)

    GNOME_VFS_XFER_PHASE_COPYING

    GNOME_VFS_XFER_PHASE_MOVING

    GNOME_VFS_XFER_PHASE_READSOURCE

    GNOME_VFS_XFER_PHASE_WRITETARGET

    GNOME_VFS_XFER_PHASE_CLOSESOURCE

    GNOME_VFS_XFER_PHASE_CLOSETARGET

    GNOME_VFS_XFER_PHASE_DELETESOURCE

    GNOME_VFS_XFER_PHASE_SETATTRIBUTES (setting the target file information)

    GNOME_VFS_XFER_PHASE_FILECOMPLETED (ready for the next file)

    GNOME_VFS_XFER_PHASE_CLEANUP

    GNOME_VFS_XFER_PHASE_COMPLETED

- source_name (gchar *): Source URI.
- target_name (gchar *): Target URI.
- file_index (gulong): Current file number.
- files_total (gulong): Total number of files in the transfer.

- `bytes_total` (GnomeVFSFileSize): Total number of bytes in the transfer.

- `file_size` (GnomeVFSFileSize): Current file size.

- `bytes_copied` (GnomeVFSFileSize): Number of bytes transferred from the current file so far.

- `total_bytes_copied` (GnomeVFSFileSize): Total number of bytes copied in the transfer so far.

- `duplicate_name` (gchar *): Set this to avoid a duplicate file.

- `duplicate_count` (int): The number of copies of the file so far; helps build a unique name like *copy 2 of file*.

- `top_level_item` (gboolean): If TRUE, the transfer function call explicitly named the current item; it is not part of a recursively traversed subdirectory.

8.6.1 Additional Transfer Functions

Now that you've seen the particulars of transferring a single item, you are ready to see the other transfer utilities at your disposal:

- ```
  GnomeVFSResult gnome_vfs_xfer_uri_list(const GList *src_uri_list,
                                         const GList *target_uri_list,
                                         GnomeVFSXferOptions options,
                                         GnomeVFSXferErrorMode error_mode,
                                         GnomeVFSXferOverwriteMode overwrite_mode,
                                         GnomeVFSXferProgressCallback callback,
                                         gpointer data)
  ```
  Like gnome_vfs_xfer_uri(), but transfers each URI in src_uri_list to its corresponding URI in target_uri_list.

- ```
  GnomeVFSResult gnome_vfs_xfer_delete_list(const GList *src_uri_list,
                                            GnomeVFSXferErrorMode error_mode,
                                            GnomeVFSXferOptions options,
                                            GnomeVFSXferProgressCallback callback,
                                            gpointer data)
  ```
  Deletes the items in *src_uri_list*.

- ```
  GnomeVFSResult gnome_vfs_async_xfer(GnomeVFSAsyncHandle **handle_addr,
                                      const GList *src_uri_list,
                                      const GList *target_uri_list,
                                      GnomeVFSXferOptions options,
                                      GnomeVFSXferErrorMode error_mode,
                                      GnomeVFSXferOverwriteMode overwrite_mode,
                                      GnomeVFSAsyncXferProgressCallback afunc,
                                      gpointer adata,
                                      GnomeVFSXferProgressCallback callback,
                                      gpointer data)
  ```
  Like gnome_vfs_xfer_uri_list(), but in asynchronous mode, so that your program can perform other tasks during a transfer. For regular status reports, GnomeVFS invokes

---

afunc(*handle_addr, info, adata)
  ```

The type definition for *afunc* is

```
typedef
gint (* GnomeVFSAsyncXferProgressCallback) (GnomeVFSAsyncHandle *handle,
                                            GnomeVFSXferProgressInfo *info,
                                            gpointer data);
```

For synchronous requests that require an answer, GnomeVFS makes the usual call to

```
callback(info, data)
```

8.7 File Types

After extracting a MIME type (for example, image/png) from a URI or file, you can ask GNOME for more information about the type with these functions:

- gboolean gnome_vfs_mime_type_is_known(const char *mime_type)
  Returns TRUE if GNOME recognizes *mime_type*.

- GnomeVFSMimeActionType gnome_vfs_mime_get_default_action_type(const char *mime_type)
  Indicates how GNOME normally opens the type; the return value is one of the following:

    GNOME_VFS_MIME_ACTION_TYPE_NONE: Undefined.

    GNOME_VFS_MIME_ACTION_TYPE_APPLICATION: Opens the file with an application.

    GNOME_VFS_MIME_ACTION_TYPE_COMPONENT: Opens the file with a component.

- GnomeVFSMimeApplication *gnome_vfs_mime_get_default_application(const char *mime_type)
  Returns a freshly allocated GnomeVFSMimeApplication structure containing the default application for *mime_type*. See the discussion that follows for more information on this structure.

- GList *gnome_vfs_mime_get_short_list_applications(const char *mime_type)
  Returns a list of GnomeVFSMimeApplication structures with the applications recommended for *mime_type*.

- GList *gnome_vfs_mime_get_all_applications(const char *mime_type)
  Returns a list of GnomeVFSMimeApplication structures with all applications that can handle *mime_type*.

- const char *gnome_vfs_mime_get_icon(const char *mime_type)
  Returns an icon name for *mime_type*. Do not attempt to deallocate or change the name.

NOTE *This is not a full path, just a name. If the icon is in several formats, the name does not include a suffix, and in that case, you should add your own, such as .png. The images are independent of your current Nautilus theme.*

- const char *gnome_vfs_mime_get_description(const char *mime_type)
  Returns a short description of *mime_type*. Do not attempt to deallocate or change the description string.

- gboolean gnome_vfs_mime_can_be_executable(const char *mime_type)
  Returns TRUE if you might be able to execute files of *mime_type*.

GnomeVFSMimeApplication structures fields include the following:

- id (char *): The application identifier.

- name (char *): The full application name.

- command (char *): The application executable name.

- can_open_multiple_files (gboolean): TRUE if the application can open more than one file at a time.

- expects_uris (GnomeVFSMimeApplicationArgumentType): Indicates how the application expects command-line file parameters. Possible values include the following:

  GNOME_VFS_MIME_APPLICATION_ARGUMENT_TYPE_URIS
  URIs only.

  GNOME_VFS_MIME_APPLICATION_ARGUMENT_TYPE_PATHS
  Local paths only.

  GNOME_VFS_MIME_APPLICATION_ARGUMENT_TYPE_URIS_FOR_NON_FILES
  Local paths for local files; URIs for everything else.

- supported_uri_schemes (GList *): The application's supported URI access modes (*http*, *ftp*, and so on).

- requires_terminal (gboolean): The application must run in a terminal window.

You can manage GnomeVFSMimeApplication with these utilities:

- GnomeVFSMimeApplication
  *gnome_vfs_mime_application_copy(GnomeVFSMimeApplication *application)
  Returns a copy of *application*.

- void gnome_vfs_mime_application_free(GnomeVFSMimeApplication *application)
  Deallocates the memory for *application*.

- void gnome_vfs_mime_application_list_free(GList *app_list)
  Deallocates the memory for *app_list* and all applications inside.

- gboolean gnome_vfs_mime_id_in_application_list(const char *id, GList *app_list)
  Returns TRUE if the application for *id* is in *app_list*.

8.7.1 Declaring MIME Types

For GNOME to realize that your application supports a certain MIME type, you must declare the type and then declare the application. To declare the type, create *$(PREFIX)/share/mime-info/name.mime*, where *name* is your application identifier or application suite. For example, if your MiracleText program is part of MiracleOffice; your *miracleoffice.mime* file might look like this:

```
application/x-miracletext
        ext: mtx

application/x-miraclecalc
        ext: mcl

application/x-miracleoffice-plugin
        regex,2: ^miracle-.*-plugin.so$
```

Declarations start with a MIME type and end with an empty line, and `ext:` directives map a fixed file extension to the type. However, `regex:` directives try to match an entire filename to a regular expression.

The `,2` after regex in the preceding example specifies the priority level. Higher numbers mean higher priority; the default is 1.

In addition, the example makes sure that GNOME recognizes MiracleOffice plug-ins. Without the third rule, GNOME would recognize MiracleOffice plug-ins using the dynamic library declaration for *.so* in *$(PREFIX)/share/mime-info/gnome-vfs.mime* that reads like this:

```
application/x-shared-library
        ext: so
```

8.7.2 Declaring Application Support for a MIME Type

After declaring the type as described in Section 8.7.1, you can tell GNOME what application goes with the type. Enter this information into another configuration file, *$(PREFIX)/share/mime-info/name.keys*; *miracleoffice.keys* might look like this:

```
application/x-miracletext
        category=Documents/Word Processor
        [de]category=Dokumente/Textverarbeitung
        [es]category=Documentos/Procesador de textos
        description=MiracleText document
        [de]description=MiracleText-Dokument
        [es]description=Documento de MiracleText
        icon_filename=miracletext-appicon.png
        default_action_type=application
        short_list_application_ids=miracletext
        use_category_default=no

application/x-miraclecalc
        category=Documents/Spreadsheet
        [de]category=Dokumente/Tabellenkalkulation
        [es]category=Documentos/Hoja de calculo
        description=MiracleCalc spreadsheet
        [de]description=MiracleCalc-Arbeitsblatt
        [es]description=Hoja de cálculo de MiracleCalc
        icon_filename=miraclecalc-appicon.png
```

```
        default_action_type=application
        short_list_application_ids=miraclecalc
        use_category_default=no

application/x-miracleoffice-plugin
        category=System
        [de]category=System
        [es]category=Sistema
        description=MiracleOffice plugin library
        [de]description=MiracleCalc-Plugin-Bibliothek
        [es]description=Librería compartida de MiracleCalc
        icon_filename=miracle-pluginicon.png
```

The keys are as follows:

- category: A category identifier that people can read. GNOME can sort MIME types according to the category; look in *$(PREFIX)/share/mime-info/gnome-vfs.keys* to see if it contains any that you can use.
- description: A short description of the type.
- icon_filename: The icon filename; do not include an extension if there are several versions of the file in different formats.
- default_action_type: How GNOME should open the file (application or component).
- short_list_application_ids: A comma-separated list of programs that the user should run to view the type.
- use_category_default: If this is yes, GNOME opens the file type with the default category application. If the application is the only program that can open files of this particular type in the category, set this to no (for example, your default word processor document application may be OpenOffice, but it may not be able to open *.mtx* documents).

You can specify keys for different locales by placing the locale identifier in square brackets just before the key (for example, [es]category). If you want intltool to do the work for you, do the following:

1. Add a *.in* extension to your *.keys* file.
2. Place an underscore before each key to translate in your *.keys.in* file.
3. Add your *.keys.in* filename to *po/POTFILES.in*.
4. Add directives to your top-level *Makefile.am*:

```
keysdir = $(datadir)/mime-info
keys_in_files = miracleoffice.keys.in
keys_DATA = $(keys_in_files:.keys.in=.keys)
@INTLTOOL_KEYS_RULE@
```

5. Generate your Makefiles; then regenerate your *.pot* file.
6. Add the appropriate lines to your *.po* files.

8.8 URI Structures

As described earlier, the GnomeVFS API has many functions that operate on GnomeVFSURI structures; some don't have corresponding functions that operate on URI strings. GnomeVFSURI structures contain hierarchical address information, and, therefore, you will find that they are much easier to manipulate than URI strings.

To create a URI structure from a URI string, call

```
GnomeVFSURI *uri;
gchar *uri_string;

uri = gnome_vfs_uri_new(uri_string);
```

Other URI structure allocation-related functions include the following:

- GnomeVFSURI *gnome_vfs_uri_ref(GnomeVFSURI *uri)
  Returns a new reference to *uri*.

- void gnome_vfs_uri_unref(GnomeVFSURI *uri)
  Removes a reference to *uri*. When the reference count in *uri* goes to 0, this function deallocates *uri*.

- GnomeVFSURI *gnome_vfs_uri_dup(GnomeVFSURI *uri)
  Returns a duplicate of *uri*.

- gboolean gnome_vfs_uri_dup(GnomeVFSURI *uri1, GnomeVFSURI *uri2)
  Returns TRUE if *uri1* and *uri2* are the same.

8.8.1 Building URI Paths

Use these functions to create URI paths:

- GnomeVFSURI *gnome_vfs_uri_append_string(GnomeVFSURI *uri, const gchar *str)
  Appends *str* to the end of URI, returning a new URI structure; inserts a new path separator if necessary.

- GnomeVFSURI *gnome_vfs_uri_append_path(GnomeVFSURI *uri, const gchar *path)
  Appends *path* to the end of URI, returning a new URI structure; inserts a new path separator if necessary. This function translates any special characters in *path*.

- GnomeVFSURI *gnome_vfs_uri_append_file_name(GnomeVFSURI *uri, const gchar *filename)
  Appends *filename* to the end of URI, returning a new URI structure; inserts a new path separator if necessary. This function translates any special characters in *filename*, including # and /.

NOTE *The reason for separate functions for pathnames and filenames is that GnomeVFS cannot otherwise determine when it should translate path separators (# in particular) for strings, multiple paths, or filenames.*

8.8.2 Extracting Path Information from a URI

These functions extract various pieces of the path:

- `gchar *gnome_vfs_uri_to_string(GnomeVFSURI *uri, GnomeVFSURIHideOptions hide_options)`
  Returns a newly allocated string corresponding to *uri*; `hide_options` is a bitwise OR of any of these constants:

  > `GNOME_VFS_URI_HIDE_NONE`
  >
  > `GNOME_VFS_URI_HIDE_TOPLEVEL_METHOD`: Does not include the first access method in the URI (at the very start, before the colon).
  >
  > `GNOME_VFS_URI_HIDE_HOST_NAME`
  >
  > `GNOME_VFS_URI_HIDE_HOST_PORT`
  >
  > `GNOME_VFS_URI_HIDE_USER_NAME`
  >
  > `GNOME_VFS_URI_HIDE_PASSWORD`
  >
  > `GNOME_VFS_URI_HIDE_FRAGMENT_IDENTIFIER`: Hides any access method specified with #.

- `gboolean gnome_vfs_uri_exists(const GnomeVFSURI *uri)`
  Returns TRUE if *uri* exists.

- `gboolean gnome_vfs_uri_is_local(const GnomeVFSURI *uri)`
  Returns TRUE if *uri* is on a local file system.

- `gboolean gnome_vfs_uri_has_parent(const GnomeVFSURI *uri)`
  Returns TRUE if *uri* has a parent URI (that is, if / does not appear in its namespace).

- `GnomeVFSURI *gnome_vfs_uri_get_parent(const GnomeVFSURI *uri)`
  Returns the parent URI of *uri*.

- `gboolean gnome_vfs_uri_is_parent(const GnomeVFSURI *parent, const GnomeVFSURI *uri, gboolean recursive)`
  Returns TRUE if *parent* is the parent of *uri*. If *recursive* is TRUE, this function recursively searches the directory hierarchy above *uri*.

- `const gchar *gnome_vfs_uri_get_path(const GnomeVFSURI *uri)`
  Returns the full path of *uri* as a string. Do not deallocate or alter this string; it is a part of *uri*.

- `const gchar *gnome_vfs_uri_get_fragment_identifier(const GnomeVFSURI *uri)`
  Returns a fragment identifier in *uri* (for example, *#section*).

- `const gchar *gnome_vfs_uri_get_scheme(const GnomeVFSURI *uri)`
  Returns an access scheme in *uri* (for example, *gzip*).

- `gchar *gnome_vfs_uri_extract_dirname(const GnomeVFSURI *uri)`
  Returns a newly allocated string containing the directory name in *uri*. The string terminates with a path separator.

- gchar *gnome_vfs_uri_extract_short_name(const GnomeVFSURI *uri)
  Returns a newly allocated string containing the path filename in *uri* (with no access method). The result can be a local pathname, a filename with no path, a hostname, or a single path separator (for the root).

- gchar *gnome_vfs_uri_extract_short_path_name(const GnomeVFSURI *uri)
  Same as the preceding function, but never returns a hostname; in that case, it returns a single path separator.

8.8.3 Accessing URI Connection Information

These functions extract parameters relevant to the connection used to access remote URIs:

- const gchar *gnome_vfs_uri_get_host_name(const GnomeVFSURI *uri)
  Returns the hostname in *uri*. Do not deallocate or alter this string.

- void gnome_vfs_uri_set_host_name(const GnomeVFSURI *uri, const gchar *hostname)
  Sets the hostname in *uri* to *hostname*.

- guint gnome_vfs_uri_get_host_port(const GnomeVFSURI *uri)
  Returns the port in *uri*.

- void gnome_vfs_uri_set_host_port(const GnomeVFSURI *uri, guint port)
  Sets the port *uri* to *port*.

- const gchar *gnome_vfs_uri_get_user_name(const GnomeVFSURI *uri)
  Returns the username in *uri*.

- void gnome_vfs_uri_set_user_name(const GnomeVFSURI *uri, const gchar *user_name)
  Sets the username in *uri* to *user_name*.

- const gchar *gnome_vfs_uri_get_password(const GnomeVFSURI *uri)
  Returns the password in *uri*.

- void gnome_vfs_uri_set_password(const GnomeVFSURI *uri, const gchar *password)
  Sets the password in *uri* to *password*.

8.8.4 URI Lists

There are several functions that manipulate lists of URIs:

- GList *gnome_vfs_uri_list_ref(GList *uri_list)
  Increments the reference counts in every URI in *uri_list*; returns the list pointer.

- GList *gnome_vfs_uri_list_unref(GList *uri_list)
  Decrements the reference counts in every URI in *uri_list*; returns the list.

- GList *gnome_vfs_uri_list_copy(GList *uri_list)
  Completely copies *uri_list* and returns the copy.

- GList *gnome_vfs_uri_list_free(GList *uri_list)
  Completely deallocates *uri_list*.

8.9 Miscellaneous Utilities

The functions in this section don't fit anywhere else in this chapter:

- `char *gnome_vfs_get_local_path_from_uri(const char *uri_string)`
  If *uri_string* is a file on the local file system, returns a newly allocated string with just that path.

- `char *gnome_vfs_get_uri_from_local_path(const char *full_path)`
  If *full_path* exists, prepends `file:///` and returns the result as a newly allocated string. Otherwise, this function returns NULL.

- `gboolean gnome_vfs_is_executable_command_string(const char *command)`
  If *command* is in the current search path (the PATH environment variable), or if *command* is a full executable pathname, returns TRUE.

- `GnomeVFSResult gnome_vfs_get_volume_free_space(const GnomeVFSURI *uri, GnomeFileSize *bytes_addr)`
  Writes the number of free bytes in *uri*'s file system into **bytes_addr*. This function works only if *uri* is on a local file system.

- `char *gnome_vfs_icon_path_from_filename(const char *filename)`
  Returns the full path of the icon file *filename* or NULL if GnomeVFS can't find the icon. This function can find files only in *$(PREFIX)/share/pixmaps*.

8.10 Result/Error Codes

All of the GnomeVFSResult values in this section are greater than or equal to 0 and smaller than GNOME_VFS_NUM_ERRORS:

- GNOME_VFS_OK: Operation successful.
- GNOME_VFS_ERROR_NOT_FOUND: File or directory does not exist.
- GNOME_VFS_ERROR_GENERIC: Unknown/undefined error.
- GNOME_VFS_ERROR_INTERNAL: Internal error; probably a bug in GnomeVFS.
- GNOME_VFS_ERROR_BAD_PARAMETERS: Invalid function parameters, such as NULL instead of a URI string.
- GNOME_VFS_ERROR_NOT_SUPPORTED: Operation or access mode not supported.
- GNOME_VFS_ERROR_IO: Error when reading or writing.
- GNOME_VFS_ERROR_CORRUPTED_DATA: Invalid data in the file system source (such as an archive).
- GNOME_VFS_ERROR_WRONG_FORMAT: File system source does not match the access method.
- GNOME_VFS_ERROR_BAD_FILE: Invalid file descriptor.
- GNOME_VFS_ERROR_TOO_BIG: File too large (to read, write, or manipulate).
- GNOME_VFS_ERROR_NO_SPACE: Target file system is out of free space.
- GNOME_VFS_ERROR_READ_ONLY: Target file system is read-only space.
- GNOME_VFS_ERROR_INVALID_URI: URI format error.
- GNOME_VFS_ERROR_NOT_OPEN: Tried to access file data with a closed descriptor.

- GNOME_VFS_ERROR_INVALID_OPEN_MODE: Invalid GnomeVFSOpenMode parameter when opening a file.

- GNOME_VFS_ERROR_ACCESS_DENIED: Permission denied.

- GNOME_VFS_ERROR_TOO_MANY_OPEN_FILES: Process cannot open any more open file descriptors.

- GNOME_VFS_ERROR_EOF: Attempt to access past the end of a file.

- GNOME_VFS_ERROR_NOT_A_DIRECTORY: Attempt to access a regular file as a directory.

- GNOME_VFS_ERROR_IN_PROGRESS: Operation failed because another operation is pending.

- GNOME_VFS_ERROR_INTERRUPTED: Something stopped the file access.

- GNOME_VFS_ERROR_FILE_EXISTS: Attempt to create a file that already exists.

- GNOME_VFS_ERROR_LOOP: Infinite symbolic link loop detected.

- GNOME_VFS_ERROR_NOT_PERMITTED: Operation not allowed (for example, a URI with "unsafe" characters was specified).

- GNOME_VFS_ERROR_IS_DIRECTORY: Attempt to access a directory as a regular file.

- GNOME_VFS_ERROR_NO_MEMORY: GnomeVFS has run out of memory.

- GNOME_VFS_ERROR_HOST_NOT_FOUND: Host in URI not found.

- GNOME_VFS_ERROR_INVALID_HOST_NAME: Invalid hostname in URI.

- GNOME_VFS_ERROR_HOST_HAS_NO_ADDRESS: Could not determine the address from the URI hostname.

- GNOME_VFS_ERROR_LOGIN_FAILED: Username or password invalid.

- GNOME_VFS_ERROR_CANCELLED: User interrupted the operation.

- GNOME_VFS_ERROR_DIRECTORY_BUSY: Attempt to access a directory that has a read lock.

- GNOME_VFS_ERROR_DIRECTORY_NOT_EMPTY: Attempt to remove a directory that is not empty.

- GNOME_VFS_ERROR_TOO_MANY_LINKS: Attempt to create too many hard links to a single inode.

- GNOME_VFS_ERROR_READ_ONLY_FILE_SYSTEM: Attempt to write to a read-only file system.

- GNOME_VFS_ERROR_NOT_SAME_FILE_SYSTEM: Attempt to perform an operation that requires its items to be on the same file system, using items on different file systems.

- GNOME_VFS_ERROR_NAME_TOO_LONG: Filename too long.

- GNOME_VFS_ERROR_SERVICE_NOT_AVAILABLE: Requested service is not available (perhaps not implemented).

- GNOME_VFS_ERROR_SERVICE_OBSOLETE: Requested service is obsolete and unusable.

- GNOME_VFS_ERROR_PROTOCOL_ERROR: Network error.

To get a string corresponding to an error code, call

gnome_vfs_result_to_string(*result_code*)

WARNING   *Do not attempt to deallocate or alter this string. You can place the function call directly inside* g_printerr(). *If you want to manipulate the error message, make a copy with* g_strdup().

8.11 Portability Notes

Position values (offsets) and file sizes vary from system to system; some platforms support very large files requiring larger integers.

Although GnomeVFS encapsulates the sizes with GnomeVFSFileSize and GnomeVFSFileOffset, you can still encounter problems with file sizes and offsets. The following macros and function can help you write a more portable program:

- GNOME_VFS_OFFSET_IS_LONG_LONG: Always defined on systems where the Gnome-VFS offset type uses long long rather than long.
- GNOME_VFS_SIZE_FORMAT_STR: Use this macro behind the % in printf() format strings when printing the file size.
- GNOME_VFS_OFFSET_FORMAT_STR: Use this behind the % in printf() format strings when printing file positions.
- gchar *gnome_vfs_format_file_size_for_display(GnomeVFSFileSize *size*) Returns size in a newly allocated string in human-readable form (for example, "180 bytes" or "1.8 GB").

8.12 File Information Example

The final example in this chapter prints all information about a file that GnomeVFS can find. Not only do you see the file information structure from Section 8.3.3, but MIME types (Section 8.7) pop up, as do some portability issues.

Run this program on the command line, using a URI string as a single argument.

```
/* -*-coding: utf-8;-*- */
/* file.c -- retrieve and summarize file information */

#include <string.h> /* for strlen() */
#include <time.h> /* for ctime() */
#include <libgnome/libgnome.h>
#include <libgnomevfs/gnome-vfs.h>
#include <libgnomevfs/gnome-vfs-mime-handlers.h>

#ifdef LINUX
# include <linux/fs.h> /* for MAJOR() und MINOR() */
#endif /* LINUX */

int print_file_error(GnomeVFSResult code, const gchar *uri_string)
{
  const gchar *error_str;

  error_str = gnome_vfs_result_to_string(code);
```

```
      g_printerr("%s: file error (%d): %s\n", uri_string, code, error_str);

      return 1;
}

int main(int argc, char **argv)
{
  gchar *file_uri_str;
  GnomeVFSResult result;
  GnomeVFSFileInfo *info;
  GnomeVFSMimeApplication *application;
  gchar *icon_name, *icon_name_tmp, *icon_path, *tmp;

  if (argc != 2)
  {
     g_printerr("Usage: %s <uri>\n", argv[0]);
     exit (1);
  }

  /* initialize GnomeVFS */
  if (!gnome_vfs_init())
  {
     g_error("%s: could not initialize GnomeVFS\n", argv[0]);
     exit (2);
  }

  /* determine URI */
  file_uri_str = argv[1];

  /* load a new file info structure with information about the URI */
  info = gnome_vfs_file_info_new();
  result = gnome_vfs_get_file_info(file_uri_str, info,
                             GNOME_VFS_FILE_INFO_GET_MIME_TYPE);
  if (result != GNOME_VFS_OK)
  {
     exit(print_file_error(result, file_uri_str));
  }

  g_print("URI: %s\n", file_uri_str);
  g_print("base name: %s ", info->name);

  if (info->valid_fields & GNOME_VFS_FILE_INFO_FIELDS_TYPE)
  {
     switch (info->type) {
        case GNOME_VFS_FILE_TYPE_UNKNOWN:
           g_print("(unknown type)\n"); break;

        case GNOME_VFS_FILE_TYPE_REGULAR:
```

```
                    g_print("(normal file)\n"); break;

            case GNOME_VFS_FILE_TYPE_DIRECTORY:
                g_print("(directory)\n"); break;

            case GNOME_VFS_FILE_TYPE_FIFO:
                g_print("(FIFO/named pipe)\n"); break;

            case GNOME_VFS_FILE_TYPE_SOCKET:
                g_print("(socket)\n"); break;

            case GNOME_VFS_FILE_TYPE_CHARACTER_DEVICE:
                g_print("(character device)\n"); break;

            case GNOME_VFS_FILE_TYPE_BLOCK_DEVICE:
                g_print("(block device)\n"); break;

            case GNOME_VFS_FILE_TYPE_SYMBOLIC_LINK:
                g_print("(symbolic link)\n"); break;
        }
    }

    if (info->valid_fields & GNOME_VFS_FILE_INFO_FIELDS_SYMLINK_NAME)
    {
        g_print("- symbolic link points to %s\n", info->symlink_name);
    }

    if (info->valid_fields & GNOME_VFS_FILE_INFO_FIELDS_PERMISSIONS)
    {
        g_print("- Permissions: O%o\n", info->permissions);
    }

    if (info->valid_fields & GNOME_VFS_FILE_INFO_FIELDS_FLAGS)
    {
        if (info->flags & GNOME_VFS_FILE_FLAGS_LOCAL)
        {
            g_print("- is on a local file system");

#ifdef LINUX
        if (info->valid_fields & GNOME_VFS_FILE_INFO_FIELDS_DEVICE)
        {
            g_print(" (device %d, %d)",
                    (int)MAJOR(info->device), (int)MINOR(info->device));
        }
#endif /* LINUX */

        if (info->valid_fields & GNOME_VFS_FILE_INFO_FIELDS_INODE)
        {
            g_print(" (inode %"\
```

```c
GNOME_VFS_SIZE_FORMAT_STR")", info->inode);
            }
        }
        g_print("\n");
    }
    if (info->valid_fields & GNOME_VFS_FILE_INFO_FIELDS_LINK_COUNT)
    {
        g_print("- %d link%s\n",
                info->link_count, (info->link_count == 1) ? "" : "s");
    }

    g_print("- user id (UID): %d\n",info->uid);
    g_print("- group id (GID): %d\n", info->gid);

    if (info->valid_fields & GNOME_VFS_FILE_INFO_FIELDS_SIZE)
    {
        tmp = gnome_vfs_format_file_size_for_display(info->size);
        g_print("- size: %s ", tmp);
        g_free(tmp);
    }

    if (info->valid_fields & GNOME_VFS_FILE_INFO_FIELDS_BLOCK_COUNT)
    {
        g_print(" (%"\
GNOME_VFS_SIZE_FORMAT_STR" 512-byte blocks)\n", info->block_count);
    } else {
        g_print("\n");
    }

    if (info->valid_fields & GNOME_VFS_FILE_INFO_FIELDS_IO_BLOCK_SIZE)
    {
        g_print("- optimal read/write buffer: %d bytes\n", info->io_block_size);
    }

    if (info->valid_fields & GNOME_VFS_FILE_INFO_FIELDS_ATIME)
    {
        g_print("- last access:        %s", ctime(&(info->atime)));
    }
    if (info->valid_fields & GNOME_VFS_FILE_INFO_FIELDS_MTIME)
    {
        g_print("- last modification: %s", ctime(&(info->mtime)));
    }
    if (info->valid_fields & GNOME_VFS_FILE_INFO_FIELDS_CTIME)
    {
        g_print("- last change:        %s", ctime(&(info->ctime)));
    }

    if (info->valid_fields & GNOME_VFS_FILE_INFO_FIELDS_MIME_TYPE)
```

```
{
    g_print("- MIME type: %s (%s)\n", info->mime_type,
            gnome_vfs_mime_get_description(info->mime_type));

    switch (gnome_vfs_mime_get_default_action_type(info->mime_type))
    {
        case GNOME_VFS_MIME_ACTION_TYPE_NONE:
            g_print("- no default action\n");
            break;

        case GNOME_VFS_MIME_ACTION_TYPE_APPLICATION:
            application =
                gnome_vfs_mime_get_default_application(info->mime_type);
            g_print("- default action: open with application %s\n",
                    application? application->name : "");
            gnome_vfs_mime_application_free(application);
            break;

        case GNOME_VFS_MIME_ACTION_TYPE_COMPONENT:
            g_print("- default action: open with a component\n");
            break;
    }

    /* somewhat roundabout way of finding an icon */
    icon_name = g_strdup(gnome_vfs_mime_get_icon(info->mime_type));
    if (icon_name)
    {
        g_print("- icon name: %s\n", icon_name);

        icon_path = gnome_vfs_icon_path_from_filename(icon_name);

        /* path doesn't exist? try with .png extension */
        if (!icon_path)
        {
            icon_name_tmp = g_strconcat(icon_name, ".png", NULL);
            icon_path = gnome_vfs_icon_path_from_filename(icon_name_tmp);
            g_free(icon_name_tmp);
        }

        if (icon_path)
        {
            g_print("- icon path: %s\n", icon_path);
            g_free(icon_path);
        }
        g_free(icon_name);
    }
}

/* clean up GnomeVFS, exit */
```

```
    gnome_vfs_file_info_unref(info);
    gnome_vfs_shutdown();

    exit (0);
}
```

8.13 Further Topics

GnomeVFS is a modular system, so writing your own GnomeVFS module is a logical way to provide a new data access method for your GNOME application. This procedure is fairly involved and does not appear in this book. However, GnomeVFS already supports so many access methods that you likely won't need to write your own.

Another topic not covered here is the GnomeVFS API for changing the MIME type database at run time. The user can override the system *.mime* and *.keys* files with the application registry (select **Desktop Preferences > Advanced > File types and programs** in the GNOME menu). As an application developer, you rarely need to dig around in a user's application registry.

This book also does not touch on Bonobo, including the MIME support for Bonobo components.

9

WHERE TO GO FROM HERE

After reaching this point in the book, you should have a fairly good idea of how to develop software with GNOME. This chapter departs from the programming discussion by answering questions that a potential GNOME developer might pose:

- How do I stay up-to-date with any changes to GNOME?
- How can I contact other GNOME developers?
- How can I contribute to the GNOME community?
- What does the future hold?

9.1 Reading, Discussing, and Collaborating

You can begin your foray into the GNOME community by digging up more GNOME information and finding ways to communicate with other GNOME enthusiasts.

Perhaps you feel obliged to give something back to the GNOME Project in return for all of this software available under a free license. Or you may have a practical reason to work with GNOME — maybe a piece of software that you're using doesn't work quite right, or something is missing.

Whatever your goal, there are many ways to start exploring the GNOME community. Check out *http://www.gnome.org/resources/*.

9.1.1 Real Life

GNOME Project volunteers and several companies are regulars at large computer trade shows, especially those that pertain to free software. In addition, a GNOME Users and Developers Conference (GUADEC) takes place every year.

For more details, see the GNOME website; check out the event calendar at *http://www.gnome.org/resources/calendar.html*.

9.1.2 WWW

Most of the available GNOME resources are on the World Wide Web. Because of GNOME's broad international base and the range of component projects, countless GNOME-related sites are spread across the Internet.

The primary GNOME website is *http://www.gnome.org/*, and this is where you should start to find other resources, such as the GNOME FAQ, information on how your company can support GNOME, and a list of developers.

GNOME Foundation

The GNOME Foundation is a nonpolitical, nonprofit, democratic group registered in California. Take a look at the charter and by-laws at *http://foundation.gnome.org/* to get an idea for what the foundation does. If you get deeply involved with GNOME, you can become a voting member and run for official posts.

News

FootNotes (*http://www.gnomedesktop.org/*) is a semi-official user-maintained GNOME news site. In addition to the latest general announcements, you'll find weekly summaries, CVS activity statistics, and Bugzilla activity.

Software Downloads

The central GNOME software distribution site is *http://download.gnome.org/*. Refer to Appendix D for information on how to choose software.

For a directory of all third-party GNOME software, go to *http://www.gnome.org/softwaremap/*. If you're looking for something particular, this is the first place to start, and if you're writing an application, you should add an entry here.

RDF site summary (RSS) information is available from *http://ftp.gnome.org/pub/GNOME/LATEST.xml*. Use a program such as Straw to view this information.

GNOME Bugzilla

One of the most important resources for GNOME users and developers is the GNOME bug-tracking system, GNOME Bugzilla (*http://bugzilla.gnome.org/*). If you have perused *ChangeLog* in any package, you may have already seen entries such as "Fixes #88325" and "fix mem leak (bug #72976)." The numbers here are Bugzilla indices that you can look up in Bugzilla.

You get a new bug number when you submit a problem report with GNOME Bugzilla or Bug Buddy (**Applications > Programming > Bug Report Tool**). To help manage the report, Bugzilla creates these fields:

- **Product**: The package containing the problem (for example, nautilus).

- **Component**: The piece of the package with the problem. The component depends on the product; for example, Documentation is a component of the Nautilus package, and General is a default, catch-all component.

- **Short Summary**: A very short summary of the problem.

- **Opened by**: The person who reported the bug.

- **Long Description**: A detailed description of the problem, including how to replicate the issue. You can add to the description later and include files (as attachments similar to an email attachment).

- **Status**: One of the following:

   UNCONFIRMED: No one has confirmed that this is actually a bug yet. Bugzilla users with sufficient privileges can change this status to NEW if they confirm the bug or to RESOLVED if they address the problem immediately.

   NEW: Someone confirmed the bug, but no one has taken responsibility for it yet.

   ASSIGNED: Someone has decided to fix the bug.

   NEEDINFO: There's some trouble in fixing this bug, and the person who originally reported the bug needs to provide more information.

   RESOLVED: Someone fixed the bug, and the person who reported the bug should verify the fix.

   REOPENED: There are still some issues involving a bug that was resolved.

   VERIFIED: Someone has verified that the bug fix works.

   CLOSED: The bug is completely dead (there is no reason for further action).

- **Severity**: Indication of how bad the bug is:

   Blocker: The problem prevents a new release of the package.

   Critical: This is a severe problem that leads to crashes and data loss.

   Major: The problem makes most of the package unusable.

   Normal: The problem makes only a small part of the package unusable.

   Minor: The package is usable, but the bug is still visible enough to cause errant behavior.

   Trivial: The problem doesn't affect the way the package works; it's just annoying (a typographical error, for example).

   Enhancement: This isn't a true problem, but rather, a suggestion on how to make the package better.

- **Priority**: Indication of how quickly the bug should be fixed:

  Immediate: As soon as possible.

  Urgent: Before the next release.

  High: Before the next major public release.

  Normal: Soon.

  Low: Whenever.

- **Target Milestone**: The version release that should include a fix.
- **Resolution**: A hint on a resolved bug:

  FIXED: Someone fixed the bug.

  WONTFIX: No one can or will fix the bug, ever.

  LATER: Later versions will include a fix.

  REMIND: The bug will probably reappear in later versions.

  DUPLICATE: Someone already reported the bug (supply this bug's number in the duplicate's description).

  INCOMPLETE: No one could reproduce the bug.

  NOTGNOME: This bug has nothing to do with GNOME.

  NOTABUG: "That's not a bug, it's a feature!" There's no reason to "fix" this, especially if it's not a problem.

- **Operating System/Details**: The platform and version where the bug appears.
- **Assigned To**: The person responsible for fixing the bug.
- **Depends**: If the bug can't be fixed until other bugs are fixed, this is a list of the other bugs.
- **Blocks**: Numbers of bugs that can't be fixed until someone fixes this bug.

A large portion of GNOME development is channeled through Bugzilla because it manages all problems and most smaller ideas. The person who reports a bug gets any changes and additions to the original description via email. If you want to work on GNOME, you should register with Bugzilla; it requires nothing other than a valid email address.

For more information on Bugzilla, see [Barnson].

Developer Home

The GNOME Developer's Site is *http://developer.gnome.org/*. Here, you can find news, documentation, current projects, and more. Here are some projects that may especially interest you:

- **GNOME Documentation Project** (*http://developer.gnome.org/projects/gdp/*): This project provides GNOME documentation of every kind, including a table listing current package documentation status.
- **GNOME Usability Project** (*http://developer.gnome.org/projects/gup/*): In addition to the GNOME usability guidelines and standards, this project provides a testing system that runs through GNOME's CVS tree and extracts information about user interfaces.

- **GNOME Accessibility Project** (*http://developer.gnome.org/projects/gap/*): This project provides GNOME access to those with disabilities.

- **GNOME Translation Project** (*http://developer.gnome.org/projects/gtp/*): This project aims to translate GNOME software to other languages. It includes a status report with an entry for each package; the goal is to make each entry "100% translated."

- **GNOME Webhackers** (*http://developer.gnome.org/projects/gwh/*): Here, GNOME Webhackers build and maintain the various GNOME websites.

GTK+

If you're a GNOME enthusiast, you should visit the GTK+ website (*http://www.gtk.org/*) from time to time.

9.1.3 Mailing Lists

The most important channels for GNOME discussion are perhaps mailing lists. Go to *http://mail.gnome.org/* and see if the lists there interest you.

NOTE   *Use the Web interface to subscribe to lists — it's easier and not as error prone as other methods. In addition, before subscribing to a list, look at the list archive to see if the actual discussion is what you have in mind.*

Announcement Lists

These lists serve only to distribute information and are not meant as a means of discussion. Don't reply to mail that you may get from one of these lists, and don't try to send anything to the lists.

- **gnome-announce-list**: General GNOME announcements, such new package releases. GNOME summaries come across this list as well.

- **foundation-announce**: GNOME foundation announcements.

- **cvs-commits-list**: Alteration logs for everything in the GNOME CVS source tree.

WARNING   *Subscribing to **cvs-commits-list** causes an enormous amount of mail to flow to your inbox. You may want to browse the list archives instead, and if you do choose to receive all of the messages, you will probably want to filter them.*

Discussion Lists

- **gnome-list**: General GNOME discussion.

- **gnome-love**: General discussion for those who are interested in getting involved with GNOME.

- **gtk-list**: General GTK+ discussion.

- **gtk-app-devel-list**: GTK+ application development.

- **desktop-devel-list**: General discussion of desktop applications and related areas.

- **gnome-accessibility-list**: Discussion of accessibility issues (ATK, interface development, and so on).

- **gnome-doc-list**: Documentation issues.
- **gnome-il8n**: Internationaliztion discussion.
- **garnome-list**: Discussion for those who use the GARNOME (A GNOME distribution; see Appendix D).

9.1.4 IRC

There are Internet relay chat (IRC) channels for real-time GNOME discussion. The GIMPnet server at *irc.gimp.org* has discussions on GNOME, GTK+, and GIMP. The following channels are always available:

- **#gnome**: General GNOME topics.
- **#gnome-help**: Help with GNOME.
- **#bugs**: Interactive problem hunt. If you find a bug in GNOME and have some time, come here and see if the experts that hang out on this list can fix it. Sometimes there are Bug Days — meetings where everyone is asked to report as many bugs as possible. Look on GNOME news pages for announcements.
- **#gtk+**: General GTK+ discussion.

9.2 The Future

No one and nothing is perfect, including GNOME. Version 2 contains many improvements introduced since the GNOME 1 days. However, backward binary compatibility is very important to GNOME, so you don't have to worry about your version 2 executables breaking; any program that works under GNOME 2.0 works with GNOME 2.2, and so on, up until GNOME version 3.0. In addition, your source code should compile without a problem. Progressive releases after a major release improve usability and fix bugs rather than expand the API.

9.2.1 libegg

GNOME 2 has an auxiliary library called libegg, for testing new features. Everything in libegg is supposed to go back into the main GNOME release; however, it's sometimes difficult to tell exactly when a change actually does make it into an upcoming release.

9.2.2 Toolbars

GtkToolbar will have a replacement widget sometime in the future. The main reason is that the items inside **GtkToolbar** aren't really child widgets; you need special functions to manage them. In addition, the toolbar has some other problems that need to be fixed, such as the mixing of buttons with and without labels and the interaction of the toolbar with windows that are narrower than the toolbar itself.

9.2.3 Trees and Lists

The powerful **GtkTreeView** widget is getting a makeover. Plans include better cell rendering (for data types such as images), better keyboard operation, support for context menus, support for drag-and-drop operation for multiple entries, the ability to sort entries based on certain criteria, and the ability to save the tree view configuration (that is, the node position and currently expanded nodes).

9.2.4 Date/Time Widgets

There's plenty of work to do on **GnomeDateEdit**. Current problems include GNOME's inability to store a 24-hour time and week start preference for the user and its inability to get or set dates before 1970 because the API works with Unix time. In addition, you can get only a full date; you can't pick out an individual piece such as the local time or a year. A new, more flexible widget should show up in libegg soon.

9.2.5 Icon Themes

As you can see from Section 8.7, the mechanism for finding an icon that corresponds to a MIME type isn't terribly powerful. This is mostly because each MIME type can have several icons (several sizes in PNG format, an SVG version, and a set for each theme). Nautilus organizes its icons according to theme and current size, choosing the correct one for the user's settings; gnome_vfs_get_icon(), on the other hand, always returns the same name.

   Work is currently in progress to resolve icon themes systemwide, not just in Nautilus.

9.2.6 Recent Files

A systemwide API for a list of recently opened files may make it into GNOME 2.6. There are some programs that already use this functionality in the GNOME CVS tree; of course, they must link against libegg.

9.2.7 File Browser

The GTK+ file browser is a nagging topic among GNOME developers. The browser is unsatisfactory, but not so awful that it screams for replacement. However, a long discussion has provided many ideas on how to improve the file browser. Therefore, a new widget may appear sometime in the future, most likely in GTK+ 2.4. This rework of the GTK+ widget will be able to plug in to the GNOME infrastructure (GnomeVFS and MIME type icons in particular), but will also stand on its own for pure GTK+ applications.

   Still being debated is how the new file browser dialog should actually appear. There are as many opinions as there are people discussing the matter, and the proposals are far from similar.

9.2.8 System Sound

At the moment, GNOME uses the Enlightened Sound Daemon (ESD) to play system sounds. It works, but that's about the only nice thing that you can say about ESD.

ESD replacement is as persistent a topic as creation of a new file browser dialog. The current discussion includes GStreamer (a GNOME sibling project) and the new X11 Media Application Server (MAS). Both are modular systems that can do quite a bit more than play sounds.

9.3 Conclusion

Now, after substantially more pages than originally planned, the author's task is complete. I tried to write the book that I would like to have been able to buy years ago; a chain of fortunate circumstances has made this book possible.

For you, however, the fun, hopefully, is only just beginning. Perhaps you're a seasoned software developer charged with adding proper GNOME support to a package or building an entirely new application. Then again, you may be an enthusiastic volunteer developer or maintainer, serving only your imagination (and the GNOME Project, of course). Or maybe you are somewhere in between.

In every case, I hope that you happily reach for this book whenever you need it. Its publication represents the fulfillment of my personal GNOME 2 dream. I hope that your GNOME 2 dreams come true, too.

A

STOCK ITEM REFERENCE

GTK+ Stock Items

Macro	Identifier	Label	Icon
GTK_STOCK_ADD	gtk-add	Add	
GTK_STOCK_APPLY	gtk-apply	Apply	
GTK_STOCK_BOLD	gtk-bold	Bold	
GTK_STOCK_CANCEL	gtk-cancel	Cancel	
GTK_STOCK_CDROM	gtk-cdrom	CD-Rom	
GTK_STOCK_CLEAR	gtk-clear	Clear	

Macro	Identifier	Label	Icon
GTK_STOCK_CLOSE	gtk-close	Close	
GTK_STOCK_COLOR_PICKER	gtk-color-picker	*none*	
GTK_STOCK_CONVERT	gtk-convert	Convert	
GTK_STOCK_COPY	gtk-copy	Copy	
GTK_STOCK_CUT	gtk-cut	Cut	
GTK_STOCK_DELETE	gtk-delete	Delete	
GTK_STOCK_DIALOG_ERROR	gtk-dialog-error	Error	
GTK_STOCK_DIALOG_INFO	gtk-dialog-info	Information	
GTK_STOCK_DIALOG_QUESTION	gtk-dialog-question	Question	
GTK_STOCK_DIALOG_WARNING	gtk-dialog-warning	Warning	
GTK_STOCK_DND	gtk-dnd	*none*	
GTK_STOCK_DND_MULTIPLE	gtk-dnd-multiple	*none*	
GTK_STOCK_EXECUTE	gtk-execute	Execute	
GTK_STOCK_FIND	gtk-find	Find	

Macro	Identifier	Label	Icon
GTK_STOCK_FIND_AND_REPLACE	gtk-find-and-replace	Find and Replace	
GTK_STOCK_FLOPPY	gtk-floppy	Floppy	
GTK_STOCK_GOTO_BOTTOM	gtk-goto-bottom	Bottom	
GTK_STOCK_GOTO_FIRST	gtk-goto-first	First	
GTK_STOCK_GOTO_LAST	gtk-goto-last	Last	
GTK_STOCK_GOTO_TOP	gtk-goto-top	Top	
GTK_STOCK_GO_BACK	gtk-go-back	Back	
GTK_STOCK_GO_DOWN	gtk-go-down	Down	
GTK_STOCK_GO_FORWARD	gtk-go-forward	Forward	
GTK_STOCK_GO_UP	gtk-go-up	Up	
GTK_STOCK_HELP	gtk-help	Help	
GTK_STOCK_HOME	gtk-home	Home	
GTK_STOCK_INDEX	gtk-index	Index	
GTK_STOCK_ITALIC	gtk-italic	Italic	
GTK_STOCK_JUMP_TO	gtk-jump-to	Jump to	
GTK_STOCK_JUSTIFY_CENTER	gtk-justify-center	Center	
GTK_STOCK_JUSTIFY_FILL	gtk-justify-fill	Fill	
GTK_STOCK_JUSTIFY_LEFT	gtk-justify-left	Left	

Macro	Identifier	Label	Icon
GTK_STOCK_JUSTIFY_RIGHT	gtk-justify-right	Right	
GTK_STOCK_MISSING_IMAGE	gtk-missing-image	*none*	
GTK_STOCK_NEW	gtk-new	New	
GTK_STOCK_NO	gtk-no	No	
GTK_STOCK_OK	gtk-ok	OK	
GTK_STOCK_OPEN	gtk-open	Open	
GTK_STOCK_PASTE	gtk-paste	Paste	
GTK_STOCK_PREFERENCES	gtk-preferences	Preferences	
GTK_STOCK_PRINT	gtk-print	Print	
GTK_STOCK_PRINT_PREVIEW	gtk-print-preview	Print Preview	
GTK_STOCK_PROPERTIES	gtk-properties	Properties	
GTK_STOCK_QUIT	gtk-quit	Quit	
GTK_STOCK_REDO	gtk-redo	Redo	
GTK_STOCK_REFRESH	gtk-refresh	Refresh	
GTK_STOCK_REMOVE	gtk-remove	Remove	
GTK_STOCK_REVERT_TO_SAVED	gtk-revert-to-saved	Revert	
GTK_STOCK_SAVE	gtk-save	Save	
GTK_STOCK_SAVE_AS	gtk-save-as	Save As	

Macro	Identifier	Label	Icon
GTK_STOCK_SELECT_COLOR	gtk-select-color	Color	
GTK_STOCK_SELECT_FONT	gtk-select-font	Font	
GTK_STOCK_SORT_ASCENDING	gtk-sort-ascending	Ascending	
GTK_STOCK_SORT_DESCENDING	gtk-sort-descending	Descending	
GTK_STOCK_SPELL_CHECK	gtk-spell-check	Spell Check	
GTK_STOCK_STOP	gtk-stop	Stop	
GTK_STOCK_STRIKETHROUGH	gtk-strikethrough	Strikethrough	
GTK_STOCK_UNDELETE	gtk-undelete	Undelete	
GTK_STOCK_UNDERLINE	gtk-underline	Underline	
GTK_STOCK_UNDO	gtk-undo	Undo	
GTK_STOCK_YES	gtk-yes	Yes	
GTK_STOCK_ZOOM_100	gtk-zoom-100	Zoom 100%	
GTK_STOCK_ZOOM_FIT	gtk-zoom-fit	Zoom to Fit	
GTK_STOCK_ZOOM_IN	gtk-zoom-in	Zoom In	
GTK_STOCK_ZOOM_OUT	gtk-zoom-out	Zoom Out	

GNOME Stock Items

Macro	Identifier	Label	Icon
GNOME_STOCK_ABOUT	gnome-stock-about	About	
GNOME_STOCK_ATTACH	gnome-stock-attach	*none*	
GNOME_STOCK_AUTHENTICATION	gnome-stock-authentication	*none*	
GNOME_STOCK_BLANK	gnome-stock-blank	*none*	*none*
GNOME_STOCK_BOOK_BLUE	gnome-stock-book-blue	*none*	
GNOME_STOCK_BOOK_GREEN	gnome-stock-book-green	*none*	
GNOME_STOCK_BOOK_OPEN	gnome-stock-book-open	*none*	
GNOME_STOCK_BOOK_RED	gnome-stock-book-red	*none*	
GNOME_STOCK_BOOK_YELLOW	gnome-stock-book-yellow	*none*	
GNOME_STOCK_LINE_IN	gnome-stock-line-in	*none*	
GNOME_STOCK_MAIL	gnome-stock-mail	*none*	
GNOME_STOCK_MAIL_FWD	gnome-stock-mail-fwd	*none*	
GNOME_STOCK_MAIL_NEW	gnome-stock-mail-new	*none*	
GNOME_STOCK_MAIL_RCV	gnome-stock-mail-rcv	*none*	
GNOME_STOCK_MAIL_RPL	gnome-stock-mail-rpl	*none*	
GNOME_STOCK_MAIL_SND	gnome-stock-mail-snd	*none*	

Macro	Identifier	Label	Icon
GNOME_STOCK_MIC	gnome-stock-mic	*none*	
GNOME_STOCK_MIDI	gnome-stock-midi	*none*	
GNOME_STOCK_MULTIPLE_FILE	gnome-stock-multiple-file	*none*	
GNOME_STOCK_NOT	gnome-stock-not	*none*	
GNOME_STOCK_SCORES	gnome-stock-scores	*none*	
GNOME_STOCK_TABLE_BORDERS	gnome-stock-table-borders	Table Borders	
GNOME_STOCK_TABLE_FILL	gnome-stock-table-fill	Table Fill	
GNOME_STOCK_TEXT_BULLETED_LIST	gnome-stock-text-bulleted-list	Bulleted List	
GNOME_STOCK_TEXT_INDENT	gnome-stock-text-indent	Indent	
GNOME_STOCK_TEXT_NUMBERED_LIST	gnome-stock-text-numbered-list	Numbered List	
GNOME_STOCK_TEXT_UNINDENT	gnome-stock-text-unindent	Un-Indent	
GNOME_STOCK_TIMER	gnome-stock-timer	*none*	
GNOME_STOCK_TIMER_STOP	gnome-stock-timer-stop	*none*	
GNOME_STOCK_TRASH	gnome-stock-trash	*none*	
GNOME_STOCK_TRASH_FULL	gnome-stock-trash-full	*none*	
GNOME_STOCK_VOLUME	gnome-stock-volume	*none*	

B

GLOSSARY

A

abstract *(class)* An abstract class cannot be *instantiated*; it serves only as a *parent class* to *derive* other classes.

access function A function (or *method*) that allows read or write access to a field inside an *object*. In the *GObject* convention, the function name usually contains _get_ or _set_. The GObject *property* system abstracts and unifies access functions.

accessibility (also A11y) For disabled persons. For example, an accessibile application might have an interface to represent text in Braille, offer a screen reader, and have interfaces for alternative input methods such as voice input and head/mouth sticks. Many organizations require accessibility features for software. In *GTK+* and *GNOME, ATK* provides accessibility.

accumulator (signal) During *signal emission,* many *signal handlers* may each return values. However, GSignal can return only one value to the code that emitted the signal. An accumulator is a special *callback* that GSignal invokes after each signal handler to collect and/or process the handler return values, passing the final result back after the emission.

alpha channel The part of an *RGBA* value in a bitmap that determines transparency. Images without alpha channels have no transparency information and therefore cannot contain features such as translucent areas.

antialiasing   Edge smoothing. With no special help, a *bitmap* representation of a diagonal line exhibits "jaggies" at edges between bright and dark pixels. Text displayed on a monitor is especially prone to this phenomenon due to an especially large number of shapes crammed into a small area. Antialiasing attempts to ameliorate this situation by filling neighboring pixels with interpolated colors, and in some cases, the results can significantly improve legibility. However, antialiasing can also distort characters badly, especially without the use of font hinting.

API   Application programming interface. The API is the part of a software package that a programmer uses. An API consists of exported constants, variables, functions, *classes*, macros, and more. In the C programming language, header files normally define API elements.

application identifier   A *GNOME* application's symbolic name (for example, gnome-terminal for GNOME Terminal). Use the application identifier in any place where you must represent the application in a pathname: for example, in executable names, application-specific installation directories, help files, and menu item files. Several GNOME library functions use the application identifier.

asynchronous   Offline; the opposite of *synchronous*. In asynchronous I/O, program execution is not blocked during system access, but rather, the I/O access runs in the background. The main program can retrieve the result later, or the I/O system can interrupt the main program with a *callback* function when the operation completes. Some programs that use asynchronous I/O interact much better to user input — in particular, *Nautilus* and any usable Web browser — because the window does not freeze when waiting for user input. *GnomeVFS* offers asynchronous I/O for *GNOME*.

ATK   Accessibility Toolkit. The library supporting accessibility features in *GTK+* and *GNOME*. ATK receives information about the user interface structure and then allows the user to operate the interface with tools such as touch screens and magnification windows.

atom   A block of data, usually small and one of several similar blocks; *memory chunks* are efficient means of creating atoms.

attribute   1. In *object-oriented programming*, a part of a *class* that defines a piece of data inside a class; see *property* for GObject-specific information. 2. In *XML*, a key-value pair that expands the information inside *tag*: For example, sauce=worcester.

B

base class   The class at the root of a *class hierarchy*; all other classes in the hierarchy inherit their properties and methods from this class. In GObject, the base class is named **GObject**.

bitmap   1. In general (not quite correct), any arbitrary raster (consisting of pixels) image; a rectangular two-dimensional array of pixels. 2. In the *X Window System*, a special image format called XBM with a one-bit depth (black and white), used now primarily for masks on color images.

Bonobo The *GNOME* component object model. An open specification for an object model and the name for its *GTK+*–based reference implementation. Bonobo is based on *CORBA* and draws strongly from Microsoft's OLE. The main purpose of Bonobo is to embed content (documents, or rather, *components* or *controls*) into other content (documents or applications).

C

callback A function that the programmer does not call directly; rather, the system calls the function in response to an event. You must define and register a callback with the system. A C callback function must strictly conform to a predefined prototype so that the arguments and types match, but usually, there is a customizable argument called a *(user) data pointer.*

canvas A *widget* that displays structured graphics. Canvas widgets play a large role in the interfaces for several applications; the background for word processors, spreadsheets, and *vector graphics* programs usually consist of canvas widgets. The *GNOME* canvas widget is quite powerful (with architecture borrowed from the Tk toolkit). A canvas widget has its own coordinate and object management systems. An application often displays only a piece of the whole canvas, which you can scroll and zoom.

child (widget) A *widget* packed into a *container* is called the container's child. A *widget tree* represents the relationships between many connected containers and children.

child class (or subclass) A class *derived* from a *parent class* that *inherits methods, signals*, and *properties* from the parent.

class The type of an *object*: that is, the definition of an object's *methods* and *attributes*. See also *object-oriented programming*.

class hierarchy The tree-structured hierarchy of classes formed by their *inheritance* relationships.

class structure In *GObject*, a data structure that holds various class-related items, primarily function pointers for working with *properties* and *signals*.

closure An anonymous "frozen" function with some parameters and variables already initialized. You can invoke something inside a closure later to reuse these parameters (similar to the way you can use a static variable in C). *GLib* uses the GClosure implementation for *signals*.

component In general, a reusable piece of code that implements a certain interface that you can load into a program at run time.

constructor A *method* called during *instantiation* of a class.

container (widget) Any *widget* that can hold another widget. A system of several nested containers and the widgets inside is a *widget tree*. To make a widget visible, you must place the widget inside at least one special container such as a program window or *dialog window*.

control   In *Bonobo*, a compound widget that you can activate and operate as a single widget (for example, in one line of code). See also *components*.

controller   The *C* in MVC. A controller is a (normally user-accessible) element that manipulates a *model*. The controller often also picks up the job of a *view*.

CORBA   Common Object Request Broker Architecture. A system for communication between software modules. Unlike earlier remote procedure call methods, CORBA is object oriented, where programs define interfaces to their objects with the *IDL*. The so-called broker handles the requests and parameters between these interfaces. The idea is that the entire process is abstract, so that you can exchange data between programs in different programming languages and over a network with the *IIOP* protocol, if necessary. Unlike its competitors such as *COM*, CORBA is an open standard.

CVS   Concurrent Versioning System. This package manages source code tree access to distributed developers. CVS helps prevent conflicts, supports source code rollbacks, can concurrently manage different versions of the code, and more. Nearly all large open-source software projects use CVS.

D

derive (a *class* from another class)   To define a class based on another class. The new class *inherits* the original's *properties* and *methods*.

destructor   A *method* that an *object* system calls when you destroy an object (or the object is otherwise no longer needed). The destructor is responsible for cleaning up after the object, returning its memory to the free pool in the process. For example, a *class* for a TCP connection might have a destructor that closes the connection.

detail   You can attach an extra string when you bind a *signal handler* to a *signal*. Any code that *emits* the signal can include a detail as well; only handlers installed with this detail run.

dialog (window)   A *window* that interacts with the user in one particular situation and is visible only until its job is complete; therefore, it is a so-called transient window. In the *X Window System*, there is a difference between transient and program windows; for example, the *window manager* handles them differently.

DocBook   A document structure (now *XML* based) for technical documents, software documentation in particular. DocBook is enormous and it is now the standard for most open-source software, including *GNOME*.

E

em   In typography, a length equal to the point size of the current type. This is usually roughly the length of an uppercase *M*.

emission *(signal)*   The entire procedure that takes place when *emitting* a signal.

emission hook   Like a *signal handler*, but bound to an entire class, not just to one object at a time. Use a hook if you don't particularly care about the signal emission's object.

emit (a *signal*)   Emitting a signal on an object causes all *signal handlers* bound to that signal on the object to run. These handlers return values; normally, the last handler's return value goes back to the code that called the signal. If you need more than one return value, use an *accumulator*.

event   1. In general, an event is something that happens, such as a *signal emission*. 2. In *GTK+*, events primarily come from the user's input stream and go to *windows*. Events are not the same as signals (however, GTK+ does use signals to send events to **GtkWidget** objects).

event-driven programming   In the classic programming model, you write a program that executes from start to finish; the user may enter data along the way if necessary, possibly changing program flow somewhat. In event-driven programming, the program primarily reacts to user input, doing little when the input stream is inactive (that is, there are no *events*). In general, *GUI* applications are event driven.

F

finalize   To clean up after a data structure; usually, this process involves calling a *finalizer*.

finalizer   A function that runs when cleaning up after a data structure. *GType* has a base finalizer that reclaims the *class* memory allocated by the base *initializer*, as well as class finalizers (which normally are not necessary). The finalizer runs when the last *reference* to an *object* disappears.

floating reference   A reference that does not (yet) have an owner pointer. A newly created *widget* in *GTK+* has a floating reference; when *packed* into a *container*, the container takes control of the reference.

focus (input)   The target of input *events*. The focus decision usually happens on two levels. First, the *window manager* manipulates the focus on a per-window basis; in certain cases, it can automatically change the focus from one window to another. Then the application window must determine which of its *widgets* receives the focus. *GTK+* marks the focus target with a dotted line around widgets or with an active cursor inside entry boxes and text widgets.

font description   The *Pango* format for describing a font; it starts with the font name, followed optionally by slant, variant, weight, width, and point size. Examples are Times Normal 36 and Charter Bold Italic Condensed 10.

framebuffer   1. A region of memory containing arrayed pixel values, where each value corresponds to a pixel on a display; in computer graphics, the framebuffer is the last stop on the way to the monitor. 2. In a narrower sense, especially pertaining to the Linux kernel, framebuffer graphics refers to certain graphics that are rendered directly, without going through layers such as the *X Window System*. As of version 2.0, *GTK+* can write directly to the framebuffer.

GDK   GTK+ Drawing Kit. *GTK+* calls GDK to draw *widgets* on the display. *GDK* is independent of a back end such as *X11*, Windows, or *framebuffer*, making it easier to port *GTK+* to other platforms.

GIMP   The GNU Image Manipulation Program. A powerful image-processing package that uses (and originated) *GTK+*. GIMP was one of first popular high-performance open-source user programs.

Glade   A graphical application for building graphical user interfaces. Glade supports widgets and components from *GTK+*, *Bonobo*, and *GNOME*.

GLib   A low-level library used by many other libraries, including *GTK+* and the *GNOME* system. GLib offers efficient platform-independent modules for relatively low-level system tasks, such as multithreading and memory block access, as well as conventional data structure support (lists, trees, and so on).

GNOME   GNU Network Object Model Environment. This acronym is now somewhat irrelevant, because GNOME was originally a network-transparent object model (now *Bonobo*). GNOME is three things: a set of development libraries for software development, a desktop software environment package, and the community that uses and develops the system.

GNOME-Print   The GNOME interface for printing and anything related to printing. GNOME-Print supplies a number of graphics primitives for drawing on a virtual canvas and then takes over the hard part of guiding a document through the maze of software and hardware required to put an image on real paper.

GnomeVFS   GNOME Virtual File System. A network-transparent library for file access; it supports asynchronous access, coupling of *MIME* types to actions, and other common file operations.

GObject   The *GLib* object system; an *object-oriented* implementation for programming languages that have no native object support. GObject manages all object information and operations at run time.

gravity   Describes the behavior of a *mark* in a text buffer (for example, the cursor) when text is inserted at the mark. Left gravity means that the mark goes before the new text; right gravity means that the mark moves after the text.

GSignal   The *GObject signal* implementation.

GTK+   GIMP Toolkit. Originally a part of *GIMP* as a free replacement for the *Motif toolkit*, this library soon took on a life of its own. GTK+ is now ranks with Qt as one of the most popular toolkits for programming applications in the *X Window System*.

GType   The *GObject* type system. GObject uses GType to advertise the types that exist, the properties that the types have, and the relationships between types.

GValue   An encapsulation system for values of various types. You can use a `GValue` in any place where you might use an *untyped pointer* but do not wish to lose the type information.

GUI   Graphical user interface.

H

handler   A term in *event-driven programming*; a function that processes an *event*; often a synonym for *callback*. See also *signal handler*.

hints (window manager)   *X Window System* applications can ask for special treatment from the *window manager*. Examples of hints include specification of where windows should appear on the display, that the window should not be obscured, and the layer order. Earlier, *GNOME* and *KDE* used a set of incompatible hints, but they now use a unified hint system called NET_WM Hints [XDG].

hook   See *emission hook*.

I

IDL   Interface Definition Language. You must define *CORBA* object interfaces in this C++-like language so that the *ORB* can export the objects.

IIOP   Internet Inter-*ORB* Protocol. The IP-based protocol that *CORBA* uses to transfer information over the network.

index (in a **GtkTextBuffer** object)   The distance between two positions in a text buffer, measured in bytes (not characters).

inherit   See *derive*.

inheritance   The feature in *object-oriented programming* that allows you to *derive* one class from another.

initializer   A function that initializes a data structure. *GType* has several initializers: a base class initializer for dynamically allocated *class variables* and any number of class initializers to set initial values and install *properties* and *signals*.

inode   A data structure in a Unix file system that contains details about the file (permissions, access times, data block location, and so on).

instance   An incarnation of a *class*; that is, the in-memory runtime details of an *object*.

instance structure   The data structure for *instances* of a *class* in *GObject*.

instantiation   The act of creating an *instance* of a *class*, reserving memory and calling the *constructor*.

interface   In *GObject*, a collection of *methods* that apply to a number of classes that are not necessarily *derived* from the same *parent class*. Any class that has the required methods is said to implement the interface. The interface system is the GObject substitute for *multiple inheritance*.

iterator   A data structure that represents a position in another, composite data structure. For example, a tree iterator points to a specific node in a tree. In *GTK+*, iterators assist in the management of text buffers and tree *widgets*.

K

KDE   K Desktop Environment. On the surface, KDE is similar to *GNOME*, but the underlying architecture is quite different. The GNOME and KDE projects tend to cooperate in areas where the implementation is not too difficult, or where a pressing need exists (for example, shared mime associations).

L

link count   On Unix systems, each filename links to a file in the underlying file system (this is sometimes called a hard link). You may have more than one filename per file; the number of names that link to one file is call the file's link count.

locale   A collection of settings related to a user's location, such as language, character encoding, date/time format, numeric format, and paper size.

M

main (event) loop   The loop that an *event-driven* program enters after initializing its user interface and binding its *handlers* to *events*. The main loop occasionally asks the windowing system for new events to distribute to the handlers, draws widgets, and performs other miscellaneous tasks.

mark   An object that represents a position between two characters in a text buffer and that remains valid even when the text in the buffer changes. Marks have *gravity*.

markup language   A language that decorates text (for example, with a series of *tags*) that give specific pieces of the text a meaning or style. *XML* is a prominent markup language.

marshaller   In *GObject*, a function that carries the parameters of a *signal emission* to the handler and transports the return value back. Every *signature* needs its own marshaller; you can generate a marshaller with the `glib-genmarshal` program.

memory chunk   A block of memory allocated at one time and then split into small pieces called *atoms* for use by a program. The *GLib* memory chunk data structure is `GMemChunk`; it is useful for simultaneously allocating tiny pieces of evenly sized data.

method   A piece of code (a function) that works only with a particular *object*; methods declarations are in the *class* of an object.

MIME   Multimedia Internet Mail Extensions. A series of header extensions and encodings and a bundling style that allows email transmission of data that isn't necessarily plain text.

MIME type   A *MIME* file classification description (such as text/html). Many desktop environments now use MIME types to make sense of file types.

modal   When an application opens a modal window, the user cannot operate any other window in the application until the modal window closes.

model   The *M* in *MVC*. An internal data structure displayed by the *view* that the user changes with the *controller*.

Motif   A *GUI toolkit* for the *X Window System*, written in C; it was at one time popular with commercial applications, but now is less popular due to an unpleasant programming interface and years of proprietary licensing.

multiple inheritance   A form of *inheritance* where a class has more than one *parent class*. *GObject* does not support multiple inheritance, but does have an *interface* system as a substitute.

MVC   Model/View/Controller. A way of thinking about software design (in particular, *GUI* applications) in which programs consist of *models*, *views*, and *controllers*.

N

Nautilus   The GNOME desktop shell; a file manager that can do quite a bit more than manage files.

O

object   In the narrow sense, an object is an *instance* of a *class*.

object-oriented programming   A programming style (often with specific programming language support) that features encapsulation of data and algorithms, *inheritance*, and polymorphism.

offset   1. The distance, in bytes, between the start of a data structure and a certain field in the data structure. 2. In a **GtkTextBuffer** object, the distance between two positions in the text, in characters (not bytes).

OMF   Open Metadata Framework. A standardized *XML* format for document metadata. *ScrollKeeper* uses OMF to describe help files.

OOP   See *object-oriented programming*.

ORB   Object Request Broker. The *CORBA* server that manages the message transfer between clients and servers.

ORBit   The *ORB* implementation in *GNOME*.

P

pack   To place a *widget* inside a *container*, usually with the help of a special function to control the placement, size, and other geometric widget behavior.

Pango   The library that *GTK+* uses to render text. Pango can display nearly any kind of writing, not just writing that runs left to right.

parent class   The *class* from which a *child class* derives its *methods*, *properties*, and *signals*.

pathname   A filename specified along with its complete path.

pixmap (XPM)   In the *X Window System*, a specific *bitmap* format for color images.

point   A typographical unit of length equal to 1/72 of an inch. Normal text is roughly 10 points tall, but with *GTK+* and *Pango*, the actual height depends on your monitor's resolution.

property   Data storage in a *GObject* object; a property has an identifier, name, description, domain, initial value, and code to read and set the value.

R

reference count   A counter associated with an *object* that keeps track of the number of references to the object. When the reference count goes to zero, the memory manager removes the object. Every *GObject* instance has a reference count.

renderer   An object that displays a cell in a tree view. A renderer is active over an entire column in the view; a column may have more than one renderer.

RGBA   Red/Green/Blue/Alpha. The normal format for a color value of a monitor pixel with transparency.

row reference   A permanent marker on a node in a tree model; row references are the tree equivalent of text buffer *marks*.

S

schema   In GConf, a key that does not have an associated value but, rather, describes another key-value pair. A schema describes the application that created and uses the key, the default value of the key, and the purpose of the key.

ScrollKeeper   The *GNOME* system for managing help documents and their associated *OMF* files.

session management   In the *X Window System*, a means of saving the current desktop state for a desktop session upon logout. The idea is that the desktop environment should be able to restore the session to its previous state when the user logs in again.

signal   In *GObject*, a message that an *object* receives. A signal has a string identifier; you can bind a *signal handler* to the signal to react to the message. See also *accumulator*.

signal detail   See *detail*.

signal handler   A callback function invoked upon emission of a *signal*; a fundamental concept of *event-driven programming*. In *GSignal*, a signal handler has at least two arguments: a pointer to the object and a *data pointer*. Any additional arguments go between these two.

signature   A function's argument types along with its return value type. In ANSI C, a function's prototype represents its signature; this is important in the implementation of *signal handlers* and *marshallers*.

small caps   A type font that represents lowercase letters as smaller versions of the capital letters; they're easier to read than exclusively capital letters.

snapshot   A developer's archive of a source code tree. In comparison to an archive of a tested package neatly prepared with make dist, a snapshot receives no special treatment and may be a little rough around the edges. Although most snapshots configure well with no additional help, you must sometimes run the GNU autotools with autogen.sh before building the package.

subclass   When one class is *derived* from another, this is the resulting class.

SVG   An open-standard format for *vector graphics*, based on an *XML* document type.

synchronous   Any program using a synchronous I/O operation suspends execution during I/O access; synchronous programs are easy to write but are sometimes not suitable for *GUI* applications. The opposite of *asynchronous*.

T

tag   1. In *XML* documents, a marker that denotes new meaning or style for the following text, or one that signifies the end to a previous tag (for example, <tag>text</tag>); can have *attributes*. 2. In a *GTK+* text buffer, a group of text attributes that can be applied to any pieces of the current text.

toolkit (GUI)   A function or class library that contains the building blocks for creating graphical interfaces. Most operating systems other than Unix come with only one dedicated toolkit, making the term somewhat specific to the *X Window System*. Example toolkits include *GTK+*, *Motif*, Qt, and Microsoft Foundation Classes.

U

UCS-4   Universal-coded Character Set, 4 bytes. A *Unicode* encoding that uses exactly four bytes to represent a character.

Unicode   An international-standard character set that can represent any character in any language. See [TUC] for more information.

untyped pointer   A pointer that does not know its target type. In C and many other programming languages, most pointers correspond to a type so that the compiler can compute offsets for data sizes and offsets. Untyped pointers (void * in plain C and `gpointer` in *GLib*) simply point to a piece of memory; it is up to the programmer to do something with the memory (for example, cast the pointer to another type and ensure that this type is actually behind the pointer).

URI   Uniform Resource Identifier, a term that covers *URL* and *URN*; because URNs are rare, this term nearly always means URL. *GnomeVFS* uses URIs to denote a file path, with specific extensions: for example, to decompress a file with *gunzip*.

URL   Uniform Resource Locator. The old term for a resource path, now no longer used in technical documents.

URN   Uniform Resource Name. Either a guaranteed permanent *URL* or a *URI* with the method *urn:* that does not point to a location but, rather, to a location-independent resource.

user data pointer   An *untyped pointer*, normally the last argument in the prototype of a *callback function*, that allows you to pass arbitrary data along with the other arguments. You can employ user data pointers when you want to use one callback function for slightly different *events*, where only one small piece of data is different for each event.

UTF-8   UCS Transformation Format, 8 bits. A *Unicode* encoding that is backward compatible with ASCII; with non-ASCII text, characters do not have a constant width in bytes.

UTF-16   UCS Transformation Format, 16 bits. A *Unicode* encoding that uses two bytes to encode each character.

V

vector graphics   Unlike *bitmap* graphics, vector graphic files consist of specific objects, such as lines, curves, circles, and text, that you can scale, translate, and transform without losing any data.

view   The *V* in *MVC*. A view displays a *model*. In principle, you can have as many views of a model as you like; all should change simultaneously when you alter the model.

W

widget   A general term for *GUI* user elements, including windows, buttons, entry boxes, and labels. Widgets are the smallest pieces of a GUI *toolkit* and normally fall into a *widget tree*, where widgets are *packed* into *container* widgets.

widget tree   A treelike hierarchy of *widgets*, where widgets are the children of *containers*, and containers can hold other containers. *Glade* has a special window where you can view the widget tree of the current project.

window   1. In general, a clearly marked (usually rectangular) semiautonomous area on a display that you can manipulate in a number of ways (for example, by moving the window). *Window managers* add standard decorations to windows. 2. In the *X Window System*, any area that receives *events* from the X server. One window can contain dozens of other windows: one for each *widget*.

window manager   In the *X Window System*, a program that oversees the position, layering, and decoration of windows. The window manager also provides the user with window controls to manipulate windows. Normally, the controls on all windows have a uniform look. Windows can request special treatment with window manager *hints*.

X

X Window System (or X11)   A portable, network-transparent windowing system. The system consists of an X server dedicated to drawing on a display and receiving input *events*, and X clients that talk to the server in order to draw graphics or get input data. The X Window System is enormous but still the universal standard on most Unix systems.

XML   Extensible Markup Language. A widespread standard for creating document structure specifications. HTML and *DocBook* are XML-based formats. GNOME uses `GNOME-XML` to interface with XML.

BIBLIOGRAPHY

Amundson, Shawn T., Emmanuel Deloget, and Tony Gale, "GTK+ Frequently Asked Questions," http://www.gtk.org/faq/ (accessed December 2003).

Barnson, Matthew P., Steenhagen, Jacob, and The Bugzilla Team, "The Bugzilla Guide," Release 2.17.5 (November 2003), http://www.bugzilla.org/docs/html/ (accessed January 2004).

Brown, Preston, Jonathan Blandford, and Owen Taylor, "Desktop Entry Standard," Version 0.9.4, http://www.freedesktop.org/standards/desktop-entry-spec (accessed December 2003).

Bunks, Carey. *Grokking the GIMP*. Indianapolis: New Riders, 2000.

Cormen, Thomas H. *Introduction to Algorithms*. 2nd ed. Cambridge: MIT Press, 2001.

FSF 1991 (Free Software Foundation), "GNU General Public License," Version 2, http://www.gnu.org/licenses/gpl.html (accessed December 2003).

FSF 1999 (Free Software Foundation), "GNU Lesser General Public License," Version 2.1, http://www.gnu.org/licenses/lgpl.html (accessed December 2003).

Fogel, Karl, and Moshe Bar. *Open Source Deleopment with CVS*. 3rd ed. Phoenix: Paraglyph, 2003.

GDSC Contributors, "GNOME Documentation Style Guide," Version 1.3 (2003), http://developer.gnome.org/documents/style-guide/ (accessed December 2003).

GUP (GNOME Usability Project), "GNOME 2.0 Human Interface Guidelines," Version 1.0, http://developer.gnome.org/projects/gup/hig/ (accessed December 2003).

Johnson, Michael K., and Erik W. Troan. *Linux Application Development*. Reading: Addison-Wesley, 1998.

Kernighan, Brian W., and Dennis Ritchie. *The C Programming Langugage*. 2nd ed. Upper Saddle River: Prentice Hall PTR, 1988.

Knuth, Donald. *The Art of Computer Programming*. 3rd ed. Reading: Addison-Wesley, 1997.

Mason, David, Daniel Mueth, Alexander Kirillov, Eric Baudais, and John Fleck. "The GNOME Handbook of Writing Software Documentation," Version 1.0.2 (2002), http://developer.gnome.org/projects/gdp/handbook.html (accessed December 2003).

Mor, Ralph, "X Session Management Library," Version 1.0; X Consortium Standard: X Version 11, Release 6.4, ftp://ftp.x.org/pub/R6.4/xc/doc/hardcopy/SM/SMlib.PS.gz (accessed December 2003).

Mueth, Daniel. "Writing Scrollkeeper OMF Files," Version 1.0 (2002), http://scrollkeeper.sourceforge.net/documentation/writing_scrollkeeper_omf_files/ (accessed December 2003).

Pennington, Havoc. *GTK+/GNOME Application Development*. Indianapolis: New Riders, 1999. http://developer.gnome.org/doc/GGAD/ggad.html (accessed December 2003).

TUC (The Unicode Consortium). *The Unicode Standard*. Version 3.0. Reading: Addison-Wesley, 2000. http://www.unicode.org/unicode/uni2book/u2.html.

Tredinnick, Malcolm, "Porting Applications to the GNOME 2.0 Platform," http://developer.gnome.org/dotplan/porting/index.html (accessed December 2003).

Vaughan, Gary, Ben Elliston, Tom Tromey, and Ian Taylor. *GNU Autoconf, Automake, and Libtool*. Version 3.0. Indianapolis: New Riders, 2000. http://sources.redhat.com/autobook/ (accessed December 2003).

Walsh, Norman, and Leonard Muellner. *Docbook: The Definitive Guide*. Sebastopol: O'Reilly & Associates, 1999.

Wexler, Mike, "X Session Management Protocol," X Consortium Standard: X Version 11, Release 6.4, ftp://ftp.x.org/pub/R6.4/xc/doc/hardcopy/SM/xsmp.PS.gz (accessed December 2003).

Wirth, Niklaus. *Algorithmen und Datenstrukturen*. *Pascal-Version*. Stuttgart: Teubner-Verlag, 2000.

XDG (X Desktop Group), "Extended Window Manager Hints," Version 1.3, http://www.freedesktop.org/standards/wm-spec/ (accessed December 2003).

GETTING THE GNOME
DEVELOPMENT SOFTWARE

To make any sense of this book whatsoever, you need to acquire and install the
GNOME 2 development environment. This appendix describes how to do just that.

System-Specific Packages

Reasonably current GNOME binary packages are available for almost every operating
system: RPMs, Debian packages, Solaris packages, FreeBSD ports, and so on.
Unfortunately, it is impossible to say just how current these packages are at any given
moment. The Ximian Red Carpet system also offers automatic updates for GNOME 2
packages.

GARNOME

One of the most popular (and certainly most convenient) ways to install the GNOME
development environment from source code is to use the GARNOME system
available at *http://www.gnome.org/~jdub/garnome/*. Install GARNOME on your system
using the following instructions:

1. Download the newest package from the website (the filename is *garnome-version.tar.bz2*, where *version* is the version number).

2. Unpack the source code with

```
bunzip2 -dc garnome-version.tar.bz2 | tar xvf -
```

As of yet, you do not have any source code on your system; GARNOME retrieves the packages on demand.

3. Go to the new *garnome-version* directory and edit *gar.conf.mk* with your favorite text editor. The most important setting here is in the line that contains main_prefix ?=; replace the default $(HOME)/garnome with the installation prefix of your choice.

4. (Optional) If you have already downloaded some of the GNOME source code archives and want GARNOME to recognize them, remove the # in front of GARCHIVEDIR =. Then, add the directory containing the tarballs.

5. Run

```
cd meta/gnome-desktop
make install
```

6. Wait a long time while GARNOME downloads the core packages, verifies the packages against checksums, and then unpacks, compiles, and installs the packages. If everything went well, you will now have a complete GNOME core system at the prefix you specified in Step 3.

7. (Optional) Run make install in *meta/gnome-fifth-toe*, *meta/gnome-hacker-tools*, *meta/gnome-office*, and *meta/gnome-power-tools* if you wish to install any of these sets.

8. (Optional) If you set GARCHIVEDIR earlier, you can run make garchive to copy your freshly downloaded tarballs to that directory.

9. Run make clean in the top-level directory if you need to free up some disk space.

NOTE *These instructions assume that your system is permanently connected to the Internet. If this is not the case, run* make paranoid-checksum *in the top-level directory to download all of the packages so that you can then disconnect your network.*

If you installed GARNOME outside of a regular system directory, you need to set several environment variables so that the programs can find their libraries and data. The easiest approach is to use a script like the one shown here to start a GNOME session (set *YOUR_PREFIX* to your GARNOME prefix):

```
#!/bin/sh
GARNOME=YOUR_PREFIX

# executable path
PATH=$GARNOME/bin:$PATH
```

```
# shared libraries
LD_LIBRARY_PATH=$GARNOME/lib:$LD_LIBRARY_PATH

# Python libraries
PYTHONPATH=$GARNOME/lib/python2.2/site-packages

# pkg-config .pc files
PKG_CONFIG_PATH=$GARNOME/lib/pkgconfig:/usr/lib/pkgconfig

export PATH LD_LIBRARY_PATH PYTHONPATH PKG_CONFIG_PATH

exec $GARNOME/bin/gnome-session
```

Place this script in your X startup sequence and restart your X session. This procedure makes the GNOME development environment available during your new GNOME session; however, you cannot use the environment outside of your session (for example, when using a remote shell).

CVS

GNOME development takes place on the *cvs.gnome.org* server, where you can retrieve the latest developer's version of any package at any time. You can read about CVS at *http://www.cvshome.org/* and in [Fogel]; here is a summary of how to use it:

1. Set your CVSROOT environment variable login to the anonymous GNOME CVS server:

```
export CVSROOT=:pserver:anonymous@anoncvs.gnome.org/cvs/gnome
```

2. Run cvs login. When asked for a password, press Enter. This step creates a *.cvspass* file in your home directory that tells CVS how to access *cvs.gnome.org*.

To check out a package, make sure that you have the CVSROOT variable set as described and run cvs checkout *package*. For example, to get the Nautilus source code, you would enter

```
cvs checkout nautilus
```

The reply should look something like this:

```
cvs server: Updating nautilus
U nautilus/.cvsignore
U nautilus/AUTHORS
U nautilus/COPYING
U nautilus/COPYING-DOCS
  ...
  ...
```

If you already have a source tree, use cvs update *package* to update the package to the current version.

To see what packages you need for the GNOME installation, look up the release notes of the latest GNOME desktop and developer package.

NOTE *Getting software via CVS usually means that you are interested in the latest versions. The commands provided here work with the newest branch of the source tree. Therefore, do not expect them to be bug free. In addition, you need all of the GNU autotools described in Chapter 6, and you must run the* autogen.sh *script to create a valid* configure *script and compile the package.*

JHBuild

GNOME developers on the GNOME CVS server tend to use a system called JHBuild to retrieve and build the GNOME code. Here's how it works:

1. Set up CVS as described in the previous section.
2. Get the JHBuild package:

```
cvs checkout jhbuild
```

3. You now have a jhbuild directory. Change to this directory.
4. Read the README file.
5. Look at Makefile to see if you need to change anything on your system.
6. Install JHBuild:

```
make install
```

7. Copy sample.jhbuildrc to a dot file in your home directory:

```
cp sample.jhbuildrc $HOME/.jhbuildrc
```

8. Edit your $HOME/.jhbuildrc file to suit your system.
9. Build and install the preliminary configuration:

```
jhbuild bootstrap
```

10. Build and install everything else:

```
Jhbuild
```

NOTE *To build a single module and its dependencies, use the* build *command:*

```
jhbuild build module
```

Conventional Source Archives

If you really want to do everything on your own and for whatever reason do not want to use CVS, you can go to *http://download.gnome.org/* for tarballs of each package. Choosing this path means that you need to unpack, configure, and compile each package by hand.

This isn't the easiest way to install the system; GARNOME provides a much easier and preferable alternative in most cases. However, if you are *really* determined, you can go to *http://www.karubik.de/gig/* for guidance on how to install the packages and for the current release notes for the library installation order.

CREATIVE COMMONS NONCOMMERCIAL-SHAREALIKE LICENSE

NonCommercial-ShareAlike 1.0

License

1. **Definitions**

   a. **"Collective Work"** means a work, such as a periodical issue, anthology or encyclopedia, in which the Work in its entirety in unmodified form, along with a number of other contributions, constituting separate and independent works in themselves, are assembled into a collective whole. A work that constitutes a Collective Work will not be considered a Derivative Work (as defined below) for the purposes of this License.

   b. **"Derivative Work"** means a work based upon the Work or upon the Work and other pre-existing works, such as a translation, musical arrangement, dramatization, fictionalization, motion picture version, sound recording, art reproduction, abridgment, condensation, or any other form in which the Work may be recast, transformed, or adapted, except that a work that constitutes a Collective Work will not be considered a Derivative Work for the purpose of this License.

   c. **"Licensor"** means the individual or entity that offers the Work under the terms of this License.

   d. **"Original Author"** means the individual or entity who created the Work.

   e. **"Work"** means the copyrightable work of authorship offered under the terms of this License.

   f. **"You"** means an individual or entity exercising rights under this License who has not previously violated the terms of this License with respect to the Work, or who has received express permission from the Licensor to exercise rights under this License despite a previous violation.

2. **Fair Use Rights.** Nothing in this license is intended to reduce, limit, or restrict any rights arising from fair use, first sale or other limitations on the exclusive rights of the copyright owner under copyright law or other applicable laws.

3. **License Grant.** Subject to the terms and conditions of this License, Licensor hereby grants You a worldwide, royalty-free, non-exclusive, perpetual (for the duration of the applicable copyright) license to exercise the rights in the Work as stated below:

   a. to reproduce the Work, to incorporate the Work into one or more Collective Works, and to reproduce the Work as incorporated in the Collective Works;

   b. to create and reproduce Derivative Works;

   c. to distribute copies or phonorecords of, display publicly, perform publicly, and perform publicly by means of a digital audio transmission the Work including as incorporated in Collective Works;

   d. to distribute copies or phonorecords of, display publicly, perform publicly, and perform publicly by means of a digital audio transmission Derivative Works;

The above rights may be exercised in all media and formats whether now known or hereafter devised. The above rights include the right to make such modifications as are technically necessary to exercise the rights in other media and formats. All rights not expressly granted by Licensor are hereby reserved.

4. **Restrictions.** The license granted in Section 3 above is expressly made subject to and limited by the following restrictions:

    a. You may distribute, publicly display, publicly perform, or publicly digitally perform the Work only under the terms of this License, and You must include a copy of, or the Uniform Resource Identifier for, this License with every copy or phonorecord of the Work You distribute, publicly display, publicly perform, or publicly digitally perform. You may not offer or impose any terms on the Work that alter or restrict the terms of this License or the recipients' exercise of the rights granted hereunder. You may not sublicense the Work. You must keep intact all notices that refer to this License and to the disclaimer of warranties. You may not distribute, publicly display, publicly perform, or publicly digitally perform the Work with any technological measures that control access or use of the Work in a manner inconsistent with the terms of this License Agreement. The above applies to the Work as incorporated in a Collective Work, but this does not require the Collective Work apart from the Work itself to be made subject to the terms of this License. If You create a Collective Work, upon notice from any Licensor You must, to the extent practicable, remove from the Collective Work any reference to such Licensor or the Original Author, as requested. If You create a Derivative Work, upon notice from any Licensor You must, to the extent practicable, remove from the Derivative Work any reference to such Licensor or the Original Author, as requested.

    b. You may distribute, publicly display, publicly perform, or publicly digitally perform a Derivative Work only under the terms of this License, and You must include a copy of, or the Uniform Resource Identifier for, this License with every copy or phonorecord of each Derivative Work You distribute, publicly display, publicly perform, or publicly digitally perform. You may not offer or impose any terms on the Derivative Works that alter or restrict the terms of this License or the recipients' exercise of the rights granted hereunder, and You must keep intact all notices that refer to this License and to the disclaimer of warranties. You may not distribute, publicly display, publicly perform, or publicly digitally perform the Derivative Work with any technological measures that control access or use of the Work in a manner inconsistent with the terms of this License Agreement. The above applies to the Derivative Work as incorporated in a Collective Work, but this does not require the Collective Work apart from the Derivative Work itself to be made subject to the terms of this License.

c. You may not exercise any of the rights granted to You in Section 3 above in any manner that is primarily intended for or directed toward commercial advantage or private monetary compensation. The exchange of the Work for other copyrighted works by means of digital file-sharing or otherwise shall not be considered to be intended for or directed toward commercial advantage or private monetary compensation, provided there is no payment of any monetary compensation in connection with the exchange of copyrighted works.

5. **Representations, Warranties and Disclaimer**

a. By offering the Work for public release under this License, Licensor represents and warrants that, to the best of Licensor's knowledge after reasonable inquiry:

i. Licensor has secured all rights in the Work necessary to grant the license rights hereunder and to permit the lawful exercise of the rights granted hereunder without You having any obligation to pay any royalties, compulsory license fees, residuals or any other payments;

ii. The Work does not infringe the copyright, trademark, publicity rights, common law rights or any other right of any third party or constitute defamation, invasion of privacy or other tortious injury to any third party.

b. EXCEPT AS EXPRESSLY STATED IN THIS LICENSE OR OTHERWISE AGREED IN WRITING OR REQUIRED BY APPLICABLE LAW, THE WORK IS LICENSED ON AN "AS IS" BASIS, WITHOUT WARRANTIES OF ANY KIND, EITHER EXPRESS OR IMPLIED INCLUDING, WITHOUT LIMITATION, ANY WARRANTIES REGARDING THE CONTENTS OR ACCURACY OF THE WORK.

6. **Limitation on Liability.** EXCEPT TO THE EXTENT REQUIRED BY APPLICABLE LAW, AND EXCEPT FOR DAMAGES ARISING FROM LIABILITY TO A THIRD PARTY RESULTING FROM BREACH OF THE WARRANTIES IN SECTION 5, IN NO EVENT WILL LICENSOR BE LIABLE TO YOU ON ANY LEGAL THEORY FOR ANY SPECIAL, INCIDENTAL, CONSEQUENTIAL, PUNITIVE OR EXEMPLARY DAMAGES ARISING OUT OF THIS LICENSE OR THE USE OF THE WORK, EVEN IF LICENSOR HAS BEEN ADVISED OF THE POSSIBILITY OF SUCH DAMAGES.

7. **Termination**

a. This License and the rights granted hereunder will terminate automatically upon any breach by You of the terms of this License. Individuals or entities who have received Derivative Works or Collective Works from You under this License, however, will not have their licenses terminated provided such individuals or entities remain in full compliance with those licenses. Sections 1, 2, 5, 6, 7, and 8 will survive any termination of this License.

b. Subject to the above terms and conditions, the license granted here is perpetual (for the duration of the applicable copyright in the Work). Notwithstanding the above, Licensor reserves the right to release the Work under different license terms or to stop distributing the Work at any time; provided, however that any such election will not serve to withdraw this License (or any other license that has been, or is required to be, granted under the terms of this License), and this License will continue in full force and effect unless terminated as stated above.

8. **Miscellaneous**

a. Each time You distribute or publicly digitally perform the Work or a Collective Work, the Licensor offers to the recipient a license to the Work on the same terms and conditions as the license granted to You under this License.

b. Each time You distribute or publicly digitally perform a Derivative Work, Licensor offers to the recipient a license to the original Work on the same terms and conditions as the license granted to You under this License.

c. If any provision of this License is invalid or unenforceable under applicable law, it shall not affect the validity or enforceability of the remainder of the terms of this License, and without further action by the parties to this agreement, such provision shall be reformed to the minimum extent necessary to make such provision valid and enforceable.

d. No term or provision of this License shall be deemed waived and no breach consented to unless such waiver or consent shall be in writing and signed by the party to be charged with such waiver or consent.

e. This License constitutes the entire agreement between the parties with respect to the Work licensed here. There are no understandings, agreements or representations with respect to the Work not specified here. Licensor shall not be bound by any additional provisions that may appear in any communication from You. This License may not be modified without the mutual written agreement of the Licensor and You.

Creative Commons is not a party to this License, and makes no warranty whatsoever in connection with the Work. Creative Commons will not be liable to You or any party on any legal theory for any damages whatsoever, including without limitation any general, special, incidental or consequential damages arising in connection to this license. Notwithstanding the foregoing two (2) sentences, if Creative Commons has expressly identified itself as the Licensor hereunder, it shall have all rights and obligations of Licensor.

Except for the limited purpose of indicating to the public that the Work is licensed under the CCPL, neither party will use the trademark "Creative Commons" or any related trademark or logo of Creative Commons without the prior written consent of Creative Commons. Any permitted use will be in compliance with Creative Commons' then-current trademark usage guidelines, as may be published on its website or otherwise made available upon request from time to time.

Creative Commons may be contacted at http://creativecommons.org.

INDEX

about windows. *See* **GnomeAbout**

abstract class. *See* class, abstract

accelerators, 184–185. *See also*
    GtkAccelGroup

access methods (versus properties),
    82–83

accessibility. *See* ATK

AC_CONFIG_FILES, 331–332

AC_CONFIG_HEADER, 330–331

AC_CONFIG_SRCDIR, 330–331

accumulators. *See* signals,
    accumulators

AC_DEFINE_UNQUOTED, 331–332

AC_HEADER_STDC, 330–331

AC_INIT, 330–331

aclocal.m4, 329, 336

AC_OUTPUT, 331, 333

AC_PROG_CC, 330–331

AC_PROG_INTLTOOL, 331–332

AC_SUBST, 331–332

AH_TEMPLATE, 331–332

alignment containers. *See*
    GtkAlignment

ALL_LINGUAS, 331–332

AM_GLIB_GNU_GETTEXT, 331–332

AM_INIT_AUTOMAKE, 330–331

AM_MAINTAINER_MODE, 330–331

application identifier, 249

application windows. *See* **GtkWindow**;
    GnomeApp

arrays. *See* GArray

assertions, 29–30

assistants. *See* druids

asynchronous file access
    canceling operations, 393, 398
    description, 393–394

example, 398–410
    file information, 396
    opening and closing files,
        394–395
    reading and writing, 395
    searching for directories,
        396–397
    symbolic links, 397–398

ATK, 114, 244, 323

atom, 11–12. *See also* memory chunks

attributes, 62

autoconf, 329, 336

autogen.sh, 338

autoheader, 329, 336

automake, 329, 336

Autotools. *See* GNU Autotools

base class
    definition, 64
    methods, 72–74
    properties and, 73, 80
    utility macros, 71–72

Battlestar Galactica, 124

binary data, 37

Bonobo, 248

Boolean values, 8

box containers. *See* **GtkBox**

Bradley, John, 113

Bugzilla, 432–434

button boxes
    description, 141
    example, 141–145

buttons. *See* **GtkButton**

C++ compatibility, 69

casting macro, 67–68

cell renderer. *See* **GtkCellRenderer**

check boxes. *See* **GtkCheckButton**; **GtkCellRendererToggle**; **GtkMenuItem**

child anchors. *See* **GtkTextBuffer**, child anchors

child properties, 147–148, 152

CLAMP(), 125, 140, 402

class

    abstract, 64, 70

    base (*see* base class)

    creating, 66–83

    definition, 62

    hierarchy, 64

    initializer, 70, 75–77, 79–80, 87–89, 102–104

    properties (*see* properties)

    signals (*see* signals)

    structure, 66–67, 70, 74, 101

    type identifier (*see* type identifier)

    utility macros, 67–69, 102, 107

clipboard, 165, 241

color choosers. *See* **GtkColorSelection**; **GnomeColorPicker**

color, GDK, 296

combo box. *See* **GtkCombo**

compiling, difficulty with, 325–326

config.h.in, 329, 336

configuration systems, traditional, 345–346

configure

    options, 337

    standard targets, 337

configure.ac (configure.in), 329–333

constructor, 62, 72–73

containers

    child, 114

    definition, 114

    value (*see* GValue)

    widgets (*see* widget, containers; **GtkContainer**)

context menus, 151, 271

controllers. *See* MVC

credits windows. *See* **GnomeAbout**

cursor, 234

CVS, 329

data pointer

in objects, 135–138

    user (*see* user data pointer)

date and time widgets. *See* **GnomeDateEdit**

debugging using flow control, 29–30

decorations. *See* **GtkArrow**; **GtkFrame**

desktop files, 333–334, 338–339

destructor, 73

details. *See* signals, details

developer home, 434–435

dialogs. *See* **GtkDialog**; **GtkColorSelection**; **GnomeColorPicker**; **GtkFontSelection**; **GnomeFontPicker**; **GtkFileSelection**; **GnomeFileEntry**

directory operations, 391–393

DISTCLEANFILES, 333–334

dividers, 176–180. *See also* **GtkFrame**; **GtkSeparator**; **GtkMenuItem**

docked elements, 259

drop arrow, 193

druids, 288. *See also* **GnomeDruid**; **GnomeDruidPageEdge**; **GnomeDruidPageStandard**

dynamic module loader (GModule), 60

emission hooks. *See* signals, hooks

emission. *See* signals, emitting

entry box. *See* **GtkEntry**; **GnomeEntry**

error codes

    GConfClient, 366–367

    GnomeVFS, 385, 422–424

    Unicode, 24–25

error diagnosis. *See* message; GError

event–driven programming, 116

events

    definition, 114

    signals and, 116, 119–120

example

    asynchronous file access, 398–410

    attaching signal handlers, 95–97

    button boxes, 141–145

    child properties, 148

    class initializer, 76–77, 79–80, 87–89, 104

example, *continued*
  class utility macros, 67–68, 102, 107
  containers, 141–145
  displaying help, 256
  displaying URL, 255
  GArray, 46–48
  GConfClient application, 370–376
  GConfClient data access, 356–357
  GConfEntry, 362–364
  GConfValue, 359–360
  GdkPixbuf, 134–139
  GError, 31–34
  getting source code, 4
  GHashTable, 55–59
  Glade–assisted program, 319–323
  GList, 39–45
  GNOME program skeleton, 250–251
  GnomeAbout, 286–287
  GnomeApp, 259–264
  GnomeClient, 302–303, 406–408
  GnomeColorPicker, 272–277
  GnomeDateEdit, 272–277
  GnomeDruid, 288–294
  GnomeDruidPageEdge, 288–294
  GnomeDruidPageStandard, 288–294
  GnomeEntry, 272–277
  GnomeFileEntry, 272–277
  GnomeFontPicker, 272–277
  GnomeHRef, 283–284
  GnomeIconEntry, 272–277
  GnomePixmapEntry, 272–277
  GnomeVFS file information, 424–429
  GNU Autotools, 330–343
  GString, 36–38
  GTimer, 25
  GTK+, 116–120
  GtkAdjustment, 159–163
  GtkArrow, 177–179
  GtkBox, 141–145
  GtkButton, 153–157
  GtkCellRenderer, 194–197, 217
  GtkCheckButton, 153–157

GtkColorSelection, 172–176
GtkCombo, 159–163
GtkDialog, 188–191, 288–289
GtkEntry, 159–163
GtkFileSelection, 172–176
GtkFontSelection, 172–176
GtkFrame, 177–179
GtkImage, 124–128, 134–139
GtkLabel, 124–128
GtkListStore, 194–197
GtkMenu, 259–264
GtkMenuBar, 259–264
GtkMenuItem, 259–264
GtkMenuShell, 259–264
GtkNotebook, 141–145
GtkOptionMenu, 159–163
GtkPaned, 141–145
GtkProgressBar, 124–128
GtkRadioButton, 153–157
GtkRadioMenuItem, 266
GtkScale, 134–139, 159–163
GtkScrolledWindow, 186–187
GtkSeparator, 177–179
GtkSpinButton, 159–163
GtkStatusbar, 259–264
GtkTable, 141–145
GtkTextBuffer, 219–226
GtkTextIter, 219–226
GtkTextView, 219–226
GtkToolbar, 259–264
GtkTooltips, 181–183
GtkTreeIter, 212–219
GtkTreeStore, 212–219
GtkTreeView, 194–197, 212–219
GtkTreeViewColumn, 194–197
GtkWindow, 116–120
GTree, 49–53
interface base initializer, 108
interface initializer, 109–110
interface method, 110
locating files, 252–253
Makefile.am, 333–335
marshallers, 92–94
memory chunks, 11–13
message logging, 26–27
MIME types, 417–418
print handler, 28
quarks, 14

example, *continued*
    references, 85–86
    signal definition, 87–89
    signal details, 97
    signal handlers, 89–90, 95–96
    signal hooks, 98–99
    signal listing and printing,
        100–101
    structure, 4
    synchronous file access, 383–385
    temperature converter, 305–323
    type identifier function, 69,
        102–103, 109
    using objects, 84–86, 105–106
exception handling. *See* GError
executing programs, 253–255
EXTRA_DIST, 333–334
fatal errors, 26–27
file browsers. *See* **GtkFileSelection**;
    GnomeFileEntry
files
    accessing (*see* GnomeVFS)
    locating, 251–253
    management (*see* synchronous
        file access, file management)
finalizer, 73–74
focus. *See* input focus
font choosers. *See* **GtkFontSelection**;
    GnomeFontPicker
fonts, 129–130
functions and macros, difference
    between, 4
GArray, 46–48. *See also* GList
g_array_append_vals(), 47
g_array_free(), 48
g_array_index(), 46–47
g_array_insert_vals(), 47
g_array_new(), 46
g_array_prepend_val(), 47
g_array_prepend_vals(), 47
g_array_remove_index(), 48
g_array_remove_index_fast(), 48
g_array_set_size(), 47
g_array_sized_new(), 46
g_array_sort(), 48
g_array_sort_with_data(), 48
g_ascii_dtostr(), 17
g_ascii_strcasecmp(), 14

g_ascii_strtod(), 17
g_assert(), 30
g_assert_not_reached(), 30
GBaseFinalizeFunc, 70–71
GBaseInitFunc, 70–71
g_blow_chunks(), 12
GBoxed, 111
GByteArray, 59
g_cclosure_marshal_*(), 91–92
GClassFinalizeFunc, 70–71
GClassInitFunc, 70–71
g_clear_error(), 31–32
GClosure, 93, 111
GCompareFunc, 44–45
GConf
    configuration editor, 347–348
    data types, 347
    keys, 347
    overview, 346–347
    path, 346–347, 353–354
    programming with (*see*
        GConfClient)
    schemas, 347–348, 368–370, 376
    user programs, 347–352
GConfClient
    accessing directories, 361–362
    accessing keys and values,
        361–362 (*see also* GConfEntry)
    accessing values, 354–360 (*see also*
        GConfValue)
    application skeleton, 353–354
    cache, 366
    error handling, 366–368
    example, 356–357
    example application, 370–376
    initializing, 352–354
    value change notification,
        364–366
gconf_client_add_dir(), 353–354
gconf_client_all_dirs(), 361
gconf_client_all_entries(), 361–362
gconf_client_clear_cache(), 366
gconf_client_dir_exists(), 361–362
gconf_client_get(), 358
gconf_client_get_bool(), 355, 357
gconf_client_get_default(), 353–354
gconf_client_get_entry(), 361
gconf_client_get_float(), 354

gconf_client_get_int(), 354, 356
gconf_client_get_list(), 355–356
gconf_client_get_pair(), 355
gconf_client_get_string(), 355, 357
gconf_client_key_is_writable(), 356
gconf_client_notify_add(), 365
GConfClientNotifyFunc, 365
gconf_client_notify_remove(), 365–366
gconf_client_preload(), 366
gconf_client_remove_dir(), 353–354
gconf_client_set(), 358
gconf_client_set_bool(), 355, 357
gconf_client_set_error_handling(), 354,
    364, 367
gconf_client_set_float(), 355, 357
gconf_client_set_int(), 355, 357
gconf_client_set_list(), 356–357
gconf_client_set_pair(), 356–357
gconf_client_set_string(), 355, 357
gconf_client_suggest_sync(), 366
gconf_client_unset(), 362
GConfEntry, 361–364
gconf_entry_free(), 361, 364
gconf_entry_get_key(), 361, 364
gconf_entry_get_value(), 361, 363
gconf_entry_steal_value(), 361
gconftool-2, 349–352
GConfValue
    example, 359–360
    operation, 357–358
gconf_value_copy(), 359
gconf_value_free(), 358, 360
gconf_value_get_bool(), 358
gconf_value_get_car(), 359
gconf_value_get_cdr(), 359
gconf_value_get_float(), 358
gconf_value_get_int(), 358, 360
gconf_value_get_list(), 359
gconf_value_get_string(), 358
gconf_value_new(), 358–360
gconf_value_set_bool(), 358
gconf_value_set_car(), 359
gconf_value_set_car_nocopy(), 359
gconf_value_set_cdr(), 359
gconf_value_set_cdr_nocopy(), 359
gconf_value_set_float(), 358
gconf_value_set_int(), 358–359
gconf_value_set_list(), 359

gconf_value_set_list_nocopy(), 359–360
gconf_value_set_list_type(), 359–360
gconf_value_set_string(), 358, 360
gconf_value_to_string(), 359–360, 363
g_create_hash_table_new(), 54–55
g_critical(), 26–27
GDestroyNotify, 49
g_direct_equal(), 55
g_direct_hash(), 55
GDK, 113, 132–134, 244
gdk_color_parse(), 291, 293, 296
GdkPixbuf, 132–139
gdk_pixbuf_add_alpha(), 133
GdkPixbufAnimation, 245
gdk_pixbuf_composite(), 133
gdk_pixbuf_copy(), 132
gdk_pixbuf_copy_area(), 132
gdk_pixbuf_fill(), 134
gdk_pixbuf_get_has_alpha(), 133
gdk_pixbuf_get_height(), 132
gdk_pixbuf_get_width(), 132
GdkPixbufLoader, 245
gdk_pixbuf_new_from_file(), 132
gdk_pixbuf_saturate_and_pixelate(),
    133–134
gdk_pixbuf_scale(), 133
gdk_pixbuf_scale_simple(), 133, 136
GEqualFunc, 54–55
GError
    defining error domains and
        codes, 32–34
    description, 30
    example, 31–34
    setting error conditions, 33–34
    structure, 30
g_error_free(), 31–32
g_error_matches(), 31–32
gettext, 329, 331–332, 335, 341–343
GETTEXT_PACKAGE, 331–332
g_extension_pointer(), 253
g_filename_from_uri(), 24
g_filename_from_utf8(), 24
g_filename_to_uri(), 24
g_filename_to_utf8(), 24
g_free(), 9–10
g_free_list(), 45
GFunc, 43
GHashFunc, 54–55

GHashTable
    creating, 54–55
    deleting, 59
    deleting entries, 58
    description, 54
    example, 55–59
    finding size, 56
    hash function, 54–55
    hash value, 54–55
    inserting and replacing entries,
        56
    iterating through, 58–59
    lookups, 57
g_hash_table_destroy(), 59
g_hash_table_foreach(), 58–59
g_hash_table_foreach_remove(), 58
g_hash_table_foreach_steal(), 58
g_hash_table_insert(), 56
g_hash_table_lookup(), 57
g_hash_table_lookup_extended(), 57
g_hash_table_new_full(), 55
g_hash_table_remove(), 58
g_hash_table_replace(), 56
g_hash_table_size(), 56
g_hash_table_steal(), 58
GHFunc and GHRFunc, 58
g_int_equal(), 55
GInterfaceFinalizeFunc, 109
GInterfaceInitFunc, 109
g_int_hash(), 55
G_IS_OBJECT(), 72
G_IS_OBJECT_CLASS(), 72
Glade
    clipboard, 313
    creating a project, 306
    description, 305
    example use of libglade, 319–323
    interface file (.glade), 314–317
    making room for widgets in
        containers, 311–312
    property editor, 308–312
    signals, 318–319
    starting, 305–306
    user interface integration into
        applications, 317–319
    widget palette, 307
    window titles, 310
glade_get_widget_name(), 319

glade_get_widget_tree(), 319
glade_xml_get_widget(), 318, 322
glade_xml_get_widget_prefix(), 318
glade_xml_new(), 317, 322
glade_xml_signal_autoconnect(), 319
glade_xml_signal_connect(), 319
glade_xml_signal_connect_data(), 319,
        323
GLib
    naming conventions (see naming
        conventions)
    overview, 7
    types, 8–9
glib-genmarshal, 92–94
GList
    adding elements, 39–40
    concatenating, 45
    copying, 45
    creating, 38–39
    deallocating, 45
    example, 39–45
    iterating through, 43–45
    navigating, 40–42
    removing elements, 42–43
    reversing, 45
    sorting, 44–45
g_list_append(), 39
g_list_concat(), 45
g_list_copy(), 45
g_list_find(), 40
g_list_first(), 41
g_list_foreach(), 43–44
g_list_index(), 41–42
g_list_insert(), 39–40
g_list_insert_before(), 40
g_list_last(), 41
g_list_length(), 41–42
g_list_next(), 41–42
g_list_nth(), 41
g_list_nth_data(), 41
g_list_nth_prev(), 41
g_list_position(), 41–42
g_list_prepend(), 39, 42
g_list_prev(), 41–42
g_list_remove(), 42
g_list_remove_all(), 42
g_list_reverse(), 45
g_list_sort(), 44

g_list_sort_with_data(), 45
g_locale_from_utf8(), 24
g_locale_to_utf8(), 24
G_LOG_DOMAIN, 26
g_log_set_always_fatal(), 27
g_log_set_handler(), 59
g_malloc(), 9–10
g_malloc0(), 9–10
GMemChunk. *See* memory chunks
g_mem_chunk_alloc(), 11–13
g_mem_chunk_alloc0(), 12
g_mem_chunk_clean(), 12
g_mem_chunk_create(), 13
g_mem_chunk_destroy(), 12
g_mem_chunk_free(), 12
g_mem_chunk_info(), 13
g_mem_chunk_new(), 11–13
g_mem_chunk_new0(), 13
g_mem_chunk_print(), 13
g_message(), 26–28
g_new(), 10–11
g_new0(), 10
GNode, 60
GNOME
        application menu files
            (*see* desktop files)
        file domain, 251–252
        Foundation, 432
        future of, 436–438
        learning about, 431
        libraries, 247–248
        license, 2
        opposition to, 248
        software downloads, 432
        Usability Project, 434 (*see also*
            user interface guidelines)
        utility functions, 251–256
        widgets in Glade, 307
GNOME application
        compiling, 251, 326–328
        initializing, 249–250
        windows (*see* **GnomeApp**)
GnomeAbout
        example, 286–287
        operation, 285–286
gnome_about_new(), 285–287
GnomeApp
        description, 259

        example, 259–264
        titles, 259
GnomeAppBar, 304
gnome–app–helper, 304
gnome_app_set_contents(), 263
gnome_app_set_menus(), 263, 268
gnome_app_set_statusbar(), 263, 270
gnome_app_set_toolbar(), 263, 270
GnomeClient
        example, 302–303, 406–408
        operation, 300–302
GNOME_CLIENT_CONNECTED(), 300–301
gnome_client_save_any_dialog(), 302
gnome_client_save_error_dialog(), 302
gnome_client_set_clone_command(),
            302–303
gnome_client_set_current_directory(),
            302–303
gnome_client_set_discard_command(), 302
gnome_client_set_environment(), 302
gnome_client_set_restart_command(),
            302–303
GnomeColorPicker
        example, 272–277
        operation, 280 (*see also*
            GtkColorSelection)
GnomeDateEdit
        example, 272–277
        future of, 437
        operation, 282–283
GnomeDruid
        description, 288
        example, 288–294
        operation, 298–299
gnome_druid_append_page(), 293, 298
gnome_druid_insert_page(), 299
gnome_druid_new_with_window(), 293, 298
GnomeDruidPage. *See* **GnomeDruid**,
        description
GnomeDruidPageEdge
        description, 294
        example, 288–294
        operation, 294–296
gnome_druid_page_edge_new_with_vals(),
            291, 294–295
gnome_druid_page_edge_set_bg_color(),
            291, 293, 295

gnome_druid_page_edge_set_logo_bg_
        color(), 296
gnome_druid_page_edge_set_textbox_
        color(), 293, 296
gnome_druid_page_edge_set_text_color(),
        293, 296
gnome_druid_page_edge_set_title_
        color(), 291, 293, 296
GnomeDruidPageStandard
    description, 294
    example, 288–294
    operation, 297–298
gnome_druid_page_standard_append_
        item(), 292–293, 298
gnome_druid_prepend_page(), 299
gnome_druid_set_page(), 299
GnomeEntry
    example, 272–277
    operation, 277–278 (*see also*
        GtkEntry; **GtkCombo**)
gnome_entry_append_history(), 277
gnome_entry_clear_history(), 277
gnome_entry_get_max_saved(), 278
gnome_entry_prepend_history(), 277
gnome_entry_set_max_saved(), 278
gnome_execute_async(), 254
gnome_execute_async_fds(), 254
gnome_execute_async_with_env(), 254
gnome_execute_async_with_env_fds(), 254
gnome_execute_shell(), 254
gnome_execute_shell_fds(), 255
gnome_execute_terminal_shell(), 255
gnome_execute_terminal_shell_fds(), 255
GnomeFileEntry
    example, 272–277
    operation, 278–279 (*see also*
        GtkFileSelection)
gnome_file_entry_get_full_path(), 273,
        278–279
GnomeFontPicker
    example, 272–277
    operation, 279–280 (*see also*
        GtkFontSelection)
gnome_font_picker_uw_set_widget(), 275,
        279
gnome_gconf_get_app_settings_
        relative(), 353–354
gnome_gtk_widget_add_popup_items(), 271

gnome_help_display(), 256
GnomeHRef, 283–284
GnomeIconEntry
    example, 272–277
    operation, 280–281
GnomeIconList, 304
GnomeIconSelection, 304
gnome_master_client(), 300, 303
GnomePixmapEntry
    example, 272–277
    operation, 281–282
gnome_pixmap_entry_get_filename(), 274,
        282
gnome_pixmap_entry_new(), 276, 281
gnome_pixmap_entry_set_pixmap_subdir(),
        282
gnome_pixmap_entry_set_preview_size(),
        282
gnome_popup_menu_append(), 271
gnome_popup_menu_attach(), 271
gnome_popup_menu_get_accel_group(), 271
gnome_popup_menu_new(), 271
gnome_popup_menu_new_with_accelgroup(),
        271
gnome_prepend_terminal_to_vector(), 254
GnomeProgram, 249
gnome_program_init(), 249–250, 261
gnome_program_locate_file(), 251–253
gnome_score_get_notable(), 258
gnome_score_init(), 258, 285
gnome_score_log(), 258
GnomeScores, 284–285
gnome_scores_display_with_pixmap(),
        284–285
gnome_sound_play(), 256
GnomeThumbnail, 304
gnome_triggers_do(), 257–258
gnome_url_show(), 255
gnome_url_show_with_env(), 255
gnome_util_home_file(), 253
gnome_util_prepend_user_home(), 253
GnomeVFS
    asynchronous access (*see*
        asynchronous file access)
    directory operations (*see*
        directory operations)
    error codes (*see* error codes,
        GnomeVFS)

GnomeVFS, *continued*
    executable information, 422
    file access types, 380
    file information example,
        424–429
    file permissions, 386
    free space, 422
    icons, 422
    initializing and shutting down,
        381–382
    local file access, 422
    MIME types (*see* MIME types)
    portability notes, 424
    purpose, 379
    synchronous access (*see*
        synchronous file access)
    transfers, 411–415
    URI, 379–381
    URI structures (*see* GnomeVFSURI)
GnomeVFSAsyncCallback, 395
gnome_vfs_async_cancel(), 393, 398, 401
gnome_vfs_async_close(), 395, 401–403
GnomeVFSAsyncCloseCallback, 395, 401
gnome_vfs_async_create(), 394
gnome_vfs_async_create_symbolic_link(),
        397–398
gnome_vfs_async_create_uri(), 395
GnomeVFSAsyncDirectoryLoadCallback, 398
gnome_vfs_async_find_directory(), 397
GnomeVFSAsyncFindDirectoryCallback, 398
gnome_vfs_async_get_file_info(), 396
GnomeVFSAsyncGetFileInfoCallback, 396
GnomeVFSAsyncHandle, 393
gnome_vfs_async_load_directory(),
        396–397
gnome_vfs_async_load_directory_uri(),
        397
gnome_vfs_async_open(), 394, 405
GnomeVFSAsyncOpenCallback, 395, 403
gnome_vfs_async_open_uri(), 394
gnome_vfs_async_read(), 395, 403–404
GnomeVFSAsyncReadCallback, 395, 402
gnome_vfs_async_set_file_info(), 396
GnomeVFSAsyncSetFileInfoCallback, 396
gnome_vfs_async_write(), 395
GnomeVFSAsyncWriteCallback, 395
gnome_vfs_async_xfer(), 414–415
GnomeVFSAsyncXferProgressCallback, 415

gnome_vfs_check_same_fs(), 390
gnome_vfs_close(), 384, 386
gnome_vfs_create(), 384–385
gnome_vfs_create_symbolic_link(), 391
gnome_vfs_create_uri(), 386
gnome_vfs_directory_close(), 392
gnome_vfs_directory_list_load(), 392
gnome_vfs_directory_open(), 391
gnome_vfs_directory_open_from_uri(),
        391
gnome_vfs_directory_read_next(), 392
gnome_vfs_directory_visit(), 392
gnome_vfs_directory_visit_files(), 392
gnome_vfs_directory_visit_files_at_
        uri(), 392
GnomeVFSDirectoryVisitFunc, 392–393
gnome_vfs_directory_visit_uri(), 392
GnomeVFSFileInfo, 387–390
gnome_vfs_file_info_clear(), 390
gnome_vfs_file_info_copy(), 390
gnome_vfs_file_info_dup(), 390
gnome_vfs_file_info_list_free(), 392
gnome_vfs_file_info_matches(), 390
gnome_vfs_file_info_new(), 390, 404
gnome_vfs_file_info_ref(), 390
gnome_vfs_file_info_unref(), 390, 405
gnome_vfs_find_directory(), 393
GnomeVFSFindDirectoryResult, 397
gnome_vfs_format_file_size_for_
        display(), 424
gnome_vfs_get_file_info(), 387, 404
gnome_vfs_get_file_info_from_handle(),
        390
GnomeVFSGetFileInfoResult, 396
gnome_vfs_get_file_info_uri(), 389
gnome_vfs_get_full_path(), 404
gnome_vfs_get_local_path_from_uri(),
        422
gnome_vfs_get_uri_from_local_path(),
        384, 404, 422
gnome_vfs_get_volume_free_space(), 422
GnomeVFSHandle, 385
gnome_vfs_icon_path_from_filename(),
        422
gnome_vfs_init(), 381–382
gnome_vfs_initialized(), 382
gnome_vfs_is_executable_command_
        string(), 422

gnome_vfs_make_directory(), 391

gnome_vfs_make_directory_for_uri(), 391

GnomeVFSMimeApplication, 416

gnome_vfs_mime_application_copy(), 416

gnome_vfs_mime_application_free(), 416

gnome_vfs_mime_application_list_free(), 416

gnome_vfs_mime_can_be_executable(), 416

gnome_vfs_mime_get_all_applications(), 415

gnome_vfs_mime_get_default_action_type(), 415

gnome_vfs_mime_get_default_application(), 415

gnome_vfs_mime_get_description(), 416

gnome_vfs_mime_get_icon(), 415

gnome_vfs_mime_get_short_list_applications(), 415

gnome_vfs_mime_id_in_application_list(), 416

gnome_vfs_mime_type_is_known(), 415

gnome_vfs_move(), 390

gnome_vfs_move_uri(), 390

gnome_vfs_open(), 385

gnome_vfs_open_uri(), 385

gnome_vfs_read(), 387

gnome_vfs_remove_directory(), 391

gnome_vfs_remove_directory_from_uri(), 391

GnomeVFSResult, 422

gnome_vfs_result_to_string(), 423–424

gnome_vfs_seek(), 387

gnome_vfs_set_file_info(), 389

gnome_vfs_set_file_info_uri(), 390

gnome_vfs_shutdown(), 381–382

gnome_vfs_tell(), 387

gnome_vfs_truncate(), 391

gnome_vfs_truncate_handle(), 391

gnome_vfs_truncate_uri(), 391

gnome_vfs_unlink(), 390

gnome_vfs_unlink_from_uri(), 390

GnomeVFSURI

    building, 419

    connection information, 421

    description, 419

    extracting path information, 420–421

    lists of, 421

gnome_vfs_uri_append_file_name(), 419

gnome_vfs_uri_append_path(), 419

gnome_vfs_uri_append_string(), 419

gnome_vfs_uri_dup(), 419

gnome_vfs_uri_exists(), 420

gnome_vfs_uri_extract_dirname(), 420

gnome_vfs_uri_extract_short_name(), 403, 421

gnome_vfs_uri_extract_short_path_name(), 421

gnome_vfs_uri_get_fragment_identifier(), 420

gnome_vfs_uri_get_host_name(), 421

gnome_vfs_uri_get_host_port(), 421

gnome_vfs_uri_get_parent(), 420

gnome_vfs_uri_get_password(), 421

gnome_vfs_uri_get_path(), 420

gnome_vfs_uri_get_scheme(), 420

gnome_vfs_uri_get_user_name(), 421

gnome_vfs_uri_has_parent(), 420

gnome_vfs_uri_is_local(), 420

gnome_vfs_uri_is_parent(), 420

gnome_vfs_uri_list_copy(), 421

gnome_vfs_uri_list_free(), 421

gnome_vfs_uri_list_ref(), 421

gnome_vfs_uri_list_unref(), 421

gnome_vfs_uri_new(), 403, 419

gnome_vfs_uri_ref(), 419

gnome_vfs_uri_set_host_name(), 421

gnome_vfs_uri_set_host_port(), 421

gnome_vfs_uri_set_password(), 421

gnome_vfs_uri_set_user_name(), 421

gnome_vfs_uri_to_string(), 420

gnome_vfs_uri_unref(), 403, 419

gnome_vfs_write(), 384, 387

gnome_vfs_xfer_delete_list(), 414

GnomeVFSXferProgressCallback, 412

gnome_vfs_xfer_uri(), 411–412

gnome_vfs_xfer_uri_list(), 414

gnome_window_toplevel_set_title(), 259

GNU Autotools

    description, 328–329

    example, 330–343

    outfitting source code with, 329–330

GObject, 62

G_OBJECT(), 72

g_object_add_weak_pointer(), 85–86

G_OBJECT_CLASS(), 72
g_object_class_install_property(),
        79–80
g_object_get(), 84–85
g_object_get_data(), 135
g_object_get_property(), 85
g_object_get_valist(), 85
g_object_new(), 83–84
g_object_ref(), 85–86
g_object_remove_weak_pointer(), 85–86
g_object_set(), 84
g_object_set_data(), 137–138
g_object_set_property(), 85
g_object_set_valist(), 85
g_object_unref(), 85–86
GParamSpec, 75–77
g_param_spec_*(), 75–76
g_print(), 27–28
g_printerr(), 27–28
g_printf_string_upper_bound(), 17
GPrintFunc, 29
g_propagate_error(), 34
GPtrArray, 59
g_qsort_with_data(), 59
GQuark. *See* quarks
g_quark_from_static_string(), 14
g_quark_from_string(), 14
g_quark_to_string(), 14
g_quark_try_string(), 14
GQueue, 60
graphical user interfaces,
        programming. *See* toolkits
gravity, 234–236
g_realloc(), 10
g_renew(), 10
g_return_if_fail(), 30
g_return_if_reached(), 29
g_return_val_if_fail(), 30
g_set_error(), 33–34
g_set_printerr_handler(), 28–29
g_set_print_handler(), 28–29
GSignalAccumulator, 94
g_signal_add_emission_hook(), 99
g_signal_connect(), 95–96
g_signal_connect_after(), 96
g_signal_connect_data(), 101
g_signal_connect_swapped(), 96
GSignalEmissionHook, 98

g_signal_emit(), 90–91
g_signal_emit_by_name(), 90–91
g_signal_emitv(), 91
g_signal_emit_valist(), 91
g_signal_handler_block(), 100
g_signal_handler_disconnect(), 96
g_signal_handler_find(), 101
g_signal_handler_is_connected(), 96–97
g_signal_handlers_block_by_func(), 101
g_signal_handlers_block_matched(), 101
g_signal_handlers_disconnect_by_func(),
        101
g_signal_handlers_disconnect_matched(),
        101
g_signal_handlers_unblock_by_func(),
        101
g_signal_handlers_unblock_matched(),
        101
g_signal_handler_unblock(), 100
g_signal_hook_remove(), 99
GSignalInvocationHint, 94–95
g_signal_list_ids(), 100
g_signal_lookup(), 100
g_signal_name(), 100
g_signal_new(), 88–89
g_signal_newv(), 101
g_signal_query(), 101
g_signal_stop_emission(), 100
g_signal_stop_emission_by_name(), 100
g_signal_valist(), 101
GSList, 59
g_snprintf(), 16
GSpawn, 254
g_stpcpy(), 16
g_strcanon(), 16
g_strchomp(), 16
g_strchug(), 16
g_strcompress(), 15
g_strconcat(), 15
g_strdelimit(), 16
g_strdup(), 15
g_strdup_printf(), 15
g_strdupv(), 17
g_strdup_vprintf(), 15
g_str_equal(), 55
g_strerror(), 29
g_strescape(), 15
g_strfreev(), 17

g_str_hash(), 55

GString
  adding, removing characters and data, 36–37
  comparing, 37–38
  creating, 36–37
  deallocating, 38
  description, 35
  example, 36–38
  typical operation, 35–36

g_string_append(), 36
g_string_append_c(), 36
g_string_append_len(), 37
g_string_append_printf(), 38
g_string_append_unichar(), 36
g_string_assign(), 35–36
GStringChunk, 59
g_string_equal(), 37
g_string_erase(), 37
g_string_free(), 38
g_string_hash(), 38
g_string_insert(), 36–37
g_string_insert_c(), 36
g_string_insert_len(), 37
g_string_insert_unichar(), 36
g_string_new(), 35
g_string_new_len(), 36
g_string_prepend*(), 36
g_string_prepend_len(), 37
g_string_printf(), 38
g_string_set_size(), 37
g_string_sized_new(), 35–36
g_string_truncate(), 37
g_strjoin(), 15
g_str_joinv(), 17
g_strndup(), 15
g_strreverse(), 16
g_strrstr(), 16
g_strrstr_len(), 17
g_strsignal(), 29
g_strsplit(), 17
g_strstrip(), 16
g_strstr_len(), 16
g_timeout_add(), 226
GTimer, 25–26
g_timer_*(), 25–26
GTK+
  compiling programs, 118, 326–328
  components, 113–114
  example, 116–120
  program behavior, 118
  program structure, 119
  terminating programs, 119–120
  themes, 115–116, 246
  widgets in Glade, 307
gtk_accelerator_valid(), 184
GtkAccelGroup, 184, 261, 265, 271
gtk_accel_groups_from_object(), 184
GtkAdjustment
  example, 159–163
  operation, 167–168
gtk_adjustment_changed(), 167
gtk_adjustment_get_value(), 167
gtk_adjustment_new(), 160, 167
gtk_adjustment_set_value(), 167
GtkAlignment
  description, 141
  operation, 152
GtkArrow
  description, 177
  example, 177–179
  operation, 180
GtkAspectFrame, 245
GtkBox
  child properties, 147–148
  creating with Glade, 311–312
  description, 141
  example, 141–145
  properties, 147
gtk_box_pack_end(), 146–147
gtk_box_pack_end_defaults(), 147
gtk_box_pack_start(), 146–147
gtk_box_pack_start_defaults(), 143, 147
GtkButton
  description, 153
  example, 153–157
  properties and signals, 157–158
GtkCalendar, 245. *See also*
    GnomeDataEdit
GtkCallback, 146
GtkCellRenderer
  description, 194
  example, 194–197, 217
  operation, 208–209

GtkCellRendererPixbuf, 208–209
GtkCellRendererText, 208–209
gtk_cell_renderer_text_new(), 195, 197, 217
GtkCellRendererToggle, 208–209
gtk_cell_renderer_toggle_new(), 217
GtkCheckButton
    description, 153
    example, 153–157
    properties and signals, 157–158
GtkCheckMenuItem. *See*
        GtkMenuItem
gtk_check_menu_item_new_with_label(), 266
gtk_check_menu_item_new_with_
    mnemonic(), 265
GtkClipBoard, 241
gtk_clipboard_get(), 241
GtkColorSelection
    description, 163
    example, 172–176
    operation, 170
GtkColorSelectionDialog. *See*
        GtkColorSelection
gtk_color_selection_is_adjusting(), 170, 173
GtkCombo
    description, 158
    example, 159–163
    operation, 166–167
gtk_combo_set_popdown_strings(), 161, 166
GtkContainer, 145–146
gtk_container_add(), 118–119, 142, 145–146
gtk_container_child_get_property(), 148
gtk_container_child_set_property(), 148
gtk_container_foreach(), 146
gtk_container_remove(), 145
GtkCurve, 245
GtkDialog
    creating with Glade, 307
    description, 188
    example, 188–191, 288–289
    operation, 191–193
gtk_dialog_new_with_buttons(), 189–192
gtk_dialog_set_default_response(), 190, 192

GtkDragDestIface, 204
GtkDragSourceIface, 204
GtkEditable (interface), 165–166
gtk_editable_copy_clipboard(), 165
gtk_editable_cut_clipboard(), 165
gtk_editable_delete_clipboard(), 165
gtk_editable_delete_text(), 165
gtk_editable_get_chars(), 165
gtk_editable_insert_text(), 165
gtk_editable_paste_clipboard(), 165
GtkEntry
    description, 158
    example, 159–163
    methods, 165–166
    properties, 164–165
    signals, 165
GtkEventBox, 244
GtkFileSelection
    description, 164
    example, 172–176
    operation, 170–171
gtk_file_selection_get_selections(), 172
GtkFixed, 245
GtkFontSelection
    description, 163
    example, 172–176
    operation, 170–171
GtkFontSelectionDialog. *See*
        GtkFontSelection
GtkFrame
    description, 176
    example, 177–179
    operation, 179–180
GtkGammaCurve, 245
GtkHBox. *See* button boxes
GtkHBox. *See* **GtkBox**
GtkHPaned. *See* **GtkPaned**
GtkHScale. *See* **GtkScale**
GtkHScrollBar. *See* **GtkScrollBar**
GtkHSeparator. *See* **GtkSeparator**
GtkImage
    example, 124–128, 134–139
    manipulation (*see* image
        manipulation)
    memory leaks, 136
    properties, 131–132

GtkImageMenuItem. *See* **GtkMenuItem**

gtk_image_menu_item_new_from_stock(), 261–262, 265

gtk_image_menu_item_new_with_label(), 266

gtk_image_menu_item_new_with_mnemonic(), 265

gtk_init(), 117

GtkLabel

    creating with Glade, 310–311

    example, 124–128

    markup language (*see* Pango, markup language)

    properties, 130–131

GtkListStore

    accessing nodes, 198–200

    creating, 198

    description, 194

    example, 194–197

    iterating through, 200

    removing nodes, 199

    setting and adding nodes, 198–199

gtk_list_store_append(), 195, 197–198, 199

gtk_list_store_clear(), 199

gtk_list_store_insert(), 199

gtk_list_store_insert_after(), 199

gtk_list_store_insert_before(), 199

gtk_list_store_new(), 195, 197–198

gtk_list_store_prepend(), 199

gtk_list_store_remove(), 199

gtk_list_store_set(), 195, 197–198

gtk_list_store_set_value(), 198

gtk_main(), 118–119

gtk_main_quit(), 117, 119

GtkMenu

    creating and installing (summary), 267–268

    description, 264

    example, 259–264

GtkMenuBar

    description, 264

    example, 259–264

    operation, 267–268

GtkMenuItem

    description, 264

    example, 259–264

    example of **GtkRadioMenuItem**, 266

    operation, 264–268

gtk_menu_item_new_with_label(), 161, 266

gtk_menu_item_new_with_mnemonic(), 262, 264–265

gtk_menu_item_remove_submenu(), 267

gtk_menu_item_set_submenu(), 262, 267

GtkMenuShell

    description, 264

    example, 259–264

    operation, 266–267

gtk_menu_shell_append(), 161, 262, 266

gtk_menu_shell_insert(), 267

gtk_menu_shell_prepend(), 267

GtkMessageDialog, 245

GtkNotebook

    description, 141

    example, 141–145

    operation, 150–152

gtk_notebook_append_page(), 151

gtk_notebook_append_page_menu(), 144–145, 151

gtk_notebook_insert_page(), 151

gtk_notebook_insert_page_menu(), 151

gtk_notebook_prepend_page(), 151

gtk_notebook_prepend_page_menu(), 151

gtk_notebook_remove_page(), 151

GtkOptionMenu

    description, 158

    example, 159–163

    operation, 164

gtk_option_menu_get_history(), 164

gtk_option_menu_set_history(), 161, 164

GtkPaned

    description, 141

    example, 141–145

    operation, 150

gtk_paned_add1(), 143, 150

gtk_paned_add2(), 144, 150

gtk_paned_pack1(), 150

gtk_paned_pack2(), 150

GtkProgressBar

    example, 124–128

    operation, 140

gtk_progress_bar_pulse(), 127–128, 140

GtkRadioButton
  description, 153
  example, 153–157
  properties and signals, 157–158
GtkRadioMenuItem. *See*
  GtkMenuItem
gtk_radio_menu_item_get_group(), 266
gtk_radio_menu_item_new_with_label(),
  266
gtk_radio_menu_item_new_with_
  mnemonic(), 265–266
GtkRange, 168, 185. *See also* **GtkScale**;
  GtkScrollBar
GtkRuler, 245
GtkScale
  description, 158
  example, 134–139, 159–163
  operation, 168–169
GtkScrollBar, 185. *See also*
  GtkScrolledWindow
GtkScrolledWindow
  description, 185–186
  example, 186–187
  operation, 188
gtk_scrolled_window_add_with_
  viewport(), 186, 187
GtkSeparator
  description, 176
  example, 177–179
  operation, 180
GtkSeparatorMenuItem. *See*
  GtkMenuItem
gtk_separator_menu_item_new(), 266
GtkSignalFunc, 269
GtkSizeGroup, 245
GtkSpinButton
  creating with Glade, 311
  description, 159
  example, 159–163
  operation, 169
GtkStatusbar
  example, 259–264
  operation, 270–271
gtk_statusbar_pop(), 270
gtk_statusbar_push(), 270
gtk_statusbar_remove(), 270
gtk_statusbar_set_has_resize_grip(),
  271

GtkTable
  creating with Glade, 310
  description, 141
  example, 141–145
  operation, 148–150
gtk_table_attach(), 149
gtk_table_attach_defaults(), 144
GtkTextBuffer
  accessing text, 229
  child anchors, 240
  deleting text, 228
  description, 219
  emitting signals, 229
  example, 219–226
  extracting text information,
    230–231
  indices, 226
  inserting text, 227–228
  modifying text, 228
  offsets, 226
  requirements, 226–227
  searching text, 233–234
  signals, 241–242
  text styles (*see* **GtkTextTag**)
  user actions, 228–229
gtk_text_buffer_apply_tag(), 238
gtk_text_buffer_apply_tag_by_name(),
  223, 238
gtk_text_buffer_begin_user_action(),
  228
gtk_text_buffer_copy_clipboard(), 241
gtk_text_buffer_create_child_anchor(),
  224, 240
gtk_text_buffer_create_mark(), 234–235
gtk_text_buffer_create_tag(), 224, 236
gtk_text_buffer_cut_clipboard(), 241
gtk_text_buffer_delete(), 228
gtk_text_buffer_delete_interactive(),
  228
gtk_text_buffer_delete_mark(), 235
gtk_text_buffer_delete_mark_by_name(),
  235
gtk_text_buffer_delete_selection(), 228
gtk_text_buffer_end_user_action(), 229
gtk_text_buffer_get_char_count(), 229
gtk_text_buffer_get_end_iter(),
  224–225
gtk_text_buffer_get_insert(), 235

gtk_text_buffer_get_iter_at_child_
    anchor(), 240
gtk_text_buffer_get_iter_at_mark(), 235
gtk_text_buffer_get_line_count(), 229
gtk_text_buffer_get_mark(), 235
gtk_text_buffer_get_modified(), 228
gtk_text_buffer_get_selection_bound(),
    235
gtk_text_buffer_get_selection_bounds(),
    220
gtk_text_buffer_get_slice(), 229
gtk_text_buffer_get_tag_table(), 239
gtk_text_buffer_get_text(), 229
gtk_text_buffer_insert(), 227
gtk_text_buffer_insert_at_cursor(), 228
gtk_text_buffer_insert_interactive(),
    227
gtk_text_buffer_insert_interactive_at_
    cursor(), 228
gtk_text_buffer_insert_pixbuf(), 225,
    240
gtk_text_buffer_insert_range(), 228
gtk_text_buffer_insert_range_
    interactive(), 228
gtk_text_buffer_insert_with_tags(), 238
gtk_text_buffer_insert_with_tags_by_
    name(), 238
gtk_text_buffer_iter_at_line(), 229
gtk_text_buffer_iter_at_line_index(),
    230
gtk_text_buffer_iter_at_line_offset(),
    230
gtk_text_buffer_iter_at_offset(), 230
gtk_text_buffer_iter_get_bounds(), 230
gtk_text_buffer_iter_get_end_iter(),
    230
gtk_text_buffer_iter_get_selection_
    bounds(), 230
gtk_text_buffer_iter_get_start_iter(),
    230
gtk_text_buffer_move_mark(), 235
gtk_text_buffer_move_mark_by_name(),
    235
gtk_text_buffer_new(), 223, 227
gtk_text_buffer_paste_clipboard(), 241
gtk_text_buffer_place_cursor(), 234
gtk_text_buffer_remove_all_tags(), 238
gtk_text_buffer_remove_tag(), 238

gtk_text_buffer_remove_tag_by_name(),
    223, 238
gtk_text_buffer_set_modified(), 228
gtk_text_buffer_set_text(), 227
GtkTextCharPredicate, 233
GtkTextChildAnchor. *See*
    GtkTextBuffer, child
    anchors
GtkTextIter
    acquiring, 229–230
    description, 227
    example, 219–226
    extracting text information,
        230–231
    scrolling to, 243
    searching text, 233–234
    setting position, 231–233
    used with GtkTextTag, 239
gtk_text_iter_backward_char(), 232
gtk_text_iter_backward_chars(), 232
gtk_text_iter_backward_cursor_
    position(), 232
gtk_text_iter_backward_cursor_
    positions(), 232
gtk_text_iter_backward_find_char(), 233
gtk_text_iter_backward_line(), 232
gtk_text_iter_backward_lines(), 232
gtk_text_iter_backward_search(), 234
gtk_text_iter_backward_sentence_
    start(), 233
gtk_text_iter_backward_sentence_
    starts(), 233
gtk_text_iter_backward_to_tag_toggle(),
    233
gtk_text_iter_backward_word_start(),
    233
gtk_text_iter_backward_word_starts(),
    233
gtk_text_iter_begins_tag(), 239
gtk_text_iter_can_insert(), 231
gtk_text_iter_ends_line(), 231
gtk_text_iter_ends_sentence(), 231
gtk_text_iter_ends_tag(), 239
gtk_text_iter_ends_word(), 231
gtk_text_iter_equal(), 220–222
gtk_text_iter_forward_char(), 232
gtk_text_iter_forward_chars(), 232

gtk_text_iter_forward_cursor_
    position(), 221, 232
gtk_text_iter_forward_cursor_
    positions(), 232
gtk_text_iter_forward_find_char(), 233
gtk_text_iter_forward_line(), 232
gtk_text_iter_forward_lines(), 232
gtk_text_iter_forward_search(), 234
gtk_text_iter_forward_sentence_end(),
    233
gtk_text_iter_forward_sentence_ends(),
    233
gtk_text_iter_forward_to_end(), 233
gtk_text_iter_forward_to_line_end(),
    233
gtk_text_iter_forward_to_tag_toggle(),
    233
gtk_text_iter_forward_word_end(), 233
gtk_text_iter_forward_word_ends(), 233
gtk_text_iter_get_buffer(), 230
gtk_text_iter_get_bytes_in_line(), 231
gtk_text_iter_get_char(), 229
gtk_text_iter_get_chars_in_line(), 231
gtk_text_iter_get_child_anchor(), 240
gtk_text_iter_get_line(), 230
gtk_text_iter_get_line_index(), 230
gtk_text_iter_get_line_offset(), 230
gtk_text_iter_get_offset(), 230
gtk_text_iter_get_pixbuf(), 240
gtk_text_iter_get_tags(), 239
gtk_text_iter_get_toggled_tags(), 239
gtk_text_iter_get_visible_line_index(),
    230
gtk_text_iter_get_visible_line_
    offset(), 230
gtk_text_iter_has_tag(), 221–222, 239
gtk_text_iter_inside_sentence(), 231
gtk_text_iter_inside_word(), 231
gtk_text_iter_is_cursor_position(), 231
gtk_text_iter_is_end(), 231
gtk_text_iter_is_start(), 231
gtk_text_iter_set_line(), 231
gtk_text_iter_set_line_index(), 232
gtk_text_iter_set_line_offset(), 232
gtk_text_iter_set_offset(), 231
gtk_text_iter_set_visible_line_index(),
    232

gtk_text_iter_set_visible_line_
    offset(), 232
gtk_text_iter_starts_line(), 231
gtk_text_iter_starts_sentence(), 231
gtk_text_iter_starts_word(), 231
gtk_text_iter_toggles_tag(), 239
GtkTextMark
    cursor and, 234
    description, 227
    manipulating, 234–235
    scrolling to, 243
    selection, 235
gtk_text_mark_get_buffer(), 236
gtk_text_mark_get_deleted(), 235
gtk_text_mark_get_left_gravity(), 236
gtk_text_mark_get_name(), 236
gtk_text_mark_get_visible(), 236
gtk_text_mark_set_visible(), 235
GtkTextTag
    description, 236
    operation, 236–239
    used with GtkTextIter, 239
gtk_text_tag_get_priority(), 238
gtk_text_tag_set_priority(), 239
GtkTextTagTable, 227, 239–240
gtk_text_tag_table_add(), 239
GtkTextTagTableForeach, 240
gtk_text_tag_table_foreach(), 240
gtk_text_tag_table_get_size(), 240
gtk_text_tag_table_lookup(), 239
gtk_text_tag_table_new(), 223, 239
gtk_text_tag_table_remove(), 239
GtkTextView
    creating, 242
    description, 219
    example, 219–226
    methods, 243–244
    properties, 242–243
    relationship with **GtkTextBuffer**,
        242
gtk_text_view_add_child_at_anchor(),
    224, 240
gtk_text_view_backward_display_line(),
    244
gtk_text_view_backward_display_line_
    start(), 244
gtk_text_view_backward_starts_display_
    line(), 244

gtk_text_view_forward_display_line(), 244

gtk_text_view_forward_display_line_ end(), 244

gtk_text_view_get_editable(), 227

gtk_text_view_move_mark_onscreen(), 243

gtk_text_view_move_visually(), 244

gtk_text_view_new_with_buffer(), 224, 242

gtk_text_view_place_cursor_onscreen(), 243

gtk_text_view_scroll_mark_onscreen(), 243

gtk_text_view_scroll_to_iter(), 243

gtk_text_view_scroll_to_mark(), 243

gtk_text_view_set_buffer(), 242

GtkToggleButton, 245. *See also* **GtkCheckButton**

GtkToolbar

    example, 259–264

    future of, 436

    operation, 268–270

gtk_toolbar_append_item(), 269

gtk_toolbar_append_space(), 269

gtk_toolbar_append_widget(), 269

gtk_toolbar_insert_item(), 269

gtk_toolbar_insert_space(), 270

gtk_toolbar_insert_stock(), 263, 269

gtk_toolbar_insert_widget(), 269

gtk_toolbar_prepend_item(), 269

gtk_toolbar_prepend_space(), 269

gtk_toolbar_prepend_widget(), 269

gtk_toolbar_remove_space(), 270

gtk_toolbar_unset_style(), 268

GtkTooltips

    example, 181–183

    operation, 180–181, 183

gtk_tooltips_disable(), 183

gtk_tooltips_enable(), 183

gtk_tooltips_set_tip(), 180–181, 182

GtkTreeCellDataFunc, 207

GtkTreeIter

    description, 197

    example, 212–219

    operation, 201–202

GtkTreeModel (interface)

    description, 193–194

    methods, 198–202

gtk_tree_model_foreach(), 200

GtkTreeModelForeachFunc, 200

gtk_tree_model_get(), 198, 215

gtk_tree_model_get_iter(), 201, 214, 216

gtk_tree_model_get_iter_first(), 202

gtk_tree_model_get_iter_from_string(), 201

gtk_tree_model_get_path(), 200

gtk_tree_model_get_value(), 198

gtk_tree_model_iter_children(), 202

gtk_tree_model_iter_has_child(), 202

gtk_tree_model_iter_n_children(), 202, 214

gtk_tree_model_iter_next(), 202

gtk_tree_model_iter_parent(), 202

gtk_tree_model_nth_child(), 202

GtkTreePath, 200

GtkTreePath. *See* **GtkTreeStore**, navigating

gtk_tree_path_append_index(), 200

gtk_tree_path_compare(), 201

gtk_tree_path_copy(), 200, 214

gtk_tree_path_down(), 201

gtk_tree_path_free(), 200, 215–216

gtk_tree_path_get_depth(), 201, 214

gtk_tree_path_get_indices(), 201, 214

gtk_tree_path_is_ancestor(), 201

gtk_tree_path_is_descendant(), 201

gtk_tree_path_new(), 200

gtk_tree_path_new_first(), 200

gtk_tree_path_new_from_string(), 200, 216

gtk_tree_path_next(), 201

gtk_tree_path_prepend_index(), 201

gtk_tree_path_prev(), 201

gtk_tree_path_to_string(), 200

gtk_tree_path_up(), 201, 214

GtkTreeRowReference, 202

gtk_tree_row_reference_free(), 202

gtk_tree_row_reference_get_path(), 202

gtk_tree_row_reference_new(), 202

gtk_tree_row_reference_valid(), 202

GtkTreeSelection, 209–212

GtkTreeSelectionForeachFunc, 211

GtkTreeSelectionFunc, 212

gtk_tree_selection_get_selected(), 210

gtk_tree_selection_get_selected_rows(), 211

gtk_tree_selection_get_view(), 210

gtk_tree_selection_iter_is_selected(), 211

gtk_tree_selection_path_is_selected(), 211

gtk_tree_selection_select_all(), 211

gtk_tree_selection_selected_foreach(), 210–211

gtk_tree_selection_select_iter(), 211

gtk_tree_selection_select_path(), 211

gtk_tree_selection_select_range(), 211

gtk_tree_selection_set_mode(), 210

gtk_tree_selection_set_select_ function(), 212

gtk_tree_selection_unselect_all(), 211

gtk_tree_selection_unselect_iter(), 211

gtk_tree_selection_unselect_path(), 211

GtkTreeStore
    accessing nodes, 198–200
    creating, 198
    description, 194
    example, 212–219
    extracting information, 199–200
    navigating, 200–202
    removing nodes, 199
    setting and adding nodes, 198–199
    traversing, 200

gtk_tree_store_append(), 199, 214–215

gtk_tree_store_clear(), 199

gtk_tree_store_insert(), 198

gtk_tree_store_insert_after(), 199

gtk_tree_store_insert_before(), 199

gtk_tree_store_is_ancestor(), 199

gtk_tree_store_iter_depth(), 200

gtk_tree_store_new(), 197–198, 216

gtk_tree_store_prepend(), 199

gtk_tree_store_remove(), 199

gtk_tree_store_set(), 198, 216

gtk_tree_store_set_value(), 198

GtkTreeView
    description, 194
    example, 194–197, 212–219
    future of, 437
    manipulating, 203
    properties, 204

    selection (*see* **GtkTreeSelection**)
    signals, 204

gtk_tree_view_append_column(), 196, 205, 218

gtk_tree_view_collapse_all(), 203

gtk_tree_view_collapse_row(), 203

GtkTreeViewColumn
    cell renderers and, 204–208
    description, 194
    example, 194–197
    manipulating, 205–208
    properties and signals, 207–208

gtk_tree_view_column_add_attribute(), 205

gtk_tree_view_column_clear(), 205

gtk_tree_view_column_clear_ attributes(), 205

gtk_tree_view_column_new_with_ attributes(), 196, 197, 205, 217

gtk_tree_view_column_pack_end(), 205

gtk_tree_view_column_pack_start(), 205

gtk_tree_view_columns_autosize(), 206

gtk_tree_view_column_set_attributes(), 205

gtk_tree_view_column_set_cell_data_ func(), 207, 217

gtk_tree_view_expand_all(), 203

gtk_tree_view_expand_row(), 203

gtk_tree_view_get_column(), 206

gtk_tree_view_get_columns(), 206

gtk_tree_view_get_cursor(), 203

gtk_tree_view_get_selection(), 210

gtk_tree_view_insert_column(), 206

gtk_tree_view_insert_column_with_ attributes(), 206

gtk_tree_view_insert_column_with_data_ func(), 206–207

gtk_tree_view_move_column_after(), 206

gtk_tree_view_remove_column(), 206

gtk_tree_view_row_activated(), 203

gtk_tree_view_row_expanded(), 203

gtk_tree_view_scroll_to_cell(), 203

gtk_tree_view_set_cursor(), 203

GtkVBox. *See* button boxes

GtkVBox. *See* **GtkBox**

GtkViewport, 186

GtkVPaned. *See* **GtkPaned**

GtkVScale. *See* GtkScale
GtkVScrollBar. *See* GtkScrollBar
GtkVSeparator. *See* GtkSeparator
GtkWidget
    description, 120
    destroying, 121–122, 146
    disabling, 121
    displaying, 120–121
    hiding, 121–122
    methods, 120–121
    properties, 121–122
    signals, 122
gtk_widget_add_accelerator(), 184
gtk_widget_destroy(), 118–120, 121
gtk_widget_hide(), 121
gtk_widget_hide_all(), 121
gtk_widget_hide_on_delete(), 119
gtk_widget_show(), 120
gtk_widget_show_all(), 118–119, 121,
    268
gtk_widget_show_now(), 121
GtkWindow
    creating, 119
    destroying, 124
    icons, 124
    positioning, 123
    properties, 123–124
    resizing, 123–124
    titles, 122–123
gtk_window_add_accel_group(), 184, 261
gtk_window_remove_accel_group(), 184
gtk_window_set_default_icon_from_
    file(), 124
gtk_window_set_icon(), 124
gtk_window_set_icon_from_file(), 124
gtk_window_set_icon_list(), 124
GTraverseFunc, 53
GTree
    adding and replacing nodes,
      50–51
    creating, 48–50
    deleting nodes, 52
    description, 48
    example, 49–53
    finding nodes, 51–52
    gathering statistics, 53–54
    traversing, 53
g_tree_destroy(), 54

g_tree_foreach(), 53
g_tree_height(), 53
g_tree_insert(), 50–51
g_tree_lookup(), 51–52
g_tree_lookup_extended(), 51–52
g_tree_new(), 49
g_tree_new_full(), 49–50
g_tree_new_with_data(), 49
g_tree_nnodes(), 53
g_tree_remove(), 52
g_tree_replace(), 50
g_tree_steal(), 52
g_try_malloc(), 10
g_try_realloc(), 10
g_type_add_interface_static(), 108–109
G_TYPE_CHECK_CLASS_CAST(), 67–68
G_TYPE_CHECK_CLASS_TYPE(), 67–68
G_TYPE_CHECK_INSTANCE_CAST(), 67–68
G_TYPE_CHECK_INSTANCE_TYPE(), 67–68
G_TYPE_FROM_INTERFACE(), 110
GTypeInfo, 69–71, 107
G_TYPE_INSTANCE_GET_CLASS(), 67–68
GTypeInterface. *See* interfaces,
    creating
G_TYPE_OBJECT. *See* type identifier,
    base class
g_type_register_static(), 69–71
g_ucs4_to_utf16(), 23
g_ucs4_to_utf8(), 24
g_unichar_digit_value(), 20
g_unichar_isalnum(), 18
g_unichar_isalpha(), 18
g_unichar_iscntrl(), 19
g_unichar_isdefined(), 18
g_unichar_isdigit(), 18
g_unichar_isgraph(), 19
g_unichar_islower(), 18
g_unichar_isprint(), 19
g_unichar_ispunct(), 18
g_unichar_isspace(), 19
g_unichar_istitle(), 18
g_unichar_isupper(), 18
g_unichar_iswide(), 19
g_unichar_isxdigit(), 18
g_unichar_tolower(), 20
g_unichar_totitle(), 20
g_unichar_toupper(), 20
g_unichar_to_utf8(), 24

g_unichar_type(), 19
g_unichar_validate(), 18
g_unichar_xdigit_value(), 20
g_utf16_to_ucs4(), 23
g_utf16_to_utf8(), 23
g_utf8_casefold(), 22
g_utf8_collate(), 22
g_utf8_collate_key(), 23
g_utf8_find_next_char(), 21
g_utf8_find_prev_char(), 21
g_utf8_get_char(), 21
g_utf8_get_char_validated(), 20
g_utf8_next_char(), 21
g_utf8_normalize(), 22
g_utf8_offset_to_pointer(), 21
g_utf8_pointer_to_offset(), 21
g_utf8_prev_char(), 21
g_utf8_strchr(), 22
g_utf8_strdown(), 22
g_utf8_strlen(), 21
g_utf8_strncpy(), 21
g_utf8_strrchr(), 22
g_utf8_strup(), 22
g_utf8_to_ucs4(), 23
g_utf8_to_ucs4_fast(), 23
g_utf8_to_utf16(), 23
g_utf8_validate(), 20
GValue, 77–79
GValueArray, 111
g_value_dup_string(), 78
g_value_get_*(), 78–79
G_VALUE_HOLDS_*(), 78–79
g_value_set_*(), 78–79
g_value_set_static_string(), 78
g_value_unset(), 79
g_vsnprintf(), 16
g_warning(), 26–27
hash table. *See* GHashTable
header file
    GConf, 352
    Glade, 317
    GLib, 8
    GNOME, 249
    GnomeVFS, 381
    GTK+, 116
help
    displaying GNOME documents,
        256

generating documentation,
    339–340
widget tooltips (*see* **GtkTooltips**)
high scores. *See* scores; **GnomeScores**
hooks. *See* signals, hooks
hyperlinks. *See* **GnomeHRef**; URL,
    displaying
icons
    choosing (*see* **GnomeIconEntry**)
    GtkWindow (*see* **GtkWindow**,
        icons)
    themes, 437
images. *See* **GtkImage**; **GdkPixbuf**;
    GtkTextBuffer, child
    anchors;
    GnomePixmapEntry
include file. *See* header file
indexing, arrays and lists, 4
inheritance
    defining subclasses, 101–106
    description, 63–64
    multiple, 65
input focus, 121–122, 311
instance
    definition, 62
    structure, 66–67, 70–71, 81, 101
interfaces
    base initializer, 108
    creating, 106–111
    description, 65–66
    implementing and installing,
        108–110
    using, 110–111
intltool, 329, 331–332, 335, 343
INTLTOOL_DESKTOP_RULE, 333–334
IRC, 436
iterators
    text (*see* GtkTextIter)
    tree (*see* GtkTreeIter)
keyboard operation, 183–184. *See also*
        mnemonics; accelerators
keys
    GConf (*see* GConf, keys)
    hash, 38 (*see also* GHashTable)
    sorting, 22–23
Kimball, Spencer, 113
label, 124. *See also* **GtkLabel**
libbonobo, 248

libbonobo–activation, 248

libbonoboui, 248

libegg, 436

libgconf–2, 346

libglade, 314–322

libgnome, 247, 249

libgnomecanvas, 247

libgnomeui, 247, 259

libgnomevfs, 247

libtool, 335

limits, of this book, 2

line splitting, 3

list box. *See* tree and list widgets

lists. *See* GList

locale, 22, 24–25, 130. *See also* gettext;
    intltool

log domain, 26

m4, 330, 336

mailing lists, 435–436

main event loop, 116

Makefile templates. *See Makefile.am*;
    Makefile.in

Makefile.am, 329, 333–335

Makefile.in, 329

marks. *See* **GtkTextMark**

markup language. *See* Pango, markup
    language

marshallers. *See* signals, marshallers

Mattis, Peter, 113

membership relations, 63–65

memory chunks
    creating and deallocating, 11–13
    diagnostics, 13
    example, 11–13
    used in a tree, 49–52

memory management, 9–14

menu bars, 259. *See also* **GtkMenuBar**

menus
    GTK+ (*see* GtkMenu;
        GtkMenuItem;
        GtkMenuShell;
        GtkMenuBar)
    option (*see* GtkOptionMenu)
    popup (*see* context menus)

message logging, 26–29, 59

methods
    access (*see* access methods)
    creating, 74

definition, 62

MIME types
    declaring, 416–418
    determining, 415–416

mnemonics, 130, 162, 183–184,
    264–265

modal windows, 123

models. *See* MVC

multiple inheritance, 65

MVC, 159, 185, 193, 203, 219

naming conventions, 8, 62

news, 432

notebooks. *See* **GtkNotebook**

numeric data entry. *See*
    GtkSpinButton

object–oriented programming, 61–66

objects
    creating, 83–84
    data pointer, 135–138
    definition, 62
    using, 83–86

OMF files. *See* help, generating
    documentation

option menus. *See* **GtkOptionMenu**

packing (widgets), 114–115, 145–151,
    308–309

paned widgets. *See* **GtkPaned**

Pango
    description, 114
    GtkTextTag and, 236–237
    markup language, 129–130

parameters
    command–line, 250 (*see also*
        session management)
    GObject (*see* GParamSpec)

paths. *See* **GtkTreeStore**, navigating

PKG_CHECK_MODULES, 331–332

pkg–config
    compiler and linker options,
        327–328
    package status, 327
    purpose, 325–326
    with Makefile, 328

PKG_CONFIG_PATH, 326–327

platform, for this book, 3

pointers
    required knowledge, 1, 4
    untyped, 8–9

popup menus. *See* context menus
preferences. *See* GConf
prerequisites, for this book, 1–2
print handlers, 28–29
progress bar, 124. *See also*
    GtkProgressBar
properties
    and the base class, 73, 80
    child (*see* child properties)
    declaring in classes, 75–83,
        104–106
    definition, 74–75
    in Glade (*see* Glade, property
        editor)
    installing in classes, 79–82
    internal access, 80–82, 104–105
    justification, 82–83
    using, 84–85, 105–106
quarks, 13–14
radio buttons. *See* **GtkRadioButton**;
    GtkMenuItem
reference counts, 62–63
references
    example, 85–86
    floating, 120, 145
    strong, 85–86
    weak, 85–86
renderer. *See* **GtkCellRenderer**
resizing. *See* **GtkWindow**, resizing
saving program state. *See* session
    management
scores, 258. *See also* **GnomeScores**
scrolling, 185. *See also*
    GtkScrolledWindow;
    GtkTreeView; **GtkTextView**
ScrollKeeper, 340–341
searching
    GtkTextBuffer, 233–234
    strings, 16–17
    Unicode strings, 21–22
selection
    text buffer (*see* **GtkTextMark**,
        selection)
    trees (*see* **GtkTreeSelection**)
session management, 248, 300. *See*
    also **GnomeClient**
shell, using to execute programs,
    254–255

signal handlers
    attaching, 95–97, 101
    defining, 87–90
    description, 86–87
    example, 89–90, 95–96
signals
    aborting emission, 100–101
    accumulators, 87, 89, 94–95
    blocking, 100–101
    cache array, 87, 91
    dash and underscore in names,
        119
    defining, 87–90, 101
    description, 86–87
    details, 97
    emitting, 86, 90–91
    events and, 116, 119–120
    extracting identifiers, 100–101
    Glade and (*see* Glade, signals)
    handler (*see* signal handlers)
    hooks, 91, 98–99
    listing and printing, 100–101
    marshallers, 87, 89, 91–94
    property change (notification),
        74
    using (*see* signals, emitting; signal
        handlers, attaching)
signature, 90
sliders. *See* **GtkScale**
sorting
    GArray, 48
    GList, 44–45
    quicksort, 59
sound, 256–258, 438
spin button. *See* **GtkSpinButton**
standard event handlers, 117, 119
status bars, 259. *See also* **GtkStatusBar**
stock items, 132, 139–140, 288
strings
    array operations, 17
    converting to and from numbers,
        17
    copying, 15–16
    creating, 15–16
    GString (*see* GString)
    quarks (*see* quarks)
    searching, 16–17
    splitting and joining, 15, 17

strings, *continued*
    translating, 16–17
    Unicode (*see* Unicode)
strnfill(), 15
subclasses. *See* inheritance
SUBDIRS, 333–334
synchronous file access
    description, 382–383
    example, 383–385
    file information, 387–390
    file management, 390–391
    opening and closing files,
        385–386
    reading, writing, seeking,
        386–387
    relationship to Unix file
        operations, 382–383
table containers. *See* **GtkTable**
tabs. *See* **GtkNotebook**
tag tables. *See* **GtkTextTagTable**
tags. *See* **GtkTextTag**
text styles. *See* Pango, markup
    language; **GtkTextTag**
text widgets. *See* **GtkTextBuffer**;
    GtkTextView; **GtkEntry**;
    GtkCombo; **GnomeEntry**
threads, 60
timeouts, 226
timer. *See* GTimer
titlecase, 18–20
titles. *See* **GtkWindow**, titles;
    GnomeApp, titles; Glade,
    window titles
toolbars, 259. *See also* **GtkToolbar**
toolkits, 113
tooltips. *See* **GtkTooltips**
transfers. *See* GnomeVFS, transfers
tree and list widgets, 193. *See also*
    GtkTreeModel
trees. *See* GTree; **GtkTreeModel**
type identifier
    base class, 72
    creating objects with, 83–84
    function, 69–71, 102–103
    in type identifier function, 69–70
    in utility macro, 67–68
    parent class, 102
typographical conventions, 2–3

Unicode
    character encodings, 18
    converting strings and characters,
        20–25
    encoding conversion, 23–25
    error codes, 24–25
    extracting string information, 21
    GString and, 36
    GTK+ and, 120
    identifying, 18–20
    in **GtkTextBuffer**, 227
    operations, 17–25
    searching and navigating strings,
        21–22
    UCS–4, 18
    UTF–16, 18
    UTF–8, 18
    validating, 18, 20–21
URI. *See* GnomeVFS, URI
URL, displaying, 255. *See also*
    GnomeHRef
user data pointer
    iteration and, 43–45
    signal handler example, 154–156
    signal handlers and, 96
user interface guidelines
    combo boxes, 167
    dialogs, 193
    druids, 294
    entry boxes, 278
    frames, 180
    GtkLabel, 131
    menu bars, 264
    modal windows, 123
    option menus, 158
    origin, 114
    preferences, 377
    sliders, 169
    sound, 256
    status bars, 271
    toolbars, 268
    tree view selections, 212
    widget arrangement, 153
    window titles, 122–123
user interfaces, graphically creating,
    305. *See also* Glade
value containers. *See* GValue
views. *See* MVC

watermarks, 295, 297

widgets

    containers, 140–141 (*see also*
        GtkBox; button boxes;
        GtkPaned; **GtkTable**;
        GtkAlignment)

    data entry, 158–176 (*see also*
        GtkOptionMenu; **GtkEntry**;
        GtkCombo; **GtkScale**;
        GtkSpinButton;
        GtkColorSelection;
        GnomeColorPicker;
        GtkFontSelection;
        GnomeFontPicker;
        GtkFileSelection;
        GnomeFileEntry)

    date and time (*see*
        GnomeDateEdit)

    default, 122

    definition, 114–115

    display, 124 (*see also* **GtkLabel**;
        GtkImage; **GtkProgressBar**)

    drawing, 115

    in text buffers (*see*
        GtkTextBuffer, child
        anchors)

    operations (*see* **GtkWidget**)

    tree, 114, 313

    windows (*see* **GtkWindow**)

windows. *See* **GtkWindow**; **GnomeApp**

wizards. *See* druids

HOW LINUX WORKS
What Every Super-User Should Know

by BRIAN WARD

How Linux Works describes the inside of the Linux system for systems administrators, whether they maintain an extensive network in the office or one Linux box at home. While some books try to give copy-and-paste instructions for how to deal with every single system program out there, *How Linux Works* shows the reader how the Linux system functions so that they will have the knowledge to solve any problem that comes up.

APRIL 2004, 392 PP., $37.95 ($55.95 CAN)
ISBN 1-59327-035-6

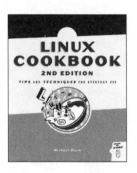

THE LINUX COOKBOOK, 2ND EDITION
Tips and Techniques for Everyday Use

by MICHAEL STUTZ

The Linux Cookbook, 2nd Edition shows you the best ways to do things on Linux, so that you can get your work done, quickly and easily. Organized by the general things that you use your computer for, the book gives you "recipes" for each task, each one with simple, step-by-step instructions, and an example that shows how to use the technique in practice. Covers the major Linux distributions.

APRIL 2004, 576 PP., $39.95 ($57.95 CAN)
ISBN 1-59327-031-3

THE LINUX ENTERPRISE CLUSTER

by KARL KOPPER

The Linux Enterprise Cluster is a practical guide for building and installing an enterprise-class cluster for mission critical applications using commodity hardware and open source software. Includes information on how to build a high-availability server pair using the Heartbeat package, how to use the Linux Virtual Server load balancing software, how to construct a reliable printing system in a Linux cluster environment, and how to build a job scheduling system in Linux with no single point of failure.

MAY 2004, 456 PP., $49.95 ($72.95 CAN)
ISBN 1-59327-036-4

WICKED COOL SHELL SCRIPTS
101 Scripts for Linux, Mac OS X, and UNIX Systems

by DAVE TAYLOR

This cookbook of useful, customizable, and fun scripts gives you the tools to solve common Linux, Mac OS X, and UNIX problems and personalize your computing environment. Among the more than 100 scripts included are an interactive calculator, a spell checker, a disk backup utility, a weather tracker, and a web logfile analysis tool. Examples are written in Bourne Shell (sh) syntax.

JANUARY 2004, 368 PP., $29.95 ($43.95 CAN)
ISBN 1-59327-012-7

THE SPAM LETTERS

by JONATHAN LAND

From the man behind TheSpamLetters.com comes a collection of humorous and entertaining correspondence and one-shot replies to people who send out mass junk emailings (a.k.a. spam). Compiled from the nearly 200 entries on the website, *The Spam Letters* brings together the best of these letters in one convenient little book. If you hate spam, you'll love *The Spam Letters*.

MAY 2004, 336 PP., $17.95 ($26.95 CAN)
ISBN 1-59327-032-1

PHONE:
1 (800) 420-7240 OR
(415) 863-9900
MONDAY THROUGH FRIDAY,
9 A.M. TO 5 P.M. (PST)

FAX:
(415) 863-9950
24 HOURS A DAY,
7 DAYS A WEEK

EMAIL:
SALES@NOSTARCH.COM

WEB:
HTTP://WWW.NOSTARCH.COM

MAIL:
NO STARCH PRESS, INC.
555 DE HARO ST, SUITE 250
SAN FRANCISCO, CA 94107
USA

UPDATES

Visit http://www.nostarch.com/gnome.htm for updates, errata, and other information.